THE TRANSCENDENT YEARS

Circle Theater Company 1970 (later Circle Rep)
1 – Marshall W. Mason, 2 – Unidentified, 3 – Robert Frink, 4 – Tanya Berezin, 5 – Rob Thirkield, 6 – Lance Taylor, 7 – Burke Pearson, 8 – Beth Bowden, 9 – David Starkweather, 10 – David Stekol, 11 – Stephanie Gordon, 12 – Marina Stefan, 12-a – Doric Wilson
Photo by Sharon Madden

THE TRANSCENDENT YEARS

Circle Repertory Company & the 1960s

MARSHALL W. MASON

Founding Artistic Director

Copyright© by Marshall W. Mason

For

Rob Thirkield,
whose generous spirit was the very soul of Circle Rep,

Tanya Berezin,
whose courage sustained Circle Rep for a second generation,

and

Lanford Wilson,
who, by taking it as a sanctuary, gave Circle Rep the best reason for being.

Introduction

Revelations

Americans in the 21st century are starved for meaning in our lives, something hard to come by as significance is increasingly eroded by technology. What's good today is obsolete tomorrow and antiquated the following week. We devour novelty at such a rate that meaning appears expendable; we discard the past as we tear into the future. Context has become a rare commodity.

Art does not emerge from a vacuum, but from a specific social and historical context. Theater lovers can take comfort that the art of theater was born amid the greatest explosion of political, philosophic, and creative innovation in the history of civilization – the Golden Age of Greece, in the fifth century B.C.

If it were not for the turbulent spirit of the Renaissance almost two-thousand years later, putting humanity rather than God at the center of concern, could Shakespeare's depiction of human complexity have been so richly articulated?

Without the stirrings of Russia's economic revolution and Freud's equally revolutionary psychological theories, would Chekhov and Stanislavski have felt the need to dispense with the artificial theatricality of the 19th century to focus on the reality of everyday suffering, both comic and tragic?

Without the surge of hope in the years following the Great Depression, when Roosevelt's New Deal promised a just democracy helping rich and poor alike in pursuit of life, liberty and happiness, might the Group Theater of Harold Clurman and Clifford Odets have remained unrealized?

Similarly, it's difficult to imagine how Circle Repertory Company could have been conceived without the "mystic, crystal revelations" that characterized the adventurous decade called the 60s. Those same revelations played a part in the ubiquitous expansion of 21st century communications envisioned by people like Bill Gates and Steve Jobs.

From the buoyant prospects stirred by the election of John F. Kennedy in 1960 to the disgraced resignation of Richard M. Nixon more than a decade later, an eruption of societal forces drastically changed perceptions of the world. Bob Dylan prophesied, "The times, they are a-changin'." The use of hallucinogenic drugs, accompanied by the eastern religious influences of Buddhism and Hinduism, guided by the Tibetan Book of the Dead, focused attention on the seemingly limitless possibilities of the human spirit.

A belief emerged among many of this generation in the harmony of the universe and the common currency of love. These spiritual awakenings were given expression in music (Dylan, Donovan, the Beatles, the Rolling Stones, and Cat Stevens, for example), politics (the stirring rhetoric of Martin Luther King, Jr. and the driven idealism of Robert F. Kennedy), and the visual arts (the psychedelic world of Peter Max and the myth-busting irony of Andy Warhol, among others).

We criticized the values passed down by our parents and rejoiced in "the mind's true liberation."

Ambitious artistic principles were inspired that resulted in a living theater that transcended the limitations of the theater we'd inherited. The "fabulous invalid," as it was called, needed resuscitation. *The New York Times* annually issued an anguished complaint: "Where are the new playwrights?" We became devoted to putting that question to rest.

The term "The Sixties" is used nostalgically by those who participated in the counter-cultural revolution of the decade and pejoratively by those who perceive the era as one of irresponsible excess. Although I will cite contemporaneous events on the world stage to help the reader understand the context of our artistic progress, it's beyond the purview of this book to analyze the forces that shaped the decade. My depiction of that seismic time will be necessarily subjective and anecdotal. As Jefferson Airplane's Paul Kantner wryly observed: "If you can remember anything about the Sixties, you weren't really there." Well, I was there, but I will try.

Julian Barnes in his book *The Sense of an Ending* defines history as "that certainty produced at the point where the imperfections of memory meet the inadequacies of documentation." He also wrote: "If I can't be sure of the actual events anymore, I can at least be true to the impressions those facts left. That's the best I can manage." Me too, Mr. Barnes, so here goes.

"Once upon a time," Matt Friedman intones in Lanford Wilson's *Talley's Folly*, "there was a hope throughout the land." Matt was referring, of course, to the period that preceded the Second World War, the fervent years of Clurman and Odets. But when we produced the play in 1979, the phrase reverberated in the naïve, but ardent hope of those amateur revolutionaries in *Fifth of July*, who cried, "You have no idea of the country we almost made for you!"

The ambition to create a better America was a result of the inspiration we took from the election of President Kennedy, for whom I cast my first vote. "The torch has been passed to a new generation," he declared at his inauguration, and then he challenged Americans to make a selfless commitment to a virtuous cause, with the assurance that we had the power to improve a world of poverty and ignorance. The Peace Corps and his visionary Space Program were conduits for this kind of challenge. With his patrician, bilingual First Lady, he embraced a sophistication that established New York at the center of the world stage. When this regal couple ascended to the White House, they invited classical cellist Pablo Casals to play. The President appeared in white tie. Jacqueline Kennedy's impeccable taste upgraded popular fashion to haute couture. We were proud of this newfound American elegance. Art and intellectual pursuits were welcomed at the highest levels for the first time in my life.

Then his silver-throated eloquence was stilled by assassination and his successors were determined to return America to a more conservative path. The attempt of the Warren Commission to explain the murder seemed to me unconvincing. More than fifty years later, I remain a skeptic of the official story and its "single bullet" theory. I had learned to question the establishment whenever it seemed justified.

One person who held President Kennedy in highest regard was Joe Cino. I will describe Joe's influence on me and the eventual Circle Rep in more detail in the second chapter of this book, but at this point, I will say only that it was at the Caffé Cino I first experienced many aspects of a world of transcendence. The Cino waiter Johnny Dodd was the first man I ever saw with long hair and an earring. It was Joe Cino who first said, "Do what you have to do," which later evolved into: "Do your own thing."

Another icon for Joe was Marilyn Monroe, whose flagrant sexuality invited us to celebrate our senses. As a skinny kid from Texas, I cowered in shame from a self-image that could not compete with the prowess of football heroes, whose muscular physiques kicked sand in the faces of wimpy beanpoles like me. Then, miraculously, along came Mick Jagger and sexy was redefined. I was desirably lithe and slim —exactly what turned my generation on.

Joe Cino gave young artists in Greenwich Village a place to vent their passions and explore what they had to say, and soon he was joined by Ellen Stewart and her La MaMa Experimental Theater Club, "dedicated to the playwright and all aspects of the theater." Theater Genesis and the Judson Poets Theater (with Al Carmines) rounded out the quartet of pioneers of off-off-Broadway theater, and we were given our chance to shine.

Before long, Joseph Chaiken founded The Open Theater with Jean-Claude van Itallie; and Ellen Stewart sent her La MaMa Troupe to travel throughout Europe (under the direction of Tom

O'Horgan) to flaunt an exhilarating American re-invention of theater. Edward Albee, Sam Shepard, Lanford Wilson, John Guare, and Paul Foster enunciated new theatrical languages that expanded theater beyond the constraints of a linear narrative.

At the same time, Michael Smith and Michael Feingold at the *Village Voice* championed off-off-Broadway and started recognizing achievements with Obie Awards. New critical voices like Mel Gussow of *The New York Times* began to encourage the vibrant theatrical visions emerging in America.

At the movies, we were watching Stanley Kubrick's double-edged view of the future in *2001: A Space Odyssey* and *A Clockwork Orange*. "Happenings" were the precursor of "Raves," and many followed Timothy Leary's advice to "turn on, tune in, and drop out." Some idealists fled the polluted urban environment to form experimental rural societies called communes.

The Stonewall Riots gave rise to Gay Liberation and, hand in hand with the bra-burning emancipation of Women's Lib, young people were changing the way we saw ourselves. Of course, this new surge toward personal freedom could not have happened without the Civil Rights Movement and Dr. King, who spoke so powerfully of dreams denied. The courage of African Americans demanding equality roused people to raise their voices in protest against society's other injustices, like the unnecessary and deadly war that erupted in the Far East. These protests, sometimes reaching five-hundred-thousand strong, created a chaotic climate of change. Here was a ringing response to President Kennedy's challenge to do something for our country. Unfortunately, by the time of the Vietnam War in 1964, President Johnson denigrated these idealistic protesters as "nervous Nellies," using the slur of effeminacy to question our patriotism.

Concurrent with these political and social events was the introduction of Moore's Law, an important moment in the development of computer hardware. Moore's Law posits that the number of transistors that can be placed inexpensively on an integrated circuit increases exponentially, doubling approximately every two years.

So, important forces that govern our 21st century lives also were born in the Sixties.

In 1969, my father died. Before he passed, I rushed to the ICU. Beneath a jungle of tubes and wires, he smiled up at my hippie image and said, "I like your hair." He never pretended to understand me, but he accepted me. He was buried on the 5th of May, a date that resonates in the opening line of my first production at Circle Rep, *Three Sisters*: "Father died a year ago today, on the 5th of May." With his death, I felt the turn of destiny's wheel, putting me next in line for extinction. It was time to discover what my fate was meant to be, and how I might contribute to the world.

A month later, I took LSD for the first time. It was a life-changing event. At the risk of an uncomfortable (although I hope, not unwelcome) level of intimacy with the reader, I must describe the experience. As I was approaching a sexual climax with my partner, I experienced a sensation that my entire nervous system was hard-wired into a cosmic electronic master board; in an instant all connections were abruptly unplugged, and my essence was inundated with a blinding white light. It was a personal experience of the singularity that is thought to be the genesis of our universe – a Big Bang, indeed! My perceptions expanded vastly and instantaneously, as I acquired a celestial wisdom. It was as though I knew with certainty the answers to Eternal Questions. From a sense of peace and enlightenment, a clarity of purpose emerged that focused my consciousness on a path for a transcendent future.

A thesaurus defines transcendent as "inspiring, inspirational, uplifting, awe-inspiring, moving, and magnificent." These are words that describe the years that led up to Circle Rep's nascence.

Dictionary definitions could be seen as a description of Circle Rep's goals:
1. Better: superior in quality or achievement.
2. Beyond the limits of experience, therefore unknowable intellectually.

3. Beyond categories: a philosophy above all known beliefs.
4. Independent of the world: existing outside the material universe, and so, not limited by it.

Synonyms include:
- Passionate: fervent, ardent, zealous, obsessive, fanatical, loving, fiery.
- Spiritual: sacred, devout, divine, mystical, psychic.
- Searching: penetrating, probing, pointed, thorough, sharp, incisive.
- Believing.
- Adventurous: daring, bold, audacious, brave, risky, exploratory, courageous.
- Inspiring: uplifting, awesome, moving, magnificent.
- Evolutionary: developing in small increments that accumulate to bring about significant change.
- Experimental: new, untried, investigational.

"Ever to be best and stand above all others," is said to be Alexander the Great's favorite quotation from Homer. We strove to be that.

I'll pick up the story from this point later, but first I must retrace my steps and relate some of the events that preceded our beginning, and set us on a "magical mystery tour" that would culminate in the founding of Circle Rep on Bastille Day –July 14, 1969.

It was quite a trip.

Part One
Before The Beginning

Chapter 1

Aspirations

"I am training you for a theater that does not exist." The story of how Circle Repertory Company came into being begins with this declaration from Alvina Krause, the legendary acting teacher at Northwestern University. She fixed us with the kind of gaze an eagle focuses upon its prey.

"I am training you to be artists in a profession that prizes fame and success over artistic achievement. Always keep in mind that apart from what nature has endowed, talent is the ability to learn and grow."

We were in awe of A.K., as we called her behind her back. To her face, she was always "Miss Krause." She was a woman small in stature, but with a towering presence. Her silver hair was swept up in a chignon that crowned her head like a diadem. She almost invariably wore purple. Her eyes were a piercing steel blue that seemed able to read your very thoughts. With the assurance of Athena, she used brutal honesty in a relentless quest for truth. No compromise would be considered. She could (and did) wound deeply.

Studying with her was a privilege, not a right, and toward the end of freshman year, students were obliged to ask Miss Krause for permission to take her sophomore acting class. This was a terrifying moment, because your whole future seemed to dangle on a single thread, waiting for her acceptance. "Why?" she would demand.

My answer was: "Because I intend to devote my life to the theater, and I want to be the best actor I can be, and you're the best teacher to help me reach my goals." I was accepted.

We were more than her students; we became a Spartan army of would-be artists, dedicated to mastering acting techniques that could bring to life the great themes of dramatic literature. A.K. believed in the power of theater to enrich and change society through an illumination of the human experience. She frequently cited the Hungarian Revolution of 1956 to stir our sense of social responsibility as artists.

The "we" I refer to were her acting students, and included Paula (Ragusa) Prentiss, Richard Benjamin, Tony (Dave) Roberts, Lawrence (David) Pressman, Penny Fuller, Marcia Rodd, Stuart Hagmann, Laird Williamson, Larry Kamm, Jerry Zeismer, Russel Lunday, Jane Lowry, Nancy Killmer, Jake Dengel, Claris Nelson, Rob Thirkield, and me. Karen Black was also in my classes at Northwestern, but Miss Krause didn't like her, so she studied acting with Dr. Robert Schneideman, the default teacher for those not making the cut with A.K.

At Arizona State University, where I taught for ten years in the 1990s, my students seemed to grow younger and more culturally ignorant as each year's class rolled by. William Hurt won an Academy Award as Best Actor, and was for a time among the top box-office attractions. But by the mid-nineties, my classes were dimly aware of him, as Brad Pitt emerged for their generation. Soon, we'll be asking, "Brad *who?*"

Nevertheless, Google exists for just such a purpose, so I'll resist an impulse to fill in the impressive résumés of my classmates. Many in our class of student actors, inspired by Miss Krause to adopt the highest standards for the art of acting, achieved successful careers, but often in vehicles of entertainment that didn't fulfill their artistic potential. I joke that all my classmates became famous before me.

But my aspiration to excel was not born in A.K.'s class at Northwestern; she only articulated what began for me years earlier in a small town in southern Texas.

Discovering Excellence

In 1949, I was living with my paternal grandparents in Luling, Texas, a town of about 4,500 people, nestled between two rivers, about forty-five miles from Austin and sixty miles from San Antonio. My mother left me with my grandparents a couple of years before, when she, her new husband, and my newborn half-brother Sammy were transferred by the Air Force from Amarillo, where I was born, to New Orleans. I was meant to finish second grade in Luling before rejoining Mother, once she was settled. As it happened, I preferred my life with my grandparents and begged to continue school in Luling with my new friends. I never lived with my mother again.

Every Saturday I went to the Stanley Theater to see a double feature, complete with previews of coming attractions, a newsreel, an animated comedy, and a serial. On one of these Saturdays when I was in the fourth grade, there was something about the featured movie that deeply moved me and awakened a new level of awareness.

The film was called *Pinky*, and it was about a young, light-skinned black woman from Mississippi who passed for white when she went north to finish nursing school, and fell in love with a handsome white doctor. The essence of the film was about discovering who you really are and being true to your identity. It featured Academy Award-nominated performances from Jeanne Crain, Ethel Barrymore and Ethel Waters. But there was more to the film than the sum of its parts; so I waited through the previews, the newsreel, Bugs Bunny and an episode of *Zorro* to watch the credits roll by again as the movie started its next showing, trying to understand why this movie affected me so intensely. The final credit was "Directed by Elia Kazan." Even though I had no real concept of what a director did, I instinctively knew that Mr. Kazan was responsible for making this film so exceptional. His work set my standards for excellence at the age of nine, and they served me throughout my life in the theater.

As I entered my teen years, I went to live with my father, because the larger city of Amarillo could offer more artistic opportunity than the small town of Luling. My freshman year, I won an award for Best Actor at the regional competitions playing the role of a poet named Robert in a slight one-act comedy called *Antic Spring*. I feel sure that one reason I impressed the judges was my intuitive immersion in the circumstances of the play. I remember creating imaginary grass on which we had a picnic on the bare floor of the stage.

Seeing Marlon Brando's searing portrayal of Mark Antony in the 1953 Joseph L. Mankiewicz film of *Julius Caesar* provided an embodiment of the artistry in acting to which I aspired. Brando brought Shakespeare to life with an emotional reality that shook both me and the foundations of ancient Rome. I also belatedly saw his unprecedented Stanley Kowalski in *A Streetcar Named Desire*, (directed by my idol, Elia Kazan). These two performances are for me paragons of artistic achievement.

A year or two later, this exemplary standard was joined and even elevated by James Dean's incandescent Cal in Elia Kazan's *East of Eden*. Coupled with *Rebel without a Cause*, Dean defined teenage angst for a generation in what is recognized as one of the most influential performances in movie history.

Kazan directed two of the four performances that signified for me what the art of acting could achieve, so naturally, I was curious about his other accomplishments. At the Amarillo High School library, I discovered the *Burns Mantle Best Plays Theater Yearbook*. Inside, the plays chosen as the best of each Broadway season were summarized. I was hungry for any morsel of information about the theater, so I devoured them volume by volume.

Here I discovered the plays that Kazan directed on Broadway, so I was introduced to the work of Arthur Miller and Tennessee Williams. *Death of a Salesman* and *All My Sons* expanded my world. Based on the films I'd seen of Kazan's work, I imagined how each play he directed must have come to life. The same was true for *A Streetcar Named Desire* and especially *Cat on a Hot Tin Roof*. I enjoyed the film version of *Cat* (directed by Richard Brooks), but when I read the summarized play in the *Best Plays Yearbook*, I imagined how Kazan's direction electrified the life of the play on stage. I could sense how palpable the performances of Barbara Bel Geddes, Ben Gazzara and Mildred Dunnock must have been, based on the evidence of Burl Ives and Madeleine Sherwood, Kazan's original cast members who repeated their roles in the movie. Imagining Kazan's stage version inspired me to direct my first production at Northwestern a couple of years later.

A School of Stars

As I approached graduation, I expected to study acting at the University of Texas, where I had a small scholarship. But one Sunday afternoon, a high-school friend spotted me in my front yard and stopped to chat. He asked about college and I told him my plans. He said he intended to go to Northwestern University, "because Northwestern has the best school of theater in the country."

Intrigued by this claim, the next day I went to my high school drama teacher, Mrs. Whitworth, and asked her what she knew about Northwestern. It turned out she received her Master's Degree from N.U. and she provided me with catalogues that described everything I needed to know.

I discovered that many famous stars of stage, television and film studied at Northwestern, including four Academy Award winners: Charlton Heston (*Ben-Hur*), Jennifer Jones (*Song of Bernadette*), Patricia Neal (*Hud*) and Cloris Leachman (*The Last Picture Show*). Other Northwestern alumni included the distinguished Broadway director Gerald Freedman, Tony Award-winning writer George Furth and Pulitzer Prize-winning critic, Walter Kerr. I immediately applied for admission. Even though many of these accomplishments were achieved long after I was reading the Northwestern catalogue, there were plenty at the time to whet my desire for the best.

It was well past the February 15th deadline for applications, and even worse, Northwestern was very expensive. There was no way I could go there without a substantial scholarship. Nevertheless, shortly before graduation in May, I received a letter of acceptance, along with a full academic scholarship that covered tuition, room and board. My dream of pursuing my dreams was coming true.

The train trip from Amarillo to Chicago aboard the San Francisco Chief traversed more than mere miles. The curves of Lake Shore Drive delivered me to Sheridan Road and the lush green campus of Northwestern on the edge of Lake Michigan. My life as a freshman was precisely the expansion of experience that college promises. I met people from all over the country, detected that my accent needed correction, discovered that there was such a thing in America as anti-Semitism (which had been unknown to me in Texas), and encountered the joys of philosophic thought from Plato, through Hume, to Nietzsche.

Freshmen had to focus on orientation to the new life of academia, so participation in the university theater productions on the Main Stage was discouraged. Instead, I spent my first year ridding myself of an unbearably nasal West Texas drawl. I learned to aspirate my vowels, enunciate my consonants and find the true timbre for my voice, which was far lower than my teenage tension was producing. By the end of my freshman year, my origins were undetectable from my speech.

I managed to squeeze in a couple of stage appearances. I played a small role in a student-directed workshop of Ugo Betti's *The Queen and the Rebels*. Dr. Lee Mitchell was the Chair of the Theater Department and he cast me as a servant in his production of Philip Massinger's 1827 comedy *A New Way to Pay Old Debts*. I doubt either of my performances impressed anyone.

Although Miss Krause was the dominant presence at Northwestern and her spirit hovered over all dramatic activities, the first production I saw on the main stage was Dr. Schneideman's *Waiting for Godot*, with Jake Dengel and Wayne King. It was a wondrous experience and, in my mind, it brought Beckett's masterpiece definitively to life. It was followed by *A Servant of Two Masters*, where I first saw the luminous talent of Nancy Killmer. Northwestern was living up to its hype.

Excellence Across The Stage

In Miss Krause's sophomore class in acting, she addressed us by our last names (Pressman, Roberts, Ragusa, etc.), and trained us in Stanislavski's basic principles of acting: relaxation, concentration and using the creative imagination. We learned public solitude, the "Magic If," and how to identify imaginary circumstances (who, what, where, when, why and how). It was in this class I first heard Miss Krause's ruthless dismissal of untruthful acting: "Cut! Flunk! *Next!*"

I began my second year appearing in the main stage production of Anouilh's *Legend of Lovers*, playing the small part of Louie, the poor company manager of an acting troupe who couldn't manage very well. James Gousseff, a doctoral student who was Miss Krause's assistant, directed the production, which featured Ragusa opposite Paul Hardy as the young lovers, with Roberts and Delphi Nikopoulos (Harrington) as the older, morally corrupt stars of the company. The set was an extremely raked stage (one-inch rise for each foot). The excitement of playing on such a steeply angled set influenced many design choices after I became a director.

Then I had the good fortune of being cast as the Station Master in Miss Krause's production of Chekhov's *The Cherry Orchard*. The Station Master is one of the party guests in the third act and has no written lines; but in a stage direction, Chekhov has him recite Tolstoy's *The Magdalene* during a pause in the dancing. We rehearsed for months. My wife was played by Michelle Formberg and we improvised our life together, creating a marriage that lasted for decades. We decided we were now elderly and that I had advanced from being a peasant boy, working his way up as a railroad employee, until I was named manager of the railway station when my supervisor passed away. I imagined that the only distinction in my entire life came in grade school, when I'd won a prize for reciting Tolstoy's poem. Our scenario was that now we'd been invited to the big mansion for the first time. Naturally, I felt obligated to bring something to the party.

The act begins with all the guests waltzing. The Station Master dances with Varya, the eldest daughter of the house (played by Jane Lowry). When there was a break in the music, I saw my opportunity to make my small contribution. Climbing onto a chair, I proudly began to recite Tolstoy's poem in the cadences of announcing destinations at the departure of trains ("Kiev! Minsk! Vilnius! Riga! All aboard!"). I was so wrapped up in my recitation I failed to notice that as the orchestra began to play again, my audience dispersed, resuming the waltz. My wife tugged at my coat, and I blushed (I am told) as I realized my situation. I climbed down, replaced the chair and, covering my embarrassment, threw myself into waltzing with my wife.

It was a splendid production. The process by which we explored the life of the play provided a pattern I have followed in all my subsequent work in the theater. My book, *Creating Life on Stage: A Director's Approach to Working with Actors* describes it in detail. (Heinemann Press, 2006.)

Particularly, I remember two extraordinary performances in *The Cherry Orchard*: Rob Thirkield's touching characterization as the ancient servant Firs, who is forgotten, left behind to die as the final curtain falls; and Pressman's charismatic portrayal of a neighboring landowner, Pischik. In the fourth act, Pischik realizes that the orchard has been sold, and that his friends will be leaving forever. His blustery reassurance, "Never mind, never mind," was capped at his exit with involuntary tears, as he choked out, "My daughter, Dashenka, sends her regards." Now excellence in acting was visible across the stage from where I stood.

As my first year of study with Miss Krause came to a close, I faced another crossroads in my artistic development. Every summer since 1945, A.K. took her best and brightest students to a summer theater called The Playhouse in Eagles Mere, Pennsylvania, which she operated with Lucy McCammon, her companion of many years. It was at Eagles Mere that Jake Dengel's fabled performance of *Hamlet* occurred, and where Patricia Neal played Ruth in *Blithe Spirit*.

After making A's in Miss Krause's acting class, I asked her if she'd be taking me to Eagles Mere, along with the best of my classmates. Her reply stunned me: "I don't think so."

Since I had implicit faith in Miss Krause's judgment, I suddenly perceived that I was not going to be a great actor. Of course, my reaction was magnified by teenage insecurity. As the quarter ended, I determined that my best course of action was to leave the theater altogether, because if I could not be the best, I didn't want to delude myself any further. Since I excelled as a debater in high school, I thought maybe I should transfer into pre-law to study a profession in which I thought I might do well.

The Joy Of Rep

In May, Jim Gousseff gave an end-of-the-term party in his off-campus apartment. I recall there was a good deal of Rhine wine. As kids celebrated the conclusion of another year of college, Jim cornered me and asked if the rumor he'd heard was true: was I planning to leave the theater?

I explained that unless I could be the best at acting, I didn't think I should continue. Jim said forcefully that the theater needed people who believed in it as I did. "Maybe you should try another role. Have you thought about directing?"

In the previous spring quarter, Stu Hagmann directed a mesmerizing production of Tennessee Williams' *Suddenly Last Summer* and I served as his assistant director. I learned a great deal from this experience, especially from Stu's use of music to frame the mood of the play. I thoroughly enjoyed being part of the directorial process.

"Well," I answered Jim hesitantly, "there *is* a play I'd like to direct." What I had in mind was to fulfill my imagined production of *Cat on a Hot Tin Roof*. It had no parts in it that I could play – even though I identified with Brick, Maggie, Skipper, Big Mama and even Big Daddy. I felt that if I *could* write a play, *Cat* was the play I'd want to write. It was about things that concerned me personally: sexual identity, alcoholism, suicide, death, hypocrisy, even being poor and desperate. Although I enjoyed the film with Elizabeth Taylor and Paul Newman, I longed to deal with the truth of Brick's tortured sexuality, which was all but invisible in the film.

Jim advised me to try out for Northwestern's summer theater program, which mounted four great plays in repertory outdoors on a festival stage erected adjacent to the theater building. Jim assured me that I'd get at least one good role; then, I could direct *Cat* in the fall in a student workshop production. If I still felt I didn't belong in the theater, I could reconsider my options. This sounded like an appropriate plan, and I knew my friend Rob Thirkield had elected to stay for the summer rep, rather than return to Eagles Mere. So, I agreed to audition.

The summer repertoire was to be:
- Sophocles' *Oedipus Rex*, directed by Dr. Schneideman,
- Shakespeare's *A Midsummer Night's Dream*, directed by Jim Gousseff,

- Shaw's *Saint Joan*, directed by Jack Clay, and
- Sheridan's *The Rivals*, directed by John Van Meter.

Laird Williamson and I were cast in the chorus of *Oedipus* (Rob played the seer, Tiresias). I was Philostrate, the Master of the Revels in *Dream* (Rob played Peter Quince, and Laird, Oberon). I was double cast in *Saint Joan* as Courcelles and the Gentleman from the Vatican (while Rob played Bishop Cauchon, and Laird, Brother Ladvenu). My plum part was Faulkland, the comic romantic lead in *The Rivals,* opposite Laird as Jack Absolute and Ardyth Hamburg as Mrs. Malaprop.

Evanston, Illinois is a perfect place to spend a summer by the lake, doing what you love best. Every morning, I woke up, looked at the calendar and discovered *who* I was to *be* that night!

All the productions were good. Paul Hardy was a credible Oedipus and Delphi, a regal Jocasta. The costumes for *Dream* were by Northwestern's brilliant designer Paul Reinhart, in the style of the French renaissance, with flowing yards of drapery on every character. *Saint Joan* was also well done and *The Rivals* was a romp. By donning an eighteenth century wig, I discovered how handsome I might have been in an earlier era. The melodic undulations of Sheridan's elaborately structured dialogue were both a joy and a challenge: cascades of verbiage that required exquisite diction and firm breath-control. I received a good review from the campus newspaper.

The outdoor stage was at the side of the theater building in a garden setting, surrounded by lilac shrubbery. A faux-Elizabethan stage was erected, a lower deck reached by ramps and an upper deck reached from the first level by a symmetrical pair of stairways. The apron thrust into the audience, who were seated in bleacher-like seats, situated between banks of lights elevated on telephone pole-like stanchions. Because I was on stage every night, I can only imagine that the audience experienced a delightful summer evening of theater. We were sold out every performance.

There can be no doubt that the experience of playing rotating rep profoundly influenced my vision of what theater should be. All the great theaters in history, from the ancient Greeks to the nineteenth century in Europe, played a schedule of rotating rep. Only in America did it seem we had forgotten one of the fundamentals that kept theater fresh and alive throughout the ages. Not surprisingly, when I created a theater some ten years later, it was a repertory company.

Distinction In Directing

When classes resumed, I applied to direct one of the student productions. These workshops featured three short productions (we were limited to fifty minutes each, a rule I brazenly broke), directed by three different students for one night only. The performances were on the main stage, on a Monday night after a University Theater production had closed. Following the presentation of the three plays, Miss Krause conducted an immediate public evaluation of each production, giving detailed critiques of the actors' and the directors' work. These critiques were sometimes rather harsh and no one in the audience ever left his seat until Miss Krause finished her critique. It was akin to a blood sport.

When I told A.K. that I wanted to direct *Cat*, she wrinkled her nose and questioned why I wanted to do such a distasteful play. She thought Big Daddy's elephant joke in the third act was obscene. I explained that my cutting of the play included only the first two acts, and that I thought *Cat* was an important play for our time, with its blistering attack on hypocrisy. She gave me the go-ahead.

My readings for Maggie included Karen Black and Marcia Rodd, but I selected Ardyth Hamburg. Ardy had been Anya in *The Cherry Orchard*, Mrs. Malaprop in *The Rivals*, and played the Judy Holiday role in *Born Yesterday* at Eagles Mere, apparently to dumb-blonde perfection. She had the wholesome, cheerleader qualities that would give Maggie a balance of strength, determination and vulnerability. After the auditions, Karen accosted me: "You didn't cast me because you think I'm too neurotic." There was some truth to that.

For Brick, I found Larry Kamm, who, although he was small, matched well with Ardy. He was well built and looked good in a towel, so I could believe him as a football player, albeit on a Doug Flutie scale. A large, affable student named Weldon Bleiler, had the qualities to make an effective Big Daddy. Robin Deck was perfect for Sister Woman, and Marvin Gottlieb was sympathetic casting for Gooper.

Our rehearsals were in fluorescent-lighted classrooms, requiring considerable imagination to transform their sterility into a sumptuous bedroom on Big Daddy's plantation. I plunged into rehearsals with the conviction of a young Stanislavski. The goals of the production were high: we were going to *live* the parts. I detested "blocking" in the mechanical sense of a director assigning movement to actors. I passionately believed that *all* movement should be organic, based on actors' impulses, arising from belief in the circumstances of the play. I insisted on the highest standards of discipline and this included learning the lines for each beat of the play in advance, to use as a "map we could explore." I broke the play down into "beats" of action, the foundation of a dramatic structure. We spent the first week improvising background situations and relationships.

At one rehearsal, an actor arrived ten minutes late. I indignantly announced that the creativity of the rehearsal had been irreparably damaged by his implicit lack of concern. Following Stanislavski's lead, rather than carry on in a dispirited atmosphere, I dismissed the cast and walked out in a dudgeon. I wandered about the campus for about ten minutes, cooling down, and then returned to the rehearsal room to see what the actors decided to do in my absence. Fortunately, they conscientiously remained and proceeded to run their lines, chastened and unwilling to waste any more rehearsal time. I was pleased with their conscientiousness and we had an exceptionally creative rehearsal that night. A couple of years later, I tried this again in my first New York production. With professional actors, I was stunned when I returned ten minutes later: they'd all gone home!

At the age of nineteen, for me art had a capital "A" and my approach was certainly serious with a capital "S." My cast, accustomed to Miss Krause's domineering personality, rose to my every challenge, as I spurred them on with encouragement. We worked together tirelessly and joyfully to achieve a living play. I somehow managed to get each actor to believe in my vision, which set our goals high, aiming for the best each of us had to offer. This would be the performance of our lives!

At the penultimate rehearsal (our first time on stage), Miss Krause sat in the back row of the theater, watching the dress rehearsal. At the end, I went over for her assessment. All she said was, "It's very well-staged." The anger I nursed from her rejection the previous spring flared. "What do you mean, 'staged?'" I demanded. "The blocking," she replied. "It isn't blocked at all!" I hotly informed her. "The movement is *all* organic," which implied that *my* standards were higher than *hers*.

The next night the three productions played their one and only performance. The first two plays were performed, and then, finally, my *Cat on a Hot Tin Roof* played for the only audience who would ever see it. The two prior productions were each within the fifty-minute regulation, but my *Cat* ran seventy minutes. I was nervous that I would be called on the carpet for breaking the rules.

Miss Krause strode down front at the conclusion of the productions and prepared to give her oral critique of the work. These always were awaited anxiously, and the mood resembled that of a crowd at an execution by guillotine.

Miss Krause gave evaluations for each actor and director in the previous productions, and then launched into her appraisals of *Cat*. She praised each of the actors, giving thoughtful consideration to the progress each had made in the process of learning. She was especially appreciative of the work of Ardy as Maggie, Larry as Brick, and Weldon as Big Daddy, saying it was the best work each of them had done and that they'd achieved a new plateau of artistry.

Then she paused and fixed the audience with that eagle eye that put the fear of God into us. "I suppose," she said carefully, "you all noticed the superlative direction."

The entire audience leapt to their feet in thundering agreement. I was stunned. I had never seen a standing ovation at Northwestern, and I couldn't believe it was for me.

Following my auspicious debut, I was eager to direct again. In the spring, I was approved to stage Euripides' *The Trojan Women*. I wrote original music to which the choruses were sung, as if they were familiar folk songs of the people. Although I did not have a strong personal attachment to the play, I was passionate about the urgent anti-war theme, which gave the production power. It, too, was well received.

I asked Miss Krause if now she wanted me to come to Eagles Mere. This time she said yes. I would play a number of roles but more importantly, I would direct Friedrich Schiller's *Mary Stuart*. Penny Fuller was to play Mary and Paula Ragusa was to be Elizabeth. But before the quarter ended, a talent scout from MGM came to Northwestern and whisked Paula away to become a movie star (Paula Prentiss in *Where the Boys Are*). She was replaced by Claris Nelson, one of my most constant collaborators over the next fifty years.

At the end-of-year convocation, I received an award for best student director of 1959. The award was a book by the historic director Gordon Craig, inscribed by the faculty.

Merit At Eagles Mere

The Playhouse was founded in 1945 by Alvina Krause and Lucy McCammon to use students from Northwestern (and also outstanding actors from other universities) to perform a series of great plays, classical and contemporary, for a summer-subscription audience of vacationers in the mountains of Pennsylvania.

Apart from The Playhouse, Eagles Mere had few other enterprises. There were some lakeside cottages, a filling station, a post office and a general store. Across the lake loomed the faded elegance of once-posh resorts: the Lakeside Hotel, the Crestmont Inn and the Edgemere Hotel, all popular from the 1880s to the 1960s, but in decline since the 20s.

A.K. and Lucy owned a house on a street near an old-fashioned soda fountain called The Sweet Shoppe. Between the two was a rambling Victorian house with about twenty bedrooms where the students were housed. The Lodge, as it was called, had an enormous dining room with two long tables covered with oilcloth that could accommodate the thirty members of the company. There was a large kitchen and pantry, and the only paid professional was a cook. We each drew "KP" on a rotating basis to pay for our room and board. Lucy must have done the grocery shopping when she wasn't out in her rowboat, fishing. There was a small living room with worn furniture and an adjoining room with a pay telephone, mailboxes and a bulletin board, on which our rehearsal schedules could be found, as well as the written critiques Miss Krause posted in a "blue book" after each production. There was no television. The screened-in back porch had been transformed into a costume shop. Behind the house, a dilapidated garage was adapted into a shop where we produced silk-screen posters to advertise each show.

In addition to KP, we spent time (when not in rehearsal) on the crews for publicity, costumes, set-construction, props, or lighting. The sets were built in a series of old sheds near the theater, which provided storage as well as building space. The prop room was a lean-to attached to the backstage of the theater. Lighting equipment was stored in a loft above the rear of the auditorium. The students performed all the chores at Eagles Mere, from household duties to box-office staff to construction and running crews. We had only Sundays off, but even then, we wouldn't stray far – most of the time only next door to The Sweet Shoppe to enjoy a mug of crystal clear birch beer and to listen to a favorite song on the radio ("Once there were green fields, kissed by the sun; once there were valleys, where rivers used to run..."). Once or twice in the course of the summer, a group piled into the "company car," a rattle-trap jalopy, and drove over to Laporte, the Sullivan County seat, to catch a movie like *Psycho*, which was released that summer.

The Playhouse offered nine productions, from mid-June to late August. They each played a week for four performances. Although the productions were performed sequentially, rehearsals were conducted in repertory fashion. The production that was scheduled to open two weeks away rehearsed in the mornings, from nine to noon. There was a two-hour lunch break, and then the production that opened the following week rehearsed in the afternoon from two to five. There was a two-hour dinner break, then the current play had a tech rehearsal on Monday, a dress rehearsal on Tuesday, and afterwards, performed Wednesday through Saturday nights at eight.

The intense daily routine started with breakfast at 7:30 A.M. and ended frequently as late as midnight. This grueling schedule wore out even young people in the prime of endurance. By the end of August, most students swore they'd **NEVER AGAIN** come back to Eagles Mere, a protestation often forgotten by the following spring.

The Playhouse itself was a drafty old building with a cramped, eccentric proscenium stage and tiny retiring rooms on each side backstage. The make-up room was in the basement and an exterior stairway led from the dressing rooms below to the backstage wings. There was no interior crossover, so if one exited Stage Left and had to enter Stage Right, it required a trek through the woods at the rear of the theater. The Playhouse accommodated about two hundred patrons, as well as a friendly family of bats, who made an occasional appearance during performances.

The repertoire during the twenty seasons A.K. operated The Playhouse included the great playwrights from the Renaissance to the twentieth century. After offering eight challenging plays, she scheduled a light comedy or musical that might make a little at the box-office and be less taxing to an exhausted company.

The Transcendent Years

My first summer at Eagles Mere in 1960, we opened with Shaw's *Pygmalion*, in which I played Freddy Eynsford-Hill. Madly in love with Eliza (played by Linda Radley), I used Freddy's song from *My Fair Lady*, "On the Street Where You Live," as my subtext. Lerner and Lowe's musical adaptation was still the biggest hit on Broadway at the time. Wayne King (whom I'd admired so much in *Waiting for Godot*) was a charmingly eccentric Higgins. Dave (Tony) Roberts both directed and played Doolittle. I don't know how good the production was; Miss Krause had reservations about our ability to deliver Shaw's wit with the requisite

"...rapidity and clarity, building involved sentences to brilliant climaxes that are aimed straight at a target and never miss."

But I had a wonderful time in my first juvenile role. Miss Krause praised my

"vibrant joy in interpreting the character of Freddy, not freely enough in Act I, but excellent in Act III."

Up next, Stu Hagmann directed a lovely *Streetcar Named Desire*, for which Miss Krause had nothing but praise:

"A triumph in acting and directing. The total performance of this drama will be memorable always."

My recollection of J.M. Barrie's *Quality Street* is dim, due no doubt to the fact that as we were performing it, I had begun morning improvisations for *Mary Stuart*.

Meanwhile in Los Angeles, far from the "Pocono Endless Mountains" of Eagles Mere, J.F.K. received the Democratic nomination for President. Sans television, we read about it the next morning in the local paper, little aware of the changes in store.

I remember even less about my supporting role in Maxwell Anderson's *Barefoot in Athens*. I was in my second week of rehearsals, staging *Mary Stuart* in the afternoons. Wayne King was a splendid Socrates. As A.K. put it:

"Much of the credit must go to Wayne for his ability to embody the Socratic ideal in human form; to present it in so rational a way that it becomes a living thing. Laird did his best acting to date. He made his points with the energy required and no excess. Marshall did the same, with excellent pointing of ideas. He needs to watch that pieces of business are not studied. It is sometimes a little too evident that he has sought a particular effect. He is right in what he achieves, but it could happen more easily and naturally."

The following Monday we had our tech rehearsal for *Mary Stuart*. The complicated sets were designed by my long-time colleague, extraordinary lighting designer and close friend, Dennis Parichy. The action alternates between Westminster Palace and Mary's prison in Fotheringay Castle, with one interval in a park inserted in the middle. The set was one large wall that pivoted back and forth, Westminster on one side and the prison on the other. As with many tech rehearsals, all did not go smoothly and, in what was typical of her Monday night critiques, Miss Krause demanded: "So! What are you going to *do* about it?" It's surprising that rather than discourage us, this familiar gauntlet always fueled new resolve to fix the problems.

The dress rehearsal went somewhat better. The costumes by Mary Strachan were opulent and perfect in period detail. Claris looked like an Elizabethan portrait come to life, awash in pearls and brocades. Penny glowed with an inspirational radiance, whether in severe black, topped with Mary's heart-shaped bonnet, or in the dazzling white gown she wore to her death. There were several other notable performances, particularly Roberts as Leicester, the dashing favorite of the Queen; Pressman as Talbot, Keeper of the Seal; and Laird as the romantically doomed Mortimer. Wayne King, who played the Sheriff of Northampton, used a long white staff ceremonially to accompany Mary to her execution and, with each step, the sound of his staff striking the deck reminded the audience of the blade about to fall on Mary's neck.

A.K.'s critique said:

    "Our production was distinctive; first, because it had clarity of purpose, which gripped the audience in what they might call 'suspense,' but which we recognize as 'inevitability.' Secondly, it was distinctive because we found the music of the drama, not only the cadences of the verse which, with a few exceptions, was exceedingly well-spoken; but also, the over-all music, rhythm, surge of the whole. There was a flow of sequence to sequence; a current of sound, movement, reverberation that flowed from scene to scene...The performance of Saturday night came closest to sending people home in the right frame of mind: they were moved by tragic events, but a sense of good theater exalted them *above* the realities. And that is the ideal theater experience."

During the run of *Mary Stuart,* Richard Nixon received the Republican nomination for President in Chicago.

Sunrise at Campobello slipped by me almost unnoticed (I was rehearsing Malvolio), except for the vibrant performances of Pressman as F.D.R. and of Killmer's Eleanor. Miss Krause:

    "Pressman's work is amazingly complete, yet like Nancy's, unstudied. He creates, he believes in what he creates, and so do we."

I had the time of my life playing Malvolio in *Twelfth Night.* I had the pleasure of playing opposite Penny Fuller as Viola and the lovely Gretchen Walther as Olivia. Miss Krause's evaluation curbed my self-esteem a bit:

    "Marshall's difficulties are technical. He created a character admirably. But having created Malvolio, he doesn't quite permit him to respond freely to the situations, and so he is sometimes studied; *or* he lets go too completely, and the situation and character go out of control. Marshall's line delivery is not sure: he drops words, or fails to land the line. He, like most of you, has not yet learned how to snap a line at the end so that it *releases* laughter."

I would play Malvolio again twenty years later at Circle Rep under the direction of David Mamet to (I hope) better effect.

Nancy Killmer was Claire Zachanassian in *The Visit*, with Wayne King as her nemesis, Anton Schill. These roles were created on Broadway by the great Lynne Fontanne and Alfred Lunt, and I was fortunate to have seen them on tour in Chicago. The standard of excellence the Lunts established is legendary. She, in particular, was unforgettable; but as much as I admired Miss Fontanne from the audience, I was equally thrilled with Killmer across the stage from me. Krause's critique:

"The play became the drama of a *town*, not of individuals in a town... It was hard hitting every moment, yet it was always theater to be enjoyed. Everyone played in the same style, everyone was in an ensemble. Everyone contributed to the whole: Mason's walk off after preventing Schill's escape – the epitome of 'We have done the right thing.' Nancy's work and Wayne's work can only be spoken of in superlatives. Nancy's creation of Claire was true art... a real triumph."

I learned how much easier it is to act well when your acting partner is brilliant; it's as though she gives you your performance.

In a display of versatility, the following week Killmer was *Auntie Mame* and I played Mr. Babcock. We were so exhausted by the summer's end I doubt I had the energy to be "studied." As the final play of the season, *Mame* had no critique from Miss Krause, but I can certify that Nancy was as hilarious as Mame as she had been blood-curdling in *The Visit*.

There was barely time to recover before we were back at Northwestern, and I was busy with my senior year. There had been an international competition to select the best new play from Latin America, and the winner of the Rosamond Gilder

Award was an Argentine play, *The Bridge at Rio Campana* by Carlos Gorostiza. Northwestern agreed to present the winning play as a University Theater production. For the first time in memory, an undergraduate was selected to direct on the main stage. This singular honor was mine. The play was a social drama about the inequity of classes in Argentina, with a rather melodramatic plot. I think we performed it well. On November 8th, during our rehearsals, John F. Kennedy was elected the 35th President of the United States.

Glimpses Of The Future

In early December, I made my first trip to New York City, where I was to be interviewed for a Fulbright Scholarship. The airplane flew up the Hudson River, giving me a breathtaking introduction to Manhattan before we landed at La Guardia. At the audition, actors were provided for me to demonstrate my directorial skills. I came prepared to direct the paperboy scene from *A Streetcar Named Desire*. When I walked in, I was introduced to the panel who would appraise my work; they included a director named Stuart Vaughn, and the great actress from Kazan's productions of *Death of a Salesman* and *Cat on a Hot Tin Roof*, Mildred Dunnock. The panel watched as I worked on the scene, supplying the actors with a running commentary about the environment: the heat, the humidity of the rainy summer evening, the sounds of life outside in the French Quarter, the aroma of Blanche's perfume, the taste still on the boy's lips of the cherry soda he's just enjoyed. Altogether, I felt good about how the actors responded to my subliminal coaching, even though I felt pretty silly auditioning: directing is *not* a performing art.

At the conclusion, the panel evaluated what they'd seen. Stuart Vaughn was aggressively hostile. "What were you trying to do, hypnotize the actors?" I hated him on the spot, perceiving that his directorial approach was at polar opposites from mine. Mildred Dunnock, on the other hand, was warm and appreciative, and I felt no matter what the results, I achieved something worth more than the scholarship: the acknowledgement in Miss Dunnock's approving brown eyes. She recognized a fellow artist.

Then I saw my first Broadway show. *Camelot* had just opened and I walked up to the box-office five minutes before eight and innocently inquired if they had a single ticket. Amazingly, there was an unclaimed house seat, so I saw the second performance of *Camelot* with Richard Burton, Julie Andrews, Roddy McDowell and Robert Goulet from the orchestra in a second-row center-aisle seat. It was, and remains, the most spectacular show I ever saw on Broadway. The opulent gold sets, gracefully changing from the sleepy snowdrifts of winter to the expectant buds of May, would cost millions in today's economy. And of course, hearing Julie Andrews effortlessly trill those lilting tunes right before my very ears was an indescribable treat. I practically levitated up the aisle for intermission, thrilled by the glorious soliloquy Burton delivered in Shakespearean style that ended the act.

I didn't get the Fulbright, which was probably the proverbial disguised blessing, because if I'd got it, I'd have gone to England for a year, missed my productions at the Caffé Cino, and perhaps never met Lanford Wilson. The theater for which Miss Krause trained us might never have come into existence.

In January, President Kennedy gave his memorable inaugural address, asking us what we could do for our country. In March, he founded the Peace Corps, and in May, he set the nation's goals for putting a man on the moon within the decade.

In the winter quarter, Miss Krause directed *King Lear* with the twenty-year-old Pressman in the daunting title role. He remains the best Lear in my experience, having seen a dozen (and directed my own production). Pressman's timeless characterization of the tragic king was honest and deep. His catastrophic rashness destroyed him, and he spoke the part with eloquence. Claris played his Cordelia, Roberts, his Kent and, since I was only in the first scene as Burgundy, I could watch the rest of the play from the wings. I never missed a moment of Pressman's performance. It was a towering achievement that raised a bar.

In her acting classes, Miss Krause sometimes demonstrated the art of acting by giving us a glimpse of a character that totally took over her being. If a student brought in the Messenger's speech from *Medea*, A.K. would leap on stage, lift a knee, press her back against the proscenium, and transform into Medea; her body writhing with pleasure, devouring every word of Jason's demise, pulling the story from her partner with electrifying sexual energy. She was revenge incarnate. It made the hair on the back of your neck stand in awe of the power of retribution.

Or, revealing the treasures hidden in the verse of Shakespeare, she would *become* Cleopatra, her voice trembling with the might of a monarch but revealing the ache of a mortal, singing the vowels and consonants, each image thrillingly articulated and filled with feeling:

"I dreamed there was an emperor, Antony:–
O, such another sleep, that I might see
Such another man!"

The spinning world seemed to stop at this woman's sorrow. You held your breath in wonder at the depth of feeling she could pour into the words: the onomatopoeic clash of consonants, crashing on waves of the emotion flooding the elongated vowels.

One of the best demonstrations came from a scene in Anouilh's *Becket*. Pressman and Dennis Longwell were working on Henry II and Becket. In the scene, the two men meet after years of separation in which they've come to personify completely opposing forces. In their youth, these two were the closest of blood brothers, indulging in the dissolute revelry of youth, all raging hormones, drunken orgies and wild blood, even sharing the beds of the women they deflowered. Then the King made the mistake of appointing his buddy to become the Archbishop of Canterbury, casting his best friend in the role of his mortal enemy. In the scene, they meet some twenty years later in frigid opposition in the middle of a battlefield on a frozen plain, their respective armies chafing at their backs with impatience to destroy each other.

Miss Krause watched the two students skim lightly over the dialogue, which has a smooth, indifferent surface. She decided to demonstrate how the scene was all about the hidden subtext, the bitter longing for lost love that lay beneath the casual words. She joined Pressman on stage and proposed an improvisation. She set the circumstances as ten years after Pressman's graduation. Pressman was her favorite: clearly the deepest, most honest actor of our class, and the one with the most potential to become a great artist. The improv went something like this:

"Hello, Dave."
"Hello, Miss Krause."
"You're looking well. Quite handsome, in fact."
"Thank you."
"I've followed your career."
"Yes?"
"I understand you'll have a new series this year."
"Yes, on NBC."
"I'm sure it will be successful."

All the while, with a frozen half-smile on her lips, she fixed on him her penetrating gaze. Her subtext was, "What became of that great artist in you? Why have you settled for so little?" Pressman felt the burden of the future weighing against him, and although he was in agony, he was too proud to admit the failure he could read in her critical, stony stare.

I learned more about subtext in this simple demonstration than in any other moment in school. Ironically, Pressman remembers this as the most despicable manipulation he ever experienced; he was humiliated by the unspoken prediction that he would sell out his talent to commercial success. I'm sorry that it took his suffering to teach me an essential artistic lesson. Forty years later, after a television career that included playing the father of Doogie

Howser, he had the sweetest revenge on Miss Krause's uncharitable prophesy when he played Tyrone in my *Long Day's Journey into Night,* rich in subtext. He eventually became the consummate artist promised in his youth.

Later in my life, I had the honor of directing Jessica Tandy, who was the best actor I ever worked with; but moment for moment, Miss Krause was her equal. What separated them was Ms. Tandy's miraculous ability to create her role freshly night after night as if it had never been done before, and yet at the same time, repeat it exactly in perfect detail. At Eagles Mere, Miss Krause played several roles prior to my arrival. I'm sure her portrayals of the Dowager Empress in *Anastasia* and Miss Moffat in *The Corn Is Green* were high points in the history of Eagles Mere. She always insisted she didn't like to act; it was too nerve-racking. But for a few moments in class, she could and did throw herself fully into some of the greatest characters in drama, with spontaneous relish and absolute mastery.

In the spring quarter, I directed another student workshop, this time of Ibsen's beautiful play *The Wild Duck.* I cast Laird as Hjalmar and Stu as Gregers, and they were both magnificent. It's a play I wish I could have done again.

My mother, my stepfather, Otis, and my half-brother, Sammy, came from California to Evanston for my graduation, as did my proud father from Texas. When I brought my father to meet Miss Krause, she was every inch a dowager empress. When we came into her living room she was seated on a high-backed chair that resembled a throne. She rose regally and approached my father with one arm extended, as if she fully expected him to kiss her hand. When he shook hands with her, she pulled him close and whispered something in his ear. I was thrilled with this royal display of her powerful persona. Afterwards, I asked my father what she had whispered to him and he told me: "She said, 'Your son is going to be a great director!'" My belief in Miss Krause endowed this oracular pronouncement with conviction. If she said it, it was undoubtedly true. I had a destiny to fulfill.

During my years at Northwestern, I was keenly influenced by the new wave of foreign films that came to the art cinemas of Chicago. Ingmar Bergman's masterpiece *Wild Strawberries* and Federico Fellini's starkly existential *La Strada* both offered additional visions of excellence. But my new god was the French film director Francoise Truffaut. His indelible portrait of a young man's struggle to survive an indifferent world in *The 400 Blows* defined the heights of artistry I hoped to achieve. It was (and still is) my favorite film of all time.

Eagles Mere Reprise

Then suddenly, I graduated from college, and was returning to Eagles Mere for my final summer. I was to direct Shaw's *The Doctor's Dilemma* and Rostand's sweeping romance, *Cyrano de Bergerac*. I'd also play Belcredi in Pirandello's *Henry IV*. As Chubby Checker put it so astutely: "Let's twist again, like we did last summer!"

Laird and Ellen Tucker made a lovely couple in *Green Grow the Lilacs*, the Lynn Riggs play that the musical *Oklahoma!* was based on. This play was perhaps the origin of "lyric realism," the style for which Circle Rep became famous.

I loved directing *The Doctor's Dilemma*. My production featured a cast-full of fine characterizations, including Dennis Longwell as Dr. Ridgeon, Vance Jeffries as the dying artist Dubedat, and a lustrous Nancy Douglas (related to Supreme Court Justice Douglas) as Jennifer, the artist's wife. A.K.'s critique summed it up:

> "Brilliant Shaw: good to look at, good to listen to; Shaw played with audacity, intelligence and passion. Brilliant style, clarity of idea, clarity of speech, a clear, straight line of action, clear objectives, excellent ensemble – all add up to brilliance."

Cyrano was celebrated as the 150th production at Eagles Mere, and I was honored to be directing it. *Cyrano* was an ambitious undertaking for a summer theater with a small stage, but Tom Foral's set was a small-budget miracle.

"Foral's framework for the proscenium, highly decorative, colorful, sweeping, was most successful in its invitation to enter a different world... It telegraphed that the action would be heroic... and the production ultimately fulfilled the promise of the design. You created romantic tragedy in the best tradition with color, vitality. For the duration of the play, you believed in the world you created – and the audience participated in your belief... The performances had the sweep, the surge, the conviction that romantic tragedy must always have. It has its own kind of theatrical exaltation."

Dennis Longwell scored a tour-de-force as *Henry IV.*

"Dennis' work was brilliant, in every sense: acting, interpretation, grasp... Dennis has the ability to conceive a character in his mind and instantly this character becomes a complete physical entity... Belcredi was an excellent creation, too – a Pirandello figure. Perhaps there was still too much life in him, too much participation in life, and Marshall sometimes over-emphasizes, but he kept the conflict of the drama motivated from Belcredi's angle, and he kept it progressing to his death... Remember your first night, and recreate this joy of acting in all you do."

As our season ended, the Berlin Wall was being erected in Germany, but we were putting up Mary Roger's musical *Once Upon a Mattress.* I worked in the box-office for the last two plays, and enjoyed the productions from an increasing distance. My sheltered artistic life under Miss Krause's sharp eye was ending. It was time for the eaglet to leave the aerie and spread his wings.

Excellence in the future would have to be earned on my own.

CHAPTER 2
OPPORTUNITIES

I arrived in New York City Labor Day weekend, on a warm Friday evening, September 1, 1961. I stayed the first few days at the Sloane House YMCA on 34th Street. The first thing I did was to call Jane Lowry, the Varya I danced with in *The Cherry Orchard*, who'd come to New York the previous year. Jane said she was in a play in Greenwich Village and invited me to see it. She gave me directions and I promised to come for the Sunday night performance at 9 P.M.

I took the A train to West Fourth Street, the stop for Washington Square, the heart of Greenwich Village. I'd heard tales about the infamous Village, but the bizarre behavior I anticipated on the streets did not materialize. I was almost disappointed. I found a little street off Avenue of the Americas that angled to the left, stretching just one block to Bleecker Street. The sign on the corner indicated Cornelia Street, which was my goal. Near the far end of the block, I found an open door at number 31 that displayed a poster in the storefront window advertising a play: Doric Wilson's *Now She Dances!*

This was the Caffé Cino. I stepped through the doors like Alice passing through the looking glass. My life would never be the same. The room was a-twinkle, illuminated only with Christmas lights. The walls were covered in a colorful collage of posters and pictures, from flexing body-builders clad in posing straps, to glamor shots of Marilyn Monroe, Jane Russell and Jacqueline Kennedy, leavened by the sweet countenance of Pope John XXIII.

The room was small, no more than sixteen feet wide and about fifty feet long. A pressed-tin ceiling floated high overhead and, apart from Christmas lights, the only light in the room was from a Tiffany-style lamp hanging over a brass espresso machine behind a service counter in the far left corner of the room, and from the rainbow lights of a jukebox, diagonally across the room in a corner near the entrance. About twelve tables of various sizes were scattered about, some outfitted with ice cream-parlor chairs with scrolling wire backs. An area about eight by eight feet was cleared in the middle of the room where the play would be performed, lighted by PAR lamps on wire clips.

I sat at one of the small tables, and was greeted by an elfin creature with Greta Garbo cheekbones. His dark hair fell to his shoulders and he sported a gold earring. His lithe frame moved with supple sensuality, as gracefully as an ice-dancer. He wore tight black pants, a white shirt open to mid-chest, with an abbreviated white apron around his hips. This was the waiter Johnny Dodd, whose dark Gypsy eyes spread enchantment wherever they glanced. I took the oversized menu and studied the extravagant calligraphy. I settled on a cappuccino. Flashing a Mona Lisa smile, Johnny whirled away. I was impressed: I'd never seen a man with long hair, much less an earring. This was 1961, after all!

At nine, a cherubic-faced man with dark curls rang some silver chimes and announced the performance would commence. The Christmas lights dimmed, the PAR lights went up on the stage area, and we were treated to a play by Doric Wilson about Salome and John the Baptist, as Oscar Wilde *should* have written it; that is, in the style of *The Importance of Being Ernest*. There was a Maid in a black uniform, starched white apron and frilly headpiece (played by Jane Lowry), and a Butler in pinstripes and tails (Tom Lawrence, also from Northwestern). The funniest moment in the play was when John the Baptist's head was presented quite properly on a silver tray in a tea cozy.

Afterwards, the actors passed a basket to receive contributions from the audience in appreciation of their work. I was delighted, and stayed to see the second performance at 11 P.M. Between the shows Jane introduced me to the angelic man whose name graced the Caffé, Joe Cino. A dancer who'd retired from the stage when he reached the thickening years of his early thirties, Joe was an Italian-American who was a free soul. He was happy to meet a director, and immediately invited me to bring him a show. I said I'd try to think of something to do. Like Christmas itself, the spirit of the Caffé Cino remains as vivid in my memory as it did twinkling fifty years ago.

That same week that Roger Maris broke Babe Ruth's home-run record, I found an apartment on West 74th Street, a block off Central Park, and got a temporary job, which soon became steady employment. I worked for a theater club called the Play-of-the-Month Guild, as assistant to the founder, Helen Thompson. Our business was to guide groups of theatergoers to prime seats at the best shows on Broadway. My job was to assign the subscribers' seats. As a result, I found myself working very close to Broadway, albeit at the outer edges. I was privileged to see all the shows soon after they opened, most notably the Pulitzer Prize-winning *How to Succeed in Business without Really Trying*, starring the gap-toothed charm of Robert Morse and the legendary Rudy Vallée. I saw it the night after its opening at the 46th Street Theater from, I must add, very good seats.

More importantly, I saw Kim Stanley's electrifying performance as Freud's first patient in *A Far Country*, which confirmed that excellence can appear on Broadway. I also caught the stage adaptation of the Pulitzer Prize-winning novel *All the Way Home*, where for the first time I was warmed by the radiance of Colleen Dewhurst.

My first Christmas in New York, I gave my friends (all four from Northwestern) matinee tickets to the play that impressed me the most: Paddy Chayefsky's *Gideon*, with magnificent performances from Douglas Campbell in the title role, and Frederick March as the Angel of the Lord. Directed by the renowned Tyrone Guthrie, *Gideon* lured me back four times, as I tried to unravel the secrets of the ingenious staging, in which the Angel apparently materialized out of ether. At my fourth visit, I willfully forced myself to concentrate on the area of the stage where the Angel appeared, rather than get carried away by the action, as happened three times previously. I discovered there was no technical apparatus involved in his magical appearance; he merely walked on from the wings to the place he "appeared" while the audience was riveted by the action on the other side of the stage. I added "misdirection of attention" to my repertoire of staging tricks. Guthrie's direction was a new high water mark. Never before had I witnessed such magic on the live stage.

The following month I saw the Broadway premiere of Tennessee Williams' late masterpiece *The Night of the Iguana*. It starred the magnetic film star Bette Davis and the sensitive British stage star Margaret Leighton. Directed by Frank Corsaro (with whom I soon would study at The Actors' Studio), it featured a spectacular first act curtain, with a deluge of rain thundering down on stage, with the declaration: "There is your God, Shannon!"

Only a month after my arrival, I saw *One Way Pendulum* at the Off-Broadway Phoenix Theater. I went backstage to ask if they needed any help, and they hired me as an assistant stage manager. The job lasted only two weeks because, in typical New York fashion, the production closed prematurely. A month later, the startling novel *Catch 22* was published, establishing that *irony* was something we'd have to learn to live with. In December, Adolph Eichmann was convicted of war crimes and sentenced to death; justice is sometimes realized, no matter how delayed.

Shortly after the New Year, I looked around the office and realized that every employee at the Play-of-the-Month Guild (most of them in their forties) started out to be in the theater – a dancer, an actor, a stage manager. I suddenly recognized the danger of a comfortable job *near* the theater, but not *in* it. I quit on the spot, even though I had no idea how I'd support myself. If necessary, I'd live on belief in myself. After all, Jacqueline Kennedy was giving viewers the first televised tour of The White House and, by example, the First Couple exhorted us to be persistent in pursuit of our dreams.

In March, my friend from Northwestern, Claris Nelson joined me in New York and I introduced her to the Caffé Cino, where we became habitués. We saw work by madcap avant-garde playwright Harry Koutoukas and by the versatile actor/director Neil Flanagan, who seemed to be a sort of Peter Ustinov of the Cino. At Northwestern, Claris wrote a couple of one-act plays in a style reminiscent of Giraudoux. We talked to Joe about mounting one of them for the Cino.

When the summer came, I sublet an apartment at One Christopher Street with a Murphy bed that folded up into the wall.

A Debut

In July, we began rehearsals for Claris' charming fantasy *The Rue Garden*. I cast Lin Kennedy from open auditions, where I also discovered off-beat Linda Eskenas, who became a star in the off-off-Broadway firmament. Also in the cast were Ronald Willoughby from Northwestern, and the author herself. The production opened at the Cino on July 29, 1962. Critic Michael Smith wrote one of the first favorable reviews of off-off-Broadway for the *Village Voice*, August 16, 1962. He declared the play:

> "Almost pure magic and director Mason did an admirable job with it."

So, my Caffé Cino debut offered some promise.

During the run of our play, Marilyn Monroe was found dead at her Brentwood bungalow of an over-dose of sleeping pills, an apparent suicide. Something of America's innocence was beginning to unravel. Paradoxically, we were heartened by the loving nature of Pope John XXIII, who ordered a Second Vatican Council to liberalize some repressive strictures of the church.

When my summer sublet ended, I rented an apartment in a curve-cornered, red-brick building called The Van Gogh at 14 Horatio Street. The building was one of the new breed of "luxury" apartment buildings with a doorman that were springing up in the Village. It was seventeen stories tall and featured a reproduction of a Van Gogh masterpiece in the lobby. My apartment on the third floor overlooked the beginning of Eighth Avenue, where it converges with Hudson Street. It was a large L-shaped studio space with beautiful parquet floors. The rent was $159 a month, way beyond my means but, with my father's help, I managed to live there the next four years.

We followed the success of *The Rue Garden* with another fable by Claris called *The Clown,* about the loss of innocence in a corrupt world. Again, Ron Willoughby and Claris were in the cast, this time joined by Paul Hardy and Jim Haire, two more actors from Northwestern. *The Clown* opened on September 23rd, 1962 and became one of Joe Cino's favorite plays.

Paul's day job was working as secretary to Edward Albee, whose October premiere of *Who's Afraid of Virginia Woolf?* rocked and shocked staid old Broadway and promised a new era of excellence. At last, there was an American writer on Broadway, which had been dominated by British writers for a decade.

Meanwhile, Ellen Stewart, a fashion designer who loved the Cino coffeehouse-theater concept, decided to start one of her own. She began in a basement on East 9th Street in July 1962, calling it Café La MaMa. Al Carmines soon established the Poets Theater at the Judson Memorial Church and Ralph Cook founded Theater Genesis at St. Mark's Church. This quartet of experimental theaters became known as off-off-Broadway.

In November, Claris and I completed our hat trick at the Caffé Cino with her re-telling of *Medea,* dismissed by the *Village Voice* reviewer Michael Smith as:

"... not a success, although Miss Nelson has a far from ordinary ear for language."

The show was notable primarily for the fact that Rob Thirkield played Jason. It was the first time he and I worked together in New York and it was, in the words of *Casablanca*: "the beginning of a beautiful friendship."

Co-Founders Converge

Robert Leeming Thirkield was born in Glen Cove, Long Island on July 29, 1936 to a wealthy Brooklyn family. Rob's maternal grandfather Thomas Leeming took the patent on a product developed in Paris by Dr. Jules Bengué. Mr. Leeming brought it to America in 1898 and sold it under the brand name Ben-Gay. Rob's mother, Helen, inherited the company along with her siblings and had sold it to the Pfizer Corporation by the time we were beginning our careers in New York. Rob's paternal grandfather was an Episcopal bishop.

Rob was a graduate of the Choate Academy (also attended by President Kennedy) and took his B.A. at Wesleyan University. He came to Northwestern to get his Master's Degree and stayed for several years. Rob had a stocky, well-proportioned physique, fine, silken dark hair and the most exquisite hands I've ever seen on a man. He was handsome in a James Mason kind of way, emanating a self-effacing, modest demeanor. But he was uncomfortable as a leading man; his forte was character work, ranging from the ancient servant Firs in *The Cherry Orchard* to the grizzled bum Skelly in *The Rimers of Eldritch*.

Following my Northwestern directing debut with *Cat*, Rob became one of my most ardent fans. He took me under his wing, broadening my world by exposing me to the cultured life he knew. He introduced me to opera by playing the recording of Maria Callas and Tito Gobbi in *Tosca*. Rob described the story as we listened and pointed out the marvelous acting that was evident even in the recording. I became totally involved in Callas' performance and was a converted fan forevermore. I moved into a small bedroom in a large off-campus apartment adjacent to the rattling El, which Rob shared with me and two other students. He quietly paid the bills because he knew none of us could afford to pay for the electricity or the telephone.

I served as Rob's uncredited acting coach when he played Caesar in Miss Krause's opulent production of Shaw's *Caesar and Cleopatra* opposite Paula Ragusa as Cleopatra, Richard Benjamin as Apollodorus and David Pressman as Pothinus.

After receiving his Master's Degree, Rob enlisted in the army and served in the rank of SP4 for two years. When I got to New York, he was still in the army, but his father, who was a vice-president at Manufacturers Hanover Trust, helped me get settled in, cashing checks from my father, opening a bank account and getting a telephone. When Rob was discharged, I cast him to play Jason in Claris' *Medea*. His parents came to see him perform, even though the racy Cino was a long way from their Metropolitan Opera box in the center of the Dress Circle.

Historical Asterisk

In January, 1963 I saw Sir John Gielgud's production of *The School for Scandal* at the Majestic Theater on Broadway. A classmate from Northwestern named Richard Sterne worked with Gielgud briefly the previous summer, so I was bold enough to send him a note introducing myself and asking permission to come backstage afterwards. The production, directed by Gielgud, also starred Sir Ralph Richardson and Richard Easton in fine performances; but it was Gielgud himself as Joseph Surface that held me mesmerized. I secured seats on the center aisle in the first row, as close to the actors as one could get without actually being on stage. From this intimate perspective, I could see Sir John's every impulse. Even in the Restoration style of the play, Gielgud was as *real* in his role as Marlon Brando in *Streetcar*. He behaved with total honesty within his imaginary circumstances. He took snuff, not as a piece of period business, but as an addictive need to calm his nerves, much like the modern equivalent of smoking a cigarette. Utterly besotted, I trained my eyes on him exclusively. But Sir John listened to his acting partners with such concentration that I was forced to follow his focus. It was a lesson in true ensemble playing. Afterwards, I went backstage, agog with my opportunity to question the great man. Gielgud received me graciously, fielding my intense questions as he removed his make-up. I'm sure I was a bore. After half an hour, Sir John changed from his dressing gown into a suit and an overcoat, bid me goodnight and left me standing stock-still in shock from my first personal encounter with a legend of excellence.

Inspired to accomplish great things, I felt frustrated, in spite of our success at the Caffé Cino. I was trained to act and direct in the finest plays of the Western canon, and off-off-Broadway offered only one-act opportunities. I began to envision an Off-Broadway theater where we would be able to show what we could do. On April 6, 1963, I gathered nine recent graduates of Northwestern into my apartment on Horatio Street to talk about this idea. In addition to Rob, Claris and me, the most committed person in the group was Brenda Solnick, who was not only one of my classmates from Northwestern, but also graduated from Amarillo High School a year before me. We were joined by Ron Willoughby, Jim Haire, Dennis Parichy, Marvin Gottlieb and Ardyth Hamburg.

We decided to form a production company called Northwestern Productions and bundle three productions into a single investment. We hired Alfred Geller as our attorney and he drew up legal documents to enable us to raise money. We met frequently for several months, first trying to decide what plays we wanted to present. There was a list of a dozen or so, and we all read them and discussed their advantages and drawbacks. In those days, it was uncommon for a producing team to be comprised of nine partners. I was designated both the lead producer and the director of the first play. Leading them was a bit like herding meerkats. We decided by secret ballot to mount Ibsen's rarely-produced *Little Eyolf*, followed by Shaw's *Arms and the Man* and then *The Mask and the Face* by Luigi Chiarelli.

We set our fund-raising goal at $50,000. Investors were required to invest in all three projects, protecting our artistic goals from the hit/flop dangers of commercial production. Mindful that this was a considerable sum in the early 1960s, we reserved the right to proceed with only two productions after we'd raised $33,000 if the whole investment seemed beyond our means. Such turned out to be the case. After trying to raise money for a year, we elected to drop the third play. But that did not entirely solve our problem; we were still $10,000 short of the minimum we'd need to produce both plays required by our contract with investors.

In early November, Rob and I went to see the closing performance of the Broadway production of Bertolt Brecht's *The Resistible Rise of Arturo Ui*, starring Christopher Plummer in an unforgettable performance, during which he literally seemed to *grow* on stage before our very eyes from a Chaplin-esque little man into a giant Chicago gangster. It was a tour-de-force by an actor who has always been an icon of artistry. The mogul David Merrick produced and Tony Richardson directed. But despite this pedigree, the critics didn't *care* for the production, comparing it unfavorably to one at the Berliner Ensemble; so this extraordinary production closed after only eight performances. Even Tennessee Williams was falling on hard times. His eccentric play *The Milk Train Doesn't Stop Here Anymore* failed at the start of 1963 and when David Merrick attempted to mount a revival in January of 1964, starring the fabled Tallulah Bankhead and Hollywood heartthrob Tab Hunter, it lasted only five performances. Broadway was a hostile place for challenging theater.

As we struggled to reach the level of funding that would allow our ambitious project to go forward, President Kennedy was shot and killed in Dallas on November 22, 1963. It's hard to convey to those born since that fateful date the profound effect it had on the country. It was a national patricide. And then, the presumed assassin himself was killed. It left us shaken and vulnerable, unlike anything since the surprise attacks on Pearl Harbor on December 7, 1940, and unmatched again until September 11, 2001. The slow replays of the Zapruder film, inflicting the deadly wounds again and again, haunted us like the Eumenides for years to come. It was difficult to focus on abstract things like dreams of art.

By the end of November, it was clear that the Northwestern Productions project was in jeopardy. We decided to commission a new translation of *Little Eyolf* because, of all the great writers, Ibsen was the most neglected in translation. Most of his plays existed only in nineteenth-century British versions, almost unspeakable by an American tongue. We found a Norwegian writer named Val Forslund who agreed to undertake a new translation for a nominal fee. Through this Norwegian connection, we were alerted to the existence of a wealthy man named Johann Fillinger, who was capable of helping us reach our goals by investing the final $10,000. He had a friend with an ambition to be a director, and in return for helping us, we would have to give this fellow a chance to direct. I was already set to direct the Ibsen but *Arms and the Man* was not yet assigned. Desperate to get our project off the ground, we agreed to let this Norwegian direct the Shaw. It seems absurd in retrospect, but we were blinded by our needs.

Finally capitalized, we rented the Actors Playhouse in the Village for *Eyolf*. We cast the play around our little company of actors as well as we could. Brenda was to play Eyolf's mother, Rita Allmers, the role played by the great Nazimova in the 1910 production on Broadway. Claris was cast as Asta Allmers, Eyolf's aunt, and Ron Willoughby played Engineer Borgheim. Rob designed the sets, Claris designed the costumes and Dennis Parichy designed the lights. Auditions were required for the rest of the cast because we needed an older character actress to assay the age-old Rat-Wife, a child to play the title role, and a leading man for the pivotal role of Alfred Allmers. We found the wonderful Dorothy Peterson for The Rat-Wife, and Scott Moore, Jr. was a talented kid for Eyolf. For the lead role of Allmers, we found an actor named Mark Lenard, who had a couple of credits on Broadway, several television appearances, and had recently played in an Off-Broadway production of *Exiles*. He was tall, dark and ruggedly handsome, with a tortured inner spirit that suited the role of Eyolf's father, torn by a sense of responsibility for the death of his child, which he feels is punishment for his incestuous attraction to his sister, Asta.

Rehearsals went reasonably well right up to the dress rehearsals, at which point we reached an artistic impasse with the dour Mr. Lenard, who seemed unable to deliver enough warmth for an audience to care about the main character. Days before the scheduled opening, he abandoned the project. This meant we had to delay our opening, putting our fragile financing in peril. We begged Mark Lenard to return to the production. He agreed to come back for two weeks only at double the salary, but it allowed us to open. Again, we were backed into a corner that had no other solution. To protect our investors, we *had* to get the show opened. We agreed to his exasperating terms, and on March 16, 1964, we opened to mixed reviews.

In *The New York Times,* Howard Taubman greeted us with extravagant praise:

> "The production has power commensurate with that of the writer. Chief credit for this accomplishment must go to the director... It's obvious that Northwestern is training talented people, and Mr. Mason must be regarded as one of the ablest."

Northwestern alumnus Walter Kerr, writing for *The Herald Tribune,* did not see it that way, writing the most negative review I would receive for many years:

> "Mr. Mason's actors quickly become lost in their own living room, strutting about the stage like so many stuffed bears taught to intone prose."

The remainder of New York's seven daily papers was equally divided.

Still, with the encouragement of *The Times* we ran for thirty-three performances, not bad for an obscure Ibsen, but hardly comforting to our investors. Their money yielded little more than a boost to our egos, yet it launched our professional careers. At 24, I was the youngest member of the Society of Stage Directors and Choreographers, the recently formed labor union that I would one day lead as president.

Meanwhile, an artistic revolution began in the most unlikely of fields: popular music. The Beatles debuted on the Ed Sullivan Show, and released "She Loves You (Yeah, Yeah, Yeah)" and "I Want to Hold Your Hand," a double whammy of delight. Reeling from the tragic events of the previous fall, America embraced the lively spirit of this rock and roll phenomenon. Bob Dylan began spinning imagery in ways we'd never heard before, warning that "the answer, my friend, is blowin' in the wind," and arousing a passion among the young to get out from under the hard rule of adults (those over 30), and make changes that could benefit all mankind. By mid-April, these musicians were joined by The Rolling Stones, assuring us that time was on our side. Youth would never be the same.

We began previews in April for *Arms and the Man* at the East End Theater at 85 East 4th Street. No actors from Northwestern were involved. While truth in performance was not a priority of the Norwegian director, it was still a handsome rendition of a witty and wise play. The previews went well – the audiences roared with appreciation of Shaw's satire of the absurdity of backward countries determined to fight wars. Then the reviewers came. Almost unanimously, the press dismissed the production as mediocre. At the next performance, the audience fell silent. They no longer thought it was hilarious; they'd been told it wasn't funny. We closed after a shortened run of twenty-four performances and again lost all the investment. Northwestern Productions became only a footnote in history, an asterisk at best in the development of Circle Rep.

Though I gained experience as a producer, I'm not sure a case can be made that I gained much expertise in financial matters, given the difficulty I continued to have juggling fine arts and deficits at Circle Rep. Perhaps I learned something about inspiring artists to work together to achieve something larger than our individual efforts, but my aspirations for excellence were flickering rather dimly.

Miss Krause's artistic theater would have to wait.

Heroic Endeavors

There were several attempts at establishing an artistic theater in America in the twentieth century. In 1926, Eva Le Gallienne founded the Civic Repertory Theatre. Her goal was to present classics and important foreign plays at low admission prices. Her productions introduced American audiences to the works of Chekhov and Ibsen, among others. She directed, translated and starred in most of her theatre's presentations. Hard hit by the Great Depression, the Civic Rep closed in 1935.

Harold Clurman, Cheryl Crawford and Lee Strasberg made a determined effort with the founding of The Group Theater in 1931. These pioneers were devoted to the same artistic principles as the Moscow Art Theater, whose founder Stanislavski influenced them. Mr. Clurman details the saga of The Group Theater in his retrospective *The Fervent Years*, to which the title of this book pays homage. The idea of The Group was to create an American ensemble devoted to honestly depicting America. Their principal playwright was Clifford Odets and their most significant accomplishments were the plays he wrote for the company (like *Awake and Sing*, *Golden Boy* and *Waiting for Lefty*). Torn apart by its own success when Hollywood capitalized on their individual talents, The Group closed its doors in 1941. American theater was left to drift from one commercial success to the next.

The remnants of The Group founded The Actors Studio in 1947, principally among them, Elia Kazan. The actors who served as exemplars in my pantheon of excellence all trained at The Studio: Marlon Brando, James Dean, Kim Stanley, Barbara Bel Geddes, Kim Hunter, Karl Malden, Lee J. Cobb, even Marilyn Monroe. By the time I was in New York, Lee Strasberg was the chief mentor at The Studio, while Kazan, the founder, pursued his prodigious film and stage career. But The Studio was a training ground for actors, not a producing organization. From 1948 to 1964, they presented only seven productions, which hardly qualified it as a permanent theater.

In 1960, the multi-talented Ellis Rabb formed the A.P.A. With his wife Rosemary Harris, Nancy Marchand, George Grizzard, Clayton Corzatte, Keene Curtis, Donald Moffat, Helen Hayes and Will Geer, among others, Rabb led a collective of artists who produced classic plays in repertory. In 1964, the A.P.A. merged with another Off-Broadway institution, Norris Haughton's Phoenix Theater, to form a producing partnership that prospered as the APA-Phoenix. Their production of *You Can't Take It with You* in 1965 was a high point and they moved their Off-Broadway enterprise to Broadway's Lyceum Theater. They dominated Broadway with artistic class for the next five seasons, until they disbanded in 1970, just as Circle Rep was beginning.

The most promising development in the hopes for an artistic American theater began around the same time. John D. Rockefeller III wanted a theater contingent for his urban renewal Project, Lincoln Center, so the Board of Directors hired Elia Kazan, Robert Whitehead and Harold Clurman to form the Repertory Theater of Lincoln Center. Strasberg bitterly remained at The Studio; he never forgave the slight he felt when he was passed over in the formation of Kazan's new theater.

With the help of Robert Lewis, Kazan spent a year training a company of talented actors to form the core of an acting company. While the granite and marble edifice of Lincoln Center was being constructed on the Upper West Side, a marvelous wooden structure was erected in the Village to serve as its temporary home. It was called the ANTA/Washington Square Theater on the campus of New York University. On January 23, 1964, the Repertory Theater opened with the premiere of Arthur Miller's *After the Fall*, directed by Kazan and starring Jason Robards, Jr. It was a stunning production of a remarkable play depicting the author's marriage to Marilyn Monroe. It seemed as if the dream of a real American art theater at last was being realized.

Unfortunately, the Lincoln Center Board of Directors was just as addicted to hits as the most crass of commercial producers. After a season that couldn't match their spectacular opening, the Board dismissed Kazan, Whitehead and Clurman, just as the company was about to move into its monumental home uptown. The Board replaced them with Herbert Blau and Jules Irving, who brought their own actors with them from San Francisco, and the Repertory Theater Company was disbanded.

The founding of Circle Rep five years later was strongly influenced by these Lincoln Center events. One of our formative ideas was that a theater should be governed by artists, rather than a board of directors with a corporate mentality.

Meeting The Future

The spring and summer of 1964 brought the opening of the New York World's Fair, as well as the first protests in the streets of New York and San Francisco against the war in Vietnam. *Hello, Dolly!* was the biggest Broadway hit, *Jeopardy!* debuted on television, and at the movies, *From Russia with Love* competed with *Mary Poppins* for popcorn consumption. Irony confounded Americans: three civil rights workers were murdered in Mississippi, yet Dr. Martin Luther King, Jr. was awarded the Nobel Peace Prize.

As for me, I read a review in the *Village Voice* in which Michael Smith raved about a remarkable *coup de théâtre* in a new play at the Cino. Intrigued, I went to catch the closing performance on a Sunday night in April.

The play was a slight piece entitled *So Long at the Fair* by a young writer recently arrived in New York named Lanford Wilson. Michael Smith was right: the play had a shocking conclusion, in which a young man fresh from the South is being pursued by a New York City girl who's trying to seduce him. She manages to get his convertible sofa opened up to a bed, where a great deal of the action takes place. Faithful to his hometown sweetheart and frantic to avoid seduction, he accidentally smothers his stalker with a pillow. Panicked, he folds her lifeless body up into the hide-a-bed, replaces the cushions and sits on the sofa. The phone begins to ring and we realize it must be the girl's father, who knew where she was going. The terrified young man stares at the phone, frozen by guilt as the lights go down.

What made the conclusion so electrifying is that it challenged our "suspension of disbelief;" you *can't* fold a live human being up into a sofa, we thought, so the illusion that she was dead seemed tangibly *real*. It was a clever juxtaposition of the realities of a living performance with fictional circumstances, a tension exploited by much of Lanford's work. It was exhilarating when the sofa was unfolded for the actress to tumble out cheerfully to take a curtain call.

As clever as the play was, though, what impressed me most was the honesty of the performance. The young man was played by handsome Michael Warren Powell and I felt his acting was at a level of honesty I had not seen before at the Cino. I came away impressed more by the charisma of the actor than the cleverness of the writer.

Within a month, Michael was featured at the Cino in another play by the same author and I couldn't wait to see him again. But this time, it was the writing in *Home Free!* that captivated me. Cino royalty Neil Flanagan directed Michael and Maya Kenin as two lovers in a cloistered relationship. The couple is lost in a fantasy world they have built to protect themselves from the harsh realities on the other side of the door. Joanna is teeming with the promise of life in her swollen belly. She and Lawrence have invented two imaginary playmates, Edna and Claypone, whom they use to misdirect any conflict between themselves. Written with a poetic language unequalled in contemporary drama by anyone except Tennessee Williams, the play created a world of alternative reality worthy of Ionesco. The lights came up on Lawrence gazing in wonder at a spinning gyroscope, a device whose orientation remains fixed regardless of all motion outside itself. It was an image that captured perfectly the metaphor of the characters ignoring a chaotic world. At the end, as Joanna suffers the pain of her imperiled pregnancy, she is unable to persuade the agoraphobic Lawrence to leave the apartment to get a doctor. In the final moments, the writer dropped a bombshell that was as shocking as the *coup* in his first play: Lawrence and Joanna are brother and sister. Their baby, conceived in incest, brings imminent death crashing into their protective cocoon.

In my estimation, this writer was the best contemporary playwright I'd encountered, an heir to the lyricism of Tennessee Williams, who'd inspired my career.

During his early days at the Cino, Lanford worked as a clerk for the Americana Hotel, where he used their typewriter to write plays during the mostly uneventful night shifts. Having had a successful collaboration with Neil Flanagan on *Home Free!*, Lanford called him one night about a new play he was working on at the Americana. He asked Neil whether he thought a play about an outrageous drag queen could be produced. How bold dare he be? Neil told him not to worry, just to write it, and then they'd see. When Lanford finished *The Madness of Lady Bright*, he gave it to Neil, who quickly read it and gave Lanford his response. He would not direct it, he told Lanford. "I'm going to *play* it."

The Madness of Lady Bright debuted at the Cino May 18, 1964. It was directed by Dennis Deagan and Neil Flanagan played the title role, with Michael and Maya in the supporting roles of multiple characters in Leslie Bright's imagination. This play broke through theatrical boundaries in both style and substance. It was the first openly unapologetic dramatization of an effeminate homosexual, a drag queen at home by himself on a miserably hot summer evening and his gradual descent into madness. The audience was transported inside the mind of this exotic creature; we empathized with his hilarious disintegration and felt his anguish at the end, as he begged imaginary saviors: "Take me home. *Please take me home.* TAKE ME HOME, SOMEONE! TAKE ME HOME! Take me home. Take me home. Take me home. Take me home...."

The lights went down, and a stunned audience cheered both the bravura performance by Neil and the dazzling pyrotechnics of Lanford's writing. No one who'd seen him would ever forget the character of Leslie Bright. In a subsequent revival, *Lady Bright* became the longest-running play in off-off-Broadway history, with more than 250 performances.

In August, the same month *A Hard Day's Night* captured the élan of our times, the Cino was doing something unprecedented: they were going to offer a *revival* of a new play they'd premiered. This *Home Free!* was directed by William Archibald, author of *The Innocents*, an adaptation of Henry James' *The Turn of the Screw*, which ran for four months on Broadway back in 1950 and had been made into a film with Deborah Kerr in 1961. Archibald was also a member of The Actors Studio; he brought fellow Studio member

Joanna Miles with him to play the Joanna in the play. Michael was still playing Lawrence.

The new production was a marked departure from the original. Gone were the warm, cozy elements of a fantasy world, replaced by the harsh realities of peeling wallpaper, dingy laundry, bare light bulbs and the naturalism of The Actors Studio. The magic of the gyroscope had been transmuted into more substantial symbols: a toy Ferris wheel being constructed by Lawrence, and a Surprise Box, where the couple left unexpected delights for each other. But the biggest change was in the text itself. In the first few lines of dialogue, the audience learns that Joanna and Lawrence are siblings. The entire action of the play was now experienced through the lens of incest. I was thrown by the change.

At the end of the performance, Joe Cino came by my table to see how I'd liked the play. I told him I still loved it, but that I was troubled by the rewriting. "Have you told Lance?" he asked. "I haven't met him," I replied. "You haven't *met Lanford?*" He was incredulous. "Come over here." He led me to a long table in the corner near the jukebox. Sitting alone was a slender man in his early twenties with a shock of floppy brown hair that fell over his forehead. But his hair could not hide the most alarming blue eyes I'd ever seen; like Paul Newman's eyes, they seemed to stand out about a foot in front of his face, piercing in their intensity. After Joe introduced us, he told Lanford I'd seen his plays, then whisked away, leaving us alone.

"Oh?" Lanford replied with interest at meeting a new fan. "You saw the original production of *Home Free!?*" I said, "Sure I've seen them all." "I've really improved the script, don't you think?" he boasted. In blunt, undiplomatic fashion I replied, "No, I think you've ruined it." He was startled by my honesty. I explained that I felt that by revealing the incestuous relationship at the opening of the play, he'd removed an element of suspense that sustained the audience's curiosity about the couple. The power of the play seemed diminished by losing the explosive revelation at the end. (Of course, I was accustomed to such dramatic devises in the work of Ibsen.) He explained that he wasn't writing about *incest;* he wanted the audience to contemplate the way we contrive inventions to avoid reality. I answered that his solution was like using an atomic bomb to defoliate a jungle; I felt there must be a simpler way to accomplish his aims while preserving the powerful ending. But to Lanford the last-minute revelation was a cheap trick and he hated it when the audience gasped. We courteously agreed to disagree. There was little in our first encounter to suggest we would become artistic partners for life.

Our Most Admired

Lanford Eugene Wilson was born in Lebanon, Missouri on April 13, 1937. His mother, Violetta had been a nurse's aide, but during the Second World War she worked in a garment factory. Ralph, his father, was not a faithful husband and his roving led Lanford to blame him for his mother's emotional stress that resulted in a baby sister being stillborn. Ralph left Missouri for Southern California and Violetta married Walt Lenhard, who was a dairy inspector. Lanford's school years were unremarkable, but he never forgot an English teacher, Mr. Klapp, telling him he would never amount to anything. It served as a spur for Lanford to prove him wrong. In school, he saw a production of *Death of a Salesman*, which attracted him to the theater and he soon played Tom in *The Glass Menagerie*. Slim and handsome, Lanford's pointed nose and thin lips were eclipsed by his silky chestnut hair and electrifying blue eyes.

After high school, Lanford went to San Diego to rejoin his father, who also had remarried. Lanford discovered he had two delightful half-brothers, little Jim and John, as well as a sympathetic stepmother, Tommye, who became a pal. While working a day job as a riveter at Ryan Aeronautical where he was nicknamed "Oz," he enrolled at San Diego State. The events of the six months with his new family are chronicled in *Lemon Sky*, the autobiographical play Lanford was struggling to write when I first met him and which he would not complete for another four years.

He left Southern California and his unconventional family of friends: Tony, Joan, and LoVerne Brown and their sidekick Tanya (not the actress from Circle Rep), about whom he wrote *The Sandcastle*, to go to Chicago, hoping someday to become a painter. Once there, he utilized his talent for drawing to get a job as a commercial artist at an ad agency. He lunched sometimes with his boss Beth Turnbull and her friends Hugh Hefner and Mies van der Rohe, Lanford having no idea at the time who his illustrious lunch partners were. On breaks, he wrote short stories, and one day he realized that a story he was working on probably would work better as a play. He had not written more than a few lines of dialogue before he suddenly recognized that he was a playwright. He enrolled in night school at the University of Chicago to learn more about playwriting. He met Michael Warren Powell, a design student at the Art Institute of Chicago's Goodman Theater, and they became roommates. As Lanford was discovering his talent for playwriting, Michael itched to leave design behind to try his skills as an actor. So, the two young men took a bus to New York City.

In New York, Lanford and Michael worked at various jobs: Michael as a design assistant for home decorator, Leona Kahn, and Lanford as an assistant in the publicity departments to both Liz Gordon at the Phoenix Theater and Allison Harper at the New York Shakespeare Festival. After staying with friends for a while, the boys took a room at the Broadway Central Hotel at 673 Broadway (which collapsed in August 1973, killing several people). The hotel was erected in 1869 and housed a theater at the rear of its premises on Mercer Street, where *One Flew over the Cuckoo's Nest* played for over a thousand performances. The hotel served as the model for Lanford's breakthrough play *The HOT L BALTIMORE*.

One night Lanford met Bill Hoffman, a young editor for Hill & Wang publishers. When Bill and his friend, the composer John Corigliano, learned Lanford was a playwright, they insisted he *had* to go down to the Caffé Cino. When he did, Joe Cino immediately offered him a date to do a play. Lanford had a script called *So Long at the Fair*, which he thought might be ready for production.

Joe suggested a director named Glenn Dubose and the play gave Michael his first chance to act in New York. Actually, Lanford wrote *Home Free!* first, but Bill and John had given the script to Gian Carlo Menotti to consider for his Spoleto Festival, so it couldn't be produced until he heard back from Menotti (who, it turned out, had lost the script on a plane). So, his Cino debut was *So Long at the Fair.*

Claris and I became fast friends with Lanford, whom everyone called "Lance." With his connections to the Phoenix Theater, he could get me in to see productions of the APA-Phoenix, where I was stimulated by the graceful staging of Ellis Rabb and the elegant style of his company. During one such excursion, we had a conversation that had a significant effect on the future. Like Ellis Rabb, I'd been trained in the classics, and to my mind, they were the ultimate beacons of excellence. But Lanford pointed out that dead playwrights always have artists devoted to reviving the past. It was *living* playwrights that reflected the times we lived in. Surely, their work was more important to the survival of the theater and deserved the best possible productions: living ensembles and dynamic direction to give life, not to the musty masterpieces of yesterday, but to vibrant, critical examinations of the present. This concept became one of the founding principles of Circle Rep.

Claris and I returned to the Caffé Cino with her new play *Neon in the Night,* a two-hander about a girl's crush on an unavailable young man, based in part on the captivating waiter, Johnny Dodd.

One admirer of that production was a Cino regular named Bob O'Connor, a poet who was a native of Roswell, New Mexico. He'd just finished writing his first play, *The Haunted Host,* and he asked me to direct it. As an author, Bob decided to use only his first and middle names, becoming Robert Patrick. The Host in the play is an accomplished writer who is visited by a young man from the Midwest who wants to be a writer, too. The Guest is unaware that he bears a strong resemblance to the writer's late lover, a recent suicide. The play displayed an original intelligence, a clever wit, and dexterous dialogue on a par with the best of Oscar Wilde.

Since no one could articulate the host's zingers better than the author himself, I cast Bob in the title role. From the time I'd met Lanford I'd been aware of his sometime boyfriend, Bill Hoffman, the young editor from Hill & Wang. He was a hunky, handsome strawberry blond, who also aspired to write, and he was perfect typecasting for the Guest. So, these two important American writers were first seen as actors *playing* writers in credible, moving performances. The most powerful line was the Host's confession to the Guest, "I don't want to *buy* you; I want to *be* you." *The Haunted Host* was a very satisfying experience and the success of the production was one of the factors that led Lanford to invite me to work with him.

One chilly night in October, unable to get to sleep, I was wandering the streets of the Village when I encountered Lanford. We stopped at Whelan's Drug Store at the corner of Eighth Street and Sixth Avenue to sit at their counter and warm up with a cup of hot chocolate. Lanford was very animated because he'd just finished his first full-length play. I told him I'd love to read it sometime. "What are you doing *now*?" he nudged. So, I followed him back to the Broadway Central, sat on the day-bed that served as a sofa and without pause, read *Balm in Gilead* from start to finish.

The play was phenomenal. Lanford created a world of low-life characters, some thirty-eight or so: prostitutes (both male and female), drug users (pushers and addicts), and the dissolute denizens of an all-night coffee shop on Manhattan's Upper West Side. These characters vividly came to life in an unprecedented whirlwind of over-lapping dialogue (later emulated by film director Robert Altman). The innovations in the play were astounding: for the first time in dramatic literature, several scenes erupted simultaneously. The concurrent action was scattered about the interior of the coffee shop and on the street corner outside, each thrilling vignette vying to outdo the others, and yet all somehow harmoniously complementing each other. The fabric of the dialogue, interwoven at break-neck speed, was sheer poetry disguised as naturalistic speech. Despite the documentary style of the action, characters stepped forward to break the fourth wall, delivering asides and monologues in direct addresses to the audience, erasing the boundary between fiction and the urgent reality of the present tense. Nothing like it had ever been written, although the multitude of characters and the seamy world they inhabited were reminiscent of Gorky's masterpiece *The Lower Depths.*

When I finished reading the play, I hardly knew what to say. I mentioned that it was like a contemporary version of *The Lower Depths* (a reference that went right over Lanford's head since he'd never read Gorky), and I earnestly warned him: "You'll need a brilliant director for this."

About a week later, I ran into Michael Powell at the Cino and he said that Lanford told him I'd hated the play. Mystified, I explained to Michael that I thought I'd been very clear about my admiration: I'd compared it to a masterpiece and, by suggesting that the piece needed a brilliant director, I was subtly trying to offer my services.

Lanford and Claris were sitting together at a coffee shop when Michael reported my clarification. He recounted that I'd told him *Balm in Gilead* was the best original play I'd ever read. Lanford snorted, "How many original plays has he *read?*" To which, Claris shot back, "Well, all of *mine*, for a start."

Joe, Michael, Claris and I lingered late one night at the Cino, as we often did after closing, to participate in Joe's casual ritual of Greek dancing, and Lanford read his latest play *The Sandcastle* to us. It made even smoother use of both overlapping dialogue and simultaneous action; I liked the characters and the story enormously. Within the month, Lanford also rewarded us with his charming new one-act play, *Ludlow Fair.*

Following a performance of *The Haunted Host,* Lanford approached me and conducted a quick review of my directorial background. After considering my qualifications and based on the evidence of the production he'd just seen, he asked if I would like to direct *Balm* at La MaMa, where he'd been given a production date. Crisply, I accepted on two conditions: first, that he would not interfere in my process with the actors (he had a reputation of being meddlesome); and secondly, that he allow me to direct *The*

Sandcastle as a follow-up. A little taken aback by my take-charge demeanor, Lanford agreed.

Ellen Stewart's La MaMa was first located in a small basement that seated only thirty people and like the Cino, no admission was charged and a basket was passed for the actors. Ellen sold coffee and cake. The first production was Tennessee Williams' *One Arm*, directed by Andy Milligan, who became a famous footnote to the film industry for his sexploitation and horror movies. The first time I went to La MaMa was to see a production of Tennessee Williams' *Auto da Fe*, directed by Joe Cino himself. I met the alluring, enigmatic Ellen Stewart, with her smooth honey-colored Belgian chocolate skin, her Medusa-like hairstyle and her French accent, presumably a Creole patois that thickened or lightened from one occasion to another. If the Sphinx were to come to life, she probably would be Ellen Stewart.

Ellen was accused of running a bordello, so she moved the operation to a second floor loft at 82 Second Avenue, where the space was considerably larger and seated seventy-four. Fifty cents admission was charged. In an attempt to side-step city restrictions, Ellen re-named it La MaMa Experimental Theater Club. Paul Foster made his debut with *Hurrah for the Bridge*, during which Ellen Stewart began her ritual of ringing a bell at the start of every performance and announcing that La MaMa was "dedicated to the playwright and all aspects of the theater." She produced the early works of Julie Bovasso, Tom Eyen (later famed for his *Dreamgirls*), Leonard Melfi, Megan Terry, Jean-Claude Van Itallie, Jeff Weiss, and also introduced directors Tom O'Horgan, Jacques Levy, Lawrence Sacharow and Joseph Chaiken.

There was a kind of friendly rivalry between the Cino and La Mama, but most of the original off-off-Broadway artists moved back and forth freely between the two venues. Sometimes popular shows from the Cino moved to La MaMa for a second run and some of the plays presented first at La MaMa were repeated at the Cino.

In November 1964, La Mama moved again, this time down the street to 122 Second Avenue. Still on the second floor, the new space could seat up to 115 people. A pressed-tin ceiling was twelve feet overhead and an elevated stage twenty-three feet wide by twelve feet deep was at the back. Near the stage, small tables were on the floor level, then on two platforms of increasing height behind, offering better viewing. Admission was raised, first to seventy-five cents and then to a dollar. This is where we would premiere *Balm in Gilead*, with the luxury of an elevated stage twenty-three feet wide.

History Begins

Memory is a lake wherein a reflection of a day in a life, whether of blue skies or rain-laden trees, can be rippled away by a single stone of fact. A recollection is as insubstantial as rings of water, spreading ever wider, refracting reality through a prism of emotion, unreliable in assaying the depths at the center.

Lanford recalled that he and I sat in a coffee shop (probably the one we called the Red Booths, whose actual name has evaporated into the mist above just such a lake) for *four hours* while I described to him in exhaustive detail what *Balm in Gilead* meant to me. Apparently, I dissected the structure and marveled at how the tumultuous surface suggested meaning hidden in the depths. I told him, he said, that the play was about commerce: the buying and selling of bodies, drugs and of commodities like self-respect, love and honor. The play could have just as easily been written about Wall Street, I said, as about the derelicts on the corner of Broadway and 78th Street. I have no memory of this specific event, but Lanford's version of this critical juncture at the beginning of our collaboration is a satisfying fable, rich in particulars.

At our auditions for the many characters, it became evident that Lanford and I shared the same ideas of excellence in acting. The auditions were an exposition for a sizeable collection of talent from Northwestern. Considering how many parts there were, I was lucky to have such a resource to supply some of the talent we needed. We also made use of the best actors from the Caffé Cino and from the wealth of artists in other disciplines (like models and painters) who were attracted to the off-off-Broadway theater scene, and in whom we found colorful talent that could offer types not typically found among actors.

For the leading roles of Darlene and Joe, we were blessed to attract a member of The Actors Studio, Avra Petrides (who'd been slated to play *Electra* for Kazan before the Lincoln Center Company was disbanded). She brought to the play unvarnished honesty with spectacularly invisible technique. For Joe, we found Gregory Rozakis, a Golden Globe nominee from Kazan's 1963 autobiographical film *America, America*. For the important role of Ann, we found Mary Tahmin, a film actress who made a living dubbing foreign stars like Anna Magnani into English.

The only conflict between Lanford and me was a brief debate about the casting of Fick, the mumbling derelict whose non-stop, heartbreaking plea for a protector is a key poetic element, providing contrapuntal rhythms underlying much of the play. I preferred Rob, but Lanford wanted the more theatrical Neil Flanagan. Appreciative of Neil's masterly performance in *Lady Bright*, I agreed to let him play Fick, provided that Rob played the smaller but ominous part of The Stranger and understudied Neil as Fick. This compromise worked out perfectly since Neil was in some professional demand and he would have to miss a couple of performances. Rob's rendition of Fick on those occasions inspired Lanford to write for him the role of Skelly in *The Rimers of Eldritch* the following year.

The first rehearsal was held in my apartment on Horatio Street, whose capacity was challenged by the crush of twenty-eight actors. After I described the importance of the play and the artistic excitement we could look forward to, I talked about discipline and the unusual requirement that the cast needed to come to rehearsals with their lines learned. I emphasized the collaborative nature of our work and then gave them character/beat breakdown charts that specified which actors were involved in each beat of action. A rehearsal schedule was printed on the reverse side that outlined a carefully wrought plan to achieve our goal of creating a living play by the opening performance. I took the cast through the script and told them where to mark each beat of action.

Lanford was intrigued; he had never worked with anyone who approached a play by identifying beats of action. He quickly grasped the concept and surreptitiously began to thumb ahead in the script, playing a little game of guessing where I'd mark the next beat. To his surprise, in his estimation I'd hit them exactly, even when the beat began in the middle of a speech, as they sometimes do. I believe an enduring trust emerged from Lanford's appreciation of this process, which demonstrated my thorough understanding of the play. Trust is a fundamental reason for the success of our collaboration, which would be recognized as the longest collaboration between a writer and director in the history of the American theater, a fact noted by *Playbill* in 1983 after only nineteen of our forty years together.

Rehearsals of *Balm in Gilead* were burdened by the lack of a consistent rehearsal space; we were required to shift the rehearsals to different locales several times, as we ferreted out free spaces that could accommodate our large cast. We secured space in the Bouwerie Lane Theater basement for several rehearsals; a cast member had a contact with an ABC studio mid-town that was available for a couple of nights; and because Lanford and I were participants in the Directors Unit and the Writers Unit at The Actors Studio, we were able to have occasional rehearsals there.

Some of the first week was spent on research, going to a coffee shop on the Upper West Side to observe the behavior of the all-night habitués, which included the streetwalkers and drug dealers and drag queens we were going to impersonate. As this was a potentially dangerous mission, we went in groups to ensure our safety.

I rehearsed the overlapping scenes separately, giving each scene a chance to explore an uninterrupted through-line, and only when we had found strong and clear actions for each did we begin to blend them together. Many scenes essentially featured two cues for each line of dialogue: the give and take *within* the action of the scene itself, and the line of dialogue that was the *actual* cue from another scene playing simultaneously. As there was no precedent for this kind of bizarre double-consciousness, we struggled our way through the play with some difficulty. The scenes could play separately with well-grounded truth, but Lanford's interlocking dialogue created a musical score when two scenes, like different sections of an orchestra, played at the same time. My background included years of playing in concerts from sixth grade through college, and that experience helped me to orchestrate the contrapuntal music of the dialogue. Everyone in the cast was devoted to both things: the *truth* of performance within their scene and to the *music* the interlocking dialogue created when the scenes were played together. We treasured the symphonic nature of Lanford's dialogue. But it was as difficult to achieve, as it was unprecedented.

We took our rehearsals of the play to two sessions of The Actors Studio for help. The policy at The Studio (which was rarely heeded) stipulated that participants should bring in unfinished work so that Strasberg (or Clurman) could offer suggestion to improve it. Lanford and I took the policy literally, so we brought in *Balm*'s third week of rehearsal while we were still struggling with our problems.

In the Directing Unit, we presented part of the first act with me whispering sub-textual reminders to Avra Petrides, pointing out elements of the café as the buzzing hive of life unfolded. In the open critique that followed our presentation, members of The Studio were outraged; how *dare* a director talk to an actor (especially a Member!) while she was *working!* Lee Strasberg came to my defense. He said working on the sensory subtext of the actor with a stream of subconscious suggestion was a valid technique that he used himself. When he asked what kind of guidance we needed, I told him of our dilemma: how could we solve the challenge of responding truthfully to cues within the scene and at the same time listen for a literal cue coming from a scene across the stage?

Strasberg gave me the best directorial advice I'd ever received: "You can have the actors perform *truthfully*," he told me, "*or* they can perform the mechanical task of picking up the cues from across the stage. You cannot ask them to do *both*. As the director, you must choose which is more important, the *effect* of the musical dialogue, or the *truth* within each scene." I had no hesitation in choosing the truth as being more important to the life of the play than the music. "Then you must release the actors from the *obligation* for each cue to fall exactly right and trust that the author has written the music with such authority the effect will remain."

As soon as the actors were released from obligation and simply devoted themselves to playing the truthful actions within their scenes, they discovered an ability to hear the cue from across the stage *and* to play the dialogue exactly as written. The key to their ability to do so was based on several things. First, when they strained to hear the literal cue in another scene, it interfered with their concentration; a tension was introduced that was counterproductive to the truth of their performances. We were reminded of Stanislavski's precept that *relaxation* is the first essential principal of truthful acting. Secondly, all actors possess a *dual consciousness*: of the fictional reality in which they are immersed and the *actual* reality of performance: vocal projection, repeating the blocking, to be in the light, etc. And thirdly, we found that the simultaneous dialogue had to be spoken at a moderate volume and never compete with the other scene. We had to hear ourselves think.

When released from the obligation, the actors' relaxed and tuned in to that dual consciousness. They could *hear* the cue without interrupting their own scene. Miraculously, the precision we'd strived to achieve effortlessly fell into place. We had truth and beauty simultaneously.

Harold Clurman also made helpful suggestions when we presented part of the play in the Writers Unit. His critiques always were as insightful as they were entertaining.

The technical aspects of the production were a true "do what you have to do" experience. Lanford and I went to restaurant supply stores on Lafayette Street and managed to beg, borrow and bargain for the restaurant equipment we needed, from counter stools to coffee machines, napkin holders to neon signs, and menus of "daily specials" to a cash register. Within our tiny budget, Lanford and I built the booths from second-hand lumber and upholstered them with red vinyl, edged with metallic strips. I designed the ground plan of the set and Lanford's visual gifts were helpful in decorating the all-night café. Dennis Parichy lit the production in a magical yet unmerciful light, a mixture of saturated colors and stark white.

The script called for a musical opening with four black singers performing a number, only to disappear from the scene, not to be used again. This was a luxury we could not afford; but I was determined to preserve what Lanford intended for the beginning of the play. Through one of the cast members, I found a 45-RPM record that was a demo disk for a doo-wop style pop tune by Jerry Ragovy. It was fully orchestrated and had just the funky sound of rhythm and blues (rather like Fats Domino's) that Lanford wanted to begin the play.

The production opened at La MaMa Experimental Theater Club in a second-floor loft on Second Avenue Friday, January 22, 1965, two days after Lyndon B. Johnson was sworn in for his own full term as the 36th President of the United States, proclaiming his intention to build a "Great Society," a goal derailed to a degree by leading us deeper into the war in Vietnam.

As the rhythm and blues song blared its catchy tune, from the rear of the audience our cast of twenty-eight actors marched down the side aisle, mounting the stairs to the stage and forming a line that filled the stage from wall to wall. The sheer number of bodies facing the audience was a stunning effect; this was the largest event ever to happen off-off-Broadway. The play suggests that the action of the first act should be seen from one perspective and then in the second act, from the opposite side. This required the set to rotate without the help of a revolving stage. So when the line of bodies across the stage broke, the cast picked up the booths (bolted together as a unit), the counter and the stools that comprised the restaurant, and in a circular motion turned the café around. This dance/scene-shift ended as the first lines of dialogue began and the audience was thrown into the turbulence of life that characterizes this play. The set was turned again at the beginning of the second act, restoring us to the initial perspective, and again at the end. The circular imagery captured the restless lives trapped in a rut of relentless repetition.

Especially memorable was Michael Warren Powell as Dopey with his delivery of an uproarious gripe about cockroaches, their ancient history and how they'll survive even a nuclear disaster, which begins, "You know, though, what?" Also notable was John Kramer's joke on how Chicago's obsession with masculinity leads people there to disdain umbrellas, ending: "Consequently, people get rained on a lot in Chicago."

One of the most stunning moments was when Fick, whose continuous mumbling in the drug-ravaged haze that underlay much of the cacophony throughout the first act, finally wound down. His helpless plea for a protector, perhaps a balm to alleviate his suffering, went unanswered and the stage fell quiet. Then an almost comatose Savannah Bentley, who as Babe teetered on a stool at the end of the counter, moved for the first time in the play. Lifting her head from a heroin-induced stupor, she took in Fick's emptiness, then turned slowly and looked to Dopey, her dark, wounded eyes a silent plea for relief. Dopey turned to the audience and said, Michael's voice brimming with emotion, "I think we'll call an intermission here." And the audience choked back a gasp as the stage went black.

The tour-de-force belonged to Avra's eighteen-minute monologue in the second act, as Darlene relates the story of her marriage to Cotton. It was delivered to Mary Tahmin, as Ann, hanging in there at the counter between tricks; her occasional responses, "Yeah, I know what you mean" gradually dissipated into the distraction of silence as Darlene's epic recounting un-spooled.

Balm in Gilead sold out every performance and was extended for a second week. There were literally lines down the block on Second Avenue; it was the hottest ticket in town. In a later era, the production would have transferred to Broadway, but at the beginning of 1965, it played its two weeks of performances and drifted over the lake of memories of the few who saw it, never to be forgotten.

Here's an excerpt from Michael Smith's lengthy review (February 11, 1965) in the *Village Voice:*

"Wilson's most ambitious play to date. Basically documentary, it adds a series of innovations, making theatrical statements about an entire milieu. Wilson's kaleidoscopic technique...is given shape – not quite successfully – by its focus on a particular story...Much of the play is brilliant and all of it is entertaining. Marshall W. Mason did a fine job of staging the play, keeping its focus clear and the relationship between the many elements alive and persuasive. It is to be hoped that *Balm in Gilead* will get a more extended run."

In *Backstage* (February 26, 1965), Judith Gayle Harris wrote:

"Under the fine direction of Marshall W. Mason the various denizens of an all-night coffee shop on New York's Upper West Side come to life in Lanford Wilson's new play, making it a genuinely exciting theatrical experience."

Although favorable, these reviewers seemed unaware of the revolutionary nature of what we did. One person who understood we had created an extraordinary ensemble was Lanford Wilson. He was awed by seeing his play come to life every evening, the rich characterizations of his script realized in vibrant performances. Toward the end of the run, he urgently grabbed my arm. "We really must keep this cast together. We could form a company and create our own theater."

There was an example of Joe Chaiken doing just that with his newly formed Open Theater. But I didn't want to struggle along in basement theaters on miniscule budgets. I hoped some enterprising producer would whisk us away to fame and fortune. I was still smarting from Northwestern Productions and understood the perils of doing it yourself. I told Lanford: "Oh, no, I'm too young for that!" I was twenty-four years old.

There has been speculation about the literary influences on Lanford's writing, with particular comparisons made between

Lanford's lyrical sensibilities and those of Tennessee Williams. Even more has been suggested about Lanford's debt to Chekhov; he has even been called "the American Chekhov." The truth is that Lanford's vision of theater came from watching live performance, not from reading plays or from lectures in a classroom. It was playing Tom in *The Glass Menagerie* in high school after he'd seen a moving production of *Death of a Salesman* that generated his love of theater. In New York, Lanford saw the Joan Littlewood production of Brendan Behan's *The Hostage* and this became the most important influence on his ideas of what a play should be (and what a production should do, I might add: it was an exemplary ensemble effort).

After *Balm* closed, we saw Peter Brook's Broadway production of Peter Weiss' *The Persecution and Assassination of Marat as Performed by the Inmates of the Asylum of Charenton under the Direction of the Marquis de Sade*, much praised for its ensemble acting; but Lanford was not impressed. He had seen a true ensemble and he was not persuaded by this synthetic British version.

The idea of a permanent ensemble of actors that he could write for became a reality with the creation of Circle Rep four years later. Lanford must be given credit for first envisioning the opportunities such a theater might offer.

Chapter 3

Transitions

Edward Albee used the financial harvest of his Broadway hit *Who's Afraid of Virginia Woolf?* to invest in the future of the American theater. Together with Richard Barr and Clinton Wilder, they financed a new project called Theater 1965, a professional showcase for new American writers to be produced at a professional Off-Broadway theater.

It would be difficult to overestimate Edward Albee's importance to the theater in the second half of the twentieth century; but apart from his groundbreaking plays, he seldom receives recognition for sponsoring the professional debuts of many important playwrights. Theater 1965 created a Playwright's Unit in the fall of 1964, and Edward had been a frequent visitor to the Caffé Cino and La MaMa. Barr-Wilder-Albee selected three plays from these venues for the inaugural New Playwright Series at the Cherry Lane Theater: *Balls* by Paul Foster from La MaMa, *Up to Thursday* by Sam Shepard from the Playwright's Unit, and *Home Free!* by Lanford Wilson from the Caffé Cino.

Lanford was having a hard time deciding who should direct his professional debut. Neil Flanagan, who had directed the first production of *Home Free!* at the Cino, was already busy directing Lanford's newest one-act *Ludlow Fair*, so he wasn't really considered. Albee proposed Milton Katselas, who had directed the original production of *The Zoo Story*; but Lanford was experiencing the most successful collaboration of his young career with me on *Balm in Gilead*.

I was at La MaMa one afternoon when Ellen Stewart handed me a message from Lanford that said he needed to talk to me. I called him from the pay phone. He explained how torn he felt in choosing a director for *Home Free!*, but that he thought he should take Edward's advice and work with Katselas for his debut; he earnestly promised that I definitely would direct his *next* play. I responded bluntly that if the first production were not a success, who could say whether there would ever *be* a second production? I reasoned that if he was having trouble choosing between a "nobody" like me and a famous director of Milton's stature, it was clear that he thought I was the better director; otherwise, there would be no conflict. Apparently, that made sense to Lanford because he agreed to let me direct *Home Free!*

During the last week of *Balm in Gilead*, Lanford and Neil went into rehearsal for *Ludlow Fair*. It was a charming portrait of two young women who shared an apartment in New York and their contrasting longings for romance. It's one of Lanford's best (and most frequently performed) one-act plays.

Balm in Gilead closed and rehearsals for *Home Free!* began the next day. Despite my misgivings about Lanford's script revisions in the second Cino production, I was excited by the opportunity to restore a lyrical mood to the play. If the audience had to know from the start that the relationship of the characters was incestuous, I would try to make the imaginary world they created so irresistible that the shock would have a minimal impact.

I kept the cast intact from the previous Cino production, with Michael Warren Powell as Lawrence and Joanna Miles as Joanna. The actors had a symbiotic chemistry and they had built a layered relationship. I was pleased to inherit their honest performances, especially because my rehearsal period would span only ten days, and most of my work would be devoted to re-staging the action. At the Cino, the audience was scattered about on all sides, seeing *Home Free!* from different perspectives, sharing an intimate space with the cast. These advantages disappeared once the action was confined to the singular perspective of the Cherry Lane's tiny proscenium stage. Now the audience would be shrouded in a distant darkness, as if peeking through a keyhole at the lights of another world. Even though the Cherry Lane has only 199 seats, it is a long, narrow auditorium stretching back twenty-two rows. This would be a test as to whether Lanford's work could communicate to a larger audience under more conventional circumstances.

One scenic element was vital to the play: Joanna and Lawrence are protected from the chaos of the external world by a door. On one side of that door, they have created a world of fantasy and games; on the other side, an ominous reality threatens to encroach upon the fictional universe within. The problem was that the producers had allotted small budgets, based on the concept that the plays should be performed with sparse scenic elements. We could accept that there would be no walls: the interior of the room could be suggested by a bed, the Ferris wheel, various chairs and stools, and the area could be suspended in a void with the black velour curtains that are endemic to most proscenium stages; but we *had* to have a door.

The production manager was deaf to my pleas for this essential element, so Lanford and I devised a ruse. He would come to a rehearsal and throw a royal fit, yelling at me that I should have known a door was essential. Lanford's feigned fury worked wonders. The producers, who included a fellow writer, immediately acceded to the playwright's demand, and *voilà*, they built us a sturdy stage door that could withstand the slamming and locking required by the action.

To make the world of Lawrence and Joanna special, I abandoned the seedy environment of the Archibald production and used the fanciful elements in the play to create a refuge in which the characters could barricade themselves from reality. In the intimacy of the Cino, the very *idea* of a toy Ferris wheel could suggest their imaginative world, so a two-foot high prop, assembled with the little dowels and wooden spools of a Tinkertoy set, sufficed. With the greater distance of a proscenium stage, I doubled the size of the Ferris wheel, using the metal nuts and bolts of an Erector

Set. This gigantic toy was elaborately decorated, painted gold, and encrusted with large colored-glass gems and rhinestones to endow it with a Christmas-tree-like splendor. The tilting cars of the Ferris wheel were made from the cardboard boxes for kitchen matches, with the tops cut open to make backs, and the seats upholstered in velvet and sequins. It was constructed entirely by Michael Warren Powell, who worked every waking minute during the ten days of rehearsal, using his design skills to sew, glue and accessorize this whimsical prop that projected a sense of wonder even at a distance. As the audience entered, Lawrence was already on stage, putting up colored crêpe streamers overhead to represent the constellation of the Seven Sisters. When he began his lecture about the evolution of stars to the imaginary children Edna and Claypone, he rapped on the table with a wooden hanger and as the houselights dimmed, he began with the first line of the play: "Now, if you'll only pay attention..." Then, dramatizing the powerful forces ricocheting through space, in a manic frenzy he destroyed his crêpe streamer universe before Joanna knocked at the door to be admitted.

I reasoned that if these characters were so petrified by the demands of their landlady (whom they called Mrs. Pruneface) for overdue rent, they'd probably not paid their electric bill either; so candles provided all the illumination in their room, lending an enchanted glow to the sparkle of the Ferris wheel. I hoped these changes would soften the harsh fact of incest.

Opening night was upon us before we could get scared. The first play was Sam Shepard's absurd romp *Up to Thursday*. The play had first been performed the previous November at Edward Albee's Playwrights Unit at Village South Theater. I was never quite clear what the play was about, but it involved a young man sleeping in bed under an enormous American flag, and his various friends trying to coax him into getting up. Sam says the title came from his fear of being drafted, with the pressure of a deadline on freedom. I wasn't the only one who didn't get it; the critics didn't have a clue. Sam himself says it was "a bad exercise in absurdity," and that he didn't really consider it a play at all. But it was fun to watch and it displayed some lovely performances by Stephanie Gordon and Kevin O'Connor.

Balls was Paul Foster's abstract *homage* to Samuel Beckett, with an original twist. Except for the lighting and the script, all elements of theater had been eliminated, even the presence of actors. In their place were two white ping-pong balls suspended by invisible threads; illuminated against a chasm of darkness, they swung back and forth in arcs that moved progressively closer to each other and then, almost imperceptibly, away again. This minimal action was accompanied by tape-recorded voices that suggested disembodied dead souls revisiting an abandoned cemetery. Entertaining themselves throughout eternity, the spirits represented by the ping-pong balls made wry observations on the pathetic lives of the living. I loved the play at La MaMa and I thought it even more impressive enlarged for Off-Broadway.

And the evening climaxed with our little incestuous play about the dangers of evading reality. By comparison, *Home Free!* was old-fashioned, but it was not confined by realism; it was as unconventional as an Ionesco duet, using an eccentric charm to lure an audience into dramatic circumstances that led to fatal consequences.

We opened on Wednesday, February 10, 1965, two weeks before my twenty-fifth birthday. The Cherry Lane is located on Commerce Street at one of the most beguiling intersections in the Village. Lanford and I went to the corner bar, the Blue Mill Tavern, during the first two plays and then sneaked back to hang out in the anonymity of darkness at the rear of the theater to steal a look at our own work. On stage, awash in candlelight, Michael and Joanna were luminous; the audience seemed rapt.

The opening night party was held at La MaMa. The first program of the New Playwright Series played for only 23 performances, but *The New York Times* cited *Home Free!* as the evening's major discovery:

"In baseball parlance, it may be only a single, but it's a solid hit."

Lanford Wilson's professional career was launched successfully, and his debut became another seed cultivated in our collaborations that would germinate into Circle Rep.

A Fertile Field

Home Free! closed a week after the assassination of Malcolm X. State troopers in Selma, Alabama, attacked 525 Civil Rights workers on what came to be known as Bloody Sunday. It began a year of confrontations between the authorities and civil rights protesters, who had grown by the end of March to 25,000 people marching with Dr. King from Selma to Montgomery. The first American combat troops were sent to Vietnam.

It's a bit ironic that simultaneously with these stark realities, off-off-Broadway was coming head to head with mainstream theater: a paying audience and the establishment press. Most of the reviewers found the bill so experimental they were hard pressed to evaluate it. Commercial Off-Broadway was home to *The Fantasticks* and *Little Mary Sunshine* and only rarely hosted serious dramatic works. The press didn't know what to make of the trailblazing styles of the writers to whom they were introduced in the New American Playwrights Series.

Vibrant new playwrights like David Starkweather, John Guare, William M. Hoffman and Jeffrey Weiss kept the Caffé Cino abuzz with excitement. Paul Foster became one of Ellen Stewart's most produced playwrights at La MaMa with plays like *Hurrah for the Bridge*, *The Madonna in the Orchard* and *The Hessian Corporal*. Although Paul never enjoyed quite the mainstream acceptance of his two fellow writers, his *Tom Paine* became an Off-Broadway hit in 1968, directed by Tom O'Horgan at Stage 73, where it played for 295 performances and was nominated for the Pulitzer Prize.

Theater Genesis produced Sam Shepard's first plays, *Cowboys* and *Rock Garden*, in 1964. His *Chicago* was first seen at La MaMa, and at the Cino he'd shown his *Icarus's Mother* and *4-H Club*. I saw all of Sam's early plays, but I had trouble understanding why everyone was so excited. Then I saw Jacques Levy's brilliant production of Sam's *Red Cross* at the Judson Church and suddenly I grasped his genius. A jolt of existential theatricality ran through me like an electrical current. Overnight I became one of his biggest fans. Sam went on to other professional productions, including

La Turista, produced by Wynn Handman's American Place Theater at St. Clement's Church. He contributed material for the gigantic hit *Oh! Calcutta!* and his *Operation Sidewinder* made it to Broadway when Jules Irving opened the Lincoln Center's Vivian Beaumont Theater in 1970.

But Theater 1965's other illustrious discovery was Lanford Wilson, whose equally impressive resume will be a subject central to this story, so I'll trace the events that followed his debut at the Cherry Lane.

Shortly after *Home Free!* closed, my telephone, which had been disconnected for non-payment, suddenly and mysteriously began to ring. The operator informed me, "Your theater is burning down." That could only mean the Cino. I rushed over to Cornelia Street to find my theater home a smoldering ruin.

Immediately we organized a benefit to raise money to rebuild the Cino. The benefit was held at the Writers Stage, hosted by Edward Albee. We raised enough money for Joe to re-open. He resisted suggestions of annexing the adjacent property to expand the Cino. He wanted it to stay just as it had been, and before long it was back in operation.

It was at a Saturday matinee in March of 1965 that I saw the last performance of Maria Callas in *Tosca* at the Metropolitan Opera, with Tito Gobbi as Scarpia. It was the final season at the Old Met on Broadway between 39th and 40th Streets. The audience was abuzz because of the presence of the Secret Service, who had accompanied Jacqueline Kennedy to the performance. I was watching from the Thirkields' front row seats in the center of the Dress Circle, so I could see Mrs. Kennedy seated mid-way in the orchestra. I can't be certain that Mme. Callas was aware of the presence of her rival, who would marry her long-time companion Aristotle Onassis, but it seems unlikely she was the only person who *didn't* know she was there. In any case, her performance contained an arresting piece of stage business. In the second act, following Callas' heart-breaking rendition of *Vissi d'arte*, Tosca waits for Scarpia to sign a safe conduct. Traditionally, Tosca discovers a knife on the dinner table, which she picks up and hides behind her back, fretting and fuming during an extended musical sequence until Scarpia approaches her; and then she stabs him. Callas played down the histrionics. Instead of melodramatically hiding the knife behind her back, to steel her nerves she went to the table where she poured herself a glass of wine; as she put down her glass, she *saw* the knife. She did not move a muscle, transfixed by the sight of the instrument of her salvation; the suspense was electrifying. When Gobbi finally approached her from behind for his amorous embrace, at the last possible second Callas grabbed the knife, turned and plunged it into the startled Scarpia. It was an example of great acting and provided me with an important lesson: Don't foreshadow.

On a more mundane level, I directed a trio of one-acts by Michael Matthias at the 41st Street Theater with Claris, Rob, Michael and John Kramer. I brought one of the plays to The Studio for help, but Strasberg, not remembering his previous praise for my work on *Balm in Gilead,* was harsh in his evaluation, saying: "I would never tell someone that they're not a director, but..." and he shrugged. His stinging rebuke rang in my ears as I left New York for a summer vacation with my mother in California. But rather than deterring me, his criticism redoubled my commitment to grow as an artist.

I stopped in Amarillo on my way back and my father accompanied me east to see the New York World's Fair. The same week 25,000 marchers in Washington protested the war, the demonstrations steadily growing as the U.S. became more and more involved in Vietnam, where our troops had increased to 125,000. At a teach-in at Berkeley, 30,000 young men burned their draft cards, so the burning of draft cards was banned by law. National events continued to swing from one extreme to the other. LBJ established Medicare and Medicaid, and signed into law the Voting Rights Act, only one week before the violence of the Watts race riots broke out in L.A. The "real" world was stranger than the most absurd dramas off-off-Broadway. Bob Dylan was booed at the Newport Folk

Festival for using an electric guitar, as he demanded to know in these extreme times:

"How does it feel?/ To be on your own?/ With no direction home?/ Like a complete unknown?/ Like a rolling stone?"

The Beatles rocked Shea Stadium with the first massive pop concert in history.

While I was away, Lanford wrote a new one-act and offered to let me direct *This Is the Rill Speaking* at the Cino. *Rill* is a chamber-piece portrait of adolescent dreams, smothered by the conventions of life in a small rural town. After the sophistication of *Balm, Home Free!* and *The Sand Castle*, I wasn't ready for something as countrified as *Rill*. I'd spent my life trying to get away from small-town limitations, so I said, "This one's not for me." Lanford decided to direct the play himself. The play in performance was touching and lyrical, and it was probably a mistake to turn it down. Lanford's favorite story about this play was overhearing Johnny Dodd answering the phone at the Cino, with a conversation that went something like this: "Caffé Cino...We have a new play by Lanford Wilson called *This Is the Rill Speaking*...Rill...No, Rill...R-I-L-L...I have no idea."

With the opportunities afforded by La MaMa's larger stage, I began to work more there than at the Cino. After I'd mounted Claris' *The Girl on the BBC* with former Northwestern friends Tom Lawrence and Michael Griswold (as well as La MaMa favorite Victor LiPari), I started work on the production of Lanford's *The Sand Castle*. That same week Sandy Koufax pitched his perfect game in the World Series.

We had a good cast that included Sam Shepard's girlfriend, the Open Theater actress Joyce Aaron as Sasha, Claris as Joan, John Kramer from *Balm in Gilead* as Calvin, and Mike Griswold (from Northwestern) in the sensitive role of Owen. Our casting included some people new to La MaMa, like Angela Wood, who played Irene, and Beeson Carroll as her lover Clint. I designed the set, which was a rambling beach house in San Diego and Dennis Parichy did the lighting.

But a funny thing happened on the way to the performance. *The Sand Castle* is subtitled "or *There is a Tavern in the Town,* or *Harry Can Dance."* The almost nonsensical subtitle is a clue about the unconventional style of the play. This autobiographical piece is about a family of bohemian friends Lanford encountered in San Diego during the brief period he was living with his father. The plot is dangerously close to soap opera: Irene's daughter, Joan, seduces Clint, her mother's boyfriend. The saving grace is an irreverent, light-hearted style that contrasts sharply with the melodrama, as the characters sometimes break into song-and-dance. The play is influenced more by Brendan Behan's *The Hostage* than by O'Neill.

To accommodate the abrupt changes of style in the script, I tried to find "organic movement" that was more theatrical than usual. During a realistic stretch in the play, I asked Joyce to perch on the downstage edge of a table, in preparation for a sudden shift in style to a bout of song and dance. She felt uncomfortable with that staging, and Lanford deferred to Joyce, agreeing that the moment could play just as well *behind* the table. That little compromise signaled a bow to realism from which my production never recovered. The melodrama of the play predominated and the lighthearted Brechtian self-parodies seemed forced. I was frustrated that my production didn't match what I loved on the page. Lanford was satisfied enough; the performances were honest. But I couldn't wait to remount the play a year later, when I finally got it right.

Despite my own reservations about this first production of *The Sandcastle,* Michael Smith wrote in the *Village Voice* (September 30, 1965):

"I found much pleasure in it. [It] receives an effective production under Mason's carefully modulated direction."

Pope Paul VI, following the lead of The Beatles, held a Mass at Yankee Stadium while I was directing Rob Thirkield in a production of *Krapp's Last Tape* at The Actors Studio to warm praise from Strasberg. Once again, he forgot his previous criticism when he'd come close to suggesting I give up theater.

Maybe Strasberg was distracted, because just the night before, the dazzling lights of the metropolis had gone out, plunging the City into darkness for the first time in history. Electricity was disrupted all over the East Coast. Since that first power failure, there have been several more, so they've lost the impact of the Blackout of 1965 when Mayor John Lindsay and the rest of us were stunned by this apparent singularity. The 18th century architecture of Greenwich Village, lighted only by the flickering of candles in the windows transported us to the early days of New Amsterdam. It was as enchanting as it was unimaginable that such a thing could happen!

Off-off-Europe

During the previous six months, I'd supported myself working at various box-office jobs and continued directing at the Cino. While I was treasurer for the box office of *The Zoo Story*, both Lanford and Michael Powell left New York. The Dramatists Guild initiated a program that provided financing for a young playwright to audit the entire rehearsal process of a Broadway play. Lanford secured an appointment as an observer of Frederick Knott's thriller *Wait until Dark*, directed by Arthur Penn and starring Lee Remick and Robert Duvall. When the company left for their Boston tryout, he traveled with them. I'm sure he learned a lot from watching a director, cast and writer struggle with out-of-town adjustments for Broadway.

Ellen Stewart formed two acting troupes to take the experimental work of off-off-Broadway to European audiences. Tom O'Horgan and Ross Alexander were the directors of the two troupes. Tom's troupe played in Copenhagen for six weeks, while Ross' group played in Paris; then the two troupes were to switch cities. When Ross' troupe failed to attract audiences in Paris, they returned to New York; but after being well received in Copenhagen, Tom's troupe went on to Paris, where they enjoyed some success.

Michael Warren Powell left for Europe as a member of the Tom O'Horgan Troupe, along with Kevin O'Connor, Victor LiPari, Mari-Claire Charba and Jacque Lynn Colton. They performed *Chicago* by Sam Shepard (in which Kevin O'Connor sat in a bathtub and dealt with his life from there); *This Is the Rill Speaking* by Lanford Wilson; *The Recluse* by Paul Foster; *Thank You, Miss Victoria* by William Hoffman (a monologue in which a man at work in a private office has phone sex with a dominatrix, and strips from his suit and tie down to his boxers); *Birdbath* (a miniature Gothic horror story) by Leonard Melfi; *War* and *America Hurrah* (an abstract satire of American values in which oversized puppets destroy a motel room) by Jean-Claude Van Itallie.

Left alone in New York, which had just been surpassed by Tokyo as the world's largest city, I managed to get uptown despite a subway strike to see Edward Albee's fictional yet autobiographical adaptation of *Malcolm* on Broadway. I was very moved by it, but the critics did not share my enthusiasm. It played only seven performancesand was followed a month later by Tennessee Williams' stimulating double bill *Slapstick Tragedy*, which also lasted only seven performances. Much safer at the Cino, I opened David Starkweather's hilarious dark comedy *The Love Pickle*. The play involves a fellow and his girl on a date who go to a restaurant so crowded that they're seated at a table for two in the men's room. It was fun, a good beginning for the new year of 1966.

Following up on the success of *Home Free!*, a commercial producer optioned *Ludlow Fair* and *The Madness of Lady Bright* for Off-Broadway. Unfortunately, the producer, William Hunt, opted to direct the productions himself and changed the casts from the popular runs at the Cino. In *Lady Bright*, he decided to cut the two actors who played a variety of people in Leslie's life, replacing them with recorded voices, transforming the three-character play into a one-man show. He typecast an effeminate actor who played the role for pathos but found little of the humor that had made the play so successful. The result was an embarrassment. *Ludlow Fair* was the curtain raiser, and the cast was Sasha von Scherler and Anne Wedgeworth, both capable actors who suffered under inept direction. The double bill opened at Theater East to almost universal pans. The only positive thing the critics noted was Lanford's gift for colorful dialogue, but they scolded that it takes more than good dialogue to make a good play. Fortunately, Lanford had already seen the plays well directed and acted at the Cino, so his ego was not bruised by the failure, which closed after fifteen performances.

One good thing came from Lanford's receiving his first advance against royalties: he was able to rent an apartment of his own for the first time. With Roy London, an actor he'd met from the Open Theater, he moved into a one-bedroom third-floor walkup on West 4th Street, which had a small living room with a dining room alcove that could serve as a second bedroom. He lived in this Bob Dylan-esque "pad" for a couple of years, mostly by himself because much of the time Roy was away on a national tour. It was in this apartment Lanford experienced a prolific period of writing, generating the scripts of *The Gingham Dog*, *Lemon Sky* and *Serenading Louie*.

While The Beatles were declaring themselves "more popular than Jesus," Ellen Stewart introduced her troupe to New York audiences with the La MaMa Repertory Series, following their lengthy out-of-town tryout in Europe. The Circle-in-the-Square's Paul Libin and Ted Mann presented *Six from La MaMa* at the Martinique Theater, which included Lanford's *This Is the Rill Speaking*, Bill Hoffman's *Thank You, Miss Victoria*, and Leonard Melfi's *Birdbath* in the first program; followed by Sam Shepard's *Chicago*, Paul Foster's *The Recluse*, and Jean-Claude van Itallie's *War* as the second program. After the first three nights, three plays were dropped, and *Chicago*, *Rill*, and *Birdbath* were combined to finish the last thirteen performances.

Meanwhile I continued to improve my theater skills by working at The Studio. I directed a touching project of Tennessee Williams' *The Mutilated* with Bill Jordan and Sasha Von Scherler. Again, Strasberg was helpful and supportive.

As U.S. troop levels reached 250,000, tens of thousands of protesters picketed the White House and rallied at the Washington Monument. Dr. King made his first speech against the Vietnam War and was joined within a week by New York's Senator Robert Kennedy.

The threat of being drafted was never far from consciousness. Lanford wrote a little sketch called *Wandering (a Round)* that reflected these concerns. Lanford, Zita Litvinas and I acted in its New York premiere at the Caffé Cino in June 1966. This five-minute play is an abstract satire of the life of a man (Him) harassed by his parents:

She: Where have you been?
Him: Out.
He: What were you doing?
Him: I was just wandering around.

He's examined for the draft, psychoanalyzed, falls in love and marries, divorces and dies, all in five quick minutes. It was produced subsequently at the Mark Taper Forum in Los Angeles as part of an omnibus program called *The Scene*. In 1968, *Wandering* became part of a Café au GoGo production called *Collision Course*, a revue put together by Edward Parone that also included sketches by Jules Feiffer, Israel Horowitz, Jack Larson, Terrence McNally, Leonard Melfi and Robert Patrick.

The summer of 1966 dramatized wildly different elements of our society. Civil rights activist James Meredith was shot in Mississippi; Richard Speck murdered nine student nurses in their Chicago dormitory; sniper Charles Whitman holed up in the tower at the University of Texas, from which he shot and killed thirteen people at random; and the Boston Strangler was finally captured. But some social progress was being made. The Supreme Court issued the Miranda ruling, requiring that defendants must be informed of their rights prior to being questioned by the police. The National Organization of Women was founded, which proved a powerful force in the struggle for women's equality. Along with civil rights and the protests against the war, women's liberation became another cause for which people were willing to defy the establishment to achieve their goals.

Off-off-Broadway continued to be vital: Jeff Weiss premiered his defiantly autobiographical one-man show at La MaMa called

And That's How the Rent Gets Paid, providing a prototype for confessional drama that would reach its apex years later in the work of Spalding Gray. Bob Dahdah created his camp musical spoof *Dames at Sea* at the Cino, starring young Bernadette Peters. It ran for sixteen weeks, joining *Lady Bright* as a huge off-off-Broadway hit before it transferred for a commercial run Off-Broadway of 575 performances.

Lanford completed his second full-length play *The Rimers of Eldritch,* which had a cast of seventeen (in style, an expansion of his one-act *This Is the Rill Speaking*). Lanford continued to experiment and innovate with *Rimers*; it completely departs from chronological order in telling its story. The main plot of the play begins with a jury's verdict ("Not Guilty") and then skips back and forth in time until at the climax of the play, the crime itself is revealed (Skelly being killed with the blast of a shotgun). Lanford decided to direct it himself. *Rimers* was effective at La MaMa in a production with minimal scenery, but I thought it lacked the dimensions that I'd found in *Balm in Gilead*. His productions of *Rill* and *Rimers* proved that Lanford had the talent to stage his own plays, but he also discovered that he didn't like doing so.

When Barr-Wilder-Albee decided to produce *Rimers* at the Cherry Lane for a commercial run, Lanford asked me to take over the direction. My vision for the play was more elaborate than Lanford's spare staging at La MaMa. There is a dead character in the play whose absence hovers over the whole town. He was a teenage boy called Driver Junior, and he'd been killed in an auto crash a year before. I wanted his wrecked car to be a centerpiece to the action of the play and to create a whole town with an environment as rich as the language. Once again, the producers were reluctant to provide a budget big enough to accommodate such a set. They reasoned that Lanford's sparse staging, with minimal scenic elements, helped the action of the play move along. We met and I declined to direct *Rimers* if they wouldn't support my vision. The producers hired the fine director Michael Kahn, who did a superb job of preserving Lanford's simple staging when it opened at the Cherry Lane. Although it ran only thirty-two performances, *Rimers* earned Lanford his first prize, the Drama Desk's Vernon Rice Award.

Between the La MaMa and the Cherry Lane productions of *Rimers,* Michael Powell went back to Europe with the La MaMa Troupe for their second tour. This time their repertoire was limited to *Chicago, Rill, America Hurrah,* and *Tattoo Parlor* by Tom Le Bar. In addition to Michael, Kevin, Victor, Mari-Claire and Jacque Lynn, they were joined by Marilyn Roberts and Katena Mandas. They returned to the United States in early December and mounted Paul Foster's new play *The Hessian Corporal* at La MaMa.

That fall, actor Ronald Reagan became Governor of California, while Truman Capote's White Ball was the sensation of the New York social scene. In Los Angeles, Walt Disney died at the age of sixty-five of lung cancer, ending a formative era of animation that influenced our generation. And the River Arno flooded its banks in Florence, Italy, endangering many priceless works of art.

A Super Nova And A Black Hole

The 1967 New Year got off to a lively start with a Be-In at Golden Gate Park in San Francisco, a preamble for what would come to be known as the "Summer of Love." The first Super Bowl was played in the Los Angeles Coliseum, with Green Bay defeating Kansas City. Within the first two months, The Doors debuted, lighting our fires as few had done before; and Aretha Franklin requested our *Respect,* launching an anthem for the feminists' movement.

There was an explosion of activity in the off-off-Broadway arena. The La MaMa Troupe created several new productions for their repertoire: Rochelle Owens' *Futz,* about a man enamored of his pet pig; *Tom Paine (Part I)* by Paul Foster, an abstract biography of the American patriot, narrated by ensemble re-enactments that included a colossal Marie Antoinette in a gown that covered the entire stage; *Times Square* by Leonard Melfi, an encounter between an obsessive young man and a murderous young woman; and

Melodrama Play by Sam Shepard, in which two brothers scuffle over the copyright theft of a song. Lanford was in rehearsal for the second production of *Rimers*.

I was directing a little slice of realism by Donald Kvares called *One Room with Bath* at the 13th Street Theater, with Claris and Michael playing two strangers who meet while looking for an apartment and almost have a relationship. We had one review, *Show Business* (February 11, 1967) John Camilla:

> "A poignant study of two lonely people. With the sensitive staging by Mason and the acting of Powell and Erickson, one becomes aware of professionalism not seen regularly off-off-Broadway."

I received my first offer to direct from a producer outside my immediate circle of friends. Holly Solomon was a wealthy woman with a love for the arts, who'd admired my work at La MaMa and the Cino. She was producing Jerome Max's *The Exhaustion of My Son's Love* at Temple Emanu-El, located on Manhattan's Upper East Side, across from Central Park on a site formerly occupied by the John Jacob Astor mansion. I received a telegram with the offer: it paid $500, a considerable fee in those days. Remembering my delight of seeing Walt Witcover's premiere production at the Cherry Lane, I eagerly accepted. The cast was made up of members of the congregation, who enjoyed the chance to perform in their amateur theater program. Rehearsals went well and when we opened, the show was a success for both the cast and their friends and family in the audience.

Meanwhile at the Caffé Cino, Joe initiated a series of revivals of Cino favorites: *Ludlow Fair*, then *The Madness of Lady Bright*, to be followed by *The Clown* and *This Is the Rill Speaking*. Tragically, Joe's lover, John Torrey, had been killed in a freak electrical accident. Joe asked me to revive *The Clown*, which was John's favorite play, to open on John's birthday in April. We decided it should be an all-star Cino event. I convinced many of the Cino's best-known playwrights to participate in this memorial revival. Lanford was cast as the Prince,

David Starkweather was the Circus Manager, Ron Link played the Philosopher, Robert Patrick was Cecil and I was the Superintendent of the Theater. Claris was the Headsman, and Jane Harris was The Boy. In addition to playing the Duke, Michael Warren Powell designed and constructed the costumes in what would be the most opulent production ever to play the Cino. Michael was rehearsing for *Futz* and I was rehearsing *The Exhaustion of Our Son's Love*, both simultaneously with *The Clown*.

The Cino had evolved from a little-known coffee shop at an obscure location to a prominent position in the new theater movement. In the early days, whenever no audience showed up for a performance, which sometimes happened, Joe would insist that we go ahead and, "Do it for the room." These performances were always something special for those of us who participated in them, especially since the room included Joe Cino and the staff: Johnny Dodd, Kenny Burgess and Joe Davies. The regulars who came were remarkably gentle people, like the gorgeous Hope Stansbury who had posed for Salvador Dali, and Esther who read tarot cards, and Mary Boylan who had an interesting career playing senile old ladies in films. Also Cino regulars were poet and muse Magie Dominick, scholarly Robert Heide and quietly magnetic John Gillman. The Cino also derived outrageous energy from the irrepressible Harry Koutoukas and the flamboyant diva Charles Stanley. We were a family of artists and though we wore our eccentricities on our sleeves, they were actually pretty tame.

As the fame of the café grew, Johnny Dodd became more and more in demand as a professional lighting designer, but he continued to be the waiter at the Cino. Kenny Burgess was a fine artist, whose paintings are in the collections of a number of well-known people, but he made sandwiches, while Joe Davies (who'd played Johnny Appleseed in a national tour) washed dishes.

The Cino became a magnet for avant-garde artists of all stripes. Robert Patrick was the doorman/host, ushering the sometimes-swelling crowds to their tables. Particularly visible were celebrities from Andy Warhol's Factory, who began hanging out at the Cino as regulars, sometimes even appearing on stage. Lanford and I both were impressed with the relaxation and honesty of performers like Warhol's film star Ondine, who acted in a number of plays at the Cino.

I was unaware that this crowd also signified that drugs had become common currency at the Cino. Bob Patrick, who was there every night, saw the growth of this phenomenon with some alarm. I don't mean to sound naïve, because hallucinogenic drugs were a feature of the Cino from its very inception. Johnny Dodd gave me my first joint of marijuana, which sent me panicked to the library the next morning, since all I knew about pot I'd learned from sources like *Reefer Madness*. I was sure I was hooked for life, until the encyclopedia clarified that marijuana was not known to be habit-forming. Most of the people at the Cino indulged in grass and some hallucinogens, like mushrooms, peyote, mescaline and even LSD. One notable exception was Lanford, who did not like losing control, so he resisted even the mildest forms of drug ingestion. I was a reluctant participant at first, but by the end of the 60s I conquered temptation in the manner recommended by Oscar Wilde and yielded to it. That summer, Grace Slick of the Jefferson Airplane observed on "Surrealistic Pillow" that:

"One pill makes you larger/ and one pill makes you small/ And the ones that your mother gives you/ don't do anything at all/ Go ask Alice, when she's ten feet tall."

But the Warhol crowd also brought with them more sinister drugs like cocaine, methamphetamines and heroin. I don't know the extent to which Joe partook in these more dangerous drugs, but it wouldn't be surprising. The amazing thing is that many of us remained unaware of the extent of this narcotics invasion. Our ignorance was partly because we'd begun to work in a variety of venues, and partly due to the extended run of *Dames at Sea*, during which we dropped by the Cino less frequently.

Still, we were excited to return to the Cino with the memorial revival of *The Clown*. Neil Flanagan was starring in the revival of *The Madness of Lady Bright*, while we were in the midst of rehearsals.

In the late-night hours during the final week of *Lady Bright*, Joe put on a recording of Maria Callas' mad scene from *Lucia di Lammermoor* and, perhaps grieving for John Torrey, perhaps irrational from drugs, he committed hara-kiri (Japanese ritual suicide by disembowelment). Apparently, during the process he tried to call Johnny Dodd, but instead got Michael Smith, who was living with Johnny at the time. Michael hurried to the café, found Joe with severe injuries and called for an ambulance to rush him to St. Vincent's Hospital.

Everyone soon heard about Joe's act of desperation and we were stunned with disbelief. The halls of St. Vincent were crowded with artists from the Cino keeping vigil, hoping to be helpful with blood transfusions. Joe was first in surgery and then intensive care; none of us were permitted to see him or talk to him, but the doctors issued bulletins, reassuring us that he would recover. They were wrong. On Sunday night, April 2, 1967, Joe Cino, the father of off-off-Broadway, died of self-inflicted wounds.

The devastation we felt was worse than anything any of us had ever experienced. Our muse-on-earth, our inspiration and nurturer had abandoned us for eternity. The void he left is inexpressible. It was Robert Patrick's lot to mop up the viscera and blood that stained the walls and floors of the Cino, so life might return to the place. We had been scheduled to open *The Clown* just two days later on Torrey's birth date; but it seemed inconceivable that we could go on. Nevertheless, since the production had been planned as a memorial, it also seemed important that we not abandon it. So we decided to delay the opening for a week. *The Clown* became a memorial for both John and Joe, a signal that the Caffé Cino would live on.

On April 20, 1967, Michael Smith noted in the *Village Voice*:

"[The Cino] presented Claris Nelson's brief, light fantasy *The Clown*. I found it charming. Mason's staging was showy and frivolous."

And in *Show Business,* James Moss wrote:

> "*The Clown* is playing to large houses at the Cafe Cino for good reason. This charming play is a sensitive and funny rendering of the classic confrontation of innocence and evil. [It's] refreshing to see a play consistent in writing form, acting and direction, which was in large measure the work of [director] Mason. The costumes were the most opulent ever in a coffee-house production."

What would happen to the Cino? We all felt it should be a living monument to him, continuing to present new life in the theater. Eventually, by consensus we drafted Charles Stanley, the prima donna of the Cino, who perhaps most nearly represented the free spirit Joe embodied, to assume responsibility for re-opening the Cino and keeping its mission alive. By the end of the year, Charles was exhausted by the burden. He turned the responsibility over to Wolfgang Zuckerman and former *Village Voice* critic, playwright and director Michael Smith. They kept it open another couple of months until March 1968, when the liability of dealing with city regulations overwhelmed them and it finally ended.

Paint It Black

Since I passed up directing *Rimers*, I planned to produce Lanford's new play *The Gingham Dog* at La MaMa. It was a searing drama about the divorce of a racially mixed couple; although conventional in form, it was an incendiary subject. We'd seen a project by LeRoi Jones at The Studio that depicted vengeful black militias beheading white people at random and hoisting their heads on pikes. It was a device familiar in Shakespeare, but extremely unnerving when applied in the present tense to race relations. It was easy to imagine one's own head impaled on a pike. Lanford's play on the subject of race relations, *The Gingham Dog*, was his answer to that violent vision.

In spite of the "Summer of Love," race riots were rampant: in Tampa and Buffalo in June, Newark and Detroit in July, and

Washington, D.C. in August. Yet in a sign that change was coming, Thurgood Marshall became the first black Justice of the Supreme Court and by the end of the year, Cleveland's Carl Stokes became the first black mayor of a major American city. In June, the Supreme Court ruled that laws prohibiting interracial marriage were unconstitutional; yet in September when *Love Is a Many Splendored Thing* became the first soap opera to deal with interracial relationships, CBS fired the show's creator. It would have been a good time to produce a play on that subject, but we realized we couldn't cast *Gingham Dog* to our satisfaction.

Before Joe's death, Ellen was enlarging her vision with an ambitious plan to send the La MaMa Troupe out on their third European tour. This extensive excursion featured a repertoire that required a larger company. Ellen asked me if it would be all right to include two of "my actors" in her troupe. I was happy for Claris, Rob and Michael Powell to head off to Europe for an artistic adventure. They would play in Germany at Frankfurt, Heidelberg and Munich; in Italy at Spoleto; in Sweden at Stockholm and Malmö; in Copenhagen; then in Amsterdam, Edinburgh and London.

To top it all, their repertoire included a new play Lanford had written for them, so he was going too. They all left in June, and suddenly I found myself isolated. With Joe Cino gone as well, it was very lonely.

I'd begun working in the New York Shakespeare Festival offices for Allison Harper, a job I enjoyed that paid the bills; but the job lasted only a month. So I went on unemployment and asked Ellen to let me remount *The Sand Castle*. This was just the break I wanted to rescue the play from my botched production. This time I'd get it right.

Before he left with the La MaMa Troupe, Rob Thirkield had met a young actress with flaming red hair in summer stock who'd become his girlfriend. Being protective of Rob (and his considerable fortune), at first I was suspicious. He swore she was a brilliant actress; so when everyone left us behind for Europe, I asked her to come to my apartment to read a few lines of Irene from *The Sand*

Castle. Although she was fifteen years too young for the part, she had a kind of ageless maturity. Her simple, deep honesty blew me away. I cast her at once and we began to work together for the first time. Her name was Tanya Berezin.

The Fourth Cornerstone

Harriet (Tanya) Berezin was born March 25, 1941, in Philadelphia to Russian Jews, Moe and Betty Berezin. Her father owned a clothing store. She idolized Betty Hutton and decided to become an actress. At Boston University, her roommate was Faye Dunaway. Before moving to New York to pursue an acting career, she changed her name to Tanya, a happier match with her Russian heritage. Tanya met Rob Thirkield at a summer theater in 1966. Their summer romance deepened after they returned to New York. Since I was Rob's closest friend, I soon was introduced to her. She also met my almost-constant companions, Lanford, Michael and Claris. Rob brought her into his artistic haunts, the Caffé Cino and La MaMa.

Lanford was directing Rob in *The Rimers of Eldritch* at La MaMa and, two days before opening, an actress dropped out of the production. Rob's new girlfriend was quickly drafted to fill the role. She claims she was terrible, but she couldn't have been too bad, because when Lanford revived *This Is the Rill Speaking* at the Cino, he used Tanya again. I formed no opinion of Tanya's talent until she read for me for *The Sand Castle* revival. We became good friends and I was Best Man at her wedding to Rob. Our friendship survived many challenges.

The most impressive thing about Tanya was her talent. Small in stature, she is a giant on stage. By no means conventionally beautiful, with frizzy (or at best, curly) red hair and freckles, Tanya's sheer talent radiates an inner magnificence that can convince an audience she is lovely. Her work is an illustration that acting is behaving truthfully in imaginary circumstances. Her confidence allows her to behave *as if,* exuding that air of languid self-acceptance that truly beautiful women possess. I've rarely worked with anyone who equals her honesty. She's also one of the most courageous artists I've encountered, as you'll see. How Tanya become a cornerstone of Circle Rep and succeeded me as Artistic Director is one of the stories this chronicle will tell.

This second *Sandcastle* was the first time I'd directed one of Lanford's plays without the author present. I wanted to cast the production with engaging people. For Joan, I cast my sexy companion Zita, best described as a quicksilver girl. In the role of Sasha, for the first time in my career I cast a black actor in a part written as white, and beautifully black Robbie MacCauley was a good fit for the character. I found an appealing hunk to play Clint named Alan Feinstein. Tanya played Irene, John Kramer repeated his role as Calvin from the earlier production and for the pivotal role of Owen, I found a charismatic young actor named Michael McClanathan. Michael's sensitivity was reminiscent of James Dean's. He had curly blond hair and, although he was small, he was powerfully built. An ex-Marine, he had USMC tattoos on his arms, which embarrassed him greatly. He had to cover them with make-up on stage. His shy demeanor illuminated the role of Owen, based on Lanford's adolescent friend Tony Brown in San Diego. Tony was a poet and he wrote this bit of haiku that I treasure:

"Trembling I watched the blood re-touch
The ring of white where I gripped your wrist
Too tightly in my anger."

Michael McClanathan convinced an audience that Owen could write that.

The Beatles released their revolutionary *Sgt. Pepper's Lonely Hearts Club Band*. It was the summer The Monterrey Pop Festival popped and the first live international satellite production featured the debut of The Beatles' song "All You Need is Love." The British Parliament even decriminalized homosexuality, so now British gays were free to join in this "Summer of Love."

Rehearsals were fun. The ensemble rivaled that of *Balm in Gilead*. The play sprang to life, complete with song-and-dance interludes that flowed naturally from the exuberant fun. Yet serious moments had as much impact as moments Eugene O'Neill ever wrote. One strand of the plot deals with Owen's moonstruck puppy love for Jill, the pregnant wife of their neighbor Calvin, an oceanographer. Late in the play, after Calvin has forbidden Owen from visiting Jill anymore, Irene, herself aching with the loss of her lover to her promiscuous daughter, comforts Owen in his bereavement. Enveloped by the incoming fog, they stood huddled together, mother and son, isolated in the universe, marooned on the empty shore of an ocean of time. The moment lingers in my memory as vividly as any I've directed: the acting, the writing and the staging came together in perfect harmony.

The opening performance (ironically on the 5th of July) was attended by the immortal poet W.H. Auden, who lived in the Village. He came backstage and, virtually unable to speak, embraced Tanya and me; every wrinkle of his wizened face filled with a river of flowing tears. This memory is the kind of treasure in the heart to which Blanche refers in *A Streetcar Named Desire*, making me feel rich indeed.

After our two-week run at La MaMa, we transferred the production to the Cino for another week. It's a shame Lanford never saw it. I'm sure he would have loved it.

Dan Sullivan wrote in *The New York Times* (July 28, 1967):

"*The Sandcastle* handles its materials directly and honestly, and gets a sensitive performance at the Cino – especially from Tanya Berezin as the mother."

Near the end of July, Rob and Lanford were missing Tanya and me; so they arranged for us to join them in Europe. Neither of us had ever been outside the United States; but Jimi Hendrix was asking: *Are You Experienced?* We were definitely ready. Rob sent us money for tickets, so Tanya and I boarded a KLM Royal Dutch Airliner for Copenhagen.

A New Old World

During the seven-hour flight to Denmark, Tanya and I bonded in a rare way. We shared every level of every subject – our lives, our loves and, most importantly, our dreams. This interchange of souls followed a month of intimate work together, in which we both reached a new pinnacle of artistic achievement. This bond survived a divorce from my best friend and paths that have taken us in almost opposite ways in our post-Circle Rep lives. She became my most trusted ally. I continued to rely on her honesty, strength and courage through years of challenges, triumphs and despair.

We landed at Kastrup Airport, thought by many to be the most pleasant in the world, greeted by Rob, Michael and Lanford, who came to pick us up in the La MaMa van. They drove us to a compound in the Danish countryside that was the home of the notorious author Elsa Gress and her husband, painter Clifford Wright.

Elsa Gress was considered an *enfant-terrible*, either a gadfly or the conscience of Denmark, depending on your point of view. She attacked Danish architects for their "soul-less" buildings, lacking the imagination of the designers of cathedrals. Clifford was an American artist whose work was exhibited at the Seattle Art Museum and the Museum of Modern Art. He'd lived in New York where he met and married Elsa Gress, and he moved to Denmark to live with her and their children on the Island of Mon, south of Copenhagen. He designed for the Royal Danish Opera and also illustrated books.

Their house was a rambling rural estate, riotous with flowers, with clean fresh air under the bright blue skies of summer. Multiple bedrooms accommodated the troupe and the Wright family, with room to spare for guests like us. A spacious living room opened onto an enormous dining room, with a long, thick wooden table that seated twenty or more. In some respects, it reminded me of my days in the Lodge at Eagles Mere. Across the six-car driveway was a barn, where the Troupe rehearsed.

While the Troupe was in rehearsal, Tanya, Lanford and I visited the landmarks of Copenhagen. The Royal Danish Theatre was a special pleasure. Built in 1748 as the theater of the king and then as the theater of the country, it's both intimate and grand, with colonnades and crystal chandeliers embracing a miniature auditorium. The most memorable event in Copenhagen was seeing Marlene Dietrich perform at the Tivoli Gardens. This enchantress of stage and screen mesmerized us all. She sang in a direct, personal style, making eye contact with individuals in the audience. It felt like she singled *me* out and aimed her performance to me alone. Her rendition of Pete Seeger's anti-war anthem "Where Have All the Flowers Gone?" was evidence that art could influence minds.

It was apparent, however, that by the time the Troupe retreated to rehearsals in Elsa's barn, our friends were less happy than when we saw them last. The Troupe operated on a tight budget that afforded few luxuries. The travel from city to city, country to country in two vans was exhausting. The accommodations when they arrived at a destination were meager. The way these artists were herded across Europe influenced my notions of how I would treat members of my own company when we formed one.

Lanford was particularly disillusioned. He had written his most experimental piece especially for the Troupe. But it was apparent that Tom O'Horgan didn't like him and he refused to begin rehearsals on it. Lanford was eager to get away from life with a company where he felt unappreciated and to see Europe from a better perspective. As requested, I had booked us an itinerary to see the highlights of the Continent.

After Vienna (where we saw the works of Breughel and Bosch) and Venice (where we enjoyed the Byzantine splendor of St. Mark's), we flew to Florence where we met up with our young playwright friend, Kenny Pressman. We stayed in a fifteenth century hostel that backed onto the Gallery of the Accademia di Belle Arti, which houses Michelangelo's incomparable David. This masterpiece is indescribably moving. No copy or photograph can capture its magnificence. The marble is like living flesh, to be viewed from every angle. In the hall leading to David are Michelangelo's unfinished Captives, struggling to free themselves from their blocks of stone.

If one could have only one artistic experience in life, this exhibit of David and The Captives would be my choice.

But the hard beds, strong coffee, and dry rolls at the *pensione* breakfast spurred us to find more comfortable lodging. I found an old hotel on the River Arno that we could afford. Our room had walls two feet thick, with a tiny window overlooking the Ponte Vecchio.

While we were standing one evening in the Piazza della Signoria, a scene not unusual for the late 60s unfolded. A hippie with flowing shoulder-length hair and a beard reminiscent of Christ was arrested. Half naked and struggling like a martyr, he was escorted by the police into the Palazzo Vecchio, which still serves as Florence's prison. Perhaps he was hallucinating the immolation of Savonarola, who was punished with death in 1498 for his Bonfire of the Vanities in this very square. Nearby, on the banks of the River Arno, groups of hippies camped out for the beautiful summer evenings, strumming their guitars and practicing the age-old generosity of spreading *amore*.

I had a unique personal experience at the Bargello Museum, home to Donatello's David. Familiar with the statue only from photographs, I'd always been rather scornful of the effeminate naked youth depicted by Donatello; it's a vivid contrast to the manly strength I admired in Michelangelo's David. As I stood criticizing Donatello's statue, with the shepherd boy's shoulder-length locks spilling from a feathered hat and a complete lack of muscularity, I was in the middle of saying, "How could such a little wimp kill Goliath?" when I suddenly burst into tears as I perceived Donatello's message. "Oh, my God!" I cried out. "It was a *miracle!*" The giant was killed not by the ineffectual sword of an adolescent, but by the hand of God. For a Texas boy, overly hung-up on masculinity, it was a divine revelation.

By now Lanford was tired of flying, so we took a train to Rome. Ever since I'd studied Latin in the eighth grade I had a love of Roman antiquity and everything Caesar. I soaked up the ancient glories of the Forum Romanum, the beauty of the Pantheon, the fragments of statuary on the Palatine Hill and the eeriness of the catacombs. I relished saltimbocca and veal scaloppini at the open-air restaurants on the boulevards. Everywhere we went we could hear Procol Harum's haunting melody "A Whiter Shade of Pale", providing a soundtrack for our Roman holiday. Back then, people were permitted to wander through the ruins of the Coliseum even late at night. It was spooky to walk along the winding paths within that ghostly wreckage, but it was a beehive of activity; people were looking for companionship, even for a few minutes. The air tingled with anonymous danger. Deep in the shadows cynical local boys mocked the restless action by whistling: "The worms crawl in, the worms crawl out, the worms play pinochle in their snout."

The Vatican and its incomparable museum are artistic marvels. Michaelangelo's Sistine Chapel ceiling is an achievement that rivals his statue of David. The graceful tapestries of Raphael, the painter's painter, are breathtaking in their serenity. For art lovers like Lanford and me, Rome was a feast of blessings, which we gratefully devoured.

One incident framed our visit to Rome as somewhat historical. Lanford had been commissioned by composer Lee Hoiby to write a libretto for his operatic rendition of Tennessee Williams' *Summer and Smoke*. Lanford wrote the libretto in an artist's sketchbook. The evening he completed the Prologue to the opera, I had the privilege to watch him inscribe at the bottom of the page: "Rome, August 1967".

We flew on to Amsterdam, where the press was notified by our hotel that we were coming and they sent reporters to conduct a news conference with Lanford upon our arrival. Apparently the fame of off-off-Broadway was spreading. Again, it was the museums that captivated us: the Rijksmuseum with the Dutch Masters, the Rembrandt House Museum and the Van Gogh Museum, which houses the world's largest collection of Van Gogh's paintings and drawings. The liberal atmosphere of Holland was lovely after the more traditional cities of Italy, but it was cold and damp. Chilly walks along the canals gave opportunities for reflection.

We met up again with the La MaMa Troupe in Edinburgh. After being the season's sensation with their repertoire in the Fringe Festival, they were appearing in Paul Foster's *Tom Paine* at the city's principal theater, the Churchill. The city of Edinburgh was the most charming capital I visited. Crowning the city is Edinburgh Castle, dating back to the 12th century. The city has many small stone-paved culverts that span upper and lower passages, lending a medieval atmosphere. Yet you can walk in almost any direction no more than a dozen blocks before finding yourself in the company of sheep grazing in the green, damp countryside.

We traveled with the Troupe in their vans down to London, leaving behind the gloomy waters of the Firth of Forth, passing through the picturesque shires of rural England and hobbit country to the great capital of the British Empire.

Both Lanford and I were genuine Anglophiles, so arriving in London was like coming home. So many familiar names: Charing Cross, Baker Street, Victoria Station, Piccadilly Circus, St. James Park, Buckingham Palace, the Tower of London, the River Thames, Big Ben, Westminster Abbey, Covent Garden, Trafalgar Square, the Royal Albert Hall. These legendary names were actual places. While in London, I was thrilled to see my old college friend Lawrence Pressman playing opposite Donald Pleasence in the Harold Pinter production of *The Man in a Glass Booth*. It was an auspicious start to what I hoped would be Larry's glorious career.

Jean-Pierre Voos was the producer of the International Theatre Club, which was hosting the La MaMa engagement at the Mercury Theatre (another legendary name!) on Kensington Park Road.

The La MaMa Troupe was very successful in London, as they had been throughout their European tour. Jean Pierre was excited to discover that with Lanford and me he had in hand another American playwright and director. With hopes that the London excitement over the La MaMa Troupe could translate into an ongoing hunger for more Americana, he asked us to consider mounting a couple of one-acts to follow La MaMa's run at his theater. We suggested that *Home Free!* and *The Madness of Lady Bright* might fill the bill. Although pleased with the idea, Lanford was tired of his long journey, so he left for New York. Claris was eager to leave the La MaMa Troupe behind and Michael was excited to play Lawrence again.

Our plans were cut short by the La MaMa Troupe's intention to remount *Tom Paine* on the West End. There was confusion about whether the production would materialize, whether the money could be raised or a theater secured; so we began rehearsals for *Home Free!* But then, Tom O'Horgan asked Michael to come to a meeting of the Troupe, at which he threatened that if Michael didn't continue with the show, the production would fall through and Michael would bear the responsibility of failing the entire Troupe at their moment of triumph. The show, he was told, could not go on without him.

I thought this was pure psychological blackmail, and I tried to persuade Michael that it was hardly credible that the Troupe's West End engagement depended on him, whereas our enterprise centered on Michael in *Home Free!* Faced with the dilemma of letting down the Troupe or betraying his oldest friends, Michael was tortured. But in the end, Tom's guilt-trip worked; Michael agreed to stay with *Tom Paine*. Annoyed by the manipulation, for which I held Ellen Stewart ultimately responsible, I told Jean-Pierre we could not mount the plays at this time. He was disappointed, but he optimistically asked us to return the following spring to bring *Home Free!* and *Lady Bright* to London. We promised to do all we could to come again in the coming year.

We returned to a country still in the throes of controversy. The guerilla leader and pop-cultural hero Che Guevara was executed. Tens of thousands marched on Washington to protest the war and Allen Ginsburg chanted "OM" in an attempt to levitate the Pentagon. He was later arrested in New York, along with Dr. Benjamin Spock, for protesting LBJ's policies. Senator Eugene McCarthy announced his candidacy for President, challenging the incumbent over the issue of the war. In keeping with the times, the Off-Broadway production of *Hair* opened at Joseph Papp's Public Theater.

When I called Ellen to confront her with my disgust about the way things had unfolded in London, she apologized and offered me the chance to go into rehearsal immediately. She introduced me to an African-American playwright named Donald Julian. She had scheduled his *A Coffee Ground among the Tea Leaves* for production. I accepted the occasion to immerse myself in new work.

I am baffled when I'm accused of being a director mired in a realistic style. Much of my work has been experimental in nature, in a variety of styles that range from the formalism of ancient Greek drama, through the exuberant sweep of Elizabethan plays, to the absurd and abstract worlds of the avant-garde. *A Coffee Ground* was written in a mélange of styles, requiring a sumptuous production and a multi-talented, multi-racial cast. Our production was an enormous success at La MaMa and I received the best reviews I'd yet been given. The *Village Voice* compared my work, involving climax after climax, to the composer Gustav Mahler, a comparison meant to praise that really irked me because I hate Mahler (yes, even the "Second.").

A Phoenix Arises

Lanford had been shaken by Tom O'Horgan's refusal to rehearse the piece he wrote for the Troupe. The play examines the principal cause for war: patriotism. It was not only the most experimental play *he'd* ever written, it was more experimental than anything I'd ever *read*. It was dangerously experimental, mixing theatrical fiction with reality.

The characters in the play are named the same as the actors who play them. The work was called *Untitled Play*, a dark play on the meanings of "play." It was written for a cast of twelve, who progress from childhood games to personal abuse to an abstract depiction of a bloody war.

Two childlike characters representing a kind of Pierrot and Pierrette watch the action develop. The play begins innocuously, as they witness the taunts of children playing primitively cruel games in a driveway, and develops incrementally into the social pressure that demands conformity to the rules of society. In the middle of the play, as civilization develops, the entire cast performs a delicate and intricate pavane, ending as one actor fails to execute correctly the graceful formality of the steps. In a stage direction, the author requests the cast to depart from written lines to improvise at this point, using their own words to express disgust for the errant individual, heaping abuse upon him, using anything they know about the *actual* actor to make him experience genuine humiliation, and to strip him naked. The actor who is thus disgraced is left sobbing, as the cast retreats to the edges of the playing area.

Interspersed with the action are monologues that shine a Brechtian clarity, cutting through theatrical illusion and setting the audience straight about what they are seeing. There ensues an abstraction of excessive patriotism, as the cast divides into sides that each touts its superiority. After marching, strutting, waving banners and singing anthems, an abstract war breaks out, with the cast hidden beneath the huge silk banners of each side, red against white, which cover the entire stage. Accompanied by a cacophony of music, the silk colors attack and retreat with increased frenzy, until the battle climaxes. In eerie silence, Pierrot and Pierrette slowly pull back the silk, revealing the twisted bodies of the victims on the battlefield.

The Poets Theater at the Judson Memorial Church offered to present the orphaned play. Reverend Al Carmines, associate pastor of the church and a brilliant musician, agreed to compose the score. It was fun putting together a substantial ensemble, largely made up of people I'd worked with repeatedly over years of off-off-Broadway. In a way *Untitled Play* was the origin of what someday would become a formal company of artists.

Our rehearsals were conducted in the church gymnasium and the work was among the most stimulating I'd known. The actors were trained like recruits in an army of artists to be disciplined and uncompromising. We shared personal facts about our most profound fears and dangerous impulses. It was important that every member of the company discover, confront and reveal the raw potential for murder that lurks within each of us. We established a collective trust within our rehearsals that was tantamount to the Islamic extremism of the twenty-first century. Our devotion to the play, our work and each other was unreserved, with the single-mindedness of a suicide mission.

Sensitive to the dangerous psychological territory we were exploring, I delayed rehearsing the critical scene of humiliation until we staged the rest of the production. Concentrated discipline was required to learn the graceful steps of the pavane, which had to be executed perfectly by all except one. We spent vital time on the monologues that were interspersed with the action. I worked with Zita to mimic the icy heat I'd seen in Marlene Dietrich, addressing individuals in the audience so personally that each one felt singled out by her indictment of the cruelty of war. The abstract battle scene had to be choreographed and performed with precision. We did many improvisations to build group trust, based on the integrity of each artist.

About two-thirds the way through our rehearsal period, I decided we were ready to tackle the free-fall improvisation of real feelings and actions that required the humiliation of one member of the group. I chose the angelic Michael McClanathan to be the victim of the abuse. I knew from his sensitive work as Owen in *The Sand Castle* that he would be a vulnerable receptacle for the scorn of his peers. The first time we unleashed the company on Michael was one of the most gut-wrenching experiences of my life, in or outside the theater. Using every bit of knowledge they had about Michael's weaknesses, the company skillfully and incisively dissected his persona, cutting away the exterior charm and sweet demeanor, to expose to the air the bowels of pride and egotistical superiority he had hidden deep within. The company was unsparing. They stripped him, both physically and psychologically. The effect on Michael was devastating. When they had finished their physical, verbal and psychological evisceration, Michael was left naked, sobbing pitifully in abject disgrace. The company retreated silently to the sides of the gym, as Michael recovered himself as much as he could and, gathering his clothes to cover his nakedness, withdrew.

This perilous experiment succeeded. We had crossed an artistic Rubicon perhaps never before braved. The company, compelled to perform the humiliation, were as overwhelmed by recognizing their own inhumanity as Michael was in being their victim. A few days later, we repeated the scene, apprehensive whether we could go again to the depths of that terrible place. Once more, the company was superb in its appalling task.

But next time, the scene turned into an astounding breakthrough. As before, the actors stripped Michael naked and threw at him the damaging insights and invectives they'd previously discovered. Once again, Michael collapsed, sobbing. But as the company withdrew to the sides of the stage, Tanya Berezin stopped midway and turned back to Michael. Savagely approaching him, she screamed: "You son of a bitch! You're not humiliated! You're faking! Just like everything else in your life!" Michael blushed a deep scarlet and began to cry in earnest. Satisfied, Tanya emptily dragged herself to her corner. It was the most courageous artistic moment I've ever witnessed. On artistic courage like that we could build a theater.

Unfortunately, when the production left the confines of the gymnasium for the larger sanctuary of the Judson Church, much of the intensity was dissipated. To represent the world of the play, we erected an enormous tent made of parachute silk that contained both audience and stage, eliminating the presence of the church itself. This required hours and hours of many sewing machines piecing together enormous sections of the silk tent. It was rigged to rise around the audience as the play began, an engineering challenge. The walls of the church disappeared behind the silk cocoon that confined the audience in the world of the play.

But the spectacular nature of the setting, combined with the theatricality of the lighting, diminished the harsh honesty of our experiment. Under the unchanging glare of the gymnasium lights, there had been no "effects." The focus was on the reality of the actors' experience. In retrospect, I wish we could have brought the audience into our gymnasium/rehearsal room, and sat them about on the floor to experience the play.

While I'm not sure the audience was ever as morally demolished as we were in rehearsal, the playing of the humiliation scene was never compromised again after Tanya's bold confrontation. They really *did* humiliate Michael at every performance. It was such a torturous experience that neither Lanford nor I could bear to watch what we had created. After the first performance, we watched the production only until that scene came up. Then we would retreat into the choir-room behind the sacristy, and wait until the singing signaled the scene was over. Even off-stage, we felt pangs of guilt about what we made these artists do. Following this production, Lanford never published the play for fear that in less professional hands it could impart psychological damage on unsuspecting amateurs.

Michael Smith in the *Village Voice* (February 1, 1968):

> "*Untitled Play* is Lanford Wilson's plunge into the avant garde, and he goes extravagantly deep. Director Mason's successes are the climaxes, which are numerous and spectacularly effective."

Untitled Play was an important turning point. We now had the fortitude it takes to create a theater with the artistic goals Miss Krause had envisioned. We were talented enough; now we were also strong enough.

Chapter 4
Journeys

The year 1968 began with a surprising declaration of liberty in Czechoslovakia by Alexander Dubček known as the Prague Spring. But on the other side of the world, the Viet Cong launched the deadly Tet Offensive, offsetting any sense of moving toward peace. The infamous My Lai massacre soon followed, in which American troops killed scores of innocent civilians, a shameful event in the history of United States forces that has not yet been forgotten.

Following *Untitled Play* (which dramatized our feelings about war), we turned our attention to the racial strife that was ripping our nation apart, and began rehearsals for *The Gingham Dog*. I'd retrieved the script a year before from a drawer where Lanford had retired it. At that time, there were six characters and the drama was in a three-act format. He was despondent about the unwieldy way the plot unfolded, so we got out scissors and Scotch tape. We sat on the living room floor of his West 4th Street apartment and cut and pasted the script into a new form. We excised two of the characters, focusing on the four at the center of the drama. We restructured the events to tell the story in two movements with one intermission. A plot that seemed cumbersome now flowed smoothly to a dynamic first act curtain, followed by a poignant second act in which the alienated lovers unsuccessfully try to span the abyss that's opened between them.

The New Dramatists gave Lanford a date to mount a workshop production at their theater on East 4th Street, across from where La MaMa is located today. We found Lea Scott, a forceful, honest actress from the Negro Ensemble Company to play the incendiary role of Gloria. Michael Warren Powell played her vacillating husband Vince, an architect, and beautiful Gretchen Walther (who'd played Olivia opposite my Malvolio at Eagles Mere) played his ignorant Southern sister Barbara. David Gallagher played the gay next-door neighbor Robert, a role that re-appeared to better effect as the character Larry in *Burn This*. I designed and built the set, using the cardboard from enormous refrigerator boxes to make flats that, when taped together and painted white, depicted the bleak, modern apartment the couple shared in the latter part of their marriage. I also designed the lighting.

The play begins with the couple dividing their belongings into moving boxes. Naturally, that chore is laden with emotional memories, as they carve up the life they've created together. While they pack, happier times are evoked when they were young lovers, setting out on a road of idealism that knew no color barriers. At the beginning of their marriage, they shared a romantic nest above the Waverly Theater on Sixth Avenue. Vince played basketball across the street with neighborhood kids of all races, and when he came home, sweaty and tired, Gloria lavished on him the unsullied love of newlyweds. As the marriage has gone on, they've moved into a trendy new apartment and the couple has developed interests that have taken them on divergent paths. Gloria, a social worker, has become active in radical black politics, while Vince is designing a new housing unit, part of an urban redevelopment that Gloria dismisses as prison-like slums, perpetuating poverty and despair. Their ideological differences have splintered the bonds they've shared and left them implacable foes.

Lanford began writing the play after seeing a LeRoi Jones project at The Actors Studio. The Jones play contained violent rhetoric by black militants, railing against all white people and blaming them for the subjugation of the past. Lanford wrote a scorching reply to that narrow point of view, lashing out at the hate in these rants. At first, he didn't know what he'd written. Was it an essay? Was it dialogue? If it was the latter, who was saying it and what were the circumstances? Then, typical of Lanford's writing methodology, a couple of days later he wrote a blistering rebuttal to the first speech. It was immediately clear that the second speech, defending the ferocious emotions of blacks toward whites, was spoken by the black wife of a white man. It was also clear their relationship was irreparably torn. So, here were the beginnings of a play; the task was to retrace how these people came to this impasse.

The play was blazingly relevant at the time. It was also the first straightforwardly realistic play Lanford wrote, which meant it might speak to the wider audience a commercial production could provide. We were aware of that possibility as we worked on the play, but that was not our goal. We were dedicated to discovering the truth of these people and to giving them a voice.

We realized our artistic goals. The performances sizzled with honesty, matching the rhetoric of the dialogue. Audiences were deeply moved. I was particularly proud of the second act where, with all emotion spent, Vince comes back to the empty apartment in the middle of the night and finds Gloria experiencing the same hollowness he's discovered in himself. After the things they've said to each other, there is no possibility of reconciliation. At the end, Vince quietly closes the door, leaving Gloria looking out the window as the first light of dawn illuminates the plume of smoke from her cigarette. The play ends with a full minute of silence, this nebulous image, lingering like a bleak Hockney print. A minute is a long time in stage-time, unconventional for a play with such a conventional structure.

As for the commercial potential, no offers were forthcoming. However, Lanford did receive a proposal from Artistic Director Davey Marlin-Jones to mount a regional production at the Washington Theater Club, an opportunity he gratefully accepted. Lanford went to the Capital for the final rehearsals and the opening. New York producer Haila Stoddard saw Davey's production in Washington and gave Lanford his first shot at Broadway.

Lanford and I executed a written agreement that if he was offered a professional production, I was guaranteed the right to be the director. I'd asked Lanford to sign it because I'd seen colleagues (like Neil Flanagan, Michael Powell and Rob Thirkield) left behind when plays they were in advanced from off-off-Broadway to professional productions. As the months went by and Lanford didn't mention any progress on his expected Broadway debut, I asked what was happening. Lanford told me the producers felt they couldn't risk a Broadway investment on both a new playwright *and* an untried director. I could understand their hesitation, but it was never my intention to prevent the play from receiving the bigger production it deserved. The producers were insisting on Broadway veteran Alan Schneider, who directed *Virginia Woolf.* I admired Alan's work, so I offered to step aside and allow him to direct the play; but I held Lanford to a provision in the agreement that in the event I did *not* direct a future production, I'd receive a percentage of his royalties in recognition of my work on the script. He agreed, so plans for the Broadway production went forward.

The Gingham Dog opened at the John Golden Theater a year later, in April of 1969. The Broadway production initially starred Cicely Tyson, but when she couldn't remember her lines, she was replaced by Diana Sands. Playing Vince was George Grizzard; Roy London and Karen Grassle played Robert and Barbara, respectively.

Unfortunately, the Broadway production missed the subtle subtext in the play. Rather than witnessing painful memories being packed into moving boxes, the audience saw actors executing mechanical "business" that the director assigned. The actors complained the boxes were only half-filled, but Schneider dismissed their concern. The play turned into little more than a shouting match. The critics were not kind, even though they recognized the playwright's potential. It closed after five performances, so I never saw any royalties. The best thing to come out of his Broadway debut was that Lanford and Roy moved to a stylish two-bedroom apartment on Bank Street, just across from

Rob and Tanya. The floors were highly polished hardwood, and Lanford bought a blue Persian rug that he centered in the living room. The apartment's contemporary chic proclaimed that the country boy from Missouri had passed through his Village hobo days to New York sophistication.

But all this transpired a year after our production at the New Dramatists the year before, when we achieved an artistic success, if not a commercial transfer.

We'd promised Jean-Pierre Voos that we'd return to the International Theater Club in London in the spring of 1968 with two new American plays. So, as soon as our *Gingham Dog* opened, we began rehearsals for *Home Free!* and *The Madness of Lady Bright*.

Voyage To The Future

At some point the previous year, Neil Flanagan had been unable to appear for one performance of *Lady Bright*, so Cino diva Charles Stanley filled in for him. The difference between the two actors was striking. Neil had the chunky physique of a mature man who'd never lost his baby fat. His performance of Leslie was a triumph of playing against type. By contrast, Charles was tall and lean, with sculpted cheekbones and enormous eyes. I wanted Charles for Leslie. In spite of my criticisms of how Lanford dumped his friends for professional advancement, I justified my choice with artistic reasons. The bravura of Neil's performance was a solo accomplishment and Charles offered a clean slate to explore the interplay with the other two characters. I cast Tanya and a hunky actor named David Groh to play the Man and Woman, representing all the men and women in Leslie's life. David was especially suited to embody the all-important image of Adam, Leslie's unfulfilled fantasy of love. I was careful not to steal anything from the Cino production, but the music was hard to top. When Leslie throws himself into a frenzy of dancing to rock and roll, the Cino production used the Rolling Stones' "Let's Spend the Night Together," a perfect choice. I found something that worked almost as well: Mitch Ryder and the Detroit Wheels' "Devil with a Blue Dress On."

For *Home Free!* I wanted Michael to continue playing Lawrence because he shared my desire to base the behavior of the character in clinical psychology. Opposite him, I cast Claris to play Joanna. She'd played everything for me from Queen Elizabeth in *Mary Stuart* to the most aggressive little dyke imaginable in *Balm in Gilead*. I was keen to see how her honesty affected the role of Joanna. Concerned that my first production was perhaps a bit too sweet, I wanted to explore the play as a dark gothic tale, perhaps closer to the author's intention.

While we were in rehearsal at the New Dramatists, every free hour we also were engaged constructing the costumes Michael designed for the Off-Broadway production of the La MaMa Troupe's *Tom Paine*. On March 25, 1968, *Tom Paine* opened uptown at Theater 73, where it continued for 295 performances. Unlike in London, this time Michael chose to appear in *Home Free!* and somehow, *Tom Paine* managed to open without him. I enjoyed the opening night, sure it would be a hit and it was.

We did a run-through at New Dramatists after two weeks of rehearsal so Lanford could see what we'd accomplished so far. I was nervous because I knew that the shows needed another two weeks before they'd be really ready. As usual at this point in my rehearsals, the pace of the plays was intentionally slow. Fortunately, Lanford was familiar with my rehearsal process, so he could imagine how much they would improve, and he was pleased with what he saw. At an emaciated six-foot-two, Charles was closer to the image Lanford originally envisioned for Leslie Bright. My only disappointment was that the author would not see the finished productions.

We were told by our London hosts that we needed to get workpapers approved by British Equity that allowed us to perform in Great Britain. In order to shore up our credibility, I came up with a name that improved our chances: the American Theater Project. The name was both grand, utilizing the term "American" to underline our national importance and at the same time humble, since the word "Project" implied that we were new, with potential to grow. Our ploy worked! We were approved to appear at the Mercury Theater in London and the Traverse Theater in Edinburgh.

I burned bridges in order to make this trip happen, skipping out on my rent, phone and utilities bills. I was risking all my chips on this single spin of the wheel. Our dream of forming a professional ensemble of artists was on the brink of becoming a reality. The American Theater Project was launching an English invasion, immediately following the disastrous London debut of The Actors Studio. Their production of *Three Sisters* had been a success on Broadway. I was thrilled by the first act, although the subsequent acts suffered from what appeared to be less rehearsal time. It starred Kim Stanley as Masha in a memorable performance, Shirley Knight and Kevin McCarthy, both of whom I later directed. But the London critics scorned The Studio's offering as self-indulgent and inaudible. Dared we hope that London critics could appreciate American acting?

On March 28th, we boarded the luxury liner *RMS Queen Elizabeth* for our voyage to England. Recalling how the actors in the La MaMa Troupe were treated, I was determined that my company felt cared for, so they could give everything on stage without worrying about off-stage necessities. Tanya and David were going to fly to London. Meanwhile, Charles, Michael, Claris and I rehearsed during our six-day crossing.

The departure was a thrilling event. All our friends came and toasted our embarkation with champagne. We hated to leave Lanford behind, but he was terrified of boats even more than airplanes and he'd already been to Europe. He was pleased the way rehearsals were going and he entrusted his plays to us.

The steward arranged for us to have access to the Board Room of the *Queen Elizabeth* for several hours every day. Our rehearsals went well, inspired by the magnitude of our undertaking and the magnificence of our surroundings. The ship was a city unto itself, with four cinemas, four swimming pools and a plethora of bars and entertainment. The cuisine was delicious and plentiful, even though we were traveling in steerage class at the bottom of the boat. We had bunk beds in each cabin that converted into a divan when not in use.

There was a small desk, upholstered chairs and a miniscule bathroom, complete with a shower. The Art Deco grand public spaces of the *Queen Elizabeth* were spectacular: great staircases descending to enormous lobbies, deck chairs on breezy promenades, a dining room with an immense chandelier and white linen-covered tables, served by a platoon of waiters all dressed in black tie formality. On the promenade decks, we watched the endless swell of the sea, a profound experience that influenced our work.

We transferred from Southampton to London, where we stayed with Jean-Pierre Voos and his wife Deanna in the Notting Hill Gate area, near the Bayswater Road that runs along Hyde Park. The Mercury Theater's small proscenium stage was about the size of the Cherry Lane's in New York. There was a slightly religious feeling to it, because windows on the side walls were embedded with narrow gothic arches that had to be covered for matinees. Our coming to London was delayed a year, but finally we were ready to make our magic.

Earning Existence

During our Atlantic crossing, President Johnson announced that he wasn't seeking re-election, bowing to the opposition to his conduct of the Vietnam War. Essentially, he ceded the likely nomination to the recently announced candidacy of Robert Kennedy, the charismatic brother of our slain president. RFK eloquently opposed the war and championed racial equality.

Only two days into our London rehearsals, terrible news came from our homeland: Dr. Martin Luther King, Jr. was assassinated in Memphis, Tennessee. The dramatic newspaper photo of people pointing from a balcony to where the shots came from was like a frieze of tragedy, the people's loss etched on their faces. As we followed the news from afar, riots broke out in major American cities for several days afterward. In a eulogy for Dr. King, Bobby Kennedy quoted from Aeschylus:

"He who learns must suffer. Even in our sleep, pain, which cannot forget, falls drop by drop upon the heart until, in our own despair and against our will, comes wisdom by the awful grace of God."

He knew of what he spoke.

There was little we could do except to continue our work, which was going well. Charles was not entirely happy with the producers, who paid us only fifteen pounds a week, about $45. But London office workers and clerks often earned only five pounds a week, so actually we were doing pretty well. Michael was upset that there wasn't more publicity about our impending arrival and opening, but actors seldom feel there's enough publicity. I felt confident that Jean-Pierre knew his business and that we would have audiences to fill the small Mercury Theater.

What I was not prepared for was the casual, almost disinterested way in which the professional stage crews went about their business of building the sets and hanging the lights. No matter how far behind we were in our schedule, they always managed to take an inordinate amount of time for a tea break. I was accustomed to the frantic pace and energy of American backstage workers, hell-bent to be ready, and it was difficult to accept that the British crews were giving it their full effort. Nevertheless, tea breaks and all, we got the tech work done, and we were prepared and eager for our opening on April 15, 1968. Both plays had realistic sets with walls, and for *Home Free!*, a door! The flats were double-sided so that they turned from Lawrence and Joanna's dark cocoon to reveal the white walls of Leslie's apartment in *Lady Bright*, with the colorful signatures of all the men who've passed through, leaving their autographs behind.

We had the distinction of being the last play censored by the Lord Chamberlain, whose oversight of decency on the British stage was abolished the week we opened. His office ruled that no mention could be made of the incest at the heart of *Home Free!*. So, ironically, I was granted my wish to circumvent seeing the play through the lens of incest. We subtly let the audience learn their relationship by having both character refer to their shared parents, so by implication, that they were siblings. The censorship caused something of a stir in the newspapers, since the British were always scandalized by the attempts by the Crown to censor what they were able to watch. The notoriety didn't hurt our box-office. Strangely, of the two plays, *Lady Bright* was far more shocking to an American audience, uncomfortable with overt homosexuality; but the censors made no fuss at all over the outrageous queen the play depicted. Apparently, the censors were quite comfortable with flamboyantly effeminate men, but not an incestuous heterosexual relationship!

I was pleased with the opening night performances. We decided that since Lawrence never left the room, he'd have no reason to change from his bed clothes; so Michael, a strapping adult with muscular legs, was shockingly sexy in an abbreviated nightshirt that reached only mid-thigh. His performance was grounded in clinically accurate schizophrenic behavior. Claris was heartbreaking as the trusting Joanna. Like a doomed doe facing a hunter's bullet, her panic came too late. She realized Lawrence was incapable of leaving the room to fetch a doctor who might save her life. The play never before attained the impact of horror we achieved in England.

The production of *Lady Bright* stunned London. Charles was poised and willowy as Leslie, an ardent admirer of *Giselle*. His long, expressive limbs moved with such grace that at the end, discarded by society and abandoned even by his fantasies, his descent into the loneliness of madness was devastating. Tanya played all the women in his life, from an unforgiving mother to a chatty manicurist to a competitive rival for the handsome men Leslie has pined for. David Groh was a commanding muscular presence in his white t-shirt and his tight black dungarees, playing all the men who'd drifted through Leslie's life: beginning with Adam, the unrequited object of unquenchable desire, who left as a souvenir the large scrawl of his autograph on Leslie's freshly-painted apartment wall; followed by all the others who'd left their names behind, each signature a memento of a sexual encounter with varying degrees of significance to Leslie.

Philip French, the critic for *The New Statesman,* raved:

> "Not to be missed. As Leslie Bright, a subtle, sinuous Charles Stanley is giving the finest performance currently to be seen in London. Enormous credit must go to director Marshall W. Mason for a lucid, sensitive, detailed production."

In *The Spectator* (April 26, 1968) Hilary Spurling wrote:

> "Although we've admired before the professional virtuosity, the visual and technical brilliance of American companies, we have seen nothing so far quite so entrancing or so imaginatively ambitious as this double bill. *Home Free!* has clarity and wit, some uncommonly fine acting, and Mr. Mason's subtle, precise and innovative direction."

And a review in *The Stage* (April 28, 1968) opined:

> "One of the most invigorating evenings of theatre to have appeared in many months."

The other reviews were also warm, some preferring the first play, others the last. But the overall critical response established the American Theater Project as an ensemble of theater artists whose work was not to be missed. Our entire run was sold out for every performance. The London press endowed our American Theater Project with authentic existence. We were praised, therefore we *were*.

Our London debut coincided with the explosion of a cultural revolution in London. All the groovy rock and roll bands were from Great Britain. The fashion industry was centered on Carnaby Street and while we were there, I bought a new wardrobe of bell-bottom trousers, billowing-sleeved pirate shirts and high-heeled boots that zippered up the side. I was the very model of Edwardian flair. On Saturdays, there was an open street fair just northwest of our Notting Hill Gate area at the Portobello Road Market, where all kinds of antiques, second-hand clothing and trinkets were sold by street merchants, whose stocks came from surpluses of previous eras, people's closets and bartered goods. We could walk there from our house on Ladbroke Terrace up Kensington Park Road to Westbourne Grove and go from stall to stall looking for treasures. I bought a heavy black Bobbie's cape of thickest wool for thirty-five pounds that I wore relentlessly over the next few winters. It weighed as much as it cost. My hair grew longer to crown my new image.

During our London run, we met the celebrated actresses Lila Kodrova and Judi Dench, who were playing in a West End engagement of the musical *Cabaret*. Lila was staying on the South End of Hyde Park and we became good friends. I frequently went to a matinee performance and, while waiting to escort her home, enjoyed watching these two actresses perform again and again.

Unfortunately, we'd scheduled a limited run. Having no idea of the degree of excitement we would stir, we'd already committed to going on to the Traverse Theater in Edinburgh. It was painful to cut short the experience of being the toast of the Capital to fulfill a pledge in Scotland. We knew that by leaving, we surrendered the momentum our success had gathered. Our triumph was sweet, but all too short.

A Hazy Shade Of Success

Tanya flew back to New York at the end of the London engagement because she bought her ticket at a special price restricted to a five-week stay. We hired a van to transport our company of five to the royal seat of Scotland. Michael did most of the driving and as luck would have it, we literally ran out of gas just short of our destination. Charles and I were elected to walk off into the night to find a petrol station. It was shortly before dawn and the Scottish countryside was enveloped in a thick fog drifting over the moors from the Firth of Forth. We walked a mile or so, having no idea where we were and we had imbibed a good smoke of hashish before we left our comrades snoozing in the van. Suddenly, appearing out of the fog like the very image of Brigadoon was an apparition of a London taxicab: one of those big, boxy black autos that are as unmistakable as they are endemic to their city. We were sure we were hallucinating! We hailed the approaching vehicle, which, much to our amazement, pulled up and we clambered aboard. Charles and I stumbled all over each other, trying to explain our plight to the driver, who answered in a dialect I'd never heard before. It was inconceivable that under the driver's thick brogue lay our own mother tongue. Although we had no idea what he'd said, the driver took us to a service station, where for a few pounds we borrowed a can that we filled with petrol and then he drove us back to find our stalled compatriots. Apparently we were at the very edge of the suburbs when we'd run out of gas, not in the middle of the moors as we surmised. It was with stoned hilarity that we arrived at dawn's first light in Edinburgh. It should have served as an omen.

The Traverse Theater was nestled at the base of Edinburgh Castle on Castle Rock. In a corner at the top of a cobblestone street known as the Royal Mile, one ascended a narrow stone staircase to a second floor that contained a lively, atmospheric pub, a small art gallery and a tiny theater tucked into a dark, damp space between them. The theater was more or less a miniature thrust stage, not unlike the Cino, so we needed to restage both plays from the proscenium configuration of the Mercury.

The Traverse was being run by Max Stafford-Clark, who later achieved stature on the world stage as Artistic Director of the Royal Court Theater and for introducing many new playwrights, including David Hare and Caryl Churchill. At our arrival, Max had just been appointed Artistic Director of the Traverse, so we were one of his first offerings.

It took only a couple of days of restaging during tech rehearsals to adjust to the confines of the Traverse and we opened on May 9th to generally favorable reviews in the local papers.

The *Scottish Daily Mail* (May 10, 1968) said:
"The Traverse picks the best from New York's richest orchard, off-off-Broadway."

The Scotsman said:
"Difficult themes are handled with great sensitivity."

The Glasgow Herald said:
"Both plays were directed by Mason, to whom must go much of the credit for the impeccable balance and atmosphere of difficult, but well-worthwhile productions."

The main element that helped us endure the cold of a Scottish spring was that we'd brought along a sufficient supply of hashish from London. I should emphasize that neither Claris nor David ever partook in our indulgences, but Charles, Michael and I regularly drew comfort from the consolation it offered.

One evening after a performance, Michael, Claris, Charles and I were proceeding merrily home, cutting through a park called Jaw Bone Walk because at one end of the path, two enormous whalebones formed an arch. Suddenly, our jocularity was interrupted by the awareness that we were being followed by two policemen, terrifying in their high-domed black helmets. Charles quickly tossed the small pipe, but one of the Bobbies searched among the bushes until he located the incriminating evidence. We were placed under arrest and taken to the precinct, where we were kept for several hours, nervously awaiting our fate. Charles claimed that the "cannabis," as they called it, was his and that the rest of us were innocent. A search of our bodies confirmed his claim. Claris was particularly annoyed at being frisked by a stocky, matronly policewoman, since she was guilty of nothing more than being in our company. Finally, long after midnight, we all were dismissed except for Charles, who was booked and detained in a jail cell overnight. We were told to return the following morning at ten to attend the trial.

We showed up at the royal courthouse the next day as instructed and found seats in the gallery. The judge actually wore a shoulder length white wig, just like in *Witness for the Prosecution*, and the solicitors all wore short little periwigs. Were it not for the solemnity of the occasion, it would have been hilarious. Charles was ushered into the courtroom, wearing handcuffs. He was a tall, thin, pathetic figure with a stubble of overnight whiskers. He stood in the dock to face his accusers (like Sydney Carton in *A Tale of Two Cities*). The evidence was presented. Charles pleaded guilty. The defense counselor pointed out that he was a distinguished foreign actor appearing in an engagement at the Traverse Theater and that the run was scheduled to end shortly. The judge peered down from his high bench of wigged eminence and directed Charles to leave town at the conclusion of the run. He fined Charles thirty-five pounds. He was released and we met him outside in a joyous celebration of his freedom, with relief that the sentence was no more stringent. We pooled our money to pay the fine and entered the final weeks of our engagement.

Zita arrived in Edinburgh to see the show, then she and I left Edinburgh together on the train. I lingered for a couple of weeks in London, frustrated that our brief blaze of fame could not be re-kindled. I finally traded airline tickets with Zita (in those days one could do that). Hers was a limited-return ticket, whereas mine was open-ended. I was eager to go back to the United States and she was happy to remain abroad. I took a ferry to Amsterdam, where I boarded a plane for New York. Inside my luggage, I carried clippings of effusive English praise for our American artistry.

In March of 2011, about a year after I wrote this account of our Edinburgh experience, I received an email from the United Kingdom. Dan Morgan sent his unsolicited recollection of that long ago time and I asked his permission to copy it here. This is his unexpurgated communication to me forty-three years later:

The Transcendent Years

"Hello, Mr. Mason:

It was interesting to recently view your comments on YouTube regarding productions of Lanford Wilson's *Home Free!* back in the 1960s. I was the stage manager at the Traverse in Edinburgh in the spring of 1968 when you brought the American Theater Project's productions of *Home Free!* and *The Madness of Lady Bright to* Scotland, and I was completely blown away by the plays and by your New York company. I had recently arrived myself at the Traverse after a year and a half with the Royal Shakespeare Company at their then London base at the Aldwych Theatre, where my first introduction to contemporary American drama was assistant stage-managing Jules Feiffer's *Little Murders*. At first I found my transition to the Traverse rather dull – despite the exciting environment of the jewel-like Traverse itself set in the rather moribund setting of grey Edinburgh, the first few productions I worked on struck me as, well, not terribly exciting (I was 26 years of age at the time). And then you and your company arrived! With two extraordinary plays! And a company of extraordinary players! It was as though the lights had come on for the first time (stage lights, life lights). I fell in love with the plays and I think I fell in love with all of you guys (I recall, vividly, dancing on the first-night party – or was it just a party? – with a beautiful young woman called Zita who was attached to your company but whose role was unclear to me) – in fact, when there was some talk of the productions moving to Paris I talked to Michael Warren Powell about my accompanying them as stage manager and he wisely advised me to stick with my contract with the Traverse.

Anyway. Well, that was all a long time ago and maybe because it's old stuff you may not care to be reminded of. But I just wanted to thank you from an old guy now who tends his garden in England and as he digs and hoes finds old sweet (and bitter-sweet) memories getting unearthed.

I hope this communication finds you in good cheer and good health.

Best wishes, Dan Morgan"

Converting Our Currency

I arrived home to learn that Andy Warhol had been shot by Valerie Solanas, a radical feminist playwright. Two years before, this same woman rang the bell of my apartment on Horatio Street and gave me her play to read. The script, entitled *Up Your Ass,* was the most appalling piece of excrement I'd ever read, but I rationalized that perhaps I couldn't appreciate its non-linear style. When she came to pick up her script, I suggested that she needed a more avant-garde director and suggested Michael Kahn. A week later, Michael called to ask why I'd sent him such a crazy writer. I apologized, but neither of us knew how close we'd come to being victims of her violence. Warhol survived the attack, but it was a close call for all of us.

It was difficult fighting my despondence, fearing the value of our enterprise was evaporating. If it were not for the reviews, it was hard to believe any of it happened. Tanya and Rob were wonderful to me, buoying me up with love, friendship and good company. We went to see Stanley Kubrick's film of Arthur C. Clarke's *2001: A Space Odyssey,* which was leaving audiences agog with a vision of the future that almost *required* psychedelic drugs to comprehend. I was staying with Rob and Tanya at their apartment on Bank Street, just across the street from the apartment Lanford shared with Roy London. We'd had dinner and I was about to retire on the pull-out bed from their sofa when television reports came ripping into our lives. Robert Kennedy, our hope for the future of our country, had been shot at the Ambassador Hotel in Los Angeles. We'd been following television reports of his victory in the California Democratic primary. Suddenly, our world was turned upside-down again by assassination. What had become of America?

The Transcendent Years

I saw Bobby Kennedy at a rally in Sheridan Square in March just before I left for London. His words were an inspiration:

> "Only those who dare to fail greatly can ever achieve greatly."

The throngs that filled the square were electrified by his charisma; he was a golden god of hope. Bobby paraphrased George Bernard Shaw and made his words immortal:

> "Some men see things as they are and say 'Why?' I dream things that never were and say, 'Why not?'"

He also said:

> "Each time a man stands up for an ideal or acts to improve the lot of others or strikes out against injustice, he sends forth a tiny ripple of hope."

I took these words to heart.

President Kennedy's assassination in 1963 was a brutal shock to the world, the nation and, of course, to his idealistic brother. Bobby served as Attorney General under President Johnson for nine months and then he was elected a Senator from New York. He was eloquent in his opposition to the Vietnam War and he championed civil rights. Bobby questioned what kind of life we envisioned for ourselves: whether privileged Americans earned the wealth they enjoyed and whether we have obligations to those who have so little.

His brother, Senator Ted Kennedy, eulogized him with these words:

> "My brother need not be idealized or enlarged in death, beyond what he was in life, to be remembered simply as a good and decent man, who saw wrong and tried to right it; saw suffering and tried to heal it; saw war and tried to stop it."

On June 9, President Johnson declared a day of national mourning. But half a century later, I mourn the loss of the nation we might have become under his leadership.

In the last week of August, the dissatisfaction of antiwar protesters reached dramatic proportions at the Democratic National Convention in Chicago. The convention ignored the supporters of Robert Kennedy and Senator Eugene McCarthy by nominating LBJ's Vice-President, Hubert H. Humphrey, a bastion of the establishment that prolonged the war. The vociferous protests in the streets were met with a show of force by the Chicago police. We were shocked to watch on television the bloody beatings the authorities rained down upon Americans who disagreed with our nation's policies.

Jacqueline Kennedy fled the country to marry billionaire Aristotle Onassis in Greece. At the Olympics in Mexico City, the defiant "black power salute" was given by the winners on the victory podium, which caused a lot of controversy.

Tanya, Lanford and I spent weekends all summer with our friend Marilyn Sutter at her house in North Haven, near Sag Harbor. I began trying to persuade people that the American Theater Project could bring distinction to any institution that provided us with sponsorship. I made appointments with the Public Theater and Lincoln Center to promote this idea. Jules Irving listened with genuine interest as I made my pitch. There was a theater in the basement of Lincoln Center called The Forum (now the Mitzi Newhouse) that seated 299, and was a lovely, intimate space with an extreme thrust stage that assured no member of the audience was more than eight rows away. It remained empty while Irving struggled to make Lincoln Center a leading force in New York. He had an empty theater; I had a homeless company with bona fide credentials from London. It seemed like a perfect juncture to join forces.

In the meantime, I became close again to Bill Hoffman. I directed his one-act *Goodnight, I love You* at the Old Reliable Tavern Theater in the East Village. Billy wrote this autobiographical play about his relationship with Lucy Silvay, with whom he conversed every night on the telephone before going to sleep. The play is a touching depiction of a gay man and his intimate relationship with a straight woman, as they share a nightly reverie of their disappointments in love, their fantasies, indeed their very souls, before ending each conversation with the title line of the play. It played at the Cino in 1965 with my Northwestern friend Mike Griswold (who'd played Owen in the first *Sand Castle*) and Linda Eskenas. Now, I cast the part of the gay man with Michael McClanathan, my sensitive Owen from the second production of *The Sand Castle*, and opposite him my own soul mate of intimate sharing, Tanya Berezin. Although there were no reviews at the Old Reliable, it was so popular that it moved to the Playbox Theater for another three weeks.

In September, Jules Irving finally approved the American Theater Project presenting a play on the stage of his Forum Theater at Lincoln Center. This was a dream perilously close to becoming a reality: my little theater company introduced on the stage of the foremost theater complex in America.

We decided to produce William M. Hoffman's *Spring Play* for our first production. The play had been done in March the previous year at La MaMa, directed by Lee Hickman. I saw it there and thought there was more potential in the play than had been realized. The play is a portrait of young artists in New York and their complicated relationships. It centers on a poet played by Rob Thirkield, and featured the great Lois Smith, and from my London *Lady Bright*, Tanya Berezin, Charles Stanley and David Groh.

Lincoln Center gave us a large rehearsal space in a building across Tenth Avenue from the theater and we rehearsed diligently, deeply committed to our mission. It was a beautiful play written by a poet and we gave it our all. I wanted the staging to be as fluid as the poetry and it was. The music was written by John Corigliano and was as inspiring as the lyrical dialogue of the text. We were scheduled to open at the Forum on November 11th.

Then Actors Equity Association notified us that they were prohibiting the production from opening at the Lincoln Center. I was astonished! This was, after all, the union for actors and we'd been *given* the theater and the rehearsal space gratis by Lincoln Center. It was an opportunity to showcase our work, which had received a fantastic reception in London.

I was granted a hearing before the Council at Actors Equity, the governing body of the union. They explained that they were in the middle of contract negotiations with Lincoln Center and that they could not agree to a showcase performance in any part of the complex without a Broadway-level contract. It was a matter of setting a precedent. Understanding our dilemma, AEA promised to find a substitute theater where we could present our production. It was a hollow compensation, but the only avenue available to us. Two weeks passed with all plans suspended. Finally, Equity found a space where we could do two performances.

Meanwhile, Richard M. Nixon was elected the thirty-seventh president of the United States. In spite of our despair over this turn of events, we went back into rehearsal.

The theater AEA came up with for our performance was the New Theater on 54th Street, where Bruce Jay Friedman's *Scuba Duba* was playing. Unfortunately, because the theater housed a hit show, we could not access the stage until after the Sunday matinee performance, which gave us only two hours on stage before our audience began arriving. The poetic atmosphere of the play inspired me to dramatize it with nearly one-hundred light cues but we were restricted to using the lights already hung for *Scuba Duba*. It would have been wise to simplify our light plot and let the audience fill in the magic with their imaginations. Regrettably, I did not do that. I spent our two hours frantically trying to give the electrician my complicated cues. At the opening performance, every time a light was meant to go down the lights came up and vice-versa. I neglected a basic principle of directing: it's a pragmatic art.

Worse, we rehearsed the play to be performed in The Forum, where there were no more than eight rows. There were twenty-six rows in The New Theater. We had no opportunity to adjust the volume at which the actors were speaking, so no one in the last eighteen rows heard a word of dialogue. It was a disaster. There was a second performance on Monday night at which the light cues went better, but audibility remained a problem.

Based on our London reviews, which the Lincoln Center Theater supplied to their subscribers, every seat was taken at both performances. The first night, the audience was polite, if puzzled. The second night, as they realized they weren't able to hear, the audience began streaming up the aisles to escape the debacle. It's a wonder Bill and I weren't trampled, hiding in the dark at the top of the aisles.

Wandering The Wilderness

I had no job for eight months after I returned from London and few prospects. I was feeling that perhaps I could make my way through life without being in the theater. I was ready to leave it behind, at least for a while. Only seeing the gripping performances of Jane Alexander and James Earl Jones in the Broadway production of *The Great White Hope* provided any inspiration. Ironically, in *La Bohème* fashion, in spite of my penurious existence, my personal life was hitting new highs, both literally and figuratively. I had a new lover, a wealthy young artist studying at Cooper Union, and we were living in an apartment on Washington Street in the Village, which we turned into a Victorian palace. We discovered that the gas fixtures in the ceiling still worked, so we disconnected all the electricity, bought Victorian chandeliers and lived for six months by gaslight. We frequently saw Zita, who introduced us first to mescaline, then mushrooms and finally, LSD.

My hopes for money were pinned on the success of *The Gingham Dog*, which was scheduled to open on Broadway in April. As noted, that didn't exactly pan out.

The new year of 1969 began with the fabled victory of "Broadway Joe" Namath and the New York Jets over the Baltimore Colts in Super Bowl III. Nixon and Yasser Arafat both took office. The last issue of *The Saturday Evening Post* hit the newsstands, which, coupled with the death in March of President Eisenhower, marked an end of an era. Sirhan Sirhan and James Earl Ray admitted killing Kennedy and King. Golda Meier became the first female prime minister of Israel.

I got a call from Texas that my father had been taken to the hospital in critical condition. I was advised to fly to Amarillo immediately. In spite of the trauma of a ruptured gall bladder, he seemed to be making a steady recovery. After a week or so, he was able to leave the ICU for a regular hospital room. We planned for his release from the hospital. I arranged for him to go to California, where he could be near my mother and live in one of the apartments he'd bought as an investment. Then he suddenly took a turn for the worse: he contracted pneumonia. He was transferred back into Intensive Care, where he received a tracheotomy. When I told my mother about this turn of events, she flew in to be with me. We were keeping an all-night vigil in the waiting room when the doctor came out to tell us that my father died while they were performing a routine cleaning of his tracheotomy. I arranged for his funeral in Amarillo, and then my mother and I boarded a plane to transfer his body to Luling, Texas, where I'd grown up as a child and where my father's adopted parents were buried. He was laid to rest on the 5th of May and I put these words from *Hamlet* on his tombstone:

"He was a man; take him for all in all, we shall not see his like again."

I drove back to New York in my father's Oldsmobile and it was at this point that I took the LSD trip and saw the white light I've described in the introduction. Zita left to go back to Europe. My love affair with the art student faded away. I moved in with an old college friend, Rod Nash, who'd been my assistant on *Balm in Gilead,* and who had an apartment on Charles Street.

In Vietnam, the Battle of Hamburger Hill raged, while in Montreal John Lennon and Yoko Ono conducted their "Bed-In" to "Give Peace a Chance." Near the end of June, at a bar in the Village named the Stonewall, homosexuals confronted the New York Police Department on Christopher Street, refusing to be arrested and launching the first strike for gay rights. I cheered them on from Sheridan Square, but remembering the bloodied heads at the Chicago convention, I didn't get personally involved.

And then one afternoon in June, Lanford and I went to join Rob and Tanya for dinner at their Bank Street apartment as they were making final plans for their wedding. Lanford was helping Tanya prepare dinner in the kitchen, while Rob and I chatted in their backyard garden over a glass of wine, when we received a life-changing phone call. Dr. Harry Lerner was a psychotherapist who'd been treating Rob for a number of years. I was also his patient for a while. He called to say that he'd found a big hall on the second floor of a building on Broadway between 83rd and 84th Streets. He knew my itinerant company needed a home. He thought this space might be suitable.

Tanya continued to prepare dinner, but Rob, Lanford, and I took a taxi uptown to inspect the place. We got to the address at 2307 Broadway, and found that the space was above a Thom McCan/Red Goose Shoe store. It seemed an improbable location for a theater. Still, we climbed the stairs and found a large cobalt-blue room about seventy-five feet long and thirty feet wide. At one end was a platform, sufficient for a dais, but not large enough to be called a stage. The ceiling was very high, and there was a distinct echo in the room when I clapped my hands to test the acoustics. The room originally was a lodge hall, but more recently, an illegal pornographic cinema.

I was not impressed. This was nowhere *near* an adequate place to perform plays. It certainly wasn't Lincoln Center. It wasn't the Mercury Theater, or even La MaMa. It wasn't a *theater*. It was a big, cavernous blue room with a hollow echo.

We went back downtown and called Dr. Lerner. I explained it wasn't what I had in mind. Dr. Lerner was the head of an anti-nuclear organization and he thought the space might serve as his headquarters. The rent was only $500 a month, so even if we didn't want it, he thought he'd take it.

"Oh, well!" I responded, "If you're going to take it anyway, we might meet there for a while until we find a real theater space." He agreed to let us do that.

Over dinner, we began to make plans for throwing a party in the big blue room to announce our intension to form a permanent company of artists. We thought it would be a kick to throw a party on Bastille Day, so we settled on July 14th. Who could guess that the party would last for twenty-seven years?

Part Two
A Big Bang

Chapter 5
Incarnation

I've always thought it fitting that Circle Rep began with a party. Throughout our history, we had the best parties (Christmas and openings) of any theater I ever worked at. The big cobalt blue room was a perfect place for dancing and celebrating. Our sound system filled the space with the joyous noise of rock and roll: The Rolling Stones, Jimi Hendrix, The Beatles, Donovan and Cat Stevens. It was a bonus that our inauguration was on Bastille Day, the start of a rebellion whose motto was: "Liberty, Equality, Fraternity."

The Age of Enlightenment offered new solutions to oppression: rationalism, revolution and democracy. In the nineteenth century, the Industrial Revolution supplanted political tyranny with economic subjugation. The twentieth century sought answers to age-old problems in ideologies, such as capitalism and communism. The Group Theater spent its fervent years enthralled with the promise of socialist solutions.

The turbulence of our generation produced a different yearning. The clash of ideologies had produced two global wars, as well as Korea and Vietnam, assassinations and national unrest. With the advent of psychedelic drugs, we turned to the transformative potential of love, peace and spiritual evolution. If the godfather of The Group Theater was Karl Marx, our inspiration was the humanism of Chekhov and Stanislavski. Of course, our influences also included a dash of Timothy Leary and Crosby, Stills, Nash & Young.

As naïve as it might appear now, we believed in a spiritual evolution that could transform human existence, just as our physical bodies evolved from apes. Belief in a new era (an "Age of Aquarius") was widespread, shared by many of us at the Cino and the nascent Circle Rep. Remember the famous picture showing an antiwar protester tucking carnations in the rifle barrels of soldiers guarding the Pentagon? The kid with the flowers was teenage actor George Harris III, part of the Harris family of actors who appeared in scores of plays off-off-Broadway. He was making a nonviolent gesture to the soldiers, who were braced for trouble as they faced 250,000 demonstrators protesting the Vietnam War with "Flower Power."

"All you need is love," was more than a pop song; it was a creed by which we lived. We embraced the unity of humankind, sharing the essence of God within us all. As John Lennon put it: "Imagine."

On that fateful acid trip I described in the Introduction, I experienced the White Light. My new consciousness transcended all I'd learned on the mundane plane of everyday life and awakened in me an artistic mission. For the next year or so, clarity of purpose endowed me with a charisma that compelled people to listen. They came for guidance and I led them on a journey of self-realization. We believed that by exploring ourselves, our artistic work deepened. I discarded the chic wardrobe of Carnaby Street for white translucent shirts of Indian cotton, leather fringe vests and velvet pants. With shoulder-length blond hair, ascetic cheekbones and a 27-inch waist, I looked the part of a transfigured guru.

Celebrations

For our Bastille Day party, we invited all the artists we admired and sixty-five or seventy of them showed up. After allowing the group to heat up with dancing, drinking and toking, we paused in the middle of the evening, turned off the music, and gathered everyone around. Rob and I stood on a table in the center of the room, and I announced our intention to create a new theater company.

I outlined the core beliefs on which we would found the theater:

- It will be a company of artists, free of a board of directors and answerable only to the dictates of artistic principles.
- It will be made up of an ensemble of actors who train in the classics to sharpen, deepen and improve our skills.
- We will use the latest theories of experimentation to explore new horizons within ourselves and our work.
- We'll make this company of highly trained actors available to contemporary American writers, who will write roles specifically for the members of the company, just as Chekhov wrote for the Moscow Art Theater, Molière for the Comédie-Française and Shakespeare for the Lord Chamberlain's Men.
- Because theater is a collaborative art, we'll break down the barriers that separate playwrights from actors, actors from directors and directors from playwrights. All disciplines will learn to work together and to appreciate the creative contributions of fellow artists.
- Our goal is to create productions in which the action of the play becomes the experience of the audience.

We were greeted with cheers; then we resumed dancing and drinking and toking.

About a week after the party, Rob, Tanya, Lanford and I traveled down to Philadelphia for Rob and Tanya's wedding-rehearsal dinner. As Best Man, I was obliged to propose a toast, wishing the couple a happy future. Everyone was aware during the banquet that the Apollo 11 mission landed on the moon at 4:17 in the afternoon. Television coverage was continuous until the hatch opened around ten o'clock and Neil Armstrong started his descent down the ladder, stepping for the first time onto the surface of the moon. Cheers filled the ballroom of the Bellevue-Stratford Hotel; then we had dessert and champagne. When the time came for my tribute, I included the historic event in my congratulations to Rob and

Tanya. It seemed a fortuitous omen, both for their marriage and for starting a theater that dreamed as boldly as President Kennedy's vision for the exploration of space.

The following week, the wedding was conducted on the rooftop terrace of the San Moritz Hotel on Central Park South, with a magnificent view of the expansive summer green that is the emerald jewel of the City. The service was conducted by a minister of the Ethical Culture Society, so the ceremony was neutral between Rob's Episcopal and Tanya's Jewish backgrounds. They wrote their own vows, which included reading a bit of poetry. Rob recited e.e. cummings': "who knows if the moon's a balloon..." which ends: "...where it's always spring and flowers pick themselves." And Tanya quoted: "somewhere i have never traveled..." which ends:

"(i do not know what it is about you that closes and opens; only something in me understands the voice of your eyes is deeper than all roses) nobody, not even the rain, has such small hands"

One couldn't have asked for a more graceful wedding. After the ceremony, Rob and Tanya drove up to Woodstock, New York for their honeymoon, where Rob had purchased a newly constructed house on a wooded hill.

The following weekend, I joined the blissful couple at their airy two-story country home with a stone fireplace, scenic decks, a huge living room encased by sliding glass doors, and bedroom-lofts above the vaulted living room. It was a wonderful place and over the next year, it served as a restful getaway for me, as well as for Rob and Tanya, who let me to use it whenever I needed.

Refreshed by our weekend in the clean country air, we returned to the smog of New York and on August 4th, we began our series of workshops. The sessions met twelve times a week on a varied schedule to accommodate both those who were working day jobs and those appearing in performances at night. Everyone was requested to attend four workshops a week in two contrasting disciplines. My workshop met six times a week, as did Rob's, Mondays through Saturdays. And then, typically, we'd pile into our cars and head to Woodstock for the weekend.

The second week after we began our workshops, Rob and Tanya decided to forego their weekend in Woodstock because there was "some kind of music festival" happening upstate and they feared the roads would be clogged with traffic. So, like the rest of New York, we followed the news of the extraordinary event from radio and television reports. At first, we were glad we'd missed the turmoil; then gradually, we realized we'd missed one of the seminal experiences of our times.

Yes, the first summer of Circle Rep coincided with the Woodstock Festival in Bethel, New York, where thousands gathered to celebrate the image of warplanes over our nation turning into butterflies. The song "Woodstock" by Joni Mitchell, made famous by Crosby, Stills, Nash & Young, expressed our sense of wonder:

> "Well maybe it is just the time of year
> Or maybe it's the time of man;
> I don't know who I am,
> But you know, life is for learning:
> We are stardust, we are golden
> We are ten billion year-old carbon
> And we've got to get ourselves back to the garden."

The weight of our responsibility contravened the clichéd image of the carefree hippie. Our spiritual quest was founded on understanding the necessity of hard work. We knew we had to have a code we could live by and that the answer to the complaint: "I can't get no satisfaction!" was not only: "Love is all you need" or "Give peace a chance," but also: "Teach your children well."

Our strategy was to give our company a common vocabulary, to share different solutions to artistic problems, and to unify our goals. We offered two contrasting approaches to explore both traditional and experimental theater: actors, directors, playwrights and designers, all training together.

Rob's workshop was called Exploration, incorporating the techniques of Grotowski, the great Polish innovator, as Rob learned them from Grotowski's disciple, Eugenio Barba, while on tour in Denmark with the La MaMa Troupe. Rob also used psychological techniques to stimulate self-realization and to discover the mythic archetypes buried within.

My workshop was called Methods and used exercises to attain Stanislavski's goals of creative, truthful acting. The plural form of "Methods" assured that we didn't limit ourselves to the techniques of the Stanislavski system, but explored whatever might make our acting deeper and more truthful. Soon after we began to work, I became aware of the contributions the Meisner Techniques made to the art; his exercises enriched our arsenal of methods and became an important part of our study.

Re-Christened

Early in August, we met with Dr. Harry Lerner to discuss the relationship of our theater to his organization. Dr. Lerner was the President of something called the Council for International Recreation, Culture, and Lifelong Education, a group that sought to promote world peace by opposing nuclear proliferation. As a not-for-profit organization, C.I.R.C.L.E. acquired an exemption from paying federal taxes. In order to raise funds for our incipient theater, we needed to operate under the umbrella of its non-profit status.

I would have preferred to be known as the American Theater Project at the C.I.R.C.L.E. Theater because our name had a history worth building upon. But Dr. Lerner insisted that if he was to act as our sponsor, we should be known as the Circle Theater. I was sure this was a mistake, because it created confusion with the already-well-established Circle-in-the-Square. Faced with our need to raise donations, we agreed to Lerner's terms and became the Circle Theater Company. Now we could pursue tax-deductible contributions and grants immediately, rather than waiting two years to acquire our own tax exemption.

Until we began to receive those gifts, though, we were dependent on Rob's generosity for our sole source of income. Fortunately, he came from a wealthy family because Circle Theater Company could not have existed without Rob's money, just as Stanislavski's Circle Theater in Moscow depended on his. I was unaware that we shared a name with Stanislavski's first theater company or I would have been thrilled by the coincidence. Stanislavski also came from a wealthy family that financed his fledgling Circle Theater. C.I.R.C.L.E.'s non-profit status meant that whatever Rob spent was now tax-deductible.

During our first eight months, we had no need for a staff. Essentially, Rob paid the rent for the space and the electrical bill, which were the sum total of our expenses. I couldn't hold another job since my time was spent teaching our workshops. When I needed money, Rob gave it to me. I had few expenses, but Rob covered my rent (I was staying in a seedy hotel in the Village near Washington Square) and made sure I had money to eat. By January, he settled on a stipend for me of $100 per week, with no taxes withheld. I naïvely declared that I could be happy to earn $100 a week for the rest of my life! (I understood nothing about inflation or the inevitable creep of necessities to sustain a "lifestyle.") Sometime that winter, unable to cope with the responsibilities of maintaining a car, I abandoned my father's Oldsmobile to the streets of the City, its windshield flocked with parking tickets I could not afford to pay. I began taking the Trailways bus to Woodstock for the weekends.

Preparations

I attended Rob's workshops and he attended mine. We expanded each other's concepts of acting. In Rob's Exploration workshop, I learned to do The Cat Exercise, a complicated series of physical maneuvers that begins with the kind of stretching a cat does upon awakening and concludes with a standing back-arch, in which one must bend backwards from a standing position until the hands reach the floor. I never fully mastered that part. I learned a great deal about myself and my body from Rob's leadership. Rob's byword was "OPEN." In his view, there could be no higher goal than to achieve total openness. We explored every inch of our bodies and every remote corner of our imaginations. All Rob's exercises were conducted in bare feet. We explored the inter-connected nature of our musculature and how relaxation in the shoulders was assisted by swinging the legs. We imagined ourselves as little chicks hatching from eggs and then learning to fly. We worked on expanding our vocal equipment by giving memorized speeches as a cow, an ape or a lion. We incorporated some formal ballet exercises, using the fifth position and pliés to stretch our muscles. We took imaginary journeys transiting our blood streams, traveling through our bodies from extremity to extremity. Rob taught us a relaxation exercise with tension-and-release of each part of the body. This technique became the basic warm up I used for rehearsals throughout my career.

In my Methods workshop, we began with Stanislavski's essential elements of acting: relaxation, concentration and the imagination. To explore these, I devised several exercises. Once we'd used Rob's tension-release warm-up to achieve relaxation, we explored Stanislavski's concept of "Public Solitude" in an exercise I called "Alone in My Room." In this workout, each actor spent time observing the sensory elements of his/her bedroom. Then using only imagination (no props allowed), re-created the room on stage. Intense concentration was required to create that environment, which left the actor free from the tension of performing so that he/she could experience *living* in the imaginary environment, producing uncensored, unconscious impulses.

I invented a series of exercises designed to engage one's imagination in given circumstances, using both public situations that everyone knew, such as: "If I were waiting in a dentist's office..." plus private circumstances whispered to each actor, like: "If I've just lost my wedding ring," or "If I just found a hundred dollar bill." Armed only with their imaginations, the actors sat on a row of chairs facing the audience, doing nothing more than *believing* in their circumstances. The audience observed their behavior and then commented on what they *saw*. The public nature of the circumstances avoided any need to speak; the action involved merely *waiting* among strangers. This exercise offers many variations by changing the locations to: "a psychiatrist's office," "a bus station," "a police station," or "an abortion clinic." The inner circumstance also could deepen to: "If I've just had my first homosexual experience," or "If I've just killed someone," or "If I'm a terrorist with a bomb." The key thing was to do nothing more than believe the circumstances were *yours* and leave yourself alone to *experience* the situation. I wanted everyone to see that an actor never needs to *show* an audience anything. He/she just needs to *believe* and unconscious behavior will reveal the circumstances in an honest way. This simplicity proved Stanislavski's advice that an actor should cut 90%.

We then started introducing characters to our exercises, using Chekhov's *Three Sisters* as our text. We began to use props while creating a character from the play alone in his/her room. I have used this exploration in my rehearsals for every play since. It's a wonderful way for an actor to imagine himself/herself in the circumstances of a character, without any pressure to *act*.

I employed some exercises I learned from Miss Krause, such as observing an animal from the zoo whose behavior suggests a character's physicalization. We also worked on her exercise of bringing a statue to life. Seeking insights from Michael Chekhov's "Psychological Gesture," we performed a dance to a love song in our bare skin. We even experimented with playing a scene after smoking a joint. We discovered that marijuana adversely affects concentration. Although it stimulates the imagination, it wreaks havoc on tempo. So, it was prohibited from our stage work.

Over the doors to the theater, I hung a banner, quoting Stanislavski: "Lighter, higher, gayer." No double-entendres were intended; we accepted his observation that: "All art is striving to become music."

We began with about fifty artists – actors, playwrights, directors and designers – signing up to participate in the workshops.

By the end of five months, this number was distilled down to thirty-one: twenty-five actors and directors, and six Company playwrights. Some of the most memorable exercises in the Methods and Exploration workshops were performed by our playwrights, particularly David Starkweather.

As autumn unfolded, there were significant signposts of our times and the times to come. The year 1969 is thought to be when the first strain of the AIDS virus (HIV) migrated to the United States via Haiti. The "Chicago Eight" were put on trial for their disruptions of the 1968 Democratic convention. Colonel Muammar al-Gaddafi came to power in Libya, a country soon to be recognized as a terrorist state. Five-hundred thousand people demonstrated in Washington against the war in a symbolic "March Against Death," while Vice-President Spiro Agnew denounced the President's critics as "an effete corps of impudent snobs and nattering nabobs of negativism." The first ATM machine was installed in Rockville Center, New York; retail giant Walmart was incorporated; and the first message was sent over what became the internet. And of course, baseball pitcher Tom Seaver led New York's "Miracle" Mets to win the World Series, making Met fans of us all. We were flying high, intoxicated by devotion to our artistic and spiritual growth.

The Power Of Art

Today, it may be hard to acknowledge the effectiveness of hallucinogenic drugs in exploring human potential. A perception has developed that drug use is exclusively recreational and destructive. Hard-earned experience (such as the Charles Manson murders and the Jim Jones cult of mass suicide) has shown how dangerous drug use can be. However, hallucinogens are not "gateway" drugs. There is a distinct boundary between these mind-expanding agents and hard drugs like heroin, cocaine, amphetamines or tranquilizers, all of which seek to shield the taker from reality. The purpose of hallucinogens was exactly the opposite: to heighten one's awareness in order to produce spiritual insights. Socrates' said our first responsibility was: "Know thyself." Hallucinogenic drugs were an effective aid in accomplishing that goal.

It's no accident that the guidelines for hallucinogenic experiences are found in the *Tibetan Book of the Dead*. An LSD trip can be a deeply spiritual experience: an encounter with nirvana, that state of grace sought by enlightened gurus like Maharishi Mahesh Yogi, the founder of Transcendental Meditation, who deeply influenced The Beatles. Hindu monks for centuries taught a path to enlightenment based on the physical discipline of yoga, coupled with an abnegation of self and a renunciation of sensual desires that bind us to the costs of earthly greed: starvation, deprivation, hatred, cruelty and wars.

A successful journey of self-discovery using LSD frees one from the limitations of fear, vanity and the intellect, all safeguards civilization uses to protect us from the fear of inevitable death. This religious insight has implications for the nature of art.

The roots of theater grew from a soil of religious ritual, born in the temple of Dionysus as a celebration of the gifts of that god, including the transformative power of wine. "In vino veritas" testified to the liberation of the spirit from the humdrum world into a kind of rapture, wherein truth spilled forth effortlessly. LSD returns the artistic pilgrim to that state of ecstasy from which the art of theater sprang.

Of the four founders of Circle Theater Company, I was the only one who used hallucinogenic drugs to expand my consciousness. Rob, Tanya and Lanford were content to receive insights from my leadership. I don't recommend that anyone else try these drugs; they can be extremely dangerous. I was lucky that I emerged from my mind-altering experiments with a clear vision of theater art and my apparent destiny to serve it.

One element of this vision was that self-realization is essential to an artist, whether playwright, director or actor. Rob used psychological techniques for self-realization that were as much a part of his Exploration workshops as the theatrical techniques of Grotowski and Barba. He used what he'd learned from studying with Blanche Evan, a dance-therapist who liberated the psyche through expressiveness of the body. Although Rob never partook of even the mildest forms of drugs, his work fulfilled my idea of how theater artists should be trained. I expressed the principles of our art and inspired people to pursue them. Rob encouraged people to trust both themselves and each other. For Rob, the *journey* was the important thing, never the *result*.

The state of the artist is paradoxical. The title of Clurman's book *Lies Like Truth* exposes its central contradiction. We uncover the truth through conjuring up imaginative falsehoods. Acting is, as Stanislavski clarified, behaving truthfully in *imaginary* circumstances, which are the fabrications of a storyteller.

This paradox echoes another: the greater the artist, the more humble the human. Sir John Gielgud, arguably the greatest actor of the twentieth century, was also the most generous gentleman I've encountered. The same is true of the incomparable Jessica Tandy, a lady as graceful in manner as she was great in artistry. Although ego is a resource for creativity, one must be selfless in service to art. Art arises from exploring a unique perspective of human nature. We are our own laboratory.

So, it's necessary to be selfish in pursuit of artistic goals, while remaining humbled by the gift of talent. No better model exists than the self-effacing Anton Chekhov, a modest doctor who insisted it was never the job of the artist to judge, but to present humanity with an image of itself. Shakespeare says much the same in Hamlet's speech to the players. At the same time, I opposed the emotional tyranny I saw in other theater groups. La MaMa Troupe members were shamed into subsuming personal interests to the "good" of the troupe. The same was true of The Group Theater and it's often the case in the commercial theater, where everything is sacrificed for the success of a show.

In my view, a theater should encourage each person to nurture the talent he finds within and never forfeit his own artistic interests. Our Company provided an opportunity for individuals to share a journey of growth with others of like mind. Self-interest is at the heart of artistic generosity. An acting teacher who was influential during our first year was Jim Tuttle, who taught both Rob and Tanya in the Meisner Technique. As he put it in his book *The Ungentlemanly Art of Acting*: "Give everything you have for your art, and *demand* everything you need."

I challenged my workshop participants to set the highest standards for themselves. Nothing short of the full expression of life on stage would do: no faking, no shortcuts, no vanity – only a devotion to the honesty of one's work. We tried any method or approach an actor found useful, whether it originated in the theories of Stanislavski, the exercises of Meisner, the psychological gestures of Michael Chekhov, the alienation of Brecht, the extremity of Artaud, the physicality of Grotowski, the literalism of Belasco, or any other resource that inspired honest acting. My workshops defined the enemies of creative acting as: ego, intellectualism and fear. We sought keys to free us from these limitations.

Our relentless pursuit for high standards in my Methods workshops was balanced by Rob's Exploration workshops, which encouraged us to accept failure without shame. These two paradoxical approaches complemented each other and together, guided our search for truth in our work.

Christmas In Woodstock

We celebrated the Christmas season and the end of 1969 at Tanya and Rob's house in the woods near Woodstock. Christmas has always been an important event in my life. Along with Lanford, Claris and Michael, we'd enjoyed the holiday in a big way through all the lean years of off-off-Broadway. When Rob married Tanya, even though she was Jewish, she joined us in observing this special season, exchanging gifts and sharing the warmth of family.

So, Rob and Tanya decorated a huge tree in the Woodstock cabin, and Lanford, Roy London, Linda Eskenas, Dr. Paul Cranefield and I joined them for a rich Christmas holiday. We got trapped in the isolated woods by a major blizzard, and our return to the City was delayed almost a week. Dr. Paul waded through waist-deep snowdrifts down the hill to inform village officials we needed snow plows to clear our road. Lanford's Christmas present to me was an Alexandrite stone handsomely set in an antique gold ring of Art Deco design. He described it as a purple bicycle reflector, and it *is* pretty gaudy. I have worn it every day for the rest of my life.

Sharing With The Public

After six months of workshops, we'd built a finely attuned ensemble of actors who spoke a common language, shared common goals, and were sensitive, responsive and supportive of each other. It was time to select a play and share our artistry with an audience.

Lanford finally finished his long-awaited autobiographical play about the traumatic experience of going to live with his father in Southern California at the age of nineteen. In June, just before we started the theater, I accompanied Lanford up to the O'Neill Festival in New London, Connecticut, where his just-finished script of *Lemon Sky* was having its first staged reading. The cast included that fine actor James Broderick (father of his soon-to-be-famous son, Matthew) as the father, Doug, and a young Michael Douglas (who soon eclipsed his famous father, Kirk) in the autobiographical role of Alan. It was a staged reading, but I was very moved by the play and the performances. Neither actor appeared in subsequent productions, but they gave Lanford the invaluable gift of seeing his play for the first time in performances that were hard to surpass.

Lemon Sky is an impressively honest work, complex in form and deep in content. But it posed a dilemma for our embryonic ensemble. One of our goals was to present new work written explicitly for us. *Lemon Sky* preceded our theater and we didn't have the ideal actors to play the roles Lanford wrote. Fortunately, he had an offer to premiere the play at the Buffalo Studio Arena, under the direction of Warren Enters.

With the success of the production in Buffalo, once again producer Haila Stoddard stepped forward to bring the play to New York. It opened on May 17, 1970 at the Playhouse Theater, a 499-seat Off-Broadway theater on 48th Street, starring Charles Durning and Christopher Walken. Lanford was thrilled with Walken, who observed Lanford's behavior and incorporated some characteristics into his performance. *Lemon Sky* received warm reviews, but the production closed prematurely after only seventeen performances. Lanford became deeply depressed. It seemed as if it hardly mattered whether the critics liked the play (as with *Lemon Sky*) or not (as with *Gingham Dog*). His plays didn't connect enough with audiences to deliver a successful run. He entered a period of writer's block from which he emerged only in the safe harbor of Circle Theater in our third season.

Meanwhile, once we decided to forego *Lemon Sky* as our opening production, I settled on a play that was written with members of the Company in mind and that utilized techniques they learned from Rob's Exploration workshop.

The play was by David Starkweather, a Cino veteran and one of our most devoted Circle participants. In keeping with the ridiculously long titles popular at the time, it was called *A Practical Ritual to Exorcise Frustration After Five Days of Rain*. It was an absurdist look from a modern perspective of the travails of the Biblical Noah, his wife and family. One son, Japheth, was a Wall Street tycoon, played by Bob Shields. Another son, Shem, was a trapeze artist, played by Spalding Gray. Pint-sized Roddy O'Connor played the youngest son, Ham. A tall, skinny but dignified actor named Robert Frink played Noah, with Tanya as Mrs. Noah. As befitted the experimental material, I asked Rob to direct our opening production, while I made plans for a follow-up production of a classic.

At the same time, we began incurring additional expenses. Dr. Lerner secured the voluntary services of an architect named John Deans to help design a thrust stage for the east end of the room, a pentagon in the shape of home plate, and Rob paid for the materials to build it. We solicited the contributed labor of local youths with carpentry skills, like Lance Taylor. We also enlisted Johnny Dodd from the Cino to design our lighting grid and help us acquire lighting instruments, the pipes to hang them on, electric cables and connectors, and a control board. Fortunately, Johnny was a partner in an electronics supply company, so we got the best breaks possible for Rob's capital investment.

Once we began producing a play, there were expenses for costumes, lighting gels, props, and a spare set that consisted of a gigantic sail and a mast to suggest an ark. A slide projector and the creation of slides were other expenses, as were masks. Rob cheerfully provided the funds needed for the production, a situation common to off-off-Broadway. For years, I provided the costs for my productions, which always exceeded the $50 to $100 provided by the Cino or La MaMa. But typical of Rob's generosity, he was equally happy to cover the costs of building a second stage at the west end of the room, a proscenium stage to accommodate more traditional fare.

By now, it was obvious that I could no longer be the sole staff member. Rob assumed the title of Managing Director, although this primarily meant paying the bills. Tanya assumed the title of Administrative Director, whose job was to keep track of expenses. When both Rob and Tanya were preparing to go into rehearsals, it became clear that we needed professional guidance. Through a member of the acting Company, we contacted a woman named Beverly Landau, who had produced a couple of Off-Broadway plays. We eagerly made an appointment to meet her for breakfast at the Greek coffee shop near the theater at the corner of 84th and Broadway.

While dressing to leave for the morning meeting, as I was transferring my change I discovered a small half-tablet, like an aspirin, in my jeans pocket. "What is that?" I thought. Then I shrugged and without a second thought, popped it in my mouth. During the taxi ride uptown, I began to feel strange, as though I might be coming down with a cold. When I arrived at the restaurant, I was bombarded by sensations. Tanya introduced me to Beverly and I joined them in a booth to discuss over breakfast our needs for professional advice. I ordered scrambled eggs with bacon, but by the time the orders arrived, I was hallucinating. The scrambled eggs were bubbling and the slices of bacon slithering across my plate.

With horror, I realized that the pill I'd thoughtlessly downed must have been a crumble of LSD. I whispered to Tanya that I needed to leave the table at once because I was in the midst of an accidental trip. My paranoia was raging, out of control.

Tanya told me to wait in the costume room of our theater next door while she telephoned an actress from the Company to come and help. She returned to her business meeting with Beverly, who I hoped was unaware of the cause for my distress. Company actress Linda Eskenas, who was experienced with hallucinogenic drugs, arrived sometime later and took me downtown in a taxi to Tanya's apartment. She prepared a bubble bath for me, which calmed my paranoia and by the time Tanya arrived home from the meeting, I was serenely happy amongst my fragrant bubbles. Subsequently, Tanya told me she'd engaged Ms. Landau to advise us on production matters. Beverly arranged for press representation and helped me draft strategies to deal with Equity.

Launching An Ark

Rehearsals for *A Practical Ritual* went well, if not always smoothly. Although he adored Rob as a teacher, David Starkweather lacked trust in Rob's directorial skills. I encouraged them to be responsive to each other's contributions; so, they were billed as Co-Directors, working side by side to develop the dark comedy. As Artistic Director, I enjoyed the confidence of both artists, so I could act as a kind of midwife to the birth of this new play.

We built a thrust stage at the east end of the room. Playwright Lanford Wilson designed the set, playwright Doric Wilson designed the masks, Marcia Lee Merrill designed the costumes, and Toby Mailman did the lighting under Johnny Dodd's supervision. Music is credited to Allan Landon. The press was handled by professional Max Eisen. I also helped by coaching Tanya as she was trying to master comedy, which was never her forte. I suggested that in order to behave honestly within the circumstances of the absurdist farce, she had to create circumstances that were ridiculous, but to which she could commit fully: for example, scrubbing the decks of the entire ship using only a toothbrush. I reminded her that it was never her job to be funny; actors must be truthful and if the material is funny, their performances will be too.

Conchata Ferrell's favorite memory of *A Practical Ritual* was of Sharon Madden's hilarious entrance as Mrs. Shem, wearing a black satin teddy, fishnet stockings, spike heels, and carrying a machine gun; at the audible audience response to her outrageous outfit, she growled: "Watch it! I'm feeling insecure." I remember Burke Pearson as the Weatherman who predicted continuing storms using a chart of the human body as his weather map, with the supporting ensemble abstractly depicting The Nervous System. In the program, the play is set as taking place: "In various locations; On a Certain Ark; Here and Now; After 15,000 years of wandering; Or at least five days of rain."

We worked under the Showcase Code Contract of Actors Equity, which required no payment to actors other than carfare, but limited us to twelve performances. The biggest expense was to acquire chairs for our audience. Our friend Marilyn Sutter obtained a catalogue from Hugh M. Keiser, an architect of office space, who had provided several of us with day-jobs in the past. I selected handsome black and chrome steel chairs that could be linked together to make stable rows and that could be stacked when not in use. The chairs cost about $35 each, and Rob purchased 100 of them. They were so sturdy they lasted Circle's next twenty years.

The debut of the Company was welcomed in the two notices we received when we opened on March 24, 1970. Here are excerpts from our first reviews:

Show Business, April 4, 1970 (Phil Zinkewiez):
"A powerfully impressive production...admirable...[it] moved swiftly and imaginatively. The entire company reached levels of performance not often seen off-off-Broadway. The involvement was total, and every move, every line of dialogue was carefully motivated."

Women's Wear Daily, April 7, 1970 (Joseph H. Mazo):

"*A Practical Ritual* serves to introduce a very fine ensemble called the Circle Theater Company. The troupe's home is on Broadway at 83rd Street, and they clearly belong on the big street. The actors are highly trained, talented and personable. They move well, speak well, and relate to one another and the audience with honesty. The play is free, witty, and very much alive. The conceits are funny, the characters real, and the techniques well employed."

As we concluded our initial season of workshops in January, we wanted to mount a classic to balance the experimental new play we chose for our opening. Nervously, I put in a call to Miss Krause to seek her advice. I told her that I wanted to do Chekhov, but I was afraid to jump the gun before I was really ready. "Do it now!" she declared. "It's never too soon to undertake a challenge. Your company will learn more from working on Chekhov than any other author you could produce." Her encouragement erased all hesitation. We followed the Starkweather comedy with Chekhov's masterpiece, *Three Sisters*.

Almost Forgotten

With our opening production behind us and *Three Sisters* going into rehearsal, the actors in our workshops shifted to using the text of Jean Giraudoux's *Ondine* for exercises. Bill Oxendine was keen to direct the play, based on the exercises in the workshop. Stuart Hagmann had directed the play at Eagles Mere the summer before I went and I'd seen photos of Stu's dreamlike production, awash in fishnets and shadows. It had been many years since Alfred Lunt directed Audrey Hepburn in the play's debut on Broadway, where it won four Tony Awards. It seemed like a good choice for our repertoire. Ondine is a mermaid that chooses to be human for the love of a man. When Bill couldn't decide between Pat Carey and Linda Eskenas for the title role, I suggested double-casting them. Both actresses attended all rehearsals, rehearsing half the time and the other half watching the director work with the alternate actress. The remainder of the cast played with both Ondines: Burke Pearson as The Old One, Carl David Jessup and Judy Kirtley as Ondine's parents, Bob Shields as the poet Bertram, with Sharon Madden, Roddy O'Connor, Marina Stefan and David Stekol in supporting roles.

The double casting was a disastrous resolution. Linda hated Pat Carey's acting and when Pat was working with the director, Linda saw no need to remain quiet or be supportive. We played only four performances and each actress played the role twice. Ron Radice designed the set and clothes. Because I was in rehearsal for *Three Sisters*, I had little opportunity to help. It wasn't a very successful project and I forgot it even had occurred until Burke Pearson reminded me. No documentation survived and Mary Ryzuk completely overlooked it in her book *Circle Repertory Company: The First Fifteen Years*.

Rep Comes To Circle

In my Methods workshop, we used *Three Sisters* for our acting exercises and everyone in the Company tackled a role. They performed many exercises delving into the hearts of the characters. The problem was we had so many devoted actors that I didn't want to divide the Company into those who would appear in a production and those who would not. In a flash of inspiration, I realized there were enough actors to fill two casts. Why not do *two* productions that gave everyone who worked on a character an opportunity to play the role? Why not follow the goals we'd set to mount experimental work side by side with traditional classics? Why not mount two productions simultaneously, utilizing everyone's workshop exercises as research, and perform the two productions of contrasting styles in rotating rep?

It was a bold concept. It united the Company into a shared vision that recognized the individual worth of each participant. At the same time, it brought into reality our idea of equal commitment to experimentation and tradition.

Until this time, to the best of my knowledge, there had never been an experimental production of the work of Anton Chekhov. All productions of Chekhov followed the indelible paradigm set by the Moscow Art Theater, branding Chekhov as the master of realism. He was an artistic revolutionary himself, breaking with tired traditions of nineteenth century Russian theater to introduce an emphasis on the inner action of the characters, rather than the external actions of a plot. By late in the twentieth century, what began as startling reality on stage had become a tired tradition, exploited by the mediums of film and television. Experimenting with Chekhov in the same way directors did experimental productions of Shakespeare was revolutionary, breaking new ground in the history of theater. Andre Serban's celebrated experimental *Cherry Orchard* at Lincoln Center followed us seven years later.

The idea of an experimental production arose from the fact that Chekhov wrote *Three Sisters* in the tumultuous years before the first Russian revolution. Russian society was beginning to unravel in ways that seemed uncomfortably familiar in 1970. The attacks against the Czars were echoed by demonstrations that were happening in the streets of Washington: the civil rights marches and sit-ins, the gay rights riot at Stonewall, the growing demands for equal rights for women, and the increasingly contentious protests of anti-war activists. Could Chekhov's insights about his pre-revolutionary society convey much-needed wisdom to our times? We seemed to be teetering on the brink of upheaval. Race riots broke out, property was destroyed, homemade bombs were detonated, and in the spring of 1970, just as we began rehearsals, the National Guard fired on American citizens and killed four student anti-war protesters at Kent State in Ohio. Was revolution far behind?

On May 9th, we joined more than a hundred thousand who bused to Washington to protest the invasion of Cambodia. With the deaths at Kent State fresh in our minds, we knew we might be risking danger, but we were inspired by Che Guevara, who died young fighting for things he believed in. Using the march in Washington as if it were a huge improvisation mixed with real-life experience, we joined the outcries aimed against our government's policies. It probably landed us on Nixon's enemy list; we didn't receive a grant from the NEA until Nixon left office.

The casting for both productions emerged organically from the workshops. Our Company was well suited to act the characters in the play. Although they are almost always cast older, as written Olga is only twenty-eight, Masha only twenty-four, and Irina only twenty at the beginning of the play. For the Traditional production, the superb work of Stephanie Gordon in the Methods workshops provided an emotional center to the play in the character of Masha, the disconsolate sister in a barren marriage, whose spirit flames to life again when she falls in love with a married man. Stephanie's life experiences gave her a keen understanding of Masha's soul.

Stephanie Gordon was born in New York City in 1936. Her father was a renowned painter, Maxwell Gordon. Her mother, Edith, managed nightclubs, among them the Village Gate on Bleecker. As a teenager, Stephanie auditioned for the High School of the Performing Arts with the death scene from *Little Women,* evoking an abundance of tears. She was accepted, and graduated at seventeen. Around this time, her parents divorced and her father retreated to Mexico City for the rest of his life. Stephanie received her BA in Theater from Hunter College and then spent a summer as an intern at a playhouse in Binghamton, New York. There, she met Leonard Melfi and Harry Koutoukas, apprentice carpenters who later became iconic off-off-Broadway playwrights. In 1958, Stephanie married Neil Jacobs, an advertising executive, who wasn't happy with her theatrical ambitions. They divorced after a seven-year marriage. At the Village Gate, Stephanie met actor Kevin O'Connor and they began a tempestuous relationship that lasted seven years. In 1964, Ralph Cook started an off-off-Broadway group called Theater Genesis at St. Mark's Church, where Stephanie appeared in Sam Shepard's first play, *Rock Garden.* It was paired with Sam's *Cowboys* featuring Kevin O'Connor. Both were cast in Sam Shepard's *Up to Thursday* when it premiered (along with Lanford Wilson) at the Cherry Lane. Stephanie appeared at La MaMa as Marilyn Monroe in Leonard Melfi's play *Niagara Falls.* She became very close to Ellen Stewart, and when the La MaMa troupe was touring Europe, Stephanie ran La MaMa in Ellen's absence. Stephanie's career at Circle Rep lasted eighteen years.

Jane Lowry, who was Varya in Miss Krause's *The Cherry Orchard*, was well suited to the long-suffering elder sister, Olga. Suzanne Pred, with large eyes and long chestnut hair stunned our Company with her work on the buoyant younger sister, Irina. David Stekol was handsome, dignified and spontaneously intellectual, a perfect combination for Vershinin, who fascinates the sisters with his speculations about the future. Robert Frink, who was wonderful as Noah, provided an anchor in the ironic role of Dr. Chebutykin. Tall, elegantly slim and yet balding, Burke Pearson was excellent for Kulygin, the schoolmaster whom Masha married in her youth. Kulygin's patient acceptance of his wife's infidelity is one of the most touching aspects of the play. For Natasha, the common girl who invades the aristocratic family and takes over, who was better casting than Tanya Berezin, who sprang from the middle-class suburbs of Philadelphia to marry my patrician partner, Rob? Michael Fesenmeier shined in the supporting role of Fedotik; short, homely Roddy O'Connor was a tragic Baron Tuzenbach, who dies in a duel; and Tony Tenuta, with his nervous hands and self-effacing modesty, was Andrei, the brother of the sisters, who has the soul of a musician, but no ambition. Rob Thirkield revived the spirit of his memorable Firs from A.K.'s *Cherry Orchard* to play aged Ferapont, who remembers the old days and mourns the pervasive loss of meaning from life.

I held auditions to cast several roles that we couldn't fill within our Company. I found a dashingly handsome actor named Lee De Ross, with a six-feet-four frame, bedroom eyes and a Byronic shock of dark, wavy hair. He brought an exotic creepiness to the egotistical Solyony, who fancies a resemblance between himself and the romantic poet Lermantov, and whose perfumed hands mask his civilian occupation as an undertaker. After his advances are spurned by Irina, he kills the Baron in a duel, leaving Irina a widow even before she is married. I also discovered the remarkable

Dawn Gray, who convincingly embodied the ancient nanny, Anfisa. Joseph de John played Rodé, and Ronald Radice and Pat Carey were servants in non-speaking roles. They all seemed impossible to improve upon.

At the second performance of *A Practical Ritual*, a big-bodied young woman came to New York from West Virginia and she came to Circle Theater to see her friend from college, Michael Fesenmeier, in a play. They went to school at Marshall University in Huntington and after graduation, she spent one semester as a high school teacher. She arrived in New York with a great hunger to learn. She wanted to be an actress. She volunteered to do anything that needed doing at our theater. She collected props, cleaned the restrooms, swept the stage – anything to learn. I decided to let her play a Maid in the Traditional production, which included lowering the chandelier to the floor during first interval, lighting the candles, and then raising it aloft to begin the second act. Her name was Conchata Ferrell; she became one of our most famous alumnae on television and in film. Playing the Maid in both productions of our *Three Sisters* was her humble New York debut.

For the Experimental production, Sharon Madden took on the difficult part of Olga; darkly mysterious Marina Stefan played Masha; and girl-next-door Beth Bowden played Irina. Jolly, chubby Bob Shields played an affable Andrei, and his soon-to-be wife in real life, Alice Tweedie, was his stage fiancée, Natasha. Tall, angular Stephen De Fluiter played Masha's husband Kulygin. All of them excelled in Rob's Exploration workshops and could apply the Grotowski techniques they learned to Chekhov's text. The army was composed of hippie-revolutionaries in the style of Che Guevara, dressed in tie-dyed fatigues.

Another person who'd been attracted to our work was Joe Butler, the drummer for the immensely popular rock band The Lovin' Spoonful. Joe wanted to explore his talents as an actor, so I grabbed the opportunity to make him our idealistic Vershinin, with his shoulder-length auburn hair and generous mustache. Playwright David Starkweather was an intense Tuzenbach, while playwright Berrilla Kerr took the role of the old servant Anfisa, and playwright Matthew Silverman played Solyony, all examples of Circle's concept of breaking the barriers between artists in different disciplines, a practice we continued for many years.

The concept for the Experimental production was to erase all traces of the realistic trappings that buried Chekhov in a remote time. There were no props; all scenery was eliminated, replaced by two large wooden A-frame ladders that could be moved into different configurations on the thrust stage to suggest the different locales of the four acts. We built a narrow runway to bridge the Experimental stage on the east end with the proscenium stage on the west. Older members of the audience were seated within the set for the Prozorov's living room on our Traditional stage, while younger audiences sat on the floor on each side of the runway, with pillows for cushions. The costumes came from the actors' closets, except for the tie-dyed fatigues that clothed our hippie army of revolutionaries, which were rendered by Henrietta Bagley.

Exercises we developed in the Exploration workshops helped us abstract Chekhov's dialogue to explore its prophetic power. For example, Olga took the High Priestess from the Tarot deck as an image, and we chanted parts of the dialogue, creating a choral interweaving of lines that overlapped and intertwined. We used exercises like Michael Chekhov's psychological gesture to transform Chekhov's inner action into physical expressions, an abstracted essence. We used direct addresses to the audience so that as Vershinin philosophizes about the future, rock star Joe Butler in a tie-dyed uniform walked along the runway smoking a joint, talking to the kids seated at either side on cushions, saying: "Just imagine (*puff*) what it will be like (*exhale*) a hundred years from now?" (*passes the joint to someone in the audience*).

The production made use of contemporary rock-and-roll music that seemed appropriate to the mood and action. We began the play with Jimi Hendrix's dissonant rendition of the "Star Spangled Banner," wrenched from his screaming electric guitar. As the soldiers were leaving near the end of the play, they sang Simon and Garfunkel's "Homeward Bound." In their final scene, Masha and Vershinin climbed the A-frame ladder placed on the runway in the middle of the audience to meet at the peak for their farewell. Then as they descended, they were physically separated by the A-frame, until Masha lost touch of his outstretched hands and collapsed in sobs at the foot of the ladder with a cry released like a primal scream.

In total contrast, the Traditional *Three Sisters* required all the trappings of a conventional Chekhovian production: completely realistic settings for four different locations, many detailed props true to the period and, most expensive of all, authentic costumes. We were fortunate that the season we began Circle Theater Company, the venerable APA closed its doors and stored all their sets in a warehouse in New Jersey. The previous season, they'd produced *The Cherry Orchard*, so all their beautiful flats, constructed of steel and velvet for Broadway, were given to us. All we had to do was hire a truck, drive to the warehouse and pick up the flats before they were consigned to be burnt (the inevitable fate of discarded Broadway sets). Rob hired the largest available U-Haul, and half a dozen of us went to New Jersey, loaded the flats into the truck, and hauled them back to Manhattan.

The velvet flats on Circle's new proscenium stage created an authentic living room and dining room of the Prozorov's country house for the first act, Andrei's study for the second act, and the sisters' bedroom for the third. The final act occurs outdoors, and one of our acquisitions from the APA was a full-stage drop, a cyclorama used in the second act of *The Cherry Orchard*. The costumes were our biggest challenge. They needed to be turn-of-the century Russian clothes and half the cast had to wear Russian army uniforms. By far the biggest cost for the Traditional production was to find suitable costumes. Inquiries at local shops led us to contact the American Costume Company in San Francisco, which built the costumes for the American Conservatory Theater production of *Three Sisters* the previous season. It cost Rob several thousand dollars to rent the costumes and have them shipped from San Francisco, but it was a worthy investment. The boots, cloaks, plumed helmets and gloves added impeccable authenticity to the heavy wool uniforms, greatcoats and beaver hats of the Russian army. The gowns were silk and lace, with exquisite period detail. In these clothes, our cast *became* the characters.

Once I decided to take Miss Krause's advice and direct *Three Sisters*, I chose a translation by Robert W. Corrigan, a version with the most colloquial dialogue I could find. Corrigan Americanized some aspects of the play to make the dialogue easy for an American audience. For example, the play begins on the 5th of May, Irina's "name day," which in Russian tradition is the birthday of the saint for whom one is named. They celebrate a name day in much the same way we celebrate birthdays, so Corrigan uses "birthday" in the place of "name day." This made sense to me, especially since we also were mounting an experimental production in contemporary clothes. While the *style* of the Experimental production was revolutionary, the *dialogue* was faithful to the script.

Even though each actor worked on the play for six months, there were some events we could explore only as a group. One of the central relationships in the play is the hollow marriage of Masha and Kulygin. It is evident that the matrimonial bleakness exposed by Masha's unfaithfulness must have had a different genesis. Surely, they entered into marriage with all the hope for a happy future we see at most weddings. It must have been a joyous occasion, for the middle daughter to be married and to such an important man in the community, the highly respected schoolmaster. So, we improvised the wedding of Masha and Kulygin, giving us an opportunity to explore Russian culture in terms of food, religion and social rituals. With an idea of unconsciously establishing a similarity between Vershinin, the Russian officer whose arrival sparks the action, and the sisters' late father, I asked David Stekol to play Prozorov for the improv and preside over the wedding with the authoritarian rule of a 19th century Russian land baron. Each actor was assigned to research Russian cooking, prepare a dish and bring it to rehearsal for the improv. The ceremony (in which I played the Orthodox Priest), the banquet and the dancing were a joyous celebration of a loving couple, a memory that lingered throughout the production, haunting the empty ruins of their marriage. My recent experience of Rob and Tanya's wedding gave us a pattern for our creation of Masha and Kulygin's union.

Another improv explored events preceding the play. As the curtain rises, the sisters and Chebutykin are awaiting a festive birthday lunch. The first line is spoken by Olga, the oldest of the sisters, who, seeing the budding trees outside the windows, interrupts grading papers to observe: "Father died a year ago today, on the fifth of May – your birthday, Irina." It seemed imperative to improvise that event, which the sisters experienced together the previous spring. Once again, David Stekol played the father in our improvisation. He was ailing from a cold he'd caught the previous week from riding horseback in a freezing rain. None of the other actors knew that I gave David a secret circumstance: during the improv, he would die. For everyone else, the improvisation was to explore what life was like when old man Prozorov dominated the household. How impotent they must have felt trying to conduct business of the estate during his illness! David was put into bed in a small backstage room and was ministered to by Anfisa, the old serving woman. We stipulated that it was a snowy day and that Baron Tuzenbach had been dispatched to the nearby town to fetch Papa Prozorov's newspaper. The family was making plans to celebrate Irina's birthday, each person harboring secret surprises to contribute to the festivities. It was hoped Prozorov would be well enough to preside at the party. Dr. Chebutykin, his oldest friend (and perhaps the actual father of the youngest daughter Irina), came to check on him. He was greeted by Irina, who was alarmed because during the night, her father developed a hacking cough. Masha stayed overnight, and she and Irina anxiously awaited the arrival of the schoolteachers, Kulygin and Olga, coming home when the school day ended. Suddenly the emptiness of the house burst into activity as tea was served to the cold arrivals, Tuzenbach came with the newspaper, and Kulygin entertained everyone with stories of colorful events at school. Dr. Chebutykin suddenly interrupted the conviviality with the news that Prozorov's condition has turned to pneumonia. One by one, the sisters were permitted in to see their dying father, who lay under an icon lighted by a flickering candle, the room infused with the aroma of incense. I drew upon my father's recent death to provide the improvisation with believable details. The actors experienced a shocking sense of reality, as they watched their father pass away. Everyone faced the death as if it were as real as their tears. Afterwards, whenever Jane Lowry spoke those opening lines, each actor revisited the memory of this event. It was an elaborate group improvisation that added enormous depth to the opening moments of the play.

We rehearsed the two productions for a little over six weeks, and then I went once more before the Council of Actors Equity. I explained that we were presenting *two* productions in rep, and therefore should be allowed to double the length of our run. Grumbling that their Showcase Code was not intended for repertory, the Council agreed to grant us an exception, allowing a total of twenty performances.

I treasure many memories of the Traditional *Three Sisters*. It ranks along with *Balm in Gilead* among the best work of my early career. The entire cast acted as a flawless ensemble, bringing Chekhov's masterpiece to life in the intimate confines of a second floor loft on the Upper West Side. Changing the complicated realistic sets for the Traditional production took considerable effort from our neighborhood volunteers. We took three intermissions to change the settings, which made the running time a full four hours. We opened in the warm month of June and we had no air-conditioning; the curtain went up at 8 P.M. and came down at midnight. We sold out all 100 seats for every performance. In spite of the heat, not one member of the audience ever left before the final curtain. Such is the power of the imagination!

The Experimental production, with no scenery, could be seen in a swift two-and-a-half hours. I was thrilled to see young New

Yorkers streaming in to experience their first Chekhovian play. It spoke to them directly in a way no conventional production could have. Of course, it helped to have a rock star playing one of the leads. I was proud of our achievement, but I would never have dared to mount an Experimental version without offering a Traditional version every other night.

The two productions played in alternating Rep (starting with the Traditional version) from June 11 to July 3, 1970. Here are excerpts from our reviews:

Women's Wear Daily, June 17, 1970 (Joseph H. Mazo): Traditional:

"The first act is well-orchestrated and full of life...The final act is even better...The characterizations are well thought out, the moods are clearly established, and the characters are constantly busy with physical activities germane to their characters and the play's action. These factors combine with honest interaction among the players to give Chekhov's people life and a full life-style, which they rarely achieve on the American stage."

Women's Wear Daily, June 24, 1970 (Joseph H. Mazo): Experimental:

"Fruit salad! There is nothing experimental about the production. It simply is an anthology of theatrical parlor tricks, currently popular among the would-be "with-its." The most interesting thing about the production is that the playwright's work manages to survive. The actors are honest and intelligent, and when they interact with one another, the characters appear in full color, like flowers budding in a field of concealing grass."

Village Voice, July 2, 1970 (Dick Brukenfeld):

"Of these two productions, I prefer the new theater version...because this show is more alive. Mason, who directed both, has managed to evoke from his actors a greater spontaneity and to create a more provocative evening. It offers a lively surface, and a very good ending when "We shall overcome" underscores Olga's speech: "Oh, dear sisters, our life isn't over yet. We shall live." Here political and personal come together splendidly."

Show Business, July 4, 1970 (Phil Zinkewicz):
"Circle Theater Company is probably one of the better off-off-Broadway repertory companies around today. It is a company – an ensemble of professional actors, directors and playwrights working together toward developing a 'creative American theater.' In the Traditional production, we see Chekhov as we have always known him. I must say that the characters did live on that stage. The situations were real and immediate and the underlying tensions were ever present. Individual performances were quite impressive. In the Experimental version, again the actors did a good job."

The Christian Science Monitor, July 3, 1970 (Alan Bunce):
"Not many repertory companies would have the courage to alternate two different versions of Chekhov's *Three Sisters,* yet Circle Theater Company has been doing just that. Mason has staged both evenings with intelligence and a strong sense of where Chekhov's real strength lies. In the end, they succeed in their stated aim to expand new techniques while encouraging the best styles of the past."

In the world outside, the Concorde made its first supersonic flight, cigarette advertising was banned from television and The Beatles announced they were breaking up. Their last album *Let It Be* was released while we were in rehearsal.

A Medley Of Mixed Metaphors

At the end of the year, the New York State Council on the Arts awarded Circle Theater Company a grant of $5000 in recognition of the excellence of our Traditional production, as well as our commitment to presenting new plays. The Peg Santvoord Foundation, which promoted experimentation in the arts, rewarded us with a grant of $5000 in recognition of our Experimental *Three Sisters*. The Executive Director of the Foundation, Donn Russell, enthusiastically saw the Experimental production several times and continued generously to fund Circle Theater Company's experimental work for the next ten years.

We threw an end-of-season party for the Company on the 4th of July, celebrating a season only ten days short of a full year. I honored Burke Pearson with an award as "Best Actor" for his rich portrayal of Kulygin, but it was a silly thing to do. We *all* were at our best, and singling out one artist over another is as futile as selecting one grape from a branch of unblemished fruit and declaring it "Best Grape."

In founding Circle Rep, we created our own Eden. For almost a year, we'd earned our manna by the sweat of our brows, toiling long, tireless hours, days on end, joyfully laboring side by side to construct a temple of art on a firm foundation of principles. Our ideals were incarnated into a body of talent that was recognized for many years as transcendent. The first phase of our future was based on the artistic productivity of sixteen founding members:

Tanya Berezin	Zane Lasky
Patricia Carey	Sharon Madden
Brad Dourif	Burke Pearson
Conchata Ferrell	David Starkweather
Michael Fesenmeier	David Stekol
Stephanie Gordon	Tony Tenuta
Berrilla Kerr	Rob Thirkield

and, of course, Lanford Wilson and me.

The Transcendent Years

I observed in an interview that for a director, having his own company is like a violinist who owns that rarest of instruments, a Stradivarius, sensitive to his slightest touch to produce the subtlest of grace notes. I now had such a Company.

The journey had been hard but the rewards were bountiful. We were flush with satisfaction, proud of our achievements. We created that artistic theater Miss Krause invoked. We knew now that our work must continue, and that the ark we built had sailed only the first league on a long voyage toward a promised land of excellence.

Chapter 6
Cultivation

Okay. Here's where I admit the downside of all those mind-altering drugs. Nowhere on the little pill that said "Eat me" were microscopic warning labels to alert that side effects may include diminished capacity for recalling details.

Memories are like scribbled notes stuffed in bottles thrown into the sea of Time. Writing about the early 70s is akin to searching a deserted beach, hoping something will float to shore. If the past is neglected for a sufficient time, many bottles littering the beach will be empty, the memories they once contained lost in that vast ocean we left behind on our voyage. There is almost no public documentation for many details of the second and third season of Circle Theater, apart from my own files. As a result, I'm relying on the collective memories of my colleagues and their scrapbooks and diaries. They've generously supplied me with forgotten particulars.

I remember little about the six weeks of summer that followed the end of our first season except that I spent it in the lush embrace of Woodstock. Shortly after the end of the season, I rented a cottage at 32 Tannery Brook Road between two babbling streams, just a five-minute walk from the heart of the village. The bungalow was identified by a small sign on the cottage as "Sunshine," so called for my landlady's nickname, not the hallucinogenic drug with the same name. She'd inherited the cabin from her grandfather and decided to realize some income by renting it out. I was her first tenant. The charming white bungalow had red shutters and a glassed-in front porch with a glider/swing and rocking chairs. The interior was one large room with kitchen facilities along one wall and a tiny closet off the back porch that contained a toilet. There were no bathing conveniences except an outdoor shower in the yard, which was fine for summer. The living room area had a wooden ladder/staircase in the center that went up to a sleeping loft that had an attic window just below the rafters. This loft would be my feathered nest for the next two years and provided a weekly respite from a demanding theater schedule. The main street of the village (Tinker Street) had a couple of bars that presented live music on weekends from the likes of the Paul Butterfield Blues Band, Odetta and Van Morrison. Bob Dylan lived on the outskirts of town. Before long, I bought a decrepit maroon Hudson that had belonged to Robbie Robertson of The Band. It was incapable of exceeding ten miles an hour. We may have missed the festival, but we were surrounded by the magic of Woodstock lore. I *was* a Sunshine Superman!

The summer in Woodstock gave us the chance to strengthen relationships, particularly with new members of the Company. I hosted weekly visits from Tony Tenuta, Zane Lasky and Brad Dourif, who formed a new core for our coming work. It was fun to introduce an urban kid like Zane to the marvels of the countryside. When I took him wading across the Mill Stream, he encountered moss for the first time, crying out in alarm: "Something's wrong with these rocks!" In a sense, he was right because, before the summer was over, I slipped on one of those mossy stones and broke my arm (for the third time in my life). Rob drove me over to the hospital in Kingston, where they set my right arm in a heavy plaster cast. Fortunately, I'm left-handed. Rob and Tanya also hosted visitors escaping the heat of the City, including Lanford, Dr. Paul Cranefield and Conchata Ferrell, whom by now we were all calling Chatty. A couple of times over the summer, I entertained weekend guests by taking an acid trip with them, with varying success in terms of expanding consciousness; but the shared experiences definitely deepened our bonds.

Rob spent the summer digging up Munch drawings that he thought were ideal to accompany his favorite play, Strindberg's *Ghost Sonata*.

I had a couple of friends who were members of a nearby rural commune. They persuaded me to lead their fellow hippies in a weekly workshop. We met in an airy barn on their farm and I introduced them to the exploratory techniques Rob developed at Circle. I took Zane with me once to observe life on a commune. He was amazed to see many of the men and women performing daily tasks in casual near-nakedness. The commune experiment, a nationwide phenomenon, showed us how their alternative lifestyle was different from our fledgling theater. Although we were spiritually united in a similar fashion, our sole sharing was in cultivating our artistic talents. Outside the safe harbor of the theater, where a spirit of communal unity prevailed, we prized our individuality. My workshops with the commune culminated in an end-of-summer avant-garde performance that took place in a farm field under a gigantic inflated blue plastic tent, kept aloft with enormous blowers. The show was intended to raise money for the commune and they sold tickets to the local communities, who came and sat on bleachers to see what these hippies were up to. It was like watching an early manifestation of Cirque de Soleil, rich with imagination but lacking their athletic skills.

I spent the yawning days of summer painting a portrait of sixteen year-old Zane Lasky in a black velvet shirt, his dark curls spilling to his shoulders like a 17th century chevalier, sitting at an as-yet-empty chessboard, contemplating moves of the future.

Abuzz In A Flurry

While our theater had been empty over the summer, Dr. Lerner permitted its use by a new group called the Film Forum. It began as an alternative screening space for independent films, with fifty folding chairs, one projector and a $19,000 budget. The project, like Circle Rep, eventually left the non-profit umbrella of C.I.R.C.L.E., incorporating as an independent non-profit institution and moving downtown to the Village South Theater on Van Dam Street.

Today, Manhattan film buffs recognize the Film Forum as one of New York's most vital institutions. I don't believe it has ever been noted that Circle Rep and the Film Forum shared a beginning of modest circumstances in an upstairs loft at 2307 Broadway.

Toward the end of August, we returned to the routines of our theater in the City, spending Tuesday through Thursday in New York, with long weekends in Woodstock. Rob, Zane and a number of others from the Company went to the Village Gate to hear Cat Stevens singing songs from his yet-to-be-released album *Tea for the Tillerman*. It was nice to return to our artistic mission, but following our inspirational first season, it was difficult to sustain the same level of intensity.

Several vital members of that first year drifted away to pursue other interests. Jane Lowry accepted acting jobs that took her touring to other cities; Spalding Gray joined Joseph Chaiken's Open Theater; Suzanne Pred married and left acting behind; playwright Doric Wilson left to engage in a more aggressive agenda for gay rights; Robert Frink just never returned. I was not the only one who found it hard to sustain the passion of our first year.

In the second year, I sidestepped leadership responsibilities by encouraging members of the Company to propose projects they'd like to work on for themselves. I reminded them our theater existed for their individual artistic progress and welcomed suggestions for personal projects. Looking back, I recognize this as a rationalization, yet I was truly committed to the concept of artists creating their own opportunities for growth. Many projects were proposed and our productions increased from four in our first season to eight in the second and from thirty-three performances to forty-seven, We also conducted two experiments in film and video. Of course, quantity is no substitute for quality but despite an absence of focus, the buzz of creative activity was stimulating, as it had been at the Cino.

A significant step forward was Edith Gordon becoming our Business Manager, a post she held for the next two seasons with tenacity and generosity. Edith was the mother of Stephanie, one of our principal actors, and she recently had retired as manager of the Village Gate. With her canny wisdom, we made progress toward professional stability. We had grants totaling $10,000 to finance our second season, so it became necessary to account for expenditures.

It also became mandatory to form a Board of Directors, but we wanted our Board to conform to the ideals we put forward at our founding party: our Board always would maintain a majority of artists. We hoped this would prevent what happened to the Repertory Theatre of Lincoln Center from happening to us. Our first Board consisted of the four founders: Rob, Tanya, Lanford and me, plus three of our best friends from the non-theater world: Hugh Keiser, Marilyn Sutter and, as Chairman, Dr. Paul Cranefield. I was elected President and Rob was Vice-President.

A Devil's Due

Dr. Paul was a renowned medical scholar with the Rockefeller University, and he came up with a proposal to present a special project as a Major Production to begin our second season. Dr. Milton Halpern was retiring in October as the Chief Medical Examiner of New York City. Dr. Paul could arrange financing from the City Department to mark the occasion with a celebratory production of Dylan Thomas' *The Doctor and the Devils*, a 1964 dramatization of the infamous grave robbers, Burke and Haire. A note in the program summarizes:

> "The teaching of anatomy in the early 19th century was made difficult by a lack of subjects for dissection. As a result, the practice of grave robbing became widespread, the grave robbers selling the exhumed bodies to anatomists. This macabre practice took a devastating new turn in Edinburgh in 1827 when Burke and Hare conceived the notion of murdering poor and lonely people to sell their bodies for dissection. Burke and Hare murdered seventeen persons; all of the bodies were sold to Robert Knox, who

was one of the most brilliant teachers of anatomy in the world at that time.

In *The Doctors and the Devils,* the story of Burke and Hare is integrated with that of Knox. The play is cast in dramatic form and contains some fictitious elements, but nearly all the details, including some of the most horrifying, are solidly based in historical fact."

Dylan Thomas wrote the piece as a screenplay, so our stage adaptation would constitute a World Premiere. Dr. Paul secured the rights and we gleefully delved into the project, using nearly every member of the Company. The murderous grave robbers Burke and Hare were played by Tony Tenuta and Burke Pearson, with Stephanie Gordon and Sharon Madden as their accomplices. Dr. Knox was played by David Stekol, his wife by Suzanne Pred, his assistant by Rob Thirkield. Michael Fesenmeier, Steve de Fluiter, Clyde Kelly and Joseph de John were his colleagues on the medical faculty. The court that tried the charges once the murderers were caught included Doric Wilson as the defense attorney and Brad Dourif as the jury foreman, with Alice Tweedie and Bob Shields as the witnesses. The supporting cast of Edinburgh citizens included Conchata Ferrell, Judith Kirtley, Tanya Berezin and Beverly Gin. The victims who were murdered to provide corpses for the doctors' dissections were played by Patricia Carey as Mary Mitchell and Berrilla Kerr as Mary Thornberry. Zane Lasky played a victim named Daft Jamie, an intriguing precursor to his portrayal of Jamie in *The HOT L BALTIMORE* two years later.

We rehearsed for several weeks in October and November, and played a preview as a special event for friends and family in our own theater before the evening of the gala (December 6, 1970) presented by the Friends of the Milton Halpern Library of Legal Medicine at the New York City Morgue, the site-specific venue for Dr. Halpern's retirement celebration. It was a great success, although it was very creepy to reincarnate the ghoulish grave robbers in such a setting. I recall Dr. Halpern afterward cheerfully giving us a tour of the morgue that included shelves of dead fetuses preserved in jars and other equally eerie curiosities. Steve de Fluiter remembers it took a raucous cast party at Judy Kirtley's apartment after the event to shake off the creepiness.

Renewing The Workshops

As the second season got underway, we conducted a brief season of workshops for the previous year's members, reviewing the principles of acting that served us so well in our first season. Rob resumed his Exploration workshops to train the new additions to the "apprentice company." My responsibilities as Artistic Director kept me too busy to sustain a similar workshop, so Company actor Tony Tenuta led the Methods workshop for the newcomers, which included seven graduates of Marshall University we dubbed "The West Virginia Contingent." As a result of Rob and Tony's workshops, these initiates learned the techniques that defined our Company and absorbed the common language we used in pursuing our shared goals.

On December 23rd, the North Tower of the World Trade Center was completed and, at 1,368 feet, became the tallest building in the world. Few were impressed with the aesthetic design of the building. It didn't have the elegant grace of the Chrysler Builder or the virile Art Deco majesty of the Empire State Building. Of course, we had no way of knowing how important the twin towers would be as symbols of American might. Despite its sterile design, the views from its Windows on the World Restaurant were unparalleled.

A European Exploration

Our second Major Production was *Princess Ivona* by Polish writer Witold Gombrowicz. It's likely this project was brought to me by Roddy O'Connor in response to my invitation to suggest personal ventures. Roddy was one of our most talented actors and received the best reviews of anyone our first season. Since he was unconventional casting for Prince Philip, his interest in the role might have been the generating force behind the proposal. It also was an attractive fit with other new members of the Company, particularly Judy Kirtley, who was perfect for the title role. I had seen an off-off-Broadway production directed by Joe Jacobs, a talented young director who showed promise; so I assigned the project to him.

The play is a tragicomedy that depicts how enslavement to form, custom and ceremony can result in despair. A young prince is pressured to marry, which he is not ready to do. Eschewing the proposed eligible matches, he wanders through a local park where he meets a homely, simple, almost-retarded peasant woman. It strikes him as an opportunity for a brilliant defiance of society to make this humble, totally unsuitable woman his bride. Ivona's ugliness serves as a mirror in which everyone who encounters her can see his own shortcomings. The prince becomes obsessed by her impenetrable nature; she's a living reproach to humanity. Eventually, the prince realizes he's trapped by his own fascination but no one can find a way out of the dilemma.

In a grotesque coincidence, Idi Amin had just become president of Uganda in a military coup, another living reproach to humanity. In Haiti, "Papa Doc" (Francois Duvalier) died and was followed by his son Jean-Claude (Baby Doc) as dictator for life, another dilemma no one could find a way out of.

Judy Kirtley recalls the production as a "joyous experience." Although Ivona is the eponymous character, it was a mostly silent role. She spoke only one word, in answer to a question about what she was knitting: "Wool." The wonderful set was by Michel Choban, with Ronald Radice as creative advisor. The style of the production was the glamorous Art Deco era of 1930s films. The cast was trained in the poised deportment of the period. Roddy O'Connor was especially effective with a flawless mimicry of Fred Astaire's walk. The costumes by Joyce Marcel helped enormously. She made Roddy look princely in his crisp white jacket, with gold buttons and epaulets. The lighting was by Lynn Carrol, with the wigs styled by Erwin Lerner. I shepherded the production, assisting with research and background, more or less in the manner of a dramaturg.

Princess Ivona played twelve performances on our proscenium stage from February 4 through March 6, 1971. Here are excerpts of two reviews:

Women's Wear Daily (undated) (Joseph H. Mazo):
"A fascinating, difficult hall-of-mirrors play. The production offered by Circle Theater Company can offer no more than intelligent competence, but that is no small blessing nowadays. Jacobs shows a fine sense of coxie invention – the farcical scenes are extremely effective. The cast is made up of talented, intelligent actors. This is not a completely satisfying production, but it is a commendable version of a play that should be seen."

Village Voice (undated) (Arthur Sainer):
"A play to be respected and one must be grateful to the Circle Theater Company for dredging it up. Kirtley has some effective moments and Pearson is quite sharp."

Not exactly glowing notices, but still offering praise for the Company. To put our modest accomplishment into perspective, it was overshadowed by Caffé Cino alumnus John Guare's triumphant success with *The House of Blue Leaves.*

In the spring, boxing champion "Smokin' Joe" Frazier (26–0, 23 KOs) and challenger Muhammad Ali (31–0, 25 KOs), AKA "The Greatest," met at Madison Square Garden in New York City in what was promoted as the *Fight of the Century.* The fight was something of a symbol of the country. Ali denounced the Vietnam War and refused induction into the U.S. Army, leading to being stripped of his title and barred from boxing for nearly four years in his prime. Ali became a symbol of the anti-establishment movement, while Frazier became a symbol of the conservative, pro-war movement. The fight exceeded even its promotional hype. Ali dominated the first three rounds but Frazier retained the title with a unanimous decision, dealing Ali his first professional defeat.

Return To Rep

Meanwhile, on a less sensational note, Rob and I were rehearsing two projects to play in rep with *Princess Ivona*. Rob was fascinated by the expressionistic masterpiece *The Ghost Sonata*, August Strindberg's dark vision of life and death. He was also struck by the expressionistic images of Edvard Munch, which he thought were ideal for illuminating Strindberg's play.

Like Strindberg, Rob was the third child of his father, who was a successful businessman (Rob's dad was Vice-President of a bank, while August's father was an industrialist). Strindberg's childhood was notoriously dark and mysterious and Rob, who had been reared by a sadistic German nanny, easily identified with him.

Strindberg despised the family as a social concept, describing it as:
> "the home of all social evil, a charitable institution for comfortable women, an anchorage for house-fathers, and a hell for children."

As a child, Strindberg went through the very hell he alludes to. As an adult, he realized he would have preferred death. Rob valued Strindberg's insight into the hypocrisy of society's gender roles and sexual morality. In *The Ghost Sonata*, Strindberg dramatizes the powerful struggle between life and death, a sinister theme that fascinated Rob. It seemed ironic that Rob, who seemed so sunny and optimistic, would be drawn to this dark vision verging on madness.

The Ghost Sonata relates the adventures of a young student who idealizes the occupants of a stylish apartment building in Stockholm. He makes the acquaintance of a mysterious old man, Jacob Hummel, who helps him insinuate himself into the apartment, only to find that it is a nest of betrayal, sickness and vampirism. He discovers a family of strangers who meet only for the sake of custom. They bask in their own misfortune, without meaning or feeling. Strindberg creates a world in which ghosts walk in bright daylight, a beautiful woman is transformed into a parrot-like mummy and lives in a closet, and the household cook sucks all nourishment out of the food before she serves it to her masters. The world, the student learns, is hell, and human beings must suffer to achieve salvation.

Munch's The Scream is a piece from a series entitled *The Frieze of Life*, in which he explored the themes of life, love, fear, death and melancholy. These themes recur throughout Munch's work. Like Strindberg, Munch portrayed women either as frail, innocent sufferers or as the cause of great longing, jealousy and despair. As you can see from the descriptions of both Munch's and Strindberg's work, Rob was on to something: a concept that united their terrifying visions of life into a single theatrical experience. The large cast included Michael Fesenmeier as The Old Man, Joseph de John as The Student, David Stekol as The Aristocrat, Roddy O'Connor as Johansson, the Old Man's servant, and Conchata Ferrell as The Cook. Judy Kirtley, Toni Edwards, Beverly Gin, Ron Seka and Brad Dourif played supporting roles.

The production put the audience in the midst of the action, with entrances sometimes coming from behind. The most memorable image (apart from the projections of Munch's drawings) was Chatty's tyrannical Cook, wearing sandals with nine-inch soles, giving her the stature of ancient Greek actors in "Buskins."

As a curtain raiser to *Ghost Sonata*, we presented our first Lanford Wilson play. *Sextet (Yes)* is a short piece of six interlocking monologues about couples and betrayals. Lanford wrote it about the same time as *Serenading Louie*, but I'm not sure when I first read it. Originally, Lanford planned to write a full-length play about the four couples, but he became bored by the realistic details. Intrigued by Samuel Beckett's exemplary economy, Lanford decided he'd rather present the characters in an abstract form and allow the audience to piece together the plot. Each character presents an accounting of his/her childhood, marriages and illicit affairs. They are united by a refrain of "Yes," reminiscent of

James Joyce. In this distillation, two of the characters remain offstage, (one is dead, the other a wife whose story is not told). The six remaining tell their stories in interlocking soliloquys. The tangle of speeches, although beautifully written, is frustrating to decipher. I directed a cast made up of Tanya, Stephanie, David Stekol and Tony Tenuta, with newcomers Beverly Gin and Clyde Kelly. The actors were seated on stools facing the audience and there was no movement except for behavioral gestures. With no interaction between the characters, it was an exercise in minimalism. The intertwined monologues alternated among the characters, so the lights came up on each isolated actor as they spoke, with the others left in darkness except when the person being spoken *about* had a faint glow of light.

Sextet (Yes) and *The Ghost Sonata* (Traditional production) joined *Princess Ivona* in rep February 11, 1971, for twelve performances. Here are excerpted reviews:

Manhattan Park West, March 4, 1971 (Aileen Jacobson):
"*Ghost Sonata* is playing at Circle Theater Company in an appropriately gripping and haunting production. Director Thirkield has molded a cast that carries through the spirit of terror and hardship...Fesenmeier as the old man is convincingly cold and single-minded...All the major performances are good. The use of Munch's paintings and graphics is extremely effective... *Sextet (Yes)* is not badly written. The language and pace are often poetic and rhythmic, but the relationships are not as deep or meaningful as the Beckett plays of which it is highly reminiscent."

Cue Magazine, April 10, 1971 (Marilyn Stasio):
"Circle Theater Company's most impressive accomplishment to date was an unusual and very successful dual production of Chekhov's *Three Sisters,* done in traditional and experimental versions which played in rep. The group's last production honored the same principle by yoking Wilson's

introspective and very contemporary playlet *Sextet (Yes)* with Strindberg's *Ghost Sonata*. It was an interesting experiment...providing ample evidence that this group is a good one to keep an eye on."

Developmental Work

Because we played only Thursdays through Sundays, the theater was available Mondays through Wednesdays for other projects. Capitalizing on the empty space, during the run of *Princess Ivona* and *Ghost Sonata*, I scheduled a Special Project of Samuel Beckett's *Waiting for Godot* that would continue our policy of encouraging theater artists to cross disciplines. Our Company designer Ron Radice had a novel idea for staging this existential masterpiece. His concept involved cross-gender casting, using Michael Fesenmeier and Sharon Madden as Vladimir and Estragon, with an outside-the-company actor (whose name is forgotten) with a huge voice to play Pozzo, and Berrilla Kerr as Lucky. Zane Lasky played the Boy, who arrives to say that Godot will not come today, but perhaps tomorrow.

One principle at Circle was that projects should be generated by an inspired vision, and Ron Radice's *Waiting for Godot* certainly was visually inspired. The barnlike interior of our loft theater-space was transformed into a desert filled with Vermiculite, a clay substance that simulated vast stretches of sand dunes, creating a barren landscape that was spot-on for the play. It was an environmental experiment, with the audience sharing the sand with the characters. Surrounding both stage and audience, huge curved sheets of translucent plastic hid the walls and ceilings of the theater, enclosing the sandy world. The plastic sheets were backlit with blue light that changed to dawn as Gogo and Didi woke up in their ditch.

This *Godot* was an appropriately senseless mirror of reality (a November cyclone in Bangladesh had just killed half a million people), and the production reverberated with imagery. The sight of Berrilla Kerr as a skinny hag with curly gray hair, enslaved by a macho tyrant jerking the chain around her neck encapsulated the image of female subjugation throughout history, just as the world was waking up to a need for women's liberation.

Waiting for Godot played for three performances March 15 through 17, 1971. I wish we could have shared Ron's vivid *Godot* with the public, but since we had not (and probably couldn't have) acquired the rights, it was doomed to be savored only by us as a special project that no critic would see. In our idealism, that seemed irrelevant. The artistic experience was sufficient.

Two Marshalls

Later in the spring, there was a workshop production of *Time Shadows* by Helen Duberstein that introduced us to the director Marshall Oglesby, who would become a key member of the Company for many years. Marshall Oglesby was born in Bossier, Louisiana in 1942 and attended Centenary College in Shreveport. After graduating, he went to work for the Dallas Theater Center, founded by the legendary Paul Baker, who became famous for directing a groundbreaking production of *Hamlet* with three actors portraying the title role. In 1969, just as we were starting Circle, Marshall Oglesby came to New York and began directing plays off-off-Broadway, where he met Helen Duberstein, one of our resident playwrights. She brought Marshall to us and by the following year, he became Managing Director and eventually Associate Artistic Director. It's hard to overestimate Marshall Oglesby's importance to Circle.

Time Shadows was a vehicle for Tanya Berezin, who gave a mesmerizing tour-de-force performance as Eleanor, opposite Guest Artist Michael Hogan as her lover, Mark, and Burke Pearson as her husband, Philip. The cast included Company members Brad, Berrilla, Judy, Zane and Mike Fesenmeier. Mark's daughter was played at the age of eight by a precocious child named Alexandra Morphet and, at the age of twenty-eight, by Chatty. It was designed by Ron Radice. We produced the play again as a Major Production the following season, but this workshop played three performances.

A Gauntlet Is Thrown

During the hyperactive schedule of our second season, I had less contact with the Company. I was splitting my time between New York and Woodstock, spending as many hours as possible in the country. I was no longer leading the Methods workshops, which in our first season brought me into continuous contact with the actors, an opportunity for a steady infusion of creative mentoring. Now, I felt inspirational fatigue. Near the end of the season, Tanya called me to task about my lackluster leadership.

When I explained that I felt I had little new to offer, Tanya bluntly told me: "Well, we're going to create a great theater, and we're going to do it *with* your leadership or without you. Which is it going to be?" Her call to action resounded like Gabriel's trumpet, summoning the dead back to life. It was just the prodding I needed to revive my passion. I rediscovered my voice and put everything I could muster into inspiring my colleagues. Not for the last time, Tanya saved the Company.

A Peter Max Molière

The final Major Production of the Second Season was my experimental staging of Molière's *The Doctor in Spite of Himself.* My concept was to mimic the artistic style of Peter Max (as the Beatles had done with their animated film *Yellow Submarine*) and use Beatles music to accompany the farcical interludes. The audience was seated on a mound of artificial grass in the middle of the theater and the action was staged all around them. I had never heard of anyone trying this reversal of theater "in the round" and I thought this romp of a comedy would be fun running around the audience. The psychedelic sets and costumes were designed by Henrietta Bagley. Chatty remembers that she designed the props, while Judy Kirtley recalls looking all over town to find a bicycle built for two.

I selected the play as a vehicle for my faithful associate, Tony Tenuta, who rescued me by teaching the Methods Workshop the second year. Our first season, he'd been a touching Andrei in the Traditional *Three Sisters* and he played one of the titular graverobbers in *The Doctor and the Devils*. Tony projected a nervous energy like some stand-up comics do. He was paired with Michael Fesenmeier as his comic servant. They were very funny together. Stephanie Gordon tried her hand at comedy for the first time as the Doctor's wife. Stephen de Fluiter was Monsieur Robert. The young lovers were played by Brad and (totally against type) Tanya.

A couple of vivid images from the production linger. I especially recall Brad dressing up in a gorilla suit and entering on a motor scooter to gain forbidden entrance to elope with his love; and Tanya with balloons attached to her wrists that allowed her to float away with him to the exuberant elation of "Lucy in the Sky with Diamonds". Rob played the mercenary hypochondriac who spoke in the insistent rhythms of an annoying television commercial for Crazy Eddy's (current at the time) that persistently repeated: "Money talks, nobody walks." Generally, the audience had a good time and it was a fun way for our Company to end the season. I wasn't sure our production would advance the reputation of the theater, so we didn't invite the critics. In retrospect, I regret this decision. It *was* fun and I suspect even critics might have been charmed. The Molière played twelve performances from late May to mid-June.

At the end of the season, celebrating the arrival of summer we participated in the 83rd Street Block Association's annual block party. It made us feel part of the community and we prided ourselves on our identity as the neighborhood theater of the Upper West Side. Sharon Madden, Judy Kirtley and Mike Fesenmeier dressed up as clowns and entertained the local children with magic tricks and juggling. I offered Tarot readings and Steve de Fluiter charted a few horoscopes. Upstairs, we dug out treasures from our closets and sponsored a fabulous rummage sale. Altogether, with the sale of baked cookies and everything, we added a substantial amount to the theater's meager coffers.

In the real world, Amtrak began passenger service, the "Pentagon Papers" were published by *The New York Times,* and Bill

Graham closed the legendary Fillmore East, the Mecca of Rock and Roll. The world's four-billionth baby was born and the 25th Amendment to the Constitution lowered the voting age to eighteen.

We joined forces with a young filmmaker from the Film Forum named Peter Polimanokos to record our performances of Lanford Wilson's *Sextet (Yes)*. Peter entered the film in a film festival in the Northwest, where it received some recognition. I recently discovered a 16mm copy of the film and had it transferred to DVD, preserving one of the earliest of Circle's performances. Seeing it all these years later, only David Stekol, Tanya and Stephanie give rich performances; the amateurism of the others is apparent.

Artistic Renewal: The Woodstock Retreat

Still smarting from Tanya's challenge to rediscover the dreams that got us to this stage, I realized we needed to re-boot our lagging inspiration. It occurred to me that a country retreat, isolated from the pressures of the City, might be a way to rekindle artistic passion. Since Rob, Tanya and I were part-time residents of Woodstock, I suggested that we invite the Company to Woodstock to resume workshop training over the summer. It was evident from our productions of Strindberg and Molière that we were taking on projects beyond our level of proficiency. Maybe the abundant beauty of the Catskill Mountains would inspire a new start. We could not pay our actors (several members of the Company returned to the city each week to collect unemployment), but we could provide them with room, board, transportation and free training. We didn't realize at the time that we were following in the footsteps of Michael Chekhov, who'd brought his company to the Byrdcliffe Arts Colony in Woodstock for a summer retreat in the 1930s.

Because Tanya was pregnant, she didn't participate in our summer workshops, but she was a sympathetic supporter, a Madonna who indulged her endless craving for Fudgesicles. Rob and Tanya had a spare bedroom for Stephanie. I had my Sunshine Cottage, where I could put up Lance Taylor and Tony Tenuta. Berrilla rented a lakeside house and could offer rooms for Ogelsby and Henrietta. Designer Ron Radice rented a cottage at the edge of the reservoir. Rob took a lease on a large, rambling two-storied farm house with six bedrooms that would accommodate the remaining members of our Company: Mike and Pat, Sharon, Judy and Chatty, Burke, Steve and David Stekol, Roddy, his wife Laurel, their young child, and Goofy (who was part English setter and part Dalmatian). It had a screened-in back porch that was shared by our two youngest members, Brad and Zane. We called it the "Big House." We also bought a "Company Car" that could be shared for local transportation. Lance Taylor volunteered to cook all the meals for the Company at the Big House, and he was assisted by rotating crews of KP duty.

The entire Company gathered every morning (except Sundays) from nine to ten for warm-up exercises outdoors on the grassy lawn at the side of the Big House, surrounded by flowering bushes of rhododendron. Members of the Company would rotate in leading relaxation exercises, sharing techniques based on their own experiences.

Our day was divided into a morning workshop in the large dining room where three days a week Rob developed his new surrealistic approach to *Ghost Sonata*. After a two-hour break for lunch, I had a three-hour workshop three days a week for a new "American" version of *Three Sisters*. Not everyone was required to participate in every workshop but some activities were designed to include the entire Company.

A variety of workshops was offered between *Ghost Sonata* and *Three Sisters*, in which the Company had opportunities to acquire an assortment of skills. Judy offered a class in basic ballet; Mike led a workshop in commedia dell'arte; Roddy and Ron conducted a workshop for developing a production of Karel Čapek's *Insect Play*; I offered a workshop in Shakespearean verse, exploring an experimental approach to *Othello*; Jim Tuttle came up several times to drill us in Meisner techniques; Tony guided Grotowski exercises; and Steve even offered a workshop in casting horoscopes.

Following a two-hour dinner break, our evening schedule was from 7 to 10 P.M. and included various activities, such as a screening of our movie of *Sextet (Yes)*, a reading of Berrilla Kerr's new play *Elephant in the House*, and an experiment in collaborative playwriting.

We also scheduled special improvisations one night each week, when some of our most intriguing experiences occurred. Especially chilling was a late night improv for *Ghost Sonata* in which the whole Company gathered around the dining room table to conduct a séance, using a Ouija Board. Everyone was willing to suspend disbelief for the purpose of an artistic exploration of the nether world. We sat around the dining room table in flickering candlelight. We asked the Ouija Board about any spirits hovering about who wanted to communicate with us. Sure enough, the plastic disk began to move urgently around the board, spelling out a message that the ghost of a little girl wanted to tell us about her untimely death from drowning in a nearby stream. Because Fesenmeier was playing the lead in *Ghost Sonata* and his fingers were among those on the disk, some suspected the answers from the Other Side might be influenced by Mike's fingertips. Still, as the girl's sad story emerged, everyone noticed a perceptible lowering of the temperature in the room, a chill that was not merely psychological but seemed to be a sensory experience. Then suddenly, although everyone in the Company was accounted for in the dining room, we all heard the heavy tread of footsteps coming down the stairs located directly above our heads. No one could have manufactured that noise; genuine chills ran up our spines.

This experiment inspired the arresting séance that started Rob's second *Ghost Sonata*. In the isolation of the countryside, the imagination is vulnerable to a degree difficult to match in the City, but this mystic experience carried over into a production with the power to spread that chill to a New York audience.

Another evening improvisation was for *Three Sisters*. We used the entire house in the late hours to create the night of the fire that's the background for the third act of the play. Rob, who was playing the Doctor, remembered how he literally drank a pint of bourbon down in the basement. When his services were needed to aid the burned victims of the nearby conflagration, he could barely focus. It was a harrowing personalization to understand Chebutykin's impotence in dealing with the tragedy.

In his classic book *On Directing*, Harold Clurman says the ideal rehearsal situation is for artists to work as if there were no opening night. Our summer retreat in Woodstock gave our ensemble the opportunity to do just that.

The Company also investigated Čapek's *The Insect Play*, a project initiated by designer Ron Radice and director Roddy O'Connor. Steve remembers Kirtley and Fesenmeier as Dung Beatles, hilariously hoarding their "pile." Nothing came of the project because by the end of the summer, Roddy needed to get a "real" job to support his family, so he left Circle Theater Company to become an arts administrator in Boston for Twyla Tharp.

Each week we were joined by the extraordinary teacher James Tuttle who led a workshop introducing the Meisner techniques. Rob and Tanya studied with Tuttle, and his work invigorated and stimulated the Company. I remember an especially touching scene in his workshop with Zane and Stephanie working on *Tea and Sympathy*. It was a tragic shock when we learned at the end of the summer that Jim Tuttle committed suicide by hanging himself. Rob dedicated the second production of *Ghost Sonata* to his memory.

Let's Go To The Videotape

Off the beaten path of orthodox rehearsals, our most intriguing experiment was a project to develop a story through improvisation. One night each week, playwright Berrilla Kerr and I met with a small ensemble of actors to improvise. The improvisations took place in the rather Gothic house Berrilla rented for the summer, which emanated an aura of mystery because none of the actors had been inside. The initial actors were Mike Fesenmeier, Zane Lasky and David Stekol. We asked each actor to invent a character. Every week, Berrilla would give each actor an objective to pursue but otherwise, they were free to create spontaneously. The premise was that Michael and Zane were college friends traveling upstate New York to visit Mike's wealthy aunt. When they got to the chalet, they encountered a mysterious stranger, David, who has taken possession of the house. We had Pat Carey and Judy Kirtley on tap to enter the scene at some point if the plot required a new element.

We planted tape recorders in every room and recorded everything that happened as the three actors (and later, the five) moved from room to room. A plot emerged slowly over weeks of chat that sometimes seemed to lead nowhere. Eventually, a devious, circuitous plot revealed a twisted Leopold and Loeb relationship between Michael and Zane, which was being subverted by the mysterious stranger. By the time the two girlfriends entered the story, they were almost superfluous to the power struggle between Mike and David over the loyalty of Zane. At one point, Zane improvised the most memorable line of dialogue (worthy of Mae West) when he informed Michael: "You're just a feather bed, Mike, and I need a hard mattress."

Once the melodrama (which is what it turned out to be) took shape, Berrilla listened to the many hours of tapes, cherry-picked the best lines of dialogue, and created a structure for the plot that materialized. She transformed the contributions of the actors into a taught little thriller. I directed the end product on videotape, using what must have been among the earliest video equipment. The huge, cumbersome camera and the reel-to-reel recording device were primitive, but we shot the story in chronological sequence, so no post-production editing was required. Berrilla called the teleplay *Kit's Play* (for what reason nobody could guess, since there was no Kit in the plot or the background). The final teleplay was probably no better than any B-grade melodrama, but the excitement was the experiment itself. I have no idea what became of the tape, so *Kit's Play* remains an ephemeral oddity of experimentation.

All in all, the Company had an enriching summer together that prepared us to return to the City to conquer our shortcomings and achieve new heights of artistry. Judy remembers the summer as a period of great liberation. Being put in touch so intensely and intimately with other human beings strengthened our bonds.

While we were in Woodstock renewing our dedication, the Kennedy Center opened in Washington, D.C. with Leonard Bernstein's *Mass,* staged by Gordon Davidson. In New York, John Guare and Galt McDermott scored a huge hit with their musical *Two Gentlemen of Verona,* which ran for 614 performances, snagged nine Tony nominations and won two, including Best Musical.

Beginning Again

As a theater devoted to the development of our artists, we resolved early on that we would begin paying our actors for their work as soon as possible. Grants were renewed and increased from the New York State Council on the Arts and the Peg Santvoord Foundation that enabled us to pay our actors a stipend of $11.72 a performance in our third season, (which was ¾ of Equity's Off-Broadway minimum of $125 per week) and $7 per diem expenses during rehearsals, long before anyone else in the off-off-Broadway arena was paying actors anything. As a result, we were able to negotiate longer runs with Equity, initially increasing to sixteen performances and eventually to twenty-five.

In the fall of 1971, I had a visit from a young woman who had just completed her studies at Yale, after graduating from Bryn Mawr. Lynne Meadow was looking for a job in the theater. I liked her immediately and wanted to encourage her strong artistic drive. I explained that our support at this point depended on unpaid volunteers, since our paltry funds were earmarked for the artists. She seemed bright, energetic and promising, so I said that if something came up, I'd call her. I told her I'd been in the same position after graduation, ready for work and no one hiring; so I'd created my own theater. I suggested she might think about doing the same.

A couple of weeks later, pondering who could fill the technical positions we would need to mount our rotating repertory of *Three Sisters* and *Ghost Sonata,* I called Lynne to see if she'd be interested in running the sound. She graciously declined and I forgot about her until the following year, when I learned she became the Artistic Director of a new group on the Upper East Side called the Manhattan Theatre Club. I guess I can stop worrying about what became of her.

We opened the third season on November 18, 1971 with our "American" version of *Three Sisters,* developed over the summer in Woodstock. It played in rotating rep with Rob's new surrealistic *Ghost Sonata.* Of the three productions I directed of *Three Sisters,* this was the least exciting to me because it was neither experimental nor traditional, but rather an amalgamation of both approaches. However, for audiences who hadn't seen either of our earlier productions, it was a fresh contemporary take on Chekhov's play. It was a wonderful showcase for our acting Company. This time, we adapted the text to contemporary language. The great symbol of yearning: "To Moscow!" became a more universal longing: "To go home again!" – an ache almost everyone experiences. We performed the play on a severely raked stage smartly designed by Ron Radice (which replaced our old "experimental" stage), using minimal props. This production attempted to extract the essence of Chekhov's play and let audiences see the characters in present-day terms. It was more an adaptation than an experiment.

Most actors in this version played roles in one of the previous productions. Some played the same role for the second or third time. Some experienced the challenge of Chekhov for the first time:

Olga – Conchata Ferrell (who'd played the Maid in
   both versions)
Masha – Stephanie Gordon (repeating her role from the
   Traditional version)
Irina – Patricia Carey (a long overdue chance to play Irina
   for the first time)
Andrei – Tony Tenuta (repeating his role from the
   Traditional)

Natasha – Sharon Madden (who played Olga in the Experimental)
Vershinin – Stephen de Fluiter (who played Kulygin in the Experimental)
Kulygin – Burke Pearson (repeating from the Traditional)
Chebutykin – Rob Thirkield (repeating from the Experimental)
Tuzenbach – Roddy O'Connor (repeating from the Traditional)
Solyony – David Stekol (who played Vershinin in the Traditional)
Ferapont – Michael Fesenmeier (repeating from the Experimental)
Fedotik – Brad Dourif (in the play for the first time)
Rode – Zane Lasky (in the play for the first time)
Anfisa – Berrilla Kerr (repeating from the Experimental)

While it was not my favorite version, it garnered the best reviews from the critics:

Manhattan Park West, December 2, 1971 (R. Lopat):
"This experimental adaptation provided one of the most absorbing and moving stage evenings it has been my pleasure to experience. Marvelous Circle Theater actors...I recommend, nay *prescribe* this production alternating in repertory. So beautifully do these actors work together that I've refrained from mentioning them by name. Just go and see for yourselves...and bring a handkerchief."

Show Business, January 6, 1972 (Harry Goldman):
"I was thrilled with Radice's stage design. I was impressed with De Fluiter, he plays amazingly well. All of the actors worked together, and all were very good. The last half of the show whirred with excitement. The audience was moved by this play and related to this adaptation."

Village Voice, January 27, 1972 (Michael Smith):
"The production succeeded and it was a pleasure to see. It was a pleasure to break out of the conventional view of this play to see the famous sisters as three stranded women."

Three Sisters was joined in repertory on December 9th by Rob's new Experimental *Ghost Sonata*, also developed in Woodstock. This time around, Rob challenged his cast boldly to explore the dark mind of Strindberg in a surrealistic style. As the audience entered, the characters in the play sat around a table in the center of the space, conducting a séance. Flickering candles and eerie music hushed the audience, intimidated by the spooky mood as they found their seats. Once everyone was in, the séance reached a climax with the appearance of a Christ-like apparition at the far end of the room, lighted from below, tangled in a fishnet: the ghost of the drowned student Arkenholz, played by Brad Dourif with a beard and shoulder-length blond hair, who staggered on stage as if he had come directly from *Night of the Living Dead*. Terrified by the success of their séance, those around the table rose and hurried offstage, before the lights came up to begin the first scene of the play. It was a chillingly effective opening, and prepared the audience for any surprise. Nevertheless, when Conchata Ferrell entered topless as the Cook, her great pendulous breasts dusted with gold flecks and her face a surreal mask of stylized black make-up (similar to the rock group Kiss), the audience was mesmerized, nailed to their seats.

Michael Fesenmeier had matured in his role as Hummel and was gripping in his wickedness. Brad's innocent reading of Arkenholz was haunted by the deathly image at the opening, foreshadowing the tragic drowning of the character. Stephanie Gordon, best known for her realistic work, was electrifying as the mummified parrot-woman, imprisoned in her closet. Burke Pearson made the servant Bengston memorable, and Zane Lasky joined the cast as a mysterious Johannson.

As with *Three Sisters*, this version was received better than the earlier one:

Manhattan Park West, December 16, 1971 (Hanna Hanani):

"Imagination, semi-nudity and Thirkield's resourcefulness have made possible a surprising, and in some ways, landmark *Ghost Sonata.* Exciting theater...All the actors helped to carry the director's interpretation of the play as the study of a mind on the verge of madness."

Show Business, December 30, 1971 (Margay Whitlock):

"This play has been haunting my dreams. [It's] exceptionally well-suited to the Grotowski-like techniques employed in this production. They illuminate the play and clarify the author's intentions. Fesenmeier gives a tour-de-force performance. The ensemble work of the company as a whole is excellent."

Mutual Radio: The World Today, December 31, 971 (Virginia Woodruff):

"Circle Theater Company provided one of the most pleasurable evenings in the theater I have had in quite some time. If you're not familiar with the absorbing work of Strindberg, this will be your perfect introduction...quite an experience! An astonishing evening. See it. It's MUST theater. Bravo!"

Village Voice, January 27, 1972 (Michael Smith):

"A very dynamic, unorthodox production under Thirkield's direction. The force and interest of Strindberg come through."

Ghost Sonata continued for sixteen performances through December 31. *Three Sisters* closed on January 16, 1972 and was followed by *The Elephant in the House,* a new play by Berrilla Kerr that opened four days later.

As the New Year approached, we could look back at an autumn of worldwide change. Great Britain joined the European Economic

Community. Intel introduced the first microprocessor, drastically altering our capacity for storing information. Kurt Waldheim became the Secretary General of the U.N. and the People's Republic of China replaced Taiwan on the Security Council. *RMS Queen Elizabeth*, on which the American Theater Project sailed to London only four years before, was destroyed by fire in Hong Kong Harbor. And during a severe thunderstorm over Washington, a man calling himself D.B. Cooper hijacked a Northwest Orient Airlines plane, parachuted from it with $200,000 in ransom money and was never seen again.

Creating New Work

Elephant in the House was the first new full-length play we presented as a Major Production since *A Practical Ritual* had introduced our theater. As eccentric as D.B. Cooper himself, the play centered on an old woman confined to her bed, guarded by the Super of the building, a large empty mansion the old woman owns on the Upper West Side. Emblematic of the turbulent 70s, people begin to invade the old lady's life, seeking shelter from a variety of problems. A teen-aged girl has run away from home. A young Marine has gone AWOL because he no longer believes in war. A zany threesome appears, comprised of a loony scientist named Horace and his two women, one of whom is pregnant and the other of whom is devoted to caring for them both. These social misfits delight the iconoclastic spinster, who mysteriously disappears from her bed at the end. The tone of the play veers from romantic comedy to outrageous farce, somewhat reminiscent of *The Madwoman of Chaillot*.

Berrilla was the first playwright who wrote roles for specific actors in the Company, fulfilling one of the main objectives of the theater. I directed the production with a cast that included Roddy O'Connor as the Super, Zane Lasky as the young Marine, with Sharon Madden, Judith Kirtley and Steve De Fluiter as the quirky ménage. I had to go outside the Company to cast the role of the old lady, Mary Elizabeth Adams. I was lucky to find Guest Artist Jane Cronin, a charismatic actress who anchored the action. And true

The Transcendent Years

to giving actors opportunities to play roles outside their "type," I cast Stephanie Gordon as the runaway teenager. I think Stephanie was inspired by the grown Julie Harris playing teenaged Frankie in *The Member of the Wedding*. We didn't quite equal that amazing accomplishment.

The Elephant in the House had sets co-designed by Henrietta Bagley and Ronald Radice, with costumes by Dina Costa and music by Ray Shackelton from Woodstock. It opened January 20th, 1972 and played sixteen performances. Most of the reviews were encouraging:

The Bergen Record, February 28, 1972 (Emory Lewis):
"A fascinating if flawed work. I vastly prefer it to many well-made and empty hits in the larger Broadway showcases. For the past three seasons, the Circle Repertory Company has produced an interesting and welcome mixture of classics and avant-garde works. The company is constantly growing in professionalism and passion. Kerr is an exceptionally promising playwright. The first act is the funniest in town. She has a wonderfully unconventional turn of mind, and her wit is fresh and unpredictable. Cronin is merely magnificent. It is one of the finest acting turns in this or any season."

Wisdoms Child, March 6, 1972 (Richard Stein):
"An ambitious and vibrant company...Kerr is a master of language and dialogue...We see the art of the Circle Theater performers come to life. Cronin was magnificent. Lasky and Madden were also quite impressive. The most innovative and interestingly executed scenic designs I have seen in a long time...a most pleasant place to spend an evening."

World-Wide News Bureau, (undated and not attributed):
"Off-Broadway theaters often produce the whole and better thing. Just an example: Kerr's new play [contains] much

thoughtful action. Cronin [is] very persuasive. The New York State Council of Arts knows whom to support!"

New Again

We followed this modest success with another new play, a timely poetic drama rich with imagery called *Time Shadows* by Helen Duberstein, a well-known feminist poet. We developed the play in a Workshop the previous season.

The play offered Tanya Berezin a chance to re-create her dynamic performance. She played a woman fighting to steady herself through a series of debilitating circumstances. The play begins with Tanya as an abandoned Eleanor, isolated in a spotlight, giving birth to a child, alone and unaided. Her screams of deliverance stunned the audience with the visceral pain of childbirth. Then the action flashes back to reveal how she arrived at this point. Her life as a feminist poet has been complicated by the strong pull of nature, as she falls in love with a famous intellectual writer (Mark, played by David Stekol) who is married to another woman (Margot, played by Conchata Ferrell). Mark is almost schizophrenic in his changeable emotional relationship to Eleanor. At times, he's warm, passionate, and encouraging to her growth as a woman. At other times, as he pursues a sexual relationship with a young man (Eric, again played by Brad Dourif), he is cold, detached, even cruel. Eleanor conceived the baby as a "perfect child," uniting Mark's intellectual brilliance with her beauty and talent, never anticipating that she would be abandoned before the baby was even born.

Marshall Oglesby guided the actors through a ponderous text, thick with poetic imagery, to performances so honest the elevated language seemed almost inevitable. Apart from Tanya's astonishing turn at the center of the play, the drama found a foil in the handsome, intelligent but cool David Stekol as Mark. The scene in which he and Brad emerged totally naked from a bed of shared passion was a stunner.

Again, the settings were by Ronald Radice, I designed the lighting and Stephen de Fluiter ran both lights and sound. Steve had never done any tech work and he found the experience a delight, "like painting." The music was by Erik Satie and Vivaldi.

Time Shadows opened April 6, 1972 and was so popular with feminist audiences that we extended it on weekends through May, for a total of twenty-five performances. Here's a sampling of what the critics thought:

Broadway Local, April 15, 1972 (Joan Firstenberg):
"A nightmare of despair... Berezin's portrayal is like a candle among the shadows. I would be surprised if any woman in the audience did not empathize with her suffering."

Village Voice, May 11, 1972 (Rosetta Reitz):
"I celebrate this play. A courageous work, like life, difficult and complex. The language is refreshingly beautiful, powerfully played by Berezin... Thank God for the New York Council of the Arts and the repertory company of the Circle Theater, that such a play can be brought to light and life."

Show Business, April 27, 1972 (Sharon Block):
"A lyrically beautiful play... well staged and well directed by Oglesby. The experimental set by Radice is excellent. [The] acting is good, especially Berezin, Stekol and Gould."

Manhattan Tribune, April 29, 1972 (Sylvia Rosales):
"Oglesby's direction is brilliant. The set by Radice is a piece of art. Mason's lighting is exactly right. The Circle actors are highly competent. Stekol is a fine and earnest player. Berezin is an actress of undeniable gifts. And that's what companies like Circle Theater are all about. With all its flaws, this is good experimental theater, well mounted

and directed and played by young, vital, dedicated actors. It's well worth seeing."

Almost Forgotten Workshops

Wedged between *Elephant* and *Time Shadows*, we presented a workshop production of *Paderewski and the Garbage Thieves* by Ronald Mele. It featured our Company actor Stephen de Fluiter and was directed by Tony Tenuta, but no one can recall who else might have been in the cast. It apparently played three performances. The rust of forgetfulness erodes all that is not gold.

Following *Time Shadows* a second, almost forgotten workshop production was mounted: *The Empire Builders* by French writer Boris Vian directed by Peter Weill. It featured Zane Lasky as the "Smurtz," a son of wacky parents who wrapped him in bandages from head to toe. Zane's entire performance could be gleaned only from his expressive eyes. Stephen de Fluiter played the Father and Trish Hawkins was the mother. It was painfully amusing to watch the dysfunctional parents taking out their rage on their son, who was little more than a mummified punching bag.

Pivotal Points - #1: A Writer Writes

In April, *The Godfather* won the Academy Award for Best Picture and instantly was recognized as one of the finest ever made. In New York, *Hair* celebrated its fourth anniversary with a free concert in Central Park, followed by a dinner for the cast at the Four Seasons, at which thirteen Black Panther protesters and *Hair* co-author, Jim Rado, were arrested for disturbing the peace and marijuana use.

But of more significance to Circle's evolution into Circle Rep, there were two pivotal events at this juncture that would change our future. The first was that Lanford Wilson, who urged me five years earlier to form a theater company, fulfilled one of our founding goals by writing a play specifically for our acting Company.

An expansion of an idea in his five-minute play *Wandering*, it transformed that "turn" into a longer, deeper work about the cycle of life. The exercise showed that no matter how everything changes, it repeats a pattern that sustains continuity. He called it *The Family Continues* and he wrote it for the Company to utilize the experimental exercises that Rob taught in his workshop. It was at the same time a parody on the kind of work the La MaMa Troupe performed in productions like *Tom Paine* and *Futz*, and it was meant to show the world that we could do this kind of self-congratulatory avant-garde as well as anyone. The published script is dedicated:

"To the members of the Circle Theater Company and their Artistic Director."

Lanford hoped an artistic home might save him from the blank pages of writer's block that crippled him since the failure of *Lemon Sky*.

The Family Continues tells the story of Steve from his birth to his death and the renewal of himself in Steve, Jr., destined to encounter the same patterns of happiness and tribulations. The plot is sketched in broad strokes and moves swiftly through twenty minutes of birth, childhood, young love, marriage, fatherhood, estrangement, old age and death, repeated with slight variations. He wrote the role of Steve for Tony Tenuta and Steve, Jr. for Brad Dourif. He capitalized on the skills he knew existed within the Company.

It was an ensemble director's delight, challenging my ingenuity to match the imaginative journey he created with rhythms and repetition. The story is told several times and one of my devices was to pivot the direction of the action 90 degrees with each re-telling, so that the audience could experience the athletic creativity of the ensemble from different perspectives. Apart from playing multiple people, the ensemble also used elastic contortions to create a human automobile, which Steve merrily races until he hits a boy in the road, at which point the actor performed an amazing back flip that captured the horror of the accident. The ensemble included

Henrietta Bagley, Patricia Carey, Stephen De Fluiter, Conchata Ferrell, Michael Fesenmeier, Victoria Levy, Sharon Ann Madden and David Stekol.

Thrilled to have our best playwright finally write something for the Company, we were eager to put it up as a Major Production, but we needed to fill out the evening. Luckily, Lanford wrote a lovely two-character play about the loneliness and loss that life sometimes deals us. The play was *The Great Nebula in Orion*, which refers to the astronomical phenomenon visible to the naked eye on a brilliant, star-lit night. The story begins with a chance meeting at Bergdorf Goodman of two former schoolmates from Bryn Mawr. Louise has become a well-known fashion designer and she invites her fellow alumna Carrie back to her apartment on West 81st Street, opposite the Hayden Planetarium, so they can catch up on where life has taken them since college. As the quiet exchange of personal histories unfolds, the regrets over paths not taken interweave with stories of professional triumphs that mask personal losses. We had the two ideal actresses for these women. Stephanie Gordon was the award-winning designer with a hidden secret, and Tanya Berezin was the genteel Connecticut society junior-matron, who has married into wealth but longs for a young astronomer she had dated in college. I staged the play in a three-sided arena, using only the simplest props and well-chosen pieces of furniture to suggest the luxurious apartment. Our work together ranks high in our ensemble creativity, bringing Lanford's touching play fully to dramatic life. This is a production I treasure and it is a pleasure to revisit it in memory. It was a jewel of perfection.

Lanford also wrote a silly little farce after he returned from Europe about a date between a sex-starved telephone operator (Melba) and her boss' son (Graham), a telephone pervert of the heavy-breathing, "what are you wearing?" variety. In Denmark, Lanford heard mothers chasing their young children, admonishing them with warnings not to pick up dirty things on the street that, to his ears, sounded like "Ikke, ikke, nye, nye, nye." Since this piece of fluff is basically a joke about nastiness that can only be given full rein in the impersonal anonymity of telephonic communication, he thought it was a suitable title for the play.

We began rehearsals on this absurd farce with Judith Kirtley playing the extravagant Melba and Rob Thirkield as the introverted Graham. After a week of rehearsal, it became apparent that Judy didn't have the experience to bring off this exaggerated style. I went to her apartment to tell her I thought the play demanded a more accomplished actress and Judy readily agreed. So I recruited Lucy Silvay, a comrade from our days at the Cino, to join Rob in this skit that would be horrendous if it weren't funny. Some found it hilarious; others found it horrendous, but I think *Ikke, Ikke, Nye, Nye, Nye* showed a side of Lanford that was silly and light-hearted, a trait obscured by his standing as one of America's most promising playwrights.

We started the evening with the subtle, poignant *Great Nebula*. After a brief interval to set up the sofa and coffee table that served as the entire set for *Ikke, Ikke*, we invited the audience to loosen up and laugh. And then we cleared the space to dazzle them with acrobatic ensemble work on *The Family Continues*.

One reward was immediately evident: we attracted our first review from the hallowed *New York Times*, where theater reputations are made and destroyed. Even though he only cautiously endorsed the evening, Mel Gussow was sufficiently intrigued to accept our next invitation to see a premiere of a Wilson play the following year, which would be historic.

3 New Plays by Lanford Wilson opened May 21, 1972 and played twenty-five performances. It was directed and lit by Marshall W. Mason, designed by Ronald Radice, Assistant to Mr. Mason was Zane Lasky. Music (for *Great Nebula*) by Rob Thirkield, Music for *Family Continues* by Michael Fesenmeier. Here are excerpts from the reviews:

> *The New York Times*, May 22, 1972 (Mel Gussow)
> "*Nebula* is an intimate and wistful portrait. This is a small play, touchingly performed by Gordon and Berezin. *Ikke, Ikke* is a broad farce, the writing is obvious, the staging is awkward, and the acting is unimaginatively

heavy-handed. *The Family Continues* is convincingly acted, particularly by Tenuta. As for the Circle Theater, it is to be encouraged for bringing theater to the movie-filled Upper West Side community."

Show Business, May 25, 1972 (Janet Barkas):
"Bravo Lanford Wilson! Here are three stimulating, engrossing plays with suspense and humor. Gordon is superb: her grace and sensitivity light up the stage. Berezin is also good. Thirkield is hilarious. Tenuta and Carey are convincing in this provocative depiction of the cyclical aspect of life. The theater needs more playwrights like Wilson."

The Bergen Record, June 6, 1972 (Emory Lewis):
"Wilson is one of America's best young playwrights. [This is] a major theatrical event at the invaluable Circle Theater. I advise you to catch this fascinating bill. *Nebula* is a sensitive and engrossing study... a small gem-like piece, and it is brilliantly acted by Gordon and Berezin. *Ikke, Ikke* is a disappointment and it is indifferently acted. *The Family Continues* is the most original and ambitious. The actors perform through perfectly timed acrobatics and experiments with sounds and word repetitions. [It's] a fascinating, powerful and haunting poem about the life cycle. It is one of the most arresting theater pieces of the season."

Women's Wear Daily, June 6, 1972 (Joseph R. Mazo):
"Circle Theater provides a home base for remarkably talented playwright Wilson. One play is interesting, one is bad, and one is very good indeed. Berezin and Gordon successfully sustain the mood and characterizations in *Nebula*. *The Family Continues* makes good use of ensemble to make this play a highly theatrical piece of work."

Village Voice, June 8, 1972 (Michael Smith):

"Wilson writes real plays. He is an innovative and adventurous craftsman. [These plays] show three aspects of his work. *Nebula* is the best of them...which at the end abruptly and shockingly confronts the void. Gordon plays Louise with a wonderfully cool, efficient, almost off-handed urbanity; Berezin as Carrie is bright and fidgety. Both settle into the play and by the end make these women movingly convincing. *Ikke, Ikke* is charmingly, sometimes hilariously played by Thirkield and Silvay. *The Family Continues* is enormously skillful and economical in its storytelling and Mason's staging is inventive and discretely purposeful."

Even though the critics were far from unanimous in endorsing all three plays, theatergoers wanted to see Lanford Wilson's new work. Readers of *The New York Times*, familiar with Mel Gussow's understated style, could read between the lines that he thought it worth the trip to the Upper West Side. It is impossible to imagine Circle's rise to prominence without the aid of Mel Gussow. He was not only our discoverer; he nurtured and promoted us throughout his career. Audiences filled the theater for nearly every performance. It felt very much like a hit.

During the run of *3 New Plays*, several mind-boggling events took place in the world at large. Governor George Wallace of Alabama was shot at a political rally in Maryland. In Rome, a madman shouting "I am Jesus Christ!" attacked Michelangelo's "Pietà" statue with a sledgehammer. The Supreme Court, in a decision that later would be reversed, ruled that the death penalty was unconstitutional. On May 28, five White House operatives broke into the offices of the Democratic National Committee and on June 17, they were arrested for burglary, beginning a saga that would take another year to play out.

The times, they *were* a-changin'. Travel altered our access to the geographic world, just as the microchip was changing our access to information. This was the first year that U.S. airlines began mandatory inspection of passengers and baggage, and it was also the year when President Nixon made his historic trip to Communist China.

In July, the Democratic National Convention met in Miami Beach and nominated anti-war activist Senator George McGovern for President. He named Senator Thomas Eagleton for Vice President, but the following month Eagleton was forced to withdraw after revealing he was once treated for mental illness. Meanwhile, the Republican National Convention in Miami Beach re-nominated President Nixon and Vice President Spiro Agnew for a second term.

Trying To Capitalize

Eager to make the most of our luck with *3 New Plays*, I booked a quick trip to London to explore the possibility of bringing Circle back to the site of our success with the American Theater Project. I knew how much European exposure helped launch La MaMa's fame, so I wanted to make the most of an opportunity to take our Company abroad with three new plays by a prominent American writer.

The productions had a cast of fourteen (which probably could be reduced to ten, if we doubled up by putting Tanya, Stephanie, Rob and Lucy into the ensemble piece). We could mount a European tour of six weeks beginning in September at a cost of $10,000, which would cover production costs, transportation, lodging and food for ten actors, plus author's royalties. Of this amount, I figured we could get $2,500 from Company contributions ($500 each from Rob, Tanya, Mike, Pat and Brad, all of whom had resources for such a contribution), another $1,000 from a rummage sale, and the remainder from booking fees in London, Edinburgh and Amsterdam.

I found a modest hotel in the Lancaster Gate area just north of Hyde Park. I went up to Notting Hill, to renew acquaintance with Jean Pierre Voos. Unfortunately, he and Deanna were having trouble just surviving. Their International Theater Club had fallen on lean times and they were no longer producing at the Mercury. I reconnected with Max Stafford Clark, who'd been at The Traverse Theatre in Edinburgh when we'd played there in 1968. He was now with the Royal Court on Sloane Square, renowned for its devotion to new work. John Osborne's *Look Back in Anger* originated there, regarded as the birth of modern British drama. Max arranged for me to see a couple of productions: *Hedda Gabler* on the beautiful jewel-box main stage and *Hitler Dances* in a small upstairs space where they presented more experimental work. He introduced me to their literary manager, Roger Coucher who, after a couple of meetings, said they would have problems with both money and schedule. I went out to Swiss Cottage to investigate the Hampstead Theatre Club, which had a sizeable main stage, a substantial subscription audience and a hit transferring to the West End. They seemed a bit more mainstream and established than we were at that time. In short, no one in England could help us. I took a ferry across to Amsterdam where the La MaMa Troupe found a sympathetic, innovative producer in Ritsaert ten Cate and his Mickery Theater, only to find that they also couldn't sponsor an American Company on such short notice.

But the trip was beneficial in one way. In Holland, I saw how the Mickery Theater's wooden modules could be stacked in various arrangements to give everyone a view of the stage. I resolved that on my return to New York my first priority would be to build similar modules that could be broken down into any audience configuration, but that would allow each patron a clear view of our work. That became a project that others, including Lanford, cheerfully joined me in doing before we opened the following fall for our fourth season.

Pivotal Points - #2: A Muse Inspires

While I was in Europe, another pivotal event occurred at Circle Theater Company. As you have seen, we were serious about encouraging artists to cross disciplines and explore another skill. Actors who complain of writers or directors can gain a new perspective from trying to write a play or to direct a production. Similarly, our playwrights acquired valuable insight into the process of acting by appearing on stage. It all seems easy until you try it.

Conchata Ferrell wrote a one-act play that she titled *Danny 405*. She timidly showed it to Lanford who told her she needed to see her script on its feet. Brad Dourif undertook to direct it in a workshop production. While it may be true that Chatty's play gave the Pulitzer Committee little to be concerned about, it was a valiant effort and a small triumph for our goals. Essentially, Chatty took an independent activity from Meisner's basic techniques and counter-posed an objective in conflict. The result was an enjoyable little drama. Tony Tenuta, with whom Chatty had a close personal relationship since the summer in Woodstock, played a man who was building a set for a fictional production. As he's attempting to measure, saw and nail together pieces of lumber, he is hounded by a fellow (played by Pinocchio Madrid), who tries to persuade the builder to quit working and join him goofing off. Tony's dedication to his job sets the theme of the play, which is a question of what endures. Pinocchio tells him that he's kidding himself to imagine that his work on the theater set is of any lasting importance. He says he saw graffiti scrawled on a wall that said: "Danny 405," and that more people will see that meaningless slogan than will come to see the play Tony is laboring on dutifully.

Chatty has never been tempted to write another play, nor Brad to direct one. Both gained a new appreciation for how vulnerable a writer and a director are when their work is at the mercy of collaborators. Chatty took us up on our offer to let any member of the Company mount a workshop production whenever the theater was free for a week. We gave them $100 for a budget. But Chatty realized she needed another play on the bill to round out the evening.

She read Lanford's one-act play *Ludlow Fair* and immediately saw she'd discovered a perfect role for herself in Agnes, the overweight roommate of pretty Rachel. She saw it was a good match for *Danny 405*. Her friend Patricia Carey would be a lovely Rachel. Lanford gave her permission to do the play, contingent on his retaining approval of a director. Concerned that she would be obligated to allow her friend Michael Fesenmeier to direct the workshop, Chatty prevailed upon Lanford to insist on Marshall Oglesby. Pat and Mike were very upset. Michael did not work with us again.

Here's the second historical pivot: Marshall Oglesby cast Trish Hawkins to play opposite Chatty. When Lanford saw the performance, he was enchanted. He would begin to write for Trish Hawkins in an artistic infatuation that spanned many years and inspired many of his most successful plays. As you follow the progress of Circle's development in the following chapters, you'll see what a significant moment Trish's introduction to the Company was. I'm sorry to have missed this performance.

When I returned from Europe, I learned how ecstatic Lanford was over Trish's work. I was surprised because I knew Lanford was never able to tolerate any kind of speech defect in actors. "But she has a lisp," I reminded him. "With Trish," he told me, "her lisp is immaterial. She's an acting genius that doesn't know *how* to lie on stage. Every moment is totally *real* and thrilling."

Trish Hawkins was born in West Hartford, Connecticut on October 30, 1945 to a father who got his PhD from Harvard in Political Science when she was two or three. He went to Washington, D.C. where he worked for a Think Tank. An admirer of philosopher George Santayana and psychological pioneer Sigmund Freud, Trish's dad also loved the theater. In the 1950s, he took his family to Vienna, Austria, where Trish spent her adolescence. She continued to study ballet in Vienna and recalls the excitement of watching her dance teacher perform at the Vienna State Opera. Trish was a member of the Children's Opera Company of Vienna and played Gretel in the Humperdinck opera *Hansel and Gretel*. Eventually, her father had enough of trying to work with retired generals of the Vietnam era, so he left government service and moved his family to Albany, where he worked as a professor of political science and public administration.

Trish also went to Harvard, where she did some acting (especially at the summer theater at Agassiz, founded by Thomas Babe and Tim Mayer) but feeling shy and awkward, she was intimidated by all the talented people there, notably Stockard Channing. At the end of her freshman year, she apprenticed at the Williamstown Theater Festival. Upon graduation from Harvard, Trish studied with Sanford Meisner in New York at the Neighborhood Playhouse. She made her stage debut in 1970 in *O! Calcutta!* While at Harvard, Peter Weill had been her classmate. Then, Peter's wife and Trish were in a production together of a musical version of *Iphigenia* at the Public Theater. When I asked Peter to direct *The Empire Builders,* he invited Trish to be in it, and since she'd seen the Traditional *Three Sisters*, she was eager to work at Circle.

With Trish as an inspiration to write for, Lanford's involvement with the Company was sealed. We became the home for one of America's most promising playwrights. We had survived three seasons and our dream of an acting company trained in the classics had become a reality. Now, our resident writers were writing for our acting Company, so another founding goal was being realized. Gradually, the creation of new work was becoming our primary focus.

We were on the cusp of bringing Circle's mission to fruition, recognized far beyond the boundaries of the Upper West Side. Although it was not clear how close we actually were, the next year provided an opportunity for a dramatic leap into making American Theater history. I looked forward to the approaching season.

CHAPTER 7
JUBILATION

For the first time, we had a sure thing to open our new season. When we presented *3 New Plays by Lanford Wilson* the previous spring, we played to nearly full houses. But many theater-lovers missed the first run, so it felt like dumb luck to be able to reprise our little hit and kick off the New York Theater season. There was no need to invite critics again. All we had to do was get word out that the new Lanford Wilson plays were back.

One of the joys of a repertory company is the opportunity to revisit previous productions. Returning a show to our repertoire was less a revival than a renewal, often with additional growth, depth and insight. The second production of *Ghost Sonata* was richer than the first, and the third version of *Three Sisters* combined and refined our previous endeavors. Now, we relished the chance to remount *3 New Plays*. We made a few replacements, but most of the key players remained. Tanya and Stephanie were better than ever in *Great Nebula*. Rob was funnier in the second play opposite a mature actress named Louise Clay, who was a fine replacement for Lucy Silvay in *Ikke, Ikke, Nye, Nye, Nye*. We reduced the cast of *The Family Continues* from ten actors to eight, with Tony Tenuta, Brad Dourif, Conchata Ferrell and Sharon Madden repeating their roles, joined in the revival by Trish Hawkins, Rob Thirkield, Eliza Miller and Pinocchio Madrid.

Our second run of the three one-acts brought renewed confidence in our mission. Apart from the comfort of slipping into familiar shoes, the greatest pleasure was knowing that this time audiences could see everything we did.

Inspiration Strikes

The stacked black boxes that gave audiences a clear view of the Mickery Theater stage in Amsterdam would transform the experience of seeing a play at Circle Theater. I wanted them built and in place for the first production. With the help of Lance Taylor and Tom Garcia, we constructed fifteen 4X8 wooden boxes that were twelve inches high. We cut hand-holes into each end, making them easy to move in order to change the configuration from proscenium, to thrust, to two or three-sided arena. We were one of the first "black box" theaters in New York. The platforms had enough width to stack them overlapping, leaving space for our sleek chrome and black Steelcase chairs, with sufficient room to get past knees and feet. These fifteen boxes gave us five elevated rows with the remaining three rows on the floor at the front, so all one-hundred seats provided a clear view of the stage. This elevated configuration came to be called stadium seating.

As we approached the opening performance, Lanford and I spent a night painting the platforms black and coating them with polyurethane to seal the paint job. Painting and sealing fifteen platforms took many hours; each platform had to dry before we could apply the polyurethane.

Knowing we were in for an all-nighter, we turned up Circle's state-of-the-art sound system and tuned in a pop music station to keep us entertained as we painted. Among the songs that filled the late night air were two that we both loved, and we sang along with gusto. The first was "House of the Rising Sun" as performed by The Animals. Lanford mentioned that this song about prostitution was one of his inspirations for *Balm in Gilead*.

Sometime later, another song came on the radio that hailed the legendary train that ran from Chicago to the Crescent City: Arlo Guthrie serenaded us with "City of New Orleans". Always inspired by music, Lanford loved this song because it captured the lost era of the railroads, before leisurely journeys by train yielded to the practicality of ubiquitous air travel. Lanford had a deep fear of flying and, except for our 1967 trip abroad, he always traveled by train. He witnessed the deterioration of the elegant palaces that once were the grand railway stations spread across America.

By this time, we were both perhaps a bit giddy from inhaling the fumes of the polyurethane, and Lanford began daydreaming out loud about how he'd like to write a play about the loss of the railroads. That loss, he said, was emblematic of our country's abandonment of the values that made it great. "Far out!" I enthused. "Write it!"

During the run of *3 New Plays*, he began to write about a decaying hotel that once had been a stylish oasis in the heyday of the railroad. Now run-down and soon to be razed, the hotel has become a seedy home to vagrants, transients, prostitutes and the elderly. I'll pick up the narrative of this creation after I tell you what happened next.

The world around us continued in turmoil. In August, the last United States ground troops finally were withdrawn from Vietnam. Then in September, word came from the Summer Olympics in Germany that eight members of an Arab terrorist group called Black September invaded the Olympic Village and murdered eleven Israeli athletes in what is remembered as the Munich Massacre.

As for me, after spending only three days a week in New York ("crashing" in Sharon Madden's tiny apartment on West 76th Street) with the remaining four days snug in my Woodstock refuge, it was time to settle down. I gave up my Sunshine Cottage on Tannery Brook Road and returned full time to the City. Sharon found a sizeable two-bedroom apartment in the Village with a thousand square feet on Christopher Street. It could easily accommodate three people, so Marshall Oglesby moved into one bedroom, I into the other, and Sharon made a nest for herself on a banquette in an alcove intended as a dining room. We each paid $125 toward the rent of $375. For the first time in a long time, I had a home in New York, which I maintained for the next thirty-six years. My focus on Circle's future improved by a factor of a zillion.

A Renaissance Fable

Some events make such an impression they seem destined to be remembered forever. The Japanese attack on Pearl Harbor on the morning of December 7, 1941 that resulted in the entry of the United States into World War II was reckoned by President Franklin D. Roosevelt to be "a date which will live in infamy." Yet, more than six decades later, the date passes almost without notice. As hard as it might be to imagine, someday we will become indifferent even to September 11th, as it recedes into history. But for fifty years, those of us old enough to remember President Kennedy's assassination can never forget where we were and what we were doing on November 22, 1963.

The nine years that followed transformed our political climate. The idealism of the "Camelot" presidency fell into disillusion, the populace exhausted by both a distant war and by the domestic protests it engendered. It was an election year and before long, the sea-changing event known as Watergate took place, requiring Nixon to assert: "Your president is not a crook."

Playwright Claris Nelson came back to New York from Edinburgh, where she earned a Master's Degree in archeology. She wrote a new full-length play that I loved right away, so I scheduled it as our second production. She wrote one of the roles for her co-star in *Home Free!*, Michael Warren Powell, who'd since spent three years in Ibiza. Claris and Michael's return re-united players from the American Theater Project with its new incarnation, Circle Theater Company. Claris called her play *A Road Where the Wolves Run*.

Claris shared my skepticism about the Warren Commission's hypothesis that a single "magic bullet" killed Kennedy and wounded Connally, a bizarre theory that was needed to justify a preconceived conclusion that Oswald was the lone assassin. Eyewitnesses testified that more than three shots were fired and that some came from a "grassy knoll" at the front of the motorcade. If *more* than three shots were fired, there was more than one assassin, and Oswald may have been no more than a patsy, set up to take the fall for unknown accomplices. The possibility of a complicated plot intrigued Claris. It was not difficult to come up with an alternative scenario at least as credible as the Warren Report's single-bullet theory. Claris set her play in the Italian Renaissance, a period famously filled with intrigue.

Claris was a lifelong vegetarian, born to vegetarian parents. One of her favorite writers, George Bernard Shaw, was also a vegetarian. Claris aspired to be as sharp, witty and as irreverently pertinent as Shaw. She prized intellect over passion, yet like Shaw, her writing has an underlying strain of romantic sentiment. Her stylistic influences are the French writers Anouilh and Giraudoux, both of whom share a keen sense of irony, leavened by more than a dollop of whimsy. A laboratory analysis of Claris' writing style would yield two parts Shaw, one part Giraudoux and one part J.M. Barry. Perhaps the work of Alfred de Musset bears the closest resemblance to her writing.

The tangled plot of *A Road Where the Wolves Run* goes something like this: A young Duke ascends to the leadership of Florence. He believes that art and learning are the best weapons to overcome the hurdles of history. Gherardo is a general in the Republic's army with a view that strength conquers all. Frustrated because there's no war to fight, he believes his duty is to defend Florence against the apathy of the new Duke. Gherardo has a lieutenant named Fabrizzio, trained to obey the order of command. Yet Fabrizzio is troubled by Isotta, an attractive young former nun who's escaped from a convent. Isotta is drawn to the virile Fabrizzio, but she is disturbed by his mindless loyalty. She futilely tries to raise his sense of personal responsibility. When Isotta discovers that Gherardo is planning to kill the Duke, she goes to the palace to alert him; but her warnings are dismissed by the fatalistic prince, determined to do nothing to defend himself. The assassination will occur in the tunnels leading from the palace to the cathedral. Gherardo employs a misfit named Arturo, who is set up to appear with a bow and arrow at the moment the Duke will be slain. When the assassination is carried out, Arturo is killed before he can reveal who is behind the plot. The death of the Duke leaves Gherardo as leader of the Republic, so Isotta, thinking she might be able to help Florence, marries him. Trapped in his marriage by a woman who knows his guilt, he is a lonely man who has achieved his goals, only to find himself at the abyss.

Claris wrote the part of the vacillating Fabrizzio for Michael. In the role of the clear-headed Shavian ingénue, Patricia Carey was the perfect stand-in for a role Claris could have played herself. In the role of the dupe, Claris envisioned the idiosyncratic behavior of Jake Dengel, the best actor we knew from Northwestern, who later joined us at Circle Rep; but for now, in Jake's absence, Rob took on the role. The aristocratic David Stekol played the idealistic Duke and Stephanie Gordon played his long-suffering wife. At the center of the play, Claris created the role of Gherardo, the brilliant yet flawed General, for Burke Pearson.

The physical production was dazzling. The Renaissance sets were designed by Ronald Radice, alternating between the rich bedroom of the Duke, the freshness of the garden and the stark grandeur of the General's villa. Dina Costa clothed the actors in luxuriant colors and velvets, and Johnny Dodd lighted the spring sunshine and the evening shadows. It was an extravagant production for an off-off-Broadway venue, and looked as opulent as any production at the much-admired APA.

A Road Where the Wolves Run opened at Circle Theater November 22, 1972 and played twenty-four performances, closing on New Year's Eve. Here are excerpts of the reviews:

Daily News, December 2, 1972 (Tom McMorrow):
"The Circle Theater Repertory Company has an outstanding technical crew, hands out the first professional-looking off-off-Broadway programs, has a beautiful girl in the box office, and onstage, alas, a poor play, poorly played....Director Mason has done his best, but better would have been to cut it in half...Patricia Carey is the best thing in the show as a convent dropout....The two sets by Ronald Radice are of Off-Broadway quality, as are the costumes by Dina Costa and the lighting of Johnny Dodd."

Show Business, December 7, 1972 (Martin Oltarsh):

"This tale has a few things to recommend it: the music is appropriate and lovely; the set and costumes are well-done and look like Italian Renaissance paintings; and Patricia Carey plays her role with direction and honesty."

Backstage, February 9, 1973 (George L. George):

"Political intrigue in 15th century Florence is the exciting fabric of Claris Nelson's cleverly plotted melodrama... The play comes to life in believably motivated characters, rich in complex, human emotions, and engaged in attractively grandiose schemes. The cast is beautifully headed by Burke Pearson and Michael Warren Powell, who enjoy excellent support. Direction by Mason is firm and well-paced. Sets by Radice are impressive."

Village Voice, December 14, 1972 (Dick Brukenfeld):

"An intelligent, incisive wit shines throughout. And much in the Shavian manner, the author gets us to believing in one side of the battle, and then shows us the other is equally just... [It] could benefit from cutting. Yet the script is in much better shape than Mason's middle-of-the-road production.... [The ending] ought to be a marvelous irony, on the order of *Three Penny Opera*.... Instead, we get a conventional clinch with just a suspicion of the whacking irony there. The best parts of this production are Radice's simple yet lushly suggestive set and Costa's rich Renaissance costumes. Off-off-Broadway is the place to develop new plays and I'm sure Mason will continue to work on this production. I want to commend Circle Theater for discovering another interesting new play, as they did last year with Berrilla Kerr's *Elephant in the House*."

I agree that the production should have been more Shavian, but to achieve crisply delivered repartee, we needed someone like

Brian Bedford as Gherardo. I'm afraid our training still had not equipped us for that level of expertise.

Nevertheless, in just three years we were being recognized for our premieres of new American plays, and that recognition was about to increase exponentially.

On The Cusp

While we were presenting *3 New Plays* and *A Road Where the Wolves Run*, Lanford was writing. Mid-fall he brought me a typed-out script of the first act of a new play. He sat nearby, smoking nervously, while I read the script. Each time I laughed he'd say, "What?" and peak over my shoulder to see what line had scored. I laughed quite a lot. This was witty stuff, full of rich characterizations. The narrative was filled with overlapping dialogue, reminiscent of *The Sandcastle*. There were more than a dozen characters coming and going through the lobby of a derelict hotel, home to old-age pensioners, prostitutes and transients, each character more colorful than the last. It was full of life, but lean in what one might call a conventional plot. When I turned the last page, he pounced. "So, what do you think? Is it a play?"

I answered enthusiastically, "Oh, it's a play, all right. It's brilliant. I love it. But something had better *happen* in the second act." He was relieved. "Oh, it will," he promised. "A lot will happen."

By the time *Road* was open, he finished two more acts. Sure enough, near the end of the second act there was an explosion of action, derived from subtle seeds he planted in the contrasting characters, clashing over conflicting dreams.

At the center of the play is a nameless Girl (she's recently discarded "Martha" and "Billie Jean") who's a fanatically romantic train enthusiast. She knows every local train's schedule, and each distant whistle brings her updates of whether the schedule is being met. An energetic, cheerful disposition puts her curiosity at the center of everything going on at the hotel. Before long, we discover this enchantingly naïve creature is actually a teenaged prostitute, who has traveled throughout the United States and knows the train stations in every city.

Bill, the desk clerk at the hotel, is a virile man who has a no-nonsense relationship to the variety of transients who come and go; the sole exception is his abject infatuation with The Girl. A bit mature to be a bachelor, his longing for The Girl is unspoken.

In contrast to the fresh exuberance of The Girl, a raucous, cynical whore named April has seen it all and enjoyed most of it. Her entrance is a bellowing complaint that there's no hot water and, although she's exhausted from a busy night of turning tricks, she stays up to have a cup of tea and shoot the bull with Bill and The Girl. A third hooker named Suzy appears before the end of the first act, sneaking in a john.

Presently we meet Millie, a retired waitress with a mystical appreciation of ghosts, and Mr. Morse, a loveable curmudgeon who keeps his life's savings in a sock upstairs in his room.

Into this unconventional "family" of hotel residents comes a brash young woman from Buffalo, dragging along her introverted younger brother. They are only stopping briefly, en route to claiming a plot of land they've bought in Utah, where they hope to strike it rich by growing garlic. And finally, a disaffected young man about The Girl's age named Paul Granger comes to the hotel in search of his grandfather, who has disappeared. When The Girl learns that Paul's grandfather was a railroad engineer, the action is set in motion for an urgent hunt to track him down in the hotel's records.

The three acts of the play span the morning, afternoon and evening of a Memorial Day, and all the action takes place in the lobby of a hotel soon scheduled for demolition.

In writing about the loss of historic architecture, the shrinking railway system and the tumultuous lives of the disenfranchised, whether hooker or pensioner, Lanford evokes a portrait of a changing America. It's a vibrant play; it was funny, it was sad, it was shocking, it was mournful, it was evocative, it was eloquent, and it was *ours*.

He wrote most of the roles for specific actors in the Company. Blonde Trish Hawkins, with her lithe figure and guileless sex appeal, was the embodiment of his lead, The Girl. Red-haired

Conchata Ferrell, with her corpulent, sensuous, down-to-earth presence and her guffawing laugh was everything Lanford imagined as he wrote the role of April. Always eager to challenge an actor whose work he admired, Lanford threw the hilariously vulgar role of Suzy to the elegant Stephanie Gordon. Appreciative of Rob's talent as a character actor, Lanford fashioned the old grump, Mr. Morse, for him. And with the role of the waif-like younger brother of the Buffalo lesbian, he offered our teenaged neighborhood kid, Zane Lasky, an opportunity to ply his quickly developing skills. There were parts for nervously harried Tony Tenuta as the hotel manager, Mr. Katz, and for Louise Clay as the sourpuss desk clerk, Mrs. Oxenham. Burke Pearson had only a few lines in his role as Suzy's John, but with the rich comic possibilities of a balding scarecrow trying to sneak across the lobby to have sex with Suzy.

But not all the casting worked out as Lanford imagined. He wrote the role of Paul Granger III for our hippie juvenile from an affluent West Virginia background, Brad Dourif, capturing that oddly alienated vibe that continues to serve Brad well in a long string of films from *Dune* to *Lord of the Rings*. But Brad had enrolled in a professional acting class for intensive study with Sanford Meisner of the Neighborhood Playhouse. Unfortunately for us, Mr. Meisner had a strict rule: he discouraged his students from taking roles in productions or risk being dropped from the class. He wanted their full attention on practicing his exercises. So, incredibly, Brad declined Lanford's gift of a role written especially for him. Fortunately, we saw how talented Jonathan Hogan was in a workshop production of a David Ives play called *Canvas*, so we quickly drafted him to play Paul.

Lanford wrote the role of Jackie, the brash lesbian gamin from Buffalo, for Tanya Berezin. Once again, Tanya's timing was off, because she was pregnant with her second child. But she knew of a feisty, wiry actress named Mari Gorman and, reluctantly, Tanya recommended Mari for her part. Tanya's forced generosity resulted in one of the most memorable performances of the year.

The Transcendent Years

Although no one in the Company was right for the visionary Millie, Lanford had the image of Helen Stenborg in his mind from the beginning. She played in his *The Rimers of Eldritch* five years earlier at the Cherry Lane and he knew she'd animate Millie with grace and style.

Not so readily apparent was the question of who could play Bill Lewis, the virile leading man. Through Roy London, we learned that Judd Hirsch was appearing in a play Off-Broadway by Jean-Claude van Itallie, one of our Cino writers. Entitled *Mystery Play*, it was playing for only fourteen performances at the Cherry Lane, so Lanford and I rushed down to see it. We met afterwards with Judd, who was a little skeptical about appearing with an off-off-Broadway company. He had, after all, a Broadway credit (albeit as a replacement) in the role of the Telephone Man in Neil Simon's *Barefoot in the Park*. Nevertheless, Judd is nothing if not game, so he agreed to come to our first reading of the play and give it a shot. He became one of our most prized assets in years to come.

We imported Guest Artist Trinity Thompson to play wheedling Mrs. Billotti, begging to retrieve her pathetic son Horse's possessions, which have been confiscated by the hotel management. Playwright John Heuer became the Postman, Howard McBride played the Cab Driver, and a young kid from the neighborhood, Marcial Gonzalez, was cast as the Pizza Boy. There was also an occupant named Rogers who's trying to escape without paying his rent, played by Peter Tripp. There were seventeen characters.

We assembled at Stephanie Gordon's apartment on Greenwich Street in the Village for the first reading. Lanford and I were concerned that the actors might read the play at a casual pace, so he and I read the first act aloud to them, demonstrating the quick, overlapping rhythms the piece was meant to have. Then we entrusted them with the second and third acts. Zane Lasky recalls that when the script called for Jackie to rub charcoal off Jamie's face, he stood to make himself available for Mari Gorman to do the action. Lanford wryly commented to him afterwards, "You were the first actor in the play on his feet."

The cast was enthusiastic. We had a terrific new comedy to work on. Rehearsals began shortly after the New Year. We all looked forward to it.

What's In A Name?

First, though, we needed to put out word that Lanford had written a new play, prepare posters, print programs, press releases and fliers. He wanted to call the play *Memorial Day*: he was drawn to simple titles that resonated with larger meaning, such as Jean-Claude van Itallie's brilliantly ironic *America Hurrah*. I thought *Memorial Day* was a flat-footed title and told him so. I was hoping for a title that could attract a large audience. He thought about that, and then said, "Well, I've always been intrigued by the suggestive neon signs you see sometimes with letters burned out." A prime example was the (ES)SEX HOUSE towering over Central Park. Lanford said he once saw a sign that pulsated with a red HOT L and he thought that might be the basis for a good joke. I thought it was sizzling for a title. So we brainstormed to come up with a name for our run-down HOT L. Since the play was set in Baltimore, I suggested we call the play *The HOT L BALTIMORE*. Lanford loved it, so we had a suggestive name sure to lure audiences. He designed a bright goldenrod poster with lettering that fanned out the title in an Art Deco emblem, warning: "One month only! February 4th to March 4th."

Creative Collaboration

We threw ourselves into the joyful process of artistic discovery. *HOT L* poses certain research challenges because it contains details most actors wouldn't know about. For example, the play begins with The Girl hanging over Bill's shoulder, questioning how he makes wake-up calls from the switchboard behind the front desk. Obviously, we had to acquire this skill, so a field trip was required. I gathered the actors playing Bill, Mr. Katz and Mrs. Oxenham, and we went to several old-fashioned, lower-end hotels, where we both interviewed and observed hotel clerks to learn everything we needed to know to run an old-fashioned hotel.

Assuming the actresses in the cast had no first-hand knowledge of prostitution, I took the actors playing The Girl, April and Suzy on a field trip to an all-night restaurant at 71st and Broadway where they could observe hookers pursuing their trade.

Lanford provides no biographical details for the characters, beyond a few intriguing particulars, such as Millie's once having served as a waitress to President Calvin Coolidge: ("He didn't pay, and he didn't tip.") Otherwise, all backgrounds of the people in the play were supplied by the imaginations of the actors. Although Lanford attended virtually every rehearsal, I discouraged the actors from asking him about their characters. It was their job to explore those questions, not his to provide answers. Lanford loved the rehearsal process and he savored watching actors create the life of his play. His presence and enthusiasm was a constant source of inspiration, providing a strong incentive to do our best to honor his work.

After a week of research, we took on the script in small beats of action, with the actors having learned their lines for each beat before we staged it. We explored each moment of the play in depth with curiosity. It was vital that our ensemble's behavior be so believable it would be impossible to detect any "acting." We wanted the audience to experience this slice of life as if it were *really* happening right now, before their eyes.

With this in mind, I staged the play in a two-sided arena, with audiences on both sides of the hotel lobby. It was necessary for the audience to cross part of the lobby to reach their seats, only a few feet from the action on stage. I wanted the audience to be IN the hotel, sharing the space with the characters.

Lanford and I constructed a front desk on the southern side of the space, with a stairway on the other side that suggested access to upper floors. We found old furniture on the streets of the Upper West Side (the streets of New York are a generous provider of detritus: one man's trash is another man's set decoration) to serve in the dilapidated lobby. We found an old carpet that unified the seating area where Millie read her newspaper and Mr. Morse and Jamie played checkers. Having our set throughout rehearsals allowed the actors to *live* in that space; we also used actual props during the discovery of movement. All that remained was for our talented set-decorator Ron Radice to paint a *trompe d'oeil* cream-colored marble surface with dark-brown veins. He was so successful at this subterfuge that one had to *touch* the wooden surface to detect it was not in fact stone.

There was one daunting problem to resolve. During the mayhem that erupts at the end of the first act, Suzy comes down the stairs wrapped only in a towel. When she becomes involved in a raging argument, impulsively she snaps her towel at her adversary, leaving her momentarily stark naked. Stephanie Gordon has a substantial mammary endowment, and public nudity was an anathema to her. This problem did not arise until we got to the dress rehearsal, when suddenly she was confronted with the reality that she would be naked. After much hand wringing, I finally convinced her that the climactic moment of the first act absolutely *demanded* this brief moment of nudity. It was no more than a quick flash, essentially a "naked lady" joke, like a *New Yorker* cartoon. The point was not the nudity itself, but that she's so hysterically angry she forgets herself and uses her towel as a weapon. It happens so fast, I told her, no one would see anything but the joke. As soon as Suzy realizes what she's done, she instantly covers up and runs screaming back up the stairs. Stephanie is a very brave actor, deeply committed to her art. So she bit the bullet and agreed. Subsequently, the audience's screams of hilarity were so gratifying that Stephanie performed the moment with relish. This outrageous business capped the first act, vaulting the audience out for the intermission delighted.

A Sober Reminder

As we approached the first preview, it was clear we had a very funny play. The actors were having the time of their lives with these rewarding characterizations, and once we picked up the tempo, the comedy ripped by with awesome spontaneity. Suddenly, I began to fear we'd ventured too far down the comic path. After a dress rehearsal, I assembled the cast for notes. I warned them not to yield to the temptation of enjoying the surface of the play too much or we were in danger of losing the depth we knew lay beneath the fun. I reminded them of the serious consequences of the events in the play: Jackie abandons her innocent brother who, at best, will be rescued by whores; the hotel will be torn down and another architectural treasure will disappear permanently; Bill will never find the courage to declare his love for The Girl, and nothing will change her darkening future, or his; Millie and Mr. Morse will soon be joining the spirits that Millie imagines haunt the hotel; all will be deprived of their homes. As funny as it is, the play has dark reverberations about how the things we value are slipping away.

The humor is not in the punch lines of a sitcom, but painfully funny because the observations are so true. For example, The Girl, commenting on the deterioration of the downtown area, complains:

> GIRL: Baltimore used to be one of the most beautiful cities in America.
> APRIL: *Every* city in America used to be one of the most beautiful cities in America.

And when the Cab Driver barks at Suzy,

> CAB DRIVER: Come on, lady! I'm double-parked.
> SUZY: Tell me about it. The whole fucking country is double-parked!

These are lines that resonate. Nailing our obsession with the present and our increasingly short attention span, there is this exchange in the first act:

> GIRL: Did you hear they're tearing down this hotel?
> SUZY: To*night*???!!!

My reprimand was a reminder delivered at just the right moment; the cast buckled down to dig deeper. We understood this extraordinary play was an artistic blessing. The ensemble was dedicated to what Miss Krause referred to as the fourth dimension of a play: in addition to the truth of individual performances, the actors have an obligation to convey the message of the author, speaking to his time, to our time.

A Curtain Of Music

The final touches of our production were to assemble clothes for the characters, light the stage and provide the music that began and ended each act. Dina Costa coordinated the costumes; I hung, focused and cued the lights; and most importantly, I added the music.

Since Lanford's writing was so influenced by music, I decided to set up a convention, using music, rather than lights, as a "curtain" to introduce and close each act. When the audience comes into the lobby, popular tunes fill the air as Bill sits at the front desk, doing a crossword puzzle. During the pre-show music, actors come and go, intermingling with the audience in a complexly choreographed introduction to the traffic of a hotel lobby. Finely timed to initiate the dialogue of the written play, as Bill sits at the switchboard to begin his chore of morning wake-up calls, he turns the knob on the radio behind the desk, and the music that has filled the whole theater contracts down into the small tinny speaker of the radio, which Bill snaps off to begin the dialogue, sucking us into the world of the play. The opening curtain was "City of New Orleans":

> "Good morning America how are you?
> Don't you know me I'm your native son?
> I'm the train they call The City of New Orleans,
> I'll be gone five hundred miles when the day is done."

At the end of the first act, there is pandemonium, with all the characters talking at once, all desperate to make their points, capped with Suzy's "naked lady" joke. To drown out the hubbub, Mr. Katz snaps on the radio and Dobie Gray's "Lovin' Arms" swells out into the house speakers, filling the theater as the actors quickly abandon the stage and the audience is left with the first intermission.

Music continued to play in the theater and lobby throughout the interval, and the House Manager signaled the audience to return to their seats when Ricky Nelson's "Garden Party" played, followed by the second act "curtain," Neil Diamond's "Sweet Caroline". Again, it fades into the radio and is snapped off by Mr. Katz to begin the action, followed by a long pause. Paul is impatiently waiting at the desk, while Mrs. Oxenham searches the records of the hotel to find if his grandfather was ever a resident, and Mr. Morse and Jamie engage in a game of checkers. The second act includes The Girl delivering a heartfelt hope for the existence of ghosts and otherworldly phenomena:

GIRL: I want a major miracle in my lifetime!

It ends with Jackie's passionate defense after robbing Mr. Morse of his savings:

JACKIE: I got dreams, goddamit! What's he got?

Catching Jackie red-handed, Mr. Katz wrestles the money from her, followed by her devastatingly embarrassed exit. Millie quietly stands on the stairs and assures Paul that his grandfather is alive.

PAUL: How do you know?
MILLIE: I don't know how I know, I never know how I know,
   but I just know he's still alive.

Underscoring this final line of Act Two, on the radio is the haunting melody of the Moody Blues' "Question":

"I'm looking for someone to change my life,
I'm looking for a miracle in my life."

The third act begins with the Rolling Stones' "Ruby Tuesday" and ends with the waif Jamie abandoned by his sister. He sits nervously waiting for her return throughout the act, and April realizes she won't be returning. She snaps on the radio and barks to Jamie:

APRIL: Off your butt! Dance with me.
JAMIE: I don't know how.
APRIL: Nobody knows how. The important thing is to move.

She pulls him to the middle of the lobby and, as the lights fade on the odd couple circling arm in arm, the music swells into the audience with the irony of Johnny Nash's "I Can See Clearly Now":

"I can see clearly now, the rain is gone,
I can see all obstacles in my way;
Gone are the dark clouds that had me blind:
It's gonna be a bright, bright
Sun-shiny day."

In keeping with the lyricism of the dialogue and accompanied by a world surrounded by music, I kept the staging as fluid as possible. While always working with the actors to discover impulses that are the genesis of organic movement, I'd learned from *Balm in Gilead* how to maintain focus in the midst of quickly paced, overlapping scenes. The smoothness of the action flowed with intricate patterns of movement that kept the audience focused on what was most important in a myriad of behavioral details.

After four weeks of working privately in an artistic world, previews demand that we share our creation with anonymous strangers. It's always a precarious moment, baring our souls, hoping the audience will share our vision. At the first preview, I give a little pre-curtain speech to mark the passage of the work from the artists to the audience, reminding the crowd that they are the final element to be added in the artistic process. I encourage them to be generous in their responses. "If you think it's funny, laugh. If you think it's sad, cry. We need your responses to gauge the adjustments we need to make in our work."

The first preview went flying by slowly, and the audience was enthusiastically supportive. The roar of the audience's laughter surprised the actors, who had forgotten during the final rehearsals how funny their serious work was. Afterwards, Lanford's agent Bridget Aschenberg met us in the lobby. Her only comment to me was, "You look tired." Not exactly the response I was hoping for. She reminded Lanford critics need not be invited if he didn't want them. Not the response we were hoping for. Buoyed by the reception of the audience, Lanford allowed that he was fine with the decision to invite the major New York critics to our opening. We played seven previews to hone our creation before we faced the critics. Our confidence grew with each preview, as we tested a variety of audience reactions. Not many changes were made in the text, but the pace tightened and the confidence of the actors increased.

Unleashing A Triumph

The opening night performance arrived on Sunday, February 4, 1973. Fully half of our hundred seats were occupied by the New York press, including a dozen or so members of the New York Drama Critics' Circle. Mel Gussow was there from *The New York Times*, Tom McMorrow of the *Daily News*, Emory Lewis of the *Bergen Record*, Martin Gottfried of *Women's Wear Daily*, William Glover from the *Associated Press*, Michael Smith from the *Village Voice*, Allan Wallach from *Newsday*, John Beaufort of the *Christian Science Monitor*, Richard J. Scholem from *NPR*, and half a dozen critics for the neighborhood weeklies. Lanford and I hid behind a black curtain masking the side of the stage where we could peek through a pinprick-sized hole to watch the audience reaction. The performance went very well and reaction was good, in spite of the predominance of notoriously unresponsive critics. As always at Circle, we had a wonderful, celebratory opening night party. Here are excerpted reviews from the Monday morning after opening:

Daily News, February 5, 1973 (Tom McMorrow):

"A crackling good evening of theater, featuring one of the most hilarious first-act curtains in town. Wilson is thoroughly original, and his people touch both your funny-bone and your heart. Director Mason has staged the interlocking, often overlapping action and dialogue with broad naturalism, and a deft choreographic touch. Strong performances were the rule, not the exception. Hawkins, Ferrell and Gordon show you people, tragic and wryly humorous. Thirkield does an exquisite portrait of an old man. ... Gorman and Lasky's sister and brother will stay with you a long time."

The Bergen Record, February 5, 1973 (Emory Lewis):

"A triumph born of the blues! It is a mournful, soulful dirge for the passing of the American dream. I liked it immensely. [It's] the most mature and luminous of Wilson's scripts. The actors, deftly directed by Mason are first-rate."

Women's Wear Daily, February 5, 1973 (Martin Gottfried):

"First class Lanford Wilson, and that is about as good as you will find in the modern American theater ... Wilson's writing is simply superb, a triumph of inspiration and craftsmanship. Mason's direction is equal to the musicality. He has assembled a company of gifted actors, [and] created a functioning ensemble of them all, something the play absolutely required, and the result is genuinely wonderful theater."

Long Island Press, February 5, 1973 (William A. Raidy):

"More than an "e" is missing. It is a character study in search of characters; a point in quest of a plot. Nevertheless, I felt [this] was a play well worth doing, and the Circle Theater Company has presented a splendid production. They have my admiration, if nothing else."

So not everyone loved us at first glance, but those who did, loved us a lot. And then on Thursday, other positive notices began to stream in:

The New York Times, February 8, 1973 (Mel Gussow):
"Wilson is a very American playwright, with a nostalgic longing for a lost sensibility. This is a play to be savored and to be cherished. Mason has responded with a harmonious production. The actors rise to the occasion. The pivotal character is played with vivacity by Trish Hawkins. Listen to her recite the American cities she has visited, making each name sound freshly minted and bracing."

Village Voice, February 8, 1973 (Michael Smith):
"Lanford Wilson is a master of playwriting crafts... [He has] a unsurpassed skill at orchestrating multiple interwoven scenes and conversations. Wilson is a real writer and [this is] a real play. [It's] being premiered in a finely crafted, occasionally inspired production. Besides Gorman, whose unflinchingly observed, subtle, strong picture of Jackie is one of the best performances I've seen in a long time, there is much to like and admire in the acting. The production is eloquent in detail. Mason, as director, achieved a complex and convincing texture, and some of the dynamic transitions are thrilling. Wilson and Mason [are] working together, making pure theatrical music."

As soon as the favorable notice appeared in *The Times*, we began to attract momentous attention. The celebrated Broadway producer Kermit Bloomgarden and the renowned director, critic and teacher Harold Clurman came. *Newsweek* booked tickets; so did Gordon Davidson, artistic director of the Mark Taper Forum in Los Angeles, and theater mogul Alexander H. Cohen. Finally, even the dean of American theater criticism, Walter Kerr of *The Sunday New York Times,* reserved seats.

Since both Lanford and I studied with Clurman at the Actors Studio, we were especially interested in his response. He had, after all, founded The Group Theater, the most influential theater in American history. We took our usual position behind our peek-hole and studied Clurman's reactions. Lanford has described Clurman as looking "like a child under a Christmas tree," because Clurman's expression was one of sublime pleasure. His review of HOT L was our favorite review we ever received:

The Nation, March 5, 1973 (Harold Clurman):

"The Circle Theater Company offers the best cast and the truest ensemble acting now to be seen in New York. What I found more important than my pleasure at this single event, is the existence of a company which has held together for four years in relative obscurity. Wilson wrote this piece for the people who act it, and it is well staged by founder and artistic director Mason. There is genuine communication between actor and actor: they live in the same world, they are integral to their environment and are expressive of it. It is difficult to achieve this coherence in the circumstances of commercial theater production. Not only is time needed, but the actors must share kindred ideals, training, and emotional or intellectual background. And they have to stay together long enough to acquire a spontaneous sense of one another. Only then will they become one with the entire fabric which constitutes the real *play* in the theater. That is what has happened with the Circle Theater in Wilson's play. One can barely distinguish between the script and the acting. Wilson's writing is salty and vivid; his observations accurate and compassionate, marked by a not entirely poisonous humor. Still, the transcendence of the play springs largely from the acting. Gorman is as touching as [she] is funny. Stenborg is eloquent in a minor key. Ferrell projects health and refreshment by the very acceptance of her own cynicism. Hawkins, in whom the light of imagination still burns, strikes a necessary note of mutilated lyricism. Thirkield is as crusty as the peeling walls, and handsome Jonathan Hogan supplies a sound note in the lunatic, melancholy discord. I was impressed by the quantity of talent that must be going to waste for the lack of means to develop it."

Kermit Bloomgarden immediately took an option to produce the play for an extended commercial run, while Gordon Davidson made arrangements, even prior to the transfer, to produce the show at the Mark Taper Forum in Los Angeles in August.

A Living Legend

Within days, Kermit summoned Lanford and me to his penthouse apartment on Central Park West to discuss his plans to produce *HOT L*. The white-gloved elevator attendant took us to the 19th floor, where the elevator doors opened onto his private apartment. After a small vestibule, we entered through the dining room, where the walls were blanketed with posters of his productions: *Death of a Salesman, Look Homeward Angel, The Diary of Anne Frank, The Little Foxes, Another Part of the Forest, The Children's Hour, Watch on the Rhine, Toys in the Attic, A View from the Bridge, The Lark, Autumn Garden, Deep Are the Roots, The Music Man* and *The Most Happy Fellow*, among others. The posters were accompanied by the awards Kermit received for them: seven New York Drama Critic's Circle Awards, three Pulitzer Prizes, three Tony Awards and six more nominations. It was a hallowed hall we were entering. This was theater history as I had learned it from the *Burns-Mantle Best Plays Annual* when I was in high school.

His servant ushered us into a spacious living room covered with a plush beige carpet, replete with some splendid artwork and a grouping of enormous eggshell-colored sofas. The room was bordered on one side by windows opening out on to a rooftop veranda overlooking the western side of Manhattan and the sparkling Hudson River. It resembled nothing so much as a movie set of a legendary Broadway producer's apartment from the musical

Manhattan Tower. We looked around at everything in awe, waiting for Mr. Bloomgarden to join us. I was scared shitless, while trying hard to be urbane and sure of myself. It felt like we had reached the mountaintop to consult the great guru.

Presently, he came in, invited us to sit and offered us coffee. At the time of our first meeting, Kermit was sixty-nine years old, gray of hair but still husky in physique. He walked with the aid of a cane because he lost his right leg to diabetes only a year before and had an artificial limb below his knee.

He was gracious in his ardent praise of both the play and the production and he was unequivocal about his desire to produce it commercially. In his youth, he was the Business Manager of The Group Theater, so he valued highly the ensemble work we created. He wanted to move the entire production, exactly as it was; in his estimation, its perfection could not be improved upon. It was refreshing to hear a producer speak enthusiastically about mounting a show without stars. He said, "I don't want anyone saying Kermit Bloomgarden came in and ruined a beautiful production with changes."

In the course of our long association, Kermit became like a second father to me; I lost my own father only five years before and Kermit's fondness for me and unwavering support taught me much about the theater. He once confided to me: "You know why I'm such a good producer?" I shook my head to elicit the answer. "Because I *know* I'm not a director!" I grew to love this wise and talented giant of theater art.

We were a little concerned with the size of the cast, but we knew two of the roles could be cut, providing more focus. The part of the Postman was superfluous because the play takes place on Memorial Day when there's no mail delivery. The other part was a fleeting cameo of a resident trying to avoid paying his bill. That incident also added little and easily could be deleted. With these characters edited out, only fifteen actors were left, still a sizeable cast, but Kermit was emphatic that nothing more should change. By the end of our meeting, Kermit shared that he was deeply moved by the character of Mrs. Billotti, pleading for her son, Horse, and her diabetic husband. I never contemplated her wheedling diatribe as anything but comic relief, but Kermit, a veteran of the disaster of diabetes, felt the woman's pain. All of the characters had a level of personal angst that shades the comedy and it was that shading that so deeply and personally touched Kermit.

All his experience had been producing on Broadway, but he was extremely concerned to maintain the intimacy that our arena staging provided. No Broadway theaters offer this kind of seating, so he was eager to hear our ideas about how to solve this problem. I pointed out that the audience basically viewed the play as one does in a proscenium production, only from two different sides. Drawing on our experience with changing perspectives in *Balm in Gilead* by reversing the direction of the ground plan from Act I to Act II, I suggested that we could achieve a similar solution on a proscenium stage with *HOT L*. He immediately got on the telephone to his General Manager Max Allentuck to arrange a run through at a small Broadway theater. Max came up with the Biltmore, which had given audiences an intimate experience with the musical *Hair*. A date was set for an afternoon so the cast could play on an empty Broadway stage and allow us to gauge the experience from a proscenium perspective.

It was thrilling to see our actors on the stage of the Biltmore, a Broadway theater with a capacity of only 903. Using rehearsal furniture of folding chairs and card tables, we performed the first act with the front desk on Stage Right and the staircase on Stage Left. Then for the second act, we reversed the direction, and then returned to the first configuration for the third act. *The HOT L BALTIMORE* is a vivid play and I thought it filled the relatively intimate Broadway space nicely.

In the meantime, Max came up with an alternative: the Off-Broadway Circle-in-the-Square Downtown on Bleecker Street in the Village. The space was a peculiar shoebox shape with three long rows along each wall and a raised audience area at one end, creating a three-sided arena that seated 299. Ted Mann and Paul Libin, the producers for the Circle-in-the-Square, recently had built a new theater in the Broadway area that increased their seating capacity to 650; so the downtown space, although still owned by them, was available for rental as an Off-Broadway venue. Even though it meant producing for the first time Off-Broadway, Kermit was excited by the prospect of maintaining the intimacy of an arena stage. We were a little disappointed not to be making the leap to the big time, but Lanford and I both could see the wisdom of Kermit's concern. It was decided: *The HOT L BALTIMORE* would transfer to the Circle-in-the-Square Downtown at the end of its run at our little uptown Circle Theater and our dream of Broadway was deferred another three years.

Meanwhile, uptown the cast continued to thrill audiences nightly in our second story loft-theater. Flattering reviews continued to pour in, adding momentum to our transfer:

> *Village Voice,* February 15, 1973 (Michael Feingold):
> "Nobody has said enough about how good Lanford Wilson's *The HOT L BALTIMORE* is, and how fine the Circle Theater's production of it is. Let me put it this way – there is finally a great new play in a great production on Broadway – and what it is doing all the way up on 83rd Street is a question for Broadway to do some serious soul-searching about."

> *Newsweek Magazine,* February 26, 1973 (Jack Kroll):
> "It's the freshest play – the best American play – I've seen this season. It is an authentic rebirth of [a] writer's spirit – open, compassionate, loving, hard-boiled, soft-boiled, scrambled. Wilson's characters are the beautiful losers, the walking wounded. The performance is one of the best ensemble efforts I've ever seen. Especially fine are Gorman, parrying life with a perpetual bob and weave; and Hawkins, simmering with sweet anguish for the too-late trains and the too-late people."

And finally the opinion of the Grand Pooh-Bah:

> *The New York Times,* Sunday, March 4, 1973 (Walter Kerr):
> "Wilson's play has justifiably been attracting attention off-off-Broadway. Wilson writes with persuasive humor and dry

accuracy, and director Mason has found for most of his players sharply defined speech patterns that function like musical counterpoint. If this were a film, Gorman's performance would get her an Academy Award. Against her winning belligerence is set Stenborg's superb composure. Trish Hawkins' ebullient daydreamer [is] soothing, flowing free, seeming to dance rings around the ruins. Just as distinctive are Ferrell's blousy and cynical laughter, Lasky's run-down battery hesitations, Hirsch's mercilessly abrupt "Seven o'clock," as he stabs at his switchboard to haul the defeated out of bed. The marriage of text and performance becomes something of an event, and though the Circle's schedule calls for a final performance this evening, I feel certain there'll be further opportunities to see it. I'd try, if I were you."

With this kind of encouragement from the press, Kermit had little trouble raising the capital needed to transfer our play to a commercial Off-Broadway run. Roping in media consultant Roger Ailes as his co-producer, Kermit quickly capitalized the production at $35,000. A bit slow on realizing the financial opportunity we'd created, we attempted to invest $5,000 in our own production for Circle, which was receiving a royalty of only 1% of the gross box-office receipts; but, of course, the investors stood to earn a lot more. Unfortunately, we were too late. Kermit told us the show was fully capitalized and he could not accept our investment. What a pity.

All Aboard!

At the end of our uptown run on March 4th, the actors had a week off before resuming tech rehearsals at our new home downtown on Bleecker Street. Of the fifteen actors who made the transfer, only Stephanie Gordon, Mari Gorman, Trish Hawkins, Judd Hirsch, Helen Stenborg and Rob Thirkield had Equity cards. The other nine were joining Equity as a result of being cast in this professional production. Trinity Thompson could not continue with the show due to previous obligations, but we easily replaced her with our wild-eyed scenic artist, Henrietta Bagley, who had promising qualities for a garrulous Mrs. Billotti.

One benefit we gained from the new, larger space was that we now had room to fashion a handsomely curved marble staircase, far grander than what we'd been able to suggest in our tiny space uptown. Once again, I feverishly managed to hang, focus and cue the lighting (my only professional credit of a craft I loved).

With the prospect of an unlimited run Off-Broadway, it was necessary to hire a professional stage manager, a resource we didn't have in our off-off-Broadway world. After a couple of interviews, I engaged a wiry woman named Andie Wilson Kingwill. She was a choice that my cast endured, rather than embraced. She never became part of our family, remaining instead an annoying stepmother to our childlike artists. Still, I suppose we owe her some begrudging gratitude. After all, we now were playing eight performances a week, with a new level of professional demands. Fortuitously, my fine artists could accommodate this responsibility without sacrificing their childish joy. They didn't love Andie, but they toed her authoritarian line.

As the senior member of the cast, Helen Stenborg took upon herself the responsibility to shepherd our inexperienced company through a lengthy run. Whenever Helen felt the pace was lagging, she rattled her newspaper and tapped her foot, as a reminder of the necessity of maintaining the musical rhythms of the dialogue. Audiences never noticed anything amiss, but the actors dreaded the distraction. The cast picked up the pace or suffered a rattling newspaper during their scenes.

The Circle-in-the-Square Downtown is located on Bleecker Street, one of the main thoroughfares in Greenwich Village, so taxis were plentiful. The large rectangular marquee offered respite in rainy weather and provided an opportunity to advertise our play with quotes from reviews that could be seen from any approach. The theater had a nice-sized exterior lobby by the box-office, although none inside. Once one came through the doors, you were directed immediately right or left to the long rows of shabby movie theater-style seats that surrounded the rectangular stage. The high tin ceiling provided a volume of space above that made for good lighting angles and a sense of former grandeur. The main adjustment for the actors was to increase their volume so they could be heard in a space three times larger than the area we occupied uptown.

The dressing rooms were located at each end of the theater, the Men's up a flight of stairs behind the audience to a room over the lobby. The Women's was at the opposite end of the theater, behind the curved marble stairway. Both dressing rooms were long, narrow spaces, with mirrors along one wall and costume racks on the other. They were fairly cramped quarters for a cast of fifteen, but as a Company, we got along and shared the threadbare amenities without much friction. The age of the old theater (it had been occupied by the Circle-in-the-Square since 1960) meant old wooden floors, frayed carpets and sagging seats, all of which added to the decrepit atmosphere of the Hotel Baltimore, where our play was set. Relative to our uptown space, it was dirty and pretty seedy, and the actors initially had a problem with mice and cockroaches, which required constant correction as we settled in for a long run.

I had to restage much of the action utilizing the corners of the stage space to create angles, so audiences in the end section didn't feel like they were watching the play from the wings. Still, this was accomplished in one week of rehearsals and by March 20th, we were ready to play two previews before our opening night.

Kermit Bloomgarden and Roger Ailes presented the Circle Theater Company production of *The HOT L BALTIMORE* at the Circle-in-the-Square Theater on March 22, 1973. The opening night was a success and afterwards the champagne flowed. Famous fashion photographer Frederick Eberstadt, who took such brilliant photos of our *Balm in Gilead* eight years before, captured the opening night for posterity. The reviews rushed in by press agents Dorothy Ross and Herb Streisfield were glowing. We were the hit of the season. Here are excerpts from the major critics, reviewing the play for the first time, almost vying with each other to be quoted:

The New York Times, March 23, 1973 (Clive Barnes):

"Herald of a new pattern. Wilson's play is delightfully old-fashioned. These are footnotes to a declining civilization – our own: a nation of transients looking for a past and a wake-up call. Wilson shows great compassion ... every single person is interesting. The direction by Mason is impeccable. It practically breathes with the play, as do the actors. What matters is the ensemble performance, which is lovely. *HOT L* could be, and should be, Wilson's first big commercial success. It is an easy play to love. Mr. Wilson knows the score – a hit, a home run. Wilson is both funny and sad about today, and the combination is an unbeatable winner."

Daily News, March 23, 1973 (Douglas Watt):

"Wilson is a gifted and appealing playwright. Hawkins has an awkward charm, and sensitive, believable work is done by Stenborg, Ferrell, Gorman, Lasky, Hirsch, and most of the others. Mason directed them, and well. You wouldn't want to room there, but *The HOT L BALTIMORE* is an interesting place to visit."

New York Post, March 23, 1973 (Richard Watts):

"For warm-hearted enjoyment in the theater, you can't do better than to go downtown and take a look at *HOT L BALTIMORE*. It provides an interesting and appealing evening, and it is certainly acted with skill and spirit. All the characters are entertaining people, and their thoughts, woes, confidences and self-revelations make an engaging and sympathetic play. Wilson has written a fine play, one of the triumphs of the season. I can imagine few people that it won't enchant."

Kermit hired distinguished graphic artist David Byrd to design an elegant poster. It was black, bordered by a bright red tube that spelled out the title at the top in a neon sign with the missing "E," and with quotes in white that shouted: "A Triumph!" "An Event: See It!" "A Hit! A Home Run! An Unbeatable Winner!" and "Best American Play!"

Our performances were sold out almost every night and suddenly, Lanford and I were making real money. My royalties averaged $200 a week and Lanford was earning more than $700. For the first time in our lives, we were going to have to pay income tax; what a privilege!

We both attended every performance for the first couple of months, and then I cut down to seeing it only a couple of times a week for the next three months. It was a joy to observe the audiences' reactions to our work and to watch the actors living their roles on stage. As an illustration of just how honest they were, here's a funny anecdote.

Midway in the first act, April decides to fix herself a cup of tea. Along with the clock on stage that showed the real time (it was reset at the beginning of each act to the appropriate hour of the day), our hotplate really worked, so she actually boiled water and made a cup of tea every performance. But one night, Conchata Ferrell started her usual business and then abandoned it. She never went back to enjoy the cup of tea blocked into her behavior. As I've noted, the staging involved intricate interactions. Taking Millie a cup of tea, for instance, brought the focus to her at the other end of the stage. The no-nonsense Helen Stenborg was upset that Chatty had changed the blocking and I arrived backstage as she was complaining. I asked Chatty why she hadn't done her business with the tea. She explained that the hot plate wasn't working, so the water never got hot. "Well why didn't you just pour the water from the kettle into a cup and *act* the temperature of the tea? The audience would never know the difference." She was dumbfounded for a moment by the very idea of faking it and then confessed: "It never even occurred to me."

These actors really lived their roles, as pictures taken of performances reveal. Lanford's favorite picture of *HOT L* is of Mari Gorman standing at the counter, deeply lost in thought about her plans; no one in the audience is meant to be watching her because the focus at the moment was on the other side of the stage. But the camera caught her total immersion in Jackie's introspection: she was the star of her own drama and every moment was full. As the critic said, if it had been a film, Mari would have won an Oscar.

As it was, she did win the Clarence Derwent Award, the award Equity gives every year for the best newcomer. She also won an Obie Award and both she and Trish Hawkins received Theater World Awards, and Trish, a Drama Desk Award.

Entering History

The production was open only a few weeks before the New York Drama Critics' Circle announced their awards for 1973: Best Musical – *A Little Night Music;* Best Play – *The Changing Room;* and Best American Play – *The HOT L BALTIMORE.*

For the next few weeks, a mysterious change came over our audience; they more or less stopped laughing. They came to see a Drama Critics Prize-winner, produced by the same man who brought them the prize-winning *Death of a Salesman.* They were coming to see "Great Drama" and it didn't occur to them it was okay to find it funny. Of course, there were several lines that could not *help* but get laughs, but the general tone of the audience reaction sobered up for several weeks. The wonderful thing is that *HOT L* is a remarkable play, whether the audience laughs or not. These serious audiences were just as thrilled and their response just as enthusiastic: just different.

By the following month, audience reaction returned to the roller coaster of laughter and tears that characterized our earlier crowds and that continued to typify the responses of audiences over the next three years.

In May, we received invitations to attend the Obie Awards at the Village Gate, given annually by the *Village Voice* to celebrate the best of Off-Broadway. While Lanford and I had been to Obie ceremonies in the past, this was the first time we were in contention. I dressed appropriately as my vision of a rock star, with a tawny skin-tight suede buckskin pull-over with long cascades of fringe adorned with bright blue beads. With my long blond hair, freshly brushed and flowing, I was ready for the "red carpet."

Lanford won the award for Best American Play, Mari Gorman received an Obie for Distinguished Performance and I won for Distinguished Direction. In my acceptance speech, I said that I had prepared myself so long for failure that I hardly knew how to deal with success. I mentioned my long association with my playwright and I thanked my co-founders of Circle Theater Company, my wonderful cast and our legendary producer. I think I can report objectively that the ovation the audience gave us exceeded that of any other awards given that day. My moment in the sun crystallized in receiving this award, and I felt less rewarded than reborn in my commitment to excellence.

Within another week or so, we went to the Algonquin Hotel to receive the Drama Critics' Award. The afternoon reception was held in an upstairs meeting room, sort of a small ballroom, with an open bar at one end and *hors d'oeuvres* served from silver salvers. It was spooky to be in a room filled with the New York Theater critics, most of whom we were meeting face-to-face for the first time.

Also in attendance were Stephen Sondheim, Harold Prince and Glynis Johns, the creators and star of *A Little Night Music.* I was particularly star-struck by the presence of Ms. Johns, whom I had adored in a film from my college days called *The Sundowners.* Producer Lester Osterman accepted the Award for *The Changing Room* because English author David Storey did not make the trip for the occasion. Because there were only three awards, it was a brief ceremony with no acceptance speeches. At the time of our winning, there were no cash awards for the prizes. My impression of the event was a roomful of critics, milling around with drinks in their hands. The casts and producers of the three productions mostly congregated in cliques and ignored the other winners. I recall it was my first meeting of the controversial *New York Magazine* critic John Simon, who only recently had been admitted to the Drama Critics' Circle. Mr. Simon later became one of our most ardent admirers.

The most curious moment was after the reception, as we were waiting for a taxi. Rob embraced me and remarked: "Now you're a *real* director." I was taken aback by this remark until I contemplated that, with winning the Drama Critics' Award, Lanford and I became part of the same theater history I read about in the Amarillo High School library.

At The Home Front

With three of Circle's founders occupied downtown with our juggernaut, our home base uptown at Broadway and 83rd Street carried on under the guidance of our fourth founder, a very pregnant Tanya Berezin, our business advisor, Edith Gordon, and our Manager Director, Marshall Oglesby.

The final two plays in our fourth season had already been chosen: Henrik Ibsen's *When We Dead Awaken* (initially to be directed by Rob, who commissioned a new translation by Michael Feingold) and *The Tragedy of Thomas Andros* by Ronald Wilcox, directed by Marshall Oglesby. We realized early in March that Rob was still playing Mr. Morse in our extended run of *HOT L,* so Marshall Oglesby took on directing the Ibsen in his place.

Eric Bentley said: "Ibsen made tragedy modern by infusing it with his sense that society is fate"; but *When We Dead Awaken* was a dream-like departure from Ibsen's social agenda. It was the last play written by Ibsen (1899). Many consider it his most challenging work: not only are his ostensibly naturalistic characters burdened with metaphysical symbolism, but also the script demands an avalanche at its climax. Some critics have maintained that the play is essentially un-producible. So, it was just the sort of thing that attracted Rob and the kind of challenge Circle Theater was founded to take on.

In a program note on his new translation, Michael Feingold wrote that he did not want to explain the play, but he insisted that it was not inexplicable.

"The history of the play's criticism is cluttered with fanciful explanations on the one hand and desperate cries of incomprehension on the other. For me, it makes sense as a series of confrontations between four people, and that's enough."

With so many of our ensemble engaged downtown, Marshall Oglesby cast the production with mostly new faces. Of our Company, only Sharon Madden and Ron Seka were cast, although Cino-veteran Karen Ludwig also was imported to play the sensual role of Maia. In the leading roles, Oglesby cast Maurice Blanc as the sculptor Rubek, and Molly Adams as his model, Irene. Marshall Oglesby and his cast went into rehearsal just as we went into previews downtown.

The sets for *When We Dead Awaken* were a blindingly white suggestion of snow, with a bleak sky surrounding the terrace of a health resort high in the mountains. They were designed by Henry Scott and the costumes were by Martha Kelly. The music was Paul Horn's haunting flute played in the echoing halls of the Taj Mahal on the album *Inside.*

This was the first production at Circle that I hadn't attended any rehearsals, so I enjoyed it as part of an opening night audience. I thought it was a very striking production of a fascinating, enigmatic play, and Oglesby introduced several arresting images, especially at the ending when Sharon Madden's nun transformed into a naked image of death before a white curtain fell to cover the actors in the climactic avalanche.

The production of *When We Dead Awaken* opened on April 19, 1973, and played sixteen performances. The reviews were decidedly mixed, although encouraging in some respects. Here are some excerpts:

Long Island Press, April 20, 1973, (William A. Raidy):
"[It's] filled with more incomprehensible verbiage than poetry. It is a play that needs strong imagination to even consider, never mind perform. The hero of the evening is Henry Scott III, who has given the production a highly imaginative setting. The acting, for the most part, is appealing. Oglesby has

directed the play as if it were a recital. Well, perhaps it is. Its theme, however evasive, deserves a better translation, even if the meaning escapes the entire audience. And escape me it did."

Village Voice, April 26, 1973 (Martin Washburn):
"It takes courage to dare the heights of Ibsen's last play, a wildly potent and awesomely unifying vision of life. The Circle Theater production does less than justice to a great play. What emerged most satisfactorily was the cold and beautiful amorality of Karen Ludwig's Maia. I want to add that my quarrels are with an effort that has the excitement of a serious production tackling a great work. I recommend it."

Daily News, May 10, 1973 (Michael Iachetta):
"An Ibsen play well worth seeing....a memorably symbolic play, simply yet effectively staged. Director Oglesby makes the most of a series of confrontations. Ludwig makes Maia a no-nonsense seductress. Adams gives the model Irene an otherworldly dimension. Sharon Madden is a buxom shadow who creates a tasteful nude tableau as a fitting climax to a marvelous mime performance. [It's] well worth the trip."

Marshall's production bravely leaped from the Victorian to the ethereal, earning comparisons to Stanley Kubrick's *2001* and Christo's abstract sculptures that wrapped monuments in white. I thought it was stunning, no matter how confused the reviews, and it maintained our goal of producing new visions of classic work, while creating the finest work of new playwrights. We appreciated Marshall Oglesby's courageous vision.

The final production of our main stage subscription season was a new play that Marshall Oglesby discovered while working at the Dallas Theater Center. One of the young writers there was Ronald Wilcox, and he wrote a musical play that dramatized the psychological struggles of 1950s morality. He called it *The Tragedy of Thomas Andros*, a title perhaps dangerously pretentious, but bold.

I can report nothing about the rehearsal process, but this production marked the first return of a *HOT L* actor to our uptown stage. Tony Tenuta left his paying job as Mr. Katz to assume the title role for only off-off-Broadway remuneration, little more than reimbursement of expenses. Once again, Company member Sharon Madden was in the cast, joined by Guest Artists Craig Heller, Michael Jeffers, Jay Gerber, Renny Temple and William Wise (who at a future date replaced Judd Hirsch as Bill in *HOT L*). The sets were by Henrietta Bagley and, apparently, I did the lighting, although I retain no memory of it and the notices suggest there's good reason for my selective amnesia. Here are excerpted reviews:

The New York Times, June 2, 1973 (Howard Thompson):
"Circle Theater Company is a fine outfit, marking time. The sure-footed professionalism of this estimable company is immediately apparent. These are gifted, purposeful theater people. The play is something else. The hero is a crashing bore. Antony Tenuta is an actor of obvious feeling and intensity. Oglesby's staging is swift and clean, and the Norman Berman-Richard Steele music is exciting. Most delightful of all is Henrietta Bagley's set, topped by a huge feminine face in Jack-o-lantern lighting by Mason."

Show Business, May 31, 1973 (Debbi Wasserman):
"[It] almost meets its potential, both as a play and as a production, but not quite. The story is interesting, most of the acting is good, the staging is effective, and the music is well-written and appropriate. However, the play is held back by unnecessary indulgence in Freudian cliché, a few poor performances, inadequate lighting, and an awkward ending. As written, [it's] a promising, workable piece; but as performed, it is entertaining, but not really a tragedy."

Staten Island Register, June 14, 1973 (Fred Stuart):
"The Circle Theater, originators of the magnificent *HOT L* and firm believers in producing wonderful ensemble acting, have unfortunately come up with a bad play. It's hard to find plays the caliber of *HOT L*, but greater care must now be given to each new production."

So, our fourth season wound up with our Major Productions drawing the attention of only a few critics, who were carefully respectful, even of plays they didn't like.

We produced a number of workshop productions, continuing our tradition of encouraging new work from playwrights, actors and directors. I've already mentioned *Canvas* by David Ives, a workshop production directed by Richard Steele with Jonathan Hogan, Richard Easley and Lucy Lee Flippin.

There were also workshop productions of Bruce Serlen's *Icarus Nine,* Richard Wolf's *Peace at Hand,* German experimental playwright Peter Handke's *Offending the Audience,* Ed Greenburg's *Smith Here* and a revival of Lewis John Carlino's *Snow Angel.*

Not all productions were happy experiences for the authors. In particular, John Heuer entrusted his new play *Mrs. Tydings' Mason-Dixon Medicine Man* to fledgling actor/director Peter Tripp. John was discouraged from attending rehearsals until the director felt they "had something to show him." When he finally came, he discovered that the director completely rewrote the play, assuring the cast that the author would have no problem. Fortunately, the play lived to see another production in a later season with a different director, so the nightmare of John's first experience eventually was redeemed.

Molting

The Company was defined in our first season by those who persevered through six months of training to form the nucleus of our first three productions. The Company evolved in the second season to include new members Conchata Ferrell, Brad Dourif, Zane Lasky, Judith Kirtley and Stephen de Fluiter. We acquired a strong director in Marshall Oglesby, and added designers Ronald Radice and Henrietta Bagley. In the third season, the actors, writers, designers and directors from the summer retreat in Woodstock became the new core of the Company. By the end of that season, Lanford began writing specifically for our actors, and Trish Hawkins became a pivotal addition to Circle.

The responsibility for defining who constituted our Acting Company was mine. I made my choices based on the degree of commitment I felt toward ongoing work with an actor. I also evaluated each actor's commitment to our vision.

Several actors left the Company for various reasons. Judy Kirtley pursued an opera career; Steve de Fluiter became a fine arts dealer; Michael Fesenmeier left, disgruntled over his perceived casting slights and returned to West Virginia. Pat Carey stayed only for our first two shows.

But there were new additions that enriched our ensemble. Our introduction to Jonathan Hogan was almost as important as the arrival of Trish Hawkins. Director Richard Steele brought Jon in for a workshop production of *Canvas* by David Roszkowski, later known as David Ives, author of *All in the Timing*). We were immediately impressed by this lanky, sandy-haired juvenile, who had the low-keyed charm of a young Jimmy Stewart. Jonathan Hogan, who was born in Chicago June 13, 1951, became one of our most accomplished Company members. Although he never achieved the fame that many less-talented stars enjoy, Jon Hogan's electrifying stage presence gained him recognition among his peers as an "actor's actor." His many memorable performances for Circle will be described as we go. We also had to find actors for a couple of roles in Lanford's new script that couldn't readily be filled by our present actors. This led us to Helen Stenborg and Judd Hirsch. We were shedding our previous plumage and evolving into a new Acting Company of fifteen members who established our identity for years to come.

Coda

There was another bright spot in this memorable season. As a result of the success of *HOT L,* we began to receive promising scripts from noted literary agents, who previously hadn't given us the time of day. Most noteworthy was a play by Mark Medoff, submitted by Gilbert Parker, his powerful agent from the William Morris Agency. It was an impressive piece of dramatic realism with resonant overtones of American mythology called *When You Comin' Back, Red Ryder?*

I found it compelling. I asked the playwright to come in to discuss our interest in producing it. When I met Mark, I was impressed with his maturity. He was nice looking, cool and confident, with a clear, sharp intelligence. Although I couldn't identify it at the time, the source of his quiet authority was professorial; he taught at a western university. After making clear how much I admired what he'd written, I admitted I had some thoughts about how the play might be improved.

Mark's play was about how the American dream had become twisted in the recent past; memories of the brutal murders of Sharon Tate and others by the Manson gang revealed a new level of terror that could materialize at any moment. It seemed nobody was safe anymore. And the play dramatized that perception by mourning the loss of a more heroic time of the mythic American West.

When the unpredictable character Teddy enters a sleepy New Mexican diner out on the Interstate highway, operated by local kids with their small-town dreams, he electrifies the very atmosphere with the power of his personality. Tongue-tied and helpless in the face of this wild stranger, the short order cook Stephen (ironically nicknamed Red Ryder) and the homely teenage waitress, Angel, are mesmerized by Teddy's amoral promise of unnamed (perhaps unthinkable) thrills. Even a sophisticated couple of travelers from the East, Richard and Clarisse, are no match for this wildly unconventional menace when they're taken hostage. Like the characters in the play, I was mesmerized by Teddy.

My advice was this: I thought that when Teddy introduces a gun to enforce his demands, the play took a turn from an astute level of psychological insight toward the more familiar form of melodrama. I tried to persuade Mark that the play could be even more effective if he trusted the mesmerizing power of his character to terrorize this community with the sheer force of his personality, rather than introducing a weapon, which reduced the conflict to clichéd circumstances. In my view, the snake-like fascination in Manson's eyes was his real menace, and I'm sure he needed no physical force to persuade his followers to attain his horrifying ends.

Mark heard me out, but he was certain the play needed the threat of the gun to corral the audience into sharing the fear of the characters. I assured him that, despite my criticism, we were ready to give the play a production just as he'd written it. I hoped that in a workshop production, Mark might come to see the wisdom of my dramaturgical advice; so we went into rehearsal immediately in June with a simple production that emphasized the script, the acting and the direction. The design aspects were minimal; we wanted to focus on the play and its potential.

Mark brought with him a director about my age named Kenneth Frankel, and it turned out we had something in common: he too was a graduate of Northwestern. Although I hadn't known him in college, the fact we shared a similar background assured me that Ken believed in the same kind of theater, so I welcomed him eagerly. As it was Circle Rep's policy, I reminded them that they needed to use members of our acting Company to the extent they could. Our Brad Dourif was especially perfect casting for the role of Steven (the ironic "Red Ryder" of the title). This time, Brad decided to risk angering his mentor Sandy Meisner, because he felt he had reached a level in his study where professional experience would do his acting no harm. Fortunately, Sandy did not follow through with his threat to drop him, although he was undoubtedly aware of Brad's success. Ken and Mark saw him read and were convinced immediately that he was their Steven, the gangly, pathetic leftover of mythic heroism.

I'm especially grateful to Mark and Ken for introducing us to the invaluable Elizabeth Sturges, who seemed a living embodiment of the character Angel. Liz became a member of Circle Rep and enriched us with beautiful performances in plays yet to be written. She was a gift, and one we valued.

The remainder of the cast was equally suited to their roles: the square-jawed, silver-haired Addison Powell was the epitome of the prototypical self-confident Western man, Lyle, accompanied by Joe Jamrog as the good old boy, easy-going Clark. Robyn Goodman and James Kiernan provided the contrasting Eastern sophistication needed for the roles of the trapped travelers, Clarise and Richard; and Kristen Van Buren was a sexy hippie accomplice as Cheryl, whose behavior added to the incipient danger.

But of special interest was the casting of the ominous leading role of Teddy. Ken found a young actor named Ted LePlat for this part, and it was, in my view, inspired casting. Blond, blue-eyed Ted was so ethereally, angelically handsome, he was threatening. His movie-star looks, combined with a feline but masculine power in his movement made his deceptive charm lethal in the context of this simple rural town. Much as Manson's hypnotic eyes were all he needed to manipulate people to do his bidding, so Ted LePlat was magnetic in a role that recalled that evil guru.

Ken staged a workshop production for us before the end of the June, with a cast that was transfixed by Ted's performance as the mesmerizing, murderous villain. The workshop production was electrifying; I thought it was a virtually perfect rendition of Mark's play. But apparently, it was not what Mark saw in his mind: he wanted a Teddy that could mine the comic potential of the part more ably. So after the workshop production, Ken and Mark told me of their plans to replace Ted LePlat. Although I was surprised by their willingness to risk losing the charismatic performance at the center of the production, I was supportive of their artistic vision. I immediately scheduled it as a Major Production to open our fifth season in the fall.

As the season at Circle ended, *HOT L* continued its sold-out run Off-Broadway and was named a Best Play in the *Best Plays Annual*. Lanford and I prepared to leave for Los Angeles, where we were remounting a new production of *HOT L* at the Mark Taper Forum in August. And we left sure in our belief that we had another extraordinary play in our pocket for next season.

And while were being feted as the toast of New York, we were joined in the winner's circle by another momentous event: on June 9th, 1973 Secretariat won the Belmont Stakes, becoming the first Triple Crown Winner of Thoroughbred Racing since 1948, the same year *A Streetcar Named Desire* won the Drama Critics' Circle Award.

Miss Krause's goal of an artistic theater had now survived four years in New York, and was celebrated by the critics for its excellence in ensemble playing. It was another year before Miss Krause actually came to New York to see our work, and I'll report on that in the next chapter.

But what a year this one had been!

Chapter 8
Escalation

"Shaky Town" is perched on a precarious Pacific shelf of the North American continent. It's hard to imagine the elite from the wealthy suburbs of Los Angeles being willing to spend forty-five minutes on the freeways to get to a deserted civic center to watch live theater. Yet, Gordon Davidson rolled his dice on just that unlikely prospect to create the Mark Taper Forum at the Music Center in the middle of a city where, as Gertrude Stein famously asserted about Oakland, "There is no *there* there."

In July of 1973, Lanford Wilson and I found ourselves "there" to create a substantially funded production of *The HOT L BALTIMORE* (scheduled *before* its commercial success or award-winning reputation). Lanford, true to form, took the train. Flying ahead, I picked him up at the 1939 architectural masterpiece that is Los Angeles's Union Station.

In addition to his fear of flying, Lanford also never learned to drive, so he was booked into the swanky Biltmore Hotel at the edge of skid row, where he could walk to rehearsal in the Taper annex by braving on foot eight blocks of urban blight. *Nobody* walked in Los Angeles except the destitute and Lanford Wilson.

I was provided a rental car (a sky-blue Chrysler Le Baron convertible, naturally) and I was housed in the shabby (at that time) Chateau Marmont in a threadbare neighborhood known as Hollywood, about twenty-five minutes from downtown L.A. Once grand, the hotel provided me with a fifth-floor corner suite containing a king size bed, a large living room, a full kitchen and a formal dining room (800 sq. ft. in all), with a balcony overlooking the gigantic billboard on Sunset Boulevard. In 1973, my suite rented for a couple hundred dollars a week; but unlike the hotel in our play, the Chateau survived any threat of demolition and was refurbished to become a celebrity icon with matching prices.

Another perquisite of bringing *HOT L* to L.A. was that my mother lived there and it was a pleasure to see her once a week. And of course, she loved bringing all her friends to the opening. Now more image conscious, I cut my straggly hair to mere shoulder-length.

Artistic director Gordon Davidson signed top-rate designers for our West Coast Premiere: costume designer Noël Taylor, who shocked Broadway by putting Bette Davis in a shirt without a brassiere, unbuttoned and tied at the waist in *The Night of the Iguana*, was now designing for us. Archie Sharp, a television art director, created an elegant Art Deco hotel, which he distressed with ablowtorch to render the disheveled look required by the text. A classic brass elevator reminiscent of those in New York's Chrysler Building was draped with a sign proclaiming it "Out of Order." Grand Moderne lighting fixtures hung in disrepair over the lobby. My colleague Dennis Parichy was brought from New York to design the lights and he had over five-hundred instruments to work with, the most I'd ever seen in my admittedly limited career.

The auditions at the Taper were different from anything I'd experienced. We saw young film talent like Sissy Spacek, whose Texas accent was too broad at that time to carry a play, but we also saw actors stumbling in from the beach to audition in their flip-flops. We ended up with a good cast, mostly from the film industry. Gordon budgeted for importing New York actors for roles we could not cast locally and much to my surprise, the one role I thought would be a cinch in California proved impossible to cast. So for the part of the estranged Paul Granger III, I brought from New York the actor who impressed me in the Circle workshop production of *Red Ryder* – Ted LePlat. Ironically, Ted was born in N.Y. but graduated from Hollywood High before he made his way east to become a serious actor. Spontaneous tears sprung into his eyes the first time he stepped onto the stage at the Mark Taper Forum. His dream came true; he was a real actor at a major American theater, and it was his home turf. How sweet is that!

I also brought Sharon Madden to stand by for several of the roles. As understudy, Sharon never got to go on, but at least the job earned her an Equity card – small compensation for someone who'd been so central to the Circle Theater and who'd been left behind when we transferred *HOT L* to a professional venue.

For the focal role of The Girl, we had Jennifer Salt, and for the part of Bill, Christopher Lloyd, who a dozen years later became a ubiquitous film star after his performance in *Back to the Future*. (Strangely enough, Chris had been our first choice to play Bill in New York, but he became unavailable, so we went with Judd.) Trying to capture the kind of offbeat casting that made Conchata Ferrell an unforgettable April, I took a different tactic and cast Ja'net DuBois, a beautiful black actress who could supply plenty of cynicism. A wonderful actress named Barbara Colby became my Suzy. And for the challenging part of Jackie, where Mari Gorman created a sensation in New York, I cast Margaret Linn, who was Miss Krause's favorite actress at Northwestern. For the part of her withdrawn brother Jamie, I found Chip Zien, who subsequently had an extensive New York theater career (most notably *Into the Woods*). Peter Brocco (whose résumé stretched over 215 films and television appearances going back to 1932) became my best Mr. Morse, and Pearl Shear was a memorable Mrs. Billotti. The famous dancer Marge Champion played the dour desk clerk, Mrs. Oxenham, and veteran television actress Irene Tedrow was a dignified Millie. Altogether, they made a splendid troupe to create anew Lanford's contemporary masterpiece. Of this cast, Ted, Chip and Pearl came to New York as replacements in our long-running Off-Broadway hit as the original actors left.

The most challenging aspect of the Los Angeles production was blocking fifteen characters on a stage with the audience surrounding it 280 degrees. The sight-line problems were a nightmare; even though the Taper seating rises sharply, the first several rows had to be able to see action happening across the stage, often behind major scenic elements. We solved this problem by putting the hotel's front desk on the same level with the first rows of the audience, with a short flight of stairs leading up to the main lobby on a higher level. The Taper is considered a relatively intimate theater; with just over 700 seats, it's the size of the smaller Broadway houses, but it was far larger than our New York venue and required real vocal projection, since some patrons were always behind the actors.

The rehearsals went well in the ample rehearsal room in the Taper Annex. For the first time, I had a first-class professional Stage Manager in Mary Michele Miner, who employed an easygoing quest for perfection.

Each night I returned to the Chateau Marmont to watch the televised hearings of the Senate Watergate Committee, which unreeled with startling new details almost every day. White House counsel John Dean called the cover-up a "cancer on the presidency." Presidential aide Alexander Butterfield told the Senate Committee that Nixon secretly recorded potentially incriminating conversations in the oval office. When an eighteen and a half-minute gap in those tapes was revealed in October, the stage was set for the end game of the scandal, which caused Richard Nixon to become the only United States President to resign from office. This was a compelling drama, an interesting counterpoint to the comedy we were creating in the rehearsal room.

We had a smooth opening night, followed by a resplendent party at the Biltmore Hotel. (For opening night presents, we were given duplicates of ornate brass door keys with a baroque "B" on them). My mother attended in a jeweled gown, looking every bit the mother of the director. I met my film idol, the great French film director Françoise Truffaut, who attended our opening with the beautiful Jacqueline Bisset on his arm, and I talked with them on a balcony overlooking the party below. Utterly agog, I incoherently stammered that *The Four Hundred Blows* was my favorite film; but Truffaut spoke no English and I spoke no French, so he graciously accepted my enthusiastic regard, then my two minutes of tongue-tied star-worship were mercifully over.

The press reception was favorable, although in competitive contrast to their New York counterparts, the critics feigned to be far from bowled over. On the whole, Lanford and I enjoyed our stay on the West Coast as a two-month paid vacation (paid to do what we loved), and we were ready and eager to return to reality in New York.

Reality, of course, was a relative phenomenon around this time. For example, male tennis player Bobby Riggs challenged female player Billie Jean King to a nationally televised tennis match at the Astrodome in Houston, Texas. On Sep 20, 1973 in what was billed as The Battle of the Sexes, King defeated Riggs 6–4, 6–4, 6–3. Things continued to change from the old order to a new age.

The most unwelcome change imaginable occurred shortly after we left Los Angeles. Our Jackie, Margaret Linn, suffered a brain aneurism one afternoon in the actors' residence at the Montecito Hotel. Sharon Madden was giving her a massage when Maggie began to shake and contort uncontrollably. Sharon called an ambulance and Maggie died on the way to the hospital. She was replaced by her understudy, Kres Mersky, but I never saw her perform the role. The American theater lost an outstanding actress.

The Family Continued

When Lanford and I arrived back in New York, we were eager to see what our little amateur production looked like, after the slick professional mounting we'd been given at the Taper. Although we knew we'd done well, it wasn't until we came back from California that we saw just how extraordinary that Circle ensemble was.

Of course, Lanford wrote the play for the members of our Company, none of whom were well known; whereas, Hollywood agents offered us the best potential film stars available. When we'd created the show off-off-Broadway, it was do-it-yourself theater in its purest form, while the Taper pulled out all stops for an impeccable professional production.

Arriving fresh from our polished Los Angeles opening, Lanford and I sneaked into a performance at the seedy old Circle-in-the-Square after the lights went down, because we didn't want our friends to realize we were there. We wanted to see the show as an average audience was seeing it.

Well, the play started and our little amateur company wandered into the hotel lobby, and began to *live*. Judd Hirsch and Trish Hawkins were talking over each other's lines in conversational tones that were amazingly real. Then, Conchata Ferrell as April stomped down the stairs in her bathrobe, complaining about the lack of hot water. She lugged her considerable figure over to a chair and plopped down, as if she couldn't move another inch. I was amazed. This was not blocking. This was a person who sat because she was exhausted from working all night.

It was difficult to imagine that Lanford had anything to do with what they were spontaneously saying or that I had anything to do with where and how they moved. It wasn't like a stage; it was like being in the lobby of a sleazy hotel.

It appeared our amateurs achieved something all the L.A. professional expertise couldn't equal: a complex ensemble that created a living play, with a depth not seen since the days of The Group Theater, thirty or forty years before. It was thrilling and humbling to watch. Whatever our contributions were, the production seemed to have taken on a life of its own. It was great to be home!

Another Juggernaut

The fall of 1973 was an unusually busy time of change. In October, the twenty-day "Yom Kippur War" was fought when Egypt and Syria attacked Israel on that holiday in both the Sinai Peninsula and the Golan Heights. Only a few days later, Vice-President Agnew resigned, pleading no contest to charges of income tax evasion. A month later, Gerald Ford was sworn in to replace Agnew. The Watergate scandal took a dramatic turn on October 20th when

President Nixon ordered Attorney General Elliot Richardson to dismiss Special Prosecutor Archibald Cox. Richardson refused and resigned; Robert Bork, third in line at the Department of Justice, then fired Cox. The event, tagged "the Saturday Night Massacre," raised calls for Nixon's impeachment. On the brighter side, October also saw Queen Elizabeth II inaugurate the Sydney Opera House, and in Istanbul, the Bosporus Bridge connected the continents of Europe and Asia for the first time in history.

I was settling back into my job as Artistic Director, preparing our fifth season. Following the success of *HOT L,* we applied for our own 501(c)(3), the government document that grants official status as a tax-exempt, not-for-profit organization. For the first four years, our ability to solicit contributions and accept grants flowed from Dr. Lerner's umbrella non-profit association, C.I.R.C.L.E. It was time for us to be independent if we were going to grow. We were granted our own non-profit status, but the charity regulators thought "Circle Theater Company" was too close in name to "Circle-in-the-Square Theater," so we were compelled to change our name. They agreed to license us as Circle Repertory Theater Company, which from this time forward, became our official name.

Turning my attention to *When You Comin' Back, Red Ryder?,* I discovered that author Mark Medoff and director Ken Frankel replaced Ted LePlat in the central role of Teddy with the well-known Kevin Conway. Although I'd been excited by Ted's charismatic performance, Mark thought the character had more comic potential. My concerns about losing power in the play with a more conventional "heavy" in the lead proved groundless, as the play succeeded on Mark's terms.

Designer Bill Stabile created the interior of a road-side diner that was realistic in every detail, from the chrome edged counter with matching stools, to red vinyl booths, to a practical coffee-heater and a vintage brass cash-register. He installed a low-hanging ceiling with fluorescent lights over the stage area, and a dingy linoleum floor that added to the oppressive atmosphere. No wonder the kids longed to escape this place! Ken directed his actors to live in

The Transcendent Years

the space and to perform the actions of operating a diner in exacting detail, just as we had done with *HOT L*. Intimacy and the high degree of realism made the play spring to life. Penny Davis was the costume coordinator, finding just the right boots, hats, bolo ties, uniforms, and paisley wraps to crystallize each characterization. The brutally practical lighting was by Cheryl Thacker.

Mark Medoff's *When You Comin' Back, Red Ryder?* opened at Circle Repertory Theater Company on November 4th, 1973, with a ticket price of $3.50, and played for twenty-six performances. In addition to Kevin Conway, the cast again included Brad Dourif, Elizabeth Sturges, Joe Jamrog, Addison Powell, Robyn Goodman, James Kiernan, and Kristin Van Buren. The stage managers were Bill Bond and Marjorie Horne, and press was handled by Herb Striesfield. It demonstrated again the power of an honest ensemble bringing to life a perceptive play. Here are excerpted reviews:

The New York Times, November 6, 1973 (Mel Gussow):
"*Red Ryder* is the second winner from Circle Repertory. This is a theater with the highest professional standards...Frankel as director, the cast (most importantly Kevin Conway) and the set, costumes, and lighting designers have treated the play with enormous understanding and affection. Conway gives a daring and scathingly humorous performance...Brad Dourif is a compelling Red Ryder, and Elizabeth Sturges is an enchanting Angel. [The play] has vitality and authenticity, and Medoff's writing is crystalline-sharp. The Circle has discovered a play and a playwright."

Newsday, November 5, 1973 (Allan Wallach):
"A brutal but impressive play. The Circle Theater has assembled another exceptional cast for Medoff's play. The production, directed by Frankel, is extraordinary...Stabile's diner setting is so real you can almost smell the frijoles and the steak and eggs. As Teddy, Conway gives one of the best performances of the season. I also admired Sturges with

her prim, piping voice, Robyn Goodman, blending emotions with great subtlety, and Dourif, his boyish bluster edged with fear. Medoff uses dialogue with a gunfighter's marksmanship."

The Record, November 5, 1973 (Emory Lewis):
"Hail an exciting new playwright! Mark Medoff is one of the most promising dramatists in several neon moons. [His play] is an arresting, offbeat, and exciting comedy of menace. Medoff can write scenes of enormous power, and he has something to tell us about the shabby state of the Union. The cast is astonishingly deft. The ensemble work is on a much higher level than one finds on Broadway. Dourif is magnificent... Sturges is another exciting discovery... Conway is explosive. They have been directed with extraordinary finesse by Frankel. Stabile's set is a marvel."

Once more, we had a sold-out hit on our hands, and the reviews, abetted by the profits from *HOT L,* attracted producers who wanted to transfer it to a commercial run. Producer Elliot Martin picked up the option and moved the entire production, without change, to the Eastside Playhouse on East 74th Street. It was billed as: "Elliot Martin presents the Circle Repertory Theater Company Production of *When You Comin' Back, Red Ryder?"* It reopened ten days after the run at Circle Rep on December 6, 1973. Here are excerpted reviews from the transferred production:

The New York Times, December 7, 1973 (Clive Barnes):
"A fascinating and commanding play. Medoff writes superbly. [He] has a grasp of contemporary imagery that is all too rare in the theater. The staging is superb. Frankel has directed with just the right sense of menace. The set by Stabile is accurate and atmospheric. Much of the excitement though is generated by the cast, who could not have

been bettered. Mr. Conway lights up the stage. This is one of the very best plays of the season and should on no account be missed."

The Nation, November 26, 1973 (Harold Clurman):
"The play has honest intention and a degree of theatrical punch. I liked the cast [because] it convinces without strain. Conway, memorable in *Moonchildren,* is even more impressive here. Dourif is altogether believable... Sturges is utterly beguiling. Frankel's direction is right."

Not all the critics were equally thrilled. Walter Kerr of *The New York Times* found it "often irritating;" Douglas Watt of the *Daily News* called it "a pointless thriller, a cheat;" and Richard Watts of the *New York Post* professed he "simply can't understand what its admirers saw in the play."

Nevertheless, *Red Ryder* played all season for 302 more performances, winning a handful of awards: a Drama Desk, an Outer Critics' Circle, and an Obie for Mark Medoff; a Drama Desk and an Obie for Elizabeth Sturges; and an Obie for Kevin Conway.

Although Brad garnered no awards for his much praised performance as Red Ryder, he earned something more valuable: the attention of Hollywood. Milos Foreman cast him in the role of Billy Bibbit in the 1975 Academy Award-winning film of *One Flew Over the Cuckoo's Nest,* for which Brad won the British Academy Award for Best Supporting Actor, a Golden Globe for Best Debut, and an Oscar nomination.

How can one account for this quick replication of the rarely seen phenomenon of ensemble acting? How can Circle Rep claim credit, especially since only one member of our trained Company was in this new cast? My only rationale is that the production of *HOT L* set a clear example of our goals and every member of this creative team had seen it. In other words, they were provided a template of excellence that they might aspire to duplicate. And so, they created the seamless fabric of a living play. Art inspires art.

Long-Lasting Additions

By the time we produced *Red Ryder*, we had to hire a staff to operate the theater, no matter where my attention might be directed. As a result of the royalties from our commercial productions, we were able to pay our staff salaries, rather than rely on volunteers. Marshall Oglesby became our Managing Director (replacing Rob who was acting in *HOT L*) and Sharon Madden was our Administrative Director, even though she was still the "pretty girl in the box office" that one of the critics alluded to. We took on a Press Representative in Herb Streisfield. And we hired a sinewy young woman named Karen Caton as our first paid Technical Director, a position previously held by volunteer Lance Taylor, who'd decided to remain in Woodstock full-time.

As we were about to begin rehearsals on *Red Ryder*, a stocky young man from Arkansas with one glass eye ventured into our theater looking for a job. Earl Hughes had just completed a summer stock job at the Barn Theater in Augusta, Michigan. One of his friends there was a young stage manager named Peter Schneider, who told him to go to New York and he would help Earl find a job in the theater. However, Peter was delayed by a case of mononucleosis back in Madison, Wisconsin, so Earl was wandering around the Upper West Side when he came across our upstairs theater.

I hired him for $50 a week as a carpenter to assist Karen in building the *Red Ryder* set and then to run lights for the show. We also sent him downtown to do some carpentry and paint touch-up on the set of *HOT L*, which now had run for six months. Earl recalls: "That is when I first saw the production and was actually exposed to the work that you and Lance were becoming famous for." Karen lasted for only one production before she found more lucrative employment, so when *Red Ryder* transferred Off-Broadway I hired Earl to replace her as Technical Director at a salary of $75 a week. He remained with Circle Rep through our ninth season in 1978, moving up to General Manager for his last two years, culminating in *The 5th of July*. Earl was an important influence on the development of Circle Rep because of key employees he introduced to us throughout his tenure. Once Peter came to New York in the fall of 1973, with the situation ironically reversed, Earl got Peter a job with Circle Repertory Company.

Peter Schneider was a slight, angular young man with a great bush of curly light-brown hair. He was a recent graduate of Purdue University with a degree in Theater. His quick intelligence, his perceptive, focused gray eyes, and most of all, his ability to listen impressed me. I was now flooded with new scripts to read and too busy to manage alone, so I hired Peter to become Circle's first Assistant to the Artistic Director. He served as both my assistant and primary stage manager for the next two years.

After he left Circle Rep, Peter became Managing Director of David Mamet's prestigious Chicago company, St. Nicholas Theater. Peter then went to London, where he became a young theater mogul, as the General Manager of the Apollo Theater Group, a large commercial enterprise controlling several West End theaters. After three years at that post, Peter returned to the United States to assume a position as Associate Director for the 1984 Olympics Art Festival in Los Angeles.

Then Peter was hired by Roy Disney to resuscitate the flagging animation division of the Walt Disney Studios. Peter was made President of Feature Animation, where he completely changed how animated films were made. Before Peter's tenure, beginning in 1985, animation artists created an illustrated story and then voices were added individually, each actor in an isolated booth, lip synching the drawn characters. Based on his experience at Circle Rep, Peter introduced the concept of bringing together creative talent to adapt a story into a screenplay, using an ensemble of actors to record the script together, and only then putting the animators to work to illustrate the action. When I first visited Peter in Los Angeles, he proudly showed me the preliminary drawings and the drafted storyboard of the first film he was creating from scratch. It was *The Little Mermaid*, and it revitalized the Disney brand. He followed this colossal success with *Beauty and the Beast, The Lion King* and many others.

In 1997, Peter introduced the idea of adapting these successful films into Broadway musicals and, with Thomas Schumacher as a creative partner, he became President also of Walt Disney Theatricals. It was Peter's idea to hire the relatively avant-garde Julie Taymor to create a wholly fresh vision for the stage version of *The Lion King*, which won six Tony Awards, including Best Musical. Riding the crest of these innovations, Peter Schneider was elevated to the position of Chairman of The Walt Disney Company in 1999.

I wish I could claim that I foresaw the glittering future that lay ahead for Peter when I hired him to be my assistant; but all I really knew was that he was the son of a prominent professor of mathematics at the University of Wisconsin, and that his mother was a talented violinist who played with the Madison Symphony Orchestra. So, fortune had deposited with me a young man with enormous potential to assist in my artistic endeavors. I am deeply grateful for the golden years Peter was at my side on my journey with Circle Rep. Peter's affectionate, ironic nickname for me was "The Big Cheese."

Back To Work

I spent six months basking in the success of *HOT L*, before I directed again uptown. The play was called *Prodigal*, written by playwright and novelist, Richard Lortz. Richard wrote four episodes for the television series *Suspense* in the 1950s, and he lived on the Upper West Side. He brought me a script that dramatized a close-knit Jewish family, steeped in traditional values, who are threatened by the return of one of three sons after an absence of several years. I was captivated by its humanity and the rich, poetic dialogue that, in my opinion, lifted the plot above melodrama.

Richard Lortz's prose can be described as a combination of "the lyricism and theatricality of Tennessee Williams and the surrealism of Max Ernst." His writing, reminiscent of Gabriel Garcia Marquez, is as carefully crafted as that of Joyce Carol Oates, and as darkly lyrical as John Hawkes.

I was moved by the sympathetic characterizations and their dramatic conflicts. For Bertha and Bernie, the long-suffering parents in the piece, I brought in the exceptional Cathryn Damon and the venerable Salem Ludwig as Guest Artists. Judd Hirsch left *HOT L* to return to Circle Rep and play their oldest son, Saul, a businessman who provides the backing for the family's neighborhood laundry business. The impressionable youngest son was played by Zane Lasky, who also left *HOT L* to return to a new challenge. The final piece of casting was Ted LePlat as the prodigal son, Willie, returning home after seven years of a life of adventure, the exact nature of which remains shrouded in mystery. Blond Ted was like a changeling in this traditional Jewish family, but I hoped that blonde Cathryn lended some credibility as his mother. Ted wore a gold earring, which at the time was so rare it screamed decadence.

The plot concerns the return of this prodigal son, who stole $50,000 from the family when he left home. His mission in coming back is to rescue his younger brother Joey from the suffocating limitations of an over-protective family; he wants to convince him to leave in order to "find himself."

The awkward setting of a living room behind a laundromat (as well as Joey's bedroom upstairs) was solved by designer Philip C. Gilliam. The evocative lighting by Tom Munn added a lyrical atmosphere. But most importantly, I worked for the first time with two artists who continued to be central to my creative process for a number of years: Jennifer von Mayrhauser (a graduate of Northwestern) created the costumes, and became Circle Rep's Resident Designer for many seasons. Norman L. Berman composed a haunting score and became Circle Rep's Resident Composer for the next ten years. It was the first time I'd worked with Stage Manager Marjorie Horne, who returned from Red Ryder and brought a new level of professionalism to that position at Circle Rep.

Prodigal opened at Circle Repertory Theater Company on December 16, 1973 and played nineteen performances. The most memorable moment in the production was Judd's enormous emotional breakdown near the end of the play, sobbing with fury as he confronts his parents, accusing them of taking for granted his years of self-sacrifice. It was a towering performance. But alas, the critics didn't hold the play in as high esteem as we did. Here are excerpts from the reviews:

The New York Times, December 18, 1973 (Clive Barnes):
"It is a conventional family melodrama with Biblical overtones. The writing and the dramaturgy never quite jell. Mason's direction proved too declamatory in a way that emphasized rather than minimized the playwright's ornate rhetoric. The performances were good. I was particularly impressed with Hirsch. LePlat carried a decently neat air of Dorian Gray sensuality. All in all, this was by no means an unrewarding attempt at a play, but it is an attempt more notable for its real promise than for its real achievement."

The Christian Science Monitor, December 19, 1973 (John Beaufort):
"Lortz has written a thoughtful, sometimes eloquent play, which is moving in its compassion. It is expressively acted under Mason's direction."

Village Voice, December 20, 1973 (Dick Brukenfeld):
"An interesting idea... (but the characters) speak in a language that undermines their authenticity, with a self-conscious symbolism that cries for surgery. Only Hirsch is thoroughly convincing."

Newsday, (Allan Wallach):
"Monotonous and self-defeatingly talky. Mason, who staged *HOT L* so sensitively hasn't done nearly as well here. *Prodigal* never comes to life."

Despite these harsh reviews, there's an interesting anecdote. The final scene contains a beautifully written passage in which the parents mourn the loss of their youngest son. On opening night, Harold Clurman stopped me as he was leaving. "The story is over when the kid leaves," he said. "Cut the last scene." I cherish the well-meant advice, although I'm not sure it would have made a difference. To put the timing of this production in context, Broadway had just seen the opening of *Find Your Way Home* with Michael Moriarty, which won him a Tony and ran for 135 performances.

A revised version of Lortz's play re-titled *Three Sons* ran twenty performances at Playwrights Horizons in January 1978. Although Richard Lortz went on to write a number of additional novels, he died unexpectedly on November 5, 1980 at the age of sixty-three.

From Actor To Author

Our next playwright was an actor, who came to writing after a long association with Lanford Wilson. Roy Laird London was born March 3, 1943 in New York. His father Robert was an attorney, and his mother Frances was a teacher. His younger brother, Chuck, was born three years later, and the brothers were very close. Roy became a member of Joseph Chaiken's Open Theater, after studying with the Royal Shakespeare Company in England.

Roy met Lanford in 1968 and they began a personal relationship that lasted until Roy left for Los Angeles in 1981. While Lanford was traveling with the La Mama Troupe in Europe, Roy flew over to join him for a weekend and they enjoyed a romantic interlude in Paris. After Lanford returned to the United States, they became roommates, taking an apartment at 240 West 4th Street. Roy was lithe, dark and handsome, with sculpted cheekbones and glossy black hair. He had a kind of Roddy McDowell charm and a sophistication utterly missing from Lanford's country-boy persona. Roy played Robert in Lanford's short-lived Broadway debut *The Gingham Dog*. He then landed a recurring role on the daytime serial *The Edge of Night,* playing a Peeping Tom. Roy accompanied Lanford to the party on July 14, 1969 when we announced our intention to start a theater, but Roy chose not to participate in our workshops. I think

Roy felt he was at a more professional stage than these strange hippie friends of Lance's, with their long hair and dirty fingernails.

After their Broadway debut, Roy and Lanford moved into an elegant apartment on Bank Street, across from Rob and Tanya. Roy went on a national tour, playing opposite Lynn Redgrave in *My Fat Friend* (1974). Undoubtedly influenced by living with a prolific writer like Lanford, always encouraging to fellow writers, Roy wrote his first play based on an adventure his little brother Chuck precipitated by running away to Hawaii at the age of fifteen. The play was *The Amazing Activity of Charley Contrare and the 98th Street Gang*. As the stage directions read: "The action of the play takes place in the present time in Charley's mother's kitchen on the Upper West Side and wherever Charley goes."

It was a relatively slight comedy/fantasy compared to the serious work we'd been doing, but I thought it offered a fun change of pace. Stylistically, it had a Pirandello aspect, in that the role of Charley was divided into four different ages, each played by a different actor. It gave Zane Lasky the central role of Charley at the age of sixteen, when the principal action of the play occurs. Jonathan Hogan (in a stretch for such a WASP to play Jewish) played Charley at the age of thirty, which was about the author's age when he wrote it. Guest Artist David Hooks was Charley at sixty; and storming around the stage in an electric wheelchair was Rob Thirkield, playing a senile Charley at ninety. There were also roles for Sharon Madden and Tanya Berezin. The play was assigned to Richard Steele to direct, who'd been developing his skills in our workshop productions. The sets and lights were by Scott Johnson, and Jennifer von Mayrhauser again designed the costumes. Roy's brother Chuck provided both sound and video for the show, and our multi-talented Jonathan Hogan, an excellent guitarist, composed his first of many scores for Circle Rep.

For the key role of Sarah, the mother, we brought in a Guest Artist, Alice Drummond. It was also our first time to work with perky Bonnie Heron and her husband Baxter Harris, both of whom played several of roles at Circle in the next couple of years.

The Transcendent Years

Charley Contrare opened January 20, 1974 and played nineteen performances. Roy's debut as a playwright was not universally appreciated. Here are excerpted reviews:

The Record, January 21, 1974 (Emory Lewis):

"Circle Rep has become in less than five years one of the most treasured acting groups in New York. However, *Charley Contrare* is a dud, tiresome and trite. The chief reason for seeing this flawed play is Alice Drummond. She is pure gold. She is one of the theater's most incandescent artists. Zane Lasky, who looks like a young Dustin Hoffman, is superb. Von Mayrhauser is a costume designer of exceptional skill."

Newsday, January 21, 1974 (Allan Wallach):

"The idea of the play has possibilities... [but] it gets bogged down in coyness and London's inability to turn it into something more than a tricky idea. [There's] a very funny and touching performance by Alice Drummond. Director Steele has done quite well to keep the play from evaporating. He is aided by the clever setting by Johnson. The play also benefits from the engagingly roguish performance of David Hooks... [but] they can't prevent *Charley Contrare* from seeming like a bright idea, with nowhere to go."

Village Voice, February 7, 1974 (Dick Brukenfeld):

"Much of what London has conceived is entertaining. Yet too much drifts by, in need of an anchor. [The play has] a satisfying finish that feels right... an interesting work that needs further work. Director Steele has given the show an easy-going tone."

Happily, the adverse reception did not prevent Roy from continuing to write, and some of his later efforts proved more successful. And that is one of the best arguments for an on-going theater company, devoted to the advancement of its artists.

A Powerhouse

At the beginning of the season, we announced we'd present a new play by Lanford Wilson that was not yet written. Whenever Lanford faced an obligation to write us a new play, it seemed to stir his creativity; so we began promising our subscribers each season that we would include "a new play by Lanford Wilson." It was a promise he could not always fulfill; but fortunately, each time we found a substitute so wonderful that our subscribers never complained that we'd failed to deliver on our pledge.

Sometime in the fall of 1973, Peter ushered into my corner office a gigantic, brawny but attractive young man with finely chiseled features and nervous blue eyes. He looked more like a linebacker than the playwright he professed to be.

His name was Ed Moore, an actor who played the beefy hunk Hal Carter in *Picnic* and the strapping cowpoke Bo Decker in *Bus Stop* a decade earlier at the Goodman Theater in Chicago. Ed made his Broadway debut in *After the Rain* (1967) and played Lt. Cutler in Alan Arkin's award-winning production of *The White House Murder Case* by Jules Feiffer at the Circle-in-the-Square (1970), neither of which I saw. But the combination of his colossal frame with his almost little boy sensitivity left little doubt that he was an actor with serious potential. More recently, Ed earned his wherewithal on popular soap operas, as Rick Latimer on *Love of Life* and Sam English in *The Edge of Night*.

Ed explained that he wrote a two-character play for himself and an overweight girlfriend, Susan. As something of a trim Adonis, Ed was fascinated by the psychological need of some people to protect themselves by adding an armor of fat to shield their vulnerability from a hostile world. The two-hander was called *The Sea Horse.*

I read the script immediately, thrilled by the articulate writing, the complexity of the characters and the good, old-fashioned story telling. It was no surprise that an actor understood the need for credible, compelling characters, but this play was also a gem of construction and finesse. I saw at once that it was a dream part for Conchata Ferrell. The play's only weakness was a danger of sentimentality that could ruin its power in the wrong hands. Chatty's down to earth honesty would provide an antidote to that hazard.

I showered Ed with heart-felt praise, which he received like a shy puppy. Then I soberly set up the terms under which Circle Rep was interested in producing his play. I was willing to take a chance on Ed playing the part of Harry Bales that he'd written for himself. That was a non-negotiable demand, understood from the start. Looking at his résumé, I saw that Ed not only had graduated from the excellent Goodman Theater in Chicago, but he'd studied with Uta Hagen, arguably New York's foremost acting teacher. His credentials made him a good risk and he'd written himself one hell of a role.

The problem, I explained, was that our interest depended on the casting of Conchata Ferrell in the equally formidable role of Gertrude. Ed knew that Chatty was a powerful actress, who could match him talent for talent. With a sheepish reluctance, he agreed to the casting, understanding that this was no artistic compromise. His reward was the instant scheduling of *The Sea Horse* as a Major Production at Circle Rep in the spring. Moreover, I would direct it myself. As compensation for his friend Susan Riskin, we hired her as the understudy.

Edward James Moore was born on June 2, 1935 in Chicago to Mary Elizabeth and Irwin Moore, a truck driver. Ed was concerned the public might think *The Sea Horse* was a vanity enterprise, so he wanted to attribute the authorship to James Irwin, a *nom de plume* that was a tribute to his father. We complied with his wish and all our publicity presented James Irwin as the author of the play. The subterfuge worked perfectly well, until the success of the play brought demands from the press to interview this latest addition to the ranks of prominent American playwrights. It was only after the praise of both his acting *and* his play that Ed finally acknowledged his authorship. Ed was a prime example of Circle Rep's philosophy that mining one's talent can yield unexpected gold.

The play is named after a rough sailor's bar on the coast dubbed "The Sea Horse" by Gertrude's father. She has inherited it and she maintains the bar with a tough style, ruling over the rowdy, hardened seamen that are her trade. Her no-nonsense, brusque manner is abetted by a baseball bat she keeps under the counter for episodes that require brute force. By no means prudish, Gertie is "one of the boys" with a lusty enjoyment of casual sex on her own terms. Harry himself has been one of her sexual liaisons in the past, and the attraction between them won him more than a one-night stand, perhaps the only exception Gertie has made in her self-sufficient life.

It was clear that the title setting was of prime importance in staging this play; the bar must hover over the action as a third character, both a prison and a refuge. Peter Schneider brought in a designer he'd known since Purdue, and who he knew would fit right in to Circle Rep's high standards of meticulously detailed realism.

David Potts was born and raised in Ohio and first entered Purdue University as a landscape architect major. After trying out for the theatre's production of *Marat/Sade* and discovering the world of set design, he changed majors, graduated and moved to New York City. He worked for the famed costume designer Patricia Zipprodt for a year and then went on to get his Master's degree in set design at Brandeis University. When David came in to meet me, he was a slender, sweet-natured, diffident young man with a positive energy and agreeable personality that I responded to right away.

He designed a set that was perfect in every aspect, using a three-sided arena space with a front section of only two rows of seats that stretched the length of the set, facing the bar on either side of a door frame that represented the bar's entrance, and with the major portion of the seating in sections on the two ends. Posts at the corners set up a feeling that no matter where you were sitting, you were peering through a wall. Just as previous audiences felt they were walking into a seedy hotel lobby or a sterile roadside diner, our patrons now found themselves in a rustic bar that might be dangerous territory when filled with boisterous, drunken sailors. One could almost smell the salt in the air.

Not only was David's set of *The Sea Horse* perfection itself, but he also became a Resident Scenic Designer for Circle Rep, a relationship that lasted the entire life of the theater and many years beyond;

he worked with me again and again after Circle Rep's demise. He won an Emmy Award for his set decorations for *Deadwood*.

The play begins with Harry Bale's enthusiastic return from a lengthy time at sea, toting his sea bag over his shoulder. He excitedly tells Gertrude he wants to leave his maritime career and settle down with her. Gertrude is gruffly indifferent to his exuberant charm, and the play proceeds to reveal the cause of the gulf between them. It's buried in a mountainous burden of the past, when Gertrude witnessed her father's murder, leaving her distrustful of any man.

The rehearsal process was inspired. Despite the obvious risk of directing an author in his own play, we worked well together. Ed was a joy to direct as an actor and, following each rehearsal after Chatty left, I asked him to put on his author's hat and let me know any problems he perceived. As the writer, he was delighted to leave the artistic process in my hands. He could sense the play coming to life more mightily than ever before. He respected Chatty's artistry and Ed was challenged by her work opposite him. As I noted earlier, when you are acting with great partners, they almost seem to give you your performance. Ed's Harry improved steadily as we worked together.

Stimulated by the success that careful attention to reality had produced in both *HOT L* and *Red Ryder*, I wanted to push the envelope even further. As the lights came up at the opening of the play, I assigned Chatty the task of mopping the floor of the entire bar. I instructed her to ignore any urges to pick up cues and to be single minded in accomplishing her task. When Harry entered with his boyish enthusiasm, Gertrude mopped relentlessly until she finished her task before replying. I wanted the audience to see right from the beginning that this was not a conventional stage fiction to be taken for granted. I wanted the *reality* to supersede their expectation of predictable timing. It was frustrating for Ed to be ignored for such a lengthy beat, and his frustration built to a point that when the dialogue finally started, it exploded with urgency.

One of the most lyrical moments is when Harry describes the instant on his lonely sea voyage when he perceives his isolation to be a trap, and decides he wants the replenishing rewards of a human relationship. Rocking on a wooden chair that creaks like the hull of a ship, Harry captures the eerie loneliness of the shipboard in the dead of night. He vivifies his tale, mimicking the sounds of the engine and the bilge pump. Ed's onomatopoetic reverberations, whooshing and chugging, cast a spell the way a fairy tale comes to life when an inventive parent supplies bedtime sound effects. He played this section with such charm the audience fell in love with his childlike imagination. We desperately wanted Gertie to see his potential as a faithful mate. Even more touching, we discover that stuffed inside his duffel bag is a wedding dress he already has bought for her.

A precarious moment in any play is when a character is required to uncover secrets of self-revelation. Gertrude recounts her father's stabbing, and the emotional cost of revisiting this traumatic event could prove fatal to the delicate balance of sentiment and ruggedness. Chatty is an actress with a resourceful depth of feeling and her emotions are dearly purchased. To counter-act any threat of crossing the line into melodrama, I constantly reminded Chatty to recount her history simply: "Just meat and potatoes; meat and potatoes." The result was that one could perceive the story was being told sparely, with much left unsaid. This allows an audience to supply the emotion they sense lurks beneath the memory. Her restraint made it profoundly moving.

I was intrigued when our research early in rehearsal turned up the fact that, in a strange reversal of nature, after mating it is the male seahorse that carries the eggs. Ed had not known this, but his intuition made the title of the play and the bar a fitting symbol for this tale of a man who longs to have children.

As an artist, it's always difficult to name a favorite production, but *The Sea Horse* ranks high on my list. It was one of those rare occasions in the theater when I can't imagine anything I would change; in my not-so-modest opinion, it was perfect.

Once again, Jennifer von Mayrhauser provided the ideal choices of fabrics and colors, and Chuck London designed the sound. The assiduously motivated lighting was by Cheryl Thacker, who'd done such a great job on *Red Ryder*. Peter Schneider was the Stage Manager. We also hired Leah D. Frank as Business Manager to replace Edith.

The Sea Horse opened at Circle Repertory Theater Company on March 3, 1974, and played a limited engagement of thirty-two performances. Here are excerpted reviews; (keep in mind that the play was billed as written by James Irwin):

The New York Times, (Mel Gussow):

"At Circle Repertory Theater, quality is getting to be customary. First *HOT L,* then *Red Ryder,* and now *The Sea Horse.* Irwin is very much a writer to remember... Mason's direction is impeccable and the performances by Ferrell and Moore are among the finest to be seen on any stage this season. If you haven't seen a play on the Circle's home ground before it is transported to Off Broadway, it is about time you did. The seedy bar is an authentic reproduction by designer David Potts. The intimacy of the set is reflected by the intimacy of the play and the performance."

New York Post, (Jerry Tallmer):

"A burst of brilliance! The Circle Theater has done it again and maybe more so. [This] stunning new drama just about blew me out of my seat. At the final resolution there was scarcely a still heart or dry eye in the house. Irwin's voice is entirely new, and his characters are living, breathing creatures in tremendous poetic tension. Mason's staging has given the play every single thing it deserves, with a cast that is powerful.... It is something not to forget. Run, do not walk."

Daily News, (Michael Iachetta):

"Irwin's excellent first play... Harry is beautifully acted by Moore. A play about despair and loneliness... played out against a marvelously realistic set by Potts. Thacker's lighting sets the mood, and director Mason sets the style...Ferrell's Gertrude is powerful....Watch for *The Sea Horse* to move either on or off Broadway. It is that good."

Long Island Press, (William A. Raidy):
"A must! An incredible love story...the latest triumph at Circle Theater....Moore and Ferrell bring this simple, but oh so beautiful play to life, and with searing dimension. Their performances are both as good as any you will find on or off Broadway this season. [It is] directed with insight and integrity by Mason...This production deserves to be seen by a wide audience. It deserves and commands a long and prosperous run."

Newsday, March 12, 1974 (Allan Wallach):
"An affecting character study of two lonely people. The play benefits enormously from the superb performances of Ferrell and Moore. Irwin has drawn his portraits with such honesty and skill that *The Sea Horse* is constantly absorbing. This is theater at its best."

The Nation, March 23, 1974 (Harold Clurman):
"Singularly well acted...a modest play [that] bears an impress of authenticity that makes it persuasive. What makes it especially worthwhile is the acting of Moore and more especially, that of Ferrell. She is moving both in comedy and in pathos because in both she is a complete woman, a true person. We shall not forget her. Mason has directed with sensitive appreciation of the play's requirements and, even better, with regard for the nature of the two actors."

Variety, March 27, 1974:
"Circle has presented some of the most interesting plays to be seen on or off Broadway the last few seasons. This author gives every indication of being a major playwright.

Ferrell plays Gertie to perfection. Moore is also excellent. The Circle has done it again."

There were many more, equally effusive, but you get the idea. Lanford was fond of remembering that on opening night he was seated next to *New York Post* critic Jerry Tallmer. At the end of the play, as the lights fade to black, the two characters are circling each other, with Gertrude repeating, "I don't trust you. I don't trust you," and Harry responding, "You will. You will." When the lights came up for the curtain calls, Lanford recalls that both he and the critic were audibly sobbing, and sharing a personal moment of: "I know, I know."

Happily, as the press demanded, Kermit Bloomgarden offered to transfer the play to a commercial run Off-Broadway. With Max Allentuck as his partner, Kermit speedily raised the money, and on April 15, 1974, billed as "Circle Repertory Theater Company presents:" *The Sea Horse* opened at the Westside Theater on 45th Street, just blocks from Broadway's Morosco Theater, where Colleen Dewhurst and Jason Robards were starring in an unforgettable revival of Eugene O'Neil's *A Moon for the Misbegotten*, directed by Jose Quintero. The performances of the two plays were widely compared by both reviewers and audiences. Colleen, Ed Flanders and Quintero won Tony Awards for their work, and their producer Elliot Martin (who'd transferred *Red Ryder*) was given a special Tony. Their production ran for 313 performances, outlasting our run of only 136.

In April, Stephen King published *Carrie*, his first novel under his own name; so James Irwin wasn't the only author with a hidden identity. Once the Off-Broadway production opened, the press unearthed the secret that Edward J. Moore was the actual author of the play and his secret was out. Nevertheless, he won a Drama Desk Award for Outstanding New Playwright, while Conchata received Drama Desk, Theater World and Obie Awards for her performance. Oddly enough, the fact that I did not win an Obie for my best production to date may have helped me to understand the serendipitous nature of awards and, as much as I enjoy the recognition, it has prevented me from taking them too seriously. It's a lesson I needed to learn in losing five Tony Awards, before receiving the 2016 Tony Award for Lifetime Achievement in the Theater. Although the reviewers equally praised the performances, some even preferring Ed's, he didn't receive an award for his splendid work, while Chatty got three. Perhaps Ed's concern that if everyone knew he'd written the play, it would affect their judgment proved valid.

From an artistic point of view, the commercial transfer of *The Sea Horse* was not a happy one. The intimacy at Circle Rep, so frequently mentioned in the reviews, was critical to an appreciation of the play. The Westside Theater has 299 seats, triple ours at Circle. A proscenium theater without an actual proscenium arch, the Westside's bank of audience rose steeply in stadium-seating style. In a rather feeble attempt to keep the audience as close to the action as possible, we put a couple of rows on each side of the set, converting the proscenium arrangement into a token version of a three-sided arena; but the vast majority of the audience experienced the play from a distance. It's a shame the play was not made into a film, wherein the camera could preserve the intimacy of the performances; but Ed's insistence that he needed to play Harry was rejected by Hollywood, who wanted to replace him with a movie star.

The play, although compared to the work of Eugene O'Neil, was slight, a small gem, utterly dependent upon an audience's involvement with the characters; so the performances were disproportionately important to the success of the play. While the critics hailed Edward J. Moore as a major new playwright, he wrote only one more play, *The Bicycle Man*, which never achieved commercial production, despite years and years of revising the script, trying to expunge inherent flaws.

Instead, I made Ed a member of the acting Company, as well as a Resident Playwright. Although we never produced his second play, I cast Ed in two more parts where his prodigious talent as an actor could shine: *Serenading Louie,* which I'll describe in a subsequent chapter and Stanley Kowalski in my production of *Streetcar* at the Arena Stage in Washington, D.C. He was brilliant in both.

Spreading The Word

Sitting backstage in one of the *Sea Horse* dressing rooms, Mel Gussow interviewed me for an article he was writing for *The New York Times* about Circle Rep's success. The article thrust Circle Rep and me into the spotlight more than ever before.

The article was published on the front page of the Arts and Leisure section of the Sunday *New York Times,* and was headlined: "Suddenly, Real Plays About Real People." There was an oversized photo of me, almost an 8x10, accompanying the article. Mel marveled at how Circle Rep produced three important, award-winning plays in a twelve-month period. I will quote excerpts of the lengthy article below, but first let me note a regretted *faux pas.*

After Mel discovered my admiration for Elia Kazan, whom I declared, "was the last great director," he asked what I thought of the work of Alan Schneider, the most prestigious director of the previous decade. You'll recall that Alan was the Broadway director of *Gingham Dog* and, in my view, ruined the play with an inept production. I tried to sidestep Mel's tricky question by replying: "I think everyone understands the emperor has no clothes." I thought I was saying in essence: "No comment," but after my response appeared in print, Alan Schneider refused to speak to me for over ten years (a reaction I well understand). Looking back, it's hard to imagine that I could have been so callous and not have realized that my "clever" remark would be seen as an attack. Now, watching a new generation of directors eclipse my work, I empathize with Alan's reaction, and my only defense is that my answer demonstrates how naïve and unused to the spotlight I was.

Here is a lengthy excerpt of Mel Gussow's historic article about Circle Rep.

THE NEW YORK TIMES, Sunday, May 12, 1974
Suddenly, Real Plays About Real People
By MEL GUSSOW

"The Circle Repertory Company has in the past year become the chief provider of new American plays. Three Circle productions have moved Off-Broadway to become critical and popular successes. After five industrious years, the Circle is receiving recognition from the critics and the public and putting a new stamp of professionalism on off-off-Broadway. One cannot imagine better productions.

The man most responsible for the Circle is the company's co-founder and artistic director, the lanky, soft-spoken, 34-year-old Marshall W. Mason. Under his leadership, the Circle has become best known for a certain style of theater, what Mason calls 'lyrical realism' – plays that deal realistically with human situations and home truths. Circle produces real plays about real people.

Although Mason is most closely identified with the works of Lanford Wilson, Williams, Chekhov and Ibsen also played important roles in his career. At Northwestern, he was the protégé of 'the great Alvina Krause,' and the first play he directed was Williams' *Cat on a Hot Tin Roof*. He came to New York with the 'dream that I would meet Tennessee Williams and someone would say to him, let this boy direct your new play.'

Part of Mason's initial interest in Williams came from his hero worship of Elia Kazan. In New York, Mason studied at the Actors' Studio with Lee Strasberg and Harold Clurman. He says unequivocally, 'Kazan was the last great director.'

Until Mason? A smile crosses his face. 'Oh, yes, I think I'm good. That may sound terribly egotistical. But I reserve the right to fail.' After Kazan, he said, 'We had the years of Alan Schneider,' adding, 'The Emperor has no clothes.'

After Mason directed Wilson's *Home Free!* Off-Broadway, the two of them and Robert Thirkield and Tanya Berezin formed their own company, the American Theater Project, and took the play and *The Madness of Lady Bright* to London, and to their surprise, they were embraced by the critics and audience. On the wave of the London success, they returned to New York, where they were met with disinterest. Dr. Harry Lerner invited them to form a repertory theater in a space he'd found on upper Broadway, and they agreed to use it until something else came along.

The Circle Rep began in July 1969. 'The theater was for the needs of the artist, based on the relation between the actors and the playwright. Everyone shared with each other.' More than half of the company, which now numbers around 20, has been with the Circle from the beginning.

From the beginning, Circle has had a faithful following. It has survived for five years with only a minimum of foundation support. $20,850 of this season's $108,000 budget was provided by the New York State Council on the Arts and by the Peg Santvoord Foundation. Until this year, it had received no money from the National Endowment for the Arts. Most of its deficit is made up for by ticket sales and private contributions. 'We have the patronage of people who believe in the arts' – mostly from the West Side.

'The Circle is a kind of phenomenon, and not because of the commercial success. That may happen again and it may not. I hope we're not a fashionable thing. The Circle is based on a real principle of art, making the action of the play become the experience of the audience.'

Curiously, the Circle's fame has not brought it much money: it receives only 1% of the gross, which means that although *HOT L* has run over a year, the Circle has made only $5,000 from it – plus another $1,000 from the run thus far of *Red Ryder*.

Today the Circle has a season's deficit of $15,000 and its five-year lease on its theater on upper Broadway ends in June. The group is looking for a new space. The plan is to stay small, at least for now. But Mason is not without a vision.

'I'm very ambitious,' he admitted, without forsaking his usual genial manner. 'I mean to create a great repertory theater.' He talked about the great theaters of the past. 'The Moscow Art Theater had 100 actors and government support.' His eyes widened. 'If you would give me 100 actors and government support...' He paused and then asked, 'Will we make it? Will Lanford Wilson be the new Chekhov and will I be the new Stanislavski?' With a smile, he gave himself the obvious answer. 'Hopefully, no. He will be Lanford Wilson and I will be Marshall Mason and we will have a living theater.' Then he said, 'Did you know that Stanislavski's first theater was called the Circle?'"

The cat had leapt from the bag.

A Rare Revival

A circus mood must have been in the air: the following month the new World's Fair, "Expo '74," was opening in Spokane, Washington. In New York we were preparing an extravagant revival of a play that premiered in 1928 for only twenty-seven performances, and enjoyed only one revival in the intervening years.

The rarely produced play was *him* by one of the greatest modern poets, e.e. cummings. Marshall Oglesby undertook to direct this eccentric masterpiece and, continuing our inter-disciplinary policy, we convinced Lanford Wilson to appear in the title role. Trish Hawkins left *HOT L* to play the role of "me" opposite Lanford.

Company members Tanya Berezin, Ken Kliban and Sharon Madden were also featured in a cast of seventeen. It marked the first time Circle Rep enjoyed the brilliant versatility of Caffé Cino star, Neil Flanagan, who quickly became a member of our Company and appeared in many future productions. We were also joined by an extraordinary comedienne, Bobo Lewis, a veteran of three Broadway shows and more than twenty television and film appearances. Bobo also became a member of the acting Company, and played many parts for us in the next twenty years.

Also in the cast were Baxter Harris, who'd been in *Charley Contrare,* and William Wise, who soon replaced Judd in *HOT L.* John Martinuzzi and Marilyn Amaral performed a dynamic dance interpretation of "Frankie and Johnny" choreographed by Charon Lee Cohen. Elizabeth Perry and Diana Malchin are others who first appeared in *him* and later were of assistance in other shows.

him by e.e. cummings opened at Circle Repertory Theater Company on April 14, 1974, and played nineteen performances. Marshall Oglesby's production was an extravaganza featuring music and dance. The sets were by Henrietta Bagley, the lighting was Dennis Parichy's first design for Circle Rep, and Jennifer von Mayrhauser designed the flapper-era costumes of feathers and spangles. Music was by Company Composer Normal Berman, with lyrics by Bonnie Schultz. Rheatha Forster was the stage manager.

I can't report on the rehearsal process, since I was preoccupied with *The Sea Horse,* which opened at the Westside Theater the night after the opening of *him,* but I can report that I thoroughly enjoyed seeing the magical if somewhat incomprehensible show, even if it did run almost four hours. Here are excerpted reviews:

The New York Times, April 20, 1974 (Mel Gussow):
"Circle Repertory's production is valuable, but it is not so much fun as it should be. Wilson and Hawkins act with aplomb. In roles that could be grating, both are ingratiating. The lines are amusing, pretentious, whimsical, and inimitably e.e. cummings."

New York Post, April 23, 1974 (Jerry Tallmer):
"More of a curiosity than an explosion. The drama seems to last for years. Wilson is no actor, which undercuts the

project...Hawkins is a pretty 'me' and Flanagan a journeyman workhorse. I liked Bobo Lewis."

Long Island Press, April 15, 1974 (William A. Raidy):
"It is a fascinating, original and utterly mad adventure, which drew both my admiration and my rage. The strange thing is that often it works. In its total madness, there is sanity. Oglesby has directed with bold strokes. The hero of the evening is Neil Flanagan. He is utterly charming. Anyway, *him*, that most unimaginable play does manage to come to life –crazy life at the Circle Theater."

Village Voice, April 25, 1974 (Michael Feingold):
"*him* plays so well and sounds so freshly on the ears that you wonder why it isn't a repertory staple. It's a huge, complicated, bellowing thing. Oglesby's production captures a good deal of what is going on. Hawkins' gives a strong performance...I don't know which to admire more about Flanagan – his versatility or his stamina. It's very, very good work."

The Nation, (Harold Clurman):
"Circle Repertory sustains its reputation for valiant and interesting work. Their staging is surely laudable. The play's duo 'him' and 'me' are the most sensitive and touching in American playwriting. Wilson is no actor, but he knows whereof cummings speaks. Hawkins is easy to look at and seems right as 'me.' Flanagan does well in a slew of parts."

Newsweek, April 29, 1974 (Jack Kroll):
"Circle Repertory reached an apotheosis with its production of *him*, giving the four-year-old company four productions running simultaneously in New York. Circle Rep is providing U.S. theater with its only ambiance for growth at the moment....*him* in spirit epitomizes Circle's positive, poetic humanism. Stark Young called *him* 'something fresh

and blessed in the theater.' So it was and is. Wilson seems like the very spirit of the 20s with his Scott Fitzgerald profile and his fine ear for cummings' lingo. Hawkins is poignant and lovely. Prodigies of stamina and memory are performed by the cast, especially by the stupefyingly dedicated Neil Flanagan who never misses a beat playing more roles than there are in some careers."

East Side, West Side, all around the town: Circle Rep was ubiquitous. This burst of creativity and recognition was unfortunate in only one respect: it was a hard act to follow.

The Origins Of Drama

We finished up this rather remarkable season with a return to the source of theater, ancient Greece. Our next new playwright was a promising fellow named Aeschylus. Although the telling of dramatic stories had been going on for centuries, this great writer is recognized as the father of tragedy. In the Golden Age of Greece in the fifth century B.C., Aeschylus introduced a second actor on stage to provide conflict, rather than only one actor interacting with a chorus, thus basically inventing drama as we know it.

Aeschylus was born around the year 425 B.C. and is thought to have written as many as ninety plays, only seven of which have survived. The earliest of his plays is thought to be *The Persians*, first performed in 472 B.C. It recounts the story of the Battle of Salamis, which occurred only seven years earlier, and was a conflict Aeschylus actually fought in. The great naval battle was fought between the ships of Greece and those of the Persians, following the disastrous defeat at the Battle of Thermopylae, in which the Greeks were ambushed and overcome. The victory at Salamis insured the survival of Greek culture, and by extension, ours. It certainly might have been a different world if Persia won, which has led some historians to postulate that Salamis is one of the most significant battles in history. One might view *The Persians* as a first play, by a veteran returning from a long and difficult war, written from his own personal experience.

Rob Thirkield directed our final production of the season, and it was a fairly straightforward, traditional rendition of Greek drama, not experimental or avant-garde in any significant respect. Rob cast our actress/designer Henrietta Bagley as the Queen of Persia, who learns of the destruction of the Persian navy from a messenger, in a powerful narrative description of the battle. The critical part of the Messenger was played by Ken Kliban, a virile, heavily muscled man with classical training, whose voice could convey a wide range of emotional subtleties. Ron Seka (from Eagles Mere) played the Ghost of Darius and for the first time, the best actress from our years at Northwestern, Nancy Killmer, joined us at Circle Rep, appearing in the Chorus. With specificity typical of Circle Rep, the program says: "The action takes place in January 479 B.C. outside the royal palace of Xerxes at Susa (actually Persepolis) by the tomb of Darius."

The Persians opened at Circle Repertory Theater on May 19, 1974, and played twenty-seven performances. The minimalist set was by Richard Hoover, the costumes by Jennifer von Mayrhauser and the lighting by Dennis Parichy. Brad Dourif recently had married a dark-haired musician named Janet and she composed the score. Lee Pucklis was the stage manager. Here are a couple of excerpted reviews:

New York Post, May 20, 1974 (Joseph Mancini):
"It's a lively play, in its way, but (also) a static play. Thirkield has made no effort at an interesting staging, and no discernable new approach to the play is attempted and performances are ordinary. The Messenger Ken Kliban is good, the members of the Chorus are competent, and the others are audible. Circle Rep will survive."

Village Voice, May 30, 1974 (Arthur Sainer):
"Circle Repertory has tackled a surly and difficult work. A challenging performance problem is the prevalence of the

Chorus. Thirkield has employed a promising device, but it's a sluggish, disconnected production. The Ghost of Darius is ably performed by Ron Seka. Hoover's set is an imaginative construct of backdrop cords in a complex of webbing and floor planks suggesting the worn stones of an ancient era, but there is little else to recommend this production."

Well, I've always believed that if one must fail (and in art, the right to fail is essential), then fail by attempting something magnificent. One final thought: if Rob cast Nancy Killmer in the role of the Queen, more life might have been perceived in the play.

Putting A Bow On It

On June 26, 1974, the Universal Product Code was scanned for the first time, to sell a package of Wrigley's chewing gum at the Marsh Supermarket in Troy, Ohio. The age of anonymity ended; the age of digital identification began.

In addition to our six Major Productions, we also produced some interesting workshop productions. David Starkweather wrote a new play entitled *Rounding Scylla, Avoiding Charybdis.* Being utterly ignorant of the situation to which these unpronounceable images alluded, I persuaded David to rethink his title. When he explained the citation (a reference to *The Odyssey*), I recalled Ulysses tied himself to a mast to prevent falling prey to Circe's song. I urged David to find a more accessible way to bring the Homeric myth to mind. He finally came up with an alternative and re-titled his play *The Straits of Messina,* only a tad less obscure. It was a play of tangled relationships, in which a young man finds himself torn between his attraction for an alluring woman and a magnetic man. Despite the epic title, it was uncharacteristically realistic in style for David's writing. We mounted the script as a workshop directed by Marshall Oglesby, but after the vibrant *HOT L* and *Red Ryder,* this rather conventional material seemed comparatively bloodless, so we never took it further. This is the likely reason we lost the active participation of David, who was central to Circle until this point.

Well-known avant-garde author Megan Terry (of *Viet Rock* fame) brought us a play called *Hothouse*. Like David's play, it was uncharacteristically realistic in style. We mounted a workshop production of it directed by Barbara Rosoff. This workshop introduced us to Jessica James (who starred in our production of *Gemini* a couple of years later); Margaret Barker, an original member of The Group Theater, who became a member of Circle Rep; Frank Geraci, who'd been at Northwestern; and our Company member Sharon Madden. It was an interesting, seemingly autobiographical drama that played for a limited engagement of six performances mid-February, between *Charley Contrare* and *Sea Horse*. Marjorie Horne was the stage manager.

I directed a workshop production of a one-act play by Robert Patrick called *One Person,* which re-united us, however briefly, with Cino and American Theater Project alumnus, Charles Stanley. On the same bill, Judd Hirsch directed a one-act play by Elaine May called *Not Enough Rope,* in which a frustrated Zane Lasky is thwarted in a suicide attempt for reasons explained by the title. Another workshop play was called *Summer Solstice,* but I have no record of the author or director. My assistant Peter Schneider tried his hand at directing, making his debut at the end of the season with a dusty naturalistic play by Patricia Quinn called *Busy Dyin'*. It was obvious that Peter possessed a special talent, but it did not yet find optimum expression in directing.

At the Circle-in-the-Square Downtown, *The HOT L BALTIMORE* continued its run throughout our fifth season, and several of our previous players replaced in key roles. Jane Cronin, who'd been so luminous in *Elephant in the House,* replaced Conchata Ferrell as April and played it for the remainder of its long run. Jane Lowry, our Olga from the first season's Traditional *Three Sisters* replaced Stephanie Gordon as Suzy and also enjoyed an extended stay. Ted LePlat and Jonathan Hogan rotated in and out of the role of Paul Granger. American Theater Project member David Groh was the first of several replacements for Judd Hirsh as Bill. Chip Zien came from the Los Angeles production to replace Zane as Jamie. The hardest to recast was Trish Hawkins as The Girl. Faith Catlin and then Heather MacCrae were good actresses, but the special magic that Trish brought to the role was missing for the last two years of the run.

When Miss Krause finally came to New York and saw the production, a cast of replacements was playing *HOT L*. I was dismayed, believing she could hardly imagine the artistic phenomenon she missed; but she was full of praise for what she experienced, and deemed it a remarkable example of true ensemble work. I am grateful that Miss Krause could see a hint of the artistic theater we created at her instigation.

During our production of *him*, Circle Rep had four productions running in New York simultaneously, which at the time, was probably some kind of record. We launched two more award-winning productions by new American playwrights, both plays chosen for the *Best Plays Annual*. Equally importantly, most of the actors that the public recognized as the heart of our Company, the players in *The HOT L BALTIMORE*, left their well-paying jobs to return to Circle Rep to create new work. In the order of their return, we had new performances from Tony Tenuta, Judd Hirsch, Zane Lasky, Jonathan Hogan, Rob Thirkield, Conchata Ferrell, and Trish Hawkins. The idea of a permanent acting Company took hold, and could not be waylaid even by success.

However, it must also be noted that we were spending more than we were earning. Our artistic priorities were a guiding principle that burdened us with financial problems throughout our existence. Circle Rep always lived beyond its means. The New York State Council on the Arts warned that we were in jeopardy of losing their support unless we organized the theater on a more professional basis. We began accumulating an operating deficit, so we needed to rethink how our business was being managed. This sharp kick spurred us to hire a professional manager who could guide us to a more responsible level of budgeting and spending. We began our next season climbing to a new tier of contracts, raising Circle Rep over the coming year to the professional level of Off-Broadway.

It was time to leave our safe haven on the Upper West Side, and move on to a new venue for our creativity. As good as it had been, better was yet to come.

Part Three
An Expanding Universe

CHAPTER 9
CONFIRMATION

In the autumn of 1974, Lanford invited me to an advance screening of *The Migrants* in a midtown office building. He wrote this television film for Hallmark, who had sent Lanford and Tennessee Williams on a research trip through the South the previous year. Lanford based his original screenplay on insights Mr. Williams noted about the migrant farmworkers they observed together during the trip. Just after the movie started, Mr. Williams slipped into the darkened room accompanied by a young man. When the screening was over, Lanford realized he was there and wanted to say hello. He offered to introduce me, but I was reluctant.

Tennessee Williams was such an overwhelming influence in my life it was hard to grasp how his colossal artistic spirit could be contained within an actual human body. Furthermore, I had heard tales about how his drug use and alcoholism wrecked his artistic life. I was afraid to meet my god, not wanting to discover clay feet. So, Lanford went over alone and exchanged pleasantries with him.

A Living Legend

But fate intervened to bring about our meeting another way. Following the debut of *The Sea Horse*, Mel Gussow's interview appeared in *The Times*, where he mentioned that I:

"came to New York with the 'dream that I would meet Tennessee Williams and someone would say to him, let this boy direct your new play.'"

Within the week, Tennessee telephoned. He was flattered by my confession and invited me to dinner. Staggered by the prospect, I accepted. It was, after all, a command appearance.

A short time later Tennessee phoned again. Embarrassed, he explained that he invited me on a night he already had promised to spend with his sister, Rose. I knew she was hospitalized as a victim of a frontal lobotomy, dramatized in *Suddenly Last Summer*. The institution was somewhere upstate and she was permitted occasional trips to the city to visit her famous brother. Tennessee admitted he'd never exposed her to anyone in his professional life. Would I mind, he asked timidly, sharing the evening with Rose? Of course, I was only too happy to meet her. Because I'd worked on *Suddenly Last Summer* in college, in a sense I felt I knew her already.

I arrived at the Hotel Élysée aquiver. I waited in the floral redolence of the lobby until the desk clerk signaled that I should go up. Tennessee met me at the door and ushered me in. The suite was intimate; there was a living room area with a sofa, coffee table and club chairs, and a small dinner table in a windowed alcove at the other end of the room. Between them was an old-fashioned phonograph and Tennessee put on a 78-rpm record, which he said was his favorite. It was the Ink Spots, who provided a rinky-dink background for the evening. I accepted his offer of a glass of white wine.

We were going to be served dinner from room service, so he offered me a menu to choose my meal. After a few minutes, the bell chimed and he opened the door to admit Rose and her companion. Rose's escort was a sweet, attentive professional who virtually disappeared unless needed, nothing like the sadistic nun in *Suddenly Last Summer*. She joined us for dinner as the fourth guest.

Rose, probably in her sixties, was a tiny creature, perhaps no more than five feet tall, but every inch was carried with dignity. She had an elegant, delicate bearing; her hair cropped short, framing the face of a gamin. She bore a strong resemblance to Dame Judi Dench. She smoked incessantly, with a fierce style reminiscent of Bette Davis. When she came in, I was struck by the accuracy of Tennessee's poem:

"You know how the mad enter the room,
Their eyes bursting on the air like roses?"

Rose chain-smoked her cigarettes with bird-like quickness, somehow defiant in her far country, impatient with our world. Her eyes never met those of her companions. Her forehead crinkled with a trace of a frown, as though she had a slight headache or was contemplating some weighty matter known only to herself. She was silent and spoke only when addressed directly and not always even then.

She sat on Tennessee's right at the small round table covered with starched white linen, I on his left, opposite Rose. Her nurse/companion was to her right, across from Tennessee. He was a gracious host. While he politely asked me questions about myself, he thoughtfully included Rose. He often turned to her with a question designed to engage her in our chat. Tennessee told me he was planning to go to England within the month. He turned to his sister and said: "Rose, would you like to come with me to England. You could meet the Queen." Rose puffed furiously on her cigarette for a split second before firing her reply: "I am the Queen!" And despite our festive laughter, she was indeed regal. It was a rejoinder I later heard him recount with glee. Rose shared some of the famous Williams wit.

Tennessee was delighted the evening went so well. He assured me that he would love to work with me and suggested we get together again soon. After our first dinner, Tennessee realized he could safely include Rose in social engagements and from then on, she accompanied him on many public occasions. I'm glad she did because it clearly meant a great deal to Tennessee.

About a week later, I visited him again at the Élysée. This time I came to talk business. Tennessee greeted me in his "at home" ensemble: a white shirt open at the neck, a pair of dark linen trousers and bedroom slippers. He was in a buoyant mood and we shared a bottle of white wine. Tennessee introduced me to Robert Carroll, his professional/personal companion. Robert was a slim blond about twenty-four years old, handsome, with a sexy surliness. Tennessee clearly enjoyed the company of this young writer; in Robert he had a companion who could keep pace with his wit. Robert opened the bottle of wine, gave us glasses, potato chips, and then more or less disappeared into the kitchen while "Ten" and I talked.

Throughout our first meeting and the jocular ease of our second, I saw nothing of the "ravaged" wreck I'd feared to meet. I never saw Tennessee more than pleasantly high on white wine. It's true that during our first several meetings, as I prepared to depart, Tennessee slyly implied that he and his companion would not be adverse to a tryst-á-trois, but it was always suggested by way of innuendo rather than an overt proposition. I was flattered, but I was determined to preserve our relationship as artistic colleagues, so I demurely sidestepped the suggestion.

I told Tennessee that the play I wanted to direct was his first full-length, *Battle of Angels*. Tennessee was surprised and more than a little alarmed. The play had been produced thirty-four years earlier (the year I was born) in Boston by the Theatre Guild. The opening performance was a disaster, because a fire that ends the play got out of hand and the audience was evacuated, choked by billowing clouds of smoke. The play closed before it opened, so it had never been produced in New York.

Tennessee was still sensitive to this terrible event. In the mid-50s, he revised the play extensively and re-titled it *Orpheus Descending*. It had a modest run on Broadway and seemed to have settled the old score. I told Tennessee I knew the later play, but I felt his revision lost some of the delicate poetry of the original. *Battle* was a fresh play that poured from the soul of its young creator; *Orpheus* was carefully crafted, overlayed with a tough, commercial veneer, a consequence of the survival instinct.

I presented my case with the fervor of an artist with a vision. Circle Rep was going to be moving in the fall to a new theater downtown and I wanted to open the new theater with the New York premiere of the first play by Tennessee Williams. Luckily, he'd seen my production of *HOT L* so he believed I could bring it off. Although he was nervous about reopening the wounds from his first failure, Tennessee agreed to let me proceed. My *New York Times* dream was coming true.

Tennessee's robust laugh was one of his most memorable characteristics. It was a kind of high-pitched guffaw, almost ridiculous in its uninhibited, child-like joy. His laugh proclaimed how much he enjoyed being alive. He was infamous for attending performances of his plays and letting loose a hysterical yelp when he appreciated a subtle irony in what others thought were the most serious passages.

A Significant Revival

In August before tackling *Battle of Angels,* I directed William Inge's *Come Back, Little Sheba* at the Queens Playhouse, a theater that stood on the grounds of the old New York World's Fair. My agents at ICM (Milton Goldman and Ed Lamata), who also represented the Inge estate, put together a "package" of their clients to create a new production of *Sheba* starring Jan Sterling. I remembered her Oscar-nominated performance in *The High and the Mighty,* a movie I'd enjoyed as a child on one of my Saturday afternoons at the Stanley Theater. Trish Hawkins was also in *Sheba* as Marie, the spirited, young tenant who's the lustful object of all the men's attention.

It was the first time I worked with designer John Lee Beatty, who became a central collaborator in my best work. I wanted to free Inge from the trap of mundane kitchen drama and help him soar with the kind of imagery he aspired to emulate in Tennessee's plays. I introduced lyrical interludes of fantasy between the naturalistic scenes, accompanied by a haunting, melancholy score that framed the realism with theatrical poetry. *Sheba* is written with jumps in time and circumstances from scene to scene. My interludes unified the action and smoothed the jagged edges of Inge's episodic structure with a dance that drew the audience forward.

John Lee designed a set for *Sheba* that revealed a huge, empty house surrounding a two-storied staircase, rising like a cross-section of a chambered nautilus, whose gloominess tortures Lola after her little dog disappears. The audience could see the front porch, the entrance hall, Marie's bedroom, the living room, the kitchen behind and the tiny back stoop, all backed by a panoramic cyclorama. The enormous staircase rose two flights to the door of Doc and Lola's bedroom (echoing another Inge image, the dark at the top of the stairs). Characters entering at the front porch went through the foyer and disappeared behind the staircase before being seen again in the kitchen. It was a sort of "peek-a-boo" conceit that John Lee used again in several of his best designs (like *Talley & Son* and *A Delicate Balance*).

The play opened to mostly favorable reviews and I was eager for Tennessee to see it. He was a champion of the young William Inge, and I knew that his influence was as important in Inge's creative life as it was in mine.

I hired a stretch limousine to ease the arduous journey from the Élysée out to the borough of Queens, and picked up Tennessee and Robert. It was a good chance to observe their fascinating relationship. Their lively humor flew around the car with alacrity, often sharp, self-critical and always, brutally honest. Robert held nothing back in noting Tennessee's voracious appetite for degradation; and Tennessee was unsparing in his assessment of Robert's opportunism. Tennessee's honesty influenced his personal life as well as his plays. Lanford was upset by Tennessee's observation about his "corrupt ambition to succeed," and I squirmed at his withering perception that, like Shannon in *Iguana*, I enjoyed my pain too much.

It was a good performance of *Sheba* and during our return to Manhattan, I anticipated hearing Tennessee's appreciation for my having served his protégé so well. What happened instead was an occasion to mature. Selfishly focused on my own transient triumph, I overlooked the effect seeing *Come Back, Little Sheba* might have on Tennessee. Flooded with memories, he became utterly quiet the whole trip back. I chattered on a bit with Robert about trivial things, but eventually we both fell silent, realizing why Tennessee was sitting so still. William Inge committed suicide on June 10, 1973, only a year before. Seeing this play, Inge's first success, plunged Tennessee into mourning the loss of his friend and fellow artist. When we arrived at the hotel, Tennessee thanked me for the evening and we made a date to get together the following week. I regretted the pain my vanity caused.

Moving Off-Broadway

My summer production at the Queens Playhouse coincided with an important step forward for Circle Theater Company. After three commercial transfers to Off-Broadway, it was time to leave behind our little theater upstairs at 2307 Broadway and make the giant step of taking our whole enterprise Off-Broadway.

We needed to hire theater professionals who could guide us through this spurt of growth. While directing at the Queens Playhouse, I met Jerry Arrow and Barbara Darwall, the producing team working for Robert Moss (the Founder of Playwrights Horizons), who was the Artistic Director in Queens. At the end of their summer season, Jerry and Barbara would be free.

I consulted with our Board of Directors and we agreed to offer Jerry Arrow the position of Executive Director. Although Jerry was not attractive physically, he had a warm and an affable energy that was persuasive. He brought Barbara with him as Company Manager. His first task was to find a suitable theater to establish a home for our future. Jerry discovered that the Sheridan Square Playhouse, a prominent Off-Broadway theater dating back to 1958, had been gutted, turned into office space and rented out to serve as headquarters for a Republican political campaign. Once the election passed in early November, it would be available for rent and we could turn the space back into a theater.

It was located at 99 Seventh Avenue South, in the heart of Sheridan Square (at the confluence of Seventh Avenue, West Fourth, Grove and Christopher Streets) and directly in front of the Christopher Street subway stop on the IRT. Prior to being a theater, the building was host to The Nut Club, a famous nightclub frequented by people such as Lionel Barrymore, Jimmy Durante, Eddie Cantor and Mae West. Jerry negotiated a lease with the owners of the building, a couple of elderly Italian sisters named Rose and Lucy Alberti, who inherited the property from their father, who'd owned it from the time it was a stable for milk delivery wagons. At the top of the building in mosaic tiles was embedded the word "GARAGE."

It was hard to imagine a better fit. The space, although irregular, was essentially a big square, which meant we could set up our stage anywhere we wanted. In addition, a Village theater landmark would be resuscitated. The entire Company joyfully gathered in October to paint the ancient façade of the building white and to install glass display boxes for advertising our productions. We hoisted a colorful banner with the new emblem for Circle Rep on it and the Company posed for an historic picture to document our momentous move.

As we prepared for our leap forward, Richard M. Nixon announced his resignation as 37th President of the United States, to be succeeded by the appointed Vice-President, Gerald Ford. Perhaps this was as positive an omen as a rebellious emergent theater company could hope for.

A Long-Delayed Debut

When I next visited Tennessee, he told me about an exceptional young actress who played Blanche in a University of Minnesota production of *Streetcar*. Debra Mooney was, in his opinion, the best Blanche he'd ever seen. She was coming to New York and he urged me to invite her to work at Circle Rep. When I met Debra, I realized she could bring a formidable strength to the last scenes of *Battle of Angels,* playing a fierce Mrs. Regan, the Woman from Waco.

Tennessee and I met several times over the next six months to work on the script. He was eager to accommodate my suggested re-writes. I wanted to cut the morbidly humorous prologue, which seemed to me less funny than symbol-laden. The prologue had been set in a "museum" a year after the action, making the main body of the play a flashback. I felt it was better for the audience to dive right into the present-time action. I transposed a couple of the better jokes from the prologue to the first scene, in which Beulah and Dotty are arranging a home-from-the-hospital party for Jabe

Torrance. Tennessee approved all my cuts and a few line changes, some of them lifted from his revisions in *Orpheus*.

Battle of Angels is a retelling of the ancient Greek legend of Orpheus. The story is set in the dry goods store in a small southern town confined by conformity, sexual frustration and narrow-mindedness. Strictly controlled by a severe sheriff, the town has only one rebel: a debauched heiress named Cassandra Whiteside, who gleefully flaunts her independence from convention. Into this tinderbox comes Val, a young man with a guitar, a snakeskin jacket and undeniable erotic energy. He takes a job in the dry goods store run by Myra Torrance, a middle-aged woman whose elderly husband is dying, confined to his room above the store. Myra finds herself attracted to Val and to the new life he inspires. It is a liberating antidote to her loveless marriage and boring small-town life. The play describes the awakening of passion and the renewal of life, as well as their tragic consequences for Val and Myra.

In our production, we gave particular attention to the end of the play, when the Woman from Waco arrives to haul Val's past misadventures into his present predicament. Pursued by this "woman scorned" from his past, Val is stunned when Jabe Torrance comes downstairs with a shotgun, discovers the lovers and shoots Myra, who dies in Val's arms. Val escapes to the basement of the store, where he is trapped by vengeful townsmen. In a horrific climax, these men, who disapprove of the vagrant poet with the snakeskin jacket and his effortless magnetism with women, burn him alive. We fired a live flame-thrower into the basement, which in our intimate theater gave Val's screams of agony a heart-stopping credibility.

I cast one of our best actresses (and my co-founder) Tanya Berezin as Myra, the tragic heroine of the piece. I knew Tennessee wanted Myra to be a woman with the fiery passions of an Anna Magnani. I was sure Tanya could make the part her own; and so she did, with a complex, sensitive and sensual performance. Walter Kerr's review in *The New York Times* was headlined: "A Williams Tigress."

I thought the role of Val required an actor with an imposing physical magnetism like Brando (who played the role opposite

Magnani in a film version called *The Fugitive Kind*). When I directed *Come Back, Little Sheba* in August, I'd cast Ron Max in the provocative role of the Milkman, who's sort of a walking wet dream in the world of Inge. During one of my fantasy interludes he wore a Speedo and flexed with a simmering sexuality in this small role; so I thought he could provide understated charisma in the central part of Val. Tennessee, having seen *Sheba*, approved. The evanescent Trish Hawkins seemed ideal for the recklessly degenerate debutante Cassandra, and so she was. Conchata Ferrell followed her triumph as April in *HOT L* with an Obie-winning performance as Gertrude in *The Sea Horse*. Now she followed that unforgettable characterization with Vee Talbot, a painter who's the Sheriff's unstable wife. Although Chatty is a woman of ample size, she has a flushed sensitivity that made her breathless Vee a hypnotic victim of Val's charm. Everyone in the cast delivered detailed and imaginative work that contributed to a true ensemble accomplishment. In addition to the comic performances that impressed the reviewers, I remember particularly Jack Davidson's quietly threatening Sheriff, Ron Seka's emaciated, demonic Jabe Torrance, and Lance Taylor's ghostly Voodoo Man.

After rehearsals began, we became aware that Chatty would have to leave the cast after the second week of performances. She was under contract for Norman Lear's television version of *HOT L*, and had to get to Los Angeles to begin taping the series. Her departure gave me an opportunity to honor Tennessee's request by having Debra Mooney replace Chatty as the Sheriff's wife. Debra was one of the best gifts Tennessee gave me. She remained a member of the Company for many years, with many wonderful performances.

Tennessee came to only four or five rehearsals. He sat in the back, observing my work with the cast, and then he'd quietly slip out after an hour or so. He seemed pleased with everything we were doing. A handsome young employee at Circle Rep named Danny Irvine was assigned to escort Tennessee around. It was bitterly cold as winter approached and Tennessee hated the winter. Danny saw him home in a taxi, bundled up in his full-length mink coat. Sometimes, they dropped. into a couple of bars along the way, indulging Tennessee's unquenchable thirst for male beauty. Once, as they left a bar they passed a well-built young man standing on a street corner clad in only jeans and a t-shirt. "My god!" Danny remarked as they climbed into the taxi, "He's going to freeze his tail off!" Tennessee laughed. "You don't have to worry about his tail, honey. He won't be out there long."

John Lee Beatty designed an atmospheric environment for the play, using most of the interior of the Sheridan Square Playhouse. The set had a unique configuration that divided the audience into three small sections, positioned among the acting areas that represented variously the front counter, the ladies' shoes section of the store, and the grape arbor-like confectionary. The lobby of the theater opened directly onto the showcase windows of Myra's dry-goods store, and the audience entered through the front door. As with *HOT L*, the audience had to cross through the store to find their seats. Dennis Parichy created languorous moods with his haunting light design. Jennifer von Mayrhauser made the artfully simple costumes, and Norman L. Berman composed an eerie, romantic score. These were my designers from *Sheba*, and they were the core of my creative team for many years.

On November 3, 1974, Circle Repertory Company presented the New York premiere of *Battle of Angels*, which played thirty-two performances. It was a rousing success, much appreciated by Tennessee at this late point in his career. As was his custom, he left for Key West the morning after opening, hearing the news of our triumph via long distance. Here are excerpts from some of the reviews:

The New York Times, November 4, 1974 (Mel Gussow):
"An evening of renewal and reclamation. A play of atmosphere and mood... [it] has a redeeming sweetness and sensitivity. Physically the production has the Circle's customary concern with detail. There are a number of first-rate performances in subordinate roles – Conchata Ferrell, Sharon Madden, Mary Ellen Flynn, and Berrilla Kerr. Trish Hawkins

comes closest, almost turning her character into a whirlwind. The Circle Repertory Company is to be applauded for rediscovery – not just of a play, but also of a theater. The newly restored playhouse has never looked better."

New York Post, November 4, 1974 (Martin Gottfried):
"*Battle of Angels* is plainly the work of Williams in full glory. There is a wealth of poetry in its language, love and passion in its heart, and master craftsmanship in its construction. A rich sense of life and glorious writing take charge. Mason directed it and the large company beautifully. [It has] a fine full set from John Lee Beatty and a superb team performance. Hawkins is dazzling. There are any number of excellent smaller performances, and altogether they bring out the true voice of the greatest playwright America has had."

Daily News, November 17, 1974 (Douglas Watt):
"A generally impressive production. The cast was well-chosen, and Mason's direction was commendable. [The play] reveals a strong and poetic playwright already in full command of dialogue. There is, besides the lovely flights of lyricism delivered so spontaneously, that wonderful conviction in what he was saying."

The New York Times, November 17, 1974 (Walter Kerr):
"An eye opener. *Battle of Angels* starts right off at something near *Streetcar* scale. The Williams panorama is there, kicking to be born. Berezin is a revelation...ferocious, straitlaced, jealous, grateful. A thunderclap couldn't have done it better, and there is scarcely a finer performance in New York just now."

The Record, November 4, 1974 (Emory Lewis):
"A major theater event. It's a poet's dark-hued, romantic rebellion against a materialistic society. The play has been

staged sensitively by Mason. He has caught the poetry of the piece. The actors are members of the Circle Rep, one of the best ensemble groups in New York. Bouquets and congratulations to Circle Repertory Company."

North Jersey Suburbanite, undated (Robert L. Daniels):
"Just as I firmly believe Marshall W. Mason will emerge as the most important director of the 70s, actress Trish Hawkins will achieve equal distinction as a major actress. She is the best thing to happen to New York since Gerry Page and Julie Harris came into our lives."

These were the kind of reviews that might have ignited a commercial transfer, but no offer was forthcoming. Kermit Bloomgarden, who'd moved two of our productions, had opened *Equus* on Broadway just as we were about to open *Battle of Angels*. Kermit had a huge Broadway hit on his hands, which won two Tony Awards (Best Play, Best Director) and ran for the next two years. Kermit was back on Broadway with a bang and we were already beneath his radar. No other commercial producer stepped forth to extend our run in another theater, so we closed and moved on to our scheduled repertoire.

Coincidentally, while we were breathing new life into a dramatic fossil from the past, the science of anthropology celebrated one of its greatest moments. On November 24, a skeleton from the hominid species Australopithecus afarensis was discovered and named Lucy. Perhaps this was an apt omen for our next undertaking, a new play about archeologists.

A Stage Misdirection

Dramatists Play Service issued a new acting edition based on the Circle Rep revisions of *Battle of Angels*, listing our cast and credits as the premiere production. Unfortunately, due to negligence in proofing, the acting edition ends with a baffling mistake. The last lines of the play are delivered by the Sheriff and a pistol-packing Mrs. Regan as Sandra leaves with Val's snakeskin jacket:

WOMAN: She's got his jacket. Stop her!
SHERIFF: Don't move. Don't move.
    (*Sandra walks out.*)
WOMAN: Stop. Stop! Stop!
    (*The Woman from Waco shoots. Sandra laughs and the lights go out.*)

Curtain

The first part of this last stage direction somehow was printed as a line of dialogue, so the last line as published reads:

WOMAN: Stop, stop! Stop! The woman from Waco shoots. (*Sandra laughs and the lights go out.*)

I'm sure Cassandra won't be the only one laughing if future productions follow the script. All those years of reading scripts, I imagined an acting edition to be the definitive version of a play. Now I wonder how many amateur productions inadvertently propagate such errors. I can hear Tennessee's howling guffaw.

I believe Tennessee had an easier time with me on *Battle of Angels* than with any director in a long time. Our working relationship was smooth, fun and free of conflict. I mainly had to convince him that what he wrote was beautiful and need not be improved. Collaboration does not have to resemble the Ali-Foreman fight that took place during our rehearsals on October 30 in Zaire. The second installment of their championship fights was tagged The Rumble in the Jungle; this time Muhammad Ali knocked out George Foreman in eight rounds to regain the title that was stripped from him seven years earlier. Tennessee and I enjoyed a much less pugilistic relationship than his famous bouts with Kazan.

At the same time we were producing *Battle of Angels*, Tennessee's long-awaited *Memoirs* was published. The press and the public professed disappointment with the book, wanting more specifics about the process behind the great plays he'd written. Tennessee felt a memoir should be about his life, not his work; so details of his complicated sexual intrigues were included. The plays were mentioned almost in passing, as markers of time. We began working together too late for him to include our collaboration in the book. I am not named, although he refers to that first dinner I shared with Rose, relating the anecdote about the "Queen of England."

I thought the book was marvelous, and too bad for the bluenoses. Tennessee autographed my copy of his *Memoirs*:

To Marshall,
This disgracefully true thing!
Love, Tennessee

As you might imagine, I treasure it.

End Of A Year, Beginning Of A Life

At our uptown offices, in September Sharon Madden, in her final act as Administrative Director before Jerry Arrow took over, hired a young man from North Carolina to be an administrative assistant. His name was Daniel Irvine, and Danny, as he insists on being called, is a central figure in Circle Rep's history. Born April 10, 1949, Danny graduated with an MFA in Theater from the University of North Carolina at Chapel Hill, where he played an important role in creating a student-run theater program. At Circle Rep, he held a variety of positions over the next twelve years, from box-office treasurer to artistic coordinator to producing director of *The Late Show* and finally, Artistic Director of the Circle Rep Lab. Sharon remained on staff as our in-house Press Representative, first assisting, and then taking over from Herb Striesfield.

After *Battle of Angels* closed on December 1st, Marshall Oglesby took advantage of our empty theater to mount a workshop production of a new musical called *Fire in the Mind House*. Written by a team that included Lance Mulcahy, Arnold Borget and Dion McGregor, the show is best remembered for its central performer, Nell Carter, who went on to have an impressive career on Broadway and in television. Although workshop productions were not meant to be reviewed, Alice Barnet of *TV News* filed a review that described it as a "pleasurable" evening. It played only a few performances the last week of the year. Afterwards, Marshall Oglesby threw a cast party at our apartment on New Year's Eve. I called Tennessee to invite him, but Robert said he was still in Key West. Robert, however, was free and would be delighted to come. And so he did.

As the party began to wind down, I cornered Danny Irvine to say that I thought Robert might have ideas about lingering, maybe to pounce. He always seemed amenable to the idea of a sexual liaison with me. I really didn't want to complicate my professional relationship to Tennessee by entertaining his boyfriend late into the night, so I asked Danny to stay until Robert left. And so he did. Robert finally got the idea that we wanted to be alone and at last, took his leave. More than forty years later, Danny and I still celebrate our anniversary on New Year's Eve. But now we have three. On June 24, 2011, the New York State Legislature finally passed the Marriage Equality Act and Governor Andrew Cuomo immediately signed it. A month later, it was legal for same-sex couples to marry. So Danny and I were married in a civil ceremony on July 25, 2011, in a chapel at the City Clerk's office. WCBS taped the entire ceremony and broadcast it on the local 5 o'clock news. We followed this up with a religious service on August 6th at the Cathedral of St. John the Divine, officiated by the Reverend Thomas Miller. It was a spectacular event, attended by two hundred of our closest friends.

A New Year In A New Theater

As 1975 rolled in, our culture continued to change. As befitted the year designated as "International Women's Year," Ella Grasso of Connecticut was elected the first female governor who hadn't succeeded a husband in the governor's chair. NBC spun out a new game show called *Wheel of Fortune*, and Michael Ovitz founded the Creative Artists Agency, destined to be the most powerful talent agency in Hollywood.

The Transcendent Years

Director Richard Steele took advantage of our empty theater to mount a bold comic/drama by David Roszkowski called *St. Freud* as a Special Event. We produced David's previous play *Canvas* in our fourth season, shortly before *HOT L*, also directed by Richard. David attended Northwestern and got his MFA in playwriting from Yale. *St. Freud* was an ambitious enterprise, with a cast of twenty-one actors playing some forty roles. The leading role of Sigmund Freud was played by James Kiernan, coming back from *Red Ryder*.

Again, although these Special Events were not supposed to be reviewed, somehow a couple of critics saw the show and reviewed it.

> Helen Gary Bishop, writing in *The Villager*, found it:
> "the kind of flawed but fascinating play off-off-Broadway is supposed to be about."

> Emelise Aleandri writing for *TV News* described it as:
> "an engrossing workshop production exhibiting considerable wit in the writing and as much expertise in the acting by an impressive cast."

Unfortunately for Circle Rep, we didn't hang on to this playwright. He changed his name to David Ives and wrote several plays that brought him deserved recognition, most notably his much produced *All in the Timing*, which won the Outer Critics' Circle Award for 1994, played eighty performances at Primary Stages, and then transferred Off-Broadway to the John Housman Theater for another 606 performances. David became Secretary of the Dramatists Guild, and I'm proud we nurtured him through his first two plays in New York.

Rehearsing The Unwritten

The previous summer when planning our new season in our new home, we once again promised subscribers our season would include a new play by Lanford Wilson. Once again, it was a promise made without a script yet having been written. We'd been incredibly lucky the previous year to have come up with a substitute as good as *The Sea Horse*, but this year we needed to deliver on our subscription incentive. Fortunately, Lanford had an idea for a new play he'd been contemplating for several months.

Not only was it daunting to follow up his success with *HOT L*, but also he'd be following a script by the great Tennessee Williams. It put him on quite a spot. But far from the writer's block he'd experienced earlier, this time he was itching to dare again.

The play began to stir his imagination in fragmented, seemingly unlinked images. Lanford was intrigued to solve the puzzle. The first image he pictured was of Trish Hawkins doing sit-ups. What if she were exercising because she was a gynecologist undergoing her own first pregnancy?

Another early image was of a group of city folk finding themselves in the unfamiliar landscape of the countryside, with unusual night sounds that are unsettling: crickets, frogs, owls, et cetera – the strange, nocturnal noises that can seem alien, even threatening, to city dwellers accustomed only to the hum of their air-conditioners.

And there was an image of hearing something in the night, perhaps a muffled encounter of whispers at a screen door, arousing paranoid concerns that lead a nervous sleeper to come downstairs barefoot to investigate a dark, creaking house with a flashlight, saying cautiously: "Hello? Is anyone there?"

These fragments developed into scenes that were themselves enigmatic. These disparate flashes suggested that they might be shards of memory, about an event in the past that had a ruinous outcome.

Having grown up in Missouri, Lanford was familiar with the mysterious mounds erected, and then for unknown reasons, abandoned by the early Indian tribes, long before white settlers came to the continent. The Early Mississippian Culture was a highly developed civilization that existed from approximately 600 to 1400 A.D. This pre-Columbian civilization left behind many unanswered questions. No one even knows for certain what these giant pyramids of earth, such as the Cahokia Mounds near St. Louis, signified. They presented our playwright with a mystery worthy of creative investigation. After almost a year of gestation, the images began to coalesce: these sophisticated people stuck in the country were archeologists on a summer bivouac, an expedition of archeological excavation, trying to piece together the riddles of the past. The play would be called *The Mound Builders*.

A story emerged that dramatized the archeologists' headlong rush to glean knowledge from their dig before the site is inundated by an artificial lake that resort developers intend to create. This established a structural clock in the play with a built-in urgency, a stratagem that intensifies dramatic conflict. Providing the antagonist for the drama is the owner of the land, an unsophisticated local guy with all-American dreams of getting rich.

Lanford wanted to write again for Trish Hawkins and pair her up with her co-star in *HOT L*, the equally honest and original Jonathan Hogan. He also wanted to write a complex character for Tanya Berezin, who hadn't been able to play Jackie in *HOT L* because she was pregnant. Tanya chalked up a success as Tennessee's heroine Myra in *Battle of Angels* and seemed ready for an even greater challenge. Lanford also wanted to write again for Brad Dourif who also had been unable to play the part written for him in *HOT L*, and who since scored a triumph in *Red Ryder*.

The fragmented scenes needed to be held together by a structural device: a narrator, recalling events of a previous summer. The narrator is the chief archeologist, August Howe, written for Rob Thirkield, and is the spine of the play. We went into rehearsal on the first act with fragments of scenes that were to be connected by an unwritten narrative, notated in our scripts as "Bridge to Come." Lanford promised that the second act and the narration would be ready in time, and he kept his promise about ten days before the first preview.

Although Lanford wrote the parts in the play for specific players, once again Brad's part had to be filled by a substitute. Brad was cast by Milos Foreman in his motion picture adaptation of Ken Kesey's novel *One Flew Over the Cuckoo's Nest*. The film was to star Jack Nicholson, and Brad was selected for the choice role of the stuttering, virginal Billy Bibbitt, perhaps the most sympathetic character in the loony bin. So I conducted a vigorous search to find a replacement for the part of Chad Jasker, the redneck owner of the land surrounding the mounds, who is an ambitious, ultimately dangerous, would-be entrepreneur.

Among the actors attracted to Circle Rep was a handsome young man with a shock of Dionysian brown locks who came in to audition for Chad. His name was Richard Gere and the moment I laid eyes on him, I knew he'd become a major movie star. At twenty-four, Richard was striking. His lithe, muscular body conveyed a sly sensuality that was spot-on for the charming yet dangerous Chad. His fine features and charismatic appeal would be magnified on the big screen. But for now, Richard was serious about his budding stage career. His audition for Chad was impeccable; I offered him the part at once, but he had to wait to hear from his agent. He'd also auditioned to play Demetrius in Edward Berkley's production of *A Midsummer Night's Dream* at the Mitzi Newhouse Theater, part of Joseph Papp's gigantic operation at Lincoln Center. The dates were a direct conflict with ours. He got the part in the Shakespeare, and so Circle Rep lost the prospect of introducing a bright new star to the cosmos.

I settled on John Strasberg to play Chad. John was, of course, the son of the famous acting teacher and co-founder of The Group Theater, Lee Strasburg (with whom I'd studied at The Actors Studio). With curly, sandy hair and hazel eyes, John was eight years older than Brad or Richard, but he had a perpetual adolescent quality that worked in counterpart to the equally boyish Jon Hogan. Jon was playing his best friend, the young archeologist who ultimately becomes Chad's victim. There is something off-center about John Strasberg, an odd sense of distrust that could be the product of a celebrated yet demanding, famously cold father; but whatever the source of his restless uncertainty, it served Chad's moral ambiguity to a tee.

So the cast was set: Rob played the elder archeologist and narrator of the play, Dr. August Howe. Stephanie Gordon played

Cynthia, his bored, sexually ravenous wife, drafted to be the expedition's reluctant photographer; and Loren Jacobs, Stephanie's daughter, appeared as their daughter, Kirsten. Jon Hogan was the younger archeologist, Dan Loggins, with Trish as Jean, his pregnant wife, a gynecologist. Tanya was given the most demanding and multi-faceted character Lanford had written, D.K. Eriksen (Delia), Dr. Howe's alcoholic, drug-ravaged sister. She is an eminent author of works of fiction so fine they've been recognized as literature. And John Strasburg, the outsider, appropriately played the interloper, Chad Jasker.

I imagine there are few parallels in history of a group of artists so trustful that they would plunge into rehearsals on a play that was being delivered a few scenes at a time. Of course, my rehearsal method, emphasizing detailed research, bought Lanford an extra week to write, because we were busy learning all we could about the subject of the play, the Early Mississippian Culture, the mounds they built and mysteriously abandoned. The play centers around slides taken by Cynthia the previous summer, so we needed to stage a number of photographs showing our cast at work on an excavation.

We persuaded Dr. Howard Winters of the Department of Anthropology at New York University to spend several hours with us, answering our many questions and sharing practical tips of how an archeologist conducts his field research. We became intimately acquainted with trowels and brushes, the terminology, and even something about the psychology of a scientist, and why one wants to pursue such a career. This research was invaluable for tackling the text Lanford was fashioning. And in fact, Dr. Winters provided Lanford with the final piece of the puzzle – the dream that his fictional archeologists could realize in the second act: the first discovery of a god-king's tomb.

Actually, except for the blank chasms headlined "Bridge to Come," we had most of the script for the first act by the time our research was done, so we could begin staging the play. Our work, along with Dr. Winters' expertise, stimulated Lanford's creativity, with the result that *The Mound Builders* contains some of his most lyrical dialogue, and became Lanford's favorite of his plays.

The play also possesses a rare quality in Lanford's oeuvre: it spins a fascinating tale of suspense. Despite criticism to the contrary, Lanford's work always contained excellent plots (the way in which events are ordered to accumulate meaning), but he seldom told a story that intensified tension as the plot progressed.

The structure of *The Mound Builders* is built on the premise that the events we see in the scenes, the race to save the archeological excavation from the flooding of the lake by commercial developers, took place the previous summer. The present tense is contained in the narration, with Dr. Howe sorting through photographic slides and dictating into a tape recorder to Diane, an unseen secretary, who will identify the slides, put them in order and provide August the evidentiary basis for a scientific report on his historic discovery.

This structure obligates a director to provide a visual experience of the activities described in the dictation. This requires staging, photographing and processing literally hundreds of slides; then to work out the technical means for projecting them onto the entire stage, so that that the audience sees the images as Dr. Howe reviews them. It was an exciting challenge and I relied on the technical expertise of a number of colleagues. Peter Schneider, my stage manager, kept the duplicate slides in order, split between two projectors that worked in sync: one on stage, operated by the actor, and the other, projected from a booth with a super-wide lens. Apart from the artistic and technical challenges, it was also an expensive burden.

Lanford told me that he had no mental picture of how the stage should look. The only thing that was clear was that the eerie sounds of a rural night should envelop the audience. Chuck London, who operated an audio-visual company, created the most amazingly realistic surround-sound of crickets, frogs, owls and cicadas ever experienced in the living theater. Chuck's all-enveloping sounds were two years before Dolby Stereo transformed the experience of sound in motion pictures, notably with the success of *Star Wars* in

1977, and twenty years before Dolby Digital reached home theaters in 1995, approximating what Chuck achieved for us in 1975.

John Lee Beatty had designed a panoramic set for my *Come Back, Little Sheba*, followed by an environmental *Battle of Angels* at Circle. John Lee became the fifth cornerstone of Circle Rep, perhaps artistically the most important addition we yet had encountered. Trish (and many other actors at Circle Rep) could inspire; but John Lee could make manifest that inspiration. Unsurprisingly, it was to John Lee that I turned to design *The Mound Builders*.

At our first meeting, there were few visual details I could offer. I spoke to him mainly about imagery: the alien, threatening atmosphere; the ephemeral nature of memory; the sweep of anthropological discovery. And I talked about the physical needs the text demanded: an upstairs; a porch with a swing; an office with a slide projector; and some way of projecting the slides for all the audience to see. Unusually for me, I could suggest no solutions that accommodated all these hurdles. But John Lee listened and absorbed both the imagery and the practical problems.

Within a week, as the time for rehearsal approached, I developed a clear vision of what the set should look like. At our first production meeting, attended by all the designers, I was excited to share my very specific visualization. The stage should be like a shipwreck, raked with different areas that don't quite fit together, like the shards of a shattered pot; there should be a refrigerator to represent the kitchen and a porch swing to indicate a porch; there had to be an upper level with stairs descending to the main area; the screen for the slides ought to be the kind of screen wire used to surround porches and should stretch behind the width of the space; there should be large poles at the rear of the set on which we could mount searchlights for the ending of the play, when the townspeople search to recover Dan's body from the lake. Suddenly, I stopped. In my exuberance I had not taken in the fact that John Lee brought to the meeting a large black portfolio, which probably contained sketches of his ideas for the set. He sat discreetly through my enthusiastic description like an imperturbable Buddha.

Flummoxed, I apologized for being so specific about what I thought the set should look like, and sheepishly asked John Lee if he had a sketch he wanted to show us. He reached into his portfolio and produced a finished rendering in full color that, in explicit detail, showed a set that perfectly fit my detailed description.

His rendering was a sea-gray construction of wooden planks, with planes that met at improbable angles; it did indeed resemble a wrecked ship or the skeletal ribs of a beached leviathan. Just off-center was an old, white refrigerator and a simple kitchen table; stage left was a porch glider and a crude chaise longue made of the same gray slats; stage right, a narrow, steep, curving stairway led upstairs; and below, a screen door separated the kitchen from a couple of wide steps down into a yard. Downstage left, isolated from the rest, was the only level area, containing a desk, a small slide projector and a reel-to-reel tape recorder. Across the back of the stage, was an expanse of screen wire, with several telephone poles bearing searchlights. It was like being present at a miracle! Apparently, I had found an artistic soul mate, whose vision exactly coincided with mine. My partnership with John Lee over the ensuing twelve years was equal in consequence to my long-time collaboration with Lanford.

Once more, my design team also included Jennifer von Mayrhauser for costumes, Dennis Parichy for lights, and Chuck London (with George Hansen) for sound and visual effects. Along with John Lee Beatty, this group, working with Lanford and me, came to be referred to at Circle Rep as "The A Team."

While *Battle of Angels* was playing in our Sheridan Square theater, our offices remained uptown at 84th and Broadway until the end of the year. Our Chairman Dr. Paul Cranefield and our new Managing Director Jerry Arrow evaluated several spaces in the Village for their suitability as offices and a rehearsal room. Eventually, they found a large undeveloped space that had been a printing factory on the fourth floor at 9 Barrow Street, only a short block behind the theater, which we could convert into offices after the first of the year. Meantime, we continued to hold our pre-production meetings, casting and rehearsals for *The Mound Builders* uptown.

In rehearsals, Tanya's work was alarming. I always encourage actors not to think in terms of results, and to explore fully all elements of character without regard for what an audience sees. But Tanya took this experimentation to new extremes; even I began to wonder if she was going to *do* it like that. Her unrestrained exploration of the withdrawal from drugs and alcohol was an uncompromising investigation of the dark and the ugly physical torture her character was experiencing. As it turned out, all this wild, raw and disgusting behavior subsided beneath a growling, irritable surface that won Tanya an Obie Award. Her portrayal of an artist at a crossroad, a degenerate trying to find a way back to civilization, was a revelation.

Trish was wonderfully sane in contrast, hiding her character's own problems. Jean's disclosure that she was a Spelling Bee Champion when she was a child intimated a pathological need for perfection that led for a time of spelling in her head every word she encountered; the words became "syllables, not sense." She was confined briefly in an institution, before her recovery, which she attributes to "juvenile resilience." Listening to her spell "Mary, go to bed" was hypnotic and moving. ("Mary. M-A-R-Y, Mary. Go. G-O, Go. Mary go. M-a-r-y-g-o. Mary go." etc.)

Jonathan Hogan's understated, folksy Mid-Western speech rendered some of the most beautiful passages in the play with an unpretentious lyricism. His impassioned defense of a common native of the ancient culture, whom the women facetiously have nicknamed "Cochise," and who they note has "disappeared without a trace," arouses from him a detailed description of the extraordinary life the ancient Indians must have lived that is both amusing and stirring.

Later, in an intimate conversation in the middle of the night with Delia, Dan describes a drunken revelry in his college days that led him to embrace a pole that bore a fire alarm box with the hilarious and profound message: "You must answer to get help."

In another scene, Jonathan's simple, colloquial delivery put the focus on the words, as he recited an ancient poem from the Early Mississippian Culture:

"Here are our precious flowers and songs:
May our friends delight in them,
May the sadness fade out of our hearts.
This earth is only lent to us.
We shall have to leave our fine work.
We shall have to leave our beautiful flowers.
That is why I am sad as I sing for the sun."

As I said, the script contains some of Lanford's most eloquent writing. My own favorite passage is August's musing on the loss of Dan:

"A man's life work is taken up, undertaken, I have no doubt, to blind him to the passing moon. I have no doubt that in an area of his almost unconscious he knows this and therefore is not blinded but only driven."

The scene we called "The Fish and the Moon" defines the kind of writing I called "lyrical realism," by which Circle Rep came to be permanently identified. One night, we were conducting a brush-up rehearsal after we'd been off for a holiday. The theater was empty except for Lanford and me, but it was a full dress rehearsal, with all elements. The scene is of a stoned Dan coming back soaking wet from a fishing jaunt with his buddy Chad, and his account to his wife Jean and the always-skeptical Delia of the extraordinary beauty he has just experienced. The three of them are sitting in the luminous glow of Dennis Parichy's moonlight, Delia smoking a cigarette on John Lee Beatty's gray glider, while Dan, drunk from consuming his share of five six-packs, lies on Jean's lap, as she sits on the porch steps in Jennifer von Mayrhauser's exquisitely rose/raspberry-colored robe. It was like Joe Cino's admonition that when an audience isn't there, just to "do it for the room." As Tanya's smoke drifted across the stage in a textbook depiction of stratification, Lanford found me in the darkened audience and whispered with hushed awe: "Have you ever in your life seen anything so beautiful?" I agreed I hadn't. The actors were completely relaxed, living their roles in the circumstances of the characters, with no thought of an audience, and the beautiful language floated into the darkness:

> JEAN: Is this the fish or is this the moon?
> DAN: Shhh. This is the moon. This is the fish and the moon. This is both... We're busy with the strikes; we don't notice it's getting dark. Another couple of strikes, nibbles – bait stealings – nothing serious. And all of a sudden, it's night. Pitch. Ink. We're two hours away, easily. Might as well turn around. So we start back – and... up... drifts... this... orange... Deep orange... unstable... major moon. (*Beat.*) The lake is like...
> JEAN: Glass.
> DAN: ... Very calm. We're rowing back – and it's just beautiful. It's important. We stopped rowing and watched it. And then I threw my line in – (*Simply.*) – just because we were stopping. And – "Galoompba." Immediately. (*Lying in her lap. Swaying with it.*) They swam up to that light like they were mesmerized by the light, dizzy on it...
> JEAN: And that's when you caught them.
> DAN: All – however many of them. Five and seven.
> JEAN: Twelve.
> DAN: All twelve of them.

Here you have sheer poetry, disguised as everyday conversation, surrounded by physical elements as exquisite as a shimmering Monet, with deeply absorbed artists living in a world of transcendent beauty.

One unbelievable detail of our technical agility is that the Sunday afternoon Clive Barnes was to see the play, I suddenly realized that one of the scenes in the second act ought to be transposed with another in the first. Normally, this easily might be assimilated by our actors, but in this case, it also meant instantly re-programming the cueing of multiple slides. I still don't know how we accomplished this feat while *The New York Times* critic waited in the lobby for ten extra minutes, but it came off in performance without a hitch. Thank God for Peter Schneider!

The critics did not universally share our delight. Some found the storytelling too confusing; others found the subject matter too intellectual to follow; some found its gentle lulling conducive to sleep. But others, like Clive Barnes, were ecstatic. *The Mound Builders* opened on February 2, 1975, and played twenty-nine performances. Here are samples of the press reactions:

The New York Times, February 3, 1975 (Mel Gussow):
"Wilson's multi-layered new play is an epic in the guise of a family drama. This is his most ambitious work. One could easily imagine it as a film. The three actresses are excellent: Gordon as the unfaithful wife, Hawkins is the embodiment of the life spirit, [and] in the meatiest role, Berezin gives an indelible portrait of a disenchanted artist and woman. [The play] is one of those rare pieces of theater whose subject has weight and resonance. Wilson leads us on an exploration that is thought-provoking and endlessly fascinating."

The New York Times, March 1, 1975 (Clive Barnes):
"Circle Repertory Company [is] presenting some of the most important drama to be found in the city today. *The Mound Builders* is a marvelous play. It is probably Mr. Wilson's most profound and resonant play to date. It is original and brilliant, and sends you out on the street with your mind spinning cartwheels. It is one of the most interesting American plays in years, and the writing is absolutely masterly. It is a gem."

Daily News, February 3, 1975 (Douglas Watt):

"A stunningly pretentious drama. Mason has staged this with all the loving care one might accord an O'Neill revival, and it is well-acted, especially by Hogan and Berezin. But the play is almost a total bust."

New York Post, February 3, 1975 (Martin Gottfried):

"Wilson's technique and poetry are so dazzling you almost forget the trouble the play has with such minor matters as plot and point. [Wilson has written] a hard-edged melodramatic story – oddly like an action movie. [But] there is a fabulous beauty in the play's writing. Structurally, it is awesome. Berezin [is] very good, and John Strasberg, superb."

The Nation, March 15, 1975 (Harold Clurman):

"Wilson's most ambitious play. [Its] idea is provocative and unmistakably felt. What weakens it is that much of its detail is diffuse and ill-digested. I found myself strangely disturbed by the density as well as the pull and tear of motivations and thoughts, evoked and left unresolved. The play is one I genuinely respect, even in my dissatisfaction with it. [It] is well acted by the entire cast and well directed by Mason. Especially memorable are Strasberg and Berezin."

Village Voice, February 10, 1975 (Dick Brukenfeld):

"Numbing is the word for Wilson's new play. The people are insubstantial, their actions unconvincing, underimagined and superficial. Berezin makes [her] scenes a welcome relief from the pervasive ennui."

After Dark, undated (Patrick Pacheco):

"Provocative and richly textured with layers of meaning, the play is certainly Wilson's most ambitious work to date – and, artistically, his most successful. Under Mason's expert direction, *The Mound Builders* emerged as a stirring and impressive new play, the major dramatic event of this season."

Lanford designed a striking poster for *The Mound Builders* that depicted an artifact resembling a somber, grey face of the moon, floating against an inky black background. He was a graphic artist before he was a playwright and, with the sometime collaboration of Daniel Irvine, Lanford designed many of Circle Rep's award-winning posters. When *The Mound Builders* was published, Lanford dedicated it to Roy London.

Although no commercial transfer followed our run at Circle Rep, PBS chose *The Mound Builders* to be preserved as part of its "Theater in America" series. The following summer, I directed it as my first movie. I'll go into more details shortly.

During the New York run of *The Mound Builders*, Margaret Thatcher became the leader of the Conservative Party in Great Britain, which led to her becoming Britain's first female Prime Minister; Charlie Chaplin was knighted by Queen Elizabeth; and just after we closed, *The Rocky Horror Show* opened on Broadway for only forty-five performances, although it proved to be just the tip of that particular titanic iceberg.

A Dramatic Return To Experimental

It can be argued that by the 1970s, Julie Bovasso was the most important avant-garde theater artist in America. Jerry Tallmer, writing in March 1969 in *Cavalier*, essentially attributes the birth of Off-Broadway to her.

> "Julie started the whole damn thing. Without Bovasso, there might not be a Jack Gelber or an Edward Albee."

He recalls her performance in Genet's *The Maids* as being:

> "the best performance I have ever seen Off-Broadway, one of the best by any actress anywhere."

The Transcendent Years

Writing again in 2005, Tallmer recalls that in the summer of 1955, "Julie Bovasso, age 21 or 22, had walked over the bridge from Brooklyn to Manhattan to build herself that playhouse on St. Marks Place where she introduced Jean Genet to the United States of America. And after Genet, Ionesco; and after Ionesco, Ghelderode."

Julie won the very first Obie Awards given by the *Village Voice* in 1956 for her much heralded performance in Genet's *The Maids* and for Best Experimental Theater at The Tempo Theater, which she founded. She also received both the Drama Desk and the Outer Critics' Circle Awards for Best Actress in Genet's *The Screens*. She received a total of five Obie Awards, including Best Play and Best Director for her 1969 *Gloria and Esperanza*, which became the first off-off-Broadway play to transfer to Broadway, where it ran for thirteen performances at the ANTA Theater. Her play *The Moon Dreamers* played at the Ellen Stewart Theater For twenty-four performances in December 1969.

A triple threat, Julie excelled alternately as playwright, director and actor. She was just the sort of person Circle Rep was founded to nurture. Julie had a gruff, Spartan bearing about her that could be intimidating, but underneath that dour exterior, she was as shy and eager to please as a little girl. She was a complex person, enormously gifted, and to be near her was to sense the torment that raged inside. Our ten years with Julie were equally complex and, ultimately, stormy. But at the beginning and for many years, Julie was a proud and eager participant in Circle Rep's writer's workshops and a Resident Playwright.

As our founding principles outlined, Circle Rep was designed both to keep traditional methods alive and to explore the experimental. Julie brought us an opportunity to keep that second half of our mission thriving. In December of 1971, Julie premiered one of her plays at the Trinity Square Repertory called *Down by the River Where Waterlilies Are Disfigured Every Day*.

Having had such a delightful time with e.e. cummings' *him* the previous season, Marshall Oglesby seemed an ideal partner for this darkly hilarious gothic fantasy. It may be that the script was first brought to us by actor Neil Flanagan, who probably knew Julie had written a role he'd be great for. It reunited Neil with Bobo Lewis, who'd also joined our Company in *him*. We also were able to bring back Cathryn Damon, who'd been so rich and moving in *Prodigal*; and we were introduced to Charles Harper, who was a loyal Company member for many years.

But as often happened, we needed to bring in several actors to play parts we couldn't fill from within the Company. This gave us the amazing luck of working with Linda Hunt in the central role of Constantine. And perhaps because of her early experience with *Escurial*, Julie was fascinated with dwarves, and wrote many roles for them. We found Ruth Hermine was an excellent little actor to play a dwarf. Julie's play also gave us the first occasion to cast black actors at Circle Rep and we found two splendid comediennes to play contrasting maids, Sissy and Missy.

I don't think I can beat Mel Gussow's concise summary of the plot:

> "The palace is under siege. The children's army is on the march. The royal couple – they won their shaky crowns in the Literary Digest Election Sweepstakes – has sought sanctuary in a room filled with blackbirds. The Prime Minister, Count Josef, has a secret yen for the leader of the revolution. His idiot son, Count Junior, is locked in the basement. The countess is in the closet, rattling the bones of the past. While the revolution is in progress, an absurd couple watches through binoculars. She wears a hoop skirt; eventually, he wears her hoopskirt. These two lunatics have lost a son in the battle (or is it a lover?) – and suddenly, he crashes through their wall trailing a parachute."

That gives an idea of the ridiculous, dark, hilarious fantasy that makes up the *Waterlilies* world.

Marshall Oglesby recalls the rehearsals as a joyous collaboration; the cast was very dedicated and concentrated on fulfilling Julie's convoluted, complicated, perilous plots and counter-plots. Julie was busy re-writing and attending rehearsals, marveling at Marshall's ingenious staging, at Cathryn Damon's regal Countess and at Linda Hunt's brilliant, Hamlet-like Constantine. Bobo and Neil (as Clement) were hilarious. I remember one scene in which Phoebe has caught Clement dressing up in her clothes, and this silly couple has a lively argument about the miscues each has been guilty of in their relationship, which has the absurd tag line:

"What watermelon?"

Julie was delighted by the production and pleased to be part of Circle Rep.

Julie Bovasso's *Down by the River Where Waterlilies Are Disfigured Every Day* opened at Circle Rep March 23, 1975, and played thirty-six performances. Marshall Oglesby directed, the set was by John Lee Beatty, the costumes by Jennifer von Mayrhauser, the lighting by Richard Winkler, the sound by Chuck London and George Hansen, the music by Norman L. Berman, and the choreography by Ginger Darnell. The critics were mystified, as usual when confronted with theater of the absurd, and their reactions were predictably mixed. Here are some excerpts:

The New York Times, March 24, 1975 (Mel Gussow):
"*Waterlilies* is a curio cabinet of a fairy tale by Julie Bovasso. It has been handsomely mounted by Marshall Oglesby at Circle Rep. One's enjoyment of it is to be measured by one's fondness for, and indulgence of Bovasso, a very talented artist with a bizarre imagination. Her plot tantalizes the audience with secrets within secrets. The experience is something like walking blindfolded through a funhouse. [Two] characters are amusingly portrayed by Lewis and Flanagan. Damon daffily doubles as the deposed queen and the ghostly countess.

One of the author's most exotic creations is a palace dwarf, delightfully played by Ruth Hermine."

New York Post, March 24, 1975 (Joseph Mancini):
"'What's it all about?' the intermission question that haunts theater lobbies of the absurd would be better phrased, 'What isn't it about?' It treats serious social questions with humor and cynicism. Herschel [is] effectively portrayed by midget actress Ruth Hermine. [It] is nimbly directed by Oglesby, who makes intelligent use of Beatty's sparse and evocative sets, and gets from his cast ensemble acting of remarkable consistency. Bobo Lewis and Linda Hunt wonderfully overplay."

Daily News, March 24, 1975 (Douglas Watt):
"Life is too short to waste time over overly theatrical excrescences as Bovasso's *Waterlilies*. A murky and interminable play, as inexplicable as its title, it was given lavish attention by Circle Rep. The cast is studded with seasoned professionals – Lewis, Damon, Flanagan and many more – and they go about their foolish business with brave conviction. Oglesby has maintained order, but the real hero is designer Beatty."

The Record, March 24, 1975 (Emory Lewis):
"Bovasso is the mad genius of Off-Broadway. She has written some of the funniest and wisest plays of the last decade. But *Waterlilies* is a distinct flop. However, there are two brilliant comics on stage. But the team of Lewis and Flanagan, magnificent as they are, cannot save this unfortunate evening."

Women's Wear Daily, March 25, 1975 (Barbara Ettorre):
"A play which cannot be taken lightly...a well-crafted effort by Bovasso, and comes armed with a sublime cast and top-rate direction. Lewis and Flanagan are convulsively

funny, Linda Hunt is excellent. A fine cast, admirable direction by Oglesby, *Waterlilies* is in glorious bloom."

Village Voice, undated, (Michael Feingold):
"Absurdist in tone, Bovasso's play is Shakespearean in scope, romantic in its language, full of complex parallels and ironies in its plot. The overall effect is oddly fascinating and disturbing; the images intrigue you, sit within you, and are hard to shake. [This is] Oglesby's most cohesive production to date. There is high-quality work from Flanagan and Lewis, Linda Hunt, and the delicate Ruth Hermine, and Verna Hobson, and Sarallen, and most particularly Cathryn Damon."

Upon re-reading them, these reviews are more favorable than I remembered; no wonder Julie was pleased with the production and the reception. While we were cavorting in Julie's mad world, Bobby Fischer was refusing to play chess with Anatoly Karpov, conceding him the championship. On April 4, 1975, Bill Gates founded a company called Microsoft in Albuquerque, New Mexico. And at the end of April, the South Vietnamese government surrendered unconditionally to North Vietnam, ending that lengthy, bloody conflict that cost 58,159 American soldiers their lives and that divided our nation more than anything since the Civil War. We live in a world crazier than anything in Julie Bovasso's imagination.

Circle-In-The-Round

It is probably apparent by now how a Company changes and grows like the organic matter of the universe. We built on the commitment of those who'd sustained us; we accepted the laws of entropy, shedding those who did not move us forward; we added and adapted to the promise of those who could raise the bar and expand our vision. Many who had some contact with Circle Rep will testify that their association with the theater was a positive influence upon their growth as both artists and human beings. Especially following our success, both opportunities and dangers increased. The arrival of Northwestern graduate Corinne Jacker as a Resident Playwright for Circle Rep was a signal advance for our potential.

Corinne was a writer who achieved prominence in both the theater and television. She'd adapted Katherine Ann Porter's apocalyptic short novel *Pale Horse, Pale Rider* for the stage. It debuted at the ANTA Matinee Series at the Theater de Lys for one performance on October 29, 1957. That production starred Northwestern's Margaret Linn, and it moved uptown to the Jan Hus Playhouse for an extended run of forty performances. Subsequently, Corinne became the head writer for the prestigious Children's Television Workshop. I assume Corinne's connection to us was initiated by her close relationship to Maggie Linn, who died during our run of *HOT L* in Los Angeles.

Although Corinne couldn't have been more than in her mid-forties in 1975, she had a grandmotherly quality. She was a little plump, with salt-and-peppered curly hair. Her brown eyes behind her wireless glasses displayed alternately a hard glint that signaled her sharp intelligence, or a twinkle that suggested Mrs. Santa Claus. In addition to her playwriting, Corinne had a scientific background, which enabled her to write scientific treatises as well. She brought me a three-act play that she'd tried out in the summer of 1974 at the O'Neill Festival in Waterford, Connecticut, initially entitled *Taking Care of Harry*. It was a piece written in a Chekhovian style that suited Circle Rep's sensibility. Both the dialogue and the characters were textured, subtle and rich. I was attracted to it immediately and offered to direct it. Being well connected in television, Corinne brought with her the actor she wanted to play the central role of Harry: Kevin McCarthy (of *The Invasion of the Body Snatchers* fame), the first major star who came to work at Circle Rep.

But understanding the nature of ensemble casting, Corinne was eager to utilize the extraordinary talent she knew we could offer from our Company. There were excellent parts for Tanya and Jon Hogan; and there was a plum role that re-united us with

American Theater Project actress, Lois Smith. By the time we went into rehearsal, Corinne settled on a new title: *Harry Outside.*

The play centers on a famous architect, Harry Harrison, who has been recently released from confinement for a mental breakdown. He can no longer accept the restrictions and second-rate standards of modern society. He cannot even bear to stay indoors and instead has set up his studio in a clearing in the woods. As he labors on a new and absorbing project, his life is intertwined with family and friends, who, in various ways, love and admire him. From the skillful and often funny interplay of characters and action, an incisive indictment of contemporary life emerges, capped by Harry's decision to destroy his secret project, lest it too become merely a "container for people," rather than the work of art it was intended to be.

For the fourth time in a row, I turned to John Lee to transform Circle Rep's space into an environment for the production. We decided that since the action takes place outdoors in a clearing in the woods (always hard to depict realistically on a proscenium stage), it might be best to stage the play in the round, so that the audience on all four sides peaked through trees that defined the border of the clearing. He made a floor for the stage that was uneven, with gentle rises and depressions that made the movement of the actors distinctly feel outdoors. Bits of green shag carpet made convincing patches of grass here and there. And over the audience's heads was a canopy of branches and leaves. Once again, the audience entered a world when they entered our theater: the world of the play.

In addition to Kevin McCarthy as Harry and Lois Smith as his wife, Gabby, Tanya Berezin was Irene, his mistress, and Jonathan Hogan was George, a sexually promiscuous young handyman who seems to service everyone. We held auditions to find Alfred Hinckley to play Fred Crosley, Harry's neighbor, Denise Lute as a young lesbian, and Shelly Batt as Lois, Harry's daughter.

The rehearsals went smoothly. Kevin, with all his experience in films and television, had no problem learning his lines before we rehearsed his scenes. His biggest problem was Corinne's eagerness to solve every problem with a re-write. As a television writer, Corinne was used to quick fixes, and Kevin reasoned that sometimes, given the opportunity to explore, an actor could find a solution to an awkward line or convoluted sentence that might shed illumination on his character. He didn't want Corinne to make Harry's journey too smooth. I often agreed with Kevin on this point, but it was difficult to restrain Corinne's enthusiasm to change anything that seemed out of sync.

Again, Jennifer von Mayrhauser found just the right colors to delineate the characters, and Dennis Parichy's dappled light changed with the sun passing through clouds. For a full, rich characterization of an eccentric genius, Kevin McCarthy was rewarded at the end of the season with an Obie Award, which was the fifth for our acting Company.

Corinne Jacker's *Harry Outside* opened at Circle Rep on May 11, 1975, and played thirty-six performances. The reviews were generally warm and supportive. We even got approval from crabby Edith Oliver! Here are excerpts:

The New York Times, May 12, 1975 (Mel Gussow):
"Jacker's absorbing new play takes its cue from Chekhov. It is a life portrait of a community of unfinished people – destructive, self-destructive, yet surviving. Jacker has a piercing gift for disconnected dialogue. Beatty's inviting birch-tree-lined clearing could serve as a setting for [Chekhov]. *Harry Outside* is the kind of naturalistic play that thrives at the Circle. Mason orchestrates it as if it were Chekhov (or Lanford Wilson). The actors are beautifully cast. In addition to Mr. McCarthy, there are outstanding performances from Lois Smith, Tanya Berezin, Jonathan Hogan, and Denise Lute. The company's work is of such a high caliber that *Harry Outside* becomes the capstone of a very successful season. Circle is a match for any institutional theater in the country."

New York Post, May 13, 1975 (Joseph Mancini):

"A healthy reminder that Circle is Off-Broadway's most skillful group. Kevin McCarthy plays Harry brilliantly, with gusto and assurance. Smith is thoroughly convincing in a complex and demanding role. Berezin is a fine actress. Hogan was dazzling. The cast compares with those of Circle's finest productions. Mason's direction is dexterous – bold, but not heavy-handed."

Daily News, May 12, 1975 (Douglas Watt):

"Circle Rep is winding up, or down, a generally disappointing season. [The play] is a lethargic and obscure three-act drama by Jacker. Like most Circle offerings, the play has the benefit of some superior acting and sensitive direction, but the work itself is cheerless and dull. [It] just doesn't play."

The New Yorker, May 19, 1975 (Edith Oliver):

"The production of Jacker's *Harry Outside* is as good as any I've ever seen Off-Broadway – one in which script and performance are so well meshed that it is almost impossible to separate them. A fine outdoor setting by Beatty. Kevin McCarthy [gives] the most accomplished performance I've ever seen him give, and Lois Smith's clear, luminous performance is a perfect match. The other actors are believable too, under Mr. Mason's magic touch."

The Nation, June 6, 1975 (Harold Clurman):

"Circle Rep continues its noteworthy record of presenting interesting pieces by (mostly) new playwrights. Jacker is clearly an intelligent, informed person. If I found the play finally unsatisfactory despite certain well-written passages, I could not fail to follow it with close attention and respect. As in most productions of the Circle Rep directed by Mason, the acting is effortlessly convincing and without false notes. The entire cast is good."

Village Voice, undated (Michael Feingold):
"Jacker's *Harry Outside* is Chekhov and Ibsen brought up to date for the Drifting '70s. Jacker is an excellent writer; every phrase falls right and many of them fall humorously. Mason's production, as always, looks and feels very right. [But] McCarthy's special brand of beefy fervor and Smith's patented line in neurotic edginess come out with the contrived polish of B-movie acting next to the breezy, relaxed quality that Berezin and Hogan bring even to their tensest moments."

Perhaps it was appropriate that as we were presenting our fifth new female playwright, Junko Tabei became the first woman to reach the summit of Mount Everest. This was also the month that India's Prime Minister Indira Gandhi declared a state of emergency and suspended both civil liberties and elections, actions that were used to justify her assassination. And outdoors in America, two FBI agents and one member of the American Indian Movement died in a shootout at the Pine Ridge Indian Reservation in South Dakota, an event known as "The Wounded Knee Incident," to which Marlon Brando referred in turning down his Academy Award for *The Godfather.*

A Special Event

In addition to our Major Productions, we continued to offer artists the chance to do projects of their own. A young director named Jan Eliasberg came to me with a passion to direct Frank Wedekind's *Spring's Awakening*. I always loved this classic on the threshold of modern theater, so I was eager to let Jan mount it. We had some down time between the closing of *Harry Outside* and the final production, so we scheduled her project to fill our stage with an exploration of this extraordinary play.

Although Jan brought her own cast to the production, she introduced us to Lisa Pelikan, who became a Company member, and it gave us a second opportunity for the talented Charles Harper. I have always been a big fan of Kevin Geer and he was memorable in this performance.

Frank Wedekind's *Spring's Awakening* was directed by Jan P. Eliasberg, the set design by Tracy Killion, costumes by Faye Fingesten, lighting by David Kissel, original music by Tom Aronis, stage managers were Susana Meyer and Anne Fishel. It opened on June 12, 1975, and played five performances.

A Playwright Directs

At this point, all scripts submitted to Circle Rep were being read by me, Peter or Marshall Oglesby. When one of us found something he liked, he passed it along to the others. One of the scripts that came in unsolicited was *Not to Worry*, written by a refined man named A.E. Santaniello. The author had previous productions at the Alliance Theater in Atlanta, and had been variously employed as a teacher, editor, landscape architect and house painter. He also had translated Ibsen and Strindberg. I liked *Not to Worry* very much, but as the season at Circle Rep wound down, I was rushing ahead to a summer engagement at the Academy Festival Theater in Lake Forest, Illinois, where I was to direct David Storey's *The Farm*. I gave *Not to Worry* to Lanford to read, and he, too, thought it a wonderful piece of writing. To continue our cross-disciplines tradition, I asked Lanford if he would direct it. Lanford had directed his own plays *This is the Rill Speaking* at the Cino, and *The Rimers of Eldritch* at La MaMa; but this was his debut as a director at Circle. I'm sure Mr. Santaniello must have been flattered that a much-lauded writer would direct his play. They had readings, and cast Rob Thirkield, Brad Dourif and Guest Artist Teri Keane in the three roles.

The play takes place in the French Quarter of New Orleans, in a sub-levee apartment that was formerly slave quarters. It concerns the off-stage dying of a local theater director named Jim, and three friends who come to his empty apartment while he is in the hospital with cancer. Rob's character (Tony) is an old friend from the director's past, now living in New York with a lover, but who has come to be with his old friend as he faces life's end. Brad was Larry, a young kid from Kansas who has been befriended by the director and is now managing the apartment complex. Teri Keane played an amateur actress (Ruth) who'd been in plays at Jim's theater. All three people seem to have a special (and different) attachment to the dying director. But the exact nature of the relationships remains unstated, told in glancing hints. It was a play of subtlety and mystery, which suited Lanford's temperament.

Lanford regretted taking on the assignment; he felt he never was able as a director to do justice to the script. Santaniello was intellectual, exacting, even withering in his observations. He was small in stature, meticulous and fastidious. He seemed pleased by the production and did not offer much in the way of participation. He resembled the character Rob played and Lanford surmised that the play might be somewhat autobiographical, although he never asked. Lanford had difficulty finding a method of work with the actors that was not result-oriented, feeling he was in over his head. "I hated what Rob was doing as an actor, but all I could think of to tell him, was like: 'Walk over there.'" Brad told him to his face he wasn't a very good director, complaining that Lanford never let them improvise or experiment with any of their moments. Altogether, it apparently was not a good experience for anyone and, since I was away in Chicago, there was no one to bridge the communication gap.

Not to Worry by A.E. Santaniello opened at Circle Rep on June 25, 1975, and played twenty performances. It was directed by Lanford Wilson, set design by John Lee Beatty, costumes by Jennifer von Mayrhauser, lighting by Dennis Parichy, sound by Chuck London and George Hansen; stage managers were Walter Wood, Cathy Rennich and Sarah Rodman. Here are samples of the reviews:

The Record, July 3, 1975 (Emory Lewis):

"The most exciting [repertory group] in the city is Circle Rep. Santaniello is a playwright to watch. [This] play is not entirely successful, but I find it more fascinating than half the hits on Broadway. [The author] is an original, charting new territory for the theater, and he deserves a wide hearing. He is a poet of nuance. Santaniello has found the perfect director in Lanford Wilson. The three members of the cast are first-rate. I was particularly impressed by Brad Dourif. Rob Thirkield is absolutely right. Teri Keane is effective."

Daily News, July 3, 2975 (Douglas Watt):
"Not to bother with."

Newsday, July 1, 1975 (Allan Wallach):
"Even Circle Rep makes occasional mistakes. *Not to Worry* is more message than play. Wilson's direction has been unable to keep the play from becoming soapy and unconvincing, and the acting is not up to the company's usual high level. But it is unlikely that even the strongest direction and acting could have salvaged a play that fulfills so few of the demands of theater."

Village Voice, undated, (Michael Feingold):
"[This is] the kind of play I wish the Circle wouldn't do. Beatty has given it a particularly attractive set, and Wilson's staging is fluid and appropriate."

I flew in for the opening from my own rehearsals in Chicago with the remarkable Jack Gwillim, Ruby Holbrook, Nancy Snyder, Debra Mooney, Kristen van Buren and Richard Gere. We were having a wonderful time with David Storey's quietly rich domestic play, *The Farm*, so I was acutely attuned to subtlety and I thought Lanford's production of this moving play was wonderfully understated.

Great Performances

Following the opening of *The Farm* in the Mid-West, PBS sent the cast and television crews from New York to St. Louis to tape *The Mound Builders* for their series called "Great Performances." Some crews and equipment were hired from the local PBS stations. I spent a day off from *The Farm* scouting locations and we found a rickety old farmhouse, a rushing river and a farm field where we could dig pits for our archeological excavations. For me, it was the opportunity I dreamed of: the chance to direct a movie, even though it was recorded on tape, not film, and was shown on television, not in theaters. I was given a crash-course in the basic elements of directing for the camera and I dove into the process with delight.

We were given only one week on location in southern Illinois, across the Missouri River from St. Louis, to get the show on tape, with four cameras all recording everything. I'd have weeks back in New York to edit what we'd shot. As I've mentioned, my rehearsal method is based on a movie-type schedule, so the idea of shooting scenes out of chronological order was no impediment to me or my actors. And the bonus was that Brad Dourif was free to play the role of Chad, which Lanford wrote for him. Otherwise, the cast remained intact from Circle Rep. Regrettably, it was the last time I had the resourceful Peter Schneider at my side, because after the shoot, he began his bright new career as a theater manager.

It was a chance to enlarge the visual storytelling that had been confined by the limitations of the stage. We could go out on the lake fishing with Chad and Dan. We could visit the archeological digs, and actually see the unearthing of the god-king's tomb. Chad could drive a real bulldozer, and the townspeople could come out to search for Dan's body at the end. On a particularly hot August day, we filmed the biggest crowd scene, wherein the townsfolk came out in droves on picnics to watch the archeologists dig. Danny Irvine, in charge of rounding up the extras, assembled hundreds of locals for the scene that ultimately wound up on the cutting-room floor.

The Transcendent Years

We worked at a feverish pace to record this suspenseful saga; it was a challenge to capture the sprawling story in only six days on location. The final night of the shoot, we were filming a scene inside the house, and as dawn approached, it was necessary to wrap the house in tarpaper to sustain an illusion of darkness. Tanya, in a dynamic re-creation of her Obie-winning performance as Delia, appropriately had the very last line of the filming: "I'm familiar with all possible transportation in and out of here."

When *The Mound Builders* aired on February 9, 1976, David Finkle wrote this review in the *Village Voice*:

> "*The Mound Builders* is proof positive that good theater can be transported to television, and more than that, that television can confirm the excellence of new or recent plays. Everything I have hoped for in good television and in good theater is present in *The Mound Builders*. [It] is a landmark along the road in television's slouch toward maturity. [It] is among the five or ten most significant American plays of the decade, and thanks to the collaborative efforts of Jac Venza, the series executive producer; Marshall Mason, who co-directed with Ken Campbell; and the Circle Rep cast, the golden age of television is really here."

As flattering as this review is, I can't quite credit his evaluation. We were rarely as good as our best reviews and seldom as bad as our worst. *The Mound Builders* is a project with decidedly mixed success, not surprising considering that we had six days to shoot a play that ran almost 2-1/2 hours in the theater. I'm satisfied with some scenes, particularly those between Brad and Trish, where the beauty and complexity of the play are accompanied by sharp cinematography, with the restless river running behind the scene. There are moments of real drama captured on camera when Tanya and Jonathan exchange ironies, or when Trish confesses her uneasiness to Tanya in intimate scenes between them. The "fish and the moon" scene only approximated the fineness we'd achieved in the theater, but it's still beautiful.

Rob's performance is stolidly wooden in the movie (as he never was on stage), which robs the story of much of its power. When Jac Venza, the Executive Producer of the Great Performances series saw my first cut, which ran two hours, he declared it the worst mess PBS ever produced, and sent us back into the editing room to make sense out of it, and to lose half an hour of screen time. I regret the loss of my *Gone with the Wind* scene of the townspeople picnicking at the archeological site, but Mr. Venza was right: it had to go.

At the climax of the story, Dan comes downstairs in the middle of the night with a flashlight (as he has before) and this time discovers a bare-chested Chad, wearing the gold mask of the god-king, and hauling away the precious artifacts the scientists have extracted. Chad ominously orders Dan:

"Come outside, there's something I want to show you."

I think we captured the climactic suspense of this scene thoroughly, followed by shots of Chad aboard a bulldozer, wrecking the archeological site. It's chilling stuff.

While the women may have been unfair in their evaluation of "Cochise," Chad's wrecking of the site means the destruction of all evidence about his life, so he has indeed "vanished without a trace." Jean spells out Dan's fate at the end of the movie, echoing the phrase "Vanished without a trace." I'm grateful that this relic of Circle Rep remains as imperfect evidence of our excellence, and that we have not suffered the fate of Cochise and Dan, and disappeared entirely.

In a grim irony, as we were making our movie, on July 31, 1975, in Detroit, Michigan, Teamsters Union president Jimmy Hoffa was reported missing. Neither he nor his remains have ever been found.

Sustaining Excellence

On July 25, 1975, about two weeks after our final production of the season closed, *A Chorus Line* moved from Joseph Papp's Public

Theater to the Shubert Theater on Broadway, where it ran for almost fifteen years, reaching 6,137 performances, the longest running Broadway show in history at the time.

Also this season, our homegrown actor Zane Lasky starred on Broadway with Cleavon Little and Barnard Hughes in *All Over Town*. This comedy by Murray Schisgal was the only production directed by Dustin Hoffman. The play has a libidinous central character named Louie, clearly the role Dustin Hoffman himself would have played if he were younger. He cast Zane in the part and Zane delivered a funny characterization that was a human approximation of the Energizer Bunny. The production played in New York at the Booth Theater for 233 performances.

Other Company members were achieving success in television and film. Brad won a Golden Globe and a British Academy Award for *Cuckoo's Nest*. Judd starred as Murray Stone in a television miniseries called *The Law*, a follow-up to an Emmy-winning movie of the same name. David Groh became a television star playing Joe Gerard in *Rhoda*. His highly anticipated "marriage" to Valerie Harper was the highest rated episode of that show's entire 56-episode run.

Chatty starred in Norman Lear's misbegotten television series based on *The HOT L BALTIMORE*. It was Mr. Lear's first flop and was cancelled after only thirteen episodes. The perception was that American audiences were not ready for a television comedy about a prostitute, but I'm convinced that its failure was due to a wrongheaded premise, for which Lanford and I must take responsibility. We eschewed involvement in the transition of the play to television, leaving the Hollywood writers mystified as to how to write like Lanford Wilson.

As for Circle Rep, *HOT L* continued running into its third year Off-Broadway. Ted Mann and Paul Libin presented us with a plaque marking the most performances in the history of the Circle-in-the-Square Theater. *HOT L*'s sustained run provided Circle Rep with support in two ways: our theater received a small percentage of the gross box-office; and as long as I was receiving a royalty as a director, Circle saved the expense of having to pay a reasonable artistic director's salary.

Our sixth season was recognized as an outstanding year by many sources. *Harry Outside* and *The Mound Builders* were named on several Ten Best lists and Tennessee Williams joined Circle as a Resident Playwright, promising us a new play the following year. At the Obie Awards, Lanford received a second Obie for Playwriting; Kevin McCarthy and Tanya Berezin were recognized for Outstanding Performances; John Lee Beatty was recognized for his sets of *Battle of Angels*, *Waterlilies* and *The Mound Builders*; while I received Obie Awards for directing both *Battle of Angels* and *The Mound Builders*. The list of our honors kept growing, and the recognition of our excellence kept increasing.

If I were to select one year that embodied the transcendent years of Circle Rep, I think it was our sixth season. The commercial success of our previous two seasons bought us a comfortable zone of creativity, freed from the doubts and struggles of our earlier years. We had professional management, so we were free to put all our energy into generating our living theater on stage. We had a new home flexible enough to accommodate our artistic ingenuity. We were in the very heart of Greenwich Village, a revered incubator of experimentation and innovation in all the arts, where Circle Rep was welcomed as an instant Village landmark.

John Lee Beatty and Jennifer von Mayrhauser designed all five Major Productions, in a dazzling display of imagination and resourcefulness. Dennis Parichy and Chuck London provided illumination and sound that broke ground in artistic innovation.

Our repertoire was an embodiment of our mission: preserving the traditional in our rediscovery of a forgotten play by America's greatest playwright, Tennessee Williams; and exploring the experimental with Off-Broadway's most innovative visionary, Julie Bovasso. We followed the success of Lanford Wilson, widely believed to offer the brightest promise for the future of American drama, with an excavation of conflicting values; we introduced two new distinctive voices that were welcomed for their fresh talents in Corinne Jacker and A.E. Santaniello, with plays flawed enough to attest to our courage, yet provocative enough to merit a hearing.

THE TRANSCENDENT YEARS

I directed three of the Major Productions, delivering performances hailed as being among the finest in New York. We enjoyed the solid contributions of Marshall Oglesby and Lanford Wilson, directing with flair and sensitivity. We were stimulated by the presence on our stage of fine Guest Artists like John Strasberg, Linda Hunt, Cathryn Damon, Kevin McCarthy and Lois Smith.

Our core Company had grown and matured in artistry, with memorable performances by Tanya, Trish, Chatty, Stephanie, Sharon, Debra Mooney, Bobo Lewis, Berrilla, Jon Hogan, Jack Davidson, Neil Flanagan, Charles Harper, Brad and Rob. These fourteen actors indeed made up the finest ensemble in the country.

Our move to Sheridan Square was a new beginning, but it also was a culmination of a fresh force in the American Theater. We never again enjoyed quite the innocence and purity of vision that peaked in our sixth season. It was a golden year.

CHAPTER 10
INTO THE FIRMAMENT

Success is a lens that distorts reality: it magnifies everything, virtues and imperfections alike. By our seventh year, Circle Rep was established as a laboratory of creativity. We had captured the public's attention; now the challenge was to sustain our growing aura.

Autumn of 1975 paraded a civilization flipping from perils to peculiarities. President Ford survived two assassination attempts in seventeen days: first Lynette (Squeaky) Fromme, a follower of the imprisoned but not disempowered Charles Manson; and then Sara Jane Moore, an amateur radical infatuated with Patty Hearst, who'd been captured in San Francisco only four days earlier. In Rome, Pope Paul VI canonized Elizabeth Seton, the first American Catholic saint. On the same day in Amsterdam, Rembrandt's *The Night Watch* was slashed a dozen times by an unemployed schoolteacher at the Rijksmuseum. One step forward, three steps back.

October brought the final installment of the Joe Frazier/Muhammad Ali trilogy of heavyweight championship bouts. This match, held in the Philippines, was dubbed *The Thrilla in Manila*, and is ranked as one of the greatest fights of 20th century boxing. Ali defeated Frazier in their climactic meeting with a TKO in the 14th round.

On a lighter note, October 11, 1975 was the debut of NBC's *Saturday Night Live*. George Carlin was the first host, while Billy Preston and Janis Ian were the first musical guests. Maybe this was a good time to schedule a kooky comedy with social commentary to open our seventh season.

Bringing Back Berrilla

Circle Rep enjoyed a modest success in our third season with Berrilla Kerr's offbeat comedy *The Elephant in the House*, but few of our present subscribers had seen it. We'd been hidden away in our second story loft on the Upper West Side, not yet "on the map." I thought Berrilla deserved a second showing in our improved circumstances. We could also welcome back Helen Stenborg with a juicy role after playing Millie in *The HOT L BALTIMORE* for the past two years. Jane Cronin, who was so spectacular in *Elephant* originally, was now ensconced as April in *HOT L*; but Helen was ready for a change.

The role was Mary Elizabeth Adams, an eccentric old invalid who rules from her bed over a bizarre and tumultuous household. Neil Flanagan played her sympathetic caretaker, Mr. Johnson (a change of pace for him). A revival allowed us to initiate Lisa Pelikan as a member of the Company to play the teenage runaway, Francesca. Stephanie Gordon, who tackled that part in the first production (a casting stretch), now shifted to the part of Jennie, with Conchata Ferrell returning from her television series to play Molly. Rob Thirkield could be a wacky Horace, replacing Stephen de Fluiter, who was no longer with the Company; and Henrietta Bagley could repeat as Gwyneth, the bag lady.

This revival was a well-intentioned mistake. The casting was off: Helen's natural nobility undermined Mary Elizabeth's quirkiness. Chatty was too substantial for the quirky kook she was asked to play. The biggest loss was Zane Lasky as the AWOL soldier Timmy, since Zane had joined *The Tony Randall Show* on television. A young actor named Terence Foley tried, but could not fill Zane's comic footprint. John Lee designed a set with flocked wallpaper that was too stodgy for this eccentric world. Jennifer von Mayrhauser's costumes were too fine for these ragtag characters. And somehow, Dennis Parichy's lighting was too lyrical for this absurd trifle. In short, I didn't direct it very well. My earthbound revival lost the light touch of whimsy that delighted the first time around. Only Lisa Pelikan achieved the right note as the gamin Francesca.

The Elephant in the House by Berrilla Kerr opened at Circle Rep on November 2, 1975 and played thirty-two performances. In addition to the above-mentioned credits, Jonathan Hogan provided the original music; Chuck London and George Hansen afforded the minimal sound design, and the stage manager was Dave Clow. Here are excerpts of the reviews:

The New York Times, November 4, 1975 (Mel Gussow):
"Mason has staged the play with his usual careful attention to atmospheric detail. The cast [made] the evening something of a homecoming. The only thing missing was a good play. Helen Stenborg, a graceful actress, keeps the invalid from being cloying. Terence Foley in his professional debut is disarming. Most convincing is Neil Flanagan, [who] finds acres of character in this sweet-tempered man. Thirkield's performance is leaden. *Elephant in the House* is an unwarranted expenditure of energies and resources of a number of talented people."

Daily News, November 3, 1975 (Douglas Watt):
"This play revealed [nothing] except a humorless, disordered, and rather tasteless approach to the craft of playwriting."

New York Post, November 3, 1975 (Sylviane Gold):
"Kerr has written an unwieldy beast of a play [with] some superbly silly lines, some inventive humor, and some nicely ridiculous characters. Stenborg [gives] a lovely performance. Mason's direction [is] dull."

Newsday, November 3, 1975 (Len Seligsohn):
"Kerr's new play starts out as a first-rate comedy and winds up as a third-rate circus. Overall, *Elephant* provides an unusual, sometimes exciting, sometimes disappointing ride."

Village Voice, November 10, 1975 (Michael Feingold):

"Kerr's [play] is a nice, friendly, conventional American play [recalling] Giraudoux and Anouilh. Circle had better buckle down to the serious business of Chekhov, Congreve, Shaw, and Sheridan. Kerr's is not a new play, but a number of old ones gracefully rearranged, and in that there is no artistic future for a serious theater."

The danger of wanting to be taken seriously is that some will take you seriously.

If At First...

We fared only slightly better with our second production. Marshall Oglesby discovered a script by Andrew Colmar that struck his fancy. It was called *Dancing for the Kaiser.* The play is set in World War I and the story centers on an Isadora Duncan-like dancer whose role as Oscar Wilde's Salome triggers a moral crisis and a political dispute in wartime London. Mel Gussow described the thick melodramatic plot this way in his review:

"The play has more than enough ingredients for a Masterpiece Theater series – intrigue, lesbianism, a case of libel, scenes that spin from tearoom to court room."

Probably the most important legacy of this elaborate production was that it introduced us to the wonderful actor Douglass Watson, who became a valuable member of the acting Company. It also reunited us briefly with Joanna Miles, who played in *Home Free!* ten years earlier. The play had a cast of twelve, playing sixteen roles, and Oglesby put together a splendid troupe of master actors that included Tom McDermott, George Hall, Peter Walker, Peter Murphy and Jacqueline Bertrand.

As Oglesby went into rehearsal on this purposefully antiquated play, fascinating events were taking place on the world stage. The 729-foot-long freighter SS Edmund Fitzgerald sank during a storm on Lake Superior, killing all twenty-nine crew on board (an event immortalized in song by Gordon Lightfoot). Former California Governor and screen actor Ronald Reagan challenged incumbent President Gerald Ford for the Republican presidential nomination. Ford beat back this challenge, only to lose to Jimmie Carter; but Reagan was back four years later to make his lasting mark on American politics. Spanish dictator Francisco Franco finally died (providing *SNL* with its longest running gag: "Franco is still dead"), ending the dictatorship that followed the Spanish Civil War. Juan Carlos was declared King, ushering in modern Spain's transition to democracy.

And on our stage, we were harking back even earlier, to 1918. *Dancing for the Kaiser* by Andrew Colmar opened at Circle Rep on December 14, 1975 and played thirty-two performances. It was directed by Marshall Oglesby, with sets by Atkins Pace, costumes by Jennifer von Mayrhauser, lighting by Dennis Parichy, Choreography by Gilda Mullette, with sound by George Hansen and Chuck London. Here are selected reviews:

The New York Times, December 16, 1975 (Mel Gussow):
"Colmar's new play is designed to resemble an old play. Pace's set design and von Mayrhauser's costumes seem scrupulously in period. [It's] a juicy fruitcake of a play, long on plot and short on style. The play wavers between pomposity and parody. The performances are good, though not inspired, with the exception of Douglass Watson, [who] has style, easily the most enjoyable character on stage. Joanna Miles is effective as the heroine, although, perhaps, she lacks a certain panache and mystery. [But the play] simply seems antiquated."

New York Post, December 15, 1975 (Sylviane Gold):
"*Dancing for the Kaiser* is brimming with sex and politics, manners and morals, and characters that belong in some endless BBC serial. [It's] a difficult play to do, but Oglesby has solved the problem cleverly with the help of Pace's sets and the Circle's versatile space. He draws uniformly good performances from a cast headed by Douglass Watson and

Joanna Miles. Despite the fine acting, Colmar's characters remain incomplete. Still, it's a cracking good gothic story, a pleasure rare enough in the theater."

Daily News, December 15, 1975 (Douglas Watt):
"Given a certain kind of sensibility, as well as writing with a flourish to match the nutty conception, I suppose this could provide some amusement. But even with all the help it gets, including Pace's admirable settings, von Mayrhauser's often impressive costumes, and Oglesby's deft staging, it doesn't come off. There's good trash and bad trash, and *Dancing for the Kaiser* can't quite make up its mind which it wants to be."

The Record, December 15, 1975 (Emory Lewis)
"A fascinating flop. The cast, within the limitations of a flawed script, is impressive. [It's] been helped tremendously by the magnificent period sets designed by Atkin Pace. Von Mayrhauser's costumes [are] dazzling."

The New Yorker, undated (Edith Oliver):
"I found the whole enterprise preposterous, but not boring."

It's hard to justify how little I remember of this production, but I think I saw it only once, on the opening night; which brings to mind the subject that follows.

A Vacuum At The Top

If you'll indulge a bit of self-criticism, I never felt I was a very good Artistic Director. I prided myself on my own productions, but I fell short when guiding other artistic activities that were also my responsibility.

When I directed *HOT L* at the Mark Taper Forum, Gordon Davidson showed me how an Artistic Director ought to influence the work created under his leadership. Gordon was warmly supportive; he attended casting sessions, an occasional rehearsal, and all of the dress rehearsals. While never intrusive, he provided a valuable third perspective for Lanford and me. He was always available to provide sage observations at crucial moments, especially toward the end of the process, when a director, exhausted from tech rehearsals, may be so lost in the thicket he cannot remember the arbor.

Apart from his direct involvement, Gordon created at the Taper an institution that was sensitive and responsive to artistic needs. His staff was knowledgeable and alert to any need: from the casting director to the dramaturg to the technical director and their staffs.

In that last regard, I did pretty well: I assembled a first-rate technical staff. My designers were the foremost in New York. My stage managers evolved into a group with high professional standards. The addition of Earl Hughes as Technical Director vaulted Circle Rep into technical artistry, and he drafted Bobby Yanez (who later succeeded Earl as Tech Director) to join him in building and engineering both the construction and instillation of the sets. This was a particularly demanding job, because at Circle Rep, we didn't just build a set for a production; we constructed a whole different theater space from one show to the next, creating an environment that became the world of the play. This meant shifting the audience seating into new configurations with each production, as the stage migrated from one location to another. Our sets were constructed in our space, during the down time between productions. The consistent amazement of the critics and their high praise is a tribute to Earl and Bobby, as well as the designers.

It was another five years before we added a dramaturg and literary manager to our artistic staff. Because we were a Company of actors, we saw no need for a casting director at this point. In the interim, these tasks were covered by a talented succession of people who served as Assistant to the Artistic Director. Following Peter Schneider's departure at the end of our sixth season, an able young man named Steve Gomer followed him as my assistant. Born in Yonkers, Steve came to me after his study at the State University of New York. He was an excellent successor to Peter and, like him, had a distinguished career in Hollywood after he left Circle.

He was followed by Carol Patella for two years, and then Glenna Clay. Still, although my assistants were uniformly capable, they hardly could compare to the expertise of the staff of the Taper. Jerry Arrow continued as Executive Director and for the first time, we hired an in-house Press Representative, a resourceful lady named Rima Corben, who remained with us for the next four years. This core staff was crucial to challenges that lay ahead.

I subsequently worked at other theaters with outstanding leaders, including Zelda Fichandler at the Arena Stage in Washington, and my experiences confirmed my belief that many other people understood and performed the job of Artistic Director better than I.

When I've made these observations to friends, I've been greeted with a host of well-meant protestations, pointing out Circle Rep's lengthy history of producing high-quality theater. I appreciate that my vision lent me a standing that perhaps I partially deserved. But during my eighteen years as Artistic Director, the productions that I directed fared better than those where my responsibility was to support my fellow directors.

I attribute this fault to an over-sensitive concern that each director at Circle Rep should have artistic freedom. As a result, I never attended another director's rehearsals. Even at critical junctures like dress rehearsals or previews, I failed to provide the support and guidance a good Artistic Director imparts.

Dancing for the Kaiser is a case in point; I didn't see the play until the first performance. I also didn't participate in the casting. I don't know why I permitted Marshall Oglesby to mount a Major Production without a single member of our acting Company, thereby violating a fundamental principle of our theater: if a play couldn't be cast mainly from within our Company, we shouldn't be doing the play. In this case, none of our actors seemed suitable for the "Masterpiece Theater" style the play required. Yet, I allowed the production to go forward, for reasons I can neither recollect nor defend. I was nevertheless pleased that Oglesby was able to attract such a distinguished cast to Circle Rep. Our acting Company continued to grow as we were introduced to inspiring fellow artists and despite a couple of disappointing plays to begin our seventh season, we stood on the cusp of a blockbuster that expanded our universe and catapulted our reputation into a new orbit. But before we get to that, during rehearsals for *Dancing for the Kaiser*, another Circle Rep milestone was reached.

End Of The Line

Kermit posted the official notice that the long journey known as *The HOT L BALTIMORE* would pull into the station for its final performance on November 30. It had been a long ride, filled with so many joys it's like counting the ties in a railroad track to recall.

I decided something special should commemorate this extraordinary event. I invited everyone who'd ever been in the production to participate in its historic final stop. I came up with a unique idea: every actor who'd ever played in *HOT L* was seated in the front rows of the theater, and the roles were passed off in tag-team fashion throughout the performance to whoever had played each role. Many alumni showed up and took part. My idea was later duplicated by the final performance of *A Chorus Line* on April 28, 1990, but we did it fifteen years earlier.

We began the performance with the original cast. At different points throughout the play, the characters tagged the actors who had followed them in the roles, and the tagged actor entered the action and continued the unbroken narrative without a pause. It was the most beautiful performance of *HOT L* ever; it was thrilling to watch the play come to life and sustain that life through each character's subsequent incarnation. It was a tribute, not only to the stalwart players who served the production through its long run, but also a tribute to Lanford, who gave us his play to bring to life, night after night for 1,166 performances.

Who's There?

Two years earlier, in the autumn of 1973 when we were presenting *Red Ryder* at Circle Rep, Kermit Bloomgarden asked me to read a play he was keen to produce on Broadway. He said that although he loved it, the play was complicated and unconventional, and he wanted to know what I thought. The play was called *Cohn of Arc,* and it was written by a renowned cartoonist, Jules Feiffer.

In his 1967 playwriting debut, Jules suffered unfavorable critical responses to the Broadway production of *Little Murders,* a biting satire starring Barbara Cook and Elliott Gould. I was lucky enough to catch one of its seven performances and unlike the critics, I thoroughly enjoyed it. Jules' faith in the script was justified soon afterwards by a well-received production at the Royal Shakespeare Company in London; and subsequently in 1969 by a successful revival Off-Broadway at the Circle-in-the-Square, directed by Alan Arkin, which ran 400 performances and won Jules an Obie for Distinguished Play.

His new play was not as dark, but it was a lot wackier. Two late middle-aged men, one a retired stockbroker (Abe) and the other a long-unemployed musician (Cohn), have retreated into an isolated cabin in the woods, away from the hypocrisy of the world. But after twenty years, their nitpicking philosophical differences are increasingly annoying. Arguing about the nature of reality, Cohn rubs an oil lamp to demonstrate there is no such thing as magic, and in a puff of smoke, a Genie appears. Suddenly, there is a knock at the door, which introduces a series of "knock-knock" jokes before they open the door to reveal a young blonde woman in shining medieval armor. She announces that she is Joan of Arc and has come to lead them to heaven, which will involve migrating in spaceships, two by two. Subsequently, she tells them she was previously Cinderella, and before long, the chauvinists have reduced her mission to scrubbing floors. Throughout the play, there is a fantastical character named Wiseman, who employs a variety of different identities to dramatize the old men's shortcomings. At the end of the play, Joan rapturously ascends to heaven, departing with a plethora of sardonic platitudes worthy of Voltaire.

As fanciful as Joan's mission might sound, in 1975 some members of Jehovah's Witnesses actually believed that Armageddon would arrive within the year; some were selling their houses and businesses to prepare for a new world paradise, when Jesus would set up God's Kingdom on earth. On the other hand, NASA recently launched the Viking 1 planetary probe toward Mars. Who knows what's really real? I loved the premise of the play, but it was written in a hodgepodge of styles. I told Kermit I thought it needed polishing before it would be ready for Broadway.

Independently from my chance reading of the script for Kermit, I got a call from Jules Feiffer himself. He had seen *HOT L* and he was impressed by the depth of reality the ensemble achieved. He wanted me to direct his play. I was flattered; Jules was a world-famous cartoonist, whose weekly satires were insightful, acerbic commentaries on the often-ridiculous life of our times. When I picked up the *Voice*, I always turned first to the Feiffer cartoon.

Jules Feiffer was born on January 26, 1929 in the Bronx, where he graduated from James Monroe High School. At age sixteen, he began as an assistant to writer-artist Will Eisner, whose comic strip *The Spirit* appeared in a seven-page insert in Sunday newspaper comics sections. Although from childhood, Jules wanted to be a cartoonist, as he matured he found the confines of the comic strip too limiting for his imagination. He began to want more than anything to be recognized as a playwright.

When I went to his apartment on Riverside Drive, I tingled with anticipation. This famous man wanted to work with me! Once admitted by the doorman, I rode the elevator up to his tenth floor apartment, which turned out to be rather modest: two bedrooms with hardwood floors and a small living room with a dining alcove, where Jules had set up a drawing board to do his artwork. Separated from Judith, his first wife, he lived here with his daughter Halley, a teenager who split her time between Jules and her mother. Jules had a charming girlfriend named Susan, a painter who had her own apartment.

Jules actually resembled some of the apprehensive characters in his cartoons. He is very tall (maybe 6'3") with an egg-shaped head (appropriately) and a forehead etched with wrinkles above his anxious blue eyes. His black-rimmed glasses contributed to an impression of a serious intellectual with minimal self-confidence, as if anticipating that something dreadful might occur if he relaxed for a second. It is a persona that elicits instant affection and a protective determination to see that nothing bad is going to happen to him while *you're* around.

We sat in the living room, and began to talk about the play. I enthusiastically praised its possibilities and pinpointed a few areas where I was confused. Jules was eager to hear my questions and agreed to work on the sections I noted. We made an appointment to get together again in a few weeks. Our work together was smooth and congenial, based on mutual admiration. I felt as comfortable collaborating with Jules as I had with Lanford. During our months of working on the script, he re-titled the play *Knock Knock*, which I thought was provocative and appealing. Everyone knows a knock-knock joke; they surely would be eager to hear Jules Feiffer's.

Once we had the play in better shape, we started talking to Broadway producers, beginning, of course, with Kermit. Unfortunately, Kermit strongly felt the play was so idiosyncratic it needed to be cast with stars to succeed on Broadway, an approach to casting that was an anathema to me. Still, we gave Kermit a chance: he talked to Herschel Bernardi, Barbara Harris, even Jane Fonda. But nobody made a commitment, so Kermit allowed his option to expire.

We next tried talking to Adela Holzer, but we made a quick exit when she insisted we change directors. Not long after we met with her, Adela was indicted on one hundred thirty-seven counts of larceny and falsifying records. At her trial, the charges were reduced, but she was convicted of seven counts of stealing $77,500 from her investors. She was sentenced to prison for four to six years. After her release, she was indicted again in 2002, found guilty of swindling immigrants out of $200,000 and was sentenced to nine to eighteen years in prison. She finally was released in 2010 at the age of eighty-two.

Skirting that landmine, we moved on to comedian and producer Alan King, but after several weeks, it was apparent we were getting nowhere with him; he was juggling a number of Hollywood projects at the same time.

Frustrated, I suggested that we produce *Knock Knock* at Circle Rep as part of our seventh season. I reasoned that in this way, we could cast the production with actors we felt were right for the parts and we could produce the play without artistic compromise. Both Jules and I thought the play deserved a wider audience than Off-Broadway could provide, but perhaps if our reviews were good, it could move to a commercial run, as *HOT L, Red Ryder* and *Sea Horse* had done.

Once we decided to produce the play at Circle Rep, two producers suddenly turned up who were willing to commit to a Broadway transfer, even before the reviews. This helped, because the play had technical requirements that were beyond Circle Rep's normal budgets. So in return for getting advance rights to move the play from Circle Rep to Broadway, they gave us "seed money" of $10,000, about one-fifth of Circle Rep's budget for the show, to help with extra production costs.

The two people were Broadway producer Harry Rigby, bankrolled by socialite and theater dilettante Terry Allen Kramer. Right from the beginning this was a case of "strange bedfellows," but we were eager to get the play on, so we overlooked the oddity of a left-wing cartoonist and a serious director being hooked up with a producer of schlock revivals like *No, No, Nanette,* underwritten by a Republican heiress. Harry and Terry had teamed up the previous year for a revival of *Good News,* which played fifty-one previews and only sixteen performances. *Knock Knock* would be Terry's second production, so it was going to be a learning experience for everyone.

Casting the play was a crucial ingredient to its success. The previous year I'd had conversations with Joseph Chaiken about coming to Circle Rep to direct a production of Chekhov's *The Seagull.* It would have been a coup for Circle to embrace the founder of the Open

Theater, and to give him a home after his company disbanded. But there were scheduling problems: the success of *Red Ryder* and *Sea Horse* kept me preoccupied. Then, we had the task of moving our whole operation to a new theater and new offices. Sometime during this period of our irresistible hurtle forward, Manhattan Theatre Club came up with dates that suited Joe, so his production of *The Seagull* was slated to play there. Sorry I'd missed an historic opportunity, I was eager to see Joe's production, so I was there for the opening night. The production starred Leueen MacGrath as Arkadina, a perfect piece of casting. Playing her brother Sorin was Daniel Seltzer, an actor I had not seen before. Dan was a professor of English at Princeton University and a Shakespearean scholar; but his true talent lay in his extraordinary acting. In the third act of *The Seagull* when the ailing Sorin falls asleep, he is so still that for a terrifying moment, his friends and family think he has died. When the moment came, I was certain the actor, Dan Seltzer, actually had passed away on stage before my very eyes. The audience fully shared the moment of panic felt by the cast on stage. Then he snored, and Chekhov scored his tender joke as we all sighed with relief; death has been avoided for now, though, as Chekhov intends for us to realize, not forever. Dan was so brilliant I realized how perfect he was for Cohn, the Jewish curmudgeon at the center of Jules' play. I sent Jules to see the production and he agreed. Dan was a gift from the gods of casting.

I knew I could fill the other two male roles with Circle Rep veterans Neil Flanagan and Judd Hirsch. The script does not specify that both Cohn and Abe are Jewish, but because it was written by Feiffer, that was the assumption. I didn't think it was important for Abe to be Jewish and I knew our multi-talented Neil could be hilarious yet grounded in the part of Abe. The fact that Neil is Irish suggested a line of Jesuit questioning in the part of the skeptical Abe, providing a perfect foil for Dan's Talmudic Cohn. Although he'd starred in a mini-series on television, Judd Hirsch was not yet a box-office star. In New York, he was still best known for playing Bill in *HOT L*. Extremely versatile, Judd possesses a manic liveliness that is a complete opposite of his role as Bill, more akin to the frenetic energy we associate with Robin Williams (or as some reviewers noted, Sid Caesar). I had no doubt he could portray the multiple characterizations of Wiseman. Jules knew Neil and Judd from Circle Rep productions and was pleased with the casting.

Finding Joan was more problematic. She must embody Cohn's longing for hope and common sense, as indelible as the image of Carla that haunts Guido in Fellini's *8–1/2*. Fortunately, the gods of casting smiled on us again. I was conducting auditions to replace the role of The Girl in *The HOT L BALTIMORE*, winding down in its third year. When the transcendent Nancy Snyder read for me, I knew I'd found an actress with a magic all her own that might match even Trish Hawkins. But I was not about to waste her talent in the final weeks of a long-running hit; there was something much better in store for her. She was exactly the quirky kind of *shiksa* that could inspire two old curmudgeons to believe that she actually might be Joan of Arc. Nancy, born in Kankakee, Illinois in 1949, became one of our acting Company's most luminous actresses. Apart from her stage work, all of which was exclusively with Circle Rep, Nancy went on to star as Katrina Karr on the ABC soap opera, *One Life to Live*. Tall, willowy and gorgeously blonde, Nancy was the personification of Jules' fantasy. I called him right away and arranged a solo audition for Nancy the next afternoon. When she read, Jules' was ecstatic. He could see his play coming to life even before we began rehearsals.

Turning to the challenges of the set, I posed the problems to John Lee Beatty: an isolated cabin in the woods with the reality of a working stove, but with the archetypal resonance of a fairy tale setting. Also, the set had to accommodate magical appearances: Wiseman emerges from a trunk for his first entrance, and his subsequent entrances must seem equally surprising. At the conclusion, the walls of the house are blown away, so that Cohn wanders out into the open for the first time, re-encountering the reality he has left behind twenty years before. And there is the problem of devising a means for Joan to ascend to heaven at the end, a predicament made especially challenging by the relatively low ceiling at Circle Rep. John Lee's solutions to these problems were amazing; the deceptively simple cabin we see at the beginning was in reality a complex, intricate collection of tricky devices.

Jennifer von Mayrhauser's costumes needed to cover a wide range of styles within this magical world. Particularly important was the image of Joan of Arc, which needed to be both stunning and authentic. With the help of Dennis Parichy's miraculous lighting, the sight of Nancy in shining silver armor, a sword at her side, a white banner on a standard in her hand and a white plume on her helmet was dazzling, a paradigm of hope. The dowdy clothes of Cohn and Abe were likewise exactly right, using Jennifer's acute eye for blending colors and shades to produce an effortless but ideal effect. And the multiple costumes that Wiseman requires were a designer's delight. In Jennifer's array of costumes, Judd became a prototype of each image: a turbaned genie; an ominous Viennese psychiatrist/inquisitor in a black suit; a riverboat gambler with a roué image of Gaylord Ravenal; and a Judge, whose voluminous black robes were a sight gag from the Marx Brothers.

As noted, Dennis Parichy's lighting needed to serve a variety of moods, from the domestic realism of the opening scenes, to Joan's transforming entrance, to Wiseman's mysterious appearances, to the streams of sunlight breaking through the woods to suggest a glow of heavenly radiance.

But most challenging of all were the requirements for a degree of sound design that had never before been imagined. Jules envisioned Joan's Voices as two quarrelsome noodges, constantly nagging her with contradictory advice. The recorded Voices were played by Judd Hirsch, but they needed to emanate from the common articles in the cabin; so Joan's Voices spoke to her from surprising sources all over the stage: the tea kettle spoke, and the newel post answered; the doorknob prodded her, and the toaster pulled her back; the rafters of the roof contended with the floorboards. Chuck London and George Hansen devised multiple disguised speakers and invented complex sound engineering never previously employed in a stage production. The results were astonishing and hilarious.

Our technical director, Earl Hughes, contacted a specialist in illusions named Robert E. McCarthy to suggest solutions for our magical requirements. He guided John Lee in designing tricks that provided the necessary surprises. For Joan's ascent at the end, there was a hydraulic lift hidden in the beam between the kitchen and the door with a four-foot arm invisible to the audience that fastened onto a harness hidden beneath Joan's Cinderella clothes. It lifted Nancy about five feet up, paused there with Nancy suspended in mid-air, for Joan's parting address and then, as she continued her ascent the lights went out just before her head reached our twelve-foot ceiling. The illusion, with a little suspension of disbelief, was remarkably effective.

The rehearsals were a joy. In the opening scene, I put Cohn in the kitchen, preparing a stew for dinner, stirring a fragrant pot on the stove that wafted the aroma into the audience. I wanted the audience to settle into this cozy scene of familiar domesticity so they would relax and be prepared to go along with the many surprises we had in store for them. Abe sat at the table doing a crossword puzzle. The dialogue at the beginning is comic philosophical bickering on the nature of reality. Cohn challenges Abe's perceptions by holding up two fingers and demanding to know "How many fingers?" With a dry glance at Cohn's hand, Abe replies, quite accurately, "Five." The audience is lulled into comfortable amusement with this odd couple.

When there is a knock at the door, where no one has ever knocked, the audience settles in for a series of silly knock-knock jokes, like: "Who's there?" "Joan." "Joan who?" "Joan ask me no questions and I'll tell you no lies;" or "Joan know why there's no sun in the sky." And then, when the door is flung open and we see Joan in all her shining glory, the audience experiences the same thrill of leaving behind mundane reality that the two curmudgeons experience. In a world transformed into fantastic possibilities, the comic and sometime sinister turns of Judd's myriad characterizations of

Wiseman equally astounded. By the end, the audience has been taken on a wild ride, which they thoroughly enjoyed.

As usual, I invited Jules to participate in rehearsals as fully as he desired, and he came to many of them, always excited and pleased by the work as it progressed. Few changes were made in the script, which we had labored over prior to beginning rehearsals. If ever a playwright saw his play come to life beyond even his imagining, the Circle Rep production of *Knock Knock* endowed Jules Feiffer with that rare experience. On opening night, he was delirious with gratitude and pride.

Knock Knock by Jules Feiffer previewed for seven performances at Circle Rep, before opening on January 18, 1976, playing a total of forty-eight performances; in addition to previously mentioned credits, the stage manager was Dan Hild. Jules designed a poster for the show that bears the unmistakable identity of a Feiffer cartoon, a black line drawing on a white background depicting a door, with puzzled faces peering around it, and *KNOCK KNOCK* in vivid red letters.

There were more reviews than we had ever received, so I can offer only a few representative excerpts:

The New York Times, January 19, 1976 (Mel Gussow):
"Partly a philosophical fairy tale and partly a freewheeling vaudeville, the play is a miracle comedy, a genre in which there is little competition. [It's] a wild spree of jokes, pratfalls, word games, collapsing scenery, falling bodies, and burlesque sight gags. As director, Mason does not monkey with the material. Everyone acts as if nothing has happened, until something – such as a miracle – happens. Daniel Seltzer has the frazzled look of a Burt Lahr; he is funny between the lines. Cast against ethnic type, Neil Flanagan is wryly amusing. Nancy Snyder is fetching and Judd Hirsch is a one-man fun house. [It's] a fanciful evening with helium-light laughter."

New York Post, January 19, 1976 (Martin Gottfried):

"The play is grand fun, possessed by a bright madness and its word games are salutary. Mason directed it beautifully. Flanagan has evermore been proving himself a sensitive and versatile actor. Seltzer is excellent and very comic, as is Judd Hirsch."

Daily News, January 19, 1976 (Douglas Watt):

"A miracle play to end all miracle plays. [It's] a wildly fantastic farce. Seltzer and Flanagan are great fun. Nancy Snyder makes a nice wide-eyed ingénue. Hirsch is entertaining in a variety of low-comedy parts. Some scenes are as funny as anything in town."

The New York Times, January 25, 1976 (Walter Kerr):

"A good new funny American play, literate, lively, loquacious, and lovely. For a play that is gaily, giddily, overflowingly improvisational, [it] is surprisingly substantial. It is played with a splendid seriousness by Seltzer, Flanagan, Hirsch, and of course, Miss Snyder. I wish I hadn't seen *Knock Knock* so I'd still have it lying in wait for me."

New York Magazine, (undated) (Alan Rich):

"A great deal of it is screamingly funny. [Feiffer] aims his pen into the heart of life's absurdity, and directs it unerringly to its target. I cannot praise too highly the brilliant production: the inspired work by its cast under Mason's direction, and the set by Beatty is worth the price of admission."

The Nation, (undated) (Harold Clurman):

"[It's] an improvisation on a number of themes, some of which imply the world's whacky incomprehensibility. There are several quite amusing passages, but apart from its entertainment value, the whole is of little consequence. One is hard put to judge the production: is it too 'realistic' or should it be more freely extravagant? Could it have been made more hilarious? The audience seems sufficiently pleased as it stands."

Village Voice, (undated) (Ross Wetzsteon):
"Feiffer's play is a manic masterpiece. For all its surface silliness, [it] is a deeply serious play. The genius of this play lies in the simultaneous hilarity and anguish of the totally unpredictable nature of life. The miracle of Mason's work, [is that] he's given breath and blood to what most other directors would have diminished to a cartoon."

Newsweek, February 2, 1976 (Jack Kroll):
"[Feiffer's] charming, mournfully hilarious new play is a very personal work. [It's] a laughing elegy for the gently demoralized human spirit. Circle Rep [is] one of Off-Broadway's best and warmest groups. Beatty's set couldn't be better, and Mason has gotten intelligent laughter from the acting of Flanagan, Seltzer, Hirsch, and Snyder."

Time Magazine, February 2, 1976 (Ted Kalem):
"It is our good fortune that *Knock Knock* is happily incarcerated at Circle Rep. Director Mason moves all the UFOs and the splendid cast at a rocketing speed. The words are manic, sputtering with hilarity. Get into that playhouse."

Our opening night celebration was held at "One if by Land," a swanky restaurant near our offices on Barrow Street. By the time I got there, Jules had consumed several glasses of champagne; he stood at the head of a long table and tearfully delivered an emotional testimony of his gratitude to me and Circle Rep. I treasure the memory of making an author sublimely happy, even though events in the near future make this heart-felt toast recalled with a tinge of irony.

The production was by far the biggest hit we had yet produced. It became impossible to get a ticket; we were quickly sold out for the run. Streams of celebrities, many of them Jules' buddies from sophisticated gathering places, like Elaine's uptown (which was the strongest celebrity magnet in New York), flocked to Circle Rep to see it. The most famous of the famous, Jacqueline Onassis, came with her cadre of Secret Service protection. Unfortunately, I was not at the theater that night, so I never got to meet her.

Playing *Knock Knock* at our home on Sheridan Square was a delightful experience for all of us. Circle Rep had never been so celebrated.

Broadway Bound

With our artistic success confirmed, and our popularity with audiences evident, there was immediate buzz about a move to Broadway. Of course, it was no secret that the Jules Feiffer comedy always had been aimed for a large audience. I told Mel Gussow almost two years before that I was planning to direct the play on Broadway. At that time, it was still under option to Kermit Bloomgarden, and Jules and I had been working on cutting, shaping and rewriting the play for months.

Many of the reviews made special mention of the fact the production was Off-Broadway, not on. Some of the critics were clearly abetting a transfer with their praise, while some were noting the Off-Broadway nature of the material:

The New York Times (Walter Kerr):

"We are always wishing for a good, new, funny American play so we won't have to hang our heads in shame every time we think of how beholden to the British we are for our Broadway hits, and what do we get? We get Jules Feiffer's *Knock Knock*, not on Broadway, as it happens, but tucked away in the Circle Repertory Company's little house on Sheridan Square... If it had started out in England, possibly as a collaboration between Alan Ayckbourn and Tom Stoppard, it would, I feel quite certain, have been hailed upon arrival as our theater's latest Salvation Nell."

Within a week, the press began overtly to speculate about a Broadway transfer. Rex Reed summarized the situation rather perfectly:

Daily News, February 15, 1976 (Rex Reed):
"With *Knock Knock* we have at last a truly funny – as well as literate – new comedy by an American author to do combat with the surfeit of British imports, old revivals, and musicals. Result: Broadway is doing somersaults. *Knock Knock* is a bizarre Looney Tune. You have to see it to believe it. The critics who have seen it are hugging themselves with joy. The six-week run Off-Broadway was sold out instantly. Every performance saw droves of hopefuls turned away in despair. Even Jacqueline Onassis had to pull strings to buy a ticket. Now, good news. On February 24, this zany, shaggy-dog hit moves to Broadway for what should be a long, long run."

But some critics began to express doubt about the wisdom of a move:

New York Post (Richard Watts):
"If there is any justice in the theater, *Knock Knock* should have considerable box-office success in its small and intimate home downtown; there will no doubt be a demand to bring it up to Broadway, where there would be room for larger audiences. But I think this would be a serious error. There have been too many examples when bringing a small Off-Broadway show to Broadway could cause it to lose much of the popular interest and the size of its audiences. It can be fatal."

Despite the misgivings, a transfer was announced in the papers:

Variety, February 18, 1976 (Madden):
"When *Knock Knock* closes its limited engagement at the Circle Rep next Sunday, it will transfer to Broadway under

the aegis of Terry Allen Kramer and Harry Rigby, opening Tuesday at the Biltmore Theatre."

Our producers came up with a perfect theater for our leap to the big time. The Biltmore was the site in 1968 of the most successful transfer from Off-Broadway to Broadway in history: the Public Theater's production of *Hair*, which ran for four years, with 1750 performances. It was also, ironically, the same theater where Kermit brought the cast of *The HOT L BALTIMORE* for an afternoon run-through when we were weighing whether to make our commercial move to Broadway or Off-Broadway; so I already felt a kinship to the space. Seating 900, the Biltmore was one of the smaller Broadway houses, and I was sure projection wouldn't be a problem. Judd and Neil already had appeared on Broadway, but for the rest of us (Dan, Nancy, John Lee, Jennifer, Dennis and me) it was our first experience on The Great White Way. As I said, it was a learning opportunity for all.

We decided to make the transfer directly from Circle Rep to the Biltmore without a pause, hoping to sustain the momentum we had built up Off-Broadway. So, basically we went from closing the show on Sunday, into technical rehearsals on Monday and Tuesday, and opening Tuesday evening on February 24th, my thirty-sixth birthday.

Considering the speed with which we moved, it went as well as could be expected. The most surprising aspect of our move was the apparent indifference of the backstage union crews. At Circle, we'd been surrounded by a support staff who shared our vision, and who were eager to do whatever was necessary to make the show a success. The union stagehands had been around for a long time, and would be around long after we were gone. In fact, I suspect they didn't expect us to run very long, so they didn't go out of their way. I was shocked by the reports from the actors about the noise, audible on stage (but not in the audience) of the basement poker games the crew enjoyed during the performances. In subsequent transfers, I learned from Fred Reinglas how to deal with union stage hands, the cajoling, joking and suave persuasion these seeming-tough-guys require. But at the time, there was considerable tension between the serious artistic efforts of the cast and the impersonal "it's just a job" attitude of the crew. The charming General Manager, Leonard Soloway, eased our situation with the crew, and we managed to get them quiet enough that the actors could concentrate.

Terry Allen Kramer and Harry Rigby, by arrangement with Circle Repertory Company, opened *Knock Knock* at the Biltmore Theater on February 24, 1976 to generally enthusiastic reviews, although we were not re-reviewed by the major New York press, since their initial evaluations were only six weeks old. My mother flew in from California to attend the gala opening, and the celebratory party was held after the performance at Gallagher's Steakhouse on West 52nd Street. Everyone was pleased with how everything was going; Jules had a play back on Broadway, and this time it should be a hit. No one seemed the least bit anxious. Here are a few excerpts from the new notices:

New York Post, March 13, 1976 (Martin Gottfried):
"Having moved from Off-Broadway to Broadway, Jules Feiffer's comedy is doing very well, thank you. It might have been otherwise. Some productions are perfectly fine where they originate, only to seem out of place once transferred. *Knock Knock* is just as funny uptown as it was down. It carries the bigger stage as easily as John Lee Beatty's performing scenery does."

The New Yorker, March 15, 1976 (Brendan Gill):
"On the wings of a chorus of well-nigh universal praise, Jules Feiffer's new comedy has been wafted up from Off-Broadway to Broadway, where at the Biltmore, it has found a cozy home for the rest of the decade. {It's] very funny, and remarkable for its wisdom."

The New Haven Register, February 29, 1976 (John Cochran):
"*Knock Knock* is a knockout. Mason leads Feiffer's serious message through an artful labyrinth of slapstick, pratfalls, chaos, and meaningful non-sequiturs. The cast is perfect. [It's] Feiffer's most ambitious, and certainly most profound, work to date."

Sacramento Bee, March 4, 1976 (William C. Glackin):
"*Knock Knock* is Jules Feiffer's masterpiece. This wonderful production, now uptown at the Biltmore, is the work of the distinguished Circle Repertory Company. Feiffer and Mason, who has a fine sense of pace, are aided immeasurably by Beatty's set, von Mayrhauser's costumes, and the sound created by London and Hansen. Seltzer and Flanagan are full of the revelations that first-rate actors can bring to a play."

Philadelphia Inquirer, February 23, 1976 (William B. Collins):
"This is one Off-Broadway show that will take [the move to Broadway] in stride. The four people in it are quite used to the marvelous. The infinitely tricky staging (talk about special effects!) is by Mason, who knows how to make a cartoon very animated."

But after we were open uptown, the pendulum began to swing the other way, with criticism of how this transfer had come about and whether it would prosper:

Daily News (Douglas Watt):
"*Knock Knock* represents yet another example of the circuitous routes taken by cautious producers in advancing on Broadway. In this case, the Circle Repertory Company, a non-profit Off-Off-Broadway organization, was handed the play for inclusion in the company's subscription season, the identity of its actual sponsors being confined to a reference

buried in the back of the program. Although the play was apparently earmarked for Broadway from the start, the reassurance provided by a trial run and a favorable reception by the New York critics was felt to be necessary. *Knock Knock* was indeed favorably received, and encouraged by this, the producers booked the play into the Biltmore. How it will fare uptown remains to be seen."

Mr. Watt's uninformed conclusions about the genesis of the production were wrong. As I have related, Rigby and Allen came to be involved *after* we scheduled the play for the Circle Rep subscription season, cast it, and hired our designers. They had no input to the creative process, and they did not attend a single rehearsal. In fact, the deal almost fell apart due to my trigger-hair sensitivity to commercial motives.

When I first visited Terry Allen Kramer to discuss the possibility of her involvement with our production, I reacted badly to her narrow focus on success. "I don't care if it will make money or not," I arrogantly informed her. "I just want it to be good." To which she retorted, "You're not interested in its commercial success? Then you can just buzz off!" This particular "outhouse" expression offended me (with its literal image of a fly buzzing around a pile of shit), so I stood up, gathered my possessions and headed for the door. Jules and Harry Rigby both intercepted me, calmed me down and persuaded me to continue the discussion. Terry apologized: she hadn't intended to offend me. But I think I made clear to them that my goals did not necessarily coincide with their aims. If the play was a critical success, and they could help us share it with a larger audience, then fine; but I refused to consider making a commercial transfer our objective. I made it clear that if a transfer materialized, the production had to move as a whole, with no changes whatsoever. We left that meeting with our artistic principles intact.

Nevertheless, a few critics persisted in seeing something wrong with how our commercial move came about. Martin Gottfried followed up his two favorable reviews with a lengthy article that sinisterly suggested something was not kosher about a commercial venture being hatched in a not-for-profit organization:

> "*Knock Knock* is a funny play, but it does not have a funny history. Its Broadway producers played a significant role in the original, presumably non-profit, presentation of the play. How significant a role – that is how much money and advice was contributed – one doesn't know. One does know, however, that this compromised Circle's non-profit, non-commercial, institutional status."

I fired off a response to Mr. Gottfried chiding him for this piece of careless journalism. If he wanted to know the answers to the ominous questions he posed, why didn't he call me and check the facts, instead of making assumptions with troubling innuendoes? Fortunately, his paranoid take on the relationship between Circle Rep and Rigby did not affect our support from the New York State Council on the Arts. Of all the institutions that might be criticized for mixing private investment with public funding, Circle Rep was among the least culpable.

While we were rehearsing *Knock Knock*, Jimmie Carter won the Iowa Democratic caucus, the first step in his successful run for the presidency. Some of Jules' jetsetter friends were undoubtedly aboard the Concorde when it took off for its first commercial flight just after we opened in January. And *Live from Lincoln Center* debuted with live televised productions of the Metropolitan Opera on PBS.

For the first time in my life, I was earning royalties in four figures. I felt like a rich man for the short time it lasted. Circle Rep received 2% of the gross Broadway box-office receipts, providing us with a much-needed injection of earned income.

Trouble In Paradise

About ten days after the opening, taking a page from Tennessee's routine, Danny and I took a well-deserved vacation, escaping the New York winter for a week of soaking up the golden sunshine of Fort Lauderdale. We checked into the Bahamas Hotel, a modest beach inn where Zita and I had stayed a decade earlier.

After we were there a couple of days, I received a panicky call from Jules. The show was not going well: there were complaints about audibility and for some, this unconventional comedy required too much effort to follow. Despite the rave reviews, word of mouth was not great and instead of playing to Circle Rep's standing-room-only crowds, our houses were only 60% sold. Jules was petrified that the producers were going to close the show since the ticket sales were not meeting their expectations.

Jules was indignant when he discovered that I was on vacation instead of attending to the play. He accused me of negligence. I've said this was a learning experience for everyone and this is a painful example of our author's naïveté. In the professional theater, a director's work is finished at the opening night and he has no further responsibility to the production. This is clearly stated in the contract for Stage Directors and Choreographers, explicitly absolving a director from further duties. It is the job of the *stage manager* to maintain the quality of the production. The stage manager is there at every performance, in charge of seeing that the actors' performances and the technical aspects of the show are maintained exactly as the director has designed them. Most directors never see a show once the opening is past. Now, as I've indicated with *HOT L* and *The Sea Horse*, unlike most of my colleagues, I *do* return to check up on my shows from time to time, mainly motivated by enjoying my own creations; but I was never under any obligation to see them again. This is understood industry-wide by theater professionals but, unfortunately, not our playwright.

To be sure, I shared Jules' concerns, but I tried to reassure him that I'd be back in a few days and do what I could to remedy the problems, but I was not going to get on a plane and fly back at once. He was not mollified; it was an uncomfortable, somewhat heated conversation, and it was the first conflict between us. Alas, it was not to be the last.

Upon my return to New York, I discovered that the hysteria was not confined to Jules. Terry Allen Kramer was outraged by a similar misconception. The panic Jules had reported was real, if unfair and misguided. Harry Rigby was experienced enough to know better, but he did nothing to calm his co-producer or his author. I was a convenient scapegoat. I attended a performance, called a rehearsal and encouraged the actors to speak up, but otherwise, the production was pretty much as I had left it. The audience response wasn't as enthusiastic as before, even though the cast was getting their laughs like clockwork. Several critics had predicted the show would not be able to transfer its magical charm from the cozy environment at Circle Rep to the high-priced expectations of Broadway. It was beginning to appear their dire predictions had merit.

By the end of March, Judd Hirsch had offers from Hollywood to star in a new television series called *Delvecchio*, so he was leaving. We held auditions and I cast Leonard Frey to replace him as Wiseman. Leonard performed in half a dozen Broadway shows, but his claim to fame was as star of *The Boys in the Band*, which played 1000 performances Off-Broadway in 1968–70. He was good, but Judd had left an indelible mark on this role of multiple characters, in recognition of which Judd received a Drama Desk Award for Outstanding Featured Actor. His was a hard act to follow. After Judd left, something seemed out of joint about the production. As I had learned with *HOT L*, cast replacements can cause a loss of cohesion in long runs.

The production of *Knock Knock* continued doing profitable business throughout March and April, but we were not selling out; there was plenty of sitting room available. Jules bitterly complained that something he'd counted on as his "annuity" was not likely to pay its anticipated dividends. I tried to assure him that the producers would be insane to close a production that was earning more than the break-even point; it was making money. But given the inexperience of Terry Allen Kramer, there was no telling what rash action the producers might take. As it turned out, they surpassed my most farfetched speculation.

After a number of unproductive meetings where recriminations were exchanged, I pointed out that other than the full-page ad taken in *The Times* announcing the move to Broadway, the producers did virtually nothing to promote the show; it seemed to me that was a likely explanation for lagging ticket sales.

The situation grew to a crisis in early May. The producers called us together to announce they felt the only solution was to replace the cast with box-office stars. As you may guess, I refused to consider this proposal. They informed me that they were prepared to make the changes they wanted, with or without my consent. Of course, my directorial contract protected my rights; they could make no such changes without my express approval. They had to close the show to accomplish their plan, which seemed a ludicrous course of action, shooting themselves in the foot. It made no sense to close a show that was breaking even to risk losing everything on a new venture.

Underlining the imprudence of their plan, in early May, the Tony nominations were announced, and *Knock Knock* got three nominations: Best Play, Best Director and Best Featured Actor for Dan Seltzer. It was madness to close the show at this juncture. But I underestimated how bizarre the situation had become; the producers were adamant and undeterred. They announced that *Knock Knock* would close on May 23rd, go back into rehearsal, and re-open with an all-star cast in early June. I became the only director in history to be replaced on a show after being nominated for a Tony Award.

Soon, the news emerged that the producers had engaged the great O'Neill director José Quintero to direct a new version to star Lynn Redgrave, Charles Durning and John Heffernan. The only holdover from my cast was Judd's replacement, Leonard Frey. It's hard to credit the producers' delusion that any cast could surpass the almost-unanimous critical approbation our production received; you've read the superlatives.

Late in May, the Obie Awards bestowed on me my fourth Obie for Distinguished Direction for *Knock Knock*; Daniel Seltzer received a Theater World Award; and Nancy Snyder was the recipient of the prestigious Clarence Derwent Award, given by Equity to the Outstanding New Performer. Along with Judd's Drama Desk Award, John Lee Beatty's Henry Hewes Design Award for Best Set, and three Tony nominations, we were a remarkably honored group of artists to be dismissed.

It was a thrilling experience to attend the Tony Awards as a nominee, knowing my mother in California would see my face flashed on the television screen, even though I was certain I wouldn't win. (I'd seen Ellis Rabb's brilliant production of *The Royal Family* and felt pretty sure he had the award locked up; I was correct.) The party afterwards at the Waldorf-Astoria was a glittering occasion. I met Walter Cronkite, perhaps my biggest celebrity thrill yet: he was the evenhanded voice of America itself. Jules was sadly subdued, but polite. I think he held out hope until the moment the envelope was opened that he would win; but the award went to Tom Stoppard for *Travesties,* a play I thought inferior to ours. In Dan Seltzer's category, the win went to Edward Herrmann for Best Featured Actor in *Mrs. Warren's Profession*. But all the awards for plays were overshadowed by the tumultuous adulation for *A Chorus Line*, which won nine Tony Awards. It was a pleasure to be even a small part of such a major occasion.

The Circle Rep production of *Knock Knock* on Broadway closed on May 23, 1976 after 104 performances. I wish I could have left on the Concorde myself, which began service from Washington, D.C. the following day. Ten days later, a new production of *Knock Knock* opened as promised on June 2, 1976, directed by Quintero, with the previous designers continuing, and starring Redgrave, Durning, Heffernan and Frey. In general, the notices were not very good, although here's a relatively positive one:

Village Voice, (undated) (Ross Wetzsteon):
"Each production was magical in its own way. Durning is a dumber, angrier Cohn than Seltzer, and Heffernan's Abe is more aggressively impish than Flanagan's. Frey's crazy-eyed maniacal multi-performance, and Redgrave's considerably stronger, more cheerfully solider-like Joan make the play three times broader than it was downtown – but paradoxically this 'Broadway' jazzing up helps bring out rather than bury the seriousness of Feiffer's vision. The important thing, ultimately, is that both productions honor Feiffer's intentions."

The "new" *Knock Knock,* having been knocked about by the critics, closed July 3, after forty-eight performances. The producers in their wisdom took a critical and commercial success and turned it into a disaster. I survived the trauma, returning to Broadway for a total of twelve productions. Interestingly, in spite of this rough patch in our relationship, Jules returned to Circle Rep six years later with a new play, although it was directed by someone else.

But before we get to all that, let me share with you the critics' favorite joke. At one point in *Knock Knock,* the characters play a game of "I'll give you the answer, you give me the question," not unlike *Jeopardy!* with Feiffer's inventive twist. The answer is "9 W." (It doesn't help to know that 9W is a route familiar to anyone who's ever driven through the Lincoln Tunnel, leaving New York City for the vast "garden" known as New Jersey.) Give up? The question is: "Do you spell your name with a *V,* Herr Wagner?"

A Commission Refreshes

At the end of the previous season, Circle Rep applied to the New York State Council of the Arts for a grant from a special fund set aside to encourage playwrights to venture into writing for younger audiences. We were pleased to receive one of these special grants for our playwright John Heuer.

The play was entitled *Cavern of the Jewels* and told the tale of two children who escape their insensitive parents and make friends with two happy forest gnomes, who live in a cavern filled with precious jewels. In the happy end, the "little people" win. Neil Flanagan directed the caper, with sets and lighting by David Adams, costumes by Jennifer von Mayrhauser, music by Henry Krieger. We had only one review, but it was a good one, and we sold out every matinee for a six-performance run. Here is an excerpt:

The New York Times, (undated) (Mel Gussow):
"It is refreshing to come upon such a fanciful play as John Heuer's *Cavern of the Jewels.* The playwright and his director, Neil Flanagan, keep the show from becoming cute and mawkish. The cast is nimble. David Adams's set, with flowered paths, arched bridges, a tucked-away hideout, and a babbling fountain, is an inviting playground."

The Younger Play Commission program of NYSCA accomplished exactly what they'd hoped. We got a second grant the following year, and the next serious American playwright to write a children's play for us was David Mamet. Then we also teamed up with the Dramatists Guild to present two seasons of a Young Playwright's Festival, which I'll recount in chapters ahead. It was great to participate in a program aimed at tomorrow's subscribers, hoping to make theater-lovers of them all.

In March, the majestic Metro System in Washington, D.C. began operations, while in New York, we were struggling with obnoxious graffiti in our dingy subways. And on April 1, 1976, Steve Jobs and Steve Wozniak founded a company called Apple. The confusion between the computer company and the Beatles' record company is reminiscent of Circle Rep's battle to differentiate ourselves from Circle-in-the-Square. The two Apples eventually reached an agreement that Apple Computers would not enter the music business and Apple Records would not make computers. Since both Circles were in the theater business, we could reach no such accommodation.

Circle-in-the-Square was older, so we had to distinguish ourselves by being better. To keep making that distinction, we continued our seventh season at Circle Rep with a new play by Pete Gurney.

Poetic License

Albert Ramsdell Gurney, Jr. (universally known as "Pete") was born in 1930 in Buffalo, New York. He graduated from Williams College in 1952, served as an officer in the Navy and afterwards attended the Yale School of Drama. For many years, he taught literature at M.I.T., which he was still doing when he came to work at Circle Rep. He'd won the 1971 Drama Desk Award for Most Promising Playwright for his *Scenes from American Life*, which was produced by Lincoln Center in the Forum Theater, directed by Daniel Sullivan and starring James Broderick and Christopher Walken (who'd played father and son in Lanford's *Lemon Sky*, though in different productions).

I'm not sure how Pete's script of *Who Killed Richard Cory?* came to us, although I can speculate it was Steve Gomer's recommendation. I was preoccupied with *Knock Knock*, and as previously noted, I could become negligent of my duties when I was preoccupied. Nor do I remember how we came up with Leonard Peters to direct it. Leonard was an actor with the APA/Phoenix, who was just beginning to direct. He'd recently won accolades for a revival of *Craig's Wife* at the off-off-Broadway WPA Theater, which probably brought him to our attention. The only member of the acting Company who played in *Richard Corey* was Sharon Madden, so we held auditions to cast the remaining eight roles. Actors Equity required us to hold annual open auditions and we used these for selecting new additions to the Company. A panel of three actors from the Company judged the auditions, and Bruce Grey, Joyce Reehling and Roger Chapman, were chosen for the Company in this way and became part of our ongoing future.

The experience was not an entirely happy one for Pete; I'll let him relate in his own words what went wrong:

"The play is, of course, based on the well-known poem by Edwin Arlington Robinson, which is read, or used to be read, in every high school in America. It also became a song by Simon and Garfunkel. I approached the story by turning to the episodic form I experimented with in *Scenes from American Life*, where members of the cast play many parts. In contrast, the title character of Richard Cory himself is played by one actor alone, dramatizing the fact that he is doomed to play only one role throughout his life....I discovered during previews that the director, who wasn't around much, was simultaneously directing another play at Playwrights Horizons. For whatever reason, the play didn't do very well with the critics."

Apparently, the play simultaneously being directed by Leonard Peters was *The Public Good* by Susan Dworkin, which played thirteen performances at Playwrights Horizons; it opened only ten days before our first preview. In retrospect, I'm stunned that I did not know about this conflict or that I permitted it to occur. It's another example of my poor stewardship. Even though Pete returned to Circle Rep five years later with a second play (*What I Did Last Summer*), his signature successes were at Manhattan Theater Club (*Children*, *Sylvia* and *Labor Day*), Playwrights Horizons (*The Dining Room* and *The Cocktail Hour*) and Lincoln Center (*Far East*, *Big Bill* and *The Grand Manner*); he's among the important playwrights we let slip away. Leonard Peters also returned as a director to Circle Rep three years later.

The production was an impressionistic collage, taking place on a set resembling a small-town bandstand with several levels, the uppermost covered by a canopy of stained glass. Only Bruce Gray as Richard Cory ("he glittered when he walked") was dressed in elegant turn-of-the-century costume; the other eight wore casual contemporary clothes. With Arden Fingerhut's honey-colored nostalgic lighting, it was a handsome production.

Who Killed Richard Cory opened at Circle Rep March 10, 1976, playing thirty-two performances. It was directed by Leonard Peters, with musical director Charles F. Greenburg, choreography by Bridget Leicester, set design by Joan Ferenchak, costumes by Gary Jones, lighting by Arden Fingerhut, and the stage managers were Marjorie Horne and Amy Schecter. Here are excerpts from the indifferent reviews:

The New York Times, March 12, 1976 (Mel Gussow):
"As the events accumulate, we start wondering how much the two-hour play is telling us we did not already know – or feel – from the 16-line Robinson poem. Despite its deficiencies, the evening is likeable and occasionally lilting. The actors are an attractive and ingratiating company, smoothly stepping in and out of characters. Bruce Gray smartly captures Cory's impeccable façade."

New York Post, March 12, 1976 (Sylviane Gold):
"The author supplies an ironic motive for suicide, and he does it with a fair amount of style, but it isn't enough to carry a full-length play. Still, it is being given a decent production by the Circle Rep, and it's a credit to Gurney's writing and to the talents of director Peters and the fine cast headed by Bruce Gray that there is never any confusion about who is who or what is what."

Daily News, March 11, 1976 (Douglas Watt):
"[*Cory* is] on the order of an American sampler, a sketchily embroidered idea with no fixed time or place. It is not so much unattractive as unformed. Peters has staged the piece efficiently."

Village Voice, (undated) (Michael Feingold):
"[It's] a good, decent, sensible, entertaining play, [but] its moderation and good sense are its principal flaws. It was very much worth doing, and the Circle has, as usual, done it very well."

Although Simon and Garfunkel got away with a song based on the same character, Pete was criticized for attempting what I thought was a fascinating investigation of a quintessential victim of suicide. As I've recounted, I'd been the survivor already of a number of suicides, so the play held special relevance for me. When my co-founder and best friend joined the ranks of the suicides ten years later, Rob Thirkield could be seen as a man who, like Cory, had everything; except, perhaps, peace in his heart.

A Contemporary Tragedy

The Major Production that followed *Richard Cory* likewise examined a case of suicide, but in more grim detail and expressive of deeper despair. This time the suicide included multiple murders of the victim's family. *Richard Cory* was a story of a curiously detached suicide; *Serenading Louie* was its polar opposite – filled with dark passion on a scale commensurate with that of *Medea*. Whenever we hear of a man killing his entire family, we are filled with uneasy questions: what in the world would make someone *do* that? There is the vague fear that it could happen to us, or someone we know. *Serenading Louie* takes us into the mind of a man, and details his step-by-step descent into a rage that we can understand and, in an Aristotelian sense, empathize with.

As usual, we promised our subscribers a new play by Lanford Wilson. Although he wrote *Serenading Louie* in 1968, it had never been done in New York, so it fulfilled our pledge.

The story is of two couples, neighbors in an affluent suburb, who've known each other since their college days at Northwestern. Alex is a charismatic criminal lawyer on the brink of a promising political career (rather in the mold of Robert Kennedy). He has great appeal to the young idealistic protesters of the late 1960s. He is married to Gabrielle, nicknamed Gabby for justifiable reasons, who tells Alex she has the creepy sensation she's being followed. Carl is a successful contractor who was a football quarterback during their college days, and who served in Korea before he married Mary, an elegant, sensual, former Homecoming Queen. Mary and Carl have two children, who remain off-stage; Gabby and Alex are childless by choice. The men are very close and, in an intense moment of male bonding, they share each other's secrets. Alex has a mid-life crush on a teenage girl he's met at political rallies; and Carl reveals that he knows Mary is having an affair: afternoon assignations with his accountant. Carl gives very moving expression to mourning the past, when people cared about things deeply. He recalls how years ago the nation was brought together during an incident when a little girl (Kathy Fiscus) fell down a well and many hours were spent trying to reach her. The attempted rescue, broadcast live on television, was a landmark event as the nation held its collective breath, praying for her survival. At the end of the first act, Carl is violently sobbing in Alex's arms, recalling his days overseas, surrounded by his buddies, when life was good because feelings were genuine.

In the second act, Carl finally confronts Mary about the affair, and asks her to end it. Without defending herself, Mary simply tells him she can't. At the climax of the second act, Gabby's stalker is revealed to be the father of Alex's teenage girlfriend. In an explosion of fury Gabby, walks out the door, just as Carl kills Mary in their bedroom, then their two children, and then, after an incoherent phone call to Alex, he kills himself with the last blast of the gun.

Although the play is written in the realistic lyrical style Lanford perfected, there are elements of abstraction that prevent the domestic drama from becoming "soapy." The author's concept is that the two couples live in houses so identical (as suburban dwellings often are) that one set serves as the residences for both couples. They inhabit the same space, at first alternating and then as the play progresses, sometimes they occupy different parts of the two homes at the same time.

Also, throughout the play all four characters speak occasional asides to the audience. Even though they occur in the middle of realistic scenes, it is understood that these thoughts are not shared with the other characters on stage, but only with the audience. These abstract devices enlarge an audience's sense of time and space: the asides acknowledge the present tense of the performance, while the actors simultaneously suggest fictional times in the lives of the characters.

The domestic territory of marital betrayal is the stuff of daytime television, but no television drama digs as deeply as this play into hidden urges that can accumulate into tragic inevitability. Truffaut's film *The Soft Skin* travels some of the same terrain, but in spite of exquisite cinematography, Truffaut's story remains banal, right up to the moment the betrayed wife shoots her unfaithful husband in the face. By contrast *Serenading Louie*, with eloquent dialogue, uses the trivialities of daily life to illuminate the primitive forces that lie beneath the surface, as beyond human control as the tides.

The title of the play refers to the Gentleman Songsters ("doomed from here to eternity") in the melancholy lament "The Whiffenpoof Song," the legendary chorus from Yale University of "poor little lambs who have lost their way":

"We will serenade our Louie
While life and voice shall last
Then we'll pass and be forgotten with the rest."

Although Lanford chose to make his stray lambs from Northwestern rather than Yale, the song is known and sung by drunken college students everywhere. The four characters, a little high after an evening of bonhomie and nostalgia, sing the chorus in the second act.

The roles provided challenging opportunities. Tanya is no one's idea of conventional beauty, yet she possesses a grace and depth that is enormously attractive. I reasoned that the honor of Homecoming Queen is not always bestowed only for beauty, but sometimes for vivacious popularity. For most in the audience, this stretch was not an obstacle, although for a few it was. But casting against type is necessary when casting within a Company, and I believe it offers discoveries that conventional typecasting cannot match.

By contrast, the role of Carl could have been written for our big, beefy writer/star of *The Sea Horse,* so it gave us a good occasion to get Ed Moore back on our stage. Trish was perfect casting for Gabrielle; she had the range to go from charmingly silly to the towering rage that erupts in the final scene. We didn't have anyone in the Company suited to play the political star that Alex must be; so I auditioned to find daytime television star Michael Storm, who, with his golden boy looks, was a credible political icon.

Designing one setting to represent two suburban homes, John Lee Beatty produced a golden beige set with taste and amplitude. As with many of John Lee's sets, this inviting home looked ready for occupancy, and many in the audience would have been happy to move right in. Jennifer von Mayrhauser used her delicate palette to produce rich pastel hues of silk that reeked of prosperous elegance. Dennis Parichy followed the action with subtle shifts of light that kept the audience focused on the fluidity of time and place.

Late in the second act, the abstract scene between the two men was staged with Alex in his nook of an office just under the staircase, dialing his teenage fantasy lover, while Carl moves the army rifle from the hall closet up to the bedroom at the top of the stairs. It is two o'clock in the morning; Alex is illuminated by the glow of a small desk lamp, Carl by moonlight from the window at the end of the landing. Each man almost could be talking to himself, although their dialogue answers each other. Alex turns on the radio to mask his surreptitious phone call, so the scene was accompanied by the haunting melody of Melissa Manchester's "Midnight Blue."

> "Whatever it is, it'll keep 'til the morning;
> Haven't we both got better things to do?
> Midnight Blue...
> Even the simple things become rough;
> Haven't we had enough?
> And I think we can make it, one more time, if we try
> One more time for all the old times."

This is one of my favorite plays in Lanford's body of work; but when I directed the play a second time a year later at the Academy Festival Theater in the wealthy Chicago suburb of Lake Forest, I became so involved with the action that when I directed the actor playing Carl to get the rifle from the hall closet, I suddenly burst into tears. I knew that once he moves the gun to the bedroom, we are headed for an inevitable tragedy, and that there's nothing I could do to prevent it. I don't think I could endure directing it again. Similarly, Lanford noted in his introduction to the play: "I still weep for these characters' pain. I couldn't save them, but I love them."

This play contains some of the best writing, line by line, that Lanford wrote. I'll give two examples. During the convivial party near the opening of act two, the four friends reminisce about their college days, fondly making fun of Carl, the absent-minded athlete. Mary describes how she and Carl would make love after he'd studied till midnight, and then wake up at dawn and go at it all over again. She interrupts her reverie to turn to the audience with an aside, musing:

"I don't actually think... that I loved him then. But I love him then now."

If there's a more beautifully constructed line in twentieth century drama, I don't know what it is.

The play is also the occasion for the funniest line Lanford ever wrote. In Gabrielle's fury at the end of the play, upon learning that the teenage object of her husband's lust is studying to be a botanist, and that her family has whisked her away for a Hawaiian vacation to escape Alex's sphere of influence, she quips:

"Botany. She. Must. Be. *Agog*. In Hawaii."

The rehearsals were an adventure of exploration. The text is so rich, the characters so complex and true, and the dialogue so eloquent that it is a treasure of discoveries. No one outside of Chekhov offers actors more opportunities to explore.

Serenading Louie by Lanford Wilson opened at Circle Rep on Wednesday, May 5, 1976 and played forty performances. The reviews were the sort of mixed bag we we'd come to expect when the critics first encounter a new Lanford Wilson script:

The New York Times, May 6, 1976 (Mel Gussow):
"The play is about avoidance and evasion, the tension we face, the excuses we make. The real disguised pain is psychological. The end is unsettling and unconvincing. But before the drama is played out, we have witnessed the bankruptcy of four lives. Although Berezin is unable to convince us she was a homecoming queen, she and the others in the cast are fine – particularly Moore and Hawkins. Director Mason nimbly orchestrates the characters. The set by Beatty looks extremely livable. *Serenading Louie* is a different, but still evocative, side of Lanford Wilson."

New York Post, May 6, 1976 (Martin Gottfried):
"[It's] not top drawer Wilson, but it has the intelligence, the humanity and natural rhythm of all Wilson. He remains one of our superior playwrights, even when not at the peak of his form. His grasp of female-versus-male speaking styles is impeccable; his understanding of specific vernaculars, as keen as always, sometimes escalating into the poetic. Make no mistake about it – such writing represents mastery of craft. Mason could by now be considered Wilson's directing alter-ego. He has set this world to life."

Daily News, May 6, 1976 (Don Nelson):
"Wilson's characters are burnt-out cases – and so, largely, is the play. We have met his characters before and he has orchestrated their lives toward a crescendo that fails to shake us because it is so predictable. Wilson certainly cannot complain about the actors. Berezin, Hawkins, Storm and especially, Moore ARE his people: thwarted, baffled, dull – and

believable. Mason has staged *Louie* deftly, but I daresay that many will leave the theater asking: "So, what's new?"

Women's Wear Daily, May 6, 1976 (Barbara Ettorre):
"Wilson has written a masterful play on the fragility of self-image – and what happens when reality crashes down on that personal tenuous house of cards. The cast works with consummate, thoughtful precision. Director Mason again confirms his fluency in bringing Wilson's works to life."

New York Magazine, May 17, 1976 (Alan Rich):
"Wilson is one of our most gifted and intelligent playwrights, but this play could use more revision. It's not quite dull, and some of his theatrical contrivance – especially in Mason's excellent direction – adds some semblance of freshness. Even though this is one of Wilson's lesser efforts, I can recommend it, as usual when the Circle Rep is involved, for the attractive production the work has received. Mason is a clever man indeed, his manner of movement gives the play some semblance of shape, and his excellent four-member cast form a marvelous playing ensemble, their interactions as beautifully modulated as in the best chamber music."

Village Voice, May 17, 1976 (Michael Feingold):
"If *Serenading Louie* is revived ten years from now, it will be received in awe and spoken of as 'A Classic.' Mason has staged *Louie* with the quiet exactitude that always accompanies him when he is working on Wilson's plays. Miss Hawkins has grown tremendously in skill, and gives a full portrait here. I always like Miss Berezin – I uncritically adore Miss Berezin, in fact. Moore [who is] an intelligent actor of slightly crude technique, cleverly uses the crudity here, and his immense physical stature hints of the impending violence. Storm plays with great sense and seriousness, and looks convincing. The quartet plays

together as though they had been rehearsing as long as the Budapest Strings, so that, even if the play is a soap opera, the performance touches emotions considerably deeper."

Serenading Louie was revived in New York in 1984 at The Second Stage Theater, directed by John Tillinger, and with a splendid cast: Lindsay Crouse, Jimmie Ray Weeks, Dianne Wiest, and Peter Weller. As Michael Feingold predicted, almost ten years later the play opened to unanimous raves.

Lanford and Danny designed an effective poster for our production: a silver photograph of a house of cards against a dark blue background. Aware that Rob and Tanya's marriage was beginning to fray (and an eerie, if unconscious prognostication of Rob's own brutal end), Lanford dedicated *Serenading Louie* to Rob Thirkield.

Special Special Events

Village Voice critic Michael Feingold's only previous artistic relationship with Circle was his translation of Ibsen's *When We Dead Awaken* in our 1973 season. But in the spring of 1976, he came up with an ingenious idea: he wanted to direct a one-act play by Pulitzer Prize-winning poet Richard Howard. He suggested we could do it following the performance of a Major Production as an "After-Piece." I thought it was a great concept. It inaugurated a new series of one-act plays presented after a subscription performance that we later renamed "The Late Show."

The first script Michael brought us was Richard Howard's *The Lesson of the Master*, taken from his book of verse dialogue called *Two-Part Inventions*. Michael also brought an outstanding cast: Nancy Marchand and Lenny Baker. The play was about two people in the back seat of a car, being chauffeured to a cemetery in Versailles. The aristocratic woman is Edith Wharton and the working class man is a Mr. Roseman. Wharton balances on her lap an urn containing the ashes of a mutual friend, Gerald, who was an inspiration to the woman, and the lover of the man. Their civilized conversation is distant and impersonal, but as they journey, the defenses come down and the revelations are touching. She realizes Mr. Roseman is not accompanying her so much as she is accompanying *him*. At the end, as they reach the cemetery, she hands him the ashes. We had a couple of reviews for this offering.

> *Soho Weekly News,* May 27, 1976 (William Harris):
> "This is the most intelligent, atmospheric, and provocative piece of theater I've seen in many months: witty, understated, superbly crafted, alive. Nancy Marchand exudes a quiet, magnificent dignity. Lenny Baker is an excellent counterpart, full of repressed emotion. I haven't begun to adequately describe the way it touched me. *The Lesson of the Master* is a very rare gem."
>
> *Village Voice,* June 9, 1976 (Ross Wetzsteon):
> "Rarely have I seen the nature of grief (indeed, the mystery of human relationships) explored with such powerful nuance. I urge the Circle to bring back this lovely, touching, and delicate masterpiece."

We would have loved to have given this play an extended run, but Ms. Marchand and Mr. Baker had committed only to the five performances we'd scheduled.

However, we extended the idea of the After-Piece, and invited Michael Feingold to mount a second production of Richard Howard's work taken from the same book. This piece was called *Wildflowers* and imagines a meeting between Oscar Wilde, when he was visiting the United States on a lecture tour, and the reclusive American poet Walt Whitman. Again a splendid cast helped to bring the marvelous dialogue to life: Bruce Gray as Wilde and Randall Duk Kim as Whitman. Again Michael did a lovely job of staging the piece with a delicate, smooth hand. Here's an excerpt from the only review:

Soho Weekly News, July 8, 1976 (William Harris):
"Howard's imagination is surpassed only by the beauty of his writing. Once again Feingold has directed with bold strokes, breathing life into the words and situation. Tantalizing."

We concluded the first season of After-Pieces with a play called *Listen Please* by Robert Abrami, directed by Jill Fuchs. We charged $1 to stay to see the After-Pieces, and had good audience response. We continued Feingold's idea of playing a one-act after a subscription performance as part of our regular schedule; we presented three the following season, and then nine productions the following two years.

Earlier in the spring, we presented as a Special Event a workshop production of Lee Kalcheim's *Prague Spring*. A diminutive director named John Henry Davis, who'd assisted me on the Broadway transfer of *Knock Knock*, was keen to mount this play about the tragically brief surge of hope in Czechoslovakia during the era of Soviet occupation following World War II. The Prague Spring reforms were an attempt by Alexander Dubček (First Secretary of the Communist Party) to grant additional rights to the citizens by decentralizing the economy and introducing democratic principles. The freedoms granted included a loosening of restrictions on the media, speech and travel. The Prague Spring began on January 5, 1968, when Dubček began initiating the reforms and continued until August 21st, when the tanks of the Soviet Union rolled into the city to quash the movement. Remembering Miss Krause's repeated exhortations about an artist's obligations to champion moral causes (as in the Hungarian revolution), I felt this was an important event to sponsor. It was a memorable production of a good play, which received later productions at Cincinnati Playhouse and the Goodman Theater in Chicago.

Stellar Development

Apart from Major Productions, After-Pieces and Special Events, Circle Rep continued to develop new plays in workshop productions. But because there was much less "down time" at our Sheridan Square operation, our Executive Director Jerry Arrow negotiated a short-term lease with the Wonderhorse Theater at 83 East 4th Street where we presented a workshop season of half a dozen new plays. This series included Helen Duberstein's *When I Died My Hair in Venice*, directed by Marshall Oglesby, and two new plays by Corinne Jacker: *Terminal* and *Night Thoughts*. William Esper, the foremost teacher of the Meisner Technique, directed a new play by David Epstein (one of the writers of the PBS series *The Best of Families*) called *The Dark Room*. There was also *Solo for Two* by Juliette Bowles, a black playwright, and *The Magic Formula* by Sidney Morris.

In the spring, Jerry leased the Off-Broadway Truck and Warehouse Theater at 79 East 4th Street for a couple of weeks, where we presented a second season of workshop productions, which included *The Confirmation* by Howard Ashman, directed by R. Stuart White; *Fog and Mismanagement* by Jeff Wanshel, directed by Carole Rothman, in which I appeared; and a bill of one acts: Lanford Wilson's *Home Free!* directed by Stuart White and Brian Friel's *Winners*, directed by Richard Harden.

Stuart White was one of my young students in the directing workshops that I conducted at Circle Rep in 1976–77. I thought he was very talented. Slim, with energy to burn, he reminded me of myself when I'd been his age. I encouraged Stuart by giving him a number of opportunities at Circle Rep, including naming him Artistic Director of The Lab, a year after Rob initiated that new program. Stuart's lover was playwright/director Howard Ashman, who later achieved mega-success in theater and film. A native of Baltimore, Maryland, Howard moved to New York in 1974, and Circle Rep produced his play *The Confirmation* in 1976. The following year Howard became the artistic director of the off-off-Broadway WPA Theater. Then he teamed up with composer Alan Menken to create *Little Shop of*

Horrors, which ran Off-Broadway at the Orpheum Theater for 2,209 performances and won the "triple crown:" the New York Drama Critics' Award, the Outer Critics Circle Award, and the Drama Desk Award for Best Musical. It was made into a film, for which Howard received an Academy Award nomination. But his career really took off when he joined my former assistant Peter Schneider, then president of Walt Disney Studios, to create the book and lyrics for *The Little Mermaid* (Oscar for Best Song: "Under the Sea"), and *Beauty and the Beast* (Oscar for Best Song and the only animated film ever nominated for Best Picture). Howard was also the co-recipient of two Grammy Awards and two Golden Globes. He was writing songs for *Aladdin* (1992), when he died of AIDS at the age of forty.

Howard Ashman's play *The Confirmation* was a charming, slight comedy that featured a character working as a delivery boy for a fast food restaurant who was obliged to wear a chicken costume for deliveries. I tried to convince them that the play was too slight to carry a weighty title like *The Confirmation*, but they didn't take my advice. Although the play was funny, it showed no hint of the genius that later flowered when Howard turned his talent to musicals. It's fascinating to recall Howard's New York debut as a footnote in Circle Rep's history.

Carole Rothman was a recent graduate of Northwestern and a graduate student at New York University when she joined my directing workshops at Circle Rep. Carole also went on to become one of my most successful students. She was nominated for a Tony for her direction of *Coastal Disturbances* in 1987, but her major contribution has been that she is the co-founder (with Robyn Goodman, another Circle Rep alumna) and Artistic Director of New York's Second Stage Theater. Among the many wonderful productions that Carole has produced at Second Stage are three plays by Lanford Wilson: *Serenading Louie* directed by John Tillinger; *Lemon Sky*, directed by Mary B. Robinson and starring Jeff Daniels; and *Sympathetic Magic*, which I directed for her in 1997. Now ensconced in a beautiful new home on Eighth Avenue in the Times Square district,

Second Stage has been presenting award-winning productions for over thirty years.

Carole brought me the play *Fog and Mismanagement* by Jeff Wanshel, who was one of the leading absurdist playwrights in New York. His *The Disintegration of James Cherry* was produced at the Forum by the Repertory Theater of Lincoln Center and his play *Isadora Duncan Sleeps with the Russian Navy* was produced the following year by the American Place Theater and won Marian Seldes an Obie in the title role. His *Metamorphosis in Miniature*, an adaptation of Kafka he did for Martha Clarke, won him an Obie for Best New American Play in 1982. We were excited to be producing Jeff, even in a limited, un-reviewed run.

The plot of this absurdist farce is summarized in this ad for the script:

"Aboard an enormous ocean liner, a beautiful young woman is abducted by a malignant and lecherous dwarf with supernatural powers. SEE lovely young Virginia MacKintosh sexually possessed during the dance of the serpentess. SEE magical W.B. Bogus juggle two balls simultaneously. GROAN with passenger Turner Slotpole who hasn't seen his virgin bride since the monster ran off with her!"

Carole invited me to appear in the production. I had done no acting in the seven years at Circle Rep, despite my insistence that our artists should try multiple disciplines. So I took her up on it. I played a stowaway in the depths of a hold on an enormous ocean liner. Sleeping among a cargo of cabbages, I was naked under a slicker covered with cabbage leaves, and I "flashed" to protect myself. It was fun to act again. My friend, the agent Audrey Wood, quipped: "I had no idea you had such a large talent."

A Bicentennial Tribute

For our final production of our seventh season, we commissioned Roy London to write a play in celebration of America's Bicentennial.

He wrote a charming, stylish comedy about a historic event in the Revolutionary War. He called the play *Mrs. Murray's Farm*.

The plot imagines what might have motivated General William Howe, commander of the British forces, to delay his pursuit of American General George Washington when he stopped for an evening on a farm in Manhattan, which came to be called Murray Hill. By extending his evening there, General Howe allowed Washington to escape New York with his rebel troupes, which proved to be a pivotal point in the war.

Roy's play takes a delightful look, in *Upstairs/Downstairs*-fashion, at the kitchen in the great house of Mrs. Robert Murray, where her servants are working feverishly to prepare dinner for the General. We soon learn that the servants are patriots, longing to make a difference in the war. When the scene shifts to the dining room, we are as entertained as General Howe by Mrs. Murray's clever maneuvers to keep him occupied until she gets a signal that Washington has escaped. It is a frothy comedy with a scintillating invention of what might have happened behind the historic fact of Washington's escape.

Roy wanted me to direct the play, but earlier in the year, I had been contacted by Professor James Gousseff, my former teacher at Northwestern, who was now at Eastern Michigan University. He wanted me to come to Ypsilanti, Michigan to take part in a summer festival of plays at EMU. The repertoire included Thornton Wilder's *The Matchmaker,* Tennessee Williams' *Summer and Smoke,* and Lanford Wilson's *The HOT L BALTIMORE.* Jim was the person most responsible for my becoming a director, so I really couldn't refuse. I suggested I'd love to direct *Summer and Smoke.* He agreed, so Jim directed *HOT L* under my "supervision," which amounted to attending dress rehearsals and offering last minute adjustments. But I was given the opportunity to direct Tennessee's play, a lovely piece I'd always wanted to work on.

Now my commitment came in direct conflict with Roy's play at Circle Rep. I suggested a solution: since I was commuting back and forth to Ypsilanti, I could share the directorial duties of *Mrs. Murray's Farm* with Neil Flanagan. I knew Neil was well suited to the play and I felt we would have no problem co-directing. Neil agreed; Roy agreed; it was settled. I flew to Michigan each Sunday night, rehearsed *Summer and Smoke* for two days, returned to New York for two rehearsals of *Mrs. Murray's Farm* (Tuesday and Wednesday), then back to Michigan for Thursday and Friday, and in New York again for rehearsals Saturday and Sunday morning.

As a resident playwright, Roy wrote roles for specific members of the Company, so casting was a snap. He wrote the title role for Tanya and those of the kitchen servants for Nancy Snyder, Sharon Madden, Burke Pearson, Danton Stone and Michael Ayr, whom I'd discovered at a theater conference at Southern Methodist University. There was also a part for Bruce Gray and an alluring role to bring Nancy Killmer back to our stage. It was only in casting General Howe that we needed auditions, so we reached back to the Cino for an old colleague of Neil's, the very tall and altogether agreeable James Parkinson.

Rehearsals went smoothly; Neil and I seemed to complement each other's work. The actors loved playing for Neil who, as a fellow actor, was supportive and inventive. I mainly concentrated on the staging itself.

Roy's play required music, so his friend Michael Valenti composed a score that included a harpsichord solo played by Nancy Killmer. John Lee Beatty designed a charming set that changed from kitchen to dining room, and Jennifer von Mayrhauser enjoyed designing luxurious period costumes. The lighting was designed by our old Caffé Cino buddy, Johnny Dodd, and Chuck London/George Hansen designed the sound. *Mrs. Murray's Farm* opened at Circle Rep on June 30, 1976 and played forty-eight performances. Here are excerpted reviews:

The New York Times, July 1, 1976 (Richard Eder):
"*Mrs. Murray's Farm* is history as farce, and Roy London and the Circle Repertory Company have made a dazzling and beautifully staged comedy out of it. [It's] a combination of a disciplined and delicate slapstick,

writing that is both sinewy and light, and some of the funniest and most skillful acting to be seen in New York today. The set manages to be both ingenious and comic. The acting is all splendid, but Berezin, Stone, Madden, and Snyder are outstanding."

Daily News, July 1, 1976 (Douglas Watt):

"Amiable but amateurish are the paramount qualities in Circle Rep's nod to the bicentennial. London has come up with a few amusing lines, but his play has neither style nor rhythm. The reliable Tanya Berezin plays with poise and spirit. Snyder brings an off-beat comic charm, and Madden has some amusing moments. As frequently happens with Circle Rep productions, Beatty's set is more impressive than the events. The setting and von Mayrhauser's costumes create a pleasingly authentic-looking stage picture."

New York Post, (July 1, 1976 (Sylviane Gold) :

"[It's] not exactly deathless prose. London's problems with plot and character are nothing compared to the difficulties he has with period. Berezin plays Mrs. Murray with tough but wasted charm. All that came to mind was that in 100 years, no one would know this happened."

The Record, July 2, 1976 (Emory Lewis):

"This Bicentennial comedy is an unexpected summer delight. The author has combined fact and fiction with enormous wit and style. By and large, the cast is first-rate. Beautiful, tall Nancy Snyder is deliciously droll. Madden has captured just the right earthy quality. Nancy Killmer is superlative as Gen. Howe's mistress. Stone is touching as a Jewish servant. There are good performances by Michael Ayr, Bruce Gray, and Burke Pearson. The ingenious set by Beatty is one of the best of the season, on or Off-Broadway. Visit *Mrs. Murray's Farm.*"

New York Magazine, (undated) (Alan Rich):
"London's play has a cheeky, galumphing charm. [It's] a marvelous staging by Mason and Flanagan. Berezin is a glorious, raucous, devastatingly worldly character. I also particularly admired Stone and Killmer. If I don't list the rest of the cast, that's only for lack of space; as usual, the special pleasure in the Circle's work is the splendor of its ensemble. Beatty's set is another splendid job. I must also salute Valenti's music."

Village Voice, (undated) (Carll Tucker):
"The show is so amiable, so jovially directed by Flanagan and Mason, so cozily nested in another of Beatty's pirouetting sets, so colorfully costumed and acted, that one wishes the play were terrific. It's not. It's too deliberately, derivatively well-made. Berezin plays Mrs. Murray with a winning earthy ardor. As the pretty, slender, absurdly idealistic maid, Snyder is as effective as in *Knock Knock.* Madden and Stone are gifted farceurs in this spree that wishes it were a play."

The audiences had a good time, and it was a fun way to salute the Bicentennial. Ironically, on July 4th as the nation was giddily celebrating the 200th anniversary of the Declaration of Independence, airborne Israeli commandos freed 103 hostages that were being held by Palestinian hijackers of an Air France plane at Uganda's Entebbe Airport. Two days later, the U.S. Naval Academy in Annapolis inducted its first class of women. Also in July, Barbara Jordan became the first black person to deliver the keynote address at a national political convention; then the Democrats meeting in New York nominated Jimmy Carter for president. And the Summer Olympics were held in Montreal, Canada, where Romanian gymnast Nadia Comăneci earned seven perfect scores, the first time in history the Olympic judges awarded perfect 10s. She won three gold medals.

The Transcendent Years

In May, the *Village Voice* Obie Awards Ceremony was held for the first (and only) time uptown in the vast lobby of the New York State Theater at Lincoln Center. It was hosted by Edward Albee. David Mamet won Best New American Play for *American Buffalo* and *Sexual Perversity in Chicago*. Our own Neil Flanagan was recognized for "Distinguished Contributions to off-off-Broadway theater;" and for the second year in a row, I received Obies for two productions: my fourth Obie was for *Knock Knock* and my fifth was for *Serenading Louie*. In my acceptance speech, I made some disparaging remarks about Broadway, asserting that the *real* National Theater was to be found Off-Broadway and in regional theaters. This earned a retort from Edward Albee that one could create "real theater" anyplace. Of course, he was right.

The previous month, for example, Circle Rep provided the entertainment for an event at the National Arts Club on Gramercy Park where the City of New York was honoring Tennessee Williams on his sixty-fifth birthday with the Key to the City. We performed scenes from his plays and read from his poetry. It was a special moment for him, and we were honored that Tennessee asked us to be part of it.

Like A Diamond In The Sky

I can't leave the seventh season without recounting what happened in Michigan simultaneously with our final production in New York. I was at my rope's end in Ypsilanti, trying to cast the sexy leading role of Dr. John in *Summer and Smoke*. All the guys in the theater department were simply too "light in the loafers" to embody the masculine hunk that the virginal Miss Alma must lust after. My casting of Miss Alma had gone well: I'd found a talented nineteen year-old to play the part who was, I'm sure, the first true virgin ever to assay the role. But it was beginning to look like I could not cast the young Dr. John, whose sexual magnetism must shake Alma from her prudishness. I was just about to tell Jim Gousseff that I couldn't direct *Summer and Smoke* after all, when in the final minutes on the last day of auditions, a door opened at the end of the hallway, and in sauntered a big, blond boy about 6 feet 3 inches tall, an apparent jock who looked as if he might have strayed by mistake into the building from a football field. He was a student from nearby Central Michigan University, who'd heard that a Broadway director was at EMU to direct a play. He thought he'd come audition for it. The kid's reading was a miracle. He was as natural an actor as I'd ever encountered. His name was Jeff Daniels.

After the production opened, I asked Jeff to come out to a local bar with sawdust on the floor to have a beer. I told him that I'd never encouraged anyone to become an actor, because I didn't want to be responsible for a path with such perilous risks. But I felt very strongly that this guy was born to be an actor and that I should help him grow into his potential. I told him that I could promise him nothing in New York except a lowly position as an intern at Circle Rep, a recently implemented program that paid apprentices $50 a week. Jeff listened thoughtfully and said he'd need to check with his parents, who would have to help finance such a decision. Jeff was born in Athens, Georgia, but he grew up in Chelsea, Michigan, where his father, Robert Lee Daniels, owned the local lumberyard. Soon after I got back to New York, I heard from Jeff; he was coming to Circle Rep to learn what he'd need to know to become a professional actor.

What I did not realize at the time was that Jeff had finished only his junior year at Central Michigan. I assumed he was graduating. It's a good thing I didn't know this, or I would never have suggested he leave college to come to New York for an internship.

Jeff Daniels developed into one of the most recognizable homegrown stars Circle Rep produced. Excellence is addictive, and the desire for it is contagious.

Chapter 11
Hitchhiking the Galaxy

The desire for artistic excellence was not the only thing that was contagious. The summer of 1976 saw the introduction of two deadly diseases that were a menace to the world. Delegates attending an American Legion convention at the Bellevue Stratford Hotel in Philadelphia fell ill with a mysterious flu-like illness. Immediately dubbed Legionnaire's Disease, twenty-nine people died of it within a week. A month later, the lethal Ebola virus broke out for the first time in Zaire in a mission hospital run by Flemish nuns. In a different kind of horror, this was also the summer of the "Son of Sam" serial killings, which infected the City with an epidemic of fear. It was an uneasy time.

Still, against the trend of darkness, we continued to search for the light in our eighth season at Circle Rep. We'd survived our encounter with "success," our integrity unblemished. But it was going to be difficult to find six scripts each year to meet the expectations we'd created. Among our resident writers, only Corinne Jacker was writing a new play for our actors. I needed to look further afield to find material we might illuminate with our special brand of artistry. I'd found the first one.

An International Star

We were beginning the season with the New York premiere of a play by one of the world's most highly regarded playwrights, David Storey. I planned to bring in the production of *The Farm* that I directed the previous summer in Lake Forest, Illinois.

David Storey is the son of a coal miner, born in Wakefield, Yorkshire in 1933. After completing his schooling at age seventeen, Storey signed a fifteen-year contract with the Leeds Rugby League Club; he also won a scholarship to the Slade School of Fine Art in London. When the conflict between rugby and painting became too great, he paid back three-quarters of his signing fee and Leeds let him go. His first success as a writer was his novel *This Sporting Life*, which received the 1960 Macmillan Fiction Award, and which Lindsay Anderson turned in to an acclaimed film. His second novel *Flight into Camden* won the Somerset Maugham Prize for fiction. David turned to playwriting in 1966 when the Traverse Theatre in Edinburgh produced *The Restoration of Arnold Middleton*. But his breakthrough came in 1969 when the Royal Court Theater in London produced two of his plays in the same season: *In Celebration* and *The Contractor*. When David's plays were produced on Broadway, he became a sensation, winning an amazing *three* New York Drama Critics' Circle Awards for Best Play in four years: *Home* (1971); *The Changing Room*, (1973); and *The Contractor* (1974). When he came to Circle Rep in 1976, David had just won Britain's prestigious Man Booker Prize for his novel *Saville*.

Returning to the City from my busy summer, the first thing I did was to call Richard Gere to meet me for lunch. Richard was wonderful in the Lake Forest production of *The Farm*, although he was cast against type. The play concerns a northern English farm family, in which the aging father desperately needs the help of his only son in the fields. Instead Arthur has run away to London to pursue an incongruous "career" as a poet. The son should be a big strapping farm boy. Richard was a lithe, medium-sized guy, far too credible as a poet. I knew Richard was gaining attention in Hollywood and I was certain that was where his destiny lay. So at lunch, I reassured Richard that although he'd played the part brilliantly, if he received Hollywood offers, he shouldn't hesitate to take them. I wouldn't hold it against him if he had to leave the production. Richard vowed passionately that he wanted to repeat his part. He knew his performance was impressive and was sure to catch the interest of both coasts. I told him we'd begin rehearsals within the month.

But within a week, I got the expected phone call: Richard had been offered *Looking for Mr. Goodbar,* opposite Diane Keaton and Tuesday Weld, and needed to leave for California right away. I told him I was very happy for him, wished him the best and as soon as I hung up, began looking for a big farm boy to play Arthur.

My production at the Academy Festival received near universal praise and three Joseph Jefferson Award nominations. The cast was spectacular, headed by the great Jack Gwillim. Jack did not turn to the stage until middle age after two decades in the Royal Navy, where he was an all-round track and field athlete and, while stationed in the Mediterranean, he became undefeated heavyweight boxing champion of both the Army and Navy. But once on stage, he became a notable actor on both sides of the Atlantic. At six-feet-two he possessed an uncommon authority and dignity. He was a member of the Royal Shakespeare Company and the Old Vic. His theatre credits included many leading roles in the West End, co-starring with such actors as Dame Edith Evans and Sir Ralph Richardson. In 1969, he immigrated to the United States, where his Broadway credits included playing Pickering in the Rex Harrison revival of *My Fair Lady,* and Ingrid Bergman's husband in *The Constant Wife,* directed by Sir John Gielgud. He is also known for his film work, playing supporting roles in Oscar-winning films like *Lawrence of Arabia, Patton,* and *A Man for All Seasons.* Jack brought a lifetime of excellence to the stage of Circle Rep.

Opposite Jack was Ruby Holbrook, the former wife of the actor famous for his personification of Mark Twain, Hal Holbrook. Ruby stayed with the Circle Rep acting Company for the next ten years, with many memorable performances. The old farmer who needed help in the fields was cursed with the gift of three daughters who were of little use to him. Debra Mooney played the eldest daughter and Nancy Snyder was her anarchistic youngest sister. In Lake Forest, I used Kristen Van Buren (of *Red Ryder*) for the middle sister, but in New York I wanted to replace her with our Trish Hawkins. I'd found Michael Ayr at a director's workshop at SMU and cast him as Albert, the hapless suitor of the youngest girl. So now all I had to find was an Arthur as perfect as the rest of the cast; *that* required auditions.

I soon felt I had read every young actor in New York over six feet tall. Nancy mentioned she had a boyfriend I should see; he was very tall, she assured me. And that was the way I met recent Julliard graduate Christopher Reeve. He was indeed tall enough, but much too handsome to be believed as an ordinary British farm boy. His audition was very good, so I kept his picture and résumé for future reference, and before the season was over, I found a good role for him.

Throughout the endless auditions, the new intern from Michigan, Jeff Daniels, served as my reader. It gradually dawned on me that physically Jeff was exactly what I was looking for. So after the final audition, I asked him to switch hats and read for Arthur. Once I heard him, it was clear; I had to rescind my warning that I could offer him nothing except an internship. In his first month in New York, Jeff was going to debut in a central role in an Off-Broadway play. It takes more than talent to succeed; it takes talent *and* luck, being in the right place at the right time. Jeff continued to be lucky, but more importantly, his talent continued to grow.

The rehearsals in New York were a model of how we worked on a play. At one point, a writer for *The New York Times* asked to sit in on a rehearsal. I allowed this, despite trepidation about what he might think of our unconventional process. As always, my rehearsal room was equipped with controlled lights that could be dimmed for night scenes, brightened for morning. One of the most intimate scenes in the play occurs late at night when the prodigal Arthur steals into the family home and finds his sister Wendy sitting alone by the fireplace in the moonlit living room. In the rehearsal room, we used a space heater to provide the glowing warmth of the fireplace, a carpet muted the floor, and a tape recorder provided an evocative chorus of crickets. I encourage the actors to believe that the circumstances of the scene are actually happening. At this stage, audibility is irrelevant.

I want them to believe they are whispering by the fireside in their rustic living room, hidden from the family or outside observation. Naturally, this kind of work is very intimate, and unlike traditional rehearsals. When the *Times* article appeared, we were relieved to read that the journalist (Jeremy Gerard) was as captivated by the mood and the uncanny sense of reality as the actors were. Our work was like a homecoming to a play we loved; our new additions, Jeff and Trish, provided the margin of perfection we'd lacked in Chicago. John Lee Beatty's warm, rustic hearth seemed even more on target in the intimate space of Circle Rep where we played in a three-sided arena, with the stage on the West side. The same was true of Laura Crow's costumes and Dennis's miraculous moonlight.

The story of the play centers on the arrival of the absent son Arthur, who has come back from London with a bride in tow. Allison remains an off-stage character (he's left her at a local inn), but we learn she is twice Arthur's age and has two children of her own. This arouses suspicion among the family as to what this middle-aged woman might see in Arthur. In any case, the prodigal son is not welcomed home by the bitter father and by the end, when Arthur returns to London, we can only hope that the youngest sister will marry Albert, her brawny neighborhood beau, and that his addition to the family will help the aching father manage the toiling in the fields.

The Farm opened at Circle Rep October 10, 1976 and played forty-two performances. We were thrilled that David Storey was coming from London to attend the opening. A stocky, handsome fellow of forty-three, David still retained in middle age the athletic physique he acquired as a professional rugby player. Still randy as a schoolboy, he radiated a frank sexual attraction to Ruby Holbrook; I'm not sure of the extent of his success in this heated flirtation, but it certainly gave Ruby a glow. He loved our production and, for the most part, so did the critics. Here are some reviews:

The New York Times, October 12, 1976 (Mel Gussow):
"With deep understanding and affection *The Farm* illuminates the forces beyond love that hold people together.

Beginning with a base of regionalism, it achieves universality. Mason is an excellent choice to direct *The Farm*. He is precisely attuned to the Chekhovian plangencies of the work. The Circle's three sisters are an ensemble. Mooney, Hawkins, and Snyder, all of them lovely, add immeasurably to the playwright's strong sense of family. Jack Gwillim is a commanding presence – a 'grizzled old sot' on the brink of extinction. *The Farm* enfolds us, warming us in its bower. It is a quiet play, but richly textured and resonant with life. Mr. Storey is one of our finest contemporary playwrights."

Daily News, October 12, 1976 (Douglas Watt):
"Gwillim just about acts everybody else off the stage in this longish work about lost hopes, lost chances, and maybe even lost desires. Storey's *The Farm* is as beautifully written as anything he's done. This is another superb Circle production. There are thoughtful, believable performances all around. Storey remains one of our strongest and most skillful contemporary dramatists. For that reason, for Gwillim's marvelous performance, and for the excellence of the production, *The Farm* is worth seeing."

The Record, October 12, 1976 (Emory Lewis):
"One of the best dramas of the year. This extraordinary writer is skilled in the fine art of nuance. The direction by Mason is masterly. He has found the poetry of desperation that is hidden behind the masks of these stoical farm folk. The cast is perfection."

Newsday, October 17, 1976 (George Oppenheimer):
"There are few playwrights with the skill of David Storey. His writing, the fascination of his characters, and the brooding atmosphere hold you throughout. The acting and the direction are excellent. Once again the exemplary Circle Repertory Company shows its medals."

The Nation, (undated) (Harold Clurman):

"Though not one of his best plays, and there are certain flaws in the well-directed production, I believe Circle Rep is justified in presenting it. Gwillim looks right and sounds right. Mooney, Hawkins and Snyder are attractive daughters, although their Yorkshire speech is a sometime thing. Mason directs with a sound feeling for personal relationships."

The New Yorker, October 25, 1976 (Edith Oliver):

"David Storey is a spellbinder. Circle Rep has opened its current season with a good production of Storey's *The Farm*. The play is affecting, with wit and humor and sympathy. Storey certainly can write for actors, and he is served well by Mason and his cast."

Time Magazine, November 1, 1976 (T.E. Kalem):

"Storey's family will go on as immutably as the sun rises and night falls. Despite variations in accent, the cast is splendid. Mason directs with Chekhovian sensitivity. As for David Storey, he is simply one of the most gifted playwrights alive."

On the whole, it was a lovely way to open our eighth season. Our principles were on view, our production standards remained exemplary, and our playwright was happy. Now I needed to find another script on which we could work our magic.

Star Struck: Silk Stockings, An Earring And A Tattoo

For my second selection, I traveled to Florida, where a new play by Arthur Whitney was a success for a small theater in Miami. I'd been alerted to the play by Arthur's manager, agent and lover, Dudley Malone.

Dudley was very tall (about 6'4") and he fell in love with one of his clients, a diminutive blond man named Arthur Whitney. They secured a production of Arthur's play *The Passion of Lili Lamont* at the Player's Repertory Theater in the Museum of Science of Greater Miami. Dudley insisted I must see the production, not just read the script. He offered to pay my airfare to fly down to see it; so I went.

The play is about the meeting of a fan club for a faded screen star in a movie memorabilia shop. A legend in black-and-white films, Lili Lamont disappeared from public awareness after her career waned; but the owner of the shop has recently come across an old woman in a threadbare coat, whom he recognizes instantly as the screen idol. He begs her to come to his shop, where he assembles the straggly group of die-hard fans who comprise the Lili Lamont Fan Club. Part *Ninotchka*, part *Sunset Boulevard*, part *Anastasia*, the play dramatizes the arrival of Lili and the menacing behavior that ensues when she fails to live up to the fantasies of her fanatical fans.

The production in Miami was effective, but I knew Circle Rep could do better. The actress playing the title character won a local acting award but I envisioned the potential of a *real* faded film star, and I knew just where to find one. When I discovered Dan Seltzer for *Knock Knock* in Chaiken's *Sea Gull* at Manhattan Theater Club, at the center of that production was the luminous Leueen MacGrath as Arkadina. I'd first seen Leueen many years before, playing Mrs. Alving in David Ross's 1961 production of Ibsen's *Ghosts* at the Fourth Street Theater. Leueen's beautiful performance was an inspiration. She was the perfect Lili Lamont.

Leueen MacGrath (pronounced loo-EEN mac-GRAW) was born in London July 3, 1914. She began her acting career with a small role in the British film *Whom the Gods Love*, a biopic about Mozart. She followed this playing Clara Eynsford-Hill in the classic Leslie Howard/Wendy Hiller film *Pygmalion*. Leueen made her Broadway debut in 1948 in the play *Edward, My Son* and she reprised her role in the film adaptation the following year. She married celebrated American playwright George S. Kaufman, and she collaborated with Kaufman and Abe Burrows on writing the book for *Silk Stockings*, the Cole Porter musical based on *Ninotchka*. It played for 448 performances at the Imperial Theater, and was made into a film starring Fred Astaire and Cyd Charisse. Leueen returned to acting as Cassandra in Harold Clurman's Broadway production of *Tiger at the Gates,* and with Dame Sybil Thorndike in Graham Green's *The Potting Shed.*

My agent, the suave Robbie Lantz (representative of stars like Yul Brynner, Bette Davis and Elizabeth Taylor) helped me get a script to her, and Leueen responded warmly to the play (now re-titled *A Tribute to Lili Lamont*). She came to meet me at our offices on Barrow Street, where her sleek, quicksilver sophistication could not have been in greater contrast to my rather disheveled workplace. She was indeed a great beauty, even at sixty-two. She graciously agreed to play Lili on one condition: she wanted to bring with her a stage manager she'd worked with who would protect her from any disagreeable inconveniences a fragile artist might encounter Off-Broadway. I was eager to grant her request, so her stage manager soon came to meet me.

He was a strange, slight Jewish man with a trim black beard, close-cropped hair, piercing black eyes, and a tiny gold earring. It wasn't until later that I noticed the tattoo of a concentration camp on his arm. His name was Fred Reinglas, and he became the Production Stage Manager for Circle Rep for the next eighteen years.

Fred Reinglas was born in Lodz, Poland in 1936 to a couple of actors in the Yiddish theater. They survived the Holocaust by traveling east, performing and hiding, always staying one jump ahead of the German army. At the end of the war, they immigrated to Toronto, so Fred was a naturalized Canadian citizen. He came to New York in 1964, and began stage managing Off-Broadway, where he did six plays in two years. He then jumped to Broadway, where he became the original Production Stage Manager for the smash musical *Hair.* Following the Broadway engagement, Fred traveled all over the United States and several foreign countries as "Artistic Director" of *Hair,* re-mounting Tom O'Horgan's production for the next eight years. Then Leueen brought him to Circle Rep, where he remained the rest of his life, a career that spanned thirty-eight productions from 1976 until his death in 1994. His contribution to Circle Rep ranks among the most important in our history.

In a bow to the original production of *Lili Lamont*, I brought two of the Floridian actors to play at Circle Rep. William Hindman was especially convincing in the role of Oliver Fuller, the owner of the shop where the meeting of the Lili Lamont Fan Club was being held. Bill previously played in New York at Joe Papp's Public Theater in the George C. Scott production of *Richard III*, and replaced Jason Robards as Hickey in José Quintero's famous Off-Broadway staging of *The Iceman Cometh*. Bill anchored the production of *Lili Lamont* with a firm control at the center. I also imported Francis Walsh, whose portrayal of a Hispanic drag queen that specialized in impersonations of Lili was precise and non-judgmental. But the rest of the roles were wonderful opportunities for our actors. Helen Stenborg donned a black Louise Brooks-style wig to hide her shining silver hair, thereby shedding twenty years, and became Lili's most ardent fan, Bebe. Jack Davidson played her skeptical husband, interested only in getting his wife away from these nutty people. Burke Pearson played a thread-worn autograph hound, dressed in a trench coat and carrying two paper shopping bags filled with autograph books. Most fun of all was the chance to cast Claris Nelson (under her Equity name, Claris Erickson) as a pistol-packing female sheriff who'd driven two hundred miles from a small Midwestern town to attend the meeting. It was a classy ensemble to bring this group of misfits to life.

I had an intriguing concept for the production: since the play is about a screen star from the 30s, I wanted to give it a film noir look, with overtones of German Expressionism. My first decision was that the shop should be in a deep basement, which provided a lengthy stairway for Lili's arrival; so John Lee Beatty designed a musty shop that was sunk below the sidewalks like a subterranean bomb shelter. He made abundant use of cardboard boxes, ostensibly stuffed with movie star memorabilia. Our first sight of Lili, hesitating before her entrance, was only of her shoes, seen through the shaded doorway at the top of the stairs. When Jennifer von Mayrhauser clothed Leueen in a white satin gown cut on the bias, the image was worthy of Harlow. Dennis Parichy took my stylistic concept to heart, and there were dramatic moments of light thrown from the bottom of the stairs upwards, to create ominous shadows. Norman L. Berman composed a score that was both eerie yet reminiscent of the soundtracks of the 30s. This prepared the way for the almost George Grosz-like turn of the fans near the end, threatening Lili in their disappointed hostility. These effects were subtly executed, gradually darkening the tone from the first act, when it's important for the audience to laugh at the silly antics of the characters as they gather. We see their utter devotion to a mythic creature built of sheer imagination, fed by rapturous experiences in the darkness of movie theaters, before flickering silver images enlarged beyond mere magnitude.

As we were going into rehearsal, Jimmy Carter was elected the 39th President of the United States, the first president from the Deep South since the Civil War.

The rehearsals, as usual at Circle Rep, were a pleasure. The cast worked together so cohesively they helped the audience believe in the fabled legend of Lili Lamont before she even appeared. We were aided in the production by out-takes Leueen provided us from a film she'd made with Alec Guinness, which lent authenticity to the proceedings. Having an actual former film actress added immeasurably to the anticipation of the star's delayed entrance. Danny designed an elegant art deco poster with a black curl of film stock, edged with sprocket-holes, on a silver background.

It seemed a good time for nostalgia. On November 25th, just before we opened, The Band gave its farewell concert, The Last Waltz, in San Francisco. Shortly afterwards, my favorite album of all time, The Eagles' *Hotel California* was released.

A Tribute to Lili Lamont opened at Circle Rep November 28, 1976 and played forty-two performances. Unfortunately, some critics saw through our efforts to fortify the flimsy writing. Here are samples:

The New York Times, November 29, 1976 (Mel Gussow):
"This territory – star-gazing – is so deeply furrowed that it scarcely leaves room for originality. The characters are as

pathetic as they are predictable. The evening's only interest is in the performance. Once again Mason has assembled an expert cast and directed it to inhabit a stage space, a Beatty-designed basement cinema shop. Leueen MacGrath, too rarely a visitor to the New York stage, is exactly in key with Lili, capturing the character's Garboesque smokiness and latent bitchiness. The other actors also perform honorably and with some insight. But the play is as faded as one of Lili Lamont's out-takes."

Daily News, November 29, 1976 (Patricia O'Haire):
"Circle Rep seems dedicated to coming up regularly with new and original plays by new and interesting authors, and each with something to say. And it has picked another in Arthur Whitney. [*Lili Lamont*] is a strange, often disturbing, but highly effective piece of theater. The star [is] beautifully portrayed by Leueen MacGrath. The seven-member cast under Mason's direction, is excellent. Dennis Parichy did a highly effective job of lighting. It may not be a perfect play, but it is absorbing."

New York Post, November 29, 1976 (Sylviane Gold):
"[The play], without being especially funny or especially sad [is] just especially boring. Mason's direction has not elicited any classy acting. The performances are uniformly humdrum except for Burke Pearson. As usual in Circle productions, the incidentals – set, costumes, music – are quite good. All they need is a play."

New York Magazine, December 20, 1976 (Alan Rich):
"Whitney's play has its flaws, but it is on the whole a brilliant, sometimes harrowing study of the breakdown of the dream machine. MacGrath plays Lili and she is stupendous, dazzling in her power. [She's] aided immeasurably by Mason's superlative direction and by yet another of Beatty's wonderfully observant, grungy sets."

Village Voice (undated) (Julius Novick):

"Nobody could reasonably demand a better production than Circle Rep has provided for *Lili Lamont*. MacGrath plays in the authentic grand manner, with no lack of feeling behind her extravagant gestures. I found [the play] an obsessive, implausible, sentimental wallow in dog-eared nostalgia. Why are Miss MacGrath and her colleagues wasting their talents on this dreary stuff?"

It's probably an appropriate moment to reflect on that question. Why weren't we producing our own talented resident writers? And even if we did, would the critics have liked the plays any better? In the case of Tennessee Williams, I doubted they would have.

Failing Tennessee

After *Battle of Angels,* we hoped we could present a new play by Mr. Williams. But two years passed before Tennessee offered me two one-act plays in very rough, first-draft form. They were to be called *Vieux Carré.*

The first play was a crude stab at black comedy, recounting his days as a young writer in the French Quarter of New Orleans. The chief character is a harridan of a landlady, improbably named Mrs. Wire, who delivers hysterical tirades against anything and everything. The other characters are a shy young writer and a tubercular young painter who seductively taunts the writer to admit his homosexuality. This first draft was rambling and disjointed. At the end of the play, Mrs. Wire is destroyed by boiling water. I didn't believe a word of it. Why would anyone else?

Eager as I was to produce plays by Tennessee, I thought this did not approach his best work, nor what I felt he was still capable of writing. The second play came closer. It was a tender piece about an upper-class young woman, terminally ill and tragically entangled with a dissolute brute who is the barker for a strip show in the French Quarter. This play had elements I felt I could shape into something quite touching. It was a promising companion piece for one of my favorite one-acts from Tennessee's early work. I suggested that we do the second play on a bill with *Talk to Me Like the Rain*. Tentatively, Tennessee agreed.

Then the problems began. I imagined that I could get wonderful performances from two Circle Rep actors who were involved with each other in real life. Stephanie Gordon, one of our best actresses, met Jon Hogan when they were both in *HOT L,* and they'd been a couple ever since. In real life, she was a voluptuous, sophisticated lady and Jonathan was a lithely sexy younger man. Casting them in *Vieux Carré* and *Talk to Me Like the Rain,* would unify the evening and show their impressive range.

Tennessee saw the casting differently. He wanted more animal magnetism in the part of Tye; he felt Hogan's charms (which I've described as those of a young Jimmy Stewart) were all wrong for the part of this degenerate hustler. Stephanie is a New Yorker born and bred, whom I have cast in a wide variety of roles. She's far from the conventional idea of an aristocratic Southern lady, but I felt these two actors could play anything; their talent liberated them from the limitations of "type."

It was theoretically a principle of Circle Rep that we chose plays based on their suitability for the acting Company. If we couldn't cast a play with our extraordinary ensemble, then I reasoned it wasn't appropriate for our repertoire. I can't imagine Chekhov saying to Stanislavski: "Here's my play, but I don't want to use the Moscow Art Theater actors." I believe that the benefits of using members of an acting ensemble outweigh the marginal advantages of casting "types" from general auditions or using "names."

Tennessee's objections led to an impasse. I called Tennessee with the bad news: if I couldn't cast the play with our Company, we would have to withdraw our offer to produce it. Tennessee was incensed. After the call, I realized a rejection by telephone was no way to treat America's greatest writer. Casting was a complex issue, and he deserved a fuller explanation; so I wrote him a letter clarifying my reasons. In reply, Tennessee wrote the following on stationery from the Hotel Élysée:

Dear Marshall:

Many thanks for the note, it fully assuaged my delicate amour propre.

We're leaving today for a rest in New Orleans but I'm due back May 5th. Then maybe there'll be more time to get together.

There are lots of wonderful things about your repertory company, the esprit de corps, the wonderful staging you give your productions.

However, I do feel it is essential that the playwright participate in casting with the director. Ask Lance if he doesn't agree.

A playwright needs a company like yours to feel at home in. Of course, I'm an old new comer, still an out-sider – but I'd like being in.

Love,
10.

Of course he was right that casting must be agreed upon by both director and playwright; but when there is no meeting of the minds about the goals of casting a play, there can be no true collaboration.

Vieux Carré eventually was produced the following year in England under the direction of Keith Hack, to whom Tennessee dedicated the play. He well deserved the dedication, because he blended the two disparate pieces into an effective organic whole. The play became an autobiographical study of Tennessee's young life, and it is very moving.

I regret that the idea of unifying them into one play did not occur to me. I wish I could have been more helpful to Tennessee. I think my devotion to Lanford precluded a similar relationship with Tennessee. We remained good friends over the years, but I hoped someday I could make it up to him for not producing *Vieux Carré*.

In the meantime, one of our resident writers created a new play for our acting Company. It was her second play we'd produced in two years, which demonstrated that our concept of giving writers an ensemble to inspire them could produce stimulating new work. Corinne's play seemed far more promising than Tennessee's.

A Star Cluster

Corinne Jacker's new play was a fascinating and challenging piece. It drew on Corinne's wide-ranging knowledge of science, which allowed her to put physics on stage long before Michael Frayn's *Copenhage* dazzled the critics in 2000. I thought it was boldly original, traveling back and forth in time and dealing with memory in an abstract style very different from memory plays like *The Glass Menagerie*.

The play concerns a young physicist named Edward who has discovered a new sub-atomic particle that behaves very strangely: it is apparently oldest when it is born and youngest when it transforms into a different particle (much the way a caterpillar becomes a butterfly). Edward's discovery coincides with a personal crossroad: his girlfriend, Perdita, wants him to marry her. His father, Judge Wallace Howe, has just been appointed to the Supreme Court, and the family is gathered in Washington for the occasion (including Wallace's promiscuous and somewhat mad ex-wife, Laura Howe Winchester). On the cusp of these changes, Edward recalls significant moments from his youth, vignettes that are brought to life by actors playing younger versions of the characters: Young Eddie, Mother, Father, Grandfather, and the love of his adolescence, Sally. There is a complex back story, which reveals that Sally was a militant political activist. She was sentenced to prison by Judge Howe, and she dies there of pneumonia. In a stylistic anomaly that fits into neither story, Eddie's grandfather, who died before Eddie was born, is played by a young actor because he is remembered only from a sepia photograph taken in his youth, wearing a striped turn-of-the-century bathing outfit and about to dive into a swimming hole.

Corinne wrote the militant but melancholy Sally for Nancy Snyder. Tanya would play Mother in the past, and Roger Chapman (who'd joined the Company in *Richard Cory*) would play Father in the past. The young Eddie would be played by our newest addition to the Company, Jeff Daniels, fresh from *The Farm*. Moreover, Corinne wrote the part of Judge Howe for Douglass Watson, bringing him back to our stage from *Dancing for the Kaiser*.

Apart from the Company, Corinne wrote the central part of Edward for William Hurt. I knew him only as the husband of an actress I admired, Mary Beth Hurt. Corinne's passion for the young actor's talent proved well placed. At this point, Bill was a recent graduate of the Julliard School; he was six-feet-two, blond, and classically handsome, with small wire-frame glasses over intelligent blue eyes. When I heard him read the play the first time, I knew we'd found a rare talent.

William Hurt was born in Washington, D.C., the son of Claire Isabel (née McGill), who worked at Time, Inc., and Alfred McCord Hurt, who worked for the U.S. State Department. Bill lived with his father in Lahore, Mogadishu and Khartoum. After his parents divorced, his mother married Henry Luce III (heir of *Time Magazine*). William graduated from Middlesex School in 1968 where he was vice president of the Dramatics Club and had the lead role in several of the school plays. His high school yearbook predicted, "With characteristics such as these, you might even see him on Broadway." He attended Tufts University and studied theology, but turned instead to acting and joined the Juilliard Drama School.

Corinne wrote the role of Edward's mother for a warm, mature blonde named Jo Henderson, whom she'd known from *All My Children*. Jo became another long-time member of Circle Rep. For the fiancée, Perdita, auditions guided me to a lovely brunette sylph named Claire Malis, a Theater World Award-winner and a principal on *One Life to Live*. For the boyish image of the forever-young Grandfather, I remembered from auditions for *The Farm* handsome, tall, virile Christopher Reeve.

Chris was the son of Barbara Pitney, a journalist, and Franklin D'Olier Reeve, a teacher, novelist, poet and scholar, and the scion of a distinguished, wealthy family. At fifteen, Chris was accepted as an apprentice at the Williamstown Theatre Festival. The next summer, he was hired at the Harvard Summer Repertory Theater Company where he played Belyayev in *A Month in the Country*. After graduating, Chris chose Cornell, where he planned to start his career as an actor. In the fall of his freshman year, Chris received a letter from Stark Hesseltine, a high-powered agent who had discovered Robert Redford. Hesseltine had seen Chris in *A Month in the Country* and wanted to represent him. That summer, Chris toured in *Forty Carats* with Eleanor Parker. The next year, he played a full season with the San Diego Shakespeare Festival. At Julliard, he became fast friends with fellow student Robin Williams. In the fall of 1975, he was cast in the Broadway play *A Matter of Gravity* as the grandson of Katharine Hepburn, who adored him. Following an extensive national tour in that play, Chris joined Circle Rep and appeared with us both before and after his world-wide stardom.

It's rather amazing to think that we had a cluster of young actors who became major stars all on the Circle Rep stage at the same time! Of course, William Hurt, Christopher Reeve and Jeff Daniels were all at the beginning of their spectacular careers, but their extraordinary talents were already visible.

The script presents unusual production requirements: there has to be a present-time Washington apartment where the family is gathering, plus locations from Eddie's past; and the transitional element is a swimming pool, located between the present and the past. For the peculiar demands of the set, I turned to David Potts, who'd designed a perfect setting for *The Sea Horse* that preceded John Lee's entrance into the Company by six months. I told David I wanted a steeply raked, diamond-shaped stage, with the audience divided into two sections on each side of the frontal point. The pool had to be deep enough to swim in and warm enough to keep the actors comfortable, even in January. Behind the pool, David designed a wrap-around Victorian porch with elements of gingerbread trim where the actors would enact the memories. The carpeted forestage was outfitted sparsely with chic contemporary furniture, and the pool had a deck around it that made it a convincing extension of the apartment, but with lattice-work that helped to blend it with the porch of memory behind. The thrust stage was located in the northeast corner of our space.

Working with William Hurt was like falling in love. He and I worked together so fluidly that I felt I had found my ideal collaborator; he felt the same. Bill was attuned to my every suggestion. He was thrilled with our exploratory improvisations and with my approach to the discovery of organic staging through collaboration. A true believer, William Hurt was the most committed member of the acting Company for the next fourteen years, playing many characters, from leading men to supporting roles.

Our interns understudied our principal players, but Chris Reeve was understudying Bill Hurt in the leading role; an intern named David Oisher understudied Chris. Bill and Chris had been fellow students at Julliard (along with their buddy Robin Williams), so Bill thought he'd do Chris the favor of letting him play the leading role at one performance. It was exciting for everyone, as it always is when understudies go on. Chris was terrific in this one-night-only performance, but it was also the occasion for a very funny incident. In the course of the play, Edward goes for a swim, which involves a brief moment of nudity as he takes off his pants and dons a swimsuit. We'd rehearsed putting Chris in the play in the afternoon but we hadn't done it with full costumes. So when the moment came for Chris to pull on Bill's Speedo, he tugged it up as far as it would go, which, because he was considerably beefier than Bill, was only up to mid-thigh. He had to reverse course, quickly shed the bathing suit and take a skinny-dip in the pool. So the audience was treated to an unintentional peek at Chris in the "full monty."

Having an understudy did come in handy: David filled in for Chris a whole weekend when Chris flew to London to audition for the film *Superman*. When Chris returned, he confided with amazement to his cast-mates in our crowded little dressing room: "I think I actually *got* it!" And of course, he had. When Chris had dinner the following week with his father, a professor of literature at Princeton, he shyly told him: "Dad, it looks like I'm going to play Superman." Without dropping a beat, his academic father, assuming he meant Jack Tanner in Shaw's play *Man and Superman*, replied mildly: "Oh, that's nice. Who's playing Lady Ann?"

As we were going into rehearsal for *My Life* in December, Richard J. Daley died; he'd been the Mayor of Chicago for twenty-one years. Just days before we opened, Gary Gilmore was executed by firing squad in Utah (the first execution after the reintroduction of the death penalty in the United States). On his last day in office, President Ford pardoned Iva Toguri D'Aquino (known as World War II's infamous "Tokyo Rose"). On January 20th, Jimmy Carter succeeded Gerald Ford as the 39th President of the United States, and the next day he pardoned all the Vietnam War draft evaders. The times *had* changed, Mr. Dylan. All this seemed especially pertinent since our play involved the appointment of a Supreme Court Justice, the death of a political protester in prison, and the theme of forgiveness.

It was the coldest winter I can remember in New York. A high-amplitude planetary wave pattern caused record cold temperatures over the eastern United States. On the 19th of January, Miami, Florida experienced its only snowfall in history. At the end of the month, the Great Lakes Blizzard of 1977 hit Buffalo and Niagara Falls. But at Circle Rep, we were skinny-dipping in a heated onstage pool.

As cold as the winter was, it was a splendid time for the arts. The television phenomenon *Roots* began its groundbreaking run on ABC. In Paris, President Valéry Giscard d'Estaing officially opened the Centre Georges Pompidou. And six weeks later, tenor Luciano Pavarotti made his American television debut in Puccini's *La Bohème* on the first broadcast of the PBS opera series "Live from the Met."

Our production of *My Life* is a favorite of mine. In addition to the marvelous set by David Potts, Dennis Parichy used his lighting to delineate between the stark present and the sepia-toned past, and shot the night sky full of twinkling stars. Norman Berman provided another perfect score. Unfortunately, the critics did not share my love of the play. Their notices were as chilly as the weather.

My Life opened at Circle Rep January 23, 1977 and played forty-two performances. In addition to the previously mentioned credits, the costumes were by Kenneth M. Yount, the sound by Chuck London; the stage managers were Amy Schecter and David Oisher. Here are excerpts from the (mostly) disappointing reviews:

The New York Times, January 24, 1977 (Mel Gussow):
"*My Life* is confused and contradictory. Jacker has not refined the memories or defined the characters. Much of the writing is far below the author's usual level. The actors are an improvement on their material. Mr. Watson and Jo Henderson are so strong they almost convince us of the characters' credibility. There are also helpful contributions from William Hurt and Nancy Snyder. A focal point of Mason's production is a swimming pool that cramps the stage and Mason's movement of the actors. In [this] play, the present does not refract the past, nor does the past illuminate the present."

New York Post, January 24, 1977 (Sylviane Gold):
"The play is the life-and-death struggle of the pull of the past, and it is brought vividly to life by Jacker's careful writing and the Circle Repertory Company's fine acting. Jacker has brilliantly captured a literal assault of the past on a shaky mind. The actors mesh into a real ensemble. [It] has its problems, but the journey makes for an absorbing evening of theater."

The Record, January 24, 1977 (Emory Lewis):
"*My Life* is a flawed drama but it is filled with rich insights into its fascinating characters. Jacker towers over most of today's writers. [She] is a major new talent. Mason, one of

the nation's best young directors, has orchestrated *My Life* with an enormous sense of style. The cast plays with an ensemble perfection rarely seen in New York."

The New Yorker, February 7, 1977 (Edith Oliver):
"*My Life* is a complex, difficult play. The writing, always professional, is dense with images, literary allusions, and learned references, yet the play is not always as austere or intellectual as I've made it sound; there is some feeling, there is some comedy, and a number of the scenes are theatrical. The company, under Mason's direction, does well."

The Nation (undated) (Harold Clurman):
"*My Life* is a memory play, told in a convolution of flashbacks. Nearly everyone in the cast plays well and all are well-directed by Mason in Potts's ingenious setting. [But] I was left indifferent, because *My Life* is mostly rumination."

Village Voice, February 7, 1977 (Michael Feingold):
"[There] is at once too much material for a play and not enough. The writing is worth attending to. Jacker's gift is for prose that coruscates on the ear that seems at the same time perfectly natural and wittily turned. Even when her situations sink into cliché, her phrases sparkle; this is the most fluidly speaking play I have heard in some time. And Mason's production is a nearly perfect realization of it. Parichy's lighting often makes poetry where Jacker has provided only prose. Then add some very fine acting: William Hurt is the incarnation of slightly wounded success, and he is ably helped by Watson and Henderson."

As I said, it was becoming increasingly difficult to find scripts that pleased the critics. But the next one certainly did.

A Constellation Appears

As we did every year, we advertised in our subscription brochures that the coming season would include a new play by Lanford with the projected title *The War in Lebanon*, which eventually Lanford wrote under the title *The 5th of July* (details to follow). But for now, there was no new Wilson play to present. I felt obligated to our subscribers to come up with something that pleased them as much as *The Sea Horse* had. It was time to scour the horizons.

In early December while *Lili Lamont* was playing at Circle, I went to Playwrights Horizons on 42nd Street to check out a new play that received a couple of encouraging notices. Robert Moss, the Founding Artistic Director, was a good friend of mine who'd been the producer of *Sheba* at the Queens Playhouse. He and I also served for several years on the board of the Off-Off-Broadway Alliance. The play Bob discovered was *Gemini* by a new playwright, Albert Innaurato.

Alan Rich in *New York Magazine* said:

"*Gemini* is worth noting for the obvious talent of its author. What is brilliant about the work – and it is quite astounding – is the author's immaculate control over the farcical setting into which his romance has been inserted. Your admiration must grow for Innaurato's ability to orchestrate magnificent human tangles without any sacrifice of line and clarity. The man can write."

Albert Innaurato was born in Philadelphia, June 2, 1947. After graduating from California Institute of the Arts, Albert attended the Yale School of Drama. He was awarded a Guggenheim Grant, a Rockefeller Grant and two grants from the National Endowment for the Arts. While both were students at Yale, Albert collaborated with Christopher Durang on *The Idiots Karamazov, I Don't Normally Like Poetry but Have You Read Trees*, and *Gyp, the Real-Life Story of Mitzi Gaynor*. They often appeared in plays with Yale classmates Meryl Streep, Sigourney

Weaver and Wendy Wasserstein. Now he was about to burst onto the theater world like a blazing comet.

Gemini is a funny coming-of-age play (almost *opera buffa* in style) set in the shabby back yard of a working class Italian family in Philadelphia. The showcase at Playwrights Horizons was broadly but appropriately directed by another of Albert's classmates from Yale, Peter Mark Schifter. The cast included the debut of a young actress who, like the author and director, was a recent graduate of Yale, Sigourney Weaver, in the role of Judith. The play centered on her boyfriend, Francis (played by Jon Polito) and his rather bizarre family and neighbors. His expansive father, Fran, was played by Tom Mardirosian and Lucille, his father's long-suffering girlfriend, was played by Anne DeSalvo. The outrageous neighbor, Bunny, was played by Jessica James (who'd appeared at Circle in *Hot House*), and her obese, obsessive son, Marshall, was played by Jonathan Hadary. Rounding out the cast was Judith's brother, Randy, played by Reed Birney.

Here's the situation: Judith Hastings is Francis' classmate at Harvard, and she and her blond younger brother, Randy (who are the essence of WASPs) have shown up as a surprise for Francis' twenty-first birthday. Francis is mortified, because he knows his refined friends have never seen the kind of outlandish, exuberant behavior of his Italian family and neighbors. Furthermore, Randy's presence provides added tension because Francis finds himself agonizingly attracted to both brother and sister.

I enjoyed the matinee I saw; although it was over-long and heavy-handed, it was filled with life. The characters and their antics were hilarious, and the writing showed an original voice with penetrating observations, conveyed with side-splitting humor. At the end I asked to be introduced to the author. Albert is tall, probably 6'1" with a broad, earnest face. While he is overweight, he is nowhere near the obesity he imagines for himself; his physique seems solid, heavy, like a young Robert Morley. His darting black eyes signal a sharp intelligence, and while his mien is nervously edgy, it frequently gives way to compulsive giggling. I complimented Albert on the fine writing and told him to keep in touch with me. The production at Playwrights Horizons closed after a brief run under Equity's Showcase Code, which limited off-off-Broadway theaters to twenty-one performances.

About a month later, Albert's agent, the venerable Helen Merrill, called to let me know that *Gemini* was now playing at the PAF Playhouse in Huntington, Long Island, where it was scoring huge approval with suburban audiences. Knowing that I was searching for a production to fill the empty slot in our season, she invited me to take the train out to see it. And so I did.

Jay Broad was the Producing Director for PAF Playhouse, which at the time was a 230-seat regional theater on Long Island, less than an hour away from Manhattan. Jay, a slim, affable patrician fellow of medium height, with sandy hair and twinkling blue eyes, came to PAF in 1975 after serving five years as Artistic Director of Theater Atlanta. Jay wrote and directed a musical called *Red, White, and Maddox,* which transferred to the Cort Theater on Broadway for fifty-seven performances. When a hole appeared in Jay's 1977 season at PAF, Robert Moss suggested that he take a look at *Gemini*. Jay saw the Playwrights Horizons production and decided it would fit nicely into PAF's season; so shortly after its initial run, he'd brought it to Long Island. I was now in the same situation. Jay and the cast were excited by my coming to PAF because they knew I was interested in bringing the production back to Circle Rep.

The script had been tightened a bit and there were some cast changes: Carol Potter replaced Sigourney Weaver as Judith; the central role of Francis was now played by Robert Picardo; and the father, Fran, was Danny Aiello. The remainder of the cast was intact from the Playwrights Horizons production.

In the larger theater at PAF, encouraged by roaring audiences, the actors became even broader in their performances. If we brought *Gemini* to Circle Rep, there would have to be major adjustments in the style of playing. The only problem was: the playwright and the director were not speaking! Albert and Peter both had volatile personalities, and I don't know what their problems were, but Peter had left in a huff, and Albert did not want him to return. If I brought the production to Circle, I would have to re-direct it myself. Albert seemed pleased about that prospect.

I told Jay I'd love to move the PAF Production to Circle Rep. Jerry Arrow contacted PAF's business manager Joel Warren to work out the terms of a co-production. I told them that I would use the same cast and designers in New York. I even offered to keep Peter's billing as director, although I would be going back into rehearsal, substantially restaging the play, transforming Peter's broad approach to something more resembling a Circle Rep style. I wanted to instill honesty in the performances, and pay keen attention to details. The farce had to be grounded in reality.

It was an interesting time to present a play about a young man's dilemma of dealing with his homosexuality. Crazy things were going on around the country. California repealed its law prohibiting sodomy, but James Dobson founded his anti-homosexual watch-dog organization called "Focus on the Family." *Gemini* certainly threw focus on the family, but I doubt it was the kind of focus Dr. Dobson had in mind. Also, it was the time of the Anita Bryant fiasco, in which the former Miss America and Florida Orange Juice-commercial queen launched her vitriolic antigay campaign called "Save the Children." Florida voters, bowing to Bryant's influence, overwhelmingly voted to repeal Miami-Dade's gay rights ordinance. By the end of the month, 200,000 protesters marched through the streets of San Francisco protesting her anti-gay crusade. And in October, Miss Bryant was the recipient of a pie-in-the-face delivered by gay rights activists during a press conference in Des Moines, after which she retreated from her anti-gay activism.

We went into rehearsal the week after the production closed at PAF, and while I praised the work of the cast, I indicated that our mission was to tone down their performances by re-exploring the characters' relationships and simplifying the movement. They were eager to take on this new assignment. I defined acting for them as: "Behaving truthfully in imaginary situations;" and I reminded them that it was not the actor's job to be funny. If the script was funny, and we all knew it was, then we only needed to be honest and it would be funny. We began with improvisations, just as if we were starting freshly at the outset of rehearsals. The actors responded with enthusiasm to the new discoveries they made about the depth that lay behind the lines, and they enjoyed filling in the subtle histories of their relationships. I broke the script down into beats and we re-explored every moment of movement, assuring that it was organically arising from the circumstances, rather than arbitrarily assigned for comic effect. All the actors had seen productions at Circle Rep, so they were attuned to the nature of the undertaking.

Albert attended many of the rehearsals and we did a little more tightening of the script, cutting in the text what was obvious from the performance, and deleting lines that didn't add to the central action. Throughout the process, Albert was energetic and enthused about the work. He had the same joy I'd seen other playwrights experience at Circle Rep; he was watching the play he wrote come to life and he was thrilled. Much to both his and my relief, Peter Mark Schifter was busy directing another production and did not appear during the two weeks of our rehearsal. Nevertheless, I felt it was wrong to "steal" the production from Peter; although we changed a great deal, much remained that was of Peter's invention, and I felt it was only right that he should retain his billing. My influence remained hidden for the time being, an extension of my duties as Artistic Director. By the time we opened, we had converted *Gemini* into a production that was unmistakably Circle Rep's.

In addition to being pleased with the progress on *Gemini*, Albert was elated because our production of his comedy followed within a few days the premiere of his dark, grotesque play *The Transfiguration of Benno Blimpie* at the Astor Playhouse. Starring James Coco, it was a harrowing expressionistic tale of an obese man so ravenous that he devours his own flesh. *Benno Blimpie* received stunned admiration from the critics for its savage indictment of self-image. Now within a week, our newly celebrated playwright revealed another side in a play, so far removed in tone from

Benno Blimpie that it was hard to believe it was written by the same author. It was a double-barreled debut, unparalleled in recent theater history, or perhaps, ever.

Albert Innaurato's *Gemini* opened at the Circle Repertory Company (in association with PAF Playhouse) March 8, 1977 and played sixty-three performances. The director was still listed as Peter Mark Schifter, the setting was by Christopher Nowak, costumes by Ernest Allen Smith, and lighting by Larry Crimmins. Stage managers were Fred Reinglas and James Arneman. Again, the critics responded enthusiastically.

The New York Times, March 14, 1977 (Mel Gussow):
"When *Gemini* was first presented at Playwrights Horizons, it seemed to be a grand, comic soap opera. In the play's latest and, presumably, definitive version at Circle Rep, we not only see the rambunctious and bizarre comic vision, but we also feel the heartbeat. [It] is a spiraling comedy – a cascade of human frailties, fealties and pretenses, and there is uproarious laughter. In the play's progress from [previous productions] Innaurato has clarified some plot points and altered some dialogue, generally to the play's advantage. Principally what he has done is to alter the tone of the play – to tone it down. The play is less of a caricature and more human. This is a play that comes to life in performance. All of the actors are exceptional. Innaurato is a playwright with his own extraordinary voice and the imaginative talent of a conjurer."

Daily News, March 14, 1977 (Douglas Watt):
"*Gemini*, though interesting and containing much lively dialogue, is too filled with incident for its own good. It is relieved by the humor and backyard eruptions of anger, joy, suicide threats, and such. The cast is uniformly good. Innaurato remains a playwright of considerable promise, almost certain of realization."

New York Post, March 14, 1977 (Martin Gottfried):

"Innaurato is definitely a find. *Gemini* is a decent play, though not a surprising one. The same humanity that engulfs *Benno Blimpie* is in this play too, and also the energy and musical definition. There are crucial faults, but it does present the author's strengths. The dramatic rhythm is there and the love comes through."

The Record, March 14, 1977 (Emory Lewis):

"Sound the trumpets and beat the drums. Innaurato is a major new talent. His fascinating *Gemini* opened last night at Circle Rep, and I suggest an immediate visit. Innaurato is a poet of the misfit and the psychically wounded. From the angle of the dispossessed, he offers invaluable illuminations on the state of the union. Under Schifter's inspired direction, the actors work together with a silken smoothness. Since it was founded in 1969, Circle Rep has pioneered in presenting new and important American plays. Add to this impressive list Innaurato's *Gemini*."

Newsday, March 18, 1977 (George Oppenheimer):

"Innaurato has packed *Gemini* with incidents of earthy humor and touching tenderness. I thoroughly enjoyed *Gemini*. As for Circle Rep, it once again outclasses most other acting companies by a mile."

New York Magazine, May 23, 1977 (Alan Rich):

"Much has happened to *Gemini* since I first saw it last fall at Playwrights Horizons. The dialogue throughout has been sharpened, somewhat pruned of extraneous motivations, and invested with a superior sense of rhythm. The cast has been strengthened by the arrival of Danny Aiello; the others were good to begin with, and have, under Schifter's taut direction, gotten better. It is still a rambunctious, hilarious, touching, quite beautiful play."

The New Yorker, March 28, 1977 (Edith Oliver):

"Innaurato is an original of incomparable imagination. When I saw a workshop production a few months ago at Playwrights Horizons I thought it was lively enough, but disheveled. Now at Circle Rep, it is a true comedy, its wild spirit intact, and in its own way, coherent."

The Nation, April 2, 1977 (Harold Clurman):

"Though less striking [than *Benno Blimpie*] *Gemini* is probably the sounder play. What is best is its depiction of physical and emotional turmoil. The cast has been well chosen. The temptation for the director, in such instances, is to overdo the hilarious crudities and the sentiment. Schifter, on the whole, avoids both pitfalls. Aiello is an actor who, I believe, has possibilities for roles of greater (possibly Shakespearean) dimension. DeSalvo is killingly funny, Picardo is wholly convincing. In fact I liked all the actors: Birney, Potter, Hadary, James. Applause and a respectful bow to the author. We look forward to his further writing."

Time Magazine, March 28, 1977 (T.E. Kalem):

"A zinging display of comic fireworks. In an artfully accomplished cast, Anne DeSalvo rates a golden pasta award. *Gemini* is the kind of play the early William Saroyan might have enjoyed or, for that matter, written."

The reviews were practically an invitation for a longer run with a larger audience; Circle Rep was headed back to Broadway. But this time, our Executive Director, Jerry Arrow, was determined Circle Rep should benefit more from a commercial move. Jerry raised the money from investors from both Circle Rep and PAF backers. Both theaters were listed as producers, and both received a percentage of the profits.

Back into Orbit

Jerry got us Broadway's smallest house (597 seats) for the transfer, at that time called The Little Theater, later rechristened the Helen Hayes. It was in the heart of the theater district on 44th Street, next door to Sardi's, across the street from *A Chorus Line* and Shubert Alley. It was a perfect-sized theater in a perfect location.

Since Circle Rep was directly involved as a producer, I wanted to make sure the Broadway transfer was smooth and successful. During the run at Circle Rep, Albert and Peter resolved their differences. Peter was grateful that we'd preserved his work and his credit, and that we gave him an Off-Broadway hit. He was eager to be involved in the move to Broadway, and both Albert and I were glad to have his cooperation. But I was concerned about the potential for an eruption of fresh enmity between them, so I felt it was necessary for me to hold the union contract as director of the Broadway production. I offered Peter to keep his directorial credit, and I would be billed only as "Broadway Production Supervisor." We shared equally the director's royalty of 3%. Everybody was happy with the arrangement.

Peter and I essentially co-directed the Broadway production of *Gemini*. Our work together was a genial collaboration. We agreed it was best if the cast heard from only one director, so I gave the directions to the actors, while Peter made suggestions to me when he had an idea, and I passed it on. Unlike the transfer of *Knock Knock*, I made sure we had several days to restage and for the actors to make adjustments. Peter cheerfully acceded to my prior Broadway experience in making the changes needed. For the first time, we had a proscenium arch that stretched high over the stage. I asked Chris Nowak, the original designer (who was a friend of Peter's), to design a second story for the brick duplex that housed the Geminiani family and their neighbors, the Weinbargers. Visually, this added a scale we couldn't achieve with the low ceilings over the stages at Circle Rep or Playwrights Horizons. It allowed more variety of movement, with characters like Bunny appearing in her second story window in scenes where she was not directly involved in the backyard action.

We also added a cyclorama that spanned the rear width of the stage, giving us a sky that enlarged the canvas. The fence itself became more elaborate as a means into and out of the backyard. For the first time there was a need for brick buildings at each side of the stage to give a sense of the surrounding neighborhood. And the height of the proscenium allowed us to erect a real telephone pole that could be climbed, adding genuine drama to Bunny's threats of suicide.

These expansions made the set look like it belonged on Broadway. The play settled comfortably into the Little Theater as if it had been conceived there. That was lucky because it became the home of the play for more than four years.

With Chuck London, we made a hilarious television commercial as polished as a sitcom (it was shot in 35mm). It featured skinny Anne DeSalvo poaching her meal off everyone else's plates at the birthday party, with a line that became repeated far and wide: "I'm not hungry; I'll just pick." We saturated the airwaves with the ad, which was a delightful representation of the play. It lured audiences with the promise of a rousing evening of laughs. The publicity pictures of the family gathered in pointed birthday hats to celebrate Francis' twenty-first birthday suggested a warmth of family that people increasingly missed from their own. It just looked like fun!

As for the cast, now that their performances were grounded in reality, we allowed them to grow again to fill the larger space, so a balance was achieved between Peter's *opera buffa* style and Circle Rep's sense of truth. It was a happy marriage of the comic and romantic potential of the play. Suburban audiences (the so-called "bridge and tunnel crowd") were largely responsible for the extraordinary success of *Gemini*. People recognized themselves, their neighbors and their relatives in these characters, and they rewarded the show with a run of 1,819 performances – the fourth longest run of a straight play in Broadway history. It must have been a fortuitous time in the zodiac, because five days after we opened, George Lucas' *Star Wars* began playing in cinemas, becoming the highest grossing film in history up till then.

There was little the critics could add to the momentum we'd built up Off-Broadway, and with our ubiquitous television ad, we didn't really need them. Still, here are a few samples that couldn't hurt:

The New York Times, May 23, 1977 (Clive Barnes):

"I think this season as a whole is the finest of the past decade. *Gemini*, still directed by Schifter, but with the present Broadway production 'supervised' by Mason, is an immensely likeable play. It is a well-crafted, popularly styled play that recalls the heyday of semi-serious television drama, and playwrights such as Paddy Chayefsky. What matters is the brightness of the dialogue, the crispness of the direction and the happy zaniness of the fine acting. The ensemble performance is an overdrawn but ample pleasure, and I heartily commend *Gemini*. It sends you out smiling at the essential goodness of warm people in warm plays."

Newsday, May 23, 1977 (Leo Seligsohn):

"This is a very funny play, although its underpinning is deadly serious. Since I saw the play at PAF, it has undergone minor changes. In the Broadway production, supervised by Mason, and staged by its original director, Schifter, the changes have strengthened *Gemini*. The acting is still strong. Potter and Birney are engaging as the sister-brother friends. But it is Anne DeSalvo who provides the show's most unforgettable character. She is one further bit of evidence that on Broadway Innaurato's play remains as fresh, insightful and funny as I remember it."

Variety, May 25, 1977 (Madden):

"*Gemini* is one of the most exciting and interesting works thus far this season, and unquestionably establishes

[Innaurato] as a major playwright. Splendidly written, Innaurato has captured perfectly the ethnic behavior and humor with which audiences will immediately identify. Word of mouth alone could insure *Gemini* a long Broadway stay."

The New Leader, April 11, 1977 (John Simon):
"Innaurato weaves an attractive tapestry, fraught with fine-observed behavioral mannerisms, idiosyncrasies of speech, and tricky emotional entanglements. There is a good deal of precocious wisdom here. Three performances are outstanding: Aiello's Fran is a superbly rounded characterization. Birney's Randy is splendid. And Potter is a marvelous Judith."

In addition, we had splendid notices from out-of-town papers, plus the tri-state area television stations – all of which put us in touch with what grew to be our audience.

One small change from the earlier incarnations of *Gemini* should be noted. The character Marshall Weinbarger, played by Jonathan Hadary in an enormous "fat suit," began to trouble Albert. It seems he based the character on a real person in Philadelphia, and Albert became paranoid that he might be sued; so he decided to change the character's first name to Herschel. I was glad. Two Marshalls already at Circle Rep seemed enough already! Also, Wilhelm Herschel was the discoverer of Uranus, and it seemed a better fit for this fat young eccentric genius. Peter and I continued to collaborate on casting for the next few years and we gave Kathleen Turner her first Broadway job, replacing Carol Potter as Judith. Also Wayne Knight, who gained fame as a recurring character on *Seinfeld* as well as in films like *Jurassic Park* and *Basic Instinct,* replaced Jonathan Hadary as Herschel; he didn't need a "fat suit." Although more perfectly cast for the character, Wayne was neither as touching nor as funny as Jonathan.

We opened too late in the season to attract Tony nominations, but in May, the *Village Voice* awarded Obies for Performance to

Danny Aiello and Anne DeSalvo for *Gemini* and to William Hurt for *My Life*. Albert Innaurato also received an Obie for Playwriting and a Drama Desk nomination for Outstanding New American Play.

At the Sunday matinee on May 22nd, I spotted Clive Barnes at the intermission standing across the street, gazing at the theater. Mr. Barnes always preferred seeing productions at a Sunday matinee performance, perhaps because it's easier to stay awake. I went over to say hello, and he greeted me pleasantly. Pointing to the façade and marquee, he remarked that the Little Theater would make a perfect permanent home for Circle Rep, and suggested we investigate buying it. I agreed it certainly was ideal. Having a permanent presence on Broadway would be a giant step toward fulfilling my dreams of becoming The National Theater. We would be the first Off-Broadway company to leap to a home on Broadway since the Circle-in-the-Square Theater had done it in 1972 (thereby freeing up their Bleecker Street Theater for our long run of *HOT L*). Of course, neither of us had any idea that *Gemini* would keep the theater occupied for over four years. Nor did Mr. Barnes have any idea how little support we had from our Board of Directors. Circle Rep had accumulated a deficit of over $200,000 at this point; we implored the Board with scant success to raise money to retire the deficit. Any idea they were capable of buying a Broadway theater was the stuff of pipedreams, even though in 1977 it would have cost less than a million.

Planet Earth

On the world stage, Menachem Begin's election as Prime Minister of Israel gave the Middle East the first glimmer of hope for a resolution of seemingly endless conflict. The United Kingdom was celebrating the Silver Anniversary of Queen Elizabeth II with jubilees world-wide. Spain held its first democratic elections after forty-one years under Franco's dictatorship. And in China, the Communist leader Deng Xiaoping introduced reforms that integrated a market economy into the Communist system.

Meanwhile, in our small world Circle Rep continued our After-Piece series, paying actors a flat fee of $150 per show. First up,

Danny Irvine directed a delightful comedy by Jerry L. Crawford called *The Passing of Corky Brewster*. It was a perfect vehicle for the talents of Sharon Madden, a one-person play so rich it belongs to a rare category – a monodrama that is neither autobiographical nor confessional. The character Grace Turley is caught in a terrible situation and fueling herself with slugs of whiskey to ease her bereavement, she mourns the death of the title character while talking back to her radio, where a local radio DJ chats in between country-western songs. Corky was her lover, though not her husband, and according to Grace, a lover of unparalleled gusto. His death has come about at the climax of a sexual encounter with Grace. In fact, this has just happened, and in her mind she's guilty of murder. She's consuming whiskey to steel her nerves to call the sheriff and admit her crime. Of course, we imagine that while the sheriff may be as amused as we are by her "confession," no crime has actually been committed. In fact a good time seems to have been had by all; Corky always said "That's the way to go!"

The Passing of Corky Brewster opened February 8th as an After-Piece to *My Life* and ran for five performances; it was so popular we brought it back for an additional five performances at the end of March. We had only one review:

Daily News, March 24, 1977 (Don Nelson):
"In the capable hands of Sharon Madden, *The Passing of Corky Brewster* becomes an interesting examination of guilt feelings run amok. Under Daniel Irvine's adroit direction, Madden brings enough nuance and shading to her performance to grip our attention. One-character plays are difficult to pull off, but this one certainly demands applause."

We followed *Corky Brewster* with another After-Piece during *Gemini*'s extended run. *For Love or Money* was a revue of original music by Jason McAuliffe and Jay Jeffries. It was a project of a director from my directing lab, Susan Lehman. The four-person cast included Sharon Madden, Kate Kelly, Ken Kimmins and the composer, Jason McAuliffe. It played nine performances, but no review of this revue is extant.

In May, during the previews for *Exiles,* we presented another musical revue called *Cabaret Theatre (New York Times).* It was written by Gloria Allen, Brooks Porter and James Tobin, with music by Jeffrey Nissim. It was a project of another director from my lab, Ann Raychel. It played only four performances.

There are unfortunately no reviews for our fourth After-Piece, a charming play called *What the Babe Said* by Martin Halpern, directed by Amy Schecter, one of our stage managers who'd studied with me in our directing lab. It played as an After-Piece to *Exiles* for nine performances. *Babe* took place in the visiting manager's office of a Major League Baseball team. It's a two-character colloquy between an aging manager, Sal, and his veteran centerfielder, Buck. After an argument about whether it was the Babe or Leo Durocher who said, "Nice guys finish last," these crusty old-timers, trapped long past their prime by their love of the game, argue about life, religion, winning and losing. It was a piece of good timing because only a month before, Major League Baseball expanded to include two new teams: the Toronto Blue Jays and the Seattle Mariners. *What the Babe Said* is a touching and funny piece about "America's Pastime," and Martin returned to Circle Rep the following year with another new play, *Total Recall.*

In addition to the After-Pieces, we also presented a short season of workshop productions that were the climax of the directing workshops I'd offered the past two years. Jerry rented space from the Westbeth Theater Center for three weeks in the spring of 1977. My assistant, Steve Gomer, directed an excellent production of Sam Shepard's stunning one-act *Suicide in B-Flat,* which was well attended, as Sam's plays nearly always are. It had a haunting jazz score and a strikingly minimalistic set by David Potts that defined a black void with taut white ropes. Two other plays presented in this workshop season were *Allegra* by Allan Bates, directed by Richard Gaffield, and *Fat Chances* by Charlie Peters, directed by Ron Logomarsino. The workshop season also gave us a chance to mount Company writer Claris Nelson's first full-length play since *A Road Where the Wolves Run*. This complex, melancholy piece was called *To the Land*. It was directed by Richard Mogavero. It was a drama of entangled relationships with resonance about the tangled state of the country in the post-Vietnam era. These directors all participated in my directing workshops, along with Carole Rothman, Stuart White, and John Henry Davis.

We also continued our PiP program with a second workshop of John Heuer's *Mrs. Tydings Mason-Dixon Medicine Man*. This time it was directed by Susan Lehman, and John was much happier with the result. We also did a PiP of *Celebration Off River Street* by James Tobin and Steve Gomer ended up the season with a PiP of *The Brixton Recovery* by Jack Gilhooley. It's a tender play about a broken down boxer who winds up in the Brixton section of London and finds love while being nursed back to health by a Jamaican woman. I enjoyed it, but not enough to make it a Major Production.

These productions, mostly outside the mainstream of Circle Rep, offered spice and texture to our subscription series, and our theatergoers welcomed the chance to see these bonus productions. I have no doubt that some people will remember a moment from one of these plays more than Major Productions seen the same season.

Our next journey took us to Ireland, though only figuratively; in reality, we brought Dublin to Greenwich Village.

Into Another Dimension

Co-founder of Circle Rep Rob Thirkield was finally ready to direct again after a two-year hiatus. He proposed the seldom-performed *Exiles*, the only play written by the great Irish novelist James Joyce. I'm not sure what attracted Rob to *Exiles*, but it is conceivable that suspicions about his own marriage may have drawn him to similar circumstances in the play. Anyway, it was great to have Rob directing again.

James Joyce was born in Dublin on the 2nd of February in 1882. He is considered one of the most influential writers of the early 20th century. Joyce is best known for *Ulysses* (1922), a landmark novel that used a stream of consciousness technique in constructing a modern treatment of *The Odyssey*. Other major works are the short-story collection *Dubliners* (1914), and the novels *A Portrait of the Artist as a Young Man* (1916) and *Finnegans Wake* (1939). Born to a lower middle class Irish family, Joyce excelled as a student at Jesuit schools, then at University College, Dublin. In his early twenties, he immigrated permanently to continental Europe, living in Trieste, Paris and Zürich the rest of his life. Though living abroad, Joyce wrote principally about life in Dublin. As he explained: "I always write about Dublin, because if I can get to the heart of Dublin I can get to the heart of all the cities of the world. In the particular is contained the universal."

Despite an early interest in the theatre, Joyce published only one play, *Exiles*, begun shortly after the outbreak of World War I and published in 1918. The play looks back to *The Dead* (the final story in *Dubliners*) and forward to *Ulysses*, which he began around the time of the play's composition. Joyce described *Exiles* as "three cat and mouse acts."

The exiles of the title are Richard Rowan, an Irish writer, and his common-law wife, Bertha. The couple recently has returned to Dublin from exile in Rome. The story is of a love triangle that ensues when Richard's friend Robert Hand, a journalist, overtly expresses his sexual attraction to Bertha. He invites her to come to his house later that night. After he's left, a second triangle emerges as Beatrice arrives for the son's music lesson, and Richard is clearly attracted to her intellect. In an attempt to arouse Richard's jealousy, Bertha tells him about Robert's proposition and asks if she should go. Richard tells her to decide for herself. The second act takes place in Robert's house late at night. But when Robert answers the expected knock at the door, it is Richard who has come. It's an obviously awkward situation; Richard tells Robert that he knows of the proposed assignation. When Bertha arrives, Robert discreetly withdraws to his garden, leaving the couple to discuss the circumstances. After telling Bertha about the confrontation the two men have just had, Richard goes home, leaving his wife alone with Robert. The act ends without the audience knowing whether Bertha will spend the night or not. The third act is back at Rowan's apartment the following morning, where Bertha confesses to her maid that she has not slept all night. When Richard returns from buying the morning paper, he shows Bertha a very favorable review Robert has written about his newly published book. Bertha and Robert give vague but different accounts of what happened between them the previous night. Finally, the couple is reconciled; the doubt that has come into their relationship stirs Richard's renewed passion for his wife.

The casting offered wonderful opportunities for company members. Stephanie Gordon was ideal for the voluptuous Bertha. Neil Flanagan got a change of pace with the role of the seducer, Robert. Nancy Killmer, always elegant, was the "other woman" in this double love triangle. And Rob was able to bring back handsome Alan Jordan to play Richard Rowan, after his sensitive work in *Battle of Angels*.

David Potts designed the contrasting Victorian rooms and Jennifer von Mayrhauser had the agreeable task of designing rich period gowns and proper suits for the gentlemen. Dennis Parichy enjoyed lending the glow of gaslight to the scenes. And Norman Berman wrote an appropriate score.

Exiles opened at Circle Rep May 19, 1977 (the night before *Gemini*'s Broadway opening) and played thirty-five performances. It was directed by Rob Thirkield.

The New York Times, May 20, 1977 (Mel Gussow):
"There is a beguiling air of mystery and domestic menace as these people seduce and betray one another. Except for occasional fussiness of detail, Thirkield's direction is exacting and intelligent. Potts's set ingeniously converts from a homey parlor to the bachelor's red-plush lair, and von Mayrhauser's costumes and Parichy's lighting are additional assets. There is a luminous certitude about both Thirkield's production and Joyce's tantalizing, unjustly neglected play."

The Transcendent Years

Daily News, May 20, 1977 (Patricia O'Haire):

"The play probably reads a whole lot better than it performs. Nobody moves. They just talk and talk and talk and talk. As usual, the Circle has given it a handsome production. All [the actors] do well by their roles. The settings by Potts are quite authentic looking, but Thirkield really directed with a heavy, heavy hand."

The New Yorker, May 30, 1977 (Edith Oliver):

"The play is a wonder: profound in its emotional probing, utterly convincing, and often funny. The performance under Thirkield's direction is believable and engrossing."

The Star-Ledger, May 20, 1977 (William A. Raidy):

"*Exiles* is a fascinating drama, and the Circle Rep has given it a really dazzling revival. Thirkield directed, and he has instilled such a haunting quality to the play that sometimes it makes it seem better than it actually is. I bless Circle Rep for bringing it back to life so splendidly. This production illuminates the play, and I don't think one can find better performances anywhere on the stage this season."

New York Magazine, June 6, 1977 (Alan Rich):

"The play is exceptionally tense and tender; its writing, spare and doom-haunted, is so beautiful in itself that one risks the danger of missing the slender thread of plot. *Exiles* is seldom produced; that is a mistake because it is a haunting, poetic drama. The revival at Circle Rep, directed by Thirkield, is fairly close to splendid."

The Nation, (undated) (Harold Clurman):

"The Circle Company's production has been directed by Thirkield to be more normally dramatic and much more lively than the two others I have seen. As I left the theater I felt that at last I grasped the play. But Joyce is no playwright.

One need not complain of the production. It attempts a lightness which makes the play appear more overtly dramatic than it really is. To its credit, the cast – especially Flanagan – plays with candid understanding."

The Hollywood Reporter, May 26, 1977 (Charles Ryweck):
"*Exiles* is more than a mere literary curiosity. Director Thirkield has assembled a fine cast. Gordon plays with passion and frankness. Flanagan is funny and pathetic, frequently both at the same time."

The reviewers generally applauded Circle Rep for bringing back a seldom-performed play, but they had the same reservations that dogged the play since its inception.

I'm proud of the range of plays Circle Rep produced in revivals: Chekhov, Ibsen, Strindberg, Aeschylus, cummings, Joyce, Wedekind, Shakespeare, Schiller and Hauptman. We treated these writers as if they were new playwrights, seeing their work for the first time. Our goal was to bring the plays to life in the here and now, as fresh as *Gemini*. With such ambitious goals, it is no shame to admit we did not always succeed; but we gave the plays our all and we sometimes deeply stirred theatergoers who'd never seen the classics come to life as they did at Circle Rep; some of them were even critics.

In the spring of 1977, Circle Repertory Company was awarded the prestigious Margo Jones Award for outstanding service to the American Theater.

Sparkling Time Travel

When Circle Rep presented its first musical in 1977, it was a seachanging year in the music business. Fleetwood Mac released their Grammy Award-winning album *Rumours*. The Grateful Dead appeared at Cornell University upstate in Ithaca. The Supremes broke up; they performed their final concert together at the Drury Lane in London and then they disbanded (providing a storyline for Tom Eyen's 1981 Broadway musical *Dreamgirls).* Led Zeppelin played their last concert in the United States at the Oakland-Alameda County Coliseum. Three days after we opened our final production of the year, Elvis Presley performed his last concert at the Market Square Arena in Indianapolis; and on August 16th, he died in his home at Graceland, attracting 75,000 fans to line the streets of Memphis for his funeral. The King was dead, but the emergence of punk had just begun. The Clash released their debut album of the same name on CBS records. The record giant EMI fired the controversial punk rock group the Sex Pistols; undaunted, rising like a Phoenix, they released their hit album *Never Mind the Bollocks: Here's the Sex Pistols.*

Now that Circle Rep had presented a couple of musical revues as After-Pieces, Norman Berman, our company composer, proposed a musical project for a Major Production. A couple of years earlier, Norman was involved with Betty Comden and Adolph Green in a musical revue called *By Bernstein*, produced by Chelsea Theater Center at the Westside Theater. Now Norman had a similar idea for another musical revue. It consisted of songs cut from the original musical productions by Cole Porter. We called it *Unsung Cole.* I was a huge fan of Porter's (who isn't?), so I enthusiastically gave Norman the go-ahead. After months of negotiations with the Porter Estate, Norman finally secured the rights to these discarded songs.

If you reflect on a list of Cole Porter's songs, you might wonder what material was left un-sung. I dare you not to hum along as we consider these titles: "Let's Do It, Let's Fall in Love", "What Is This Thing Called Love?", "You Do Something to Me", "Night And Day", "Anything Goes", "I Get a Kick Out of You", "You're the Top", "Don't Fence Me In", "Begin the Beguine", "Just One of Those Things", "I've Got You Under My Skin", "In the Still of the Night", "My Heart Belongs to Daddy", "Ev'ry Time We Say Goodbye", "Be a Clown", "Another Op'nin', Another Show", "Always True to You (in My Fashion)", "From This Moment On", "I Love Paris" and "True Love", to name just a few of his most popular standards.

Cole Porter was born on July 9, 1891 in Peru, Indiana, the only child of a wealthy Baptist family. His father, Samuel, was a druggist; his mother, Kate, was the pampered daughter of J.O. Cole, a coal and timber speculator who was the richest man in Indiana. Kate started Porter's musical training on the violin at age six, the piano at eight, and he wrote his first operetta at ten. He attended Yale University, where he sang both in the Yale Glee Club and in the original Whiffenpoofs. Porter wrote three-hundred songs while at Yale. After graduating, he studied at Harvard, where he studied harmony and counterpoint. In 1915, Porter's first song on Broadway, "Esmeralda" appeared in the revue *Hands Up*.

In 1917, the U.S. entered World War I, and Porter moved to Paris, where he served a stint in the French Foreign Legion. He maintained a luxury apartment in Paris, where he entertained lavishly. His parties were extravagant and scandalous, described by Porter biographer J.X. Bell as having "much gay and bisexual activity, Italian nobility, cross-dressing, international musicians, and a large surplus of recreational drugs." In 1918, he met Linda Lee Thomas, a rich, Louisville, Kentucky-born divorcée eight years his senior, whom he married the following year. However, marriage did not diminish Porter's taste for self-indulgence.

Porter reintroduced himself to Broadway with the musical *Paris* (1928), which featured one of his greatest songs, "Let's Do It (Let's Fall in Love)". Continuing with this Gallic theme, his next show was *Fifty Million Frenchmen* (1929). He started the 1930s with the revue *The New Yorkers* (1930), which included a song about a streetwalker, "Love for Sale". Next came Fred Astaire's last stage show, *Gay Divorce* (1932). It featured a hit that became one of Porter's best-known tunes, "Night and Day". In 1934, Porter wrote his greatest score of this period, *Anything Goes*. For years afterwards, critics unfavorably compared most other Porter shows to this one. *Anything Goes* was also the first Porter show featuring Ethel Merman, who went on to star in five of his musicals. Now at the height of his success, Porter enjoyed his opening nights; he made grand entrances and sat in front, relishing the shows as much as any audience member.

The Transcendent Years

But in October of 1937, Porter was riding horses in Locust Valley, New York, when his horse rolled on him and crushed his legs, leaving him crippled and in constant pain for the rest of his life. Despite his pain, Porter continued to write successful shows. *Leave It to Me!* (1938) (introducing Mary Martin singing "My Heart Belongs to Daddy"), *DuBarry Was a Lady* (1939), *Panama Hattie* (1940), *Let's Face It!* (1941), *Something for the Boys* (1943), and *Mexican Hayride* (1944) were all hits. Nevertheless, Porter was turning out fewer hit songs and many thought his best period was over.

But in 1948, Porter made a great comeback, writing his biggest Broadway hit, *Kiss Me, Kate*. The production won the Tony Award for Best Musical (the first Tony awarded in that category). *Can-Can* (1952) was another hit. His last original Broadway production was *Silk Stockings* (1955), with a book by George S. Kaufman, Leueen MacGrath and Abe Burrows. Eventually, his injuries caused a series of ulcers on his right leg. After thirty-four operations, it was amputated and replaced with an artificial limb. The operation followed the death of his beloved mother and his wife's death from emphysema. Porter never wrote another song after 1958 and spent the remaining years of his life in relative seclusion. Cole Porter died of kidney failure on October 15, 1964, at the age of seventy-three in Santa Monica, California.

If Circle Rep was going to produce a musical, we would start at the top. Norman drew on some superb talent to help him realize his vision. After doing the vocal arrangements himself, Norman engaged Leon Odenz as Musical Director and though there was a minimum of dancing, Dennis Grimaldi as Choreographer.

Norman's cast of five included three outstanding singer/actresses: Mary Louise (who'd appeared in twelve Broadway shows, including playing Irene Malloy in the 1975 revival of *Hello, Dolly!*); the incomparable Anita Morris (who played in four Broadway shows, including *The Magic Show,* and four years later starred in *Nine,* for which she received a Drama Desk Award and a Tony nomination); and Maureen Moore, who'd played June in the Angela Lansbury 1974 revival of *Gypsy* and went on to appear in another dozen Broadway musicals, replacing Bernadette Peters as Rose in the 2003 *Gypsy* and replacing Betty Buckley as Norma Desmond in *Sunset Boulevard*. So our three female singers were top quality. It was difficult to find men who could match the ladies, but Norman did well with John Sloman (who followed this engagement with seven Broadway shows) and Gene Lindsey (who had four additional Off-Broadway credits.)

Following through on Circle Rep's design policy of creating an environment for each production, we turned our theater into a cabaret space with small tables and served free champagne. The art deco set was designed by Peter Harvey, the glamorous costumes by Carol Oditz, and the flashy lighting by Arden Fingerhut.

I didn't attend rehearsals, but they seemed to go well. Mounting a musical costs a bit more than doing a straight play (or gay, for that matter). For example, our "orchestra" consisted of two pianos, which required an additional pianist, and the pianos had to be re-tuned on a regular basis.

A snag occurred during the rehearsal period. Norman was excited by the notion of having "Love for Sale" sung for the first time by a male. Considering the changing social attitudes that the 60s produced, I'm sure Mr. Porter, with his own inclinations freely expressed, would have approved. Unfortunately, the Porter Estate did not see it that way and they controlled every decision about the use of the material. Cole Porter's homosexuality, although flagrantly flaunted, was a "secret" rigorously guarded by his heirs. "Love for Sale" would have to be sung by a female, so Norman regretfully complied and noted the reason in a program note.

Up to this point in Circle Rep's history, we always closed down for three months during the summer between seasons. This meant not only that the theater was dark when it could be producing income, but also that our staff was employed for only nine months and then collected unemployment for three months. Although this was legal, we were gaming the system; but with the lack of support for artists in America, we felt entitled to draw what we'd paid for unemployment insurance. But now, with the audience appeal of a musical, if *Unsung Cole* received favorable notices we could run all summer. It worked!

The Transcendent Years

Unsung Cole opened at Circle Rep June 23, 1977 and played severty-eight performances, closing September 4th. The music and lyrics were by Cole Porter, and the show was conceived and directed by Norman L. Berman. Most of the reviewers had a good time, and I seriously doubt it was a result of the cheap champagne:

The New York Times, June 24, 1977 (Richard Eder):
"*Unsung Cole* teeters fascinatingly between delight and bareness. Without his best songs, it is Cole Porter with his right arm tied behind his back. But what a left arm he had! [The] minimal setting could have used a little elegance ... [but] we have to make do with the performers and their material. Frequently that is as good as a feast."

Daily News, June 24, 1977 (Robert Jones):
"Berman has collected 32 Porter non-hits, distributed them to a cast of five outstanding people, and came up with a perfectly delightful little revue. The cast has charm and lots of voice. Each and every Porter song sounds unforgettable for at least as long as it lasts. How many more unsung songs are there by Porter? Probably enough to make a dozen more editions of *Unsung Cole.* If they're as much fun as this one, I hope I'm there."

New York Post, June 24, 1977 (Martin Gottfried):
"The songs in *Unsung Cole* tend to have first-class lyrics and second-class melodies. Mary Louise is perfectly cast, and Berman has chosen his female singers well. Berman has staged them all smoothly, softly mimicking the Thirties club style. [This] is a show for all musical lovers, and if not overwhelming, it is certainly engaging."

The Record, June 24, 1977 (Emory Lewis):
"*Unsung Cole* offers a lovely way to spend a summer evening. Berman has brilliantly provided rare songs. For

Porter fans, this unusual entertainment is a must. The director has selected five enormously talented performers, and moves them about the stage with skill. *Unsung Cole* is a heady brew, which should be around for several semesters."

Newsday, June 24, 1977 (Allan Wallach):
"*Unsung Cole* is a diverting evening. Berman has given the revue a polished staging in an ambience suggesting a cabaret (complete with ringside tables)."

Women's Wear Daily, June 27, 1977 (Howard Kissel):
"*Unsung Cole* is a marvelous evening of discovery, performed with great taste and spirit. In a five years [it] will be remembered as New York's first major introduction of the talent of Maureen Moore [who delivers] the high points of the evening."

The Star-Ledger, August 11, 1977 (William A. Raidy):
"It is the music that makes *Unsung Cole* the happy summer refreshment that it is. Berman has shaken the Porter tree and come forth with some delicious fruit. Five talented performers sing and move with grace. The evening is a charming, heady one. Champagne, incidentally, is served to the patrons. The caviar, of course, is Porter. Cole would have loved Berman's evening. One hopes that some producer will move it, for *Unsung Cole* is 'The Top'."

Time Magazine, July 4, 1977 (T.E. Kalem):
"Maureen Moore has a blazing trumpet delivery. Mary Louise has a sultry approach, a kind of smoky torch song. Anita Morris is stunningly lovely with a delicate edge of satire in her voice that Porter would have relished."

Newsweek Magazine, August 1, 1977 (Constance Guthrie):
"[The songs] sparkle with the orphaned appeal of overlooked treasure. Moore is the outstanding member of the

company. Morris sings with the smile of a Lorelei and a voice sultry enough to light Miss Liberty's torch. Mary Louise performs feats of legerdemain. But the dazzling Moore brings down the house. For Moore – from this moment on – everything should be de-lovely."

Variety, June 29, 1977 (Madden):
"Circle Rep's production is a delightful musical evening in the theater. The bright, witty lyrics come through fine and seemed to give enormous pleasure to the capacity audience. A cast of five all come through admirably. Berman deserves high praise, not only for his staging, but for his vocal arrangements. Word of mouth, already at work, should give the show a healthy run."

The Nation (undated) (Harold Clurman):
"I hastened to see the delectable people in *Unsung Cole*, who celebrate the old New York sparkle of Cole Porter's lyrics and tunes."

Village Voice, July 11, 1977 (Julius Novack):
"[The revue] is not without its pleasures. Berman has come up with some – not gems, exactly, but they sparkle just the same. Audiences seem to love *Unsung Cole*: it sells out every night."

So for the first time, but not the last, Circle Rep had a popular hit that could play all summer, which helped prevent our deficit from growing even faster than it did.

The Uncertainty Principle

In quantum mechanics, the Heisenberg uncertainty principle states that certain pairs of physical properties, such as position and momentum, cannot be simultaneously precisely known. The more precisely one property is measured, the less precisely the other can be measured.

If, in the place of "position," we use "artistic excellence," and in the place of "momentum," we substitute "fiscal responsibility," we can formulate the basic problem of the Circle Repertory Company. With our focus entirely on the former, it seemed impossible to measure the latter. In the previous chapter, when I enumerated my failings as an Artistic Director, I tellingly omitted my most grievous fault: a minimal sense of fiscal responsibility.

When we started Circle Rep, I concentrated entirely on the artistic life of the theater, and left Rob Thirkield to pay the bills. I resisted governance by a Board that, through fiscal control, might influence artistic decisions. I finally acceded to the New York State Council on the Arts' demand that we put our fiscal house in order, and we formed a Board comprised of business people as well as artists. I transferred my expectations to them, with the hope that our Board would rescue us from deficits by raising the funds needed to sustain our art. When we moved downtown to Sheridan Square, I thought I'd found a partner in Jerry Arrow, who would take care of money matters so I could continue to spend freely on our artistic programs. In reality, Jerry never said no to me; I was a spoiled child in a position where adult accountability was essential.

When our productions began to move to commercial engagements, earning profits many times over (at least in the case of *HOT L* and *Gemini*), it seemed unfair that Circle Rep continued to accumulate a deficit. After all, it was common knowledge that the profits from *A Chorus Line* subsidized operations at the Public Theater for many years. Of course what I didn't take into account was that Joseph Papp, clever man that he was, persuaded a member of his Board, LuEsther Mertz (founder of Publisher's Clearing House), to write a check totally to finance the move of *A Chorus Line* to Broadway, thereby ensuring that *all* the profits went directly back to the Public. When we moved *Gemini* to Broadway for its long and profitable run, no such benefactor was forthcoming. As a result, Jerry Arrow, acting as Producer of the show for both Circle Rep and PAF Playhouse, solicited investments from private individuals; so profits were returned to those investors, not the institutions. Circle Rep and PAF Playhouse both received a small weekly royalty; but the 40% of the profits that accrue to producers after investors are repaid mysteriously evaporated. I'm not accusing anyone of anything, except myself; I don't *know* what happened to our producer's share of the profits. My point is that as Artistic Director, I certainly *should* have known.

I do know that Jerry Arrow assumed the position of General Manager for *Gemini*, a lucrative position in any commercial theater venture. The salary and the "office expenses" of a GM are in the budget as a weekly expense, paid before profit/losses are calculated. Jerry held this position for more than four years; he undoubtedly enriched himself in a perfectly legal way. We trusted Jerry to the extent that four years later, we partnered again with him in the Broadway production of *Fifth of July*. So, apparently I wasn't the only one asleep at the wheel; financial oversight is the legal responsibility of the Board of Directors. No one was being held accountable.

Summer In Space

While *Unsung Cole* gave New Yorkers a summer to be happy about, on July 13 the City was plunged again into darkness, suffering its second total blackout. This one lasted twenty-five hours and, unlike the enchanted Blackout of 1965 when the City became a romantic autumn evening under a full moon, this time it was a "hot town, summer in the City" and there was widespread looting and disorder.

While I was metaphorically hitchhiking around the galaxy, others were making actual space exploration an increasingly normal phenomenon. The Soviet Union launched *Soyuz 24*, with plans for cosmonauts to dock with the *Salyut 5* space station. Not to be outdone, the NASA Space Shuttle *Enterprise* made its first test-free flight from the back of a Boeing 474 Shuttle Aircraft Carrier, and the U.S. launched the *Voyager 2* spacecraft, an interplanetary space probe. In 1977, we discerned that there are rings around Uranus, the planet discovered by Herschel in 1781.

In August, while *Unsung Cole* celebrated the sparkling New York of the 1930s, our year of fear ended with the capture of David Berkowitz, the "Son of Sam." Between 1942 and 1977, Roy Sullivan, a park ranger in Shenandoah National Park, was hit by lightning on seven different occasions. After eight seasons, it was strange to reflect that in this same year, Roy Sullivan was struck by lightning for the seventh time and, like Circle Rep, had survived again.

Chapter 12
Beyond the Asteroids

By our ninth season, Circle Rep's success was having a national impact. We were exporting plays to other cities. I began attending national theater conferences, serving on panels about the state of theater in our country. One of the many topics discussed was the possibility of decreasing production costs by co-producing shows. I discovered that Bill Semans from the Cricket Theater in Minneapolis and John Lion, Artistic Director of the Magic Theater in San Francisco, ran theaters of comparable size to Circle Rep and shared our artistic aspirations, as well as budget problems. With the approval of our Board, I set out to visit Minneapolis and San Francisco to explore the viability of co-productions.

The Cricket was founded in 1971 by actor Bill Semans in an old movie theater called the Ritz in northeastern Minneapolis, and their goal was to present Mid-Western premieres of contemporary drama. The Artistic Director was Lou Salerni, a talented director whose fine sensibilities would have fit in nicely at Circle Rep. In their second season, they produced Lanford's *Lemon Sky,* a couple of years later, *HOT L* and the following season both *Red Ryder* and *Sea Horse.* In their current season, they were producing *Mound Builders* and *Lili Lamont.* Circle Rep was providing the Cricket with a substantial portion of its repertoire. They were anticipating a move in the near future to a new arts center in the downtown area where the city transformed an old Masonic temple into the Hennepin Center for the Arts. Although Circle Rep was an artistic resource for the Cricket, nothing originating there held much promise for a co-production; so I moved on to San Francisco.

The Magic Theatre originated in 1967 when John Lion, a student of Jan Kott at the University of California, directed a production of Ionesco's *The Lesson* at the Steppenwolf Bar in Berkeley. The theatre's name came from Herman Hesse's novel *Steppenwolf:* "An Anarchist Evening at the Magic Theatre, For Madmen Only, Price of Admission: Your Mind." The Magic's first success came with plays by Beat poet Michael McClure, who maintained an eleven-year residency with them. When I arrived, the Magic had just moved to a new facility at Fort Mason that provided them an expanded operation that reflected their growing influence in local theater.

It was exciting that the Cricket and the Magic theaters were becoming important artistic resources, and that they both were receiving enough support to expand operations in new premium facilities. It was also great to see my old friend Sam Shepard making his home as Resident Playwright at the Magic, just as Lanford was doing at Circle Rep.

Although no immediate co-production plans emerged, the seeds were planted for future shared productions that would transfer from the Magic to Circle Rep. In years to come both Sam's *Buried Child* and *Fool for Love* made that journey and enriched our repertoire and financial well-being.

A Missive From Pluto

While I was on the West Coast, I went out to visit the Berkeley Stage Company where Angela Paton served as their literary manager. Angie came across a script called *Feedlot*, which she highly recommended to me; but she warned me that the script came laden with controversy.

The author was Patrick Meyers, who was serving a sentence at the Atascadero State Hospital for the Criminally Insane. While high on hallucinogenic drugs, Patrick raped an eleven-year-old girl. Obviously, there was a moral question about whether a work written by the perpetrator of such a depraved crime should receive a production. I read the play with great curiosity and thought it was an outstanding piece of playwriting.

Back in New York, I called a meeting of our staff and presented them with the dilemma. Not surprisingly, several staff members opposed our presenting it. I argued that despite the objectionable parentage of the piece, based on its merits alone *Feedlot* was as good a play as we'd come by. Was it the role of a theater to sit in judgment of a matter already decided by law? I was reminded of the work of Jean Genet, another sexual predator who'd been imprisoned, but who happened to be a genius. No one seriously objected to the presentation of the plays of Genet, despite the unsavory character of their author.

After much consideration, I decided that it would be a crime to suppress a work of such talent, so Circle Rep opened our ninth season with a production of *Feedlot*. Any staff member who objected to working on the project was excused from her responsibilities to this production.

Developing A Development Process

One of my allies in the decision to include *Feedlot* was the man we had just hired to join our staff in the official role of Dramaturg. His name was Milan Stitt, and he was one of the most significant additions to the future of Circle Rep, from our ninth season all the way through to the twenty-seventh and final season in 1996.

Milan William Stitt was born in Detroit, one of two children of Howard Milan Stitt, Jr. and the former Audrien Prindle. He studied to become a priest at Albion College before changing his focus to the theater. He received his BA from the University of Michigan and an MFA from the Yale School of Drama. Milan's first play was *The Runner Stumbles*, which was produced on Broadway at the Little Theater, playing 396 performances. It closed just one week before *Gemini* transferred from Circle Rep to the same theater. Directed by my friend, the much-admired actor Austin Pendleton, *The Runner Stumbles* was named Best Broadway Play in the annual *Best Plays* book.

As Milan recalled it in an article he wrote for *The New York Times,*

"When Marshall Mason invited me to join the staff as dramaturg or literary manager, I looked on the appointment as an opportunity to expand the company's existing work with playwrights. In its first few years, the company received around a hundred scripts a year. Then in a *New York Times* interview, Marshall was quoted as saying he personally read every script submitted. The number of plays submitted immediately escalated to some 3,000 a year. When I started work at Circle Rep, I helped raise funding to hire seven readers to expedite decisions on the tremendous backlog of scripts."

As a writer himself, Milan was sympathetic to the need for playwrights to get a response to their submissions. Each entry received a written critique with the merits our staff found in the play noted, as well as its weaknesses. The more promising playwrights were invited to come in for an interview. To develop some of these promising discoveries, Milan suggested forming a Playwright's Workshop, which would meet once a week, with all the resident playwrights (Lanford, Julie Bovasso, Claris Nelson, Berrilla Kerr and John Bishop) attending.

Milan saw how Lanford wrote a scene, then grabbed actors from the Circle Rep hallways to have them read it back to him. Milan saw an opportunity to formalize Lanford's process and make it available to all Circle Rep's writers. First, we established a tradition of meeting with the whole Company every Friday afternoon to read a play. Sometimes the plays were classics, but more often, they were new plays that aroused our interest. These "Friday Readings" were a mainstay of the Circle Rep process, and enabled us to introduce new scripts. The readings were amazingly well acted; our actors became expert at reading scripts aloud so vividly and with such spontaneity that a play's potential was apparent.

Milan also applied to the National Endowment for the Arts to fund our second stage of play development, which we were calling "Projects in Progress." PiPs were staged readings, with the actors carrying their scripts, even though their lines were memorized, played on whatever set the Major Production was using. We performed the PiPs Sunday and Monday nights, offered as a bonus to our subscribers, followed by a "talk-back" with the audience to glean what worked and what didn't.

It was a developmental procedure that served us well in the years ahead. It was the way we "tried out" scripts. Our audience loved the process; they felt privileged to be part of a play's development, and many productions followed the path from Friday readings to Projects in Progress to Major Productions. Play development at Circle Rep came to be recognized as Milan's most important lifetime achievement.

In The Shadows Of Hades

Since I was going to have a busy summer directing *Tobacco Road* and *Old Times* at the Academy Festival, I thought it would be wise to find a director for *Feedlot*. A year earlier, Lanford and I had gone to the T. Schreiber Studio where Terry Schreiber's production of *The Trip Back Down* by John Bishop was playing.

Terry Schreiber was born in 1937 in Winona, Minnesota. He founded his Studio in 1969 in a loft on the Upper East Side, holding classes for a handful of students. Within a few years, Terry developed a serious off-off-Broadway venue for his acting students on East 28th Street at Second Avenue. Terry met John Bishop at a YMCA, when John was directing corporate musicals known as "industrials." As a performer, Terry appeared in a couple of John's shows and he and John became fast friends.

When we saw *The Trip Back Down* at Terry's Studio, we discovered three important additions for Circle Rep: Terry Schreiber, the dynamic director of the play; John Bishop, the super-talented author of the play; and an actor with down-to-the-bone honesty named Edward Seamon, who created many characters in our repertoire for years to come.

Returning from my West Coast trip where I acquired the script of *Feedlot*, I thought Terry Schreiber was an excellent choice to direct Patrick Meyers' dark but powerful play. I explained to Terry the circumstances of the playwright's imprisonment, and I sent him off to San Francisco to visit Patrick. Terry recalls his interviews with Patrick as being a harrowing experience because of the environment in which they took place, and the elaborate security precautions that surrounded his visits.

Patrick Meyers was born in Phoenix but grew up in Denver. He attended Colorado State University where he began acting. He subsequently moved to California and joined the Company Theatre. In Berkeley, he earned a degree in television production from Merritt College and completed his first play – a children's drama for television entitled *The Frown*. The next year, Patrick was accepted into the Advanced Training Program for drama at San Francisco's American Conservatory Theatre. It was there he completed the first draft of his second play, *Feedlot*. But his promising start as a writer was interrupted by the prison term he received for his violent crime.

Patrick was a lithe, handsome fellow with delicate features and a quiet, passive personality. He revealed to Terry that the thing that terrified him most was the fear of homosexual rape. As a good-looking guy, without much machismo in his bearing, and as a prisoner convicted of child molestation, Patrick was aware of the "short-eyes" syndrome, in which prison inmates regarded child molesters as the scum of the earth, and frequently subjected them to extreme violence as an expression of disgust. Homosexual rape was viewed in prison as appropriate retribution. The first night Patrick arrived at Atascadero, he broke his fists against the wall in order to be quarantined in the infirmary, which protected him from being raped. Interestingly, the plot of *Feedlot* turns on just such a forced homosexual rape; so he was writing from his deepest fear, which provides the play with its depth and honesty.

Terry also met Patrick's wife Irene, who stood by her husband throughout his trial and imprisonment. She would come to New York to assist on the production, since Patrick would be incarcerated for another three years.

It was a busy time in the world as we went into rehearsals on *Feedlot*. Anti-apartheid leader Steve Biko who coined the phrase "Black is beautiful" was killed while in the custody of South African police, a martyr to the cause of ending apartheid. The United States agreed to transfer control of the Panama Canal to Panama at the end of the 20th century, and signed a non-proliferation pact with the Soviet Union. International soccer icon Pelé played his last game as a member of the New York Cosmos, and Reggie Jackson was "the straw that stirred the drink" as he led the New York Yankees over the Los Angeles Dodgers in the World Series. And more importantly, smallpox was declared eradicated worldwide by the spectacular success of smallpox vaccinations.

At Circle Rep, the casting of *Feedlot* again proved an invaluable asset. In addition to tough but kindly Edward Seamon, the cast included the quietly masculine Jimmy Ray Weeks, for whom both Lanford and John Bishop would write many roles. Circle provided Jeff Daniels for a comic turn as a naïve cowpoke, and a new intern named Mark Soper was so perfect for the part of the sensitive student employed at the feedlot that we relaxed our restrictions on the use of interns, and gave Mark his professional debut. But the most electrifying performance was given by a lean, slight, cynical tough-guy actor from The Actors Studio named Joseph Ragno.

Feedlot takes place in the control room of a silo-like building, a grain tower in West Texas, as modern and antiseptic as a hospital operating room. The control room is reached by an elevator. It contains the lockers for the cowboy workers, as well as television screens to monitor the progress of the cattle being herded through on their way to slaughter. The foreman is a wizened, patient fellow who oversees a crew of four cowboys who wrangle the cattle. At the opening, all five men appear in this remote space as they change clothes and prepare to go home. Only two remain for the night shift and these two are the heart of the play. One is a bantam rooster of a brutish Vietnam vet, aggressive and abusive with his swaggering macho veneer. The other is a good-looking college student, with curly blond Byronic locks and Paul Newman-blue eyes, who is sensitive and refined (and as we discover, borderline psychotic). These two taunt each other until the college kid subdues the brute, handcuffs him, and sodomizes him in the darkened room. Holding his victim hostage, he threatens to blow up the whole operation unless the press allows him to read his proclamation that men must break the bonds of their own repression.

Feedlot by Patrick Meyers opened at Circle Rep October 8, 1977 and played fifty-five performances. It was directed by Terry Schreiber, with a set by Hal Tine, lighting by Dennis Parichy, costumes by Laura Crow, sound by Chuck London. The stage managers were Amy Schecter and Michael Herzfeld.

The New York Times, October 14, 1977 (Mel Gussow):
"*Feedlot* has a raw muscularity and a quiet intensity. It deals forcefully with some provocative subjects: heroism, cowardice, and complicity in violence; aggressive masculinity and fear of homosexuality. Schreiber and his cast give the work a tautness not always audible in the writing. The play benefits greatly from the performance and the direction."

Daily News, October 14, 1977 (Ernest Leogrande):
"The conflict over opposing interpretations of manhood has drama in it aplenty. Meyers knows how to set up a dramatic situation, and the play under Schreiber's direction moves along at an almost unflagging pace, with praiseworthy performances."

New York Post, October 14, 1977 (Edmund Newton):
"Brims with sexually wounded cowboys. The clash between the violent cowboy and a vulnerable cowboy

represents Meyer's puerile probe of the sensitivity beneath the American macho. Billy Fred [is] played by Ragno with psychopathic intensity. Daniels [is] especially good as a puckishly funny youth."

The New York Times, November 13, 1977 (Walter Kerr):
"Meyer's special talent is for hitting you right in the eye you're watching him with. Meyers believes that the stage is a combat area fenced in by electrified barbed wire. The language is taut, plausible, menacing when it means to be, quickly and effortlessly funny. The 30-year-old playwright is a dramatist to the bone, deeply, totally committed to turning character, background, idiosyncratic rhythms into *events*, eruptions that are ugly, unpredictably violent, persuasive and often riveting. Thanks to the curt intelligence of the writing and the skin-prickling control of Schreiber's staging, we believe every melodramatic moment of it. One of the most striking combinations of substance and sheer stagecraft I've run across in many a lazy moon."

New York Magazine, November 7, 1977 (John Simon):
"Meyers is a man to watch. The play holds our interest and keeps growing in stature; the dramaturgy is often compelling. The performances are strong and intelligent. If you leave this theatrical repast wanting more, it is not so much because the portions were small as because they were so tasty."

Interestingly, no one in the press pursued Patrick's identity, so his criminal situation remained hidden from then public – at least, for now.

An Historic Month

While Patrick Meyers' characters in *Feedlot* were struggling onstage with the dangerous tensions of dealing with homosexuality, St.

Paul, Minnesota repealed its gay rights ordinance after Anita Bryant's anti-gay campaign in Florida. But Harvey Milk was elected City Supervisor in San Francisco, the first openly gay official of any large city in the United States. Only eleven months later, the tensions Patrick dramatized so vividly erupted in real life with Dan White's assassination of Harvey Milk and San Francisco Mayor George Mascone. The difficulty of the public's ability to deal with homosexuality at this time was tragically dramatized when the jury accepted White's plea of diminished capacity (dubbed "The Twinky Defense" by the press) and convicted him only of voluntary manslaughter. He was sentenced to serve seven years, but he was released in five. As a final repercussion of the highly-charged tension of the conflict between the gay and straight worlds, White committed suicide in 1985. Patrick Meyers identified a pulsating problem and his treatment of it was far less savage than the events that unfolded in San Francisco.

Also in this busy month, Egyptian President Anwar Sadat made an official visit to Israel, seeking a permanent peace settlement with Israeli Prime Minister Menachem Begin. Sadat, too, was assassinated four years later for his attempts to advance peace in the world.

Creating A Belt Of Asteroids

During the run of *Feedlot*, Daniel Irvine launched a new program at Circle Rep that was a platform for the celebration of the one-act play. The series was called The Late Show and like its predecessor, After-Pieces, one-acts were staged after the performance of the subscription series. The first offering was a new one-act by Lanford Wilson, which Danny directed. A philosophic work about the nature of faith, *Brontosaurus* was written for Tanya Berezin and Jeff Daniels. The mostly silent third part, an assistant, was played by Sharon Madden. The minimalist plot concerns an antiques dealer whose sophisticated Manhattan life is disrupted by the visit of a nephew, who comes to use her apartment as a base while he begins his studies. He is representative of a younger generation, pursuing a solipsist style of epiphany that relegates the antiques dealer's cultured life to the relevance of a dinosaur.

Brontosaurus by Lanford Wilson opened The Late Show series at Circle Rep on March 4, 1977 and played twenty-three performances. The critics gave enthusiastic support to a new venue for the one-act play form and regularly reviewed The Late Shows, often preferring them to the main stage offerings that preceded them. Sample reviews:

The New York Times, October 27, 1977 (Mel Gussow):
"A giant of a one-act play. With his customary artistry, Wilson moves the play from antiques shop to apartment with one conversation flowing into another. Such is the strength and humor of Tanya Berezin's performance and Wilson's writing that we feel her anxiety and loneliness, and her disdain for society's loss of form, order, and beauty. *Brontosaurus* is pungent and incisive."

Daily News, October 27, 1977 (Rob Baker):
"The performances by Berezin and Daniels are honed to perfection, and the production proves once again that Lanford Wilson is probably our greatest functioning American playwright."

WQXR (Clive Barnes):
"The series could not have hoped to have gotten off to a better start than with this resonant study of a woman pondering her life and purpose. Berezin makes her nervous energy and chirpy cynicism extraordinarily real. What an interesting play this is! Wilson is so often a spokesman for his generation and many will identify with him."

Cue Magazine, January 8, 1978 (Marilyn Stasio):
"The play bristles with wonderfully witty dialogue and piercing insights. Berezin gives a glowing performance. Tiny,

but a perfect little beauty, the play is one of Wilson's most exquisitely written works. Cheers to Circle for giving the one-act a warm home."

Destination Moonscape

Following his phenomenal success with *Gemini*, which continued its Broadway run into a second year, Albert Innaurato wrote a new play for Circle Rep. It is notoriously difficult to follow a success, which often suffers a "sophomore curse." Such was the case with Albert's *Ulysses in Traction*.

Naturally, I was excited to direct Albert's new play. I thought it funny and insightful, despite unwieldy aspects of its structure. The first act and the second are remarkably different in tone. Albert wrote it with members of the Company in mind, so we eagerly set about mounting the play as the second offering of our ninth season.

Set in the rehearsal hall of an Arts Complex at Chapel University (a fictional college, supposedly in Detroit), the play hilariously ribs academia as the college theater department rehearses an anti-war play, pointedly reminiscent of an actual play called *Summertree*. However, outside the arts complex, an actual race riot is taking place, complete with bombs and machine gun fire. The danger of the war outside encroaches on the creation of art inside, however ineptly practiced by the collegiate thespians. The cast was made up of Jack Davidson as Dr. Stuart Humphreys, the pedantic head of the theater department; faculty member Dr. Stephen Klipstader, played by Ken Kliban, who is having an affair with a nymphomaniac faculty member played by Sharon Madden; Jake Dengel (the best actor at Northwestern when Rob and I were there) as an alcoholic gay director; and Michael Ayr as an MFA student utilizing esoteric acting techniques. The ostensible playwright, John Morrisey, was played by William Hurt, and Emma, the Stage Manager, by Trish Hawkins. Joanna Featherstone was a Guest Artist who played the lone black character, Mae, an employee of facilities management (the cleanup team).

Albert ridicules academia, with its petty faculty squabbles and clandestine romantic relationships and pokes fun at some ludicrous acting techniques fervently employed by amateurs. But in addition to the satire, Albert used an autobiographical event to counterpoint the humor. While at Yale, Albert was the victim of a medical blunder at the hands of a surgeon who, while attempting to correct a urinal problem, rendered his patient impotent. Writing about such an intimate matter was brave of Albert, but unfortunately, the impotence was dismissed by critics as a symbol.

Ulysses in Traction by Albert Innaurato premiered at the Circle Rep December 3, 1977 and played fifty-two performances. It was directed by Marshall W. Mason, with a set by John Lee Beatty, costumes by Laura Crow, lighting by Dennis Parichy, and sound by Chuck London and George Hanson. The stage manager was Fred Reinglas.

The New York Times, December 9, 1977 (Richard Eder):
"Some things are interesting and some are amusing, but the play is a mess. The problem is that none of the figures are believable people. And the situation in which they are caught is even less believable. The cast directed by Mason are all good. It is premature to say Innaurato's promise is broken. But it certainly is dispersed, no doubt temporarily."

New York Post, December 9, 1977 (Edmund Newton):
"*Traction* has the pull of reality. [It's] a brooding, farcical play. This description doesn't really do justice to Innaurato's dumbfounded, eloquently perturbed characters. [He] has a sweet satiric touch. The cast is all top quality, particularly Hurt and Dengel. The [play's] perception is unsentimental and unforgettably true."

Daily News, December 9, 1977 (Douglas Watt):
"A slapdash, though lively and occasionally amusing affair, it suffers from being irritably autobiographical, with the result that it provides a very twitchy and ultimately unsatisfactory evening. The playwright/hero [is] very well-played by Hurt. The plain female dramaturge is

gently played by Hawkins. Beatty's set is excellent. Mason has staged the piece resourcefully. Although the dialogue is facile and sometimes entertaining, the people never truly involve us, and the play does little for Innaurato's burgeoning reputation."

The New York Times, January 3, 1977 (Walter Kerr):
"If you want to know how bad your new play is, give it to the best possible company of actors. I feel pretty certain Innaurato has learned something about his new piece because it's so well done. (The Circle Rep has a habit of doing things well.) Hurt is perfect as a wandering Lazarus not quite back from the dead; the world burns in his eyes. Hawkins is equally fine. Davidson makes [his professor] readily recognizable: fatuity on the march. Everyone else is impeccable. With everything that's perceptive and well written tightly nailed down under Mason's guiding hand, Innaurato can see that after a tantalizing first act, the play simply vanishes, dissolves into irresolute running about looking for exits."

The Nation, December 31, 1977 (Harold Clurman):
"Generally well-cast and acted, Innaurato's *Ulysses* is very nearly two distinct plays. The first half is an effectively farcical lampoon of a university theater. The second is an inadequate foray into 'social significance.' But the coordination fails to register with salient force because there is a wearisome insistence on sexual hang-ups. We expect something more from Innaurato."

The New Yorker, December 19, 1977 (Edith Oliver):
"Most of [it] is original and scathing and humorous. Yet in the midst of the fun, we are never allowed to forget the unhappiness underneath. It must be said, regretfully, that Ulysses never jells. Under Mason's direction the acting by

every member of the cast is excellent, almost achieving the effect of improvisation. The actors of the Circle Repertory constitute one of the few genuine theater companies in town."

New York Magazine, December 26, 1977 (John Simon):
"Innaurato lets us down. The first act is a spoof of a typical university drama department in full swing. From this droll idea, the playwright gets ample humor nicely laced with a dash of pathos. Then comes the second act: excessive, jumbled, full of clumsily introduced set pieces. The play no longer knows whether it is comedy, tragedy, or vaudeville; whether it is realistic or surreal, symbolic or apocalyptic."

Village Voice, December 19, 1977 (Julius Novick):
"I enjoyed the comic drubbing he gave academic theater. But Innaurato means his play to be more than an in-joke. It is implausible that Innaurato could have written such malarkey in all seriousness. Mason's staging is in his characteristic vein of realistic ensemble work, appropriately broader than usual here and there, but as usual beautifully fluid and relaxed, beautifully detailed without being busy. Amid all the banalities, it is still possible to enjoy the way [the actors] work together. And it is never intolerably long between jokes."

Sadly, it took Albert three years to recover from this failure and when he finally re-emerged in May of 1980 with a new play called *Passione,* he directed it himself at Playwrights Horizons, where *Gemini* originated. But he never again wrote for Circle Rep.

A Shining Satellite

During the run of *Ulysses in Traction,* we presented a new one-act by John Bishop called *Cabin 12* in The Late Show series. It was John's first play, originally presented at the T. Schreiber Studio a year earlier.

John Bishop, the son of a foreman for Westinghouse, was born May 3, 1929 in Mansfield, Ohio. He majored in theater at Carnegie

Mellon University in Pittsburgh and began his career as an actor at the Cleveland Playhouse. He made his directing debut in New York in 1964 with a musical version of *Little Women*. Despite a tough, macho mien cultivated during his service in the Marine Corps, John sported an acerbic wit that flashed unexpectedly from his strong silent-type persona. A feral, restless turbulence seemed to churn just below his placid surface, and like Wagner's Flying Dutchman, he seemed destined for a fate of eternal yearnings that could never be fulfilled. This restlessness was surprisingly resolved in his forties with a love John discovered for Lisa Maurer, whom he married and with whom he settled into one of the best relationships I've ever seen.

After he met Terry Schreiber, he began to hang around the Studio and, tired of the silly content of the industrials he was directing, John turned his attention to writing. He brought Terry two one-act plays he had written: *Cabin 12* and *49 West 87th Street*. Terry recognized John's remarkable voice as a writer and promptly produced them.

A year or so later, John finished *The Trip Back Down*, a full-length play that recounts the travails of a famous race-car driver on the downside of his career who is revisiting the past in his home town – ex-wife, siblings, school rivals, etc. With the support of an enthusiastic review by Walter Kerr in *The New York Times*, *The Trip Back Down* transferred to Broadway where it played for eighty performances at the Longacre Theater. John came to Circle Rep with Terry Schreiber when he directed *Feedlot*. John became a Resident Playwright, served as Dramaturg from 1981–83, and remained one of our chief assets for the next eighteen years

Cabin 12 is a touching one-act drama about the death of a young man in a 16-wheeler trucking accident. His brother and father meet in a motel room in the Midwest, near the site of the accident, trying to cope with plans for his funeral and burial. In the course of the play, with the counterpoint of an unruly redneck couple in the adjoining room, they try to deal with the possibility that the accident was really a suicide. John's sinewy, muscular writing offered good roles for Jonathan Hogan as the brother, Nancy Snyder and

Michael Ayr as the boisterous young couple, and especially for our newest Company member, Ed Seamon, as the mourning father.

Cabin 12 by John Bishop opened January 3, 1978 and played thirteen performances as a Late Show. It was directed by Marshall Oglesby, with a set designed by Gary Seltzer, lighting by Ruth Roberts, costumes by Irene Nolan, and the stage manager was Joanne Seltzer. As I mentioned, sometimes our Late Shows were preferred over our main stage presentations, and *Cabin 12* was one of them.

The New York Times, January 6, 1978 (Mel Gussow):

"The play is austere. This is a work that offers intimations rather than revelations, although the climax is a surprise. The play is immeasurably aided in performance. As we watch Edward Seamon and Jonathan Hogan, a life is depicted through reminiscence and emotional collision. We feel the wounds. Both actors, as directed by Marshall Oglesby, are subtle in their evocation of character and the intimacy of kinship. In common with Bishop's play, they are gently and quietly affecting."

Daily News, January 10, 1978 (Douglas Watt):

"The same spare, clean, expressive writing that characterized Bishop's unfortunately neglected *The Trip Back Down* last season on Broadway is evident in his playlet *Cabin 12*. Grief and its expression are the author's concerns here. To tell you more would be to tell you too much. Seamon and Hogan are well matched as father and son, with Hogan particularly effective."

New York Post, January 7, 1978 (Clive Barnes):

"It is as natural as an Olympic diver. Bishop is clearly a man of talent. Slowly and skillfully, the story is unfolded. It is handsomely done and in Oglesby's staging, exquisitely acted. Seamon and Hogan are offering performances of delicate variegation. Through their acting and the play itself, we get to know them. Bishop evokes the common poetry of people. The drama leapt vividly and gracefully to life."

Village Voice, January 16, 1978 (Arthur Sainer):
"A moving one-act play. What relieves the play of its inherent gloom is Bishop's crisp, functional dialogue and the fine character shadings by Hogan and Seamon. Bishop's genre is the realistic drama of revelation with a vigorous Faulknerian ending. Oglesby's direction is properly attuned to Bishop's gentle touch."

Up till now, Circle Rep had enjoyed mostly positive, sometimes enthusiastic support from the critical establishment. Even when the reviewers did not approve of a particular script, they almost always wrote respectfully of our theater. For the first time, that was about to change.

A Cosmic Disaster

My co-founder Rob Thirkield always had a fascination with the darker sexual impulses that were hidden beneath the "normal" surfaces of our civilization. He explored those uncontrollable unconscious forces in his two productions of Strindberg's *Ghost Sonata*, particularly in his second, more surreal production, in which he introduced partial nudity to the work of the Swedish Master. Most recently, he examined the sexual temptations that pull apart a marriage in James Joyce's *Exiles*.

Equally, Rob had a continuing interest in the Expressionist forms of experimental theater that he learned while he was part of the La MaMa Troupe from Eugenio Barba. He hungered to return to those experimental roots and take Circle Rep on an adventure to shake up our ostensible image as a safe haven for realism. And so he came to me with a proposal to present a compilation of two plays by the sexual pioneer in drama, Frank Wedekind.

The German playwright Benjamin Franklin Wedekind (1864–1918) was born in Hanover. His work is critical of bourgeois attitudes (particularly towards sex), and it anticipated the style of Expressionism. He was a major influence on the development of epic theatre. Wedekind wrote two plays (*Earth Spirit*, 1895 and *Pandora's Box*, 1904) that are collectively known as the "Lulu Plays." Originally conceived as a single play, the two pieces tell a continuous story of a sexually enticing young dancer who rises in German society through her relationships with wealthy men, but who later falls into poverty and prostitution. The frank depiction of sexuality and violence in these plays, including lesbianism and an encounter with Jack the Ripper (a role Wedekind played himself in the original production), pushed the boundaries of acceptability on the stage at the time.

Rob trimmed both texts down and combined them into one evening; we called the resulting play *Lulu*. Rob's concept was to exhibit Lulu's complicated life as a circus act. John Lee Beatty designed a set that essentially turned the confines of Circle Rep into an Odeon with the walls of the theater brightly painted spectacular posters; so the audience was encircled by a circus atmosphere.

Cast in the complex central role was our leading *artiste*, Trish Hawkins, whose entrance was made on the shoulders of a circus strongman, the muscular Ken Kliban, who then donned a red tailcoat and top hat, assuming the role of the Ringmaster. The project made use of almost all the Company members, including Michael Ayr, Jeff Daniels, Jack Davidson, William Hurt, Sharon Madden, Burke Pearson, Joyce Reeling, Nancy Snyder and Danton Stone. Additional roles used distinguished Guest Artists like Jacqueline Bertrand, William Robertson, our intern Mark Soper and Rob's voice teacher, Gerard Russak.

Having lived in Vienna from the age of ten to thirteen, Trish knew Wedekind's work and loved it. She appeared as Thea in a production of *Spring Awakening* at Harvard, directed by Thomas Babe, so she was thrilled that Circle Rep was going to present *Lulu*.

She was surprised when Rob offered her the title role; she was well aware of the challenge.

Several members of the cast told me that their memories of rehearsals were conflicted; Rob loved actors, but some felt his approach was a bit too "laissez faire" for such a monumental task. *Lulu* was rooted in a foreign culture, with Expressionistic grit and sexual boldness, big tests for American actors. Not only had Rob combined the two plays, but his concept of a circus environment made the work all the more demanding. Ken Kliban recalled how the actors worked scene by scene, without any real idea of the progression of the play to its gruesome climax, in which Lulu lies in a pool of blood, her throat slit by Jack the Ripper. Trish agreed:

"With a play like *Lulu,* I think the cast and director need to do a bit of therapy along the way, to deal with the psychological issues and, of course, the style. At the time, the actors felt we were alone. Of course, that's the hard part of directing; actors want to be left alone but then we tend to be resentful if we're really left alone – what's a director to do? *Lulu* would have been much more satisfying if we had done a workshop first, rather than just plunging ahead; it would have been helpful to have a choreographer and a coach involved."

Ken recalled that once they realized the depths of their journey, the cast demanded that I attend a dress rehearsal to advise them. I do not remember this, but Ken reports that I sat through the run-through, and opined: "If it ain't broke, don't fix it." So I bear part of the blame for the disaster as well. Trish wrote:

"Looking back, I am thrilled that I actually acted the part of Lulu. How many American actresses have done that? I remember two reactions to my performance, which I know was – as usual – wildly uneven. The first was John Simon– always a nemesis of mine – who said that I played the part like the comic strip character, "Little Lulu." Boy, that was a low blow! He got his opening though from the fact that I had gotten a permanent wave for the show and so my hair was in ringlets, like Little Lulu's was. The other reaction was from Al Pacino, who really liked it!"

Lulu opened at Circle Rep February 4, 1978 and played only twenty-five performances. The translation by Frances Fawcett and Stephen Spender was directed by Rob Thirkield, the setting was by John Lee Beatty, costumes by David Murin, lighting by Ruth Roberts, with original music by Norman L. Berman and sound design by Chuck London. Here are summaries of the stinging reviews:

The New York Times, February 18, 1978 (Richard Eder):
"*Lulu* is a disaster, despite a gallant and interesting performance by Trish Hawkins. It is the only major thing that comes out right in a production that is a fratricide of talents. The production is all length – three hours – and no focus. Director Thirkield finds no way to convey the play's passion or momentum. There is no style or rhythm in the delivery, and so there is little sense, and without its manic sense, *Lulu* is a jumble."

Daily News, February 18, 1978 (Douglas Watt):
"Nancy Drew meets the perverts; at least to spare Frank Wedekind the effort of rolling about in his grave, I'd much prefer to think of it that way than to think the three-hour disaster at Circle Rep was actually *Lulu*. Neither director Thirkield nor all but a very few members of the cast of seventeen have the slightest grasp of the requisite style for this lurid study of a decadent society. What an incredibly misbegotten evening!"

New York Post, February 18, 1978 (Clive Barnes):
"The evening never quite works out. Thirkield has missed no chance at misunderstanding the essential nature

of Wedekind. This is a travesty of the play, which Marshall Mason should never have permitted."

New York Magazine, March 6, 1978 (John Simon):
"The Circle Rep's *Lulu* is an unredeemed disaster. Everything about Thirkield's mounting is sheer desolation – visually, verbally, histrionically. I have neither the space nor time to itemize the horrors. Hawkins has trouble creating the illusion of being a performer. She may actually be under the impression that she is playing Little Lulu."

A Couple Of Comets

Jerry Arrow, Rob and I reached the conclusion that it was economically necessary to cut the run short. Our productions were now playing fifty-two performances; but we were on a full Off-Broadway Equity contract, which for a cast of seventeen meant we had unusually high expenses. After the dismissive reviews, we were selling no single tickets, and even our subscribers were not coming or not staying. So we elected to stop *Lulu* after twenty-five performances and replace the second half of the subscription run by remounting two well-regarded productions that had played in The Late Show series. We called the bill *Two from The Late Show,* and it included revivals of Lanford's *Brontosaurus* with Tanya, Jeff Daniels and Sharon Madden; plus John Bishop's *Cabin 12* with Ed Seamon, Jon Hogan, Michael Ayr and Nancy Snyder. It was financially a sound decision to cut the cast from seventeen actors to only seven.

It is tempting in retrospect to see shortening the run of *Lulu* as a turning point in Circle Rep's history – a decision made on business criteria, rather than artistic grounds. It is also true that the theater's co-founder Rob Thirkield never directed another major production for Circle Rep, although he did direct a workshop production the following season. I'm sure Rob was disappointed at the fate of *Lulu,* but he remained an ardent member (and supporter) of the Company. *Lulu* marked the first across-the-board critical denigration of Circle Rep, so one might surmise it was the first frayed thread in the fabric of our "glory years." But our very next production was one of the proudest accomplishments in Circle Rep's history, with even greater acclaim than we'd received; so such a conclusion may be premature.

Meanwhile, armed with glowing notices from the critics, *Two from The Late Show* opened March 4, 1978 for twenty-six performances. The casts, directors and designers remained the same, although now that they were the main event, both productions received slightly more elaborate production values.

The New Yorker, March 20, 1978 (Edith Oliver):
"Bishop, as in his fine play *The Trip Back Down*, shows his understanding of the emotions of working people and his grasp of their speech. I don't see how better actors could have been chosen than Seamon and Hogan. Snyder and Ayr also do well under Oglesby's direction. Wilson's *Brontosaurus* amounts to a monologue delivered (with what purpose I cannot tell you) by Tanya Berezin. Wilson obviously knows what he's doing; I just wish I did."

WQXR Radio, March 4, 1978 (Mel Gussow):
"Berezin plays this exceedingly theatrical figure for every ounce of spice and vinegar. *Brontosaurus* has an emotional strength and a caustic sense of humor. *Cabin 12* is austere and quietly touching. Together [they] make a full and rewarding evening of theater."

Meanwhile, Hubert Humphrey, Vice-President under LBJ, died and lay in state for two days in the Capitol Rotunda. William Webster was appointed director of the FBI, succeeding the long-term tenure of the infamous J. Edgar Hoover. And the Dallas Cowboys (then dubbed "America's Team") won Super Bowl XII by beating the Denver Broncos. And in Mexico City, electrical workers found the remains of the Great Pyramid of Tenochtitlan beneath the center of their city.

Skipping Ahead: A Time Warp

Up till now, I've related the history of Circle Rep in chronological order, imbedded with contemporaneous world events to provide perspective. But I'm now going to depart from that approach in order to furnish a comprehensive account of our crowning achievement: Lanford Wilson's Talley plays. This requires me to skip over two productions while I continue the narrative of our ninth and tenth seasons.

Our next production was Lanford Wilson's *Fifth of July*, the first of a quartet of plays that includes the Pulitzer Prize-winning *Talley's Folly*, *A Tale Told* and *Talley & Son*. The Talley cycle epitomizes the unique collaboration between Circle Rep and our most brilliant partner, Lanford Wilson. They must be considered together to trace the genesis and evolution of this body of work over several years. In the meantime, I will summarize the end of our ninth season at Circle Rep, and relate the other events of the tenth season before we turn to the Talley cycle.

A Sizzling Summer

Our ninth season ended with the production of *The 5th of July*, performed in rep with *This Living Hand*, a one-man drama of the great romantic poet, John Keats, written by a solo artist named Mark Stevenson. Although I had not encountered this young man before, I was an admirer of Keats, and when Mark auditioned the piece for us, it seemed charming, informative and entertaining.

We also presented two more Late Shows: Robert Patrick's *My Cup Ranneth Over* and Jonathan Hadary's *Pushing Thirty*. Robert Patrick was an old friend from the Caffé Cino, where I had directed his first play, *The Haunted Host*. Bob wrote *My Cup Ranneth Over* for Marlo Thomas as part of a program of short plays she commissioned for television. But it proved impossible to blend Bob's off-off-Broadway sensibility with Marlo's Hollywood humor. Bob created an odd little comedy about two roommates (Marlo was hoping to co-star with Lily Tomlin) improbably named Paula and Yucca. Once the TV project was abandoned, the script was available to us.

The little comedy seemed a delightful fit for two members of our company, Nancy Snyder and Amy Wright (who were appearing together in *The 5th of July*), so we put the project together as a Late Show. It took an affectionate look at the frustration that emerges when a hard-working, intelligent writer, who has had little success with her highly-charged feminist writings, has to deal with her roommate's overnight success as a cabaret singer by sheer luck.

My Cup Ranneth Over by Robert Patrick opened on June 8, 1978 and ran fifteen performances. One of our seasoned Stage Managers, Marlyn Baum, wanted to try her hand at directing, so she got the assignment. The set was by Linda Hacker, the costumes by David Menkes, with original music by Henry Krieger (for Bob Patrick's lyrics). Here are a couple of reviews:

Daily News June 13, 1978 (Don Nelsen):
"A delightful one-act examination of poetic justice. It dissects [its situation] with razor wit. Patrick handles the confrontation with an ironic humor that never descends into mere invective. Snyder and Wright, in collaboration with Baum, make the characters seem exceedingly credible."

The New York Times, June 23, 1978 (Richard Eder):
"A slight but frequently charming sketch. Often funny, the play has the benefit of an admirable performance by Snyder. Wright is amusing throughout as she hops in and out of a tizzy. Snyder makes a dangerous tempest in this amiable teacup of a play."

Village Voice (June 23, 1978 (Michael Feingold) :
"A tiny play that proves even a small stone can have many facets if it's a gem. Nothing could be cleverer than the way Patrick keeps it moving along with an unending flow of laugh lines, all seeming to tumble quite by accident out of the characters and the event."

The final Late Show gave our Company member Jonathan Hadary (from *Gemini*) the chance to write and perform an ironic one-man show on the horrors of leaving behind his twenties.

Pushing 30 was roundly savaged by John Simon in *New York Magazine:*
"Supposedly a traumatic experience for the writer-performer, [it's] unquestionably traumatizing for the audience. Hadary has a flip, campy humor, roughly on the level of Rex Reed's, and he can occasionally get off a funny one. But this sort of quasi-autobiographical act does not travel well outside [one's] living room."

Fortunately, Mel Gussow differed on WNET TV:
"In 60 non-stop minutes, Hadary plays the piano, sings, shows slides, and chatters garrulously about his life in and out of the theater. *Pushing 30* is informal, good natured, and engaging."

Life continued to provide ironic realities that left fictional inventions to shame, such as the stealing in March of Charley Chaplin's remains from Cosier-sur-Vevey in Switzerland, or the paralyzing of Larry Flint, American porn publisher, who was shot in Georgia. *Annie Hall* won the Academy Award for Best Picture on the West Coast, while on the East Coast, President Jimmy Carter postponed the production of a neutron bomb that would kill people with radiation, but leave buildings relatively intact. Pete Rose reached his 3,000th major league hit. An explosion at Northwestern University on May 25, 1978 was the first attack of the Unabomber. In the United Kingdom, Louise Brown was born, becoming the world's first test tube baby.

While all this was going on, we were enjoyed a 140 performance run of *The 5th of July*, the details of which I'll soon divulge; and William Hurt received a Theatre World Award for his performances in *Ulysses in Traction, Lulu* and *The 5th of July*.

The Force Of Gravity

At the start of the tenth season, Jerry Arrow left to manage the continuing Broadway run of *Gemini*. What I needed now was a partner in leadership who could handle the business side of our show business. We were in luck: the renowned Broadway Stage Manager Porter Van Zandt agreed to succeed Jerry Arrow as my business partner.

Just as in cosmological theory we know that the force of gravity played an important role in the formation of the solar system, the arrival of Porter van Zandt initiated a similar influence on the structural formation of Circle Rep.

Porter took the title Producing Director and presided over a managerial and financial reorganization that vaulted Circle Rep into a nationally recognized institution. For thirty years he was one of the theater's most accomplished production stage managers, from *Dial "M" for Murder* to *The Miracle Worker* to *Wait Until Dark*, to cite only a couple of his long-running hits. On Broadway, he was the associate producer of *The Robber Bridegroom* and Al Pacino's *Richard III*. From 1973–1978, Porter served as Executive Director of The Acting Company with Artistic Director John Houseman.

One of the first things Porter had to do was to find new office space. Our five-year lease on Barrow Street expired and the landlord intended to convert the building into apartments. In January of 1979, Porter moved us into the gigantic NYC Port Authority Building at 111 Eighth Avenue, near 16th Street (now Google's New York headquarters). It was a little sad to leave our funky offices behind, but the space on the seventh floor of this mammoth edifice gave Circle Rep a thoroughly professional atmosphere. Porter and I had adjoining walnut-paneled office suites with a door between them. Our new rehearsal room was spacious and accommodating, with large windows pouring in sunlight from Eighth Avenue. There was even a branch of Citibank on the first floor, and a helipad on the roof.

Among many staff changes, we engaged John Bard Manulis to replace Carol Patella as my assistant. John was the son of famed television pioneer Martin Manulis and Broadway and television star Katharine Bard, and after his time with us, he became head of Samuel Goldwyn Pictures.

In the autumn of our tenth season, the Susan B. Anthony dollar coin was introduced. The Yankees won their 22nd World Series. The Shah of Iran was overthrown by militants and the Ayatollah Khomeini returned from exile, establishing the Islamic Republic of Iran. Also, the serial killer John Wayne Gacy was arrested and convicted of murdering thirty-three young men in Iowa; which brings us back to our imprisoned playwright, Patrick Meyers.

Synchronicity From Ganymede

When two unrelated events transpire simultaneously with no common cause, yet appear to share a connection, the phenomenon is known as "synchronicity." This philosophic concept was first observed in the 1920s by psychological pioneer Carl Jung, but it was not fully articulated until 1951. Jung thought synchronicity had parallels with the theory of relativity and quantum mechanics. It is a concept closely related to Jung's theory of a collective unconscious.

In the arts, there are coincidences of creative thought giving birth to similar themes while being totally unrelated. In science, this sometimes leads two independent groups of researchers to share the same Nobel Prize in their field of study.

Doesn't it seem strange that America could have three great playwrights at the same time named Wilson (August, Doric and Lanford, and that the latter two died within a week of each other)? Or that New York would have two theaters named Circle? Or that Circle Rep's two principal directors were named Marshall? And two of Lanford's closest friends were named Tanya?

Patrick Meyers had been the major discovery of our ninth season, which we opened with his much-admired *Feedlot*. Still in Atascadero Prison, thousands of miles away, how could Patrick anticipate that his new play *Glorious Morning* would be seen by critics to have a maddeningly similar theme to Michael Cristofer's

Shadow Box, (which won the 1977 Pulitzer Prize) or that acclaimed playwright David Rabe wrote a play called *Cold Storage,* both on the theme of death and dying? There is no obvious explanation for such happenstances unless one subscribes to Jung's theory of a "collective unconscious" that creates synchronicity.

I spent no time worrying about these coincidences. When Patrick's wife, Irene, sent his new script to Terry Schreiber, we were thrilled to have such a speedy dividend for our artistic investment.

Glorious Morning is Patrick's most autobiographical play, equivalent to Lanford's *Lemon Sky.* Probably every author needs to write one such autobiographical play so he or she can dispense with psychological debts and move on to more universal themes. We were amazed by the sensitive realism of Patrick's new play, in sharp contrast to the dynamic punch of *Feedlot.*

It was an easy decision to open our tenth season with a new play by Patrick Meyers. Once again, we arranged for Terry Schreiber to travel to Northern California. Terry spent two weeks visiting Patrick in prison every day and Patrick enthusiastically embraced some suggestions Lanford had made, and he provided revisions as quickly as he could write.

Glorious Morning recounts the death from cancer of Patrick's mother, and the strained reunion brought about when he returns after many years to help her accept the inevitability of death. The mother in the play (Sally) has been brought to a remote cottage in the mountains, surrounded by her favorite environment as she clings to a hope for survival. She is lovingly tended to by Frank, her devoted husband, who is a professor of philosophy. They are visited briefly by a strange, friendly forest ranger (Harvey) who is writing a novel, and explains his idiosyncratic behavior by joking that he might be from the planet Ganymede. At the end of the first act, Sally and Frank's estranged son Robbie appears at the door of the cabin sheathed in black leather, wearing a black motorcycle helmet, giving him an appearance as alien as a visitor from another planet. He is accompanied by a beautiful young woman (Alicia) who, he explains, has fried her brains on acid, and is atoning as a disciple of the avatar Meyer Baba by taking a vow of silence. She speaks only one line in the play:

"True love is not for the faint-hearted and weak; it's for those of strength and understanding."

The roles were a great fit for our Company actors. Tanya was ideal for the mother, Douglass Watson exactly right for Frank, Jimmie Ray Weeks could inhabit the role of the loony, amiable forest ranger as if it were written for him, and Jonathan Hogan and Nancy Snyder brought dynamic life to the roles of the estranged son and his weird girlfriend.

Once again, Terry enlisted Hal Tine, who'd designed such an extraordinary set for *Feedlot*. Hal created a mountain cabin so evocative of a scenic vista that several reviewers expressed a willingness to take a lease on it and move in for an extended vacation. Our lighting genius Dennis Parichy provided the required glorious glow of the mountaintops, and Laura Crow designed costumes both realistic and eerie.

Terry and Tanya were initially at a loss at how to approach the difficult role of Sally. They went to Sloan Kettering to do research. There they learned about manic bursts of energy that sometimes accompany the last hours of life. That gave them the key. Tanya was irritable, demanding, mercurial and shockingly vulgar in her attempts to distract herself from her approaching death.

Douglass Watson had a difficult assignment of going from tears to laughter to sobs when he is confronted with the revelation of the deep secret that Sally must confess before she dies: an incident of incest with her teenage son many years ago, that explains why he has disappeared so thoroughly from their lives.

On opening night, with *New York Times* critic Walter Kerr in attendance, a man in the audience was struck with a heart attack. There was nothing to do except for Terry to shout out to the actors to "freeze" while the unfortunate man was attended to by a physician who luckily was in the audience. An ambulance was called and he was rushed to the hospital. I have no idea if he survived. The actors remained on stage throughout this real-life death experience and then resumed the play from exactly where they had stopped. None of the critics mentioned this event, and it is hard to judge whether it had any effect on their reception of the play.

Glorious Morning opened at Circle Rep on October 18th, 1978 and played for thirty-five performances. The "sophomore jinx" claimed another victim with Patrick Meyers:

WQXR radio, October 27, 1978 (Mel Gussow):

"*Glorious Morning* is the latest – and the least – in what seems to be a series of plays about death and dying. [Characters] must win our concern, if not our empathy. There are occasional evocative moments, but nothing is resolved. What is laudable is Terry Schreiber's production. Berezin and Watson act as if they have a permanent lease on their roles."

The New York Post, October 27, 1978 (Clive Barnes):

"Meyers's play is very subtly about the mystique of death. It is a fairly obvious play and its characterizations seem distended beyond nature, and yet to no good purpose. Where the playwright has been skillful is in approaching the horror and desperation of death. Berezin has the task of going into the dark night, of dying with grace. And she does it, as she does everything, with passion. The play was tautly directed by Schreiber, and the handsomely naturalistic setting was provided by Hal Tine. We've had many plays about death in the past couple of seasons – this is one of the more realistic."

WOR-TV, October 27, 1978 (Douglas Watt):

"Attention arresting right away. It is excellently acted, directed, and designed – qualities we've come to expect from Circle Rep. But the play is not enlightening. Meyers creates pieces of a jigsaw puzzle which don't quite fit together. He has a gift for dialogue, but the play doesn't go anywhere. It's a bleak evening, but one with lots of talent on display."

The New York Times, October 26, 1978 (Walter Kerr):
"[It's] in the same capable production hands that did so well by the author a year ago, bringing together such fine performers as Watson, Berezin, and Hogan to make a furtively embattled threesome, and Schreiber is once again in charge of keeping the temperatures ranging from the unpredictable to the very hot indeed. The playwright is at his best handling the small, sudden explosions that could not have been predicted. But the evening's underlying situation is too simply and obviously Oedipal to carry the weight of all those fanciful, ominous suggestions. Meyers writes well, characterizes well; he's just relied too heavily on a thin answer to the questions he poses, the hostilities he generates."

New York Magazine, November 13, 1978 (John Simon):
"It looks like serious, soul-searching stuff, but much of it is clever but unbelievable melodrama. This is not as bad as it sounds, however, for Meyers' melodramatics are enlivened by rattling good dialogue, and even if the situations and motivations are apt to be unconvincing, the characters have a thumping theatricality that keeps us steadily interested, even if only intermittently involved. There are sound, solid patches of effective theater scattered throughout, and the production values are very fine. The performances are deeply satisfying. Berezin gets the utmost out of both the ugliness and the dignity of Sally's unconsenting dying; Hogan is equal to the cunning menace as well as the underlying bewilderment of Robbie; and Snyder's smiling silences have the proper mystical condescension. James Ray Weeks is perfect: funny and vulnerable and resilient. Watson's performance grows in variety, richness, and profundity, until it transports us into a

realm beyond the author's present capabilities, though not, I believe, his future ones."

The New Yorker, November 6, 1978 (Edith Oliver):
"[It's] a singularly unattractive play, which manages to be depressing without being either tragic or touching. We are all in the debt of Circle Rep, which has presented a number of interesting new playwrights over the past nine years, and has done them well. That this pretentious stuff makes any sense at all is entirely the result of the clear direction of Schreiber."

The remaining reviews were unanimously glowing in their praise of the acting, singling out each player for brilliance; some also liked the play, but the consensus was that *Glorious Morning* was far below the promise of *Feedlot*. Terry made a tape-recording of a performance, which Patrick, listening in his distant prison cell, was reportedly delighted with.

As if to demonstrate the trend of synchronicity, the real world was also dealing with death while we were dramatizing it onstage. In August, Pope Paul VI died in Rome at the age of eighty-one. After twenty days of deliberations, white smoke from the Sistine Chapel indicated the Cardinals had settled on his successor, the self-effacing Patriarch of Venice, Albino Luciano. Bridging an apparent schism between the liberal tendencies of the beloved reformer Pope John XXIII and the more conservative Paul VI, he chose his papal name to be John Paul I. His papacy was to very short lived, as he died only thirty-three days later, on September 28th. He came to be known at The September Pope, with one of the shortest reigns in history. Only two weeks later, the Cardinals chose Karol Józef Wojtyła, the Archbishop of Krakow, to become the first Polish Pope. As a salute to his predecessor, he chose the name John Paul II. Even Popes must face that glorious morning of the hereafter.

Also during the run of the play, death made a particularly ghastly intrusion into public consciousness. A "New Age" cult leader named Jim Jones led his followers (called the Peoples Temple) to commit mass suicide in Jonestown, Guyana. Nine hundred eighteen lives were lost in this mad act that ranks among the most horrific in history, including the deaths of over two hundred seventy children. The mass suicides were accomplished by drinking poisoned Kool-Aid. Shortly before, members of the Peoples Temple assassinated Congressman Leo J. Ryan. A week after *Glorious Morning* closed, San Francisco mayor George Mascone and City Supervisor Harvey Milk were assassinated by Dan White. With so much death and dying in the air, perhaps it shouldn't be surprising that three leading playwrights chose to write on this subject.

A Shower Of Meteors

For once, I have no need to stretch for a celestial metaphor; the title of the first play of The Late Show season was actually *Stargazing* by Canadian/American author Tom Cone. Danny Irvine was very attracted to his writing. The play explores the relationships of two couples scanning the evening skies for falling stars. Danny saw this piece as a delightful quartet for Circle Rep actors, so he scheduled it to open The Late Show season.

Nina Friedman turned Hal Tine's *Glorious Morning* set into a starlit exterior for *Stargazing*. As the enthusiastic stargazing couple, Danny cast Nancy Snyder (fresh from her silent role in *Glorious Morning*) and Michael Ayr. As his brother, who is the reluctant host of an evening of watching for meteor showers in the summer sky, Danny cast Tim Shelton, with Debra Mooney as his wife. The staging is extremely simple, with the four characters propped up by pillows, lying on a wooden deck, watching the heavens and, in overlapping dialogue, describing the wonders of falling stars they are observing. In the course of the play, related subjects are discussed, including questions about the existence of UFOs and astrological messages, until one of them turns the binoculars to a nearby house where a couple is observed making love.

Stargazing opened at 11P.M. on November 2, 1978 and played twelve performances. The play was directed by Daniel Irvine, with sets by Nina Friedman, costumes by Joan E. Weiss, lighting by Gary Seltzer, with sound by Chuck London. The stage managers were Michael Hertzfeld and Liz Rothberg. The reviews were mixed:

The New York Times, November 10, 1978 (Mel Gussow):
"*Stargazing* is both short (45 minutes) and slight. Cone's style is somewhat in the mode, but without the melodic lyricism, of Lanford Wilson, The talk ebbs and flows, with crosscurrents occurring simultaneously. The effect is not counterpoint, but confusion. The actors, as directed by Irvine, play with a conviction that attempts to overcome the play's aridity."

New York Post, November 8, 1978 (Marilyn Stasio):
"*Stargazing* is a slight, but inoffensive one-acter. Think of it as a kind of after-theater mint – sweet, but insubstantial. Irvine has directed with an appropriate light touch."

New York Magazine, November 20, 1978 (John Simon):
"This is a very silly, noisy, unnecessary playlet. Even if one could decipher the Babel of tongues that made it so hard to follow, one is left totally uninvolved. The big booming buzz should not be blamed on the production."

Village Voice, November 20, 1978 (Terry Curtis Fox):
"*Stargazing* is a fine first act to an as-yet uncompleted full-length play. Cone's dialogue is laced with purposeful indirection, and his characters are masters of revelation through avoidance. What makes *Stargazing* so pleasant is Cone's refusal to take these revelations over their expected course."

Circle's Sitcom

Following the grim, autobiographical angst of Patrick Meyers' *Glorious Morning,* I thought I'd found a delightful antidote in a harmless, light comedy by James Farrell called *In the Recovery Lounge*.

James P. Farrell was born in Waterville, Maine in 1950, but soon moved to Cambridge, Massachusetts, where his father went to Harvard Law School. The senior Mr. Farrell was legal counsel for an international company, so he got transferred often; as a result, like Trish and William Hurt, Jim had an international education, first at The International High School in The Hague, and then The American High School in Paris. Back in the United States, Jim attended Tufts University, where William Hurt was coincidentally a classmate. At Tufts, Jim wrote a one-act play called *Here and There*, which was produced at the University's Arena Theater. Following college, he was a script reader for Ann Jellicoe, the Literary Manager of the Royal Court Theater in London. Jim moved to New York in 1974 when the Theatre of the Riverside Church produced his first full-length play, *Old Times, Good Times* and he received his MFA in 1987 in Dramatic Writing at NYU.

Impressed with his background, we hired Jim to help us with our tremendous backlog of un-read scripts and then Jim took over as Literary Manager when Milan left to join Stanley Kramer on the filming of his play *The Runner Stumbles*.

I thought Jim's light comedy would be a welcome change of pace for our acting Company. As the title suggests, the play is the scene of a hospital day room where a zany group of misfits gather while in recovery from a variety of illnesses. The play provided splendid comic turns for Jack Davidson as Stanley Hauck, who suffers from hemorrhoids and carries about one of those little donut pillows to ease the pain of sitting; for Helen Stenborg in a bright red wig as Ruth McGinn, a salty widow retired from owning a bar, who fights off cancer with a cynical wit; for Burke Pearson, who as Mr. Zachs is a bossy and belligerent hypochondriac, seemingly indigent but who turns out to be a rich eccentric, hiding out in hospitals to get away from the boredom of luxury hotels; for Sharon Madden as the cheerful and lovelorn Alice with mononucleosis; and for Danton Stone as Jack, a manic cab-driver with his neck in a brace who harbors theatrical aspirations and is the object of Alice's affection.

There is also a nurse, played by Lani Miyazaki, and a black man with ulcers, played by Nick Smith.

Of course, where the critics are concerned a light-hearted comedy without socially redeeming ambition is fatally flawed. They imagined something ominous in that our first two plays (no matter how different) dealt with illness and dying. They were particularly unkind in citing Jim's literary credentials, considering the imperfections they found in his script.

Perhaps the most outstanding element of our production was the set. Designer Tom Lynch took our practice of totally re-creating the theater space with each production to a new height of *vérité*. The audience entered down a lengthy hospital corridor, complete with recessed fluorescent ceiling lights and a faint aroma of antiseptic. Passing the doors of an elevator, they turned to the right to go through those heavy metal doors with little windows in the middle that are endemic only to hospitals, and then across the recovery lounge into their seats in the double-sided arena seating that steeply surrounded the stage. The set captured the audience in a hospital setting that left any sense of a conventional theater space far behind.

In the Recovery Lounge opened at Circle Rep November 29, 1978 and played thirty-five performances, closing on New Year's Eve. It was directed by Marshall W. Mason with a set by Tom Lynch, lighting by Dennis Parichy, costumes by Laura Crow, and sound by Chuck London. The stage manager was Fred Reinglas.

The New York Times, December 8, 1978 (Richard Eder):

"It is a serio-comedy in form, but it is neither serious nor funny. The six patients, their quirks, troubles, and conflicts are wearisomely familiar. Stanley is played agreeably by Davidson; Stone is a funny and appealing actor but the role [of Jack] comes close to making him unbearable; as for Alice, Madden does her best, but she has all the bite of a peanut butter and banana sandwich. Mason directs the play even more heavy-handedly than it deserves; he floods what is already a bog."

New York Post, December 8, 1978 (Clive Barnes):
"I found myself, first reluctantly, then outrageously amused by this hospital farce. It is a delightful premise for humor: take a group of people, put them in a room and hold over them the omni-present threat of mortality, and potentially, you have something very funny going for you. Farrell makes the most of every scrap of potential. The playwright is helped by an exceptional production. Lynch's set has us practically living with the actors. They are, fortunately, extremely agreeable people to live with. The hypochondriac, riotously played by an outrageous Pearson has been given the biggest laughs, and the rest of them contrive sickness as a pleasure. It dispenses many a laugh."

Daily News, December 8, 1978 (Douglas Watt):
"Farrell's slice-of-life piece is stale and unamusing. The patients we encounter are either abnormally irritating or dull, and sometimes both. Mason, doubtless becoming aware of the thinness and humorlessness of the material, has permitted almost everyone to overact. A more appropriate setting for this play would have been the emergency room."

Village Voice, December 18, 1978 (Terry Curtis Fox):
"Unfortunately, Mason is not producing very good plays. As is almost always the case when Mason is directing, the production is done with a care which, had there been a text, would doubtless have been attentive to it."

During *In the Recovery Lounge,* one of our ablest stage managers, Amy Schecter, tried her hand at directing with a new play by John Calene called *In Three Easy Lessons.* We put the play into our PiP program and gave it three performances, with audience commentary helping the playwright to shape his work. The play took place on a tennis court and involved an invisible tennis ball, which was rallied back and forth across the net while three characters' relationships were revealed: the tennis pro, his student and her jealous boyfriend. Jack Davidson, who prides himself on his tennis form, played the pro.

A Celestial Ghostwriter

At this point, I had the pleasure of directing *A Streetcar Named Desire* for Zelda Fichandler at the Arena Stage in Washington, D.C. The true delight for me was working for the first time with a remarkable actress in the part of Stella. Just on the cusp of marrying the playwright David Mamet, this wonderful creature was Lindsay Crouse, daughter of famed playwright Russel Crouse.

Lindsay Ann Crouse was born in Manhattan. After graduating from Radcliffe College, she began her career as a modern and jazz dancer but she soon switched to acting and made her Broadway debut in *Much Ado About Nothing*. Lindsay's film career began in earnest when she appeared as the discontented wife of a hockey player in the comedy classic *Slap Shot*. Lindsay was nominated for an Academy Award for Best Supporting Actress for her role in the 1984 movie *Places in the Heart*. I was delighted to have the opportunity to bring Lindsay into the Circle Rep family in our Late Show during the run of *In the Recovery Lounge*. Her debut was in a play called *Total Recall* by Martin Halpern.

Total Recall is a literate script that depicts a "ghost-writer" for preachers who need help with their sermons. The title comes from the fact that this hack has total recall of the Holy Scriptures because of his photographic memory. Seedy and unshaved in a bathrobe and slippers, the role provided a welcome change of pace for the elegant Bruce Gray. Having been moved by one of his sermons, a devout young married woman seeks him out as an inspiration, only to find that he doesn't believe a word of the religious dogma he spins into words of faith.

Total Recall by Martin Halpern opened at Circle Rep in The Late Show series on December 19, 1978 and played seven performances. It was directed by Ronald Roston, with costumes by Joan E. Weiss and lighting by Gary Seltzer; the stage managers were Fred Reinglas and Susan Bushard.

The New York Times, December 28, 1978 (Mel Gussow):
"The pairing of unlike subjects is a moderately interesting idea for a play, but it operates as more of an idea than as a play. Whatever stage life the work has is less of a tribute to the playwright than to the director, Ronald Roston, who keeps the two-character drama from appearing static, and to the actors, Bruce Gray and Lindsay Crouse. Gray manages to sidestep pomposity. However, it is Crouse who lends vitality to the production. She is one of those rare actresses who can exude innocence without becoming coy. Two of Crouse's best stage performances have not been seen in New York: her Stella in *Streetcar* at the Arena Stage and in *Reunion* at The Yale Rep. *Total Recall* does not tax the actress's resources, but it does offer added evidence of her luminous talent."

The Villager, January 1, 1979 (Terry Helbing):
"Playwright Halpern shows promise. His writing is generally good, flowing, and he makes important points, even in this unlikely situation. Crouse is excellent."

This was Lindsay Crouse's first of many radiant performances to come at Circle Rep, many of them opposite William Hurt.

As we rolled into a new year, The United States and the People's Republic of China established full diplomatic relations and the Pittsburgh Steelers beat the Dallas Cowboys in Super Bowl XIII.

A Solar Return

Milan Stitt suggested that whenever one of our scheduled new scripts was not ready, we should consider reviving a deserving American play. I loved the idea of re-mounting worthy recent plays. On Milan's list were Robert Patrick's *Kennedy's Children* (which I soon directed for CBS Cable on television), Sam Shepard's *Curse of the Starving Class*, Lanford's *The Mound Builders* (which we did in fact revive in our seventeenth season), and John Bishop's *The Trip Back Down*. But I noticed one play omitted from Milan's list: his own play, *The Runner Stumbles*, which was soon going to be released as a Stanley Kramer film. The imminent release of the movie meant that we could not invite reviewers, but I thought it would be a treat for our subscribers, as well as a perfect vehicle for our increasingly recognized homegrown star, William Hurt.

Milan wrote *The Runner Stumbles* in 1974. Based on an actual event in rural Michigan in 1911, the play is about a Roman Catholic priest who is tried for killing a nun after their passion is thwarted by their vows.

About the Broadway production, Mel Gussow wrote in *The New York Times:*

> "This is no dusty court record, but a play about people who are entrapped in their own and one another's obsessions. Despite flaws, the play has a strong emotional impact. The writer avoids overstatement and melodrama. In this, his first play, Mr. Stitt has the restraint and sureness of an experienced dramatist."

For the Circle Rep revival of *The Runner Stumbles*, Milan wanted as his director an instructor from the Exeter Academy named B. Rodney Marriott. Rod soon became our Literary Manager and eventually became my Associate Artistic Director. Rod was a trusted ally and a dependable second director, a role that for the previous eight years was played by Marshall Oglesby, who now had turned his attention to writing.

B. Rodney Marriott joined the Peace Corps after graduating from college, serving in Nigeria. When he returned to the United States, he was an Instructor in Theater for The Brearley School, a prestigious private school in Manhattan. He then joined the faculty of the Drama Department at Phillips Exeter Academy in New Hampshire. He staged productions in England, Liberia, Japan and China, as well as in regional theater in the United States. His New York directorial debut was our production of *The Runner Stumbles*. Subsequently, he directed five more Major Productions at Circle Rep and a host of PiP productions. When I went on Sabbatical, I named Rod as the Acting Artistic Director and after I returned, he remained my Associate A.D. When Circle Rep became the theater contingent of the Saratoga Springs Performing Arts Center in 1981, Rod was the Theater Program Director for the New York State Summer School of the Arts.

Casting the play with our Company was easy. William Hurt created a stunning portrayal of the priest, Father Rivard, who is charged in the murder of the nun, Sister Rita. Bobo Lewis was memorable as Mrs. Shandig and Burke Pearson was wonderful as Monsignor Nicholson. Timothy Shelton was the Prosecutor, June Stein played Louise and Elizabeth Sturges was Erma Prindle. Making the most of a small but important part was Jimmie Ray Weeks as Toby, the jail-keeper. But the surprise was our casting of Joyce Reehling as Sister Rita.

Joyce Reehling was born in Baltimore. She attended the North Carolina School of the Arts. Her first Equity contract job was playing Jackie in a Seattle production of *HOT L* at Rimbaud College, where she received excellent reviews, which caught the attention of Bridget Aschenburg, Lanford's agent. When we were casting about for replacements late in the *HOT L* run, Bridget suggested we see her. Her audition was good and we hired her. Her first appearance at Circle Rep was in *Richard Corey*. Joyce's solid comic delivery inspired Lanford to write the role of June for her in *Fifth of July*, which she played all summer, and in subsequent productions in Los Angeles and on Broadway.

Following her long runs in *Fifth of July*, Joyce had become a member of the Company, but she was shocked when she won the part because she thought we regarded her only as a comedienne. She loved playing opposite William Hurt for the second time and found being with him on stage to provide "a great deal of safety." She told me she didn't think Rod was a very strong director, but he was helped by Porter Van Zandt, who essentially co-directed, although without credit.

The Runner Stumbles opened at Circle Rep January 12, 1979 and played forty performances. Written by Milan Stitt, it was directed by B. Rodney Marriott, with a set by David Potts, costumes by Kenneth M. Yount, lighting by Dennis Parichy, music by Tom Spivey, and sound by Chuck London. The Production Manager was David Bradford, the Technical Director was Robert Yanez, and the stage managers were Fred Reinglas, Michael Hertzfeld and Gary Seltzer. In the absence of reviews, we congratulated ourselves.

A Super Star At Circle

One day in January, my agent Robbie Lantz called to say that two of his clients, film star Liv Ullman and celebrated director José Quintero, had just returned from Australia where they did a production of Jean Cocteau's *The Human Voice*. Would we be interested in putting it in our Late Show series as a benefit for Off-Broadway? Would we ever!

In 1979, Liv Ullman was an international movie star who also had a legendary romantic liaison with one of the greatest filmmakers of all time, Ingmar Bergman. The famous pair had one child together, (Linn Ullman) and made ten films: *Persona* (1966), *Shame* (1968), *Hour of the Wolf* (1968), *The Passion of Anna* (1969), *Cries and Whispers* (1972), *Scenes from a Marriage* (1973), *Face to Face* (1976), *The Serpent's Egg* (1977), *Autumn Sonata* (1978), and *Saraband* (2003) – all except the last one before she came to Circle Rep. Liv won the best actress prize three times from the National Society of Film Critics, twice from the National Board of Review, three from the New York Film Critics Circle, and a Golden Globe. In 1971, Liv was nominated for the Academy Award for *The Emigrants*, and again in 1976 for *Face to Face*. Her best-selling memoir *Changing* had just been published. She was by far the biggest attraction ever to grace our stage, and in a Late Show to boot.

I was eager to heal whatever rift might remain between me and José following our curious misadventure on *Knock Knock*. José was one of the directorial stars from the early days of Off-Broadway with his acclaimed productions of O'Neill. José saw this as an opportunity to give back to his roots. So we decided to make the most of this occasion by making the five performances in our Late Show series a benefit for Off-Broadway at $100 a ticket. The proceeds were to be divided among six beneficiaries: the Actors Fund of America, Equity Library Theater, the Off-Off-Broadway Alliance, the Negro Ensemble Company, the Sanctuary Theater, and, of course, Circle Rep. Since José and Liv did *The Human Voice* in Australia in November and December, putting it up for us in January was easy to do.

The Human Voice by Jean Cocteau opened at Circle Rep in The Late Show series on January 14, 1979 and played five performances. It was directed by José Quintero in a translation by Paulette Robinstein, with a setting by Eric Head, costumes by Theoni V. Aldredge, lighting by Dennis Parichy and stage managed by Fred Reinglas.

Naturally, reviews were not allowed for the benefit performance, but I can report that Liv Ullman was mesmerizing, and the audience certainly got its money's worth. The play fit beautifully on the spare, neutral set for *The Runner Stumbles* and, by adding a bed, a bedside table, a lamp and of course Liv's co-star, a white telephone, the proper mood was set for this desperate, isolated woman who's been abandoned by her lover. In lesser hands, *The Human Voice* could be annoyingly whiney, but Liv's warmth, sexiness and variety milked the drama for all the depth it could hold. The Off-Broadway institutions received about $13,000 each.

A Melancholy Moon Rises

The spacious setting for *Runner Stumbles* accommodated two more productions: a Late Show called *Minnesota Moon* by John Olive and a PiP of John Bishop's *Winter Signs*.

Minnesota Moon is a lovely two-character elegy of two high school buddies, Alan and Larry, sitting in the moonlit yard of an abandoned farmhouse in southern Minnesota, drinking beer, laughing, sharing stories and saying good-bye: Alan leaves the next day for college. It's 1968 and Vietnam looms in their futures.

Carole Rothman, who directed me in *Fog and Mismanagement* a couple of seasons earlier made use of the open platforms of *The Runner Stumbles*, bathed them in lush moonlight and got vibrant performances from Jeff Daniels and intern Gary Berner.

John Olive's *Minnesota Moon* opened at Circle Rep in The Late Show series on January 23, 1979 and played twelve performances. It was directed by Carole Rothman, with a set by Nina Friedman, costumes by Joan E. Weiss, lighting by Gary Seltzer, and the stage manager was Fred Reinglas.

The New York Times, February 1, 1979 (Mel Gussow):

"The playwright succeeds in evoking an atmosphere of wistfulness and eagerness. A life appears to be closing down its prospects at the same time that another life is opening to experience. It is a gentle mood piece about youth at a crossroad. Berner has the proper air of confidence combined with hesitance. Daniels seems to grow steadily as an actor. Together under the restrained direction of Carole Rothman – who last season did an excellent job of directing Michael Weller's one-act play *Split* at the Ensemble Studio Theater – the two create a balance of friendship. Their encounter is as evanescent as the bright Minnesota moon that gives the play its title."

The New Yorker Magazine, February 12, 1979 (Edith Oliver):

"By the time this unpretentious, haunting play is over, we realize that their youth is over, and that their friendship has perforce come to an end. Under Rothman's direction, the acting is as modest and truthful as the script."

After Dark, February 8, 1979 (Glenn Loney):
"The power of the production's sense of truth comes from the characters the actors have generated from Olive's cues, and with director Rothman's sensitive guidance. Mood is everything here!"

Italian Tribune, February 2, 1979 (Leonard Kessler):
"A delicate balance of realism and poignancy. The language is fresh and the characters are well-meaning. Their fears are universal, which brings the spectators on their side immediately. *Minnesota Moon* has the feel and texture of Thornton Wilder."

The Outer Orbits

In March, the Voyager I spacecraft discovered the planet Jupiter had rings. President Anwar Sadat of Egypt and Prime Minister Menachem Begin of Israel signed an historic peace treaty, and would share the Nobel Peace Prize. The nuclear reactors at Three Mile Island in Pennsylvania suffered the worst nuclear power plant accident in American history. In Uganda, the brutal dictator Idi Amin was overthrown and chased from his country.

Following the success of *The Human Voice,* we put up a PiP production of John Bishop's *Winter Signs,* with outstanding performances by Stephanie Gordon, Bruce Gray and Jack Davidson.

Stanley Jack Davidson, Jr. was born Worcester, Massachusetts to a middle-class family. Jack dropped out of high school at seventeen to join the Marine Corps and was stationed for three years at 29 Palms, California. After his service, Jack went to a junior college where he took a GED test to finish his high school study. He then enrolled at the University of Massachusetts, where the theater department was mounting a production of Arthur Miller's *A Memory of Two Mondays.* When one of the actors in the production dropped out, Jack's friends urged him to take the part, since they thought he'd be perfect for the role of an Irish drunkard. Previously, Jack had entertained no notions of becoming an actor. But on opening night, after his character has been described to set up a vivid expectation of his drunken nature, Jack entered and staggered over to a chair and heaved himself into it; the audience burst into applause. In that instant, an actor was born. I've known many actors in my career in the theater, and I've never encountered anyone who enjoyed being on stage more than Jack Davidson. Jack transferred to Boston University where he met Tanya Berezin (then called Harriet) and her roommate Faye Dunaway.

Jack came to New York and played Sebastian in *Twelfth Night* and Laertes in *Hamlet* at the Helen Hayes Repertory Company. Advised by friends never to take a theater job that didn't pay, Jack avoided off-off-Broadway showcase productions until he heard about our triumph with *The HOT L BALTIMORE*. He then looked up his college friend Harriet (now called Tanya) and learned that we were about to go into production for Tennessee Williams' *Battle of Angels*. Upon meeting him, I decided he was perfect for the role of the Sheriff and offered him the part without a reading. Then I cast Jack in a supporting role in *A Tribute to Lili Lamont*, in which he played the straight-arrow husband of Helen Stenborg as a loony movie fan, and again his down-to-earth honesty scored memorably. So I made Jack a member of the Company and he became one of our most steadfast artists, creating role after role for many seasons. After he'd played good roles in ensemble productions like *Ulysses in Traction* and *Lulu,* and a hilarious turn as the hemorrhoid-sufferer in *In the Recovery Lounge*, Jack landed a leading role in *Winter Signs*.

We advertised that our tenth season would feature a new play by Julie Bovasso called *Angelo's Wedding*, but Julie could not find the ending for the play, so we were faced with the familiar problem of having to come up with a substitute on short notice. So for the only time in our history, I decided to take a play directly from its PiP production into a main stage Major Production; I took over the direction, freeing John to concentrate on whatever re-writes he might need to do.

Winter Signs is a Pinter-esque romantic triangle involving three people, one of whom may be a ghost, but the mystery is: which one? Always intrigued by the supernatural, I was attracted to the play and the performances of Stephanie Gordon as Judith, Jack Davidson as her husband Leslie, and Bruce Gray as Ken.

The play takes place on a stormy winter night when a middle-aged Broadway director pays a visit to old friends in Minnesota, where the couple teach at a local university. Leslie is a drama teacher and Judith teaches ballet. Their marriage has disintegrated into bitter quarrels based on frustration with their careers and jealousy. By contrast, Ken (an ex-lover of Judith's) is an emblem of success that underlines the couple's sense of failure. Arriving unexpectedly with a report of a dreadful car crash on a nearby highway, Ken is a catalyst for revelations about the pains of their marriage, but it soon becomes a question whether he might not be the ghostly survivor of that crash, come to haunt his old friends.

The play offered me wonderful opportunities to stage mysterious entrances and disappearances, a kind of stage magic right before your eyes. Perhaps this explains why I found the play much more compelling than most of the reviewers, many of whom saw in it a pale reflection of *Who's Afraid of Virginia Woolf?*, a comparison that never occurred to me.

Winter Signs opened at Circle Rep on February 28, 1979 and played thirty-five performances. It was written by John Bishop, directed by Marshall W. Mason, with sets by David Potts, costumes by Laura Crow, lighting by Dennis Parichy, and sound by Chuck London. Fred Reinglas was the stage manager.

The New York Times, March 1, 1979 (Richard Eder):
"The ghost theme is an attempt to pump some theatrical tension into a very flat and ordinary play. The characters are interesting neither in themselves nor in the quarrels. Their attributes are familiar and their recriminations,

dealing mostly with sex, are clinical and not at all remarkable. The performers engage wholeheartedly with their roles, without managing to do a great deal for them. Mason has directed the recriminations with competent smoothness. With the help of Parichy's lighting, he has made the ghostly bits as scary as possible, given Bishop's failure to make them either useful or convincing."

New York Post, March 13, 1979 (Marilyn Stasio):
"For a little while, *Winter Signs* looks as if it's going to be a good old-fashioned ghost story. Alas, before too long, [it] shrugs off its preternatural pretensions and stands revealed as yet another banal dramatic treatment of mid-life angst."

Daily News, March 12, 1979 (Douglas Watt):
"It's hard to believe that this prolix, portentous and empty piece of theater came from the writer of *The Trip Back Down* or *Cabin 12*, both honest and effective creations. The acting is desperate, but who can blame actors lost in themselves and literary observations broken by heavy pauses. Mason has directed them as if Bishop's play actually meant a single thing. The evening's only really commendable piece of work is Potts' setting."

Cue Magazine, April 13, 1979 (Martin Gottfried):
"Bishop is a new playwright of proven talent, and there are certain reminders of that in his new play, but not much else. It is well acted by Gray, Davidson and Gordon. But I think Circle Rep got overexcited about this talented new playwright and prematurely produced his latest, to his disadvantage."

The Villager, March 19, 1979 (Richard Nason):
"*Winter Signs* projects the exhilarating unpredictability of a wild theatrical gamble. Bishop has scratched a strange and

yet immediately terrifying landscape. He has demonstrated a capacity for lyric and literate drama that seems distinctly his own. The production is absolutely superb, under the incisive and magnificently controlled direction by Mason. The performances are equally intriguing, another example of exquisite theatrical balance."

One of the things I love about live theater is that each audience member has his own perception, and nobody can dissuade you from your experience.

One hilarious event during the run must be related. One of the clues that perhaps Ken is a ghost is that mid-play Leslie fires a gun point-blank at him and there is no apparent gunshot wound. Jack Davidson fired the gun on stage, but because it was so close, firing even a blank was dangerous. So the sound of the gunshot was covered by an off-stage gunshot executed by one of our interns, Peter Bogyo. At one performance, the backstage gun jammed. After a few frustrated seconds of trying to get the gun to fire, Peter was reduced to the most embarrassing moment of his theatrical career, and simply yelled: "Bang!" Such theater lore is priceless.

Elliptical Paths

In addition to our six major productions, my assistant John Bard Manulis proposed a script he wanted to direct. The play, which won the Samuel French Award the previous year, was Norman Beim's *The Deserter*.

I had reservations about the flat earnestness of the writing, but the subject was admittedly fascinating: Pvt. Eddie Slovik, the only American soldier since the American Civil War to be courtmartialed and executed for desertion. A television treatment on Slovik's trial and execution starred Michael Sheen, but Norman's script approached Slovik's situation in an abstract manner that posed unresolved questions. Three Company actors seemed ideal casting for the roles: Michael Ayr as the Soldier, Timothy Shelton as the Sergeant and Jimmie Ray Weeks as the Priest.

The Transcendent Years

The Deserter by Norman Beim opened at Circle Rep as part of our Late Show series on March 15, 1979 and played ten performances. It was directed by John Bard Manulis, lighting was by Gary Seltzer, costumes by Joan E. Weiss and the stage manager was Fred Reinglas. Here are quotes from two reviews:

The New York Times, March 15, 1979 (Mel Gussow):
"The author achieves a feeling of starkness, but at a certain expense. There is such a resolutely low-key quality in the script and in Manulis's production as to shadow the horror and the enormity of the event. Shelton and Weeks are restricted by their roles; Michael Ayr performs capably as the deserter, conveying his character's timidity, confusion and stoicism. Unfortunately, the playwright has added very little to our understanding of this tragic episode in American military history."

Municipal Broadcasting System, March 23, 1979 (Sy Syna):
"Manulis directed in a low key: the atmosphere in the cold chateau right before dawn is a hushed one. The play itself is too sketchy for the fuller treatment which its subject matter deserves. Ayr is compelling as the soldier."

In April, between productions we turned the theater over to Rita Gardner (the original Girl in *The Fantastiks*) for a show she was developing called *A Woman's Life in the Theater*. Rita sang and danced her way through a charming evening of autobiography. Jim Litt was her pianist. It was a nice bonus for our subscribers, and played three performances at Circle Rep.

A couple of years earlier, Playwrights Horizons presented thirteen performances of a play called *Perched on a Gabardine Cloud*. Following our success with *Gemini*, the author Steven Braunstein submitted the script, which he had re-written extensively, to Circle Rep. Rob Thirkield read it and liked it very much; he chose to direct it as a PiP, which was the last production Rob directed at Circle Rep.

The play was about Burgess Hickle, a ventriloquist whose act has become world famous, but who in fact is a charlatan. The secret of his amazing ventriloquism is that he actually uses two "little people" named Molly and Spike, who sit on his lap (hence the title), pretending to be dummies. The effect is understandably amazing and Burgess has become recognized as a great ventriloquist. But a problem has arisen: Molly has become pregnant and she wants to leave the act. Burgess is distressed by the prospect of losing everything. He visits an older ventriloquist named Maurice, from whom he stole much of his material, who knows how Burgess gets his effect. He kills Maurice to preserve his secret. But in the end, he is exposed when Molly goes into labor during a performance, and his career is ruined.

Following a Friday reading, Rob put together a splendid cast, with Burke Pearson starring in the role of Burgess, Jack Davidson as Maurice, Sharon Madden as a fortune teller, and Ken Kliban and Timothy Shelton in supporting roles.

Steve recalls the audience seemed riveted by the play, but at the first performance, he was besieged by Lanford and Milan, who were alarmed by the turgid pace of Rob's production. They urged the playwright to intervene and insist on a quicker tempo. Steve recalls Rob's relationship to the actors was quietly supportive, gently guiding the actors; but Rob welcomed Lanford's concern and subsequently the deliberate pace of the show was picked up for the remaining performances.

Although I decided against producing the play as a major production, the process enabled Steve to see his play in a new light, and important revisions followed the PiP. In 1985, it was revived at the Lamb's Club Theater midtown, re-titled *Big Time*. That production was directed by and starred Tony LoBianco. So Circle Rep's process was instrumental in helping another writer improve his play.

Meanwhile, in the larger universe, President Jimmy Carter famously was attacked by a swamp rabbit in Georgia. Margaret Thatcher was elected the first female British Prime Minister. Pope

John Paul II went to his native Poland, becoming the first Pope to visit a communist country. President Carter and Leonid Brezhnev signed the SALT II agreement in Vienna. A six year-old child named Etan Patz disappeared, launching a thirty-three-year search for him. And Saddam Hussein came to power in Iraq to begin a reign of terror that lasted three decades.

The Jewel In The Crown

Following our disappointing production of *Winter Signs,* we bounced back by creating the jewel in Circle Rep's crown. It was Lanford Wilson's new play, *Talley's Folly,* which we'll discuss later. At the moment, all I need to note is that *Talley's Folly* opened at Circle Rep April 18, 1979 and played fifty glorious performances.

Wishing Upon A Star

After we scored a success in the New York State Council on the Arts pilot program, we applied again and received a grant to commission another new play for children. This time, we tapped our newest member of the Circle Rep resident writers and newly-wed husband of our Lindsay Crouse, David Mamet. David was already recognized as one of America's most promising playwrights from the time of his work with the St. Nicholas Theater in his native Chicago, which he co-founded with William H. Macy in 1972, and where his early plays like *American Buffalo* and *The Water Engine* were first developed. In the small world that is the theater, it was St. Nicholas that my assistant Peter Schneider left Circle to join as Managing Director.

David Alan Mamet was born November 30, 1947 in Chicago to Lenore June (Silver), a teacher, and Bernard Morris Mamet, an attorney. One of his first jobs was as a busboy at Chicago's The Second City. He was educated at the progressive Francis W. Parker School and at Goddard College in Plainfield, Vermont. Multi-talented, David achieved success in a variety of fields: as playwright, essayist, screenwriter and film director. He was awarded the Pulitzer Prize in 1984 for *Glengarry Glen Ross,* for which he also received a Tony nomination. He had a second Tony nomination for *Speed-the-Plow* (1988). David dedicated *Glengarry Glen Ross* to Harold Pinter, who was instrumental in its being first staged at the Royal National Theatre in London. As a screenwriter, he received Oscar nominations for *The Verdict* (1982) *and Wag the Dog* (1997). He first gained acclaim for a trio of Off-Broadway plays in 1976: *The Duck Variations, Sexual Perversity in Chicago,* and *American Buffalo.* David's first produced screenplay was the 1981 production of *The Postman Always Rings Twice* based on James M. Cain's novel. He also wrote the screenplay for *The Untouchables.* In 1987, David made his film-directing debut with *House of Games,* starring his then-wife, Lindsay Crouse. David adapted *Glengarry Glen Ross* for the screen in 1992, writing an additional part for Alec Baldwin. In addition to co-founding Chicago's St. Nicholas Theater, David is a founding member of the Atlantic Theater Company in New York.

Accepting the commission, America's most celebrated new playwright wrote a silly farce for the very young, in which Auntie Georgie (who is pretty much the opposite of "Mr. Rogers' Neighborhood"), is pelted with a pie in her face every time she comes on stage (played by a very game Joyce Reehling). The plot, such as it is, involves a poor poet who cannot afford to pay his rent but who is saved in the end by his girlfriend, who comes up with the money.

The Poet and the Rent by David Mamet opened at Circle Rep on May 9, 1979 where it played in rep with *Talley's Folly* for an undocumented number of matinee performances. It was directed by R. Stuart White, with a setting by John Lee Beatty, lighting by Gary Seltzer, costumes by Margo La Zaro, music and additional lyrics by Andrew Mishkind, and the production stage manager was Michael Herzfeld. In addition to Joyce, other Company members included Jeff Daniels (resplendent in a Canadian Mounties' red uniform), Burke Pearson (as the poor Poet), Ken Kliban (doubling as a hardhearted Factory Owner and a Landlord), Bobo Lewis (dressed as a Keystone Kop), Tim Shelton (as the Wacko Man), June Stein, and Elizabeth Sturges; Guest Artists included Lois Foraker (in a shaggy dog suit), Maura Swanson (as the rent-paying-heroine Girlfriend) and intern Andrew Mishkind (as the Piano Man). Here are quotes from two reviews:

The New York Times, May 10, 1979 (Mel Gussow):
"Billed as an entertainment for children and adults, it may appeal to the very youngest in both categories. This is not, as one might expect from the playwright's record, a tongue-tripping exercise in verbal linguistics, but a slapstick, pie-in-the-puss, banana peel-slip of a vaudevillian turn. It is too broad for my taste, but youngsters and even some oldsters laughed heartily. Margo LaZaro's costumes look as if they had marched out of a window display at F.A.O. Schwartz, and the sets by Beatty are their own toy world. The scenery [is] the most imaginative area of the show."

The Villager, May 10, 1979 (John S. Patterson):
"It's a lively, nay, raucous, and disjointed tale ... an inspired cast of zanies. The audience loved it. I loved it. This is a very silly *commedia* piece which combines slapstick, sight-gags, and childish illogic with a sorrowfully silly tale. The result is a delightful hour of stage fun."

The Last Planet

Our final Late Show of the season (and as it turned out, of the series) was by Broadway playwright, Herb Gardner. It was three short plays collected under the title *Life and/or Death*. The plays were: *How I Crossed the Street for the First Time All by Myself, The Forever Game,* and *I'm with Ya Duke*. I am struck by what an unlikely fit Herb was for Circle Rep; he was formerly married to Rita Gardner, whom we'd just presented in a one-woman show, but I'm sure it's most likely a sign of the influence that Porter Van Zandt was having on the theater. Our Company actor Judd Hirsch also probably had a hand in bringing Herb into our writing family; he performed in two of the plays, while Company actors Joyce Reehling and Jimmie Ray Weeks rounded out the cast of the others.

Life and/or Death was presented at Circle Rep as a Special Event on May 15, 1979, and played eleven performances. Written by Herb Gardner, it was directed by Porter Van Zandt, with a setting by Andrew Ian Rubenoff, lighting by Gary Seltzer, costumes by Joan E. Weiss, sound by Chuck London, and the stage managers were Fred Reinglas, Michael Herzfeld and Peter Bogyo. Neither Judd nor Herb wanted to subject this "experiment" to criticism, so there were no reviews.

The season concluded with a one-night recital of concert pianist Van Zandt Ellis, who was born in Fort Worth, received his bachelor's and master's degrees from the Manhattan School of Music, and pursued further study in Europe on various fellowships. As a pianist, he played both in midtown concert halls and in more unusual theatrical spaces, sometimes employing dramatic lighting and dance as adjuncts to his music making. Only a few years later (in June 1988), he died of AIDS at the age of forty-four. But his pyrotechnical keyboard technique made for a memorable evening of music at Circle Rep.

A Supernova Finds A Firmament

Gordon Davidson came to Circle Rep during the enormously successful run of *Talley's Folly* and made us an offer we could hardly refuse. He proposed to bring Circle Rep's productions of *Fifth of July* and *Talley's Folly* to play in rotating repertory at the Mark Taper Forum in Los Angeles, where we'd enjoyed such a wonderful experience with *HOT L* six years before. The run of *Talley's Folly* was scheduled to end on June 3 and Gordon wanted us to open at the Taper only six weeks later. Of course, we'd have to remount *Fifth of July*, which had closed the previous September, in a completely new production, so we had to leave right away for California. We needed quickly to find something to play in our theater at Sheridan Square for the summer. Suddenly, the success of an old friend from the Caffé Cino presented us with a remarkable opportunity. Sam Shepard's play *Buried Child* was named the Pulitzer Prize-winner of 1979, and it had just closed at the Theater De Lys (now the Lucille Lortel).

Samuel Shepard Rogers IV was born on November 5, 1943 in Fort Sheridan, Illinois. In the early years, Sam, the eldest of three children, led a rather nomadic life living on several military bases. His father was an army officer and former Air Force bomber during World War II, while his mother was a teacher. The family finally settled in Duarte, California, where Sam began acting in high school and writing poetry. He also worked as a stable hand at a horse ranch for a couple of years. Thinking he might become a veterinarian, Sam studied agriculture at Mount Antonio Junior College for a year; but when a traveling theater group, the Bishop's Company Repertory Players came through town, Sam joined up and left home. After touring with them, he moved to New York City and worked as a bus boy at the Village Gate in Greenwich Village.

Sam began focusing his efforts on writing a series of avant-garde one-act plays, and eventually found his way to the off-off-Broadway scene at Theatre Genesis, a ragtag group that met in an upstairs room at St. Mark's Church-in-the-Bowery. There his first two plays were produced on a double bill: *Cowboys* and *The Rock Garden*. I first met Sam when his play *Up to Thursday* shared a triple bill with the Off-Broadway debuts of Paul Foster and Lanford Wilson. Later that year, his play *Icarus' Mother* premiered at the Caffé Cino, and Sam was a familiar face hanging around the Cino and LaMaMa with his girlfriend Joyce Aaron.

All of a sudden, Sam was all over the place. *Chicago*, (first produced at Theater Genesis and then part of the LaMaMa European tour), *Icarus' Mother* (which premiered at the Cino) and *Red Cross* (seen at Judson) meant his work blanketed the known off-off-Broadway world. He won Obie Awards for all three of these plays, an unprecedented feat. The University of Minnesota offered him a grant in 1966, and the following year Sam wrote his first full-length play, *La Turista*, an allegory on the Vietnam War about two American tourists in México. *La Turista* played Off-Broadway at the American Place Theater at St. Clements Church on West 46th Street for twenty-nine performances and he was honored with his fourth Obie.

After receiving another Obie for *Melodrama Play* (written for the La Mama Troupe), Sam received grants from the Rockefeller Foundation and the Guggenheim Foundation. He started playing drums and guitar in a rock band, the Holy Modal Rounders, while continuing to write plays. In 1969, he married O-lan Jones Dark and together they had a son, Jesse Mojo Shepard. He got a taste of Hollywood when he was one of several screenwriters on Michelangelo Antonioni's *Zabriskie Point* (1970), which led him to write his satire of Hollywood, *Angel City*. In 1971, after a high-profile relationship with singer-poet Patti Smith despite being married, Sam and his family moved to London, where he spent three years writing more plays, including *The Tooth of the Crime*, first performed at the Open Space Theatre in London. During my trip to London in 1972, following Circle's success with *3 New Plays by Lanford Wilson*, I visited Sam, who seemed content with his life as an ex-pat. *Tooth of Crime* crossed the Atlantic for its first American production at the McCarter Theatre in Princeton, and then moved to The Performance Group in the East Village, where I saw it. It won the playwright yet another Obie.

When Sam came back to the United States, he became Playwright in Residence at the Magic Theater in San Francisco, a post he held for the next ten years. I next saw Sam there on the trip west I described. In spite of his *Angel City* experience, Sam returned to Hollywood to appear as an actor, playing opposite Richard Gere in Terrence Mallick's *Days of Heaven*, thereby creating a third career. Despite his branching out into other venues, playwriting remained Sam's stock-in-trade.

Returning to the theater, Sam wrote some of his finest plays, including several about dysfunctional families that later proved among his best work. When I read Sam's *The Curse of the Starving Class*, his most realistic play to date, I begged for the opportunity to direct it, but Sam wanted the director of the original London production. When it was produced at Joseph Papp's Public Theater, it was staged by Robert Woodruff. I thought Woodie did a wonderful job, but I was sorry to have missed my chance to direct one of Sam's plays. It opened

February 14, 1978 and played sixty-two performances. Naturally, it won Sam another Obie. Sam owns the Obie record, with eleven.

Buried Child was first presented at The Magic Theater in San Francisco on June 27th, 1978, directed by Robert Woodruff. In New York, it was produced at the innovative off-off-Broadway company, Theater for a New City, founded and run by off-off-Broadway veteran Crystal Field on Second Avenue, which is where I saw it.

The play is a macabre look at a Midwestern family with a dark, terrible secret. Years ago, Tilden, the eldest of three sons of Dodge and Halie, committed an act of incest with his mother. She bore his child, a baby boy, which Dodge drowned and buried in the field behind their farmhouse. The act destroyed the family. Dodge stopped planting crops and took to spending all his time smoking, drinking and watching television from a lumpy old sofa. Halie, apparently seeking salvation, turned to religion with fervor. She spouts Christian platitudes and cavorts with the hypocritical Father Lewis. Tilden, insane with guilt and grief, spent time in jail in New Mexico, and has only recently returned to the farmstead, perhaps to set everything right. The secret is drawn out into the light of day, and the family curse apparently is lifted with the arrival of Vince, Tilden's estranged son, and his girlfriend, Shelly. *Buried Child* has timeless themes of human suffering—incest, murder, deceit and rebirth—resembling the destruction wreaked in Greek tragedy.

Buried Child debuted at Theater for the New City on October 19, 1978. The reviews indicated a major playwright had matured into the top of his form. Critics who followed his Off-Broadway career were happy for Shepard's mainstream success, while mainstream critics who were unfamiliar with the playwright were pleased with their new discovery.

The New York Times, November 8, 1978 (Richard Eder):
"In the very gifted production directed by Robert Woodruff, it manages to be vividly alive even as it is putting together a surreal presentation of American intimacy withered by rootlessness. Richard Hamilton plays Dodge as

a scrawny old fighting cock. Tom Noonan makes the hulking Tilden a moving and powerful figure. Mary McDonnell gives a splendid performance. Shepard's America has poisoned its roots and destroyed its life."

The Nation (undated), Harold Clurman:
"I am convinced that he is not only a genuinely gifted but a meaningful writer. What strikes the ear and eye is comic, occasionally hilarious behavior and speech at which one laughs while remaining slightly puzzled and dismayed (if not resentful), and perhaps indefinably saddened. Yet there is a swing to it all, a vagrant freedom, a tattered song. Something is coming to an end, yet on the other side of disaster there is hope. From the bottom there is nowhere to go but up."

Following a sold-out run at Theater for the New City, *Buried Child* transferred to the Theatre de Lys, where it opened on December 5, 1978 and played 152 performances. Ironically, within a month of its closing, it won the 1979 Pulitzer Prize for Drama.

It was Danny Irvine, in his role as Artistic Coordinator, who brought to our attention that we had an incredible opportunity here. We could re-open the Pulitzer Prize-winner at Circle Rep to fill the gap in our schedule caused by our commitment to take *Fifth of July* and *Talley's Folly* to Los Angeles. We acted on the idea at once, contacting Sam and offering a summer-long extension of *Buried Child* at Circle Rep. He was thrilled.

So *Buried Child* re-opened at Circle Rep on June 20, 1979, where it played ninety more performances. Once again, it was directed by Robert Woodruff, with a new set by David Gropman and new costumes by Joan Weiss, with lights by our Company designer, Johnny Dodd. There were a few cast changes, since there was a two month hiatus between the closing at the Lortel and the re-opening at Circle Rep. Our Company actor Edward Seamon replaced Richard Hamilton in the role of Dodge and William M. Carr (who created the role of Bradley in the original Magic Theater production) replaced Jay

O. Sanders. Otherwise, the cast, which included Jacqueline Brooks continuing her role as Halie and Mary McDonnell continuing her role as Shelly (both of whom became members of the Circle Rep acting Company) stayed the same. The bewildering Tom Noonan reprised his part as the corn-shucking Tilden and both Christopher McCann and Bill Wiley resumed their parts of Vince and Father Lewis, respectively. It is safe to say that many people who saw the Pulitzer Prize-winning *Buried Child* saw it at Circle Rep. With three Company members in it and written by our old friend from the Cino who was now named a Company playwright, it felt to us very much like an authentic Circle Repertory Company production: an import like *Gemini,* refashioned in our image

A Big Fat Hit Hit Hit

In late May, Porter Van Zandt asked Danny Irvine to check out a project in which famous actress Pat Carroll was playing the legendary author Gertrude Stein. It was playing in an off-off-Broadway showcase on the Upper West Side. Danny reported back that the little workshop production was looking for a theater to mount a full production of the play; we had a vacant week, so we booked it in as a Special Event for five performances.

The play was called *Gertrude Stein Gertrude Stein Gertrude Stein* and was written for Ms. Carroll by Marty Martin. A monodrama of about ninety minutes, it invites the audience to spend a rainy afternoon in Stein's Paris apartment at 27 Rue de Fleurus. Gertrude is surrounded by her art collection, which includes Gauguin, Cézanne and Renoir. As she waits for the return of Alice Toklas, her lifelong companion who is out shopping, Gertrude spins away the time by sharing with us anecdotes of her legendary friends, which include Picasso, Hemingway and Proust, among many others. It is a piece filled with a melancholy charm, flawlessly brought to life by Pat Carroll and her director, Milton Moss. Pat Carroll's robust laugh was infectious, and her portrayal of the opinionated Miss Stein, delightful.

The production fit perfectly into the cozy atmosphere of Circle Rep. It was obvious from our sold-out performances we should find a way to extend its run. Danny suggested that we put it in rep with *Buried Child*, which was re-rehearsing for the Circle Rep transfer. In typical Circle Rep tradition, we brought in the whole team (billed as a Sea-Ker production) to play for the summer, sharing the theater in a complicated schedule with *Buried Child*.

It proved a wise choice: Pat Carroll won the 1980 Drama Desk Award for Outstanding Actress in a Play and the 1980 Outer Circle Critics Award for Best Performance in an Off-Broadway Play.

Gertrude Stein Gertrude Stein Gertrude Stein (a solo performance in two acts) opened at Circle Rep on June 20, 1979 and played sixty performances until September 26, when it transferred to the Provincetown Playhouse where it continued its run for another 313 performances (a total of 373). The reviewers were lavish in their praise:

The New York Times, June 29, 1979 (Richard Eder):
"Martin's assemblage is anecdotal, and intelligent rather than inspired; but it works very well on the whole, and it gives scope for Miss Carroll's winning and often very moving performance. It is, all in all, a moving and splendid personified picture, a piece of cultural history that like all good history strikes us as the history of ourselves."

Time Magazine, September 17, 1979 (G.C.):
"Quickly, magically, the audience is gathered into her net of words. Martin has constructed the play so skillfully that past and present join to form an artful mosaic. [Carroll gives] a mesmerizing performance."

The New York Times, October 31, 1979 (Walter Kerr):
"I come late to Pat Carroll's solo impersonation of Gertrude Stein, but I come to praise her. I went expecting a great deal. I got more than I bargained for. [She] enthralls us (literally, irresistibly). Miss Carroll's soufflé is very choice indeed. Superb texture, body and lightness both, four-star anywhere, I'd say."

Buried Child played six performances a week: Wednesday evening, Thursday evening, two performances on Friday and two performances on Saturday. *Gertrude Stein* played four performances: Sunday matinee, Monday and Tuesday evenings, and Wednesday matinee. By carefully scheduling these two hit shows to share the playing week, Circle Rep played the summer of 1979 in rotating repertory on both coasts: *Fifth of July* and *Talley's Folly* in Los Angeles, and *Buried Child* and *Gertrude Stein* in New York.

To sum up our tenth season, Circle Repertory Company presented new plays by Lanford Wilson, David Mamet, Sam Shepard, Patrick Meyers, John Bishop, James Farrell, Marty Martin and a revival by Milan Stitt. Two of our plays were awarded the Pulitzer Prize for Drama. In our Late Show and PiP workshops, we introduced new work by Tom Cone, John Olive, John Calene, Norman Beim and Herb Gardner, with a revival for Steven Braunstein. It had been six years since *The New York Times* acclaimed Circle Rep as "the chief provider of new American plays." In 1979, we were still where theater in New York was happening.

In recognition of this, we received a special Theatre World Award for 1979.

Part Four
A New Constellation

Chapter 13
A Celestial Creation

The theater's ancient origin in the worship of Dionysus suggests religious metaphors could be useful to divine the art. I think of theater as a temple to a god of truth. The actors are its celebrants, leading an audience through a ritual of empathy that illuminates the human experience. In this analogy, it is playwrights who have the role of oracle; they examine the entrails of our civilization and decipher the omens they find. This is as true in comedy as it is in tragedy and playwrights use both to show us who we are.

From the very beginning, dramatists have been concerned about the consequences of war. Euripides wrote about them in *The Trojan Women*; Shakespeare wrote about them in *Troilus and Cressida*; and this gigantic theme also intrigued Lanford Wilson.

The 20th century was an epoch of wars. It has been estimated that 100 million people died in wars during that 100 years. In the wake of World War II, the Korean War, and Vietnam, Lanford saw a dangerous trend in American nationalism that he feared would lead us into future wars, less justifiable than the global conflicts waged to "make the world safe for democracy."

During a span of time from 1978 to 1985, Lanford wrote a group of plays that originally was to be called *The War in Lebanon*. He wanted to use the town of Lebanon, Missouri as a petri dish on which to examine the effects of war on the lives of ordinary Americans.

After he wrote the first two, he started to imagine a cycle of five plays that would begin with the Civil War, when the Talley estate (which provides the setting for the plays) is being built by slaves, then continue with the First World War, followed by a pair of plays about World War II and concluding with a coda about Vietnam. But because he began writing the cycle in reverse order, the final two plays that were meant to begin the series were never written.

I'll describe the joyous journey we shared in creating the first three, which many consider the finest achievement of our long-time collaboration, The Talley Cycle.

But he hadn't originally envisioned where the Talley plays would take him. It all started in our ninth season when Lanford stumbled into an idea for a play about the aftermath of our most recent war, Vietnam.

Roads Not Taken

Shortly after the production of *Knock Knock,* I changed agents from Milton Goldman at ICM (where Lanford was also a client with Bridget Aschenburg) to the Rolls-Royce of artistic representation, Robert Lantz. Robbie was a Berlin-born, silver-haired gentleman with a beguiling accent and old-world charm. He represented the most successful writers, actors and directors in the theater and cinema, including Milos Foreman, José Quinetero and Mike Nichols. I felt privileged to be included as one of his clients. In a way, I felt it signified a measure of success greater than reviewers or prizes could bestow on me.

Knowing I longed to direct a film and follow in the steps of my artistic model, Elia Kazan, Robbie undertook to land me a job. Robbie was so influential in the film industry he could persuade the biggest producers to do as he suggested. For me, he started right at the top. He made an appointment for us to have an introductory chat with legendary film producer, Sam Spiegel, whose *Lawrence of Arabia* and *The Bridge on the River Kwai* were high on my list of all-time favorites.

At the time of our meeting, Mr. Spiegel was seventy-five years old and emanated a worldly, gracious manner. We settled into his spacious office high above Fifth Avenue and Robbie got right to the point. "Sam, this young man (meaning me) should direct your next film." Yielding immediately to Robbie's authority, Mr. Spiegel set a date with me to discuss what kind of film we might make together.

The next time I went to his office, Mr. Spiegel was seeing to the door his previous appointment, Elia Kazan. They'd been editing their film *The Last Tycoon.* Mr. Spiegel introduced me to my hero who professed admiration for my work. Mr. Kazan told Mr. Spiegel, "This is the guy who can take over from me."

Mr. Spiegel told me he'd like to produce a film about young people coming to New York to pursue careers in the theater. I saw this as an opportunity to dramatize my experiences off-off-Broadway at the Caffé Cino and La MaMa. Mr. Spiegel loved *HOT L* and we both thought Lanford would be the perfect screenwriter for our story. I promised to return with Lanford and get him involved.

The problem was that Lanford was deeply mistrustful of the film industry. He knew the pitfalls that ensnared his predecessors like Clifford Odets, who was sidetracked by screenwriting from a brilliant start in the theater. Lanford was determined to be a life-long playwright, with an unwavering commitment to the dramatic art. He was only half joking when he'd say that films were "of the devil," whose temptations he was resolved to resist. When I told Lanford we had an appointment with Sam Spiegel, he actually asked: "Who – the catalogue guy?" But he agreed to come hear Spiegel's proposal.

On a wall in his office, Mr. Spiegel had a large framed photograph of his yacht, which he described as over a hundred yards in length, with a permanent crew of twelve. It was his custom to spend summers cruising the Mediterranean. He had a palatial home in Saint-Tropez with a number of bedrooms, outfitted with a complete staff of servants. Sam's proposal was that Lanford and I should use his house on the French Riviera over the summer to convert our ideas into a film script. He explained that he would be at sea most of the time, but he could check back with us a couple of times to monitor our progress. We could even, he suggested, come out with him for a couple of weeks on his yacht to take a break from our labors.

What Mr. Spiegel could not have anticipated was Lanford's fear of the ocean. He was more afraid of sailing than of flying. His phobias were deeply rooted and incontrovertible. Although I knew of Lanford's anxieties, I didn't think even he could resist an offer of such good fortune. (Lanford later noted to me that no mention was made of paying us a salary while we were luxuriating in the South of France, toiling away on a screenplay. Lanford never wrote *anything* on spec.)

But without going into his fears of flying or sailing or his mistrust of movie moguls, Lanford told us that he had to decline the opportunity. He explained that he had planted hundreds of lilies in his garden behind his house in Sag Harbor that spring and he wanted to see them bloom. He also was feeling the stirrings of a dramatic idea. He was planning to spend the summer trying to convert his vague impulses into characters and plot for a new play.

Our theatrical collaborations had been so successful it was hard to accept that Lanford was unwilling to "repay" me by collaborating on a film. Eventually, I came to understand his reluctance because what he was beginning to imagine was a play about a gardener who planted hundreds of lilies and was eager to see them bloom. It flowered into the play (some think his masterpiece), *Fifth of July*.

A Play About A Garden

Simultaneously with Lanford's summer in his garden, he was hired to teach a writing class at Southampton College, just a few miles from his home in Sag Harbor. Lanford was skeptical about his ability to teach creative writing, but he agreed to teach the summer course:

> "On the first day I told the class everything I knew about playwriting. And there was still half an hour left in the period."

In his class was a young man named Michael Sulsona, a Vietnam vet who had lost both legs, amputated above the knees, due to stepping on a land mine during his "tour of duty." Mike's cheerful disregard of his "disability" inspired Lanford to put just such a Vietnam vet at the center of *Fifth of July*. Combined with Lanford's high regard for teachers (underlined by his own feelings of inadequacy), he made the wounded character a devoted teacher, whose concern for how his students might react to the loss of his legs has cast self-doubt on the viability of returning to teach. This dilemma gave a core to the play Lanford was beginning to write.

A number of other circumstances helped to generate the new play. We were still in our offices on Barrow Street, where Lanford built us a green room; since he was there so much, it was in effect his living room. The offices were a beehive of activity and Lanford found that energy a vital part of his creative process. Again, Lanford describes it better than I could:

"This play was written when Circle Rep was at its most glorious. Actors were in the office all the time; I almost never left. Much of the play was written with actors blabbing away in the room, all but looking over my shoulder. Everything seemed to feed the play."

I've mentioned the importance of Trish Hawkins as an inspiration for Lanford. But in 1976–77, the Company was expanded by the arrival of several artists who rivaled Trish for her role as Lanford's Muse. One of these was the wholesome and handsome Jeff Daniels, one of Lanford's greatest admirers; and the admiration was mutual, albeit of a totally different nature.

An Inveterate Raconteur

Without being too graphic or disrespectful, it must be said that Lanford was uninhibited in his affection for young men of the Company. He was irrepressibly "touchy-feely," but Lanford's genius and his incorrigible sexual energy seemed bonded together in a way that superseded acceptable social behavior. The guys would laugh and gently remove his hand from their thigh or benevolently permit it, within limits. None of these heterosexual men was threatened by his enthusiasm. Lanford's excesses were amiably tolerated by the objects of his attention.

Today Lanford's behavior would be considered sexual harassment. But to understand this properly, several things need to be noted. First, in the rehearsal room, Lanford's behavior was unimpeachably respectful. He adored his fellow artists; he was totally supportive of their work and fully concentrated on his own. Most of this intimacy took place in a social context outside the workplace. Everyone loved Lanford and spent hours with him at our off-hours hangouts, particularly at the Lions Head, a bar-restaurant on Christopher Street just across Sheridan Square (next door to the Stonewall), where casts and crews gathered to socialize with Lanford. They delighted in his company, his wit and his generosity (he almost always picked up the check). Secondly, this was a more permissive time, when sexual liberation was celebrated as a new frontier of discovery. Thirdly, if someone objected to his attentions, Lanford respected their boundaries and didn't force himself on anyone; nor did it affect his professional relationship with them. For Lanford, the creative work came first and he would do nothing to interfere with his rapport with the people whose talents he admired so much. Fourth, Lanford was an extraordinary raconteur; people enjoyed spending time with him and a little fondling was deemed an acceptable price to pay for the joy of sharing his company. So I think he should not be judged too harshly from our present perspective, when unwanted sexual attention justifiably is condemned in the workplace. His intimacy with big, butch, unquestionably heterosexual men was amiably tolerated by his companions as part of his ebullient personality. He was universally loved, even when he was drunk.

And Lanford was an inveterate consumer of alcohol. In the early years, his drink of choice was red wine. At one point, he was so continually inebriated that he literally reeked of wine. When he wasn't in rehearsal, he began drinking early in the day and continued until he passed out each night. But in the summer of 1982,

Lanford realized he needed to make an adjustment in his life, so he resolved to give up alcohol. He didn't attend AA at that time, but stopped drinking red wine entirely on his own. After three years of abstinence, he announced that he was going to start drinking again; unfortunately, he switched from wine to gin. His imbibing of this far more potent beverage grew worse and worse until, in 2001 while Signature Theater was celebrating a season devoted to his work, he collapsed in the street and was taken to a hospital. There a doctor told him that he had a choice: he could stop drinking – or he would die. At that late date, Lanford totally gave up alcohol and steadfastly attended meetings of Alcoholics Anonymous in Sag Harbor. Until his death ten years later, Lanford considered his AA buddies lifesavers. But in a cruel irony, after Lanford stopped drinking his beloved gin, he never wrote another play.

As has been the case with many writers, it might be supposed that alcoholic consumption played a part in his creativity. But I think it was a case of the need for alcohol to dull the pain from his sensitivity to the injustices of life, a frustration that his writing also addressed. I don't think there was a direct correlation, but rather two solutions to the same problem, one constructive, the other, not.

An Actor Inspires

In addition to Jeff and Trish, another artistic stimulus arrived when Corinne Jacker brought in William Hurt for her play *My Life*. Lanford saw in Bill an excellence in acting that suggested a new dimension of artistry; so he wrote the demanding part of Kenneth Talley for William Hurt and generously provided him with a dream lover in Jeff Daniels. We first encountered Nancy Snyder in an audition for *HOT L* late in its run. During Nancy's first two seasons as a member of the Company, Lanford saw her brilliance in *Knock Knock, Mrs. Murray's Farm, My Life, The Farm* and *Cabin 12*. He originally envisioned the part of Gwen for Trish, but when she was unavailable, Nancy was the one he wrote the role for. Ever since *HOT L,* Jonathan Hogan was Lanford's go-to actor in almost every play, a perpetual inspiration. Having cherished Helen Stenborg in *HOT L,* he anchored the action by creating the role of eccentric Aunt Sally for her. He also admired a newcomer, Danton Stone, first seen in *Mrs. Murray's Farm,* so he wrote the role of Weston for him. There is a gallery of sardonic observers throughout Lanford's work (Agnes in *Ludlow Fair,* Larry in *Burn This* and April in *HOT L*) whose sharp, wry humor delivers insight, criticism and hilarious zingers, recognizing humor in any situation. In *Fifth,* the role of resident wisecracker was June, the alienated former protester against the war. Lanford loved actors who were not only truthful to the bone but also capable of delivering a punch line. In Joyce Reehling, he found an actor with the comic technique to land a line and unfailingly get the laugh. Joyce was his model in creating June.

More than merely writing for the actors of the Company, Lanford was inspired by them. The only part he hadn't written for a specific actor in the Company was June's exuberant teenage daughter, Shirley. One day on the street in front of the theater, Amy Wright introduced herself to Lanford and told him she'd recently played The Girl in *HOT L.* He asked her how she'd been and she gushed, "Brilliant!" Lanford was entranced by her big eyes and vibrant eagerness, so she was the actress he had in mind as he wrote the irrepressible Shirley. This was Amy's debut with the Company, but she stayed a member for the remainder of Circle Rep's existence.

Reflecting On The Consequences Of War

Fifth of July is the story of Kenneth Talley, a double amputee veteran of the Vietnam War and his botanical lover, Jed, who is building an English garden at the back of the rambling Victorian house they share in Lebanon, Missouri. Ken is a schoolteacher, deeply devoted to his calling; but losing his legs has undermined his confidence that he can resume his career of teaching impressionable young minds. They are being visited by Aunt Sally, the widow of a Jewish accountant named Matt Friedman, whose ashes she is carrying about in a candy box, reluctant to spread his remains as promised.

Sally lives in St. Louis with Ken's sister June, a single mom of a precocious teenager named Shirley, who have both come for the weekend to spread Uncle Matt's ashes.

The play takes place on the evening of the 4th of July and the morning after. The holiday weekend also has been the occasion for a visit by two old friends, Ken's college roommate John Landis and his wife Gwen, heiress to a copper fortune. In the course of the play, we come to realize that unbeknown to Shirley, John is her father, a product of the "free love" lifestyle of the Sixties. While maneuvering to control his wife's investments, John has encouraged Gwen to pursue a singing career. They have brought along Weston Hurley, a young slacker musician working with Gwen on trying to record a song. Gwen is unable to have children and, late in the play, it is revealed that one of the reasons John and Gwen have come back to Missouri is the hope of sharing responsibility for Shirley in the future.

Meanwhile, the principle action of the play revolves around Ken's surreptitious desire to sell the Talley house to Gwen for a recording studio, in order to escape his teaching obligations and seek a new life. Ken's hope to sell the house is unknown to June and Jed, although Aunt Sally correctly suspects what's going on. In the complex unraveling of the story, we learn that during a drug-infused collegiate life at Berkeley, Ken and June lived with John. They were planning to slip off into Canada to avoid the imminent threat of the boys being drafted. But once John met Gwen, he decided to escape the steamy, complicated relationship with Ken and June and, unaware that June was pregnant, unexpectedly eloped with Gwen to Europe.

Feeling jilted, June returned to St. Louis to live with Aunt Sally and Uncle Matt, who helped her raise her illegitimate child. Kenny, likewise feeling jilted, joined the army and was sent to Vietnam, where he suffered his injuries. All this comes out in a climactic scene when Sally outbids John for the Talley house, thereby saving it for herself and Jed and saving Kenny from his pathetic attempts to evade his responsibilities. Ultimately, the 5th of July is the day everyone must return to work. It's a metaphor for what was needed to follow the calamity of the Vietnam War, getting back to work restoring the interrupted American dream.

Love and Home

Fifth of July is an ensemble piece, virtually unmatched in contemporary theater for the richness of its multifaceted human relationships. It's a portrait of a period of American history encompassed by the tragedy of the war in Vietnam, the counter-culture that fought against it and the moral uncertainty that was the upshot of the conflict.

Actors can derive boundless joy from the depth and complexity Lanford invites his collaborators to explore: the intertwined relationships and conflicting values that characterized an extraordinary era of the American experience, set in the heartland of America. More than in his other work, *Fifth of July* offers a fictional foundation as solid as anything written by Faulkner. Its reality is imbedded in the old house that Kenny has inherited from the generations of Talleys that preceded him.

It is no accident that Lanford put a house at the center of his play, because he was hard at work restoring the dwelling that was to be his home for the rest of his life. For a couple of years in the late 60s, we went to the south fork of Long Island to visit our friend Marilyn Sutter, who purchased a summer home in North Haven, just across a bridge from the historic whaling village of Sag Harbor. Lanford fell in love with it immediately and rented an apartment at The Anchorage on Main Street (joined by Roy London, Karen Ludwig and Chuck London, in their own apartments). Before the summer was over, Lanford found a house he could afford, even though he was still so poor that he and Chuck had to hitchhike to East Hampton to bring the seller the down payment. His advance from the failed Broadway production of *The Gingham Dog*, plus regional theater productions of *Lemon Sky* at the Buffalo Studio Arena and of *Serenading Louie* in Washington, provided him with the resources at last to purchase a home of his own. He found a rather dilapidated ancient Captain's House that had been built around 1845 in the brief period of architectural design known as Egyptian Revival, a sub-stratum of American Empire. Lanford spent many years and a lot of money restoring each meticulous detail of this exotic style.

At the time Lanford bought it, the old house had deteriorated into a shabby apartment building of low-rent tenants. The first task was to evict them (a difficult chore for an empathetic person) so he could begin his restoration. One tenant was an elderly, corpulent veteran of the Second World War named John, who occupied the rear second floor apartment. John was a lonely bachelor whose main goal seemed to be to get smashed each day. Lanford took pity on him and allowed John to stay on for several years, serving as a kind of watchman for the property during the seemingly endless undertaking of restoration. John's annual moment of glory was the pride he took marching under the American flag in the Sag Harbor Memorial Day parade.

During the summer of 1971, while Circle Theater was gathered at our Woodstock retreat renewing our commitment to excellence, Lanford was hammering away at the interior walls of his house with a sledgehammer. Chuck London rented the apartment below Big John in the area that later was the kitchen, until Lanford broke through the last interior wall into Chuck's apartment. After the success of *HOT L* in 1973, Lanford was earning enough to fund the expensive renovation he had in mind and finally even Big John had to go to make way for Lanford's library and study, where he planned to write plays while overlooking the lush green lawn of his back yard. So by 1978, the dream home was nearing completion. It was natural that he put the Talley home at the center of the new play. Big John is a phantom inspiration for *Fifth of July*, with its tale of a very different veteran of a very different war.

Apart from a home of his own in a town that captured his heart, Lanford also met the man who provided the most serious romantic relationship of his life. Although Roy London was an amorous partner for nearly five years, by 1976 Lanford and Roy were no more than good friends and roommates. They moved, along with Roy's brother Chuck, into an ample apartment with three bedrooms at 46 Greenwich Avenue. The new apartment received the stylish advice of Joe D'Urso, one of the leading architectural designers of the time, who liked using industrial elements in modern apartment living. So aside from banquettes installed all around for seating, the entire floor was covered with a charcoal-grey industrial carpet.

Normally, Lanford did not like going to gay bars; the type of "straight-appearing" masculine guys that appealed to him were not likely to be found down the block at Uncle Charlie's. But sometime in the winter of 1977, Lanford went uptown to a bar on Lexington Avenue hoping to find a sexual encounter. There he met Frank Anderson, a young computer programming scientist. Frank lived in Ossining, a town in upstate New York primarily famous for its legendary prison, Sing Sing, but which is actually a historic village like Sag Harbor. Frank possessed a perpetually dour expression that was softened on the rare occasions he laughed. He had not the slightest air of effeminacy; he was good-looking in a Gary Cooper kind of way. He also shared Lanford's love of antiques (particularly Shaker furniture) and was himself a collector of antique blue–and–white porcelain from China.

In his introduction to *Fifth*, Lanford recounts how his new, severely serious lover related a story to him from a book on Eskimo Mythology that he was reading. It involved a young Eskimo warrior attempting to save his family from starvation by thawing frozen caribou meat in a manner so distasteful that the family could not eat the meat, so they all starved to death. Although Frank told the story with utter seriousness, Lanford thought it was not only hilarious, but that it was the perfect metaphor for the stench of the misguided war in Vietnam. He had no idea how he was going to use it, but he scribbled it into his notebook and stored it away until half a year later when he began to write *Fifth of July*. He saw how he could use the repugnant myth in a hilarious scene in the first act when Wes Hurley repeats the tale to the appalled amazement of the other characters (and the audience).

Not only because of this direct influence on the play, but also for embodying the lover that inspired the most authentic gay relationship yet depicted onstage, *Fifth of July* is dedicated to Frank Anderson.

Recreating An Era

The rehearsals were among the most exhilarating I ever experienced. The room fairly buzzed with excitement as the artists plunged into exploring the rich circumstances of their characters. Unlike *The Mound Builders*, this time we were starting with a complete script, even though the play evolved over the next two years, resulting in a finished version that was a considerable improvement over the script we started with.

After the first reading, Danton quietly asked me, "Is Lanford under the impression that I play the guitar?" Nearly every actor in the Company played the guitar (Jeff Daniels and Jonathan Hogan were especially gifted musicians and Hogan wrote the song that ends *Fifth of July*, "Your Loving Eyes"); so it was natural for Lanford to assume that Danton played as well. Always up to a challenge, Danny learned to play the guitar for the role of the slacker musician, Weston Hurley.

The young vet whose courage and matter-of-fact attitude toward the loss of his legs initiated Lanford's creation of Ken Talley was a vital part of our research. Michael Sulsona spent hours with William Hurt privately, generously sharing with him intimate details of his war experience, his wounds and his long journey of rehabilitation. Mike detailed for Bill the hard work that was required to overcome the "disability" and learn to walk again with artificial limbs. He advised us on acquiring the correct metal crutches and how to mimic the prosthetic devises he used to regain his mobility. Mike often attended rehearsals to monitor the accuracy of Bill's movement. In the play, Kenny reminds himself that he must walk "with the stomach, not the arms," a brief summation of the use of muscles developed in physical therapy to replace those of the legs. Bill described his success with this aspect of the part as being a kind of dance, albeit one requiring great effort. Lanford recalled that after Mike laboriously and noisily clattered across his classroom to a chair by the window, he murmured sardonically, "Cha-cha-cha."

Mike Sulsona also provided the incident Lanford used for the climactic action of the play. Mike told him the thing he feared most was falling over backwards. Lying flat on his back, a paraplegic is rendered almost totally helpless because it's difficult without leg muscles to turn over, so he could crawl to a piece of furniture and haul himself back up. Lanford incorporated this event into the end of the play, with John angrily brushing past Kenny and accidentally knocking him over backwards. It is a terrifying moment, and our job was to learn how to do it safely, yet make it as terrifying for the audience as it is for the victim.

To stage this both safely and convincingly, we needed expert advice from a fight choreographer, so we went to the best: B.H. Barry. By the time he came to work for the first time at Circle Rep, B.H. was already renowned as The Master for having provided spectacularly believable fight choreography for more than a dozen plays on Broadway. Later, he was recognized with a Special Tony Award.

B.H. taught us that the success of a fight scene is an ensemble responsibility. The reactions of everyone on stage are vital elements of the audience's empathy. The reactions must appear to be involuntary responses, accompanied by audible shock and dismay.

In designing physical danger safely, B.H. emphasized that we first must learn to do everything gradually, so each step is executed perfectly. When the choreographed action is speeded up, it gives the illusion of danger, while remaining perfectly safe. Another important element is the sound that adds to the audience's fright; so as Bill hits the floor on his butt, he slams the metal crutches to the floor as he flips his upper body down. The sound covers the two-step division of the fall, adding to the impression of a dangerous accident. When this is executed at full speed, the illusion is of falling backward in one motion because the audience cannot perceive the separate steps that happen so rapidly. Additionally, as another character jumps up in frightened response to the fall, she tips her chair over, contributing to the noise. The sharp intake of breath, as the cast reacts in horror, makes it appear to be a spontaneous accident. The noise and the reactions by the whole ensemble are what "sell" the illusion as real.

I delayed the audience's realization that Ken is disabled by beginning the play with Kenny sitting at a desk, trying to translate the garbled message of an autistic student into comprehensible speech. All the characters have entered and interacted with Kenny at the desk for fifteen minutes before Kenny moves for the first time, grabbing his crutches, painfully lifting himself up from the desk chair and laboriously crossing to the sofa to sit by John. This permits the audience to establish a relationship with the person of Ken without relegating him to the category of "the disabled." In 1978, it was enough of a challenge for the audience to take in his homosexuality, without further stigmatizing him as a cripple.

Fifth of July is perhaps the first play to deal with a pair of homosexual men whose relationship is recognized by their family and friends as perfectly acceptable, even normal. In the final version of the script, the play begins with Jed entering from working in the garden and kissing Kenny on the mouth. In 1978, this was a shocking thing to witness in public and a bold beginning to a play. It established right up front the easy nature of what was not yet considered "normal." We've come a long way from that time to the growing acceptance and legalization of same-sex marriage. I'd like to think we had a hand in changing perceptions about gay relationships.

We spent a week of research at the beginning of our rehearsal period, digging into the years of turmoil that preceded the play. I went to used bookstores and retrieved old copies of *Look Magazine* and *Life*, with copious pictures of the demonstrations of the late 60s. I posted them on the walls of the rehearsal room. Most of the actors in the cast were a couple of years too young to have gone through the student protests against the war that were part of Circle Rep's experience in 1970, when we marched on Washington, partly expressing our devastation at the Kent State killings and partly doing research for our Experimental *Three Sisters*. Nancy Snyder, for example, never experienced any hallucinogenic drugs; so her research involved interviews with those of us who had, so she could understand the physical and emotional symptoms of Gwen's freak-out near the end of the first act. Lanford's description of the rally at the National Mall, attended by Allen Ginsburg and Coretta King, was uncannily accurate (considering he hadn't been there), so Nancy had only to recall television reports she'd seen as a child. And Joyce read up on the violence that was interwoven with passionate protests in groups like the SDS and the Weathermen to get a handle on June. Naturally, Jeff read up on flora and visited botanical gardens and as I said, Danton learned to play guitar. I don't recall that the cast needed much research on smoking pot. The artificial herb we used to simulate marijuana on stage had such a convincing aroma that many in the audience were sure we were using real grass.

Helen Stenborg's exploratory work for the role of Aunt Sally was aimed at fleshing out Sally's lifelong relationship with her husband, Matt Friedman, whose ashes she carries around in a candy box. She has promised to dispose of them on this Independence Day weekend. Many elements of their life together are recounted in the play; we know how they met, where they courted, even that they had seen a UFO. It was vital to Helen that she fully understood who Matt was, because he's the motivating factor in almost everything her character does. She came to Lanford for help. Who could she use to imagine the man in her life, now only ashes in a box? Helen was married to the great character actor Barnard Hughes, so Lanford suggested she think of him. Helen rejected that idea out of hand. It was clear that Matt was Jewish, everyone hated him and impishly Irish Barney wouldn't serve at all. Remembering Helen's admiration for Judd Hirsch during the long run of *HOT L*, Lanford said he thought that Matt was probably rather like Judd. "Oh, yes! That's perfect!" Helen enthused. She now had her full image of Matt Friedman, on which she could construct an imaginary lifetime. As luck would have it, Helen's search for a model for Matt was the first spur to Lanford's imagination that resulted in his writing *Talley's Folly*; but more of that later.

Joyce told me that she created a secret circumstance to justify June's persistence about dispersing Matt's ashes. She decided that Matt's last request to her was to make sure Sally dumped his ashes, anticipating that Sally would find it difficult to let him go. Joyce wore a delicate gold necklace with tiny pearls, unseen by the audience that was a constant reminder of her mission because it was a gift from Uncle Matt. Joyce also noted that June could have ended her pregnancy but that she chose to have Shirley, the only thing she retained from her love of John. She decided that June works as an illustrator for children's books, filling in details not provided in the script. These are examples of imaginative work that help an actor ground her work, making her performance utterly believable. The illusion is that she is not acting, but is actually June to the core.

Everyone I talked to in the original cast mentioned their particular admiration for Nancy Snyder's creation of Gwen. She was so beautiful and slim that there was something heartbreaking about the heiress who had nothing left inside after a series of operations. Nancy's Gwen was a living metaphor of our wounded nation. She was surviving, but with the ever-present threat of a flashback, vulnerable to all she'd lost and all she'd hoped for. Her broken spirit moved her fellow cast members, who could observe her excellence at close range. Nancy received an Outer Critics Circle Award for her performance.

John Lee Beatty eventually designed three different sets for *Fifth of July*, but in many ways, his first set at Circle Rep was both the simplest and most effective. The first act takes place on a screened-in sun porch of a Victorian house, with painted wicker porch furniture comprised of a love-seat sofa, two arm chairs and a coffee table, arranged on an oval rag rug; there's also a wicker desk at which Kenny could sit in a rotating office chair. In the second act, the action moves to the wrap-around porch with columns and a balustrade, a glider, serving as a swing, and wide porch steps leading down to the lawn. Considering the storage limitations at Circle Rep, John used the screen wall that separates the interior room and the front porch simply to swing from a position at Stage Left to the other side at Stage Right. The audience could still see the room they knew from Act I through the screens, and likewise could see in Act II the whole porch they could glimpse though the screen before.

Laura Crow designed fiberglass shields molded to fit Bill's shins and there was a plastic ankle insert into the black shoes that helped create the rigidity of artificial limbs. His khaki pants had to be a size larger than normal to accommodate the bulk, but that also added to the semblance of prosthetic devices. Working in the garden gave us an excuse to clothe young Jeff Daniels in a pair of shorts that allowed his impressive physique to be on near-naked display throughout most of the first act.

Our usual lighting designer, Dennis Parichy, was unavailable (he was probably lighting a show in a regional theater that could pay him a better fee); so Marc B. Weiss, who assisted Dennis on several projects, took on the job of lighting the show. His lighting was reminiscent of Dennis' work and it was beautiful, from dusk to the starry night, to the brilliant morning sunshine of the second act. Chuck London provided the sound design, which principally involved crickets and the sound of fireworks and, as always, contributed to the environment we created on stage.

As for my staging, I learned a lot about discovering natural movement from actors' behavior that could at the same time subtly focus an audience's attention. Having discovered intricate movement for Lanford's complex symphonies of *Balm in Gilead* and *HOT L*, staging *Fifth of July* was a simpler challenge. The movement was restricted by Kenny's limited mobility, so his position on stage was an anchor around which the staging flowed. I utilized the passing of a joint to direct the focus in a group scene like the Eskimo Myth saga. The arrangement of the wicker furniture provided a center for the circulation of movement; it was especially useful in the scene in which John is chasing Shirley after she has caught him and Gwen "in the act." Another important element of the physical movement is the stillness of

Jed in contrast to the flights of Gwen and Shirley; Jeff made Jed's stillness a contrapuntal presence that illustrated how Jed was the heart of this unconventional family. Danton's laconic Weston was as comfortable on the floor as on furniture and Shirley also could easily sit on a pillow on the floor, accommodating a cast of eight often all on stage at the same time in a room with furniture that seated only six. Upstage Center was the staircase leading to second floor bedrooms, which gave me the opportunity for a moving image at the end of the first act of Jed tenderly carrying an exhausted Kenny upstairs to bed.

The 5th or *Fifth?*

The title of *The HOT L BALTIMORE* was an enormous success with the critics. They loved figuring out what it meant and congratulated themselves on solving the riddle. Noting the effectiveness of that missing "E," I always looked for an opportunity to set a title apart when publicizing our plays, which brought about the idea of using a numeral in the title, rather than spelling it out; hence, *The 5th of July*. It had the desired effect of drawing attention in listings and ads and to this day occasionally pops up, long after Lanford abandoned it in favor of *Fifth of July*. The change of title came about after the summer run at the Mark Taper Forum because Lanford discovered that in numerology, *The 5th of July* produced a "2"; whereas by dropping "The" and spelling out "Fifth" the result was a "3", a number considered more fortuitous by numerologists. Lanford was not unduly superstitious, but he was always eager to press any advantage, so he naturally preferred a more favorable numerological assist. And the play did fare better after the title change.

The critics correctly surmised that the title was metaphorical of the end of the Vietnam Era, but most of them read the 5th of July as the day after the fireworks, when the country suffers the consequences of a national hangover. Indeed the play begins with a literal hangover from the festivities of the night before, the reunion of Kenny, John and Gwen. But to Lanford, the 5th of July meant getting back to work and the play ends with everyone aware of the work they're going to have to undertake.

As we went into previews, my sense of the play was that it was a madcap comedy on the order of *You Can't Take It with You*. The audiences roared at the jokes, and the unconventional characters were as zany as any by Kaufman and Hart.

We had a "talk-back" in an early preview to find out how much information the audience was able to glean in the quick tumble of talk by these eccentric characters. It was Lanford's habit to bury exposition, so until we had an audience it was hard to judge whether he'd buried it so deep, it was obscure. None of the characters in *Fifth* are representative of conventional relationships: the romantic pair at the center of the play are a homosexual couple; Ken's sister June has an illegitimate teenage daughter; John and Gwen carry a back-story that is complicated, even by the standards of the 60s; stoned Weston is ephemeral, Aunt Sally is attached to ashes she's carrying around in a candy box; and to top it all, one of the homosexuals is a Vietnam vet who is a paraplegic! We asked the audience if they had any idea who Shirley was, running about in her Mata Hari disguises. Only a few people raised their hands. So Lanford added this bit of dialogue when June yells at her as Shirley is running down the stairs: Kenny calls out, "Shirley, your mother is talking to you!" And when she ignores him, June adds, "Shirley, your *uncle* is talking to you!" *Voila!* Relationships clarified in an unconventional manner.

The Sunday before we opened, *The New York Times* published an article by Lanford on his writing of the play and his association with Circle Rep under the title "Observations of a Resident Playwright." He described how he enjoyed challenging the actors in the Company to stretch their talents in a new way.

"If it isn't about learning, there's no point in hanging around. We tend to push each other off diving boards. I've always written for actors. "Whom do you write for?" Actors. "But what audience do you write for?" Anybody. One of the pleasures of being a playwright is watching an actor in the process of understanding, *believing* the part. I'm one of those writers who haunt the theater weeks after a play has opened. I poke around the dressing room, sit backstage, drink the actors' coffee, and generally get underfoot. At Circle Rep, at least they know it comes with the script."

The 5th of July opened at Circle Repertory Company on April 18, 1978 and played 140 performances through September 3. The initial reviews were disappointing:

The New York Times, April 28, 1978, (Richard Eder):
"Wilson's vocabulary of freaks, sensitive and even charming though they may be, is not the right material to construct the history of a decade. A sporadically appealing, but unworkable play."

The New York Times, May 7, 1978, (Walter Kerr):
"The metaphor is weak, unmotivated, inconclusive. The evening only marks time with set-pieces, monologues, musings. It's one thing to write a play about the loss of structure in our lives; it is another to write it with as little care for shape and form as the life that is being mirrored."

New York Post, April 28, 1978, (Clive Barnes):
"Compellingly realistic. You watch the play and listen to the noises of history. This is not one of Wilson's best plays, yet what it does present is a sort of awe-inspiring authority. It is beautiful in its overlapping dialogue, its feeling for the actors, and its handsome sense of time, space, and period. The ensemble murmurs and mutters poetry in tune with the playwright's song."

Daily News, April 28, 1978, (Douglas Watt):
"The play is entertaining and full of suggestion, yet hollow. [It's] a little like Chekhov on smack, but there's no

real high. The whole cast is excellent, but there are two especially stunning performances, one by Nancy Snyder and the other by Amy Wright. Funny as it is, the play lacks resonance."

The Record, April 28, 1978, (Emory Lewis):
"Although not entirely successful, it is his most ambitious work to date. This haunted study of blasted dreams has resonance and dimension. Wilson has mixed delicate irony with wild laughter. The cast is one of the best ever assembled by the Circle Rep."

The New Yorker, May 3, 1978, (Edith Oliver):
"Wilson's most ambitious play so far. There is no doubt he is a writer in a profession crowded with non-writers. The actors work very well together."

In other words, the usual suspects who heralded hits found plenty of faults. Then we were rescued by three unlikely sources, the first by the *Daily News's* pop-culture columnist, Rex Reed; the second by the esteemed Harold Clurman; and the third by London's most distinguished, hard-to-please critic, Michael Billington of *The Guardian.*

Daily News, undated in 1978, (Rex Reed):
"Something powerful and mesmerizing is happening at the Circle Rep. Wilson's new play is one of the most incredibly well-written, beautifully acted, profound and moving and often hilarious plays it has ever been my privilege to see in the American theater. It is profoundly original and beautiful, and Mason's direction is pure genius. Like all masterpieces, it must be experienced. *The 5th of July* is the best play in town. If you care anything at all about great writing and magnificent ensemble acting, or about the art of the theater, you'd be insane to miss it."

The Nation, May 13, 1978, (Harold Clurman):

"Nothing prevented me from liking this over-extended play! The writing is wittily deft throughout, the general tone hilariously batty; and though the insights are swiftly passed over, we have frequent intimations of their presence. The play is utterly unpretentious, but something more than simple entertainment is achieved. Wilson *sees:* his sight is cockeyed but on target. A most important contribution to the fun is the excellent cast. Mason, very knowing and humane in the direction of actors, has created out of the crazy quilt of the play's jiggling patterns, a coherent and memorable "picture." To mention the particular qualities of the individual players would make this review longer than perhaps necessary. I need only say that when the play was over, I wanted to marry them all!"

The Guardian, undated, (Michael Billington):

"If one wants to see writing, acting, and direction meshing into one glorious whole, one has to see *The 5th of July.* It seems to me the best play in town. Its run has now been extended into September, and if you're anywhere near New York this summer, don't miss it."

These reviews were dutifully blown up and posted in front on our theater on the busy Village thoroughfare of Seventh Avenue South, where they attracted a walk-by crowd that enabled us to run all summer with sold-out performances, despite the initial lukewarm reviews. The show was a hit by virtue of "word of mouth" and Rex Reed kept us alive with a new mention in his columns every week. We also were helped by Mel Gussow's mid-summer radio review:

The New York Times on WNET, August 1978, (Mel Gussow):

"The play is even better and richer in character and atmosphere than it was when it opened in June. This wry and pensive play is about the decline of an age and the loss of dreams. Certainly one of the most stimulating plays of the season."

Over the course of the next three years, during which we developed *Fifth of July* before its Broadway opening in 1981, the opinions of the critics also evolved, as you'll see.

The extension of the original subscription run meant we had to find replacements for actors whose schedules committed them to other engagements. William Hurt left the cast to go to Hollywood, beginning his distinguished film career with Paddy Chayefsky's *Altered States*, directed by Ken Russell. Amy Wright also left, as did Jonathan Hogan. They were replaced, respectively, by Timothy Shelton, Jane Fleiss and Jeffrey Pomerantz, all of whom were able substitutes. Unfortunately for the original cast, during the summer the Lincoln Center Library for the Performing Arts inaugurated a program of taping stage productions for their historical archives; *The 5th of July* was one of the first productions so preserved. At that time, the archival recording was limited to one camera. Worse, the crew had not seen the show in advance, so there was no planning of effective shots. And because of the timing, they recorded the replacement cast. Nancy Snyder, Jeff Daniels, Helen Stenborg, Joyce Reehling and Danton Stone stayed with the show the whole summer and, as a result, their extraordinary work is still preserved in the archives at Lincoln Center, a seed caught in an amber bead.

A Russian Redux

More than our disappointment with the initial reviews or our pleasure with the play's success, we were amazed by the comparison many of the reviewers made to justify either their warm or negative assessments. Here's a sampling of the many references comparing *The 5th of July* to the work of Anton Chekhov:

Clive Barnes: "Just a little like an up-dated Chekhov."
Douglas Watt: "A little like Chekhov on smack."

John Simon: "A pretty good Chekhovian play written too late."
Edith Oliver: "Only Chekhov can write Chekhov's plays."
Emory Lewis: "Chekhovian in spirit and style."
Erika Munk: "A deliberate variation on the theme of *Cherry Orchard.*"

Only William A. Raidy, writing for *The Star-Ledger* noted that:

"*The 5th of July* has an oddball, contemporary *You Can't Take It with You* quality to it."

Mr. Raidy saw the same quality in the play that I saw, and the association with Chekhov was a surprise. I suppose the plot issue of selling the estate is central to both *Fifth* and *Cherry Orchard*, but I thought the madcap style of a house full of crazies more resembled the plays of Kaufman and Hart than Anton Pavlovich. Still, this was the first time Lanford's work was compared to that of the great master and the similarity continued to be cited throughout Lanford's career. Initially meant to be disparaging, the reference to Chekhov came to be an association we treasured and I think there is legitimate insight in seeing Lanford as "The American Chekhov."

An Evolving Text

During the extended summer run of *The 5th of July*, I went back to the Academy Festival Theater, where Bill Gardner virtually established a regular summer job for me. Bill scheduled a new play for me to direct by Corinne Jacker called *After the Season*, starring Irene Worth. Then Lanford came to Lake Forest and we mounted a new production of his *Serenading Louie*, with Tony Roberts, Lindsay Crouse, Arthur Taxier and Lynn Milgram.

While we were in rehearsal for *Louie*, several young actors just out of college drove over to Lake Forest to meet Lanford and me. They had formed their own theater company in Highland Park, a neighboring suburb of Chicago's affluent North Shore.

They were in rehearsal to present the Chicago premiere of *The 5th of July*. These nice kids included John Malkovich, Joan Allen, Gary Sinese, Terry Kinney and Laurie Metcalf. The theater they formed, of course, was Steppenwolf, which grew to be one of the most important theaters in America. The kids told us that they discovered a problem in the play that easily could be solved. The suspense created by the question of *when* Aunt Sally was going to dump the ashes of Uncle Matt evaporated when she did so midway in the first act. Lanford and I both saw the wisdom of their insight, so we delayed Sally's disposal of the candy box to the second act, extending this element of suspense. We called our stage manager in New York and asked him to make the changes in the ongoing run at Circle Rep. Thanks to Steppenwolf for a valuable improvement in an evolving script.

I have already noted that the first text of *The 5th of July* is markedly different from the version we ended up with three years later on Broadway. Hill & Wang published hard-backed editions of each of Lanford's previous full-length plays, beginning with *Balm in Gilead* in 1965. Thirteen years later, they were so eager to publish the new play that they rushed it into print while it was still playing at Circle Rep. A second production at the Mark Taper Forum the following year offered Lanford an opportunity to revisit the structure of the play, resulting in a tighter script.

Principally, Lanford was bothered that Gwen's outsized hilarity dominated any scene she was in. When the play began with Gwen, as it did in the first run of the play at Circle Rep, the attention inevitably focused on *her* rather than on Kenny and Jed, the central players in the drama. Perhaps the most important change of many in the evolution of the text was delaying Gwen and John's entrance until *after* we established the relationship of Kenny and Jed. This launched the audience on a true trajectory, less likely to be hijacked by Gwen's colorful antics. The definitive version of the text of *Fifth of July* is found in the Dramatist Play Service acting edition, published as a paperback in 1982, or in the Smith & Kraus edition of Volume III of the *Collected Works: The Talley Trilogy*, published in 1999.

The Ghost of a Play in a Box

Perhaps of all Lanford's plays, none came more easily than *Talley's Folly*. Once he suggested to Helen Stenborg that her fellow actor from *HOT L*, Judd Hirsch, was the living source of the ashes of Matt Friedman she was carrying around in the candy box, *Talley's Folly* tumbled forth fully imagined.

In his introduction in the *Collected Work: The Talley Trilogy*, Lanford wrote:

"Imagining Matt and Sally on a date – this big, sexy, clumsy Jew coming from St. Louis down to Lebanon, Missouri, where nobody had ever seen a Jew before – was very exciting. I knew immediately that I wanted this to be unlike anything I had written. It would be much lighter, with a gloriously happy ending."

After we returned from Lake Forest and watched the final performances of *5th* at Circle Rep, he began to write. I was in rehearsal for *In the Recovery Lounge,* and because the play came easily to Lanford, I wasn't involved in his initial writing process. But during my rehearsals in November, we scheduled Lanford's new play to be read at one of our regular Friday readings, when the Company gathered weekly to hear new work. Judd was unavailable, so for the first reading we pressed our reliably versatile Jonathan Hogan into reading the part opposite Trish Hawkins. The company was thrilled with the beautiful writing of this incipient masterpiece and Lanford was full of himself with pride. According to Lanford, only *I* remained ominously quiet in the commentary that followed the reading. We retired to my office, where I pointed out that as written, the story was pretty brutal. An overbearing man comes down to the boathouse and browbeats a lovely delicate aristocrat for an hour and a half until she agrees to marry him. There was no suspense, because Lanford had given Matt all the cards: he knew from the get-go that Sally couldn't have children, so it was just a matter of breaking down her objections.

Rather than being deflated by my criticism, Lanford saw the potential of Matt having no prior knowledge of Sally's history, but learning her circumstances along with the audience as the play unfolds. He went back to work.

After *Recovery Lounge* opened at the end of November, Lanford brought me his revised script, in which he removed Matt's foreknowledge of Sally's barren state, thereby producing a *plot*. The action now revealed the hidden secrets that bound this unlikely pair together. Because of the torture and death of his sister, Matt has resolved never to have children. But he has assumed that Sally's secret was that she had a child out of wedlock, which would be a source of shame to her. When he discovers as we do that Sally cannot have children due to an infection of her fallopian tubes, the barriers between them come tumbling down and they are clearly meant for each other. Lanford described this plot resolution as a latch sliding into place with the satisfying click of a lock.

I was exhausted from my recent opening, but I went over to Lanford's new apartment on Greenwich Street to read the play aloud so I could see how it progressed. Naturally, I wanted to read Matt, so Lanford would read Sally. While I was delighted with the mystery and suspense that emerged in the new draft, Lanford became increasingly agitated. The part of Sally, which he was reading, needed more development. He saw that even without his foreknowledge, Matt still had all the laughs and was easily the dominant part. So, he got to work on a third draft, in which the size of Sally's part doubled. Her character became more complex and capable of matching wits with Matt.

By the end of December, the full, rich story had been captured and we scheduled a reading at Lanford, Roy and Chuck's apartment for New Year's Eve, when we heard for the first time Judd and Trish read the parts Lanford wrote for them. Now, we all knew we had something special.

In the middle of our tenth season, we moved our offices from our cozy, funky home on Barrow Street to an expansive suite of offices at the gigantic Port Authority building. The new rehearsal room had huge windows that brought in loads of sunlight, warming the spring rehearsals in our new space.

The work with the actors was a pleasure as they explored each moment fully and honestly. There was, however, a slight tension throughout because Trish and Judd had gone out together during *HOT L*. Their real-life romantic liaison was fraught with an edgy nervousness. Their personalities were, as they grew to realize, virtually incompatible. Their history as a couple reached a hard-earned and delicately maintained truce, infusing the fictional wooing with a tension that was a boon to the production. When the two of them came together in the romantic moonlight of the gazebo toward the end of the play, the script allowed them to experience a closeness they found difficult to sustain in real-life, but that suffused the fictional relationship with a heart that beat with urgency.

As usual, John Lee Beatty gave us an environment that was a dream to inhabit. His lushly romantic setting was designed to have no conventional places to sit down, yet on which we could discover cleverly hidden props that could be transformed into places to sit. The boathouse was a logical place where discarded things have accumulated over the years. One of these happened to be a half-buried buggy seat that, when turned right-side up, was a cozy place for Matt and Sally to share a smoke. The gazebo logically had benches built in, as well as steps leading up to it we could sit on. John Lee connected the two piers upstage with the arch of a romantic bridge under which the river ran, which also had steps where one could sit. So the boathouse, which on first view had nothing to do with the comforts of a conventional stage, gave the characters places where they could relax and relate to each other. The ground plan was challenging, because the raked piers were only a few feet wide, with a bridge far upstage and the elaborately ornate gazebo all the way over at Stage Right. I also asked John Lee to build me a plank that extended slightly into the audience so I could utilize it for Matt's intimate revelations: his life on the run as a European Jew and the death of his sister, resulting in his determination never to have children. This crucial disclosure needs privacy, permitting Matt to relive the untellable, hiding from Sally's scrutiny, yet revealing his pain to an audience. The boathouse resembled no ground plan ever seen before.

John Lee's design of the river itself was miraculous. The water was constructed on an imperceptible slant out of crinkled foil and Mylar. Even in the intimacy of Circle Rep, where the front row was only a couple of feet from the stage, once Dennis Parichy lighted John Lee's Mylar, the illusion was incredibly convincing. John Lee also gave us a full moon that rose throughout the play after dusk fell, reaching its apex at the climax of the love story. And finally, there was a boat in the very center, where all could be resolved after the bitter revelations of the past have been purged. The couple could sit side by side in the boat, with a glorious golden moon to frame their kiss.

It's impossible to overpraise John Lee's accomplishment with this set, the result of a challenge issued by Lanford's stage directions and the details enumerated in Matt's prologue to the audience. Much has been said about how Lanford wrote for actors, but it has passed almost unnoticed that Lanford was equally inspired by the brilliance of our design team: John Lee's soaring imagination, Dennis Parichy's subtle, fluid lighting and Chuck London's ability to bring an environment to life with sounds never heard before in a theater: a chorus of nature, recorded from nature, that made the romantic night palpable. As one reviewer said, when the actor said he smelled honeysuckle, the critic was convinced he smelled it too.

The dress rehearsals eased by after a couple of days of complex tech rehearsals and suddenly we were ready to share our Valentine with audiences. The previews went amazingly well and the overwhelmingly warm reception of the preview audiences promised satisfying rewards for our work.

Talley's Folly opened at Circle Repertory Company on May 3, 1979, where it played fifty performances. It was directed by Marshall W. Mason with Judd Hirsch as Matt Friedman and Trish Hawkins as Sally Talley. The set was by John Lee Beatty, the lighting by Dennis

Parichy, the costumes by Jennifer Von Mayrhauser and the sound design by Chuck London. It was stage managed by Fred Reinglas. This production brought us the best reviews we ever received, close to unanimous praise:

The New York Times, May 4, 1979 (Mel Gussow):
"Lanford Wilson's eloquent new play is, as promised, a 'no-holds-barred romantic story,' beautifully played by Judd Hirsch and Trish Hawkins. The scale of *Talley's Folly* is deceptively small. Actually, it is one of Wilson's most expansive works, wise with a knowledge of humanity. Mason, who over the years has been Wilson's principal directorial interpreter, has given this play an inspired production. It is clear to me that Wilson is one of our most gifted playwrights, a dramatist who deals perceptively with definably American themes. Not only has he created a large, cohesive body of work, he has also steadily grown and explored his art. *Talley's Folly* is a play to savor and to cheer."

Daily News, May 4, 1979 (Douglas Watt):
"*Talley's Folly* is a captivating romantic comedy with a marvelously incisive performance by Hirsch. It is a fibrous and funny affair. It is also completely involving and charmingly eccentric. It is beautifully composed, well-made in the best sense of the term. It is Wilson's finest work since *HOT L*. Matt and Sally are a couple whose company you hate to leave."

New York Post, May 4, 1979 (Clive Barnes):
"It is perhaps the simplest and most lyrical play Wilson has so far written – a funny, sweet, touching and marvelously written love poem. Wilson's characters paint a vivid picture of the time and of America. Mason's direction is faultless – not a beat or an inflection is missed – and the acting is a delight. You will glow with satisfaction."

The New York Times, May 13, 1979 (Walter Kerr):

"*Talley's Folly* is a lovely play. Hirsch can scarcely ever have been better, and Hawkins [is] immensely attractive, disturbingly troubled. Wilson has written it tightly, brightly, and honestly, with such an impressible ear and such a beguiling smile, you feel quite restored. A treasure."

New York Magazine, May 21, 1979 (John Simon):

"Wilson has written some of the most tender, wisely funny, chargedly understated dialogue I've heard from a stage in many a moon, dialogue fraught with the essence of the greatest drama on earth: that of two pitiful yet gloriously human beings clumsily and splendidly staggering toward each other. Wilson understands the interplay of the absurd and the miraculous and how it sustains life. Mason's direction [is] as inventively true to the text as a Balanchine choreography to its music."

The Nation, May 26, 1979 (Harold Clurman):

"It contains almost no plot in the ordinary sense of the word. Nevertheless, we are charmed. *Talley's Folly* is sustained by the engaging humor of its writing and the excellence of the acting. Hirsch is a thoroughly professional actor, he inspires confidence. Hawkins is perfect."

Variety, May 16, 1979 (Humm.):

"*Talley's Folly* is an engaging and deftly written romantic comedy. It reconfirms Wilson is a playwright of exceptional talent. [It's] a pleasantly nostalgic duet, with warmth, humor and truthful observations. It's worth the risk of a Broadway transfer by someone."

The Hollywood Reporter, May 16, 1979 (Charles Ryweck):

"Charming, witty, and altogether delightful. Mason has guided the romantic comedy completely tuned to the nuances of Wilson's work. Hirsch is commanding, by turns ebullient, reflective, philosophical. It is a stunning performance. Hawkins is luminous."

The unanimity of critical praise reflected a similar reaction from the audiences. The reviews of *Talley's Folly* vied to be the most euphoric. And the amazing thing, as you shall see, is the esteem for both *Fifth of July* and *Talley's Folly* only grew with time.

Lanford dedicated *Talley's Folly* to Harold Clurman.

Chapter 14
A Binary System

As with *The HOT L BALTIMORE*, Gordon Davidson got the jump on other producers by making us an irresistible offer. Gordon proposed that we bring *The 5th of July* and *Talley's Folly* to the Mark Taper Forum to play in rotating rep immediately after our season in New York. It was a golden opportunity to work on the plays in the safety of one of America's most productive theaters. Gordon's offer pre-empted an extended New York run for *Talley's Folly*, which likely would have been to an Off-Broadway venue. The Taper gave us a chance to test its reach and popularity with bigger audiences without the risks a jump to Broadway would incur.

Playing at the Taper also allowed us to tighten and perfect *The 5th of July*. The previous year, critics faulted the looseness of its construction, but Steppenwolf's structural suggestion gave the plot a through-line that the New York critics had not seen. Lanford also saw he needed to focus on the central relationship between Kenny and Jed. The issue at the heart of the play is Ken's surreptitious plan to sell the Talley house to escape his teaching responsibilities. But the critics had not seen that, because Gwen's scatterbrained fireworks so overwhelmed the beginning that the storyline was diffused.

For me, the opportunity offered an uneven challenge. *Talley's Folly* had just concluded its run and after a short hiatus, was remounted with the same dream cast and design team. It was more a transfer than a new production. My main chore was to restage the play, adapting it from a proscenium stage to the extreme thrust of the Taper, where audiences virtually surround the action. But apart from the actors needing to audibly project to fill a larger space, not much needed to change.

The 5th of July, on the other hand, had to be completely reimagined. There had to be some cast changes, the script was evolving and it also had to be restaged from proscenium to thrust. This last task was more complicated than *Talley's Folly*, because *The 5th of July* has a cast of eight characters, all on stage much of the time. I had to reconceive the movement so they wouldn't block each other from the different perspectives of an audience all around them.

It was a busy summer. I was scheduled to follow the two shows at the Taper with a new production of Shelby Buford's play *Slugger*. Flush with the resources of my fees for three simultaneous productions, I rented a beach house in Malibu, a two-story structure that extended out into the Pacific Ocean on pylons. The lapping of the waves under the deck that extended off the living room was a perpetual reminder of my budding success and the soothing lullaby of a sanctuary after a hard day's work.

Reviving and Revitalizing

I went to Los Angeles a couple of months earlier to conduct auditions for *The 5th of July*. The original cast members coming to the West Coast were Jeff Daniels, Jonathan Hogan, Helen Stenborg, Danton Stone, Joyce Reehling and Amy Wright. I had to find new actors to portray the demanding roles of Kenny and Gwen. With the resources of the Taper casting staff, I found Christopher Allport for Kenneth Talley and Susan Sullivan for Gwen. Susan had the beginnings of a notable television career, but she had not yet reached the starring status that came with her eight years on *Falcon Crest* or *Dharma & Greg*, a decade down the road. Chris and Susan had big boots to fill, but the Circle Rep cast was supportive so the play came through clearly, even without the exquisite nuances provided by William Hurt and Nancy Snyder. It was still that rare thing: a genuine ensemble.

Throughout rehearsals, Lanford restructured, trimmed and improved the script. There was little for him to do on *Talley's Folly*.

Perhaps the biggest challenge fell to John Lee Beatty, who had to conceptualize a stage that could transform from the sun porch and veranda of *The 5th of July* to a boathouse on the river in *Talley's Folly*. A native of Southern California, familiar with the magic of Disneyland, John Lee wanted to take advantage of the Taper's stadium seating: seats sloped down to the stage so the river could be seen from above. This meant he could use real water in a tank, on which the boat could actually float. *Real water!* I was thrilled.

John Lee solved the problem by having the deck of the Talley house in *5th* divide in the center and fold over on itself, revealing the channel between the two piers containing the river for *Talley's*. It was relatively simple to strike the back wall of the Talley house and replace it with the moonlit cyclorama, the lush surrounding of weeping willows and the delicate tracery of the gazebo that gives the play its title.

The most difficult aspect of playing the two plays in rep was the awkwardness it imposed in staging the second act of *5th*. The exterior porch (where most of the action takes place) was restricted to a five-foot-wide strip surrounding the sunroom in which the first act is set. It had to accommodate eight actors on stage most of the time. Despite my misgivings about the constricted playing area, the play somehow worked on a single set that depicted both indoors and out. A unit set has become more the rule than the exception in subsequent productions, since many theaters can't accommodate two sets. I was delighted when the later Broadway production restored the luxury of having a full second act set on which to stage my movement.

As before, Dennis Parichy doused John Lee's Valentine of a set for *Talley's Folly* with lyrical moonlight and, for the first time, he tackled lighting *The 5th of July*, creating the enchantment of twilight and the abundant sunshine of the morning after. Since Laura Crow designed *5th* and Jennifer von Mayrhauser designed *Talley*, we had to choose which would do both plays. Laura won out, partly because of

Jennifer's continuing obligations as head designer of *Law & Order*. Jennifer returned for the Broadway production of *Talley's Folly*, but in the interim, Laura designed it. As always, Chuck London's sound design became a chorus of additional characters in *Talley's Folly*, as the river comes to life with the songs of frogs and crickets.

The rehearsals again were conducted in the spacious environment of the Taper studio, with high ceilings, good lighting and a staff that provided rehearsal platforms to simulate the set being constructed in the shops across town. We were once more in the capable hands of Michelle Miner, one of the most easy-going stage managers I ever worked with. She made the labor of directing two plays at once a pleasure. As always, Gordon was supportive and helpful, with insights coming from a sympathetic yet critical eye, the hallmark of a good Artistic Director. Gordon Davidson was one of the best.

Through the Telescope of Reviews

At the back-to-back openings of the two plays, the critics responded positively to the material, validating the alterations we'd made in the script of *5th* and celebrating the special love story of Matt and Sally.

Talley's Folly opened at the Mark Taper Forum Thursday, August 23, 1979, and *The 5th of July* opened in the same theater Sunday, August 26, 1979. The top ticket price was $13.25. Here are samples of the reviews:

> *The Los Angeles Times*, August 24, 1979, (Dan Sullivan):
>
> "*Talley's Folly* is a little breath of a comedy about two private people learning to talk to each other. [It's] almost all atmosphere. Under Mason's direction, Hirsch and Hawkins give authentically charming performances. Beatty's gazebo set is an exquisite shell for the mating dance. It's a quiet play, but it leaves a lovely light."
>
> *The Los Angeles Times*, August 28, 1979, (Dan Sullivan on *The 5th of July*):
>
> "*Fifth of July* [is] a much bigger play, but not necessarily a more satisfying one. For a play soliciting Chekhovian

empathy, [it] left [me] curiously detached. Wilson wrote [it] pretty much for this cast [and] under Mason's direction everyone is solidly the sort of person he or she is supposed to be."

The Herald-Examiner, August 24, 1979, (Gardner McKay on *Talley's Folly*):

"Wilson certainly is an artist and he exercises his rights freely in [this] spare play. I can't say much for the play, but I can for the casting: Hirsch is marvelous, and so is Hawkins. Hot damn, Hirsch is good. I cannot remember a more successful set at the Taper. What a set!"

The Herald-Examiner, August 28, 1979, (Jay Reiner on *The 5th of July*):

"As a piece of Chekhovian Americana, the experience is not to be underestimated. Wilson's ability to turn sow's ear talk into silk purse drama is remarkable. The play's heart beats stoutly from start to finish. It's so true and shapeless, we can only call it life. The ensemble acting is amazingly good. Mason directs Wilson like a dream. His sure handling of Wilson's material is one of the play's deepest satisfactions."

Valley News, August 24, 1979, (Rick Talcove on *Talley's Folly*):

"One of the Taper's most beautiful sets with Beatty's evocative visualization of an abandoned boathouse. The production under Mason's quiet yet sensitive staging couldn't be better. And yet, unhappily, it *just* doesn't work [for me]. The play is handicapped by an imbalance in the roles. It's time for this talented writer to assert himself more and dig deeper into his art."

Valley News, August 28, 1979, (Rick Talcove on *The 5th of July*):

"To put it simply and succinctly, Wilson's *The 5th of July* is the best thing to happen in the Los Angeles Theater in some months, and surely the best offering at the Taper in several years. [The play] is alternately funny and touching, highlighted by a real love of people and an acute understanding of their problems. The production is a tribute to New York's Circle Repertory Company. It's nothing less than an object lesson in fine ensemble playing. The entire production exemplifies the best in good naturalistic theater. It's a definite winner."

DramaLogue, August 31, 1979, (Charles Faber):
"There are indications that in time Wilson could become an American Chekhov."

Variety, August 24, 1979, (Edwa.):
"Wilson may soon become one of the foremost chroniclers of Americana and *Talley's Folly* is one step closer to that goal. Wilson is a master of creating Midwestern characters. Hirsch plays the accountant with great charm, and with some superb directing by Mason, creates an extremely likeable person. Hawkins is also excellent. Wilson captures the essence of mid-America and capitalizes on it."

Variety, August 28, 1979, (Edwa.):
"*The 5th of July* is a wonderful, warm, moving experience. It is Wilson at his naturalistic best. He knows how to write a play with maximum emotions, humor, and depth. Mason also knows how to direct this kind of naturalism. He stages it quietly and steadily, just as Wilson wrote it. And the cast couldn't be better. This is a wonderful play. It's a moving and moveable feast of theater."

Hollywood Reporter, August 27, 1979, (Ron Pennington):
"*Talley's Folly* is an extraordinarily complex work. Wilson's dialogue is richly poetic. Mason's elegant staging of this lovely script has the grace and style of a softly romantic

musical movement. Hirsch and Hawkins, with their elaborately detailed performances under Mason's sensitive direction, are the best to be seen in Los Angeles this year. *Talley's Folly* provides an extraordinary evening of theater and further establishes Wilson as one of this country's leading contemporary playwrights. This production is not to be missed."

Hollywood Reporter, August 29, 1979, (Ron Pennington):
"*The 5th of July* is one of the more important works of this decade and offers a penetrating view of modern American society. It's a very warm play and Wilson's dialogue sparkles with humor and insight. The performances under Mason's sensitive and finely tuned direction are all superb. The marvelous ensemble playing serves to give a fully sustained life to the script. It should also be noted that Wilson has re-written [it] considerably since it first opened in New York and this new version is extremely tight in terms of structure and continuity. Completing the effects of this magnificent production are Beatty's atmospheric setting, Parichy's subtle lighting, and Crow's perfectly suited costumes. Both of these two plays should not be missed."

On the whole, the critics seemed to prefer *The 5th of July* over *Talley's Folly,* although each play had its champions. I was glad that a couple of reviewers who saw *5th* in New York a year before noted how much the script improved. One critic (Rick Talcove of the *Valley News*) even enthused that *The 5th of July* deserved the Pulitzer Prize the previous year, "ten times more than *The Gin Game.*" We as yet had no ambitions for a Pulitzer, never dreaming that in the coming year they would bestow that honor on *Talley's Folly*. What we *did* dream of was taking *Talley's Folly* on to Broadway. In addition to the virtually unanimous praise rained on it by the New York press, we had an authentic television star in the cast. So, in an interview with Ron Pennington of *The Hollywood Reporter,* (August 23, 1979), I divulged our plans to open on Broadway in February, when Judd's television schedule permitted.

In a second article with Mr. Pennington (August 31, 1979), I described our coming season in New York at Circle Rep:

"The eleventh season begins with David Mamet's *Reunion*, directed by the author and starring Lindsay Crouse and Michael Higgins. This will be followed with *Hamlet*, starring William Hurt and Douglass Watson, playing in repertory with Friedrich Schiller's *Mary Stuart*, featuring Stephanie Gordon and Tanya Berezin. Both of these productions will be directed by Mason. Next will be Milan Stitt's *Back in the Race* and a revival of John Bishop's *The Trip Back Down* playing in repertory. The final offering will be the world premiere of Lanford Wilson's *The War in Lebanon*, the third entry in a projected five-play cycle."

The first four productions opened the eleventh season as promised, but the third play in the Talley cycle took Lanford another year to write. *A Tale Told* played in our twelfth season and then, brought us back to the Mark Taper Forum in August of 1981. We abandoned our plan to revive *The Trip Back Down*, but substituted John Heuer's *Innocent Thoughts, Harmless Intentions* and concluded with a beautiful new play by William Mastrosimone called *The Woolgatherer*, another two-character drama that featured Peter Weller and Patricia Wettig. Once again, the subscribers had little to complain about. I suspect the reason Lanford could not devote his attention more fully to writing the third Talley play was the Broadway production of *Talley's Folly* mid-season, which devoured our attention.

Critic Jack Viertel wrote an appraisal in *The Reader*, (August 31, 1979) headlined "The Coming of Age of Lanford Wilson," in which he perceived not only the reverberations about American society that both plays illuminate, but also expressed his reverence for Lanford's position as an important writer and for the ensemble excellence of Circle Rep. Jack subsequently left his post as a reviewer for the *Los Angeles Herald-Examiner*, jumping into the artistic trenches as Dramaturg for the Mark Taper Forum and eventually, Artistic Director of the Jujamcyn Theater operation on Broadway.

A Broadway Baby's First Hit

Lanford's love of theater began when he was a teenager in Ozark, Missouri. He saw a production of *Death of a Salesman* and he was amazed to see dappled, leafy trees surrounding the outside of Willie Loman's house and then watch the walls dissolve to reveal the inside as a different time and place. It was the *magic* of theater that entranced him, casting a spell that captured the unicorn of his young imagination, leaving him hungry for more. That appetite was further whetted when he was cast as Tom in a school production of *The Glass Menagerie*, in which he spoke the immortal words that begin the play:

> "I have tricks in my pocket, I have things up my sleeve. But I am the opposite of a stage magician. He gives you illusion that has the appearance of truth. I give you truth in the pleasant disguise of illusion."

Lanford was hooked on magic and it was a lifelong addiction.

Nowhere is Lanford's love of theater's irresistible magic more evident than in the opening soliloquy of *Talley's Folly*. The actor playing Matt Friedman enters on a stage exposed by work-lights to the humdrum existence of everyday life. Picking up on the actual existence we have dragged with us from our work-a-day world, as we take our seats in the theater, Matt assures us that the play will take only a little over an hour and a half, but he warns there will be no intermission, so if anyone needs to heed the call of nature, she'd better do it *now*.

> "They tell me that we have ninety-seven minutes here tonight – without intermission. So if that means anything to anybody; if you think you might need a drink of water or anything..."

Lanford's stage directions describe what the audience sees as Matt enters:

> (*A Victorian boathouse seen in a blank white work light in which the artificiality of the theatrical set is quite apparent. The house lights are up.*)

Matt frames the background of the story we are about to see by describing how he and Sally first came to the boathouse together a year before when they saw a UFO land down by the river. So the audience is alerted that unexplained, extraordinary things occur in life and that the possibility of a transporting experience lies before us. He reveals some of the theatrical tricks he will use to tell this tale:

> "I'll just point out some of the facilities till everybody gets settled in. If everything goes well for me tonight, this should be a waltz, one-two-three, one-two-three; a no-holds-barred romantic story, and since I'm not a romantic type, I'm going to need the whole Valentine here to help me."

He enumerates the theatrical devices at his disposal: a rotating gizmo in the footlights to create the illusion of moonlight on the water; sound effects of crickets, frogs and dogs; artificial moonlight by the baleful. What is real, he argues, is arguable. Having exposed the tricks up his sleeve, he chuckles to the audience:

> "I know what you're thinking. You're saying if I'd known it would be like this, I wouldn't have come. Or if I'd known it was going to be like this, I would have listened. But don't worry, we're going to do this first part all over again for the latecomers."

After glancing at his watch, he mutters,

> "Oh, boy, this has got to be fast."

He then rattles off everything he's already said in a non-stop, breakneck pace that usually elicited applause for Judd's verbal pyrotechnics. We are now primed to be fooled and entertained by this story, which Matt admits has to be framed as:

"Once upon a time, there was a hope throughout the land."

With the change in Matt's tone, the house lights slowly dim, pulling us into another time and place. But it isn't until we hear Sally's voice calling him from off-stage that the stage lights change, the river begins to sparkle and the sounds of the summer night plunge us into the twilight of a Missouri evening. Sally brings the magic to life, as she did for Matt all those years ago.

The critics loved how the opening monologue set the stage, comparing it to the Stage Manager in *Our Town*. And audiences were seduced by Matt, loving him and rooting for him before the heart of the play began to beat. It gives Matt a hugely unfair advantage over Sally, an edge that Sally must overcome through honest simplicity.

Ultimately, most of us don't possess the quick wit that Matt exhibits. It is ordinary Sally with whom we identify; we share her amazement and amusement at Matt's verbal gymnastics, transfixed by his irrepressible charm.

When we created the play at Circle Rep, Judd merely came from one side in front of the stage, carefully picking his way over the feet of those seated in the first row. At the Taper, for the first time I had Matt enter from the back of the auditorium, making his way down the aisle through the audience. But it was not until Broadway that Matt mingled among the crowd finding their seats, remaining anonymous until he reached the front and began to speak. At first, his glamour-free appearance made the audience think they might be hearing an announcement from a house manager, so by the time they recognized that under that beard and behind those glasses was their adorable Alex from *Taxi*, it was too late for the traditional applause that greets a star's entrance. And oh, how they loved Judd!

During the run on Broadway, Judd's romance with the audience sometimes overwhelmed his pursuit of Sally on stage. There were nights when Judd's performance rode the laughs like a stand-up comedian, showing off the comic dexterity of a Robin Williams. Trish naturally resented it when she felt she had lost Judd to the audience and there were occasional complaints to the stage manager, echoed by his complaints that she was retreating into a shell that gave him little to play with. Their relationship off stage was a little testy; but normally, when the magic transformation began with Sally's entrance, the audience was treated to an old-fashioned love story with a perfect happy ending.

Lanford's first experience on Broadway was the failure of *The Gingham Dog* at the John Golden Theater in 1968. So the delightful reception of *Talley's Folly* was a homecoming for Lanford's love of theater. He nestled into his success with ease, seeing almost every performance, watching the effects of his artistry on the audience, hanging out before and afterwards at the bar next-door, where the bartenders, waiters and even the owner became his buddies. Lanford was destined to be a Broadway baby, fulfilling a dream that originated long before with *Death of a Salesman* and *The Glass Menagerie*, both of which had been born on Broadway.

Building the Nest

Getting to Broadway is seldom easy, and the process, rarely pretty. Now that we had a certifiable hit with a star, the wisdom of a transfer was evident to everyone. Not so clear was how.

Circle Rep, having suffered through Broadway transfers before, was now managed by a Broadway expert, Porter Van Zandt. So Lanford and I were spared the details of how this was to be accomplished, having great faith in Porter that Circle Rep would not be subjected to the kind of brutal maneuvers of the marketplace that spoiled the joy of our transfer of *Knock Knock*. Or so we thought. It was decided that Porter should represent Circle Rep and we left it in his hands to find financing. His solutions proved questionable, but perhaps inevitable.

Despite the initial success of *Talley's Folly*, backers were hard to convince that a transfer would prove profitable. But Judd was flush with the rewards of a successful television career, so he stepped forward with an investment that negated the need for enthusiastic backers. Concerned about the appearance of a vanity production, Judd asked a friend, Nancy Cooperstein, to act in his behalf. Judd supplied much of the financing, but Nancy was the erstwhile producer of record. We were assured that Judd did not want the Broadway production to be perceived as "The Judd Hirsch Show," although some of the decisions that were made seemed to belie that promise.

Nancy's only previous Broadway credit was as a production assistant to David Hays on the 1962 production of *A Family Affair;* but she was married to Jordan Charney, an actor of some standing and a friend of Judd's. In 1966, Jordan and Nancy co-produced the Off-Broadway *Viet Rock* at the Martinique Theater, where it played sixty-two performances. Nancy was a short, peppy woman who assumed the role of shadow producer for Judd.

Joining Nancy, Porter represented Circle Rep as a Producer of the Broadway production: we assumed that Circle Rep would receive the co-producers portion of management's profits. As it developed, Circle received only our usual 3% share of the gross, while Porter and Nancy pocketed the producer's substantial weekly "office" fee.

Lanford and I attended the initial advertising meeting at Serino, Coyne and Nappi, the hot ad agency at the time, where we witnessed how the marketing of our show was changing. At Circle Rep, we had a lovely blue poster with a golden full moon that used John Lee Beatty's impressionistic drawing of the boathouse. This quickly was abandoned in favor of a clearly commercial show card with a black and white photo of Judd and Trish in the boat, the only color being the credits in red. No question about it – on Broadway we were going to emphasize the presence of the famous television star of the popular hit *Taxi,* who was nominated for the Golden Globe and a Primetime Emmy Award as Outstanding Lead Actor. Judd was at the peak of his popularity in 1980, having also been nominated for an Academy Award for Supporting Actor in the

Oscar-winning film *Ordinary People*. But his ongoing TV commitments meant we'd have him for only the first four months. Despite Judd's protestations that the publicity should concentrate on the play itself as "the star," after Jeffrey Richards was hired as the press representative, virtually the only promotions for the production were interview after interview with our TV star. Little was written about Lanford, the play, Circle Rep or the unusual journey it took to Broadway by way of the Mark Taper Forum. Judd was booked onto all the popular late night talk shows, like *The Tonight Show with Johnny Carson*. Presumably, all this was necessary to scare up an audience for our little two-person romance. But the result was it indeed transformed it into "The Judd Hirsch Show," making it hard to replace him four months later.

I'm not sure exactly how the Broadway production was financed, but I'm certain that a good portion of the investment was from Judd himself, fronted by Nancy. The program billed three producers: Nancy Cooperstein, Porter Van Zandt and Marc Howard (whose billing indicated a sizable financial investment). On another line, it was noted that it was originally produced at the Circle Repertory Company and then by the Center Theater Group (Mark Taper Forum, Gordon Davidson, Artistic Director).

Nancy hired Tyler Gatchel and Peter Neufeld as the General Managers, who'd managed eleven Broadway shows prior to *Talley's Folly*, including such hits as *No, No, Nanette*, *Jesus Christ Superstar*, *Annie*, and *Sweeney Todd*, so we were in the best hands Broadway had to offer. Tyler and Peter were undoubtedly key players in procuring the beautiful Brooks Atkinson Theater for *Talley's Folly*, directly across the street from the Biltmore, where John Lee, Dennis, Jennifer and I made our Broadway debuts four years before with *Knock Knock*. I don't know if the Nederlander Organization, which owned the Brooks Atkinson, initially had any money invested in the show; but I do know that after a run of nine months, the Nederlanders offered us money to free up the theater for an incoming show (*Tricks of the Trade*, which, ironically, closed after one performance). The Nederlander payoff made *Talley's Folly* profitable, the very definition of "a hit."

John Manulis, my assistant at Circle Rep received a Broadway credit as Assistant Director and he was a useful liaison with Peter Neufeld, a family friend. We took on Jordan Charney and Michael Fishetti to stand by for Judd and Mary Hamill to understudy Trish. Circle Rep collected a week's rent for our rehearsal space, during which we reacquainted ourselves with the work we'd created nearly a year before. As I've noted, returning to an artistic work only deepens the actors in their parts; it's like riding a bicycle, only you get much better at it.

Some of the physical elements built by the union shop at the Taper were shipped to New York, so the producers saved a considerable amount of money on the set, normally a sizable production expense. Unable to use real water for the river because, except for those in the balcony, a Broadway audience looks *up* at the stage; so John Lee created once again a river the audience could see from their lower seats. This time, he constructed the illusion for a lengthy run, using sheets of Plexiglass, subtly raked beneath a patch of lily pads that could be illuminated from below, giving Dennis the opportunity to create the gentle flow of a moonlit river.

Riding the Tide

The Brooks Atkinson Theater has one balcony and seats 1,069 patrons. It's popular with theatergoers, having housed a long list of distinguished productions, and it was perfect for *Talley's Folly*. Even though it's larger than the Taper, it feels more intimate because it's a traditional proscenium house, with all the audience in front of the actors.

We began previews on Valentine's Day and we invited all members of Circle Rep to come. It was celebrated as our Company Opening, exchanging gifts, cards and solidarity. There was a party for the Company at Lanford's apartment following this performance.

After six previews, *Talley's Folly* officially opened at the Brooks Atkinson Theater on February 20th, 1980, where it played 286 performances. The top ticket price was $19.50. If anything, the critics were even more enthusiastic:

The Transcendent Years

The New York Times, February 21, 1980, (Walter Kerr):

"The first quick question: will we love it in the middle of February as we did in early May? The quick answer is: you bet. *Talley's Folly* is a charmer, filled to the brim with hope, humor and chutzpah. Hirsch's performance is surely one of the finest of this season, last season, any season. The freshly available entertainment at the Brooks Atkinson is droll, sprightly, and much, much warmer than the February weather outside. It still has May in it."

WQXR, February 21, 1980, (Mel Gussow):

"The news is *Talley's Folly* has made the transition to Broadway with ease and eloquence. The play radiates with a purity and a lyricism that can be appreciated by a universal audience. Under Mason's inspired direction, Hirsch and Hawkins offer an unerring double performance in a play that is deep and wise with the knowledge of humanity. *Talley's Folly* towers over all other plays that have opened on Broadway this season."

New York Post, February 21, 1980, (Clive Barnes):

"*Talley's Folly* is magnificent. There are some plays that you simply love, and you want everyone who is dear to you to love with the same unquestioning zeal. I feel that about *Talley's Folly*. I loved it even more than I did in its original home. It is a play that can take any space and any heart. It should be with us a long, long time. *Talley's Folly* stands all by itself as the play of the season. And the acting is superb. See this play."

Daily News, February 21, 1980, (Douglas Watt):

"To my mind, it is Wilson's finest work – funny, quirky, beautifully balanced, and altogether disarming. The flow of dialogue is perfectly timed under Mason's inspired direction. It's the kind of play to be lived in and left with regret, its figures lingering in the mind like, say, the characters of *La Bohème* or *The Marriage of Figaro,* long after the lights have dimmed."

Newsweek, March 3, 1980, (Jack Kroll):
"A sweet, tender, funny, life-embracing play. [It is] enacted with marvelous skill by Judd Hirsch, who has become one of the masterly American actors. Mason has transferred his impeccable staging to Broadway, where it gives Wilson a chance to reach the wide audience he has long deserved."

The Nation, March 15, 1980, (Harold Clurman):
"*Talley's Folly* is a breath of fresh air on Broadway. Wilson's career is of special interest because it is marked by unusual progress, not only in technical security, but in inner growth. [This] may not be Wilson's best play, but it is his most engaging. Its first-rate performance makes *Talley's Folly* soar."

Daily News (Rex Reed):
"A tender, humorous and richly fulfilling moonlight sonata. Now if we could just get somebody to resurrect *The 5th of July*! For now, it's a pleasure to settle for what we've got, which is a great deal more than you'll find anywhere else on Broadway."

The New Yorker, March 3, 1980, (Edith Oliver):
"Wilson's play is enchanting: a small, elegantly composed study of two interesting people, whom, in the course of something like an hour and a half, we come to know as we know characters in a novel. Hirsch's performance is a feat of acting that one doesn't fear to call memorable. The marvelous boathouse setting is by Beatty; the costumes by von Mayrhauser; the soft moonshine and velvety blue night – excuse me – the lighting is by Parichy; and the flawless direction is by Mason."

New York Magazine, March 10, 1980, (John Simon):

"How pleasant to have *Talley's Folly* back with us on Broadway. [It] is a 97-minute onrush of breathless delight. It works just as well in its Broadway mansion as it did in its Greenwich Village *pied-à-terre.* I need not lavish words on the acting of Hirsch and Hawkins; what can you give performances that have everything? Mason's direction is as neat as Swiss clockwork, but with a poetic skylark popping out instead of a sterile cuckoo. And Wilson's play? Everything is witty, humane, touching, sly, beautifully structured, and of a directness only a complex mind can summon forth. *Talley's Folly* makes the weather inside you, suddenly and lingeringly, spring."

Village Voice, March 3, 1980, (Michael Feingold):

"An elegantly turned light entertainment with a strikingly bitter substratum; a double delight, because it gives us enjoyment without falsity. Mason's staging has suffered no serious sea-change in moving from Circle Rep's tiny home to the Atkinson. Hirsch's acting has not lost either its warmth or its precision. Hawkins is, if anything, more firmly focused, "fuller" in the role than before."

There were many, many more, but let me quote just a few one-liners:

"It is easily one of the finest plays on Broadway."
Emory Lewis, *The Record*
"Even better on Broadway than it was off."
Martin Gottfried, *CUE Magazine*
"Just as charming on Broadway as it was last spring."
Allan Wallach, *Newsday*
"A fine evening, and a welcome Valentine for Broadway."
Edwin Wilson, *Wall Street Journal*
"In a word – Wow!" Joel Siegel, ABC TV
"*Talley's Folly* once again triumphs."
William A. Raidy, *The Star-Ledger*

"A first-class piece of writing in an impeccable production." Kissel, *Women's Wear Daily*

"A beautiful play, tender, intelligent, very funny. I heartily commend it to you." Klein, WNEWTV

"Good news – lots of fun. This is a sweet evening of theater – a delight." Jeffrey Lyons, WPIXTV

"Good theater and fills a vacuum lacking on Broadway this season." Casper Citron, WORTV

I would be remiss if I didn't include the one really bad notice:

Dennis Cunningham, CBSTV:
"A trivial little smudge of a play that should never have, even in someone's wildest dreams appeared on Broadway. Though it did, it should soon have the decency to go away, whichI'm sure it will."

Oh, well. You can't please everyone!

Basking in the warmth of these lovely reviews, we had a perfect opening night party in a perfect setting, the enchanting Tavern-on-the-Green in Central Park. Its sparkling, lighted trees brightened the winter night, and my mother, who never missed a New York opening, loved every minute of it – as did all of us – and especially, Broadway's newest Baby, Lanford Wilson.

Sparks from the Fire

Unfortunately, it was hard to sustain interest in our little gem without Judd on the stage. He was replaced by Jordan Charney, a fine actor who did well by Matt; and Trish, by our Company actress Debra Mooney, superb as Sally. Judd's schedule offered him occasional opportunities to return to our production, which was lucky because whenever he was out of it, the box-office receipts dipped noticeably. Since Judd had a substantial financial stake in the success of the play, he came back to beef up the box-office whenever he could.

We were delighted when Katherine Hepburn came to see the show; she came backstage afterwards and wistfully remarked, "I'd have been very good in that part, once."

After we had been playing a couple of months, I had a message on my home telephone from Gordon Davidson, who mysteriously congratulated me on the wonderful news I would be getting the next morning. The news turned out to be that Lanford had received the 1980 Pulitzer Prize for Drama. While I'm sure Gordon was genuinely pleased for us, he might also have been understandably a trifle disappointed, because Gordon directed a second play at the Mark Taper Forum that transferred successfully to Broadway the same season: Mark Medoff's *Children of a Lesser God*. The New York Drama Critics Award for Best Play of 1980 also went to *Talley's Folly*. Both awards were a bit of a surprise to us, since we produced *Talley's Folly* in 1979; but it had not dawned on us that its debut the previous spring was *after* the Pulitzer deadline, so we were eligible for these awards the following year. The question was, could we score a Triple Crown by winning the Tony Award?

When the Tony nominations were announced, *Talley's Folly* secured five nominations: Best Play, Best Actor, Best Director, Best Scenic Design and Best Lighting Design. We were disappointed the nominating committee slighted Trish and the Tony Awards had not yet included a category for Best Sound Design, which Chuck surely would have won. Having received both the Pulitzer and the Drama Critics Award, our chance for Best Play seemed pretty good, as did Judd's chance to win Best Actor. Always pretty realistic at handicapping my own chances, I was fairly certain the Tony for Best Director would go to Vivian Matalon for his lovely revival of *Mornings at Seven*, which it did. But to our surprise, the Tony voters gave *Children of a Lesser God* a sweep: Best Play, Best Actor (John Rubenstein) and Best Actress (Phyllis Frelich). We did score one win at the Tony's: John Lee Beatty won his first Tony Award for Best Scenic Design. A good time was had by all at the Tony Party that followed the Awards. We had a feeling we'd be back.

In April, before the Tony's, I directed Jordan Charney and Debra Mooney in the Goodman Theater production of *Talley's Folly* in Chicago, which received good enough notices to transfer for a commercial run at the Studebaker Theater. Unfortunately, it ran only a couple of weeks in that cavernous auditorium, but it enabled me to rehearse these actors in the parts, so they were fully ready to replace on Broadway when Judd and Trish left.

In 1982, I directed *Talley's Folly* at the Lyric-Hammersmith Theatre in London, starring Jonathan Pryce and Hailey Mills, who were both delightful to work with and outstanding in their performances. Hailey was definitely the sexiest Sally ever! And Jonathan, who, even though he was several years too young for the part, had seen and enjoyed Judd's performance in New York, so he was ready to pick up where Judd left off, deepening and sharpening the role of Matt.

Sadly, there has been no movie made of *Talley's Folly*, although Lanford wrote a fine, rich screenplay fitted to a treatment I wrote, combining the two Talley plays that take place the same night: *Talley's Folly* and *Talley & Son*. It may seem strange that no film was forthcoming from such an esteemed play, but there is a simple explanation. Although Dustin Hoffman reportedly was keen to play Matt in a film, Lanford had promised Judd that if he came back from Hollywood to do *Talley's Folly* on Broadway, he would not sell the movie rights without him in it. Regrettably, Judd's Hollywood standing had diminished (when he won his second Emmy, he strongly criticized the industry and Hollywood does not take criticism kindly) and even Paramount, the studio who produced *Taxi*, wouldn't take the project with Judd attached. In a classic insight to Hollywood mentality, one movie producer questioned Lanford about his contract attaching Judd to the film. Lanford explained that it was a moral commitment. "Oh!" the movie mogul exclaimed, "It's only a *moral* commitment." This was apparently a concept utterly unfamiliar in the film business.

The 3rd *Fifth*

The chief obstacle to fulfilling Rex Reed's desire to see *Fifth of July* on Broadway was the necessity of finding a box-office star who could attract a thousand people each night and two thousand on matinee days. Only a couple of years before, it was still possible for a play to run on the strength of good notices and strong word of mouth. *Gemini* made the transfer to Broadway without an over-the-title star and it was still packing them in for its third year. The "bridge-and-tunnel" crowd came in from the suburbs for a night of fun in the City. Chuck London's hilarious television ad assured them it was worth the trip and promised unbridled fun. But the fluctuations at the box-office of *Talley's Folly* when Judd was out made it clear that success on Broadway now depended on giving audiences a bona fide star. Theatergoers needed confidence that their money was well spent on increasingly expensive tickets. This trend changed Broadway from a venue for passions and ideas, which had characterized the days of *Death of a Salesman* or *A Streetcar Named Desire*, to an arena for star-gazing. That trend has continued to the present, with an occasional exception like *Angels in America*, which was pre-sold by critics who'd seen prior productions in Los Angeles and London. By 1980, it was rare for ticket buyers to consider the play itself sufficient reason to buy a ticket; to succeed in the Broadway marketplace, *Fifth of July* would require a star.

Ironically, just as Judd rose from Circle Rep to stardom on television, our original Kenny in *Fifth of July*, William Hurt, was on the verge of achieving enormous box-office appeal as a film star. But that day had not yet arrived and in any case, Bill was busy in Hollywood making the films that catapulted him onto the A-list.

However, a third actor from Circle Rep had already achieved worldwide fame when our Christopher Reeve assumed the legendary role of Superman. Although pleased with his success, Chris hungered for recognition as a serious actor. He did not want to be limited to becoming a franchise for the series of sequels preordained to follow. Chris, along with his closest buddy, Robin Williams, were classmates of William Hurt's at Julliard. Now, all three of them were rising to the top as popular stars. But while Bill was still busy in Hollywood, Chris already was eager to return to the stage. The moment was ripe with opportunity. We appealed to Chris to help us bring our worthy play to a wider audience and, grateful for his early days with Circle Rep, Chris agreed to play Kenneth Talley, Jr. in our Broadway transfer. He was appearing at Circle Rep when the life-changing opportunity to portray the Man of Steel came along. His success in that film made good on their ads, which promised: "You will *believe* he can fly!" Now the question was whether an audience could believe him as a gay, double-amputee Vietnam vet, desperately evading his commitment to teach in a Missouri high school. It was a stretch, less for Chris as an actor, but for the critics who took the occasion to compare his Kenny to the sensitive work of William Hurt only two years before. It was a challenge that might intimidate anyone; but Chris gamely put his reputation on the line and earnestly tackled the job of bringing to life this complex human being.

We also needed to replace Nancy Snyder as Gwen. Nancy was pregnant with her first child and unavailable to re-create her shimmering performance as the eviscerated copper heiress. Difficult as this seemed, we'd succeeded in Los Angeles without Nancy or Bill, and both the play and the ensemble continued to shine. So, I was sanguine about the need to replace her. All I needed was to find a brilliant actress. I had seen Swoosie Kurtz at the Manhattan Theater Club a few years before in a Pete Gurney play called *Children*. I remembered Swoosie's translucent performance in that excellent play about the conflicts of a WASP family, characterized as a dying breed. I could see her bringing that sensitivity and vulnerability to the role of Gwen. What I had not foreseen was her comic genius, which imbued the role with a new dimension. In Swoosie's hands, Gwen was not only a firestorm of uninhibited unpredictability, she was also *hilarious*. Lanford's freshest character had fresh life in a completely re-envisioned interpretation. What a treasure we had found!

The rest of the original cast continued, seasoned by a lengthy engagement at Circle Rep in the summer of 1978, followed by adapting to a new Kenny and Gwen at the Taper in L.A. The core of the ensemble remained vibrant.

But suddenly, another casting problem emerged. Lanford wrote the part of Aunt Sally for Helen Stenborg. She moored the casts of both *HOT L* and *Fifth of July,* and seemed essential to the ensemble that vaulted Circle Rep to such heights of artistry. Helen had the opportunity to co-star on Broadway opposite Roy Dotrice and Pat Hingle in Hugh Leonard's new play, *A Life.* During the extended run of the original *5th of July,* Helen left our production to replace on Broadway in Hugh Leonard's *Da,* which starred her husband Barnard Hughes in the Tony Award-winning role of his life. Torn between her loyalty to her theater home at Circle Rep and the rare chance to appear on Broadway in a starring role, Helen hardly could have chosen other than she did. But the task of replacing her in *Fifth of July* loomed as a challenge.

Our auditions for Aunt Sally brought about one of the strangest mistakes I ever made. As I've noted, my assistant John Manulis was the son of a pioneering television producer and a luminous actress named Katherine Bard. His mother was a member of The Actors Studio and starred in many deluxe television dramas. Her reading for Sally in my large office at Circle Rep was mesmerizing. Here was an artist of extraordinary talent that could make the loss of Helen bearable. Incredibly, it was her son who talked me out of casting her. He was doubtful that she could project vocally to fill a Broadway house. Foolishly, I listened to his advice and instead cast veteran Mary Carver. Mary was a fine actress and she played the role of Aunt Sally admirably; but we lost the chance for the exceptional performance that Katherine might have delivered. I regretted my decision throughout the Broadway run of *Fifth of July.* My problem with Mary was entirely my own fault; I cast her without considering how small she was and how big Chris was. Seeing them side by side on stage, it was difficult to believe they were of the same *species,* much less the same family. Apart from the problem of her size, she played Aunt Sally with aplomb. The cast loved her and she served the play very well. She was especially wonderful in her scene with Danton Stone, as they breathlessly searched the nighttime sky for UFOs.

The remainder of the cast matured in their parts: Joyce Reehling personified June, Danton Stone was lost inside the character of Weston Hurley, Amy Wright sparkled as the indomitable brat Shirley, Jonathan Hogan inhabited the part Lanford wrote for him and Jeff Daniels settled even deeper into the soul of Jed.

Deeper and Richer

Once again, Circle Rep banked a little rent money from providing the rehearsal space for *Fifth of July*. Once again, Michael Sulsona and B.H. Barry were drafted to guide Chris through the trials of playing a double-amputee who had to fall over backwards. Because Chris was so much bigger than William (a couple of inches taller and many muscular pounds heavier), these tasks were even more challenging. Nevertheless, Chris was dedicated to exploring the pain and humor of Kenny to the fullest and he absorbed all the help he got. Once again, the cast rallied around a new Kenny and Gwen, as well as a new Aunt Sally, and dutifully re-explored their roles.

A couple of changes were required. For one thing, there was Kenny's line of delicious self-deprecation: "Well, once again, Super-fag's plans fail to materialize." The line was absurdly inappropriate in the context of the current casting, so it had to go. Another change was in the timing of Jed's line at the end of the first act. In previous productions, Jeff picked up the actor playing Kenny and took him to the bottom of the stairs, where he reassured the whimpering Kenny: "Hang in there." Jeff is a big guy, beefier than his previous Kenny's, so this important bit of business worked beautifully. With Chris taller and brawnier even than Jeff, we had to reconsider the placement of the line. When delivered from the bottom of the stairs, it got a laugh at the first preview because the audience interpreted it as a commentary on the chore of lugging Superman up the stairs. We moved the line to Center Stage, just after Jed has picked Kenny up, so it was restored to its original intent, soothing Kenny's fears. Only after he calmed Chris with "Hang in there," did Jeff turn upstage and the curtain fell as he approached the stairway. It was somehow even more touching to see the perfection of Christopher Reeve rendered helpless by the war; and the deep relationship of these two beautiful men was unimpeachable.

For the Broadway production, John Lee used a turntable to move the scene from inside to out. The set was three-quarters indoors for the first act and three-quarters outside for the second. I was so delighted with the turntable solution that I tried beginning the second act with the set revolving from interior to exterior, but it looked too much like a musical. It was better to keep the audience in the dark about John Lee's solution until the curtain call. Then the curtain rose as the set revolved back to the interior, where the entire cast waited, so they slid gracefully into view as the set revolved to the audience's ovation.

The Means to an End

Jerry Arrow left as Executive Director of Circle Rep after the summer extension of *The 5th of July*. But we continued a relationship with Jerry, since he still represented us as the General Partner of *Gemini*. Jerry hired Robert Lussier as Company Manager for *Gemini* and during the run of *5th* at the Taper, they flew to California to see the production and began negotiating the means for moving it to Broadway. Jerry had a disarming, open-faced geniality about him, which made one trust him. Robert had a slick, sophisticated slyness about him that made one suspicious. Nevertheless, after the odd arrangements behind the transfer of *Talley's Folly* to Broadway, it was refreshing to deal with professional producers whose intentions were clear: they would do everything they could to ensure that *Fifth of July* made a profitable transition to Broadway. With Christopher Reeve as their star, Bob and Jerry convinced Claire Nichtern, president of Warner Brothers Theater Productions, to put up the bulk of the investment. It was becoming increasingly customary for film companies to see Broadway as a useful extension of their domain and, as producers of *Superman*, Warner Brothers was eager to help their star achieve whatever he wanted. The cost of a Broadway production is meager compared to a film budget; so it was only spare change for a self-serving cause. Unlike Judd, Chris had no fear *Fifth of July* would be perceived as a vanity production. His previous Broadway appearance with Katherine Hepburn in *A Matter of*

Gravity four years before endowed him with legitimacy. He had no reason to promote himself; he was there to serve the play.

Jerry and Bob's choice of a theater was both odd and inspired. The 42nd Street Corporation had begun an overhaul that transformed a sleazy slum district to a centerpiece of New York Theater. Part of this transition was an old theater that for years was used as a squalid 24-hour movie house, running third-run fare, usually as double features. The theater was freed from its tawdry past, refurbished by the Midtown Theater Corporation and renamed the New Apollo. With just over 1,000 seats, it was a cozy home for an extensive run.

For a change, our Broadway producers did not dump the poster design from Circle Rep, but actually improved our concept. Off-Broadway, we were looking to emphasize the edgy 60s, characterized by outrageous, acid-inspired artwork. We chose a neon orange background with magenta lettering superimposed over a faint photograph of the cast posing for a re-union picture, with Jeff Daniels seated in front holding a small American flag. For the Broadway poster, the producers came up with the idea of a desktop calendar flipped open to July fifth, with a snapshot of the cast clipped onto the date: Kenny and Sally seated on a glider, Jed and Weston seated on the ground in front, with John, Gwen, June and Shirley standing behind. It worked beautifully.

Back to the Garden

Lanford Wilson's *Fifth of July* opened on Broadway at the New Apollo Theater on November 5, 1980, where it played 511 performances. Here are excerpts from the reviews, which starts with my first outright negative notice for daring to hire a star:

The New York Times, November 6, 1980 (Frank Rich):
"Wilson has poured the full bounty of his gifts into this work, and they are the gifts of a major playwright. *Fifth of July* is a densely packed yet buoyant outpouring of empathy, poetry and humor, all shaped into a remarkable vision. [But] Mason has made some serious casting errors, starting with Christopher Reeve. While the play's beauty and giddy

spirit are still evident, an upsetting measure of passion has been lost. Kurtz almost takes over the play – she nails every laugh. Yet even this gifted actress isn't cast quite properly. But it's still hard to imagine any theatergoer passing up *Fifth of July*."

New York Post, November 6, 1980 (Clive Barnes):

"An enchanting, provocative play. The play has been directed by Mason, who follows Wilson's plays like an explorer in some unknown map of love. Mason has directed virtually all of Wilson. What would, or of course, will they be like without him? Perhaps they said that – and this is not qualitative – about Chekhov and Stanislavski. Kurtz is perfect, and Reeve is most sensitive, furtive with clumsy love and vibrant with cynical despair."

Daily News, November 6, 1980 (Douglas Watt):

"*Fifth of July* scores a joyous Talley-ho. Wilson's hip, flip, slick and tumultuous comedy has now reached Broadway. It has gained immeasurably since it was first seen. Kurtz is now ready, as far as I'm concerned, to be crowned the theater's queen of comediennes. She swoops through the full evening like a bird on uppers, filling the house with gales of laughter. Ken [is] played by Reeve with a nice blend of humor and concern. [It's] essentially the same production seen earlier, excellently staged by Mason, and atmospherically designed by Beatty, Crow and Parichy. *Fifth of July* has much to recommend it as a nifty ensemble production. But oh, that Swoosie!"

The Los Angeles Times, November 6, 1980 (Sylvie Drake):

"Reeve's name is above the title for clear, commercial reasons. If it helps to sell what has turned into one of Wilson's strongest plays, so much the better. But Reeve was a stage actor long before he was a film celebrity, and was a member of

Circle Rep. Playing the Vietnam amputee is, for him, a form of homecoming. And quite a homecoming it is. Whatever reservations we harbored about *July* have been refined out of existence. It has blossomed into a tightly written, funny and deeply moving play. It is an uplifting experience. The company is very fine. Much credit must go to Mason, who has shaped and paced and cast this show impeccably."

New York Magazine, undated in 1980 (John Simon):
"Some aspects of *Fifth of July* emerge enlarged and enriched, while others are a bit thinner. This may have to do with a bigger theater and with not quite seamless ensemble acting. Wilson has a warmly persuasive way with both sharp, witty dialogue and bizarre, riotous monologues. Wilson remains at the forefront of our playwrights. Kurtz is magnificently hilarious. Reeve is decent, but less troubled and troubling than Hurt was. Daniels, Hogan, Mary Carver, Stone, and Reehling are deeply satisfying; but Wright is getting too old and cute for the perennial wacky adolescent she seems eternally condemned to play. Mason's direction of a flawlessly designed production is only a shade less compelling than it was at Circle Rep, but neither this nor any other shade should dim your fundamental pleasure in *Fifth of July.*"

Village Voice, November 18, 1980 (Michael Feingold):
"*Fifth of July,* one of Wilson's strongest plays to date, compares very favorably to Chekhov's *Seagull.* [There is] a vivid organic quality in the writing. Mason's production has retained its essential virtues, as well as most of its cast. Carver and Reeve hold the line creditably, while Kurtz outclasses hers with a stunning display of less-is-more. And the most satisfactory surprise of the evening is the increased power of Joyce Reehling's performance as the embittered sister, etched in purest hydrochloric acid."

The New York Times, November 16, 1980 (Walter Kerr):
"To my way of thinking, everyone in *Fifth of July* seems peripheral. (At present writing, this seems to be a minority report, and I do so caution you.) There are last-minute turnabouts, but we have not really participated in – or truly understood – the struggle to arrive at them."

As indifferent as the *Times*' review was initially, Christopher Reeve's name over the titled assured ticket sales. Chris was cheerful about it, fully understanding that although he was being used as a star, he was actually a member of an ensemble. He said in an interview:

"I keep throwing the passes, and the other characters keep making the touchdowns. I don't mean to be eating humble pie, but I am trying to serve the play. It's the best piece of writing to come along in the theater in years."

I tried to help Chris make that point with the curtain call. Traditionally in curtain calls, the cast takes bows in ascending order, with the smallest role first, building up to the final bow given to the star. I wanted to emphasize the ensemble nature of the production, so as the curtain rose, the whole cast was on stage and as they took their solos, Chris took the next-to-last bow, with Jeff Daniels, playing Jed, Kenny's steady, almost silent lover whose strength is the heart of the play, taking the final bow. It was a statement to the commercial theater; stars may be necessary for marketing, but artistic success depends on an ensemble. In Circle Rep productions, we ended every call (even on Broadway or in Los Angeles) with the "Circle Rep bow," in which the entire cast joined hands and after the final bow, lifted their arms overhead like a victorious team of champions. It was a stirring trademark.

The Fun in a Run

Several prominent people visited the Broadway run more than once, including film directors Mike Nichols and Lawrence Kasdan.

I can see some influence of *Fifth of July* in Mr. Kasdan's film *The Big Chill* (1983), an ensemble movie about the reunion of former friends from the 60s that starred our own William Hurt.

Just as *Gemini* provided Jeff Daniels with a weekly salary as an understudy and Stephanie Gordon replaced Anne de Salvo, the Broadway production of *Fifth of July* gave us an opportunity to reward more of our Company members. Timothy Shelton, who replaced William Hurt in our summer extension at Circle, now was stand-by for Jed and Kenny; Jane Fleiss, who had also replaced, stood by for Shirley. Lindsey Ginter understudied John and Wes; and Tanya got her first Broadway paycheck understudying June and Gwen.

When our star had to leave to fulfill his film commitments, we were enormously fortunate with our first replacement. Fabled television star Richard Thomas came and saw one performance and the next afternoon went into rehearsals with our stage manager to learn the blocking and lines. With his vast television experience, Richard was an incredibly quick study and within a week, he was ready to go on. As a result, he took over directly from Chris, with no understudy having to fill a gap. Richard understood ensemble playing from his years of playing in *The Waltons* with Michael Lerned, Ralph Waite and Will Geer. The role of Kenny fit him like the proverbial lambskin glove. He was enthusiastically received by the reviewers, who felt the Broadway production finally had come perfectly into focus:

The New York Times, April 9, 1981 (Frank Rich):
"Thanks to a major casting change, the full beauty of this comedy has finally been uncorked. Richard Thomas not only gives a performance that gracefully builds to shattering dimensions, but he has also sparked the rest of the company to follow suit. In every case, the supporting cast is rewarding the text with greater depth. In November, *Fifth of July* was dominated by Swoosie Kurtz's hilarious performance. Kurtz's character is now in proper perspective, and her performance is even better. Ben Siegler, a newcomer to the cast, is no less funny. If

Mr. Thomas has been the catalyst for these changes, credit must also be given to the entire company, and to Mason, the director. Given the scant competition, it's probably disingenuous to say that *Fifth of July* now stands as the best American play of the Broadway season. With all due respect to *Talley's Folly*, why not throw in last season as well?"

Daily News, April 9, 1981 (Douglas Watt):
"It was positively heart-warming to return to *Fifth of July.* Wilson's richly observant comedy remains one of the few vibrant plays to greet us since the fall. Thomas [gives] a sensitive performance, and the play is more cohesive and moving than ever because of it. It certainly is one of the strongest, funniest and original pieces of contemporary American theater."

Variety, April 15, 1981 (Humm.):
"Richard Thomas is a good choice for [the part.] *Fifth of July* shows no signs of lagging. It remains among the best acted plays on Broadway, and is easily the most satisfying new American Broadway play of the season. Kurtz continues to captivate, and is a surefire Tony Award contender. Jeff Daniels is another likely Tony nominee for his eloquent under-played portrayal. *July* has some of the best writing on Broadway and makes it clear that Wilson is at the top of the list of contemporary American playwrights."

Daily News, April 17, 1981 (Rex Reed):
"Since Richard Thomas has moved into the center spotlight, a miracle has happened: an already great play has become even greater. The work unfolds like a flower, offering new colors, new levels of discovery. The balance is finally perfect, and *Fifth of July* soars magnificently. Thomas is giving the kind of emotionally charged performances few theatergoers are lucky enough to see in a

decade. Ben Siegler, the other new cast member, fits in with bewildered perfection. All of them work together as though they lived together offstage as well as on, giving the play a flow, a unity, and a karma you almost never see on Broadway. Wilson must look at his wise, endearing play under Mason's deeply loving direction and wonder if he's looking at reality, an accident, or a dream. I only wish someone would film this kind of rare, exemplary perfection right now to preserve it forever in its present form. How wonderful it would be to hold on to this kind of magic forever."

Throughout the different incarnations, the roles of Kenny and Jed have been played mostly by heterosexual actors. Jeff Daniels, who, in the course of playing Jed, performed opposite William Hurt, Christopher Reeve and Richard Thomas, was asked by a reporter whom he preferred in the part. Jeff wisely declined to name a favorite; diplomatically, he asserted they were all good and each brought something new to the role. "But," he added, "Richard was the best kisser."

About that kiss – Joyce Reehling recalls a funny incident that crystalized a Broadway audience's reaction to Jed kissing Ken in the opening moments of the play. She could hear an old lady whispering to her husband: "He must be his father."

Of course, when we played student matinees, it was irresistible for adolescents to freak out at the kiss, sometimes yelling out: "Superman's a fag!" or after Richard Thomas replaced Chris, "John Boy's a fag!" *Fag* is one of the favorite words of pubescent boys, although I suspect, little by little, that may become more rare. At least, we can hope.

We were less lucky with subsequent replacements. One curiosity was the casting of Tim Bottoms to replace Richard. He seemed a logical choice to play Kenny after his sensitive performance in *The Last Picture Show* and Tim was serviceable in the part. But he had somehow not quite realized that Kenny was gay. It didn't *say* so in the script, so like the old woman whispering to her husband, somehow he accommodated Kenny's behavior in some other way. When one of his friends saw the show and pointed out to him that he was playing a faggot, after the following performance, Tim walked off the stage before the curtain call and, without stopping at his dressing room, headed straight out the stage door, never to be seen again. Somewhat desperate, in trying to locate Tim, we called his brother Joseph Bottoms, who'd seen the show and loved it. He had no problem playing a homosexual, so he replaced his brother in the role for several months and he was very good as Kenny. Michael O'Keefe is a very fine actor (he'd been sterling in *The Great Santini*) and we thought he was well cast as Kenny. Unfortunately, a sense of comedy was not his strong suit and he was just too soft for a large theater.

Apart from Richard Thomas, who became a member of the Company and played important roles at Circle Rep (including Kostya in Circle Rep's *Seagull*), we were equally fortunate to replace Joyce Reehling as June with the brilliant Kathy Bates, who also became a Company Member and later won an Oscar. In addition to Tanya, we were able to use other members of Circle Rep to replace, including John Dossett as Jed (excellent!), Ruby Holbrook as Aunt Sally and especially Ben Siegler as Weston. In fact, Ben joined the production at the same time as Richard Thomas, so he was the only Wes Richard had ever known. When I later went back to our original Danton Stone for the television version, Richard was crushed that I was taking his precious Ben away from him. Of course, once he had a chance to see what Danton did with the part, I think he was adequately consoled.

We were not so lucky replacing Swoosie. I regularly watched *Saturday Night Live,* which was an incubator for new talent. Of all the people on *SNL*, I particularly admired Laraine Newman, who seemed more an actor than a comedienne. I was fond of her deadly serious television journalist reporting on the Jewish New Year, waiting for the ball to drop in Times Square. I thought she might be the one person who could follow Swoosie as Gwen. Unfortunately,

I was wrong. She had no previous stage experience, so her performances varied wildly. She was neither funny nor believable. Luckily Tanya was there to fill in for Laraine's frequent "unable-to-go-on" episodes, which one suspected might be chemically induced.

When awards season rolled around, we were nominated for Best Play, Best Director, Best Supporting Actress, Best Set and Best Lighting. Once again I was pretty certain the directing award would go to someone other than me, in this case Peter Hall for his beautiful *Amadeus*. We lost the play award also to *Amadeus*, but we were thrilled when Swoosie won her first Tony for Best Supporting Actress, as well as the Drama Desk Award and the Outer Critics Circle Award, Broadway's Triple Crown.

Luckily, when Laraine Newman's limited run as Gwen mercifully ended, Swoosie's agent was able to negotiate excellent terms for her to return to the production. With the Tony Award added to her spectacular reviews, Swoosie was now the legitimate "co-star" of *Fifth of July* and received the advances in billing and salary that these assets earned her. She finished the run of the show and helped us maintain a healthy box-office until the end.

A Sample of Excellence Preserved

I'm happy to report that we were able to grant Rex Reed's fervent wish "to preserve it forever in its present form" by taping *Fifth of July* for Showtime and PBS in July of 1982, six months after the final Broadway performance on January 24. While I shared his desire to capture our achievement for posterity, doing so presented a couple of challenging choices. Lanford and I were grateful for the way Richard Thomas found just the right balance between Kenny's pain and ironic sense of humor, so he was a logical choice for the role on TV. Although Richard loved playing opposite Ben Siegler as Wes, we knew that Danton's original creation must be preserved and now I also had the chance to restore to the cast Helen Stenborg, for whom Lanford wrote the part of Sally Friedman. Obviously, we would continue with the center of the ensemble: Jeff Daniels, Jonathan Hogan and Joyce Reehling, all of whom not only created the roles originally, but continued to grow in them over the four years they played them. After Swoosie won the Tony Award, it was unthinkable to do the television production without her Gwen and by now she owned the role that once had been beautifully illuminated by Nancy Snyder.

The only difficulty lay in the casting of Shirley, the fourteen year-old illegitimate daughter of June. Amy Wright created the role and played it throughout its transitions from Circle Rep to the Taper to Broadway. But what had been magical onstage would be hard to translate to the intimacy of a camera. Some reviewers complained that she was too old to be believable as a teenager even in the theater, but we stood by Amy because she brought endearing life to the part. Sad as I was to recast, my loyalty to Amy could not trump my desire to bring Lanford's work faithfully to the screen. I decided a real teenager was required for the camera. I was impressed with a girl playing the younger sister of Blythe Danner in the Lincoln Center revival of *Philadelphia Story*. I asked her to come in and read for me. She was perfect. I believe Cynthia Nixon's performance in *Fifth of July* bears out the wisdom of casting her as the rambunctious teenager. She was sixteen at the time, already an astonishing artist. No longer did the character seem shrill and bratty, but now Shirley could be appreciated as Lanford intended her: the bright-eyed hope for the future of the Talley family.

This time, WNET provided me with a genuine television genius to help me transfer our creation to the small screen. Kirk Browning was the "grand old man" of capturing live stage performances for television, most notably in his long and distinguished career directing live broadcasts from the Metropolitan Opera. Kirk was gentle and generous; he told me he would teach me everything I needed to learn about directing for television so I'd never again have to share a credit with a co-director. With Kirk's guidance, I made all the decisions on how to tape *Fifth of July*. I decided on camera placement, which cameras were to be used to capture each moment, as well as the physical staging and the final editing. Once I made these decisions, Kirk conveyed my instructions to our four cameramen and our lighting and sound technicians; and he called the live edits from the trailer. The live edits were minimally used in the final cut, since I insisted that each camera be "isolated," recording every moment of the show from every angle, so that I could make decisions in the editing room, just as a film director can. Kirk was true to his word; in two weeks, I had a cram course in directing for the camera and I never shared another credit. I'm glad the DVD remains available at Amazon so everyone in the future can see a hint of our best work.

We shot the exteriors in one week on location in Connecticut, using the lawn of a splendid old Victorian house with a surrounding porch, and a second week in a Hartford television studio for the interiors. Circle Rep's David Potts provided the Art Direction, which included inventing a fourth wall and making a photographic drop to hang outside the studio set's windows to unify it with the exterior shots. I was delighted that we were able to open up the production, showing Jed down in his garden and in the shower upstairs, and Shirley climbing the tree to spy on John and Gwen. And of course, it was great to be outdoors on the lawn in real sunlight for the second act. We had a great time re-creating our work for posterity and my two weeks in the editing room were among the happiest of my life. All the performances are exemplary and they bring the play to new life every time someone slips the disc into a DVD player. I hope Rex is happy.

Chapter 15
Third From The Sun

The tale of the Talleys had been twice rewarded and a promise of a five-play cycle was eagerly anticipated. Did Lanford have any choice but to follow the Talley tale into a third episode? I'm sure he shared the public's curiosity about what was happening up at the house on the hill during Sally's tryst with Matt down at the boathouse. He also was driven by his theme, questioning American values and how war changed them, a theme he was resolute to pursue.

He tackled the subject first in *Fifth of July*, wherein the result of the Vietnam War is suggested in the ravaged body of Kenneth Talley, Jr. The fabric of the 60s is woven from the protests to that war and the play mourns the lost hopes of a generation. June bitterly lashes out at her daughter:

> "You have no idea of the country we almost made for you. And the fact that I think it's all a crock now does not take away from what we almost achieved."

Kenny debunks heroism in war as a sham. When Shirley brags that Kenny has five medals, he sharply rebukes her:

> "You may not be proud of that."

Dying for your country is not a heroic act to be venerated. He uses Weston's scatological Eskimo myth as a metaphor for American pride that leads us into fighting wars:

"The saving grace would have been surviving. Don't choke on it, don't turn up your nose, swallow it and live, baby."

In *Talley's Folly*, it is thirty-three years earlier, and the nation is engaged in an international conflict that arrived on the heels of the First World War, the war that promised to end all wars. Matt tells us:

"Once again, this country pitched its resources and industry into battle."

And the cost of that war has been the disappearance of a hope that once spread throughout the land. Matt sees the irony:

"Once again, we are told, the country has been saved by war."

He frames the love story we are about to see by noting its context:

"Now you would think that world events would not touch this hidden place. But such is not the case. There is a house on the hill up there, and there is a family that is not at peace, but in grave danger of prosperity."

The Talley family is enjoying the fruits of wartime commerce, making uniforms for the brave soldiers at their garment factory, ringing up profits and calling it patriotism.

The Talley plays preceded the two wars in Iraq and the longest war of our history in Afghanistan, but Lanford sensed the tendency afoot. He was particularly aware of the relationship between war and profit. And that becomes the focus of the third play.

A Tale Told takes place on the same night as *Talley's Folly* and considers the effects of World War Two, a home front invaded by uncertainties that cause households to begin locking their doors at night. The Talley's youngest son Timmy has been killed in battle and his death literally haunts his family. As he will say at the end of the play:

> "America won the war today. We all go off; by the time they get back, the country's changed so much I don't imagine they'll recognize it."

The seeds for *Talley's Folly* are sown in *Fifth of July* and the embryos for future Talley plays are imbedded in both. Virtually all the characters that must inhabit a third Talley play have already been introduced: Sally's maiden aunt Lottie; her little brother Timmy; her father and mother who hosted Matt at a disastrous dinner; her brother Kenny, known as Buddy and his hyperventilating wife, Olive, who are also Ken and June's parents; Sally's old beau Harley Campbell, who's in business with her father and whose funeral she attends in *Fifth of July*. Even the Young family of poor white trash is set up in *Fifth* and the autistic child that Kenny is helping is Johnny Young, the descendant of the Talley's handyman, Emmet Young, who will appear in the third play. And Sally's description of Uncle Whistler, who built the folly/boathouse provides the central character for a fourth Talley play. All Lanford had to do is flesh out the people he already set up, but that proved harder than he expected.

Lanford's imagination was hampered by pre-determined outcomes. An outlined plot was anathema to his creative process. So, as motivated as he was to follow the Talleys into the house on the hill, he was equally stymied. He said that his intention was to write in an alternative genre of the 40s, following the sentimental comedy in the manner of *It Happened One Night*, a stylistic model for *Talley's Folly*, with the plot-driven melodrama of Lillian Hellman's *The Little Foxes*.

Try, Try Again

I've never been entirely clear about why Lanford wanted to call the new play *A Tale Told*, which he insisted had nothing to do with Shakespeare's idiot. Nevertheless, we were burdened with that image's insinuation that the play was "full of sound and fury, signifying nothing." Instead, the title was meant to refer to a phrase from the 90th Psalm in the *Bible*:

> "Thou hast set our iniquities before Thee, our secret sins in the lights of Thy countenance. For all our days are passed away in Thy wrath; we spend our years as a tale that is told."

Eventually, he tired of the mix-up and came up with the far better title *Talley & Son*.

Lanford's Broadway successes kept him occupied and he spent more time at the theaters than at his typewriter. Nevertheless, as *Fifth of July* sailed through the summer, Lanford spent more days in Sag Harbor and was free to turn his attention to those pesky Talleys up on the hill.

I have not thought about *A Tale Told* in a long time and its memory is superseded by the much-improved *Talley & Son*, which didn't appear until 1985. Preparing to write about it, I returned to the script for the first time in thirty years. I was surprised at how poorly the play reads, compared to its later transformation. I certainly don't recall any disappointment back in 1981 when Lanford brought us the script. On the contrary, everyone at Circle Rep was thrilled to have the Talleys back. So I have to think about how we felt at the time, diverted from the script's shortcomings by our joy in having it to work on.

It's no mystery why the actors of the Company were grateful; they were given complex characters to bring to life. One of Lanford's chief inspirations in developing the play was to write a part for Elizabeth Sturges, who'd been so memorable in *When You Comin' Back, Red Ryder?* nine years before. We'd had little work for her since – or at least, nothing worthy of her enormous talent. She played supporting roles in the revival of *A Runner Stumbles*, in our repertory pairing of *Hamlet* and *Mary Stuart*, and in Jim Leonard's *The Diviners*. But Lanford, always appreciative of extraordinary talent, wanted to create a role for Liz that would let her shine. Aunt

Lottie, the iconoclastic Talley old maid, is at the center of *A Tale Told*. Lanford related in his foreword to the play:

"The first image was in a house where smoking was strictly forbidden, especially in the formal parlor and nobody, certainly not ladies, swore, Liz would walk through the house, lighting a cigarette, saying, 'Oh, kiss my ass!' This had to be the Talley's front parlor and this had to be Aunt Lottie."

I think Lanford got the idea of Lottie painting radium dials on watch faces from the fact that Sag Harbor had a huge abandoned building that once housed a Bulova Watch factory. Unbeknownst to all except her brother Eldon, Lottie is now dying of cancer, a result of radium poisoning. She is the tragic and hysterical heroine of the play and Matt's ally in the wooing of Sally.

Unlike our more recent volunteer armies, in the 1940s everyone pitched into the war effort and every young man was subject to the draft. Many of them couldn't wait to show their patriotism by signing up. So the Talley family has two sons at war: Buddy in the European theater and Timmy in the South Pacific. Buddy is Kenny and June's father and June is heard offstage in the play as a baby. Olive was so riotously described by Matt that I'm sure Lanford took a wicked pleasure in writing her.

Another significant inspiration to Lanford was the incredibly talented Jimmie Ray Weeks. His simple honesty, the depth of his acting and his quiet, butch manliness were all magnets for Lanford's imagination; so pale Jimmie Ray was the perfect person to portray Sally's long-lost love of her youth, Harley Campbell.

By now, it seemed Lanford could hardly conceive of a play without Helen Stenborg in it. She was the touchstone of *HOT L* and the stealthy savior of *Fifth of July*. Lanford thought it would be great fun to let Helen play Sally's mother in the new play, so he wrote Netta for her.

The rest of the cast, if not inspiring the parts, fit the roles Lanford wrote just as if they were crafted expressly for them. Tim Shelton, who'd been a solid replacement as Kenny, was perfect for the all-American Buddy; so, like Helen, Tim got a chance to play his own parent. Patricia Wettig dazzled Circle Rep audiences with double appearances in the eleventh season as the star of both *The Woolgatherer* and *Innocent Thoughts*. Lanford's Olive exploited Patty's previously unrecognized comedic gift. Our dependable Michael Higgins seemed at first to be well cast as the dependable Eldon, Sally's tiresomely conventional father and Harley's partner in the garment factory. Sexy Lindsey Ginter nicely filled the half-buttoned overalls of the dim handyman, Emmet Young. And Helen Stenborg's daughter, Laura Hughes, portrayed Avalaine Platt, the slutty teenager, who exposes that she is half a Talley herself, being Eldon's illegitimate daughter, with just the degree of awkward malevolence the part required.

More difficult to find was the right actress for Viola Platt, Avalaine's laundrywoman mom, who long ago had an affair with the young Eldon. The part was fashioned after Violetta, Lanford's own mother, who took in washing after she left her job at the garment factory. I decided to go with the best actress from Northwestern, Nancy Killmer, who always seemed to enrich any character she played. She was delicious as Tanya's co-star in *Mrs. Murray's Farm*. In *A Tale Told*, she brought a survivor's strength (compared by one reviewer to Thelma Ritter) to what is perhaps the least rewarding part in the play. Equally difficult was the casting of Timmy Talley, the young soldier who appears in the play as a ghost. We didn't have a suitable teenage boy available in the Company, so I held auditions to find David Ferry, a Canadian actor. A bit stocky for a ghost, David was nevertheless well spoken and Lanford wrote the most poetic dialogue in the play for Timmy. It needed to be spoken well, because once the character started talking, Lanford found it hard to shut him up.

It was a delightful opportunity to cast the part of Old Man Talley, Calvin, the patriarch of the whole clan. I'd long admired Fritz Weaver, a character actor who electrified the stage whenever he was on it. I had first seen Fritz starring in the Broadway production of *Child's Play* in 1970. As the sometimes senile, sometimes treacherous Mr. Talley, Fritz was the perfect choice. He became a Company member with this production and Lanford wrote another great role for him in *Angels Fall*.

With *A Tale Told*, I had a Company of happy actors, all of whom relished digging into their juicy roles. John Lee also enjoyed designing the parlor of the Talley house in its heyday, after he'd already created the sunporch and exterior of the dilapidated house in *Fifth of July*. His set was a marvel, having two gigantic doorways with sliding doors that separated the entrance hallway from the parlor, with garden doors that led out to the side porch, and across the room, the heavy mahogany door to Mr. Talley's private office. It was Victorian grandeur with Art Deco refurbishing. As was the case during the war years, the room was dominated by a cathedral-shaped radio receiver on the fireplace mantel, where the family could gather after supper to listen to Walter Winchell.

With all this creativity bubbling around the Circle Rep offices, it's understandable that we overlooked the weaknesses in the script's structure. Although Milan Stitt and Rod Marriott were excellent dramaturges, they probably felt it was presumptuous to tell a Pulitzer Prize winner his play needed more work. And where was I, Lanford's closest collaborator, who'd given him such salient advice on *Talley's Folly*? Well, *A Tale Told* contains some of the most haunting imagery and eloquent writing of Lanford's work. I was so enamored of its virtues I was blinded to its deficiencies. Usually, Lanford is his own harshest judge. Given his sensitivity, we'd learned to be supportive rather than critical.

Even a poorly constructed Lanford Wilson play had merits other writers could only wish for. As usual, his characters were rich and his dialogue sparkled. A perception that something was amiss emerged only gradually through the first two productions.

The problems were that while the style of *A Tale Told* reached for the full-throttled melodrama of Lillian Hellman, (Netta faints Center Stage after learning of her son's death), Lanford's structure did not match the tight construction of *The Little Foxes*. Harley and Eldon quarrel endlessly over the finer points of running a factory with a government contract, a subject unlikely to engage an audience. The business talk in *Foxes* is fascinating for the revelations of character and skullduggery, while Eldon and Harley just seem to drone on without revealing anything. And the sheer size of Lanford's canvas, while inspiring, was also daunting. The twelve characters are introduced in such a tumultuous fashion it's even harder than usual to latch on to the action that drives the play.

The first act is particularly muddled. The jumbled beats don't build on each other, but wander in a Chekhovian manner that's the opposite of Lillian Hellman's well-made melodrama. In *Fifth of July*, that tumultuous non-sequitur style was appropriate; here, it is detrimental. Timmy does not speak in the first act and, once he comes onstage in Act Two, Lanford gave him beautifully written monologues that hindered the forward motion of the action. I don't know why this wasn't self-evident, but we were accustomed to supporting Lanford as he broke the rules of writing, usually advancing the art as he did so. And, as I said, we were overwhelmed by the beauty of the writing and the importance of the theme.

Of course, you must take into consideration that my current harsh assessment of the script was written through a thirty-year lens of hindsight, brought sharply into focus by knowing how much better the script grew as it evolved into *Talley & Son*.

Talley Times Three

At the time, *Fifth of July* was flying high on Broadway with Richard Thomas, and the New York Theater community awaited the opening of *A Tale Told* with eager anticipation. Harvey S. Karten, reporting for *High Points Magazine* noted:

> "At the preview performance that I saw, large numbers of hopeful ticket-buyers were being turned away. I was told that the attraction was the playwright Lanford Wilson rather than the equally impressive cast headed by Fritz Weaver."

The Transcendent Years

A Tale Told opened at Circle Rep on June 11, 1981 and played for thirty-nine performances. As usual with our "A-team," the production was directed by Marshall W. Mason, set design by John Lee Beatty, lighting by Dennis Parichy, costumes by Laura Crow and sound design by Chuck London. The stage manager was Fred Reinglas.

The critical reception of the play divided the reviewers with a gap as wide as the chasm of political debate in the first decade of the 21st century. Some thought it was his best play; others were completely lost and even derisive. Most of them caught the connection to *The Little Foxes*, some in admiration, others in dismay:

The New York Times, June 12, 1981 (Frank Rich):

"While Wilson is one of our theater's very best writers, his new play seems written out of obligation rather than inspiration. His perfect ear for American speech hasn't failed him, and neither has his crack director, Mason. But this time Wilson's lush language and Mason's flawless staging have been applied to a theatrical vacuum. The evening's plot, which involves revelations of sordid business and sexual affairs, appears to be Wilson's homage to such old-time melodrama as *The Little Foxes*. The cast, however, is uniformly strong, with the standout performance coming from Fritz Weaver. Mason and Wilson's favorite design team – Beatty, Crow, Parichy – are in fine form. It's not Beatty's fault we keep wishing we were somewhere else."

Daily News, June 12, 1981 (Douglas Watt):

"The thrice-told tale is once too often. This play is the weakest of the three. Fritz Weaver's performance [is] the only reason I can see for catching the play. *A Tale Told* hasn't been too well cast. Wettig does just fine, but Higgins is too muted and hardly credible as a rake in his youth. Wilson says he's by no means finished with the Talleys; but I have the feeling I am."

New York Post, June 12, 1998 (Clive Barnes):

"Wilson's *Tale* is told brilliantly. The new play has been wonderfully directed by Mason. The acting is also graciously exceptional. There are twelve members of this cast, and they are all excellent; they play like a family. You really feel they have created one another at birth. This is possibly, very possibly, Wilson's best play to date. It is clearly Broadway-bound, and one presumes it will get there around October of this year. Wilson is creating an image of American history, commanding to us that we will never forget."

WQXR, June 12, 1981 (Mel Gussow):

"*A Tale Told* is a richly layered family chronicle that unfolds with the confidence and comprehensiveness of a great novel. This is one of Wilson's finest plays. There are a dozen characters, and by the end of the evening, each has come vibrantly to life. For Wilson, a major American playwright, *A Tale Told* is in itself an act of fulfillment."

New York Magazine, June 22, 1981 (John Simon):

"Lanford Wilson reaffirms his position at the forefront of American dramatists. Less entertaining than *Fifth of July* and less enchanting than *Talley's Folly*, this third play is somehow more imposing, more commanding of respect than either of its predecessors. [There are] twelve characters, all of them, glaringly alive and kicking and being kicked; interacting, intriguing, injuring or getting injured. At a time when most playwrights can produce only chamber music, Wilson can write for a whole orchestra. The Circle Rep production is, once again, a collaboration of inspirednesses. *A Tale Told* belies its title: Almost everything in it is dramatized, directed, enacted to a fare-thee-well."

The New Yorker, June 22, 1981 (Edith Oliver):

"*A Tale Told* is the most accomplished of the three plays. Its performance at Circle Rep under Mason's direction is as good as any in town. The performance is near to flawless. The Talleys truly seem to be a family. The best performance of all is that of Helen Stenborg, who is a model of passion and eloquence."

Daily News, June 21, 1981 (Rex Reed):

"It is well worth a visit. It helps to have seen all three plays, but *A Tale Told* is such a rich tapestry of American family life that you can enjoy it on its own terms. Just being in the presence of such colorful, intense dramatic writing is reason enough to see it. *A Tale Told* features brilliant writing, intricately embroidered direction by Mason, illuminating ensemble acting, and first-rate production values. You go away from the Talley plays high on ecstasy or pain, but you go away knowing you have been to the theater. And the ultimate joy is the knowledge that there's more to come. I can hardly wait."

The New York Times, June 21, 1981 (Walter Kerr):

"This may be *A Tale Told* once too often. Wilson is a writer of considerable talent, but his new piece is patently unsure of itself as it gropes for a shape. One imagines that fine director Mason has simply thrown up his hands to do *anything* to keep Wilson's story on the move. There are fleeting good things to grasp at. Sally Talley, in the moth-like engaging person of Trish Hawkins, appears briefly at evening's end. Circle Rep never seems to have any difficulty rounding up fine actors. [But] the Talleys are thin, unfelt stereotypes. Sally was right to leave them. Mr. Wilson might be, too."

Time Magazine, June 23, 1981 (Gerald Clarke):

"The newest play just meanders, with no discernible destination. The only thing that is obvious in this well-directed, well-acted play is that Wilson is a very talented writer. His dialogue is sharp, and his characters have color and life. The Talleys continue to fascinate."

Newsweek, June 23, 1981 (Jack Kroll):
"No playwright of his generation has attracted the same blend of approbation and affection as Lanford Wilson. He adores and honors language and he can shape it to the music of anguish, tenderness, or nutball humor. His work has built up a powerful and ethical presence in the consciousness of American theater. Wilson plays the Talley family like a master musician; he and his longtime colleague, director Mason, make the Talley house pulsate. [But] even the intense conviction of a dedicated cast can't shake the conventionality that for the first time overwhelms the tale of the Talleys."

Village Voice, June 23, 1981 (Julius Novick):
"What an old-fashioned play Wilson has written; and what a good one! The cast are all admirable. Wilson is not a formal innovator or a deep thinker; his images of America, though evocative and cogent, are not startlingly original. But the people of his trilogy go on living, The Talleys have begun to take on the solidity of characters in a good old-fashioned novel. We have gone on fulfilling journeys with them. We sense that there are more to come."

Variety, June 24, 1981 (Humm.):
"There's an abundance of lovely writing, some memorable characters, and a few strong scenes. But the play is over-plotted and overwritten and lacks a central dramatic focus. Considerable sharpening and cutting are necessary if *Tale* is to have the commercial life of its predecessors. There's more talent in *A Tale Told* than in the majority of recent American plays, and there's no question that Wilson

is among the best of contemporary playwrights. But *Tale* is too busy and cluttered to offer full satisfaction. After a rewrite, however, it might be ready to travel."

The Hollywood Reporter, June 19, 1981 (Martin Gould):
"A noticeable lack of humor separates this play from its predecessors. The cast is excellent. Even though it is the least enjoyable of the Talley family, the play will likely find its way to Broadway in the near future."

WOR, June 12, 1981 (Casper Citron):
"A major new play", [it's] the last of the trilogy. I liked it best, and I am certain that it will move to Broadway and become a contender for the next Tony season."

In fact, we had no such plans for a Broadway move. We were already committed to follow up our run at Circle Rep with another sojourn at the Mark Taper Forum in Los Angeles. Gordon Davidson was keen to keep his audience abreast of the latest sensations in New York before they became Broadway fare; bringing the third play of the trilogy to the Taper was a logical fulfillment of the repertory of *Talley's Folly* and *Fifth of July* that had enlivened the Taper season two years before. With the mixture of opinion reflected in our New York reviews, we would have an opportunity to take a second look at the play, as we did with *Fifth of July.*

A Tale at the Taper

We needed to make a few cast changes in our transfer to California. Patty Wettig had new television obligations that prevented her from continuing, so we replaced her as Olive with our ever-reliable Joyce Reehling; so once again, an actor had the fun of playing the parent of a character (June) she'd already played. We also had to replace David Ferry in the part of Timmy; David was not a member of the Company and as a Canadian, not part of our future. So we cast a young actor I'd seen in the Humana Festival at Louisville, Timothy

Busfield, a decided improvement. We replaced Nancy Killmer in the role of Viola with a California actress, Grace Zabriskie, who was very good. And importantly, William Jordan, younger and more vital, replaced Michael Higgins as Eldon. In the smaller role of Emmet Young, an actor named Richard Holden replaced Lindsey Ginter. Otherwise, Liz Sturges, Trish Hawkins, Helen Stenborg, Tim Shelton, Jimmie Ray Weeks, Fritz Weaver and Laura Hughes continued in the roles they'd originated at Circle Rep.

So, the Taper's *Tale* was half Circle Rep and half California replacements. Perhaps some of the changes were economically motivated; paying airfare, per diem and housing for a large cast made casting some local actors advisable. And on the whole, the replacements were the equal of the originals and some were actually improvements.

The design team remained the same and again did beautiful work adapting to the larger, thrust stage. We made some adjustments in the script as we went back into rehearsal, but the biggest changes still lay ahead, when Lanford took to heart some of the advice contained in the review by Jack Viertel, the *Times-Herald* theater critic.

A Tangled Tale Re-Told

The occasion for *A Tale Told* is the return of Kenneth Talley, called by his nickname, Buddy, home from his wartime service in Italy. He's on leave because the family has been expecting the imminent death of the patriarch of the clan, Mr. Calvin Talley, an octogenarian whose health has rebounded, although he drifts in and out of senility. The play begins with a household chaotic with the preparations of a goose to accommodate Buddy's desire to celebrate Christmas dinner on the Fourth of July. Viola, the family's washerwoman appears, calling out that she urgently needs to see Eldon, Buddy's dad. Eldon's wife, Netta, all aflutter with the dinner preparations, tells Viola to return later when she brings back the laundry. Eldon has been submerged with the papers in Mr. Talley's office, where he is attempting to straighten out decades

The Transcendent Years

of complex business deals, archived in an order known only to his father. Buddy's wife, Olive, is on edge with a sexual appetite that has been starved during Buddy's absence and she wants to claim as much of Buddy's leave time as she can. Upstairs, the couple's baby June is having a crying fit and Nora, the off-stage cook, is furious with everyone running in and out of her kitchen.

In addition to this flurry of activity, we learn that about an hour earlier there's been a dramatic confrontation, in which Buddy and Harley Campbell have chased off the property Matt Friedman, a Jew from St. Louis, who's been trying to woo Sally for over a year. (Their description of the incident mirrors Matt's comic rendition of the same event in *Talley's Folly*.) Central to that confrontation was Charlotte Talley, Eldon's maiden sister, known as Aunt Lottie. She has been an ally in Matt's pursuit of Sally and she is incensed by the hostile treatment Matt has received at the end of a shotgun; she's not speaking to anybody.

Harley, whom we remember from Sally's description in *Talley's Folly*, was once engaged to Sally but has since married. He is Eldon's partner in a garment factory that is turning out uniforms for the army. They have a sweeping takeover offer from a corporate conglomerate. Harley is eager to sell; Eldon opposes it on the grounds that they would lose all quality control.

In the midst of this beehive of contention, they discover that old man Talley, has disappeared; apparently he has driven off somewhere in the family's Packard. Buddy and Harley take off on a mission to track him down.

Harley finds the old man at the cemetery, ranting gibberish. He brings him back to the parlor, where Mr. Talley sits enthroned in senile splendor. He is contemptuous of his son Eldon, whom he regards as little more than a bookkeeper and we can detect in his ravings that his disdain is due to Eldon's riotous youth, when he was a bootlegger and something of a rake. In a moment of clarity, Mr. Talley brags about how he cheated a man out of his walnut crop thirty years earlier, demonstrating his superior and crafty knowledge of business. He is the epitome of a vulture capitalist.

Viola returns, still urgently wanting a private conversation with Eldon, but he dismisses her, telling her to come by the office next week. We learn that Harley serves on the local draft board and he recently brought Viola news of the death of her bother, Vaughn. We also learn that the Talley's youngest son, Timmy, is stationed in the Pacific and Eldon hopes that when he returns he will support his father in the struggle over the fate of the garment factory. The conflict between Eldon and Harley becomes quite heated, with Buddy maintaining a disinterested ambivalence.

Harley leaves to return to his duties on the draft board, while Mr. Talley re-enters, reminiscing about his dead brother, Whistler, whose grave he has apparently visited at the cemetery. Mr. Talley is left alone in the parlor in an ostensible stupor, when Avalaine Platt, Viola's slutty teenaged daughter appears. She teases the old man by tickling his ear and Mr. Talley comes suddenly back to consciousness by belting Avalaine across the face, bloodying her nose. Avalaine's wails bring the entire household running into the parlor. At the peak of confusion, Harley appears quietly at the front door holding a telegram, which Eldon realizes must contain news of Timmy's death. Netta, upset with Viola and Avalaine's persistence, is the last to notice Harley, standing mutely with the telegram. When she realizes what it means, she faints dead away, as the first act ends.

What I have not mentioned is that Lanford has written in the stage directions the comings and goings throughout the act of a young man in battle fatigues, who does not speak. This is the ghost of Timmy and as his mother faints at the end of the act, he softens her fall to the floor, his first interaction with the living people.

In the second act, Timmy begins to deliver soliloquys to the audience, describing the military operations around the taking of the Pacific Islands, Tinian and Saipan. In his second monologue, Timmy provides the details of his death in a beautifully written rendition of the experience of dying. After the turmoil of the first act, Timmy's lengthy, poetic reflections slow the action down to an eerie pace. A melodramatic turn of events reveals Avalaine is

Eldon's bastard child. Her threats of blackmail are defused by Mr. Talley's machinations. He makes a deal with Emmet Young, the Talley handyman, to marry Avalaine in return for a job at the factory. Then, after the young rednecks have left, Mr. Talley announces that Emmet will actually never work at the factory because he is casting the deciding vote, along with Buddy and Harley, to sell the factory to the conglomerate. This action eviscerates the self-esteem of his son; but Eldon has no choice but to resign himself to the outcome. And Netta, forced to face that her marriage has been a sham, tries to absorb the death of her son. She takes down the flag in the window with the two stars indicating two sons in the war, and orders Eldon to lock all the doors in the house.

After all except Lottie have left the stage, Sally comes rushing in to get her bags to run away to St. Louis with Matt, the events of *Talley's Folly* having occurred simultaneously with the action we've been watching. Lottie hides from Sally the news of Timmy's death, determined to let nothing interfere with Sally's escape to a better life. She sends Sally on her way, and then as Eldon goes from door to door, following Netta's instructions to lock every door, Lottie sits quietly, communing with Tim, as they reflect on the decline of the Talley estate. But Lottie is at peace, because she knows that tomorrow she'll receive a phone call from St. Louis that Sally and Matt are married. She muses:

"A person could get from day to day for thirty years looking forward to a phone call."

During the rehearsals in Los Angeles, there were no significant alterations in the play; so the California critics saw essentially the same script that divided the New York reviewers.

Middle Ground

A Tale Told was presented by the Mark Taper Forum (in association with Circle Repertory Company) on October 22, 1981, where it played for forty-eight performances, with the same production credits as before. The stage manager was Michelle Miner. It had a $16.50 top ticket price. Here's a sampling of what the L.A. critics had to say:

The Los Angeles Times, October 23, 1981 (Dan Sullivan):
"This is the family play to end all family plays, best appreciated as Wilson's homage to an American genre. What the audience feels is the fun of a good old-fashioned family play, the kind they don't write anymore. *A Tale Told* isn't an epic, but a charming collectible. No one could deny that *A Tale Told* is an actors' play, and it's probably going to be an audience's play as well. The Taper audience dug into it like mince pie."

The Los Angeles Herald-Examiner, October 23, 1981 (Jack Viertel):
"The Talley family has returned in a play full of startling scenes and vivid writing. If *A Tale Told* finally disappoints, at least it does so on the highest possible level. [Wilson's] embarrassment of riches finally undoes him. It is about transition, about a slipping of values and their replacement by new ones, about a world on the brink of new dreams and new methods of manufacturing those dreams. It is a play of fascinating pieces, but not quite a play that works. [It's] certainly the most ambitious of the three, and it falls short where the others achieved virtually everything they set out to do. Still, *A Tale Told* offers so much that is admirable, thoughtful and intriguing that it can hardly be dismissed. It's a deeply flawed, affecting, frustrating work that delivers more flashes of bright light than many more successful plays."

Variety, October 23, 1981 (Edwa.):
"*Tale* is a homespun happening with Wilson's excellent ear for dialogue. Characters are also excellently laid down and developed. But getting into the meat of the play and following the events is sluggish. An evening with the Talleys

would never be dull. But this one's not as exciting as *Folly* and *Fifth*. The performances are some of the best seen on local stages in a long time. But the play itself doesn't have the fire and ice necessary to be a memorable evening."

The Hollywood Reporter, October 23, 1981 (Ron Pennington):
"Lanford Wilson is, without question, the major American playwright to emerge during the middle half of the 20th century. This is sustained by his growing body of work. This is not to say *A Tale Told* is a perfect work. It needs considerable cutting and polishing. But this is a major and important play here, once it is trimmed of unnecessary complexity. And even a flawed Wilson play is better than most works currently seen in the theater. It is an engrossing play that provides a rewarding and thought provoking theatrical experience."

The Daily News, October 23, 1981 (Rick Talcove):
"*A Tale Told* is superior theater in terms of acting, directing, and scenic design, but Wilson's script is a real paradox. It provides sensitive and sympathetic characters, yet doesn't add up to much in terms of conflict and resolution. Director Mason, a master at naturalistic drama, provides a fine interpretation of Wilson's script. It stands out as a superior theatrical event."

Contemporaneous articles described "a successful run at Circle Rep," which was gratifying because, given the negativism of a couple of critics, it didn't *feel* like a hit to us. Our disappointment was not over the failure of the play to transfer to Broadway, as several reviewers predicted. Broadway was never our aim in doing productions at Circle Rep; we were dedicated to creating art, not hits. But our disappointment lay in the gap between what we accomplished and what we expected of ourselves. Despite the appraisal of journalists that we had a successful run, the chasm between opposing opinions suggested there was more work to be done.

The West Coast critics came down more unified in the middle, appreciating the play's merits, while acknowledging faults. No one called it Lanford's best play, as they had in New York; nobody dismissed it as a disaster. Given the wide range of opinion, it might be understandable that it was confusing as to how to solve the problems in the script.

But we were struck by Jack Viertel's insight in his review; he clearly understood Lanford's goals and intentions. His was the best negative review we ever received. We followed up with some conversations with Jack and he provided Lanford with some ideas about how to improve the script. In his introduction to *Talley & Son*, Lanford doesn't mention how Jack helped, but I remember at the time he was spurred by Viertel's encouragement to return to the script and improve it. And although it took somewhat longer than expected, improve it he did.

It was another three years before Lanford's revision finally appeared. In the interim, I reached a point of exhaustion that required me to take a two-year sabbatical from the demanding job of Artistic Director. Of course, Circle Rep continued apace during the fourteenth and fifteenth seasons while I was gone and I continued to directed plays for it.

Transcendent Side Trips

Just as I was starting my sabbatical, Lanford was commissioned by the New World Festival to write a play to be presented first in Miami. Lanford agreed to write it if they brought Circle Rep down to produce it. They agreed, and Lanford, always loath to be required to create, begrudgingly wrote *Angels Fall*. So 1982 and 1983 (and half my sabbatical) were devoured by the productions of *Angels Fall*, which included:
- the initial production at the Coconut Grove Playhouse in Miami;
- summer productions at the Saratoga Performing Arts Center, where Circle Rep was the resident theater company.

alongside the Philadelphia Orchestra and the New York City Ballet;
- at Lucille Lortel's White Barn Theater in Connecticut;
- the New York premiere at Circle Rep in the fall;
- and finally, a transfer to Broadway, where although it played only sixty-four performances at the Longacre Theater, earned us Tony nominations for Best Play and Best Director for 1983.

This was followed by John Malkovich's award-winning revival of *Balm in Gilead*, a co-production of Circle Rep and the Steppenwolf Theater Company, in May of 1984. It played 109 performances before transferring to the Minetta Lane Theater for an extended commercial Off-Broadway run of 136 more. Lanford, as usual, was inspired by his own success, so he had accumulated a lot to be inspired by in the summer of 1984, when he turned his attention back to *A Tale Told*. I look forward to sharing more details of these adventures and the other successful productions at Circle Rep (including Sam Shepard's long-running hit, *Fool for* Love, and William M. Hoffman's groundbreaking Best Play of 1985, *As Is*) but they are a digression from our present subject, the development of the Talley plays. So I'll get to them in the final chapters.

A New Old Play

In *Talley & Son*, several of the structural improvements were fundamental, telling the tale in a more forceful way. First among these is Lanford's decision to begin the play with Timmy's ghost, who tells the audience in the first line:

> "America won the Second World War today. It'll be August next year before anybody knows it."

Timmy sets the stage for the scale of a drama that is meant to address huge themes, bookmarking a time in history. He also serves as the narrator for the play, clarifying what is happening and making coherent what had seemed a tumbling muddle of events. He forthrightly tells us:

> "I'm a little early here. This is the Fourth of July; I'm due here on the sixth for Granddad's funeral. I've got my pass in my pocket. And while I'm here we're gonna have this big powwow about the family business. See, Harley Campbell and Dad own this garment factory, Talley & Son. Now some big company's wantin' to buy us out."

Bingo! The audience is now up to speed at the beginning of the play on what previously had to be unearthed from layers of details somewhere in the middle of the first act. Also, he establishes the nature of his being a ghost:

> "Last thing I knew I was bumping along on a stretcher, some guy's got his hand over my eyes. I was yelling, 'I gotta see Dad, man, get me up. Everything going all right, I'm home for the sixth.' I think everything didn't go all right."

Timmy claims his legitimate presence as our narrator, in sharp contrast with the earlier version where he appeared as a silent character throughout the first act, making us wait until the second to learn who he was and why he was here.

The second inspired change was bringing Sally on as the first event of the play. Sally and Lottie's relationship, a core element of the action, is established in the first scene. It is especially vivid to experience Sally's fury about the confrontation between Matt Friedman and her family that has just occurred, with Buddy driving him off the property with a shotgun. If we haven't seen *Talley's Folly*, we are filled in on everything we need to know about what will happen down at the boathouse. If we have seen the earlier play, we are gratified to be reminded of the details that set up the circumstances of *Talley's Folly*. Everyone was delighted with Sally's appearance in *A Tale Told;* she brought on stage with her the light and charm of that beloved Valentine waltz-of-a-love story. Unfortunately, she appeared only at the end of the play. Now Lanford saw the wisdom of bringing her on at the beginning, so the doings up at the Talley house frame the events down at the boathouse. It is much more dramatic to learn of the confrontation with Matt from Sally and Lottie than to be filled in when Buddy recounts the encounter to Eldon. It provides a third perspective of the event Matt describes so humorously in *Talley's Folly*.

Only after setting these moorings for the play does the tumultuous action that began *A Tale Told* begin to unfurl. So now, the bustle of giving Buddy Christmas in July has a context and Viola's desperate calling for Eldon takes the action to the next level. Meanwhile, Timmy has been able to comment on who these people are and their relationship to him, so we are introduced to the large cast with effortless clarity.

Since I was on sabbatical, I did not play a role in making the changes to the script that I admire so much. Bruce McCarty, a young actor at Circle Rep who appeared in the hit revival of *Balm in Gilead*, was especially inspiring to Lanford. Bruce spent a good deal of the summer of 1984 in Sag Harbor, hired by Lanford as a research assistant. Fueled by Bruce's inspiration, Lanford re-imagined the third tale of the Talleys. It is a substantially different and better play; hence, the necessity of a new title, *Talley & Son*. The play is dedicated to Bruce.

The Last of the Talleys

Talley & Son unfolds like a flower; gone is the jumbled exposition hidden behind tumultuous bits of action. In his revision, Lanford wrote as perfect a play as exists in his canon. The characters are enriched. New humor is injected. More emotion is evoked. Eldon is especially well re-imagined, with new shades totally absent from the earlier script. Now it is clear from his behavior and his suggestive joking that he has a randy streak that makes Mr. Talley's accusations about his youth seem right on target. The rapport between Eldon and Lottie is deepened, so that now they have layers of a brother-sister relationship that is close yet contrary. Lottie's story of running away from the tyrannical Mr. Talley to find meaning in her life by becoming a social worker is now well defined. When her independence required her to earn a living, she took a job at a watch factory, where she acquired the radium poisoning that is now killing her. These facts are no different from before, but they are expressed with clarity and compassion. Because we see Eldon's concern for her and his futile attempts to reach his unforgiving father, we discover genuine sympathy for him, whereas previously his character seemed somewhat opaque.

Even Viola's character has been given new shadings that make her come into focus as a tragic, yet longsuffering victim of the affluent Talleys. It is now believable that she and Eldon had an affair in the distant past and that Avalaine is the product of their tryst. As a result, when Avalaine appears with her threats to expose Eldon unless he compensates her with rewards commensurate with her heritage as half a Talley, it no longer reeks of melodramatic plotting, but seems a pitiable cry of help.

The debate over the conglomerate's offer to buy out the garment factory also has been sharpened and builds convincingly to an emotional climax, as Harley and Eldon engage in a mighty struggle with high stakes for them both. The additions of Timmy and Buddy to the argument, as well as Mr. Talley's stinging comments, endow the conflict with dimensions that intrigue us and draw us in, rather than impatiently enduring their quarrel.

By spreading Timmy's monologues in smaller pieces throughout the play, we look forward to the insight his character throws on the proceedings, instead of wondering whether he'll ever shut up so the action can continue.

The second act contains even more improvements in the character of Eldon. His past transgressions are clearer in the text, openly stated instead of only hinted. As a result, the conflict with Netta is also clarified, making her announcement she'll be moving unto Timmy's room (after learning of his death and Eldon's infidelity) fully justified.

But the biggest changes are in the plot, which affect how we perceive the characters. First, Eldon outfoxes Old Man Talley in the long run by exercising a Power of Attorney, which allows him to trade off the garment factory to Harley to dispose of as he likes, in exchange for Harley's minor holdings in the Talley-owned bank. Thereby, he pulls a reversal on Mr. Talley that shows the acorn didn't fall far from the oak. Since Buddy had no interest in the factory, he'll now be eligible for a position at the bank, a goal he's always wanted. This changes our estimation of Eldon significantly: no longer a wimp, but a principled man who has been restrained only out of respect for his father until he is double-crossed.

Secondly, the complex choreography of Sally's return to the house while Eldon is locking the doors now ends with him discovering her just as she's about to leave with her suitcase. He guesses that she's running off to marry Matt. Discreetly, he doesn't tell her about Timmy's death, but instead embraces her and wishes her well. So Sally leaves with her father's blessing, which changes completely how we feel about Eldon. It also gives a rather abrasive portrait of a treacherous family a warm, forgiving outcome, which helps to unify it with the joyous ending of *Talley's Folly*.

Too Late to Triumph

By 1985, Talley-mania had faded. It was impossible to rekindle the anticipation that awaited the third play three years before. There would be no transfer to Broadway, even though I think *Talley & Son* ended up the most accomplished play of the trilogy.

In July, we mounted our production of *Talley & Son* at our summer home in Saratoga. The previous summer, we discovered that by previewing *Angels Fall* up there, it helped us to get the production in prime form for a debut in New York at Circle Rep. We hoped to repeat that pattern and we did so successfully. This production featured a couple of cast changes that improved an already lovely ensemble. Robert MacNaughton, who played the lead in our production of Jim Leonard's *The Diviners* and went on to play the older brother in Stephen Spielberg's fabled film *E.T.*, took up the role of

Timmy, the ghostly narrator of the play, which he played to eerie perfection, heartbreakingly too young to die. The role of Eldon was assumed by handsome film star Farley Granger (famed for Alfred Hitchcock's *Strangers on a Train* and *Rope*) who brought just the right mix of sensitivity and character flaws to the role. Lindsey Ginter took up a new stage name as Lindsey Richardson and he moved up to become a sterling Buddy. A former Circle Rep intern, Steve Decker, assumed Lindsey's role as Emmet. A more mature Laura Hughes moved up from the role of Avalaine to become our new Olive and she was replaced as Avalaine by Julie Bargeron. We lost the invaluable Fritz Weaver to conflicting engagements, but our own expert character actor Edward Seamon more than adequately filled those considerably large slippers. We also lost the irreplaceable Jimmie Ray Weeks as Harley, but Richard Backus proved solid in the part. In the much-improved role of the washerwoman, Viola, we now had the services of Lisa Emery, one of my favorite actresses.

Helen Stenborg grew magnificently in the role of Netta and Trish Hawkins continued to radiate as Sally, now in a much-improved part. And in Saratoga, we still had Elizabeth Sturges' luminous performance as Lottie. Working during the green summer of Saratoga Springs at their Little Theater (renamed The John Housman) was positively a joy. We played only two weeks, but it was a great way to break in a production. We always left there happier and more confident as we took on New York. My two-year sabbatical was ending and, refreshed, I was ready to return to Circle Rep for the sixteenth season, to resume my duties as Artistic Director.

Same Song, Second Verse

There was one wrinkle in bringing the production to Circle Rep. Elizabeth Sturges was pregnant, and with a difficult history of miscarriages, she was required to have complete bed rest to assure a safe delivery. We called on our trusty Joyce Reehling, who played Olive in *A Tale Told* at the Taper, to assume this pivotal part, the heroine of the play. She took over with only a three-day notice. Our assistant stage manager went to her apartment and helped her learn the lines. The next day she ran through the first act with the cast and on the third day, the second act. We went directly into tech rehearsals and then, previews. The physical staging for Lottie is uncomplicated; she mainly sits on the edge of the action at her table by the French doors, playing solitaire. And Joyce adored the character of Lottie; it's one of her favorite roles.

As for our new *Talley & Son,* one of the most frustrating things about this colorful butterfly emerging from its chrysalis was how little the critics noticed the transformation. Those who liked the play initially saw no reason for changes and couldn't identify what changes had been made. For those who didn't like it to begin with, the alterations were insufficient to change their opinions.

The New York Times, October 23, 1985 (Frank Rich):

"Wilson's revised and improved drama is, for much of its length, amusing entertainment, especially as performed by a crack Circle Rep cast. Farley Granger is superb. [But] the melodramatics are flimsily managed. Still, for all the flaws that remain, the improvements are real. What was a dull, superficial play is now a superficial play that clicks along smartly. In addition to tightening, focusing, and clarifying, Wilson has added a goodly share of funny lines. Seamon is a hilarious monster. Director Mason has also helped by lightening the production's tone. The large company is mostly exemplary. Along with outstanding contributions made by Granger, Seamon, and Reehling, there is a lovely performance from Robert MacNaughton, [who] uncovers a sweet center for his spectral role. Even so, the honorable time may have come for Mr. Wilson to give up the ghost."

The New York Times, October 27, 1985 (Mel Gussow):

"In Wilson's richly textured cycle of plays about the Talleys, generations of one family dominate a town and its inhabitants. The revisions have given *Talley & Son* a greater cogency. Eldon now has a clearer line of motivation, aided by the casting of Farley Granger. He brings to his personification a certain dignity. In the evening's other pivotal role, Joyce Reehling artfully conveys her character's order of priorities. MacNaughton instills [his ghost] with a youthful sense of idealism."

New York Magazine, November 4, 1985 (John Simon):
"Having rather liked the original version, I was not much on the lookout for improvements, though improvements, I sense, there are. Mainly, the ghost of Timmy seems now better integrated into the action of the play. Wilson's strength is in extracting the extraordinary from the ordinary, and making it psychologically and dramatically plausible. Mason has a knack of making Wilson's lives look even more lived-in. It is a pleasure to watch mostly good actors deployed over the stage with a canny strategy and to hear the rhythms and dynamics of discourse provide an actual concert."

The New Yorker, November 4, 1985 (Edith Oliver):
"When I first saw *A Tale Told,* I thought it the most accomplished of Wilson's plays; and now, revised and renamed *Talley & Son,* it still seems so. I didn't notice any drastic revisions, by the way – nor do I feel the need for any. The new production is as satisfying as the original one was. I admired Seamon, and the presence of Granger adds greatly to the performance as a whole. Reehling is very good, and so is MacNaughton. The flawless direction is by Mason."

In the spring of 1986, the *Village Voice* awarded Obies for Outstanding Performances to both Farley Granger and Helen Stenborg. It was gratifying to see them rewarded for their artistry.

Plays Not Written

It's a shame Lanford did not continue the cycle of plays he envisioned. Perhaps the reviewers who declared they'd had enough of the Talleys discouraged him from seeing it through. Terrence McNally wrote as a joke in *It's Only a Play*: "Oh, everyone's sick of the Talleys!" That probably hit the target more painfully than the responses of a few critics, even though chief among them were Frank Rich and Walter Kerr of *The New York Times*.

I think it's more likely that Lanford himself grew tired of writing about them. Revising the third play in the series proved a difficult challenge and when his efforts were not rewarded, it was disheartening. His motivation for following through was diminished by his sense of writing from obligation, rather than inspiration.

I regret that the publicity attendant upon our success with the first two plays led us to discussing Lanford's prospective epic journey. The initial excitement the press expressed about the promise of a five-play cycle raised a high bar, hailing it as a bold plan unequaled in American drama. It was a lot to live up to.

The final play that was to center on ex-slaves constructing the Talley house just after the Civil War never came clearly into focus. Lanford wanted to write it in an outrageous vaudeville style, reflecting the period. It was hard to imagine how this would tie up the long saga as he described it.

But I am especially sorry he never wrote the play about Uncle Whistler following the First World War. In that play, we would have seen the devastation to the patriarch, Calvin Talley, caused by the loss of his favored son, Stuart. He is the son referred to in the company name "Talley & Son," whose death as a doughboy left Eldon always trying to measure up to his heroic older brother. It was easy to imagine Barney Hughes as Uncle Whistler, singing and whistling "Una furtiva lagrima!" as he built his folly down by the river.

Sadly, it was not to be.

Barney Hughes passed away in 2006 and five years later, in a cruel twist of fate, both Helen Stenborg and Farley Granger died in the same week as Lanford. We must be content with the three plays we have.

Part Five
Edge Of The Galaxy

Chapter 16
An Inflationary Epoch

At the beginning of time as we know it, in the first almost infinitely small fraction of a second, Professor Andrei Linde theorizes an instantaneous expansion followed the Big Bang. In March of 2014, that theory was confirmed. He postulated that within the first flash of the cosmos, a sudden and massive expansion occurred that involved matter traveling faster than the speed of light for the only time in the history of the universe. He called this singular expansion "Inflation."

It's easy to identify when the transcendent years of Circle Rep's history began. Our big bang was a psychedelic awakening that illuminated a vision of dramatic art in the form of a clear-minded dedication to the collaborative nature of the living theater. Circle Rep's arrival was the culmination of a groundswell of fervent creativity that characterized the dawn of off-off-Broadway at the Caffe Cino and La MaMa. Circle Rep was born of a transcendent vision from its very inception.

But in the first flashes of our existence, like Professor Linde's inflationary epoch, our creation escalated infinitely with the inspired concept of presenting two productions in rotating rep of a classic play, Chekhov's *Three Sisters*. Our work on this great play embodied the founding principles of Circle Rep, celebrating simultaneously tradition and experimentation. It was unprecedented.

In the history of a Company that lasted twenty-seven years and changed the American Theater, it's more difficult to pinpoint precisely when those transcendent years faded and were succeeded by seasons that could no longer be described that way.

There is no correlation between the theater's transcendence and our success. The magical aura of Circle Rep was apparent even when we had disasters like *Lulu* or bombs like *In the Recovery Lounge*. Part of the "different experience" of seeing a play at Circle Rep was the way we transformed our theater space for each production. An audience never knew what to expect. In the eleventh season (1979–80), we stopped changing the theater's configuration and settled on a proscenium arrangement with the stage on the Seventh Avenue side, adjacent to the backstage dressing rooms. The decision was made because the strain on our technical staff was considerable and we had explored every possible arrangement of the space. We felt it was an artistic challenge to settle on one formation. In later years, the theater continued to have success in discovering new playwrights and directors, as well as contributing commercial transfers both on and off Broadway. But there was a gradual change during which motivations began to spring from sources other than the vision that guided us through the first half of our existence. One could feel bit by bit that things were changing, but exactly *how* has to be determined by hindsight.

By the time we produced a beautifully revised and handsomely mounted production of *Talley & Son* in 1985, it was apparent that Circle Rep was no longer the magical place it had been. Analyzing that transition from the perspective of thirty years, 1982 emerges as a pivotal year, after which, although Circle Rep continued to enjoy success for another fourteen years and continued to make important contributions to the New York Theater, *something* had changed.

The transition began with a return to a neglected concept: playing a repertory season of great plays. The decision to present *Hamlet* and *Mary Stuart* in rotating rep echoed that inflationary moment of inspiration from our first season. It revitalized the exalted concept of creating life on stage within classic scripts. This strategy proved so bracing that we repeated the formula over the next two seasons: *Twelfth Night* paired with *The Beaver Coat* and then *Richard II* in rep with a new experimental play, *The Great Grandson of Jedediah Kohler*.

I grouped the Talley Cycle together in order to trace the arc of its development. In a similar way, let's look at the journey of Circle Rep's transformation during the series of classical repertory productions presented from 1979 to 1982.

A Daring Maneuver

Several plays are so large in scope and impact as to pose a supreme challenge. *Hamlet, King Lear, Three Sisters, Long Day's Journey into Night, A Streetcar Named Desire* and *Who's Afraid of Virginia Woolf?* are gigantic plays that demand tremendous vision, extraordinary skill and perseverance to produce. I'm proud I tackled all six of these. In our first season, Circle Rep mounted dual productions of *Three Sisters* in rep and followed with a third production of the great play alternating with *Ghost Sonata*. Returning from our season of rep in California, I wanted to restore Circle Rep's mission of mounting great classics in repertory. I announced a bold plan to present William Shakespeare's *Hamlet* in rotating rep with Friedrich Schiller's *Mary Stuart*. I directed both and they were a paradigm of Circle Rep's recommitment to excellence.

I always hoped one day to find an actor who could embody my concept of *Hamlet,* a play that requires an unusually close collaboration between a director and the player of the eponymous role. William Hurt at the age of twenty-nine offered me that opportunity. William and I had previously worked together in mutual admiration three times: in the productions of *My Life, Ulysses in Traction* and *Fifth of July.* As Shakespeare has told us:

> "There is a tide in the affairs of men, which, taken at the flood, leads on to fortune."

I was determined to seize the moment. Outside of my long-time partnerships with Lanford Wilson and John Lee Beatty, it was the most satisfying collaboration of my artistic career.

I directed *Mary Stuart* for Miss Krause at Eagles Mere twenty years before; I thought by pairing the two plays, we could illustrate the political intrigue in both. I also saw a possibility of another casting coup in Schiller's play. Circle Rep had two artistic queens who vied to be the best: Tanya Berezin and Stephanie Gordon achieved a memorable duet in Lanford's *The Great Nebula in Orion* in our third season. Pitting them as foes was an exciting idea, Tanya as the embattled Queen Elizabeth I and Stephanie as her dangerous rival, Mary Queen of Scots. Being Jewish, my two leading ladies were not typical casting for these legendary icons of British history; but casting is always more about finding what Elia Kazan called "the inner river of experience" and it surged within these two actresses.

I believed classic plays could breathe with vitality if one ignored the traps of respect and tradition that made most productions so boring and dead. I saw *Romeo and Juliet* leap to life in Franco Zefferelli's 1962 Broadway production that starred Judy Dench and John Stride. I saw John Gielgud create thoroughly living people in Sheridan's *School for Scandal*. I had confidence that my approach to creating real life on stage (successful in contemporary plays) could ignite the classics with an urgent present tense, emulating these fine examples. My approach to the two classical plays was to treat them as if they were new scripts. Without any "fancy interpretations," I wanted to present them as though we were the Globe Theater in 1603 and the manuscripts had just been penned. Our actors needed to wear the Elizabethan garments worn by the actors of that year, not costumes; the tones must be in the muted shades that real people wore. This would be a *Hamlet* in starched white ruffs. The male actors needed to grow Jacobean beards; in sympathy with this itchy demand, I grew a beard myself.

When I was nineteen, I memorized the entire text of *Hamlet*, inspired by Sir John Gielgud, who spoke Shakespeare's immortal lines with unmatched richness. In rehearsal, the cast listened to Gielgud's definitive recording of *Hamlet* as a crash course in learning to speak the verse. As we sat and ran the lines for a scene we were about to stage, William Hurt exhibited the fluent skill he mastered in his Julliard training to speak iambic pentameter with grace and authority. But once we were on our feet, his attention turned to bringing

Hamlet's circumstances to life in organic impulses. Attention to the verse was secondary to his incarnation of Hamlet's soul.

If ever there was an actor who could make an audience believe he was real and not acting, it was William Hurt. We took the play beat by beat, imagining the fictional circumstances as if they were our own. I surrounded Bill with Circle Rep actors in synch with this approach: Lindsay Crouse was an Ophelia distraught by the behavior of her boyfriend. Michael Ayr's Laertes was a convivial brother, envious of the privileged guy above him. Burke Pearson's Polonius was a well-meaning advisor over his head in a job beyond his capacity. Charles Harper was Reynaldo, a loyal servant in the household who reared the children in the absence of a proper mother, who must have died years before. Roger Chapman and Ken Kliban were Hamlet's college buddies, with the easy relationship of fraternity brothers (no lurking, hidden, snarky motives to be seen). And Tim Shelton was the staunch best friend that Hamlet could "wear in his heart of hearts" as he does Horatio.

To endow the production with a sense of royalty, I cast Academy Award-winning Beatrice Straight, herself an heiress from a distinguished American lineage, as Gertrude, a mother more concerned with keeping her new husband happy in bed than with indulging an embarrassing son. Finally, Douglass Watson, an electrifying actor with a ton of classical experience, played Claudius, the second-largest role in Shakespeare's canon and as apparently innocent of wrongdoing as Richard Nixon tried to appear.

Of course, there are a multitude of supporting parts in *Hamlet* and many of them were filled to perfection. Elegant Bruce Grey made a stylish Osric, Jack Davidson (who loved acting more than anyone I ever worked with) was a natural for the Player King, with Elizabeth Sturges as his wife and co-star. Jack also doubled as the philosophic Gravedigger. Even the pages and the Lady-in-waiting were filled with the excellent actors Bruce McCarty, Greg Germann and Mollie Collison.

Only the soldiers on the battlement at the beginning of the play were less than all one could wish for. Tony Tenuta, Gary Berner and

William Carr were a bit cowed by the responsibility of setting up the circumstances of the play, keeping watch on a cold and bitter night, spooked by the apparition they'd seen on several watches. And as both the Ghost of Hamlet's Father and Fortinbras at the end of the play, Rob Thirkield was perhaps a bit stiff.

But if an audience could tolerate the shaky opening scene until the entrance of the court, the play became an adventurous, living experience of Shakespeare. In the court scene, Hamlet is not the only character in black, as in the traditional approach. Instead, the scene represented the occasion in which Claudius and Gertrude marked the end of the official period of mourning for the late king by divesting their black cloaks for more colorful accessories, while urging Hamlet to do likewise. After the King and Queen left the stage with their entourage, Hamlet began his famous soliloquy "O that this too, too solid flesh would melt" lying flat on his back. This very private lamentation gave immediate notice that this was a *Hamlet* unlike any predecessor.

Mounting the two plays in rotating repertory was not only a daring move artistically for a Company known for creating new work, it was a massive undertaking for a theater of 160 seats. The cast of twenty-two actors, supplemented in the play-within-the-play scene by four live musicians, gave an audience an almost one-on-one encounter with Shakespeare's tragedy. Rarely had any audience experienced the play with this degree of intimacy. Our tiny backstage dressing rooms were crammed with teeming humanity, so we made additional dressing room space in the basement.

In addition to the casting I've already related, many of the actors also played important roles in *Mary Stuart*. While neither Tanya nor Stephanie appeared in *Hamlet*, and neither Beatrice, Lindsay nor Douglass doubled in *Mary Stuart*, William Hurt relished playing alternate nights in the small but touching role of Davison, secretary to the Queen, who must decide what to do with the warrant for Mary's execution that Elizabeth has thrust into his hands. It was both comic and tragic, and Bill made the most of it. Tanya recalls her scene with him as one of the most exciting she has ever played; it was always different, always unpredictably dangerous and absolutely thrilling. Tim Shelton went from Horatio to Leicester, Queen Elizabeth's favorite, whom she called Robin, a master of the intrigue at Westminster Palace and a pivotal figure in the conflict over Mary's fate. Ken Kliban stepped up from Guildenstern to the weighty prosecutor of the Scottish Queen, Lord Burleigh. Michael Ayr's fiery and grieving Laertes fueled that passion into the tempestuous young Mortimer. Rob Thirkield played Talbot, the Earl of Shrewsbury, England's Keeper of the Seal and a bedrock of integrity. Elizabeth Sturges stepped up to the satisfying role of Hanna, Mary's devoted companion, while Burke Pearson left behind the bumbling of Polonius for the sympathetic yet unyielding Paulet, Mary's jailer at Fotheringay Castle. Tony Tenuta, Lindsey Ginter, Charles Harper, Gary Berner, Jack Davidson and Mollie Collison also played supporting roles in *Mary Stuart*, bestowing on them a genuine repertory experience.

 David Jenkins designed the unit set, constructed of rich, dark, highly polished wood, with a flight of stairs at one side leading to a second-level upper platform. The concept was inspired by a medieval architectural feature I observed in Rhodes the previous summer. To the right of the wooden stage was a stone tunnel through which the audience entered the theater space. It was from this tunnel that William Hurt began the existential soliloquy unseen, beginning "To be" in the darkness of the tunnel, then stepping forward into the light on the words: "or not to be." Norman L. Berman composed the original music, which was played by live musicians with Elizabethan instrumentation. Dennis Parichy did the lighting and we experimented with laser light in the ghost scene, at a time when lasers were an innovative technology. I asked Laura Crow to design clothes for the cast in the muted colors of the Jacobean period – clothes, not costumes. In this, I was influenced by a production of *As You Like It* in Berlin by the great director Peter Stein. Laura was rewarded with an Obie Award for her designs, highlighted by her accurate reproductions of the bejeweled gowns of Elizabeth and Mary's signature heart-shaped bonnet. Historically,

Mary went to her execution dressed in scarlet, but pleading artistic license, I wanted Mary to go to her death in pure white, like a bride. Stephanie was stunning in her final scene.

Hamlet is a lengthy play – it is Shakespeare's longest – so we performed it with two intermissions. Our first act ended with Hamlet setting "The Mouse Trap":

"The play's the thing
Wherein I'll catch the conscience of the king!"

The second act ended with Hamlet's banishment to England and his final soliloquy:

"O, from this time forth,
My thoughts be bloody or be nothing worth!"

Claudius, Laertes, Gertrude and Ophelia dominate more than half of the final act, until Hamlet returns in the gravedigger's scene, Ophelia's funeral, and the final duel with Laertes.

The duel fought with rapier and dagger in the climactic scene of *Hamlet* requires not only expert swordsmanship, a skill that both William Hurt and Michael Ayr possessed; it also required a fight choreographer who could stage the fight in an intimate arena, putting the front rows of the audience ringside to the dangerous action. Our audience would smell the sweat of the fighters when Hamlet uses Gertrude's scarf to mop his brow. Once again, I turned to the foremost fight choreographer of our time, B.H. Barry. He attended rehearsals from early on and made use of the acting nuances he saw developing in William's and Michael's characterizations to utilize in the choreography. The result was the most thrilling duel I've ever seen and I'd bet it has never been surpassed. I recognize this hardly can be proved over the march of centuries; but the intimacy of the fight, combined with the imaginative brilliance of B.H. Barry and his ingenious collaborators, William Hurt, Michael Ayr,

Douglass Watson and the company of courtiers, are a combination of factors likely unparalleled in previous productions.

Let me describe the event, so you may judge for yourself if you've ever seen anything like it. The duel was fought with the Elizabethan weapons rapiers and daggers, as specified in the text, which are often replaced in productions with single foils. Hamlet actually had a beard as noted in the script. The two combatants removed their ruffs and doublets, stripping down to their tights and opened shirts. The main area of the stage, only inches from the front row, was cleared to give the contestants room and the area was surrounded upstage by courtiers eager to see the fight. Up a flight of stairs to the right of the action, a stairway connected the combat arena to an upper platform, where the thrones of the King and Queen sat on the left, giving them a bird's eye view of the duel, premium seats indeed. The action proceeded as Shakespeare describes it, Hamlet scoring a hit on the first exchange, and Claudius toasting his stepson. The second round, more heated, ends with Hamlet's second hit, followed by the Queen descending the stairs to offer Hamlet her handkerchief and a drink of wine, which Hamlet delays accepting. She remains below for the third round, in which the intensity of the duel is escalated by Hamlet's urging Laertes to fight harder and ends in a draw. As Hamlet turns to take the drink his mother offers (which Claudius has revealed contains poison that Gertrude has already imbibed), Laertes suddenly attacks his unprepared adversary, nicking him with his dagger, drawing blood. Incensed, Hamlet wrestles Laertes' weapons from him, while Laertes is left to pick up Hamlet's. The intense hand-to-hand combat ends with Hamlet wounding Laertes with the dagger, who falls just as the Queen's attendants rush to catch her collapse to the floor, dying from the poisoned cup. Laertes confesses that Hamlet has been fatally wounded with the poisoned dagger, and that Claudius is to blame for the treachery. Hamlet exclaims:

"The point envenomed too!"

And he slowly climbs the stairs on the right that led up to the King's throne across the stage.

"Then venom to thy work."

And Hamlet, in an astonishing stage illusion, throws the dagger across the upper stage, where Claudius, grasping the blade of the knife in his stomach, cries out:

"O, yet defend me, friends; I am but hurt."

On the final word, the King lurches forward, plunging headfirst from the stage above, caught at the last moment by courtiers below before he hits the floor. Hamlet runs down to finish him off with the poisoned cup and, gagging with blood and poisoned wine, Claudius crawls toward the audience, collapsing only inches from the front row.

It is the only production of Shakespeare I've ever seen in which some in the audience were sobbing audibly at the Prince of Denmark's death, tears fueled by Shakespeare's powerfully moving epitaph,

"Good night, sweet prince, and flights of angels sing thee
to thy rest."

Hamlet opened at Circle Repertory Company December 12, 1979, followed by *Mary Stuart* on December 13th. They played in rep for a total of ninety-two performances.

Most of the critics, who arrived at Circle Rep after our first five formative years, were surprised by our turn to the classics. Unaware of the classical foundation of our theater, they saw us as devoted to discovering new plays. To an extent, they were mystified by our apparent change of course. *Hamlet* received carefully restrained reviews (generally favorable, with the exception of John Simon, who left at the second intermission). But *Mary Stuart* was received with abundant praise; it was as if they were re-discovering a forgotten treasure. I will quote only two reviews, the first at some length:

The New York Times, December 14, 1979 (Mel Gussow):
"Mason's version of *Mary Stuart* is an intelligent and direct encounter with this monumental historical tragedy. His *Hamlet* is curious, but never less than intriguing. In each case, the director underscores the intimacy of the drama. But Mason has not neglected the panoply or the language. With some exceptions, the actors are able to communicate the poetry of Shakespeare and Schiller. The paired plays share a historical period, which means they are equally at home on David Jenkin's ingenious two-level set. Laura Crow's costumes add opulence to both productions. In Miss Gordon's authoritative performance, Mary remains, first of all, noble. In direct contrast, Miss Berezin's Elizabeth is forbidding, occasionally vulgar, but in common with her rival, always a queen. Their meeting is surely one of the most powerful scenes in dramatic literature. The three principal men in their orbit are also given persuasive performances by Ken Kliban, Timothy Shelton, and Michael Ayr. This *Hamlet* – and the attribution should be divided between the director and the actor – is the most physicalized within my memory. Mason is treating *Hamlet* as a play about families and about the male-pair bonding. Among other things, Mr. Hurt is a very amusing and prankish Hamlet, the witty superior of all the less knowing knights of the realm. He delivers his soliloquys with quiet conviction, as deeply personal confidences. In the best sense, the actor is unpredictable. There are also fine performances from Douglass Watson, Beatrice Straight, Lindsay Crouse, and Michael Ayr. However, in this production, it is easy to keep one's eyes on Hamlet. The Circle's *Mary Stuart*

is admirable, its *Hamlet* is unusual. Together in repertory, they reveal an adventuresome side to this valued company."

The Record, December 14, 1979 (Emory Lewis on *Hamlet*):
"The revival of the Shakespearean classic by Circle Repertory Company is alive – original, quivering, urgent. Mason sees the play in a fresh, new light: as a look at the new humanism rising out of the ashes of feudalism. William Hurt is the best Hamlet within memory. He is surrounded by a good cast, many of whom also play roles in *Mary Stuart*. Beatrice Straight and Douglass Watson play [their roles] as passionate people. Lindsay Crouse is an uncommonly good Ophelia. Michael Ayr is an arresting Laertes, and his duel with Hamlet is brilliant. B.H. Barry, who staged the fight, rates plaudits. The scene has never been done with such fire and finesse."

The repertory fare was followed within a month by our Broadway production of *Talley's Folly*, so Circle Rep was entering the peak of recognition for our artistic excellence. Within a twelve-month period, we presented two new plays by Sam Shepard and Lanford Wilson that won Pulitzer Prizes; a new play by the latest dramatic sensation, David Mamet; new work by William Mastrosimone and Milan Stitt; and a classical repertoire that starred William Hurt, Beatrice Straight and Lindsay Crouse.

Our eleventh season had other highlights, covered in the following chapter. But to illustrate the gradual change at Circle Rep, let's look at the classical repertory presentations the following two seasons. The contrasts are instructive.

Returning to Rep

A year later, within a month of opening *Fifth of July* on Broadway, we presented *Twelfth Night* in rep with Gerhart Hauptman's *The Beaver Coat*. The desire to continue to challenge ourselves with a classic repertory was commendable, but in retrospect, the inspiration for choosing these two plays pales in comparison to our *Hamlet/Mary Stuart*. In particular, the Hauptman play seems an odd choice. It premiered in Berlin in 1893, but it's a fair assumption that it had not been seen in New York since the turn of the century. We had already decided on *Twelfth Night* and were searching for something to accompany it. Our literary staff was always on the lookout for challenging plays from the world repertoire and somehow, *The Beaver Coat* caught the attention of Milan Stitt and Rod Marriott, who recommended we give it a Friday reading. Our playwright/director John Bishop loved its dark satire and was excited about the prospect of directing. Additionally, it presented Tanya with another plum part: she was ideal casting for the starring role of Frau Wolf, a sort of comic Mother Courage who, through her ingenuity, moves up in the world, stealing, lying and cheating her way to respectability.

David Mamet directed his own play *Reunion* to open our previous season (which I'll describe in the following chapter) and he was eager to try his hand at a classic. When he suggested *Twelfth Night*, I leapt at the opportunity to repeat the role that provided my greatest success as an actor twenty years before at Eagles Mere: the Puritan steward, Malvolio. I learned a great deal about acting in the interim and I was eager to see if, now that I was of a reasonable age to play the part, I could score in my main stage debut. David was titillated by the prospect of directing the Artistic Director. His wife, Lindsay Crouse, a cornerstone of our acting Company, was ideal casting for Viola. Trish Hawkins was an easy choice for Olivia and having missed our previous classical venture, she was eager to join us. David also used several other members of the Company: Jake Dengel as Sir Andrew Aguecheek, Robert Lupone as Antonio, Charles Harper as Fabian and Burke Pearson doubled in a couple of small roles, the Sea Captain and a Priest.

For the other principal roles, David brought in actors he knew from Chicago: the delightful Colin Stinton for Feste, the wan W.H. Macy for Sebastian, and the robust Michael Lerner as Sir Toby Belch and the lively Marcell Rosenblatt for Maria. The important romantic lead of the love-struck count Orsino went to Jay O. Sanders, who recently joined us in *Buried Child*. A couple of handsome interns, Rob Gomes and David Pillard, were the servants Curio and Valentine.

The unconventional set (a mish-mash of different concepts) was designed by Fred Kolouch; the costumes, totally eclectic in period and style, were designed by Clifford Capone. Only our reliable Dennis Parichy was a Circle regular, designing the lights. Peter Nels, an assistant to B.H. Barry, staged the comic fights.

For *The Beaver Coat,* John Bishop added Tom Brennan and William Severs, while Jane Fleiss and Carol Wade played the two daughters. Several actors again had the pleasure of playing in true repertory. Charles Harper went from Fabian to the part of Motes, while Marcell Ronseblatt went from playing Maria to Frau Motes. Colin Stinton rotated between Feste and Glasenapp, while Jake Dengel and W.H. Macy were Krueger and Dr. Fleischer, respectively; and Burke Pearson played the more substantial role of Judge Wehrhahn. The set was again by Fred Kolouch, costumes by Clifford Capone and the lights by Dennis Parichy.

I can't report much about the rehearsals for *Beaver Coat* since I had my hands full playing Malvolio; but I can describe the fascinating journey we took through David's novel approach to *Twelfth Night*. David's concept was that the play should be done without regard for period or style. The set was a generic Mediterranean locale, without any distinguishing characteristics that might imply a particular time. The director wanted the costumes to be expressive of the characters, regardless of period. So, for example, as Malvolio, I was dressed in tails and top hat in the beginning, only to change into golfing knickers and a flat cap from the 20s when remaking my image to please Olivia. Some characters wore contemporary clothes, others clothes from the John Philip Sousa period of Americana. It was a strange concept, but as actors, we could have cared less; we were immersed in creating the characters that could speak this lovely language and experience these fantastical identity mix-ups.

Picking up on the fact that at Circle Rep the actors were accustomed to knowing their lines ahead of rehearsal, David asked that we memorize our whole parts. We then spent almost a week sitting around a table, speaking the play to each other, while David floated around the group, pausing occasionally to whisper an image in somebody's ear. He whispered to me: "You are the Prime Minister. Keep order." Or to Olivia, when Viola comes seeking an audience to plead Orsino's case, "She's just another Jehovah's Witness knocking on your door." Good images!

After we spent a week doing this, David suddenly announced that we were going to get up on our feet and run through the *whole play*. I was stunned. No moment-by-moment preparation; we were being tossed into the sea and told to swim. I think there was a sense of panic among the cast, but we did as we were told. We could move anywhere we liked in relation to the action, pursuing the objectives we'd defined around the table and *play* the play. It was completely contrary to the way I direct and contrary to any rehearsal procedure any of us had known. Well, the experience was exhilarating. Completely free to pursue our objectives as characters, we were swept along by the magic of the play. Instead of the disaster we dreaded, we were transported by rampant creativity. It was thrilling the way the script catapulted into life. We rehearsed this way for another week, each run-through growing richer and more complex. It was the most invigorating investigation of a play I'd experienced, a revelation of the power of Shakespeare's script to inspire.

Then came a terrible moment of reckoning. With the cast at a zenith of creativity, David solemnly announced that he was now going to *block* our stage traffic. He told us his image of the movement in the production was to be like a Swiss clock, mechanical and artificial. True to his word, every step was dictated and the rush of creativity that characterized our work to that point was drained by consternation and resentment at being physically manipulated. At one point, David asked me to step forward, say a line and then step back two steps. I protested, "Tell me where you want be to be and I'll go there. But I can find no motivation for backing up after

I've spoken." Little by little, as we saw our creativity being stomped beneath the director's dictatorial boots, the cast grew increasingly resentful. I'm not putting that strongly enough: to a person, we *hated* it. Soon we were united by one thing: we all despised our director, even Lindsay, who was married to him. But our hatred of David's hijacking of our exuberant creativity had the effect of uniting the cast. In self-defense, we had only each other to rely upon. Thus, the cast merged into a phenomenal ensemble, united not by a love of sharing the work, but by an abhorrence of being robbed of that experience. Being in the production was a mixed bag. It was delightful to share the experience of Shakespeare's lovely masterpiece with an audience, buoyed up and supported by our fellow actors; but at the same time, there was sadness beneath our playing, knowing how much better we *might* have been if our director had stuck to the creative course he started with. The transcendent joy that defined the experience of playing *Hamlet* and *Mary Stuart* was absent.

As for *The Beaver Coat,* the most memorable event was a terrible accident. In one performance, Burke Pearson, playing the Judge, banged his hand down on a table to emphasize his fury and the spike of a spindle among his papers pierced it, penetrating his palm straight through. Fortunately, the stabbing went through the soft part of his hand between two finger ligaments, causing no serious damage. A doctor in the house bound up the wound. As horrible as the accident was, Burke valiantly continued his performance. Afterwards, our stage managers rushed him to St. Vincent's Hospital, only a few blocks uptown and the wound was professionally treated and dressed. The show must go on and it did. Burke told me that in contrast to the experience of *Twelfth Night,* working with John Bishop was wonderful. He was a director who valued actors' contributions and welcomed whatever the actors brought to their roles. John's production of the play was a straightforward retelling of this social satire, set in the Victorian era. We commissioned *Village Voice* critic Michael Feingold to do a new translation, which was praised for its colloquial tone.

The plot deals with a rich squire who is robbed twice – first of several cords of firewood and then of an expensive beaver coat. The engineer of the thievery is Frau Wolf, an unprincipled but crafty washerwoman in his household. A judge who investigates the case is as blind as he is smug. He refuses to consider Frau Wolf a suspect or to listen to her attempts to incriminate others. Influenced by a scalawag named Motes, the most hated man in town, he casts suspicion on a most unlikely suspect, a civic-spirited doctor. But the doctor is exonerated, so the play ends without anything being solved. Hauptman (a Nobel Prize winner) lays this miscarriage of justice squarely on the ineptitude of the town's bureaucracy.

Shakespeare's *Twelfth Night* opened at Circle Rep on December 12, 1980 and played thirty-two performances, with *The Beaver Coat* joining the repertory a month into the run of *Twelfth Night*, opening on January 11, 1981 for thirty-five performances, with both productions closing February 12, 1981. Here are two reviews:

The New York Times, December 17, 1980 (Mel Gussow on *Twelfth Night*):

"Mamet's lighthearted *Twelfth Night* features two outstanding Shakespearean performances – by Lindsay Crouse as Viola and by Colin Stinton as Feste. Stinton is such an articulate and engaging performer that one wishes his character had an even fairer share of Shakespeare's choicest speeches. Crouse is a beacon of loveliness; while pretending to be boyish, she magically retains a feminine radiance. Exuding charm along with intelligence, she convincingly becomes the object of all affection. The primary debits of an otherwise enjoyable show are Clifford Capone's capricious costumes. Trish Hawkins is a vivacious Olivia, and W.H. Macy is bedazzled but eager as Sebastian. The scenes among the three of them are both antic and romantic. Mason is funny and properly fussy, although he lacks the pyrotechnic comic dexterity of a Brian Bedford. Mason's Malvolio is a man of high standards, sincere intentions, and pinched emotions. When he returns, riotously cross-gartered, this austere puritan amusingly abandons his inhibitions and unleashes a grin. Mamet's frothy version proves three things: some artistic directors can easily double as character actors; contemporary playwrights can be at home directing in Illyria; and Crouse and Stanton are actors to be applauded."

The New York Times, January 13, 1981 (Mel Gussow on *The Beaver Coat*):
"A subversive thieves' comedy. The heartbeat of the play is Frau Wolf, a scheming washerwoman who will not allow herself to be downtrodden. A dynamic and earthy woman, Frau Wolf is a role that seems made to order for that excellent character actress Tanya Berezin. When Bishop's production focuses on her, the evening is in confident hands. The production is hampered by Kolouch's stage design, which is only a slight improvement over his impoverished contribution to *Twelfth Night*. Even with the drawbacks of some performances and the design, *The Beaver Coat* is a worthwhile choice for the Circle and an auspicious addition to the Company's repertory. Colin Stanton, who is an articulate Feste in *Twelfth Night*, enriches his cameo role of the judge's clerk with comic fusses and fidgets. Ken Kliban is an appropriately lumbering galoot as the husband. Tom Brennan has a bluff heartiness as a barge captain, and there is helpful support from William Severs, Jake Dengel and W.H. Macy. At the center of the play, Berezin creates a picture of an extraordinary wheeler-dealer, a woman with no scruples and a mountain of determination."

Okay. Once again, a successful classical rep; on balance, this repertory had merit. But the spell of enchantment Circle Rep previously cast was fading.

A Question of Motive

William Hurt returned to Circle Rep following his film debut in *Altered States* (1980) to play Lord Byron in Romulus Linney's biographical drama *Childe Byron* (described in the following chapter), immediately after *Twelfth Night/Beaver Coat*. He stayed on to go with Circle Rep to the Performing Arts Center at Saratoga Springs in August to repeat *Childe Byron* in rep with Jim Leonard's *The Diviners*, the opening production of our twelfth season. During the time Bill was playing on our stages, two other films opened: *Eyewitness* in February and *Body Heat* in August, the latter of which firmly established William Hurt as a bona-fide A-list film star. But he was having trouble adjusting to Hollywood and the unwelcome attention attached to his success; he was a reluctant movie star.

As I began to plan our repertoire for the thirteenth season, William came to my office. He still smarted over his inability when playing Hamlet to speak Shakespeare's verse while creating a spontaneous life in the part. He wanted another chance to wrestle that dilemma, so he asked me to include a production of *Richard II* in the coming season. It is, of course, a great role, with some of Shakespeare's most eloquent poetry. It gave William an ideal opportunity to resolve his problem. Unfortunately, while I admired the character and the language, the plot itself left me cold. From a director's perspective, there's no real *action* in the play; when faced with opposition, the King merely cedes his kingship to Bolingbroke. When I expressed my reluctance to direct such an uninspiring script, Bill told me his agent, Gene Parseghian, put out an initial "feeler" to Joseph Papp's Public Theater and they were keen to include William in their summer repertoire in Central Park. William wanted to let me have first crack at it. I wasn't about to let Papp steal our homegrown star, so I agreed to include the play in our repertory season. It was easy to rationalize it as providing our artists with whatever they needed to grow.

Richard II presented me with a knotty quandary. I had to find an approach that could stir my creativity. I looked to history for inspiration. *When* had a king voluntarily surrendered his throne, without a struggle and *why* would he do so? If I could find a parallel to stir my artistic vision, I could fulfill my promise to William. Two historic events came to mind. First, there was the Aztec King Montezuma, who surrendered to Hernando Cortez in the belief that the European's arrival was the predicted return of his people's legendary god Quetzalcoatl. The second was the dramatic surrender of the Celtic King Vercingetorix to the superior Roman conqueror, Julius Caesar.

In actuality, Vercingetorix led his Celts in a battle against Caesar in 52 B.C., after which he was, like Richard, imprisoned until he was strangled. Still, it was easy to imagine that Caesar's cultural superiority might have impressed the Celtic King to adopt Roman ways, as Richard is influenced by his Italian advisors Bushy and Green, despised in the play by the English barons. According to Plutarch, Vercingetorix surrendered in dramatic fashion, riding his beautifully adorned horse out of Alesia and around Caesar's camp before dismounting in front of Caesar, stripping himself of his armor and sitting down at his opponent's feet, where he remained motionless until he was taken away. It is this self-dramatizing surrender that seems to echo Richard's:

> "What must the king do now? Must he submit?
> The king shall do it: must he be depos'd?
> The king shall be contented; must he lose
> The name of king? o'God's name, let it go:
> I'll give my jewels for a set of beads,
> My gorgeous palace for a hermitage."

While setting the action of the play in the era of the Roman conquest of Gallic Britain might seem a stretch, it saved me from the more difficult task of smearing a cast of nearly naked actors with body paint to simulate ancient Aztecs. That would have been even more ridiculous.

Having crossed the Rubicon of deciding to see the play through the lens of a period foreign to Shakespeare's vision, I decided to go

The Transcendent Years

all out with a de-constructed version of *Richard II*. In this adaptation, I freely re-arranged the text to throw an audience headlong into an adventurous re-imagining of the play. I began with Act V, Scene v, with Richard already in prison at Pomfret, contemplating how he has come to this low station:

"I have been studying how I may compare
This prison where I live unto the world."

So the story is seen in flashback, as Richard recounts all that has happened to him.

In a Celtic setting, the prophetic John of Gaunt, played by Michael Higgins, is a Druid priest ("Methinks I am a prophet, new inspir'd"), with his ally, the Duchess of Gloucester, as a priestess. Stephanie Gordon, playing the Duchess, emerges from Richard's vision in prison of how it all began and climbs a sacrificial altar bearing snakes to conjure up a prophesy of how Gaunt's son will become king.

In this version, the initial combat between Bolingbroke and Mowbray is fought in the Celtic style, naked and painted blue from head to toe. So, full body make-up was limited to only two actors, rather than the entire cast.

Meanwhile, John Bishop finished an extravagant new comedy with a cast of nineteen actors playing some twenty-four characters. It was a hilarious satire of how the vaunted heroism of the Wild West has been lost in the corporate soul of contemporary American enterprise. He called it *The Great Grandson of Jedediah Kohler* and with a canvas this large, the play invited pairing with a classic in repertory. We did a PiP of the play during the run of *Childe Byron* the previous season, directed by Geoffrey Shlaes. Although I wanted to be responsible for directing both productions, I welcomed the opportunity to co-direct *Jedediah* with my assistant, John Manulus, which might lighten the burden a bit.

Because of the experience of two previous large cast repertories in our small theater (with the economic strain they imposed) and aware that William's status as a movie star rendered the Circle Rep's 160 seats inadequate to the likely demand of his newfound fans, our Executive Director Porter van Zandt negotiated an alternative space to present the two plays. Across New York on 2nd Avenue there was an old burlesque house called the Entermedia Theater with 1143 seats. It had been used for concerts (like Talking Heads in 1978) and pre-Broadway tryouts. Porter negotiated a short-term lease of a month or so and Equity agreed to let us close off the balcony, limiting the capacity to Off-Broadway regulations. Of course, unused seats did nothing to reduce the cavernous nature of the auditorium. The interior of the theater with its vast, ornate proscenium arch was painted dried-blood red.

The Company was energized by the pairing of a new play with a classic and they gamely took to rehearsals with full commitment. Again, I had Lindsay Crouse to play opposite William Hurt in the role of Richard's Queen and Michael Ayr to double as Mowbray and Exton. Others from *Hamlet* were Ed Seamon as the Duke of York; Jacqueline Brooks (who replaced Beatrice as Gertrude) was the Duchess of York; Ken Kliban was both Lord Green and the Abbot of Westminster; Charles Harper was Bushy/Groom; and Jack Davidson was Northumberland.

The previous summer I directed Richard Cox in the premiere of *Foxfire* at the Guthrie in Minneapolis, so I imported him to play Richard's rival and conqueror, Bolingbroke (later Henry IV). Other Circle Rep veterans like Gary Berner, John Dossett, Jimmie Ray Weeks, Lou Liberatore, Roger Chapman and Jonathan Bolt provided able support. In the key role of Hotspur (though far more important in *Henry IV*), I brought back Timothy Busfield from *A Tale Told* in Los Angeles. William Carr, Tim Morse and Ellen Conway played smaller roles in a cast of twenty-one.

Jedediah spans from the 19th century cowboys of Dodge City to 20th century Manhattan in alternating realities. The master of ceremonies in the play is the role of Death, masterfully impersonated by Jake Dengel, who is trying to convince the contemporary Jed, a Madison Avenue advertising executive (Michael Ayr), that he must fulfill the glorious heritage of his great grandfather (Ed Seamon). Death argues that Jed should die heroically in an act of courage by standing up to the corrupt practices of the corporation for which he works. To help persuade Jed of his innately heroic nature, Death conjures up the tale of his grandfather, Jedediah, and his standoff with the gunslingers at the Oak Street Corral. Jed's agency is peopled with dopey portraits of contemporary ineptitude, played by Ken Kliban as Leon, Jed's malapropism-inclined boss, strapping Gary Berner as Shorty, Roger Chapman as Joe and Charles Harper as Wally. Jack Davidson doubled as a client named Jack Beck and as Coach Torsi, a celebrity hired to promote the debut of the product in Las Vegas. The product is a car that transforms into a hydrofoil when it enters a body of water. Of course, the terrible secret of the Espry, as it is called, is that it's disastrously unsafe and will result in the loss of many lives, a detail overlooked for a greedy profit motive. Trish Hawkins played Jed's wife Nancy, an impassioned environmentalist that teams up with William Hurt as Henry Jarvis, a mad scientist who's ready to plant bombs to protest the unsafe product. Meanwhile, all these actors double as the gunslingers of yore, who are conjured up by Death to make his case for heroism, but who prove to be as idiotic and incompetent as their modern counterparts: Ken Kliban as Blake, Gary Berner as Doc, Jonathan Bolt as Graham, William Hurt as Ike McKee and Lou Liberatore as Johnny Two-Deuce. Meanwhile, there is also Jimmie Ray Weeks, who shows up as Jed's Zen-like brother and moves in for a few days. He's on the run from a past haunted by his time in Vietnam and is the only character besides Jed who is conversant with Death. And there is also the leggy dancer Bobbi, who appears in the industrial show promoting the Espry and with whom Jed is having an unheroic affair, played by sexy Katherine Cortez.

I employed Karl Eigsti for the set, who designed *The Woolgatherer* for us two years before. It was a two-level affair, handsome to look at, but caused consternation because it shook with the traffic of twenty actors. The wood of the platforms was moored on a scaffolding of pipes and our interns had to work long hours to transform the set for *Richard* to the set for *Jedediah*. The fact that the set had to change was a factor in its instability. Dennis Parichy designed the lights and Norman Berman came up with a haunting original score that fulfills Richard's request in prison for music that leads us into the flashback. The costumes were by Laura Crow and she had a big job here. Because of setting *Richard* in A.D. 50, the Romanized court of the King, the Queen and Richard's Italian advisors Bushy and Green all wore tunics and togas of the Roman Empire. The Celtic tribes wore coarse leggings and the traditional Celtic torques around their necks. A lot of wigs gave the Celts long hair that flowed to their waists and the King wore a ceremonial mask of gold. The backstage life was itself an adventure, donning wigs, capes and togas.

My concept for *Richard II* was daringly original to say the least and it is to the credit of our Company that they followed me so faithfully on a risky course. But the experimental nature of the production was countered by the conventionality of a traditional proscenium stage. The cavernous auditorium made our spectacle seem small. As we began previews, I realized that an audience's experience of *Richard* under these circumstances was strange and unsatisfying. I knew with a sinking heart that if I allowed the press to see my monumental mistake, it would likely do damage to the careers of my cast, in particular to that of William Hurt. So, I assembled the cast and told them that I had decided not to open *Richard* to the press. The Company was disappointed, but they accepted my judgment.

Shakespeare's *Richard II* began previews on March 10, 1982 at the Entermedia Theater in rep with John Bishop's *The Great Grandson of Jedediah Kohler*, which opened on March 12th. They played a combined thirty-two performances. *Village Voice* critic Erika Munk was annoyed the press wasn't invited to review *Richard*, so she sneaked into a preview and printed a brief but scathing notice, which confirmed the wisdom of my decision not to chance an opening. But a heartening contrary opinion arrived in the mail from a professor at Bergen Community College, Richard Evers:

"I, and my class in Shakespeare, saw your production of *Richard II* last week. I taught my usual lesson on imagery in *Richard* before we went to the Entermedia, but your staging was so exciting, so engrossing that my little imagery lesson flew out of my students' heads as they watched, captivated by your brilliant blocking, your 50 A.D. concept, and your original touches. For them and for me, it was a night to remember. I write this to thank you for bringing such life, such energy, such electricity to this, the most poetic of his plays. I write this out of gratitude for showing my class how Shakespeare plus a creative director can communicate the most wonderful magic. I loved it and cannot stop thinking about it."

We did open *Jedediah* to the critics after playing ten previews, and it was praised warmly. Here are a couple of notices:

The New York Times, March 23, 1982 (Frank Rich):
"In Bishop's new play, you can feel Circle Rep's liberating spirit of adventure. It also proves a striking esthetic departure from the kind of naturalism that has been the company's often distinguished stock in trade. In the end, Bishop's comedy does not pay off, but you have to admire its hard-edged sassiness, its willingness to take chances, and its several dozen funny lines. It is not every play that manages to encompass such diverse phenomena as the Wild West, *Sweet Charity,* the Vietnam War, the Madison Avenue ad game, the Super Bowl, and Florida condominiums. It is not every Circle Rep production that features more than two dozen characters, popping in and out of a two-level abstract set like the cast of a Harold Prince extravaganza. The spirited and cinematically minded staging by Manulis and Mason starts off with a bang. In the large cast, the best work comes from Seamon, Hawkins, Weeks, Hurt, and especially Cortez. Dengel has the right moves, if not always the

highest inspiration. But hit or miss, the company is stretching exuberantly."

The Christian Science Monitor, March 25, 1982 (John Beaufort):
"Circle Rep has fired off a wildly funny broadside of comic iconoclasm. Bishop and his collaborators have created a lampoon on the grand scale. The intricate production, with its rapid continuum of scene changes and flashbacks, has been expertly assembled and ordered by co-directors Manulis and Mason. The Circle Rep Company is in fine comic fettle."

An article in *The New York Times* many years later attributed the monetary losses of this repertory as a major factor in Circle Rep's acquiring a $400,000 deficit, from which we never recovered. I'm not sure it was quite so simple, but whatever the cause, both financially and artistically Circle Rep was losing the special quality that marked its transcendent years. By the end of the thirteenth season, I was exhausted, creatively drained. So I started a two-year sabbatical to relieve myself of my overwhelming responsibilities as artistic director. By the time I returned in 1984, it was clear that Circle Rep had grown stronger, but less enchanted.

Our thirteenth season was also was also the end of Porter van Zandt's tenure as Executive Director. Porter's years at Circle Rep marked the institutionalization of our artistic process, which is a good thing for stability. But that institutionalization also brought the seeds of transformation and the unique nature of theater at Circle Rep changed permanently.

Before we get to the last glow of transcendence that was *Angels Fall,* let's look at the three years we've skipped through in this narrative about the Talley plays and the classical repertory.

Chapter 17
Rings, Moons and Comets

In the spring of 1979, *Voyager* discovered that Jupiter, like Saturn, had rings. In the autumn, Pioneer 11 was the first spacecraft to visit Saturn, passing the planet at a distance of 21,000 km. On Earth, the Entertainment Sports Programming Network, known as ESPN, debuted. And Pope John Paul II visited the United States.

Sandwiched between the three repertory seasons and the acclaim we received from the Talley plays were a number of productions that varied in quality and reception. These productions spanned the same period of time (1979 to 1982) and illustrate Circle Rep's complicated transition, showing the journey was not a clear-cut trend, but rather a step-by-step experience that included modest joys and disappointments.

Our New Star Writer

I described our plans for our eleventh season to the press in California while we were doing *Talley's Folly* and *Fifth of July* in rep. As promised, we started the season with three one-act plays written and directed by David Mamet called *Reunion*, starring Lindsay Crouse and Michael Higgins.

Circle Rep already counted among our resident playwrights Tennessee Williams, Lanford Wilson and Sam Shepard, three Pulitzer Prize-winning writers considered, along with Edward Albee, at the forefront of American drama. The opportunity to add David Mamet to this constellation put Circle Rep into the enviable position of home to the best writers in the theater. At this point, David had been cheered for his plays *Sexual Perversity in Chicago*, *The Water Engine*, *A Life in the Theatre* and *American Buffalo*. I had seen and admired all four.

I met David when I was directing his newly wed wife, Lindsay Crouse, in the Arena Stage production of *A Streetcar Named Desire* the previous April. Since then, Lindsay made her debut with Circle Rep in *Total Recall*, becoming a member of the Company. David and Lindsay first met when she was in a 1977 production of *Reunion* at Yale. Now David proposed to direct a new production for its New York premiere at Circle Rep.

The titular play in this trio is about an estranged father and daughter getting together after a separation of twenty years. John Lee Beatty designed a set so stripped down it was an almost invisible element: an empty platform with a heavy wooden table and two chairs center stage. It was as if David were going back to the very beginnings of the art to start fresh with the essence of theater, a script and two actors. The play had been produced previously in 1976 at the Yale Repertory Theater with the same cast, directed by Walt Jones. It was accompanied by a little curtain raiser called *Dark Pony*, about a father and his very young child driving in the dark, the girl's dad entertaining her with a story about a character named Rainboy, who could always count on his friend Dark Pony to rescue him. As Mel Gussow remarked in his review,

"This is how a bedtime story should always be told; it comforts its listeners."

For the New York production, David wrote a new short play to begin the evening called *The Sanctity of Marriage*. In this Pinteresque vignette, a married couple is breaking up and remembering a shared European holiday. Mr. Gussow thought it added nothing to the evening.

Reunion, written and directed by David Mamet, opened at Circle Rep on October 10, 1979 and played forty-two performances. The set was designed by John Lee Beatty, costumes were by Clifford Capone and the lighting was by Dennis Parichy. The stage manager was Jody Boese. It was received by the New York press with muted respect:

The New York Times, October 19, 1979 (Mel Gussow):
"This tenderly evocative play is a playwright's reflection on the renewal of faith. This short, bittersweet play is wistful, enveloping us in the isolation of two lonely people. Mamet's writing is terse but sensitive – everyday language distilled into homely poetry. Finding drama beneath the lines, Miss Crouse makes us see the desperation that is masked by confidence. Mr. Higgins enriches his character as a wryly philosophical drifter. The evening is weakened by [its] curtain-raisers. They distract us from the small, quiet pleasures of *Reunion*."

There was a significant presentation in our PiP program. Casting John Bishop and Danton Stone as a priest and an acolyte, we launched Bill C. Davis' *Mass Appeal* for four performances. When I determined that we really didn't have appropriate casting for a Major Production of this appealing play, I suggested that Bill take it to Manhattan Theater Club. He did and after its MTC run starring Milo O'Shea and Michael O'Keefe, the play transferred to Broadway where it played 212 performances and was made into a 1984 film starring Jack Lemmon and Zeljko Ivanek. A second PiP in the fall was *Some Sweet Time* by Michael Cassale.

During the run of *Reunion*, the Iran Hostage Crisis began when 3,000 Iranian radicals overran the U.S. Embassy in Tehran and took ninety hostages, demanding the United States send the former Shah of Iran back to stand trial. On the brighter side, it was announced that the smallpox virus had been eradicated, making it the only human disease driven to extinction. And as a prelude to America's longest war in the 21st century, the Soviet Union invaded Afghanistan.

Return of Comet Zane

As the new decade began, we were in the midst of our repertory of *Hamlet/Mary Stuart* and Egypt established diplomatic relations with Israel. But in the same month, Soviet scientist and human rights activist Andrei Sakharov was arrested; in protest, President Jimmy Carter announced that the United States would boycott the 1980 Summer Olympics in Moscow. The FBI targeted members of Congress with a sting operation of bribery called ABSCAM. The Winter Olympics opened in Lake Placid, where the U.S. hockey team defeated the Soviet Union in the semifinals in what was called the "Miracle on Ice." Also during our classic repertory, we presented a PiP of Jonathan Bolt's play *Threads,* which later opened our thirteenth season as a Major Production.

Our homegrown actor from his teenage years, Zane Lasky, recently completed fifteen episodes as "Mario Lanza" on *The Tony Randall Show.* I asked Zane if he had anything he wanted to do on stage. He recalled the part John Heuer wrote for him in a play we'd done as a PiP five years before. *Innocent Thoughts, Harmless Intentions* also had outstanding roles for Jonathan Hogan and Patricia Wettig. It seemed a natural next step in the development of one of our resident writers. It also provided roles for Company members John Dossett, Ben Siegler, Tim Shelton and Jimmie Ray Weeks. We worked for the first time with Brian Tarantina, an important addition to our Company. The cast was rounded out with Christopher Noth, in his only role at Circle Rep before starring on *Law & Order* and *Sex in the City.*

John Heuer's *Innocent Thoughts, Harmless Intentions* opened at Circle Rep on February 27, 1980, and played thirty-nine performances. It was directed by B. Rodney Marriott, set by Tom Lynch, Lighting by Dennis Parichy and costumes by Joan E. Weiss. The stage manager was Pamela Singer. Here's one review:

The New York Times, March 8, 1980 (Mel Gussow):
"In Heuer's *Innocent Thoughts, Harmless Intentions,* an Army private played by Zane Lasky is a loner who habitually intrudes

himself into other people's business. He is keenly observed by the playwright and Lasky makes him seem poignant as well as obsessive. The malicious squad leader (Jonathan Hogan) is his natural antagonist. This dramatic conflict, a test of manhood, is the root of Heuer's play. However, the cold wintry Alaska story is interspersed with a long monologue delivered by Patricia Wettig in an attic in Minnesota twenty years earlier. Despite a sensitive performance by Wettig, the character deflects our attention. Neither story sheds adequate light on the other. Director Marriott is unable to consolidate the two sections of the play, but the actors provide an ensemble performance. Lasky and Hogan are particularly convincing as the central combatants. The final scene has a sense of imminent confrontation that is the strength of a play that suffers from a split personality."

During the run of the main stage production, we presented a PiP of a new play written by former Associate Artistic Director, Marshall Oglesby, called *Child of the Clay Country*. Marshall had withdrawn from his job at Circle Rep to devote his time to writing this play over the previous two years. It was directed by John Bard Manulis, but I felt it was not yet ready for full production.

A Second Race

Our next Major Production was Milan Stitt's new play, *Back in the Race*, written for Joyce Reehling, who'd been an inspiration as Sister Rita in Milan's previous success, *The Runner Stumbles*.

Here's the plot of *Back in the* Race: Returning to the country house in Michigan where he spent his boyhood summers, Jonathan Edwards VII, a descendant of the famous eighteenth-century Calvinist preacher, wants to learn why his late father willed the place to the aging caretaker, Cliff, who now lives there with his half-Indian daughter, Zabrina. Sensing unanswered questions in the relationship between Cliff and his father, Jonathan seeks answers, only to be met with antagonism and the threat of violence. In the end, Jonathan and Zabrina (who may, in truth, be his half-sister) symbolically burn the Edwards family album, thereby exorcising ghosts of the past.

Back in the Race: A Family Album was directed by Leonard Peters; the set was by Bill Milkulewicz, the costumes by James Berton Harris, the lighting by John Gisondi and the sound design by David Rapkin. The stage managers were Jody Boese, Mollie Collison and Fred Reinglas. It opened at Circle Rep on April 17, 1980 and played thirty-nine performances. Here's a summary of one review:

> *The New York Times*, April 18, 1980 (Frank Rich):
> "Milan Stitt is once again thinking big thoughts about matters spiritual. In his new play, he is attempting nothing less than a sweeping re-evaluation of this country's ambiguous Puritan heritage. What's more, he has found a potentially fascinating method to attack his theme. [But] it is soon lost in a flood of cloudy talk and dubious theatrical conceits. Stitt's script is long on vague pronouncements, but short on specific details. There are little, contrived plot mysteries here and there to give the evening the illusion of movement, but it is hard to care about characters who are essentially mouthpieces for an inarticulate playwright. With the exception of the always commanding John Randolph, director Peters' cast does little to enliven the proceedings."

In the course of this run, we presented the much-admired actress Barbara Baxley's autobiographical musical revue, titled *Spooky Lady*, an evening billed as a Special Event for our subscribers. It was. We also presented a PiP of Roy London's new play *In Vienna*, which we brought back as a Major Production the following season under a new title *In Connecticut*.

Another Belt of Asteroids

Our long-time technical director Earl Hughes became our General Manager prior to our hiring of Porter van Zandt and Earl was eager to produce a one-act play festival between Major Productions. He selected the plays and directors, oversaw their casting and technical needs. The experience was valuable to Earl, who is now the producing director of the Pittsburgh Playhouse of Point Park University. He presented three new plays in his One Act Play Festival immediately following the closing of *Back in the Race*: *Box Office* by Elinor Jones, directed by R. Stuart White and featuring Burke Pearson; *On the Side of the Road* by Gordon Dryland; and Shelby Buford's *Diary of a Shadow Walker*, the latter two both directed by Daniel Irvine.

Marshal Tito, a national icon of Yugoslavia, died. The biggest volcanic eruption of my lifetime occurred when Mount St. Helens in Washington state erupted, killing fifty-seven people and causing $3 billion in damage. And signaling a whole new generation, the video game Pac-Man was released.

A Summer of Sweaters

I'm not sure how we became aware that a new playwright was being produced at Rutgers University, but we got hold of the script and immediately wanted to bring it to Circle Rep. The playwright was William Mastrosimone and his first play was a two-character offbeat love story called *The Woolgatherer*. The role of Rose, a reclusive loner who has withdrawn from the world because of its unbearable violence, was perfect for our Patricia Wettig. I contacted Bill and he was agreeable to recasting the play for its professional debut, but he insisted on retaining the director, John Bettenbender, who had done so well by the play at Rutgers. John had a good academic reputation and in 1978, his production of Eric Bentley's *Are You Now, or Have You Ever Been* transferred from Rutgers to the Promenade Theater for a run of 129 performances. It featured a letter from Lilian Hellman to the HUAC, read by a series of well-known actresses appearing for a cameo performance. Bill said the dynamic Peter Weller was interested in playing the role of Cliff.

The Woolgatherer is a two-act play, set in a small apartment in South Philadelphia. It centers on Rose and Cliff, two neurotic people searching for love. Rose is a nervous and flighty woman who is haunted by the past and obsessed with destruction. Due to her hemophilia, she's closed herself off from the world. She works at a five-and-dime behind the candy counter. She dreams of true love and how she'll meet a man one day who is perfect for her. Cliff is a foul-mouthed, wisecracking transcontinental truck driver who gets stuck in Philadelphia when his truck breaks down. While he is waiting for his rig to be repaired, he wanders into Rose's store looking for a one-night stand. Rose invites him over to her apartment and they start to argue about issues like her rundown neighborhood and her boarded up window. He soon discovers she has a weird collection of men's sweaters, which gives the play its title. Despite their differences, the two characters end up falling in love.

William Mastrosimone's *The Woolgatherer*, directed by John Bettenbender, opened at Circle Rep on May 28, 1980. The set was by Karl Eigsti, the costumes were by Joan E. Weiss and the lighting by Dennis Parichy. The stage manager was Jody Boese. The reviews were enthusiastic and permitted the production to run throughout the summer for ninety-two performances. Here are short evaluations:

The New York Times, August 8, 1980 (Frank Rich):
"In small Off-Broadway houses, there are two small plays that introduce writers of real promise. William Mastrosimone's *The Woolgatherer* at the Circle Rep features sad, fledgling lovers of the Tennessee Williams school, one of whom is played by the mesmerizing Peter Weller."

The New York Times (undated):
"Energy, compassion and theatrical sense are there."

Hollywood Reporter (undated):
"Mastrosimone has a knack for composing wildly humorous lines at the same time that he is able to penetrate people's hearts and dreams."

The Woolgatherer was joined in rep on July 29th by a one-man play called *Macready* based on the diaries of the great 19th century actor William Charles Macready (1793–1873). Written and performed by Frank Berry and directed by Donald MacKechnie, *Macready* played forty-one performances.

Stars in His Eyes

I had a call from Biff Liff, the fabled super-agent from the William Morris Agency. Biff told me he'd just come back from Washington where he'd encountered a new play that was perfect for Circle Rep. The play was *The Diviners* and it won the American College Theater Festival Award for Best Play. He urged me to get down to Washington to see it. I asked Biff to get me the script to read and meanwhile, Porter took the train down to the Kennedy Center to catch the performance. The author was Jim Leonard, Jr., a recent graduate of Hanover College in Indiana.

Porter returned enthusiastic. I read the play, Lanford read the play, Milan read the play. We were convinced we could discover another important new American playwright. I asked Biff to set up a meeting with Jim. We even paid for a hotel room (a first time for us) for the young Hoosier to come to New York to discuss a possible production of his play at Circle Rep.

I recall the meeting in his hotel room as the sort of scene you'd expect from a movie with Mickey Rooney and Judy Garland. Quiet and shy, Jim was a Midwestern farm kid, wowed by New York and meeting his literary hero, Lanford Wilson. He tried desperately to remain cool. I explained to him about our process of developing plays and suggested we could schedule a PiP of *The Diviners* right away. Jim insisted that we also bring his college theater teacher, Tom Evans, to direct the PiP and that the central character be played by John Jeter, who'd been a sensation at the Kennedy Center as the teenaged leading character, Buddy Layman. We were fine with Jim's requests and within weeks, *The Diviners* was in rehearsal for its PiP at Circle Rep, presented during the run of *The Woolgatherer*. With the success of the PiP, I scheduled *The Diviners* to open our twelfth season in the fall.

During our summer run, the Republican National Convention nominated former California Governor Ronald Reagan for President. The race was contested by the incumbent President Jimmy Carter, who beat back a challenge for the Democratic nomination from Senator Edward M. Kennedy. Meanwhile, without the participation of the U.S., the 1980 Summer Olympics were held in Moscow.

A Divine Find

Finalizing our plans to open our twelfth season with *The Diviners*, I discussed with Jim Leonard the professional support his play required for a New York debut. Having seen the PiP the previous spring, I reluctantly agreed to permit Jim's college teacher, Tom Evans, to direct again. I'd have loved to stage the play myself, but I honored the playwright's wishes, even though Tom had no prior professional experience. We could provide him with the best designers New York had to offer. John Lee Beatty designed a set of stunning simplicity, comprised of a raked platform of slats with a wooden cyclorama of barn siding. Dennis Parichy was unavailable, but Arden Fingerhut, who'd done lovely work for us on *Who Killed Richard Corey?*, could design the lights. Our ace costumer of color subtlety, Jennifer von Mayhauser, was available to design the depression-era clothes. Surrounded by these first class artists, I thought Tom would be safeguarded in his professional debut. Unfortunately, Tom had never worked with designers before. He always built his own sets and lighted his own productions. He had no idea how to collaborate. The results were lovely, but Tom was a nervous wreck.

I stood firm on one aspect of the production: I felt Jim's college friend John Jeter, although a decent young actor, was simply too old to play the adolescent Buddy in a professional situation. I was concerned that cynical New Yorkers would misread the relationship between the preacher and the boy, imagining unintended homosexual overtones because of the physicality of the relationship. John Jeter was small for his age, but he was over twenty, on the verge of becoming a man. There was too much innate sexuality in John to portray the innocence of the boy. Jim was disappointed, but he yielded to my guidance. We put out the word that we were looking for a young pre-pubescent actor for the lead in the play. Shortly after our posting in *Show Business,* Bruce MacNaughton called from Phoenix to propose his son Robert as the perfect solution to our search. He was willing to fly to New York with Robert to audition for us. I explained we had no budget for that kind of expense, but Bruce was undeterred. He was so sure we would want Robert, he was happy to pay for the trip himself. True to his word, a couple of days later Bruce showed up with a gangly red-haired thirteen-year-old kid. His audition was a revelation. Robert is that rare phenomenon, a natural. Tom Evans was impressed and even Jim Leonard was stunned to see his character brought to life by such a young kid. Disagreement disappeared. We cast him on the spot, without holding any other auditions.

The play offered wonderful roles for our Company actors. Tim Shelton was a handsome preacher as C.C. Showers; Jimmie Ray Weeks was ideal as Ferris, the single-parent widower; Jack Davidson could be a convincing farmer as Basil, while Elizabeth Sturges could play his doubting wife, Luella. Jacqueline Brooks was good casting for Norma, the sensual owner of a local diner; and Lisa Pelikan was an excellent Jennie Mae, Buddy's older sister. Ben Siegler and John Dossett were the sexy but goofy farm boys, Dewey and Melvin, while Laura Hughes and Mollie Collison were the small town girls, Darlene and Goldie, who drive the swains crazy.

The Diviners is set in Zion, a fictional small town in the early days of the depression. Buddy Layman is a mentally challenged adolescent boy whose simple, sweet nature touches most everyone he meets. When the boy was a baby, he almost drowned; his brain was deprived of oxygen for several minutes. This trauma and the loss of his mother in the same accident has left him deathly afraid of water. As a result, the kid refuses to take baths, which greatly frustrates his indulgent father, Ferris, who repairs automobiles in his garage. But Buddy's sensitivity to water endows him with the gift of locating water sources underground with a stick called a divining rod, a welcome talent in the dusty farm country of drought-stricken Indiana.

The action gets under way when a disenchanted preacher named C.C. Showers passes through Zion looking for work. C.C. is trying to break away from a long line of Kentucky family preachers and is determined *not* to do what he does best. He befriends Buddy and takes a job working as a mechanic for the boy's father. C.C. soon finds himself as Buddy's mentor and teacher. Buddy's sister Jennie Mae is attracted to C.C., but she's not the only woman in town that finds C.C. a catch. Zion doesn't have a preacher and the owner of the local diner would love to see the church rebuilt, with all the Sunday customers it would bring into her café. When the people of the town learn that C.C. is a former preacher who's given up preaching, the women of Zion try to persuade him to start a new church, while he tries to persuade Buddy to wash. The preacher finally gets the boy into the river and is bathing him, but the townspeople mistake the scene for a baptism. They descend to the river, singing hymns, and in the confusion, the boy drowns. The play begins and ends with elegies spoken by the townspeople describing what happened the day of Buddy's tragedy.

The Diviners opened at Circle Rep on October 10, 1980 and played fifty performances. It was directed by Tom Evans, with a set by John Lee Beatty, lighting by Arden Fingerhut and costumes by Jennifer von Mayrhauser. The stage manager was James M. Arnemann. The reviews were generally lovely, although the play failed to entrance our usual ally, Mel Gussow:

The New York Times, October 17, 1980 (Mel Gussow):
"The atmosphere and structure remind us somewhat of Lanford Wilson's *The Rimers of Eldritch,* but in contrast, as Leonard's story is unveiled the play goes awry. The author has allowed his desire to shape a meaningful drama to obscure his ability to evoke local color and character. The emblematic staging by Tom Evans, effective in the

beginning, becomes self-conscious. At the same time, there is talent at work – in writing as well as in performance. Leonard has a certain sensitivity for humorous details. Tim Shelton imbues the preacher with charm and dignity. There are also helpful performances by, among others, Weeks, Dossett, and Siegler. With the assistance of Beatty's bleacher-like environment and Fingerhut's subtly shaded lighting, Circle Rep has given Leonard a hospitable setting for his first New York production."

Variety: "A splendid drama by a playwright with poetic as well as human feeling."

New York Magazine, October 22, 1980 (John Simon):
"*The Diviners*, which would be meritorious from anyone, is astounding from so young a writer. Leonard renders the humor and horror of the hinterlands with staggering accuracy. ... Compelling."

The Diviners was enormously popular with audiences and following our run at Circle Rep, we brought it back for our first season in residence at the Saratoga Performing Arts Center upstate. We also produced the play on a tour of the Far East sponsored by the State Department; audiences in Kuala Lampur liked it as much as our New York crowd did.

During the New York run, Danny Irvine directed a PiP of Shelby Buford's *Diary of a Shadow Walker.* Shelby, Danny and the two actors spent a weekend in Sag Harbor at Lanford's house as part of a Playwrights Retreat, stretching the one act to a full-length version. This autobiographical play was about an alcoholic writer who runs into writer's block when his girlfriend aborts his child. It again featured lovely performances by Robert Lupone and Lisa Emery; and Danny's production was an homage to film noire, filled with striking visual imagery. But the longer version seemed stretched a bit thin, so I passed on further production. We also brought back

Barbara Baxley for another one-woman Special Event, called *On Wayward Wings*, co-written by Michael Liebman.

A record number of viewers tuned in to watch *Dallas* on television to learn who shot the series' lead character, J.R. Ewing, an international obsession. Then, in a sobering dose of reality, at around 10:50 P.M. on December 8th, former Beatle and peace activist John Lennon and his wife Yoko Ono were returning to their New York apartment in The Dakota, when Mark David Chapman shot Lennon in the back four times at the entrance to the building. Lennon was taken to the emergency room of nearby Roosevelt Hospital and was pronounced dead on arrival at 11:07 P.M. An era had ended.

When our lease at the Transit Authority Building expired, Porter found us new quarters in a former perfume factory on Avenue of the Americas at Spring Street. The cloying scents lingered during our ten years there.

There were extended readings of Shelby Buford's *Gas Station* and Peter Maeck's *The Bone Garden,* continuing our system of play development. These two scripts benefited from the process, but not enough to earn them a future production at Circle Rep. However, our PiP of Joseph Pintauro's *Snow Orchard* was sufficiently promising that it became a Major Production the following season.

While *Twelfth Night/Beaver Coat* were playing, Iran released the fifty-two Americans who'd been held hostage for 444 days. They were released within minutes of Ronald Reagan being sworn in.

Mad, Bad, and Dangerous to Know

After twelve years of introducing new playwrights, we now attracted new work from writers who enjoyed previous successes. One such was Romulus Linney. I had seen earlier plays, *Holy Ghosts* and *The Sorrows of Frederick,* so I was a fan.

Romulus had a new play called *Childe Byron,* a portrait of one of history's most fascinating figures, Gordon George Lord Byron. It had previous productions at the Virginia Museum Theatre and the Actors Theatre of Louisville; we were eager to add it to our twelfth season with our newly minted star, William Hurt, as the immortal poet.

Coming off my acting foray as Malvolio, it was a pleasure to return to directing and *Childe Byron* was a delicate piece that stirred my imagination. We could cast the play so perfectly with Company actors their parts might have been written for them. William Hurt had the soul of a poet and would have no trouble making an audience believe in Byron's genius. Opposite him was Lindsey Crouse, his co-star in *Hamlet*, in the second installment of a pairing that was becoming Circle Rep's version of Lunt and Fontaine.

These two star turns were supported by an ensemble of fine actors who contributed a full panoply of British society: Stephanie Gordon, Richard Seff, Tim Shelton, Patricia Wettig and Stephanie Musnick. Especially thrilling was having the angelic beauty of young John Dossett to embody the choirboy who was Byron's youthful homosexual liaison.

Childe Byron is set in 1852 as Byron's only legitimate daughter, Ada, is writing her will. She is the Countess of Lovelace, famed for inventing a machine that was the forerunner of the modern computer. At thirty-six years old, she is the same age at which her father died. Estranged from Byron during his lifetime, as her own death approaches, she conjures up memories of her father. In hallucinations brought on by the morphine that eases the pain of her cancer, Byron springs to life as a ghost from the Other Side, re-enacting his life for her understanding. He shows her his impetuous youth, his incestuous relationship with his sister, his homosexual escapades, the scandal surrounding his brief marriage and his castigation by society.

In order to incorporate Byron's club foot, William asked for a special shoe to be made that would twist his foot in a way that made his conscious attention to this impediment unnecessary. He had the special shoe from the beginning of rehearsal, so all his movement was created with his disability intact. Rehearsals were amazingly creative. I asked everyone in the cast to write a poem, so we would each experience the delicate nature of exposing one's soul, the cost of poetry. The six supporting actors made complete characterizations of a host of people who interacted with Byron. Lindsay had the peculiar requirement of playing his daughter as well as his sister. We studied the elegant manners of early 19th Century British society and brought the behavior of the Romantic Era to life. Romulus attended most rehearsals and glowed with delight as he saw his play taking shape. At the end of each rehearsal, I invited him to comment on anything he saw amiss, but he always declined. It was inspiring to have his full support.

For the setting, I engaged David Potts to create a lovely environment in which people magically appeared by coming through revolving panels of gathered chiffon that were backed by Mylar mirrors. The action easily flowed from one location and time to another as if invoked by imagination, accompanied by the music of Hector Berlioz. Dennis Parichy's lights helped transform time and place on the almost bare stage. But the most extraordinary design element was the clothes. Michael Warren Powell returned to his original theatrical role of designer to make the elegant wardrobe for the characters. In addition to the club-footed shoe, the material for Byron's trousers were hand woven, his collars and cuffs soft and elaborate and his frock-coat perfectly fitted. William's blond hair was curled to present a leonine mane of romantic extravagance. William's Byron was beautiful to look at.

The Circle Rep production of *Childe Byron* was effortlessly stylish. I was proud of it, despite Frank Rich's harsh assessment ("a crude bus-and-truck version of *Amadeus*"). The critics praised William Hurt's performance, but took Romulus to task for having written an over-simplified, even superficial portrait of Lord Byron. This was an example of a playwright turning on a dime, being wholly satisfied with the production until the reviewers criticized his play. He blamed the failure on William Hurt's star power. In William's defense, I plead not guilty. It's not his fault that his characterization of Byron was so rich it made the text seem sketchy.

Childe Byron by Romulus Linney opened at Circle Rep February 26, 1981 and played sixty-three performances. (Debra Mooney replaced Lindsay Crouse for the last part of the run.) It was directed by Marshall W. Mason, setting by David Potts, Costumes by Michael Warren Powell and lights by Dennis Parichy. Peter Nels provided the fight choreography and the sound design was by Bruce Kaiser and Chuck London. Daniel Irvine provided visual effects and the stage manager was Alice Galloway. Here are the critical responses in summary:

The New York Times, February 27, 1981 (Frank Rich):
"William Hurt hasn't lost any of that crazy intensity that makes him a joy to watch. What makes this talented actor so special – and inevitably, a star – is his ability to create his own reality on stage. He's prepared to be fascinating without any help from the playwright. And that's just what he does in Romulus Linney's *Childe Byron,* a comic-book version of the life of Lord Byron. Linney's choices are all aimed in the direction of melodrama and sentimentality. The chorus [of actors], as well as Mason's staging and David Potts's set, suggests a crude bus-and-truck version of *Amadeus.* Aside from Hurt, the only other performance of note comes from Lindsay Crouse, a gifted actress who keeps getting better and better. Crouse, you may recall, was also splendid playing Ophelia to Mr. Hurt's Hamlet at the Circle Rep last season. These two actors are exciting to watch, no matter what they do, but let's hope that next year they'll reunite in a real play."

N.Y. Daily News, February 27, 1981 (Douglas Watt):
"Whatever the shortcomings, we can be grateful to Romulus Linney [because] even as a ghost, Byron makes for lively company. While Hurt cuts a fine figure as Byron, neither he nor Crouse become truly engaged in acting until the lights begin to dim on the first half. Now, Linney settles down to business with a prettily written and played scene at the start of the second act. Mason, the director, has

handled all this exceedingly well under the circumstances, devising some especially amusing business for the supporting players. The production, including the costuming and lighting, is first-rate all around, but Linney has, finally, only a ghost to show us."

New York Magazine, March 16, 1981 (John Simon):
"Linney's *Childe Byron* is a civilized but essentially pointless work. The Circle Rep production couldn't be more skillfully staged by Mason or more simply yet tastefully designed, and Crouse plays with exemplary refinement and command. Hurt is a handsome, sporadically brilliant, yet finally too quirky Byron."

New York Post, February 27, 1981 (Clive Barnes):
"Unquestionably, Linney's *Childe Byron* is engrossing. I enjoyed the play enormously. This is intended as an ingenious form of historical romance and as such, it is full of charm and interest. The structure of Linney's play is adroit, with almost cinematic dissolves of scenes. The director Mason has caught this play's style and pace with unstressed precision, and the setting by Potts, handsomely and admirably anonymous, the costumes by Powell, and the lighting by Parichy, all add to the tone and the play's texture. The two leading performances provide pure delight. Hurt's voice is eloquent and resonant, his timing is perfect, and he uses gesture and expression with a subtle fearlessness. Crouse shows once more what a lovely actress, intelligent and passionate, she is. It is a good cast in a play that may illustrate more than it illuminates, is often moving and never for an instant, boring."

WOR-TV, February 27, 1981 (Casper Citron):
"Hurt and Crouse bring magic to a glossing over of the life and loves of the poet Byron. They work beautifully together, so add the clever staging, excellent lighting, and

lovely costumes, Circle Rep has created an evening to be seen!"

During the run of *Childe Byron*, President Reagan was shot in the chest by John Hinckley, but he survived the attempted assassination. Two police officers and Press Secretary James Brady were also wounded. Two months later, Pope John Paul II was shot by Mehmet Ali Ağca, a Turkish gunman, as the Pope entered St. Peter's Square in Vatican City to address a general audience. These events were quite a contrast to the beauty on our stage.

We brought back Rita Gardner in a Special Event called *Say It with Music* and Geoffrey Shlaes staged a PiP of John Bishop's *The Great Grandson of Jedediah Kohler*, leading us to include it in the thirteenth season's repertory with *Richard II*.

A Talmudic Tale

The spring production was Roy London's *In Connecticut*. Roy developed the play as a PiP the previous year under the title *In Vienna*. That title came from a Hasidic aphorism that says knowledge is in Vienna but the real treasure is at home. Roy realized that the title confused audiences, so he changed it after the PiP.

We thought he made considerable progress in his revisions, although the play was a slight slice of romantic comedy. Danny Irvine and I co-directed this production at the GeVa Theater Center in Rochester New York, another attempt at co-producing to save budget costs. In an article for the *Rochester Democrat and Chronicle*, Danny was interviewed and declared me "a visionary." *In Connecticut* played well in that cold town, but when we transferred the production to New York, we began to realize that what played in Rochester might fare poorly in the City. We postponed its scheduled opening for "artistic reasons," according to an article in *The New York Times*, Connecticut Journal, May 3, 1981.

In Connecticut is set in an 1832 house in New Preston, Connecticut that belongs to Candy Schull. Her family means to sell the old house and bring Candy to live with them in New York. Although, she has many memories of her childhood in the old house, she has never appreciated its importance to her until she's on the verge of leaving it. She comes to realize that:

"The treasure is in Connecticut and it's mine."

Roy wrote the part of Candy for his friend from the soap opera world, Rosemary Prinz, who was enormously popular for her role as Penny in *As the World Turns* from 1956–1968. (My mother was very excited to meet her.) The rest of the cast was all Circle Rep. Lisa Emery played her daughter, Irene, and Robert Lupone was Irene's husband, Andrew. Sharon Madden was Irene's sister, there along with her boyfriend, Louis, played by Jeff McCracken. The house is being sold to an Italian couple named the di Pintos, played by Circle playwright Shelby Buford, Jr. and Circle designer, Henrietta Bagley. Intern Rob Gomes played the sexy moving man, Maxie. The Mayflower Moving Company gave us moving boxes and Mayflower jumpsuits for the interns who changed the scenery.

David Potts designed the 1832 house that is meant to be an important character in the play. Joan Weiss designed the costumes, Dennis Parichy the lighting and the sound was by Roy's brother, Chuck London. Music was by Michael Valenti. The stage manager was M.A. Howard.

Lisa Emery had to play a Mendelsohn piece on a violin at one point in the play. Since she never played an instrument, she had to learn the exact fingering and bowing to make it credible. The actual recording of the violin came from speakers Chuck had hidden under the sofa she was sitting on. Even in an intimate space like Circle Rep, the illusion was thoroughly believable.

Roy was never happy about the casting. The play was rooted in Jewish culture and with the exception of Ms. Prinz, there was not a Jew in the cast. This sort of thing never bothered me. I believe good actors can play anything. But perhaps we never quite found the rhythms and tone Roy heard in his mind when he wrote it.

In Connecticut began playing April 23, 1981 for thirty-eight performances. The press was not invited to review it. During the run, an interesting play called *Charley McCarthy's Monocle* by Maxine Fleischmann was given a PiP. It was a well-written piece, but too reminiscent of *Who's Afraid of Virginia Woolf?* to succeed in the 1980s. The season ended with a delightful PiP of Terrence McNally's *It's Only a Play*, in which Terrence got off his joke about being sick of the Talleys. I'm sorry that this is the only play we mounted of Terrence's, but I kept telling him he was capable of writing an important play, such as his debut on Broadway of *Things That Go Bump in the Night*. Although we read *Lisbon Traviata* in my office and Terrence was a major participant in Circle Rep's writers' workshop, all his success came at Manhattan Theater Club, after receiving a cold shoulder from me. Eventually, *It's Only a Play* found its true home on Broadway in 2014 starring Nathan Lane and Matthew Broderick.

The Major Production of *A Tale Told* followed, opening June 6, 1981 and playing thirty-nine performances before going to the Mark Taper Forum in Los Angeles. And, of course, *Fifth of July* continued its run on Broadway. So the twelfth season was decidedly a mixed bag, highlighted by *The Diviners, Childe Byron* and *A Tale Told*.

The Centers for Disease Control and Prevention reported that five homosexual men in Los Angeles, California had a rare form of pneumonia seen only in patients with weakened immune systems (the first recognized cases of AIDS). In London, Marcus Sarjeant fired six blank shots at Elizabeth II. President Reagan nominated the first woman, Sandra Day O'Connor, to the Supreme Court. A worldwide television audience of over 700 million people watched the Wedding of Charles, Prince of Wales, and Lady Diana Spencer at St Paul's Cathedral.

Summer on Two Coasts

As Lanford and I took our cast of *A Tale Told* to Los Angeles, Circle Rep became the theater component of the Saratoga Performing Arts Center in Saratoga Springs, along with the New York City Ballet and the Philadelphia Orchestra. For our first offerings at SPAC in August, Porter van Zandt and B. Rodney Marriott remounted *Childe Byron* and *The Diviners* to play in rotating rep. William Hurt was in both productions and Debra Mooney replaced Lindsay Crouse as Ada. Some of the original casts of the two productions repeated their previous roles; so many actors in our Company were employed performing in rep on both Coasts in the summer of 1981. Circle Rep also took on the responsibility for the New York State Summer School of the Arts, in which high school seniors received guidance from our first-class professionals. A seventeen year-old Philip Seymour Hoffman was, perhaps, our most prominent alumnus.

That summer MTV was launched and Mark David Chapman was sentenced to twenty years to life in prison, after being convicted of murdering John Lennon.

Following our summer in Saratoga Springs, we brought back *The Diviners* for a second Circle Rep engagement. Re-directed by B. Rodney Marriott and Porter van Zandt, we had a few cast changes. Stephanie Gordon replaced Jacqueline Brookes as Norma; Deborah Hedwall replaced Mollie Collison as Goldie; Nancy Killmer replaced Elizabeth Sturges as Luella; William Hurt replaced Ben Siegler as Melvin; Rob Gomes replaced John Dossett as Dewey; Patricia Wettig replaced Lisa Pelikan as Jennie Mae. Otherwise, Robert MacNaughton (Buddy), Tim Shelton (Showers), Laura Hughes (Darlene) and Jack Davidson (Basil) repeated their original roles.

The Diviners re-opened at Circle Repertory Company on August 4, 1981 and played an additional thirty-two performances. John Lee Beatty did the sets, Jennifer von Mayrhauser designed the costumes, Dennis Parichy took over lighting from Arden Fingerhut and M.A. Howard took over stage-managing from James M. Arnemann. There was no need for new reviews; we just used the first notices.

Too Close to Home

We opened our thirteenth season with *Threads,* a play by Jonathan Bolt, developed in our PiP program two years before. Jonathan was an actor/writer who appeared in several Circle Rep productions (*Richard II, Jedediah Kohler* and *Black Angel*) following his debut as a playwright.

Threads is narrated by David Owens (Ben Siegler), a teenager growing up in a mill town in North Carolina; he aspires to be a painter. He tells us about the summer of 1965 when his older brother, Clyde (Jonathan Hogan), a television actor of modest success, returns home because his mother, Sally (Jo Henderson), has cancer. Their Dad is Abner (William Andrews), an inarticulate factory worker with little interest in Clyde, who has been encouraged in his artistic aspirations by his mother. Neighbors and Clyde's old friends, who toil on the assembly line at the mill, come by to see him: Pete (Roger Chapman), Janine (Patricia Wettig), next-door neighbor, Jesse Sykes (Nancy Killmer) and Nub (David Morse). They provide a funny portrait of the small-town life that Clyde has escaped. They treat Clyde like a celebrity, but Clyde admits his television career has bogged down and seems to be going nowhere. He has decided to return home and take a job at the mill. His mother is deeply disappointed by this news, but his father thinks it's a good idea. We discover that Clyde was driven from home by an incident in which his father beat his mother when Clyde was a teenager. With Sally's passing, father and son face up to the task of unsnarling the tangled threads of their relationship by confronting the long-ago episode that has estranged Clyde and the embittered Abner. They come to a compassionate understanding of their differences and accept the need to follow their separate paths in life. David sums up the encounter between his brother and his family by saying it's "just like nothing ever happened at all." Throughout the play, we hear the "clackety clack" of the factory itself in the distance.

Threads by Jonathan Bolt opened at Circle Rep on October 7, 1981 and played fifty-four performances. It was directed by B. Rodney Marriott, with a set by David Potts, costumes by Joan E. Weiss, lighting by Craig Miller, Sound by Chuck London and Stewart Werner, music by Stephen Lockwood and Patricia Lee Stotter. The stage managers were Jody Boese, Fred Reinglas and

Kate Stewart. The familiar autobiographic story was damned with faint praise by most of the critics:

The New York Times, October 26, 1981 (Frank Rich):
"As long as there is an American theater, there will always be plays about the prodigal son. It's a long evening. Jonathan Bolt is obviously a well-meaning and sincere young writer, trying to tell the truth as he sees it. But if he's going to redeem the conventional American family play, he must dismantle or refurbish its inhibiting, ready-made devices to create a distinctive vision of his own. But Bolt does not seem to have put any aesthetic or emotional distance between himself and his material."

The Christian Science Monitor, October 30, 1981 (John Beaufort):
"With the opening of its thirteenth season, the Circle Repertory Company once again displays its flair for attracting and nurturing dramas that touch the heart. Jonathan Bolt's *Threads* employs a regional milieu for its thoughtful and sensitive probing of the human condition. Its emotional ebb and flow, unfolding relationships, and mixture of comic and serious elements are admirably served in the performance staged by B. Rodney Marriott. The situations may be familiar, [but] they nevertheless grip the spectator with their intensity and honesty. *Threads* marks another accomplishment of which Circle Rep can be justly proud."

During the run of *Threads,* in the PiP program we worked on a new play by Marsha Norman that turned out to be another Pulitzer Prize-winner. *'Night, Mother* was a two-character play that had a previous production at Yale's American Repertory Theater. At Circle Rep, we cast it with our two Company actors, Kathy Bates and Bobo Lewis. It was a thrilling experience and we would have scheduled it as a Major Production immediately, but Marsha's husband, Dan Byck, already had taken an option on the script to produce it on Broadway. It opened at the John Golden Theater on March 3, 1983, directed by Tom Moore, starring Kathy Bates and Anne Pitoniak for 388 performances. It was nominated for four Tony Awards and was the winner of the 1983 Pulitzer Prize for Drama. I'm proud that this moving play was first seen in New York on the stage of Circle Rep, and that Marsha Norman joined us as a Resident Playwright.

Two other PiPs followed: James Farrell's *Bing and Walker* and A.R. Gurney's *What I Did Last Summer*, both of which were presented as Major Productions in later seasons.

Egyptian president Anwar Sadat was assassinated during a parade by army members of the Islamic Jihad that opposed his negotiations with Israel. He was replaced by Hosni Mubarak, who ruled Egypt until he was ousted in the Arab Spring of 2011. President Reagan authorized the CIA to recruit and support the Contra rebels in Nicaragua, in violation of the Boland Amendment in Congress, while selling arms to Iran in exchange for hostages. This was known as the "Iran/Contra" scandal and resulted in eleven convictions, including Lt. Oliver North.

Three for One

As the year was ending, we presented three one-act plays as a Major Production. They were Lanford Wilson's *Thymus Vulgaris*, directed by Company actress June Stein; John Bishop's *Confluence*, directed by B. Rodney Marriott; and Beth Henley's *Am I Blue*, directed by R. Stuart White.

Lanford's play was a ridiculous farce about a vulgar daughter returning to her mother in a trailer park in Palmdale, California. Ruby, a woman of indeterminate age and compliant disposition, lives amid an overgrown garden of "thymus vulgaris," an herb that smells suspiciously like a menthol chest rub. She is joined unexpectedly by her daughter, Evelyn, a warmhearted hooker who announces that her Mafioso-esque boyfriend, Solly the "Grapefruit King," has asked her to marry him. She is not so sure she wants to go through with it or, for that matter, that Solly does either. But the lure of all that money and Solly's promise to give Ruby a home as well, tug at her. A well-built young motorcycle cop arrives, sent by Solly to round up mother and daughter and whisk them off to a life of luxury. And why not? There are, as Evelyn says, the users and the used—and every once in a while the used deserve a break too.

It featured funny performances by Pearl Shear (from my Taper *HOT L*), Katherine Cortez as her daughter and a very cool Jeff McCracken as The Cop, who goes "Hollywood" when he discovers he's in front of an audience. This silly piece was originally done in Los Angeles at the Lee Strasberg Institute with Danny Irvine directing Sharon Madden and Pearl Shear, but Lanford wanted to give June a chance to direct, so she took over the assignment at Circle Rep.

John's *Confluence* was the central play and gave the evening its over-all title. I thought it was the most substantial of the three. This short but touching play had three fascinating roles for our Company: Jimmy Ray Weeks was ideal casting for Chuck, a former professional football player; Katherine Cortez was his girlfriend, Kathy; and Edward Seamon was an aging baseball star.

In *Confluence*, Chuck Janola, a former Pittsburgh Steeler and now a prosperous businessman, is visiting his fiancée, Kathy, who is acting in a summer stock company. They picnic in a rural park, overlooking the confluence of three Pennsylvania rivers. When Kathy goes off to rehearsal, Chuck stays behind, both to contemplate the view and because he knows that the park is also a favorite haunt of Earl Douchette, a former baseball star and Hall of Famer, now living out his final years in a wheelchair. Wary when they first meet, Earl gradually warms to the younger man, who idolized him as a boy. Soon both are swapping tales of their glory days and commiserating at the wrenching sadness (which only other pros can understand) that comes when time robs them of the unique excellence that set them apart from others.

Am I Blue was a light-hearted play, set in a seedy New Orleans bar in 1968. It featured Jeff McCracken as John Polk Richards, June

Stein as Ashbe, Pearl Shear as Hilda, Jimmy Ray Weeks as a carnival barker, Ed Seamon as a bum, Ellen Conway as a hippie and Katherine Cortez as a whore.

Seventeen year-old John Polk, lonely and dissatisfied with his life, is waiting for midnight when he will turn eighteen. His fraternity brothers have arranged an appointment with a prostitute to celebrate his coming of age and he is fortifying his courage with liquor. Ashbe, a strange sixteen year-old girl, is chased into the bar by an innkeeper, angry because she's stolen his ashtrays. At first, John wants nothing to do with this weird girl, but he discovers she's very street-smart. Ashbe invites John to her littered apartment that she shares with her absent father. She is as high-strung and flaky as John Polk is nervous. After goofy activities like stringing together Cheerios, Ashbe offers to make love with John Polk, but he politely declines.

Am I Blue was Beth Henley's first play, written seven years before she won the 1981 Pulitzer Prize for *Crimes of the Heart*, which was first read in my office at Circle Rep in 1980. I thought it too self-consciously eccentric, so I passed it on to Manhattan Theater Club, who then produced it in January the year before.

Confluence opened at Circle Rep on December 30, 1981 and played into the New Year, with forty-nine performances. The set was by Bob Phillips, costumes by Joan E. Weiss, lighting by Mel Sturchio and sound by Chuck London/Stewart Werner. The stage managers were Jody Boese, Fred Reinglas and Kate Stewart.

The New York Times, January 11, 1982 (Frank Rich):
"There is, sporadically, a pleasing quality to the voices of the evening's estimable playwrights: Lanford Wilson, John Bishop, and Beth Henley. They've all done better work than these trifles – and received better productions – but this program does offer a tangy whiff of their respective styles. All three writers reaffirm their bond to their spiritual patriarch, Tennessee Williams. The strongest play is Henley's *Am I Blue*. We experience Henley's wondrous gift

for creating sweet comedy out of Southern eccentricities, as well as her ability to reveal the sad loneliness beneath the spunk. The cast, directed by Stuart White, is passable at best. More skillful acting can be found in Bishop's schematic *Confluence*. In Wilson's *Thymus Vulgaris*, both in the writing and June Stein's staging, the women are campy cartoons. Still, Wilson's characteristic and touching powers of empathy break through at the end."

New York Post, January 11, 1982:
"*Am I Blue* joyously proves that [Henley's] great Broadway hit *Crimes of the Heart* was no happy flash in the pan. There is real gold in that there typewriter."

Daily News, January 11, 1982:
"Bishop's *Confluence* is a small, pure gem, its every facet shining. Lean in the writing and beautifully acted and staged, it is stunning."

The Christian Science Monitor, January 19, 1982 (John Beaufort):
"Circle Rep has assembled a trio of sensitively written and perceptively performed one-act plays. The common denominator is a kind of comic ruefulness. This three-in-one program treats several of the ages of man with theatrical freshness and honesty. John Bishop's *Confluence* is the solidest in terms of character portrayal. *Am I Blue* is a poignant comedy about two lonely innocents who meet in a squalid quarter of New Orleans [that] speaks very much with its own voice. *Thymus Vulgaris* is the slightest of the one-act threesome, nevertheless sets the tone and tenor of the evening. Like the other playlets, it is well performed."

While the three one-acts were playing, we presented three PiPs: Joyce Carol Oates' *Presque Isle*; Claris Nelson's *Cat and Mouse*, directed by B. Rodney Marriott; and John Bishop's *How Women Break Bad News,* directed by Amy Saltz. None of them made it to a Major Production. Across the ocean, Queen Elizabeth II opened the Barbican Centre in London.

Out of the Nut House

Joe Pintauro was not only a member of the playwright's lab at Circle Rep, he was an ex-priest and a Sag Harbor neighbor of Lanford's, who enthusiastically promoted his work. Once we read *Snow Orchard,* we scheduled it for a Major Production.

The play is set in the Greenpoint section of Brooklyn. Rocco Lazarra (Peter Boyle) has been in a rehab institution since a suicide attempt uncovered a manic-depressive disorder. Now, medically stabilized and calm, he returns to the family he abused for over twenty years. He brings a new hobby with him, too: orchids. His deeply religious wife, Filumena (Olympia Dukakis), who has a fear of leaving the house, is not sure what to expect from him. Sebbie, the older son (Robert Lupone), is her mainstay but there has always been bad blood between him and Rocco. Blaise, the younger son (Ben Siegler), sympathizes when he uncovers Rocco's lithium and Valium. But Sebbie accuses his father of being "cool" only because of the drugs. Rocco's response is to dump his medication into the rigatoni and to reveal to Blaise his suicide attempt. He goes on to tell him about orchids and the lessons of hope they can impart. With nothing resolved, Filumena fears that Sebbie will leave home. Sebbie tries to get her to leave with him, but she refuses. Sebbie prepares to leave for Texas with Doogan, his boyfriend. Rocco learns of his homosexuality and attempts to communicate with him but Sebbie goads his father into a fit of rage before leaving for good. There will be no forgiveness for Rocco, but in the end he and Blaise coax Filumena to step outside for the first time.

Snow Orchid by Joseph Pintauro opened at Circle Rep March 10, 1982 and played for thirty-nine performances. It was directed by Tony Giordano, set by Hugh Landwehr, costumes by David Murin, lighting by Dennis Parichy and sound by Chuck London/Stewart Werner. The stage manager was Bill Kavanagh.

The New York Times, March 11, 1982 (Frank Rich):
"We learn everything Pintauro has to say by the time [the family] has had their opening meal of pasta; all the rest is predictable and melodramatic. Or almost all. When Pintauro finally lets go late in the evening, he reveals a talent for dramatizing grand passions with almost operatic vigor. We realize this playwright might have a voice, even if he is lacking in certain essential theatrical skills. Aided by Hugh Leonard's elaborate two-story set and Parichy's lighting, Tony Giordano has choreographed the action well, with a keen appreciation for the characters' physicality. He is not afraid to whip from farce to agony in a flash; but no director could redeem the script's excesses. The acting is able, though the sexy Olympia Dukakis seems miscast as the frigid recluse. Peter Boyle is in his element as a brutal man who finds it easier to be tender with plants than people, and Robert Lupone works wonders with the problematic role of the tortured son."

New York Post, March 11, 1982 (Clive Barnes):
"No one could accuse Joe Pintauro's new play of being half-hearted. Or even less than full-blooded. The only restraint is – properly – shown by Peter Boyle as the understandably bewildered father. Robert Lupone is superb, [but] Dukakis, goes too far with style. Ben Siegler, ingenious and unwittingly comic, completes this strange family quartet with appropriate energy. I think *Snow Orchid* might prove to be one of those terrible plays that are difficult to forget."

N.Y. Daily News, March 11, 1982 (Douglas Watt):
"The theater season isn't advanced one whit by *Snow Orchid*. Pintauro, who isn't a bad hand at racy dialogue and who even supplies a few genuinely funny remarks,

has been unable to settle on a precise tone, and that's its fatal flaw. Boyle gives a very cogent performance, and Lupone offers his most effective portrayal since his creation of Zach in *A Chorus Line*. Dukakis is adequately rowdy and screwy, and Siegler brings considerable appeal to the skimpily written role of the younger son. Tony Giardano has directed with the vitality of a young Elia Kazan. Landweher has designed a remarkably comprehensive interior-exterior setting, and Parichy has lighted it effectively. But *Snow Orchid* is mostly hot air."

On the 10th of March, all eight planets aligned on the same side of the Sun, called the "Jupiter Effect," which had no noticeable effect on planet Earth. The 54th Academy Awards, hosted by Johnny Carson, were held at the Dorothy Chandler Pavilion in Los Angeles. *Chariots of Fire* won four Academy Awards, including Best Picture. Just after Aprils Fool's Day, Argentina invaded the Falkland Islands and the Falklands War was underway. During the war, I was in London directing Jonathan Pryce and Hailey Mills in *Talley's Folly*.

Stars of Tomorrow

Stephen Sondheim contacted us on the behalf of the Dramatists Guild, of which he was president. They wanted to offer a contest for teenage (or younger) playwrights to compete for a professional New York production. They asked Circle Rep to be the presenter for the winners. We jumped at the chance. The idea was to offer seven fledgling playwrights full productions under expert professional auspices. We engaged our resident designers to take part in the project. John Lee Beatty agreed to design the sets, which involved a revolving black stage in order to accommodate the demands of seven different scripts and Dennis Parichy was set to design the lights. Consummate professional artist Ann Roth designed the costumes. I signed on to direct two of the plays: Kenneth Lonergan's *The Rennings Children* and John Jacobs' *Present Tense*. Elinor Renfield took on another two: Adam Berger's *It's Time for a Change* and Shoshana Marchland's *Half Fare*. Carole Rothman directed Peter Murphy's *Bluffing*, Gerald Chapman directed Lynette Serrano's *The Bronx Zoo* and Arthur Laurents directed Juliet Garson's *So What Are We Gonna Do Now?* In addition, there were staged readings of *Coleman, S.D.* by Anne Pierson Wiese and *In the Way* by Stephen Gutwillig (both directed by Carole Rothman) and *Epiphany* by Jennie Litt, directed by Gerald Chapman, the Festival Director for the Dramatists Guild. The Administrator was Peggy Hansen.

We put together a company of actors to perform the plays of the young authors, including Trish Hawkins, Bruce McCarty, Burke Pearson, Timothy Busfield, Jonathan Bolt and Karen Sederholm from Circle Rep, with Guest Artists David Labiosa, Kate Anthony, Lucy Deakins, Wanda De Jesus, Alba Oms, James Pickens Jr., Zaina Rivera and Ted Sod.

The Young Playwrights Festival sponsored by the Dramatists Guild opened at Circle Rep on April 27, 1982 and played twenty-four performances. The sound design was by Chuck London and Stewart Werner. The stage managers were Jody Boese and Kate Stewart. The *Times* gave no ground for the writers' inexperience:

The New York Times, May 9, 1982 (Mel Gussow):
"Three of the plays deal with stereotypical adolescent anxieties. Although each author demonstrates at least a modicum of writing ability, all three efforts are blunted by self-pity and sentimentality. In direct contrast, the two plays by the youngest winners are entertaining. The two programs of plays, running in repertory, are of interest more for their psychological implications than for their theatrical value. Their concerns are serious, and perhaps in time the playwrights will be able to express them in a more artful fashion."

Despite Mel Gussow's grumbling, the New York Drama Critics Circle gave a Special Citation for the Young Playwright's Festival to Circle Repertory Company and the Dramatists Guild. We proudly hung the prestigious award in our small lobby, along with our other two for *HOT L* and *Talley's Folly*. And it should be noted that Kenneth Lonegran, following his debut in the Young Playwright's Festival at Circle Rep, went on to write the sensational *This Is Our Youth* and won the 2016 Academy Award for Original Screenplay for *Manchester by the Sea*.

In the spring, we presented a PiP of Harvey Fierstein's *Spook House* and a PiP of Shelby Buford's *Screaming Eagle*, directed by Rod Marriott. I liked both of them but serious exhaustion was fraying my ability to commit to anything. I was looking forward to a sabbatical, so neither of these excellent projects went any further. I regret missing the opportunity to take Harvey into our fold of resident playwrights.

Canada was granted independence from the United Kingdom by Queen Elizabeth II. President Reagan kicked off the 1982 World's Fair in Knoxville, Tennessee, attended by 100,000 people the first day. During its six-month run, the fair was attended by more than eleven million. The Falklands War ended with the formal surrender of Argentine forces. The Equal Rights Amendment fell short of the thirty-eight states needed to pass, defeated by Phyllis Schlafly and the Christian right.

A New Phase for Feiffer

I was delighted to welcome José Quintero to Circle Rep when he directed Liv Ulman in *The Human Voice* because it erased whatever bitter feelings still simmered after he replaced me as the director of *Knock Knock*. Now we had the opportunity to welcome back the author of that play with a new project he wanted to premiere at Circle Rep: Jules Feiffer.

In the intervening years Jules wrote *Hold Me!*, a successful revue that probed hilariously into the doubtful joys and small terrors of urban living. It was produced by the American Place Theater at the Westside Cabaret in February 1977, where it played 100 performances and was directed by Caymichael Patten. When Jules finished his new play, *A Think Piece*, he returned to Circle Rep, bringing with him his recent collaborator Ms. Patten to direct.

I was in rehearsal for *Angels Fall* (described in the following chapter) at the same time Jules was rehearsing *A Think Piece*, so I saw nothing of the rehearsal or casting process and only saw the play at the opening when we returned from Miami.

From our acting Company, Debra Mooney was cast as the principal character, Betty, and Katherine Cortez was her sister, Pam. The Guest Artists were Andrew Duncan as Bett's husband, Gordon, and Ann Sachs as Betty's other sister, Mandy. As the two bratty kids, Caymichael found Tenney Walsh for Ginny and we were introduced to Samantha Atkins, who played Lulu and became Circle Rep's youngest member of the Company. The dog, Zero, was played by a white, bushy toy poodle named Patches, who had two handlers and was paid more than any of the humans.

A Think Piece takes place in the high-rise apartment of the Castle family in Manhattan's East 80s. Betty Castle is a housewife bereft of self-respect and no one in her family takes her seriously. Worse still, she is drowning in the trivia of everyday life. Betty has a congenial husband, two competitive sisters and two bratty young daughters, but her days are defined by shopping lists, vacuuming, the arrangement of flowers about her East Side apartment and the task of taking out the dog. Betty decides that only by "going crazy" can she gain "control over events." Go crazy she does, but not before some pungent speeches that sum up her predicament. When Betty can't get anyone to take responsibility for taking care of Zero, she tosses the dog out the window of her high-rise apartment. It was hilariously horrible. It's virtually the only moment I remember from the play.

A Think Piece by Jules Feiffer opened at Circle Rep on June 26, 1982 and played forty-one performances. It was directed by Caymichael Patton, with a set by Kert Lundell, costumes by Denise Romano, lighting by Dennis Parichy and sound by Chuck London Media. The stage manager was Ginny Martino. The critics were disappointed the play was not funnier, given that it was written by America's foremost satirist:

The New York Times, June 29, 1982 (Frank Rich):

"Feiffer has something corrosive to say in his new comedy, and, as always, he has an unusual, at times daring, way to say it. *A Think Piece* falls flat, yet one keeps feeling the nagging sensation that this work may be more vigorous than the Circle Rep's production lets on. Though Feiffer is by no means blameless for the failures, it can't be easy for a writer to hone a tricky scene when it is inadequately cast and raggedly staged. If the writing is too sketchy, the acting is threadbare. The cast is competent, but the director Caymichael Patton, hasn't pushed them to the stylized yet incisive playing level that Feiffer's special, prickly voice demands."

The New York Times, July 4, 1982 (Walter Kerr):

"The dog, whose character name was Zero but whose actual name is Patches, [is] the most attractive and interesting character in Mr. Feiffer's play. *A Think Piece* is unfunny, unpersuasive and downright trying. It does have something to tell us. The author wants us to know that it isn't the serious crises in our lives that do us in. It's the endlessly recurring trivia, the little things that drive us crazy. Theatrically speaking, he certainly proves his point. On the stage at the Circle Rep, the little things drive you absolutely bonkers."

During the run of *A Think Piece*, we presented two PiPs: Claris Nelson's *Double Album* (which she renamed *Comeback*) was directed by B. Rodney Marriott; and John Bard Manulis directed Marjorie Applemann's *Foxtrot by the Bay*. A week or so later, we went on location in New London, Connecticut to tape *Fifth of July* for Showtime and PBS.

By the end of these three seasons, despite our many successes (both commercially and artistically) it was evident that Circle Rep's creativity was flagging. In the final chapter, I'll describe the glow that remained from our original inspiration.

Nevertheless, it's worth noting that in these three years, even as our inner light was fading, our Projects in Progress program developed such illustrious plays as Marsha Norman's Pulitzer Prize-winning *'Night, Mother*, Bill C. Davis' Broadway and film success *Mass Appeal*, Terrence McNally's 2014 Broadway hit *It's Only a Play*, and Kenneth Lonergan's first play, launching him on a career of writing such landmark scripts as *This is Our Youth*, another Broadway hit of 2014. Along with our earlier discoveries of David Ives and Howard Ashman, even our workshop efforts continued to confirm our leadership as the chief source of new American plays.

CHAPTER 18
A COSMIC GLOW

I think we reached the summit of Circle Rep's creativity with our production of Lanford Wilson's *Angels Fall*. The quality of transcendence was never more visible. The coming together of an important play about our times with an ensemble of dedicated collaborators marked this production as a culmination of Circle Rep's initial mission. One of America's leading playwrights wrote a script for specific members of a highly trained company and that ensemble of actors, designers and director delivered a living play that illuminated the human condition. That's pretty much what we set out to do.

At the conclusion of the series of classical plays in rep with *Richard II* and *Jedediah Kohler*, I had reached a point of spiritual exhaustion. The day-to-day burdens of running a theater overtook my inspiration. I needed to be free of administrative obligations in order to grow as an artist. I asked the Board for a two-year sabbatical, which they granted me. The beginning of my sabbatical coincided with the opportunity to direct *Angels Fall*. So as tired as I was, my newfound freedom from responsibility unleashed inspiration to a degree I had not experienced since the founding of Circle Rep.

Matching my rejuvenation, the designers John Lee Beatty, Dennis Parichy, Jennifer von Mayrhauser, Chuck London, and composer Norman L. Berman reached a pinnacle of their own; after eight years of supporting and inspiring each other, this team of artists attained a collaboration unsurpassed in contemporary theater.

As for the cast, no group of actors in my experience could rival their fusion of impulse, depth and unity. Fritz Weaver and Barnard Hughes combined for a century of expertise. Nancy Snyder, Danton Stone, Tanya Berezin and Brian Tarantina had played together in various combinations, and now they rose to the quintessence of ensemble playing. Their voices were like an orchestra, their movement like a ballet. They transcended ordinary theater. The glow from Circle Rep's creation was still evident.

Inspiration from a Vision

The city of Miami launched The New World Festival of the Arts in an attempt to boost summer tourism in Florida. As Lanford wryly noted: "I don't think it worked." This ambitious project was never to be repeated. They commissioned three new plays from Edward Albee, Tennessee Williams and Lanford Wilson to premiere in Miami at the Coconut Grove Playhouse. Edward premiered his *The Man Who Had Three Arms*, directed by the author prior to Broadway. Tennessee's play was *A House Not Meant to Stand*, which premiered earlier in 1982 at the Goodman Theater in Chicago, directed by Gregory Mosher. I saw it in Miami and found it thick with confusion. Lanford fulfilled his commission with *Angels Fall*, contingent on the New World Festival's willingness to bring in Circle Rep to produce it. They agreed.

Lanford says in his introduction to the play in *Collected Works, Volume II* that *Angels Fall* came to him in an "eye-opening flash," one of only three plays (the others were *Lemon Sky* and *Burn This*) that originated in such a manner. Although Lanford disparaged it as a "genre" play, I think it's one of his most evocative scripts.

Lanford had two especially close friends in Sag Harbor: the artist Lou Fink and his wife, Florence. Having begun as a painter himself, Lanford was very fond of Lou and appreciative of his work. The two artists shared a rare simpatico relationship. In the year before Lanford wrote *Angels Fall*, Lou died, leaving his friends grieving his loss. So Lanford put the death of an artist as one of the central circumstances in the play. The character is Ernie, who has recently passed away and his estate (including his extensive collection of paintings) is being arranged by his ex-wife Marion Clay, an art dealer who has a gallery in Chicago. Lanford wrote the sophisticated part of Marion for Tanya Berezin, who also was a friend to the late Lou Fink. Marion is accompanied on this trip to settle Ernie's estate with her "boytoy," Salvatore Zappala (Zappy), a young professional tennis player. Lanford wrote Zappy for the delightfully eccentric Brian Tarantina, who received a Theater World Award for his performance. These two characters will leave for a tennis tournament in Los Angeles as soon as Ernie's affairs are wrapped up.

Lanford's initial vision that came in a flash was seeing inside a dirt-poor adobe church for Southwestern Indians, where an agitated professor (Niles Harris) and his much younger wife (Vita) are seeking respite from the blistering sun in the coolness of the church. This odd couple is on their way to a psychiatric sanatorium in Phoenix, where Niles is to receive treatment for a nervous breakdown that erupted on the campus of an eastern university where he teaches. But they have been turned back on the highway because, presumably, a bridge is out.

The church is the abode of a jolly priest (Father William Dougherty) and his foster-son, Doctor Don Tabaha, a half-Indian who has grown up in Father Bill's care. Don has recently completed medical school and has been offered a rewarding job as a cancer researcher at an esteemed clinic in San Francisco operated by a famous expert, Dr. Lindermann. Father Bill is alarmed by the temptation for Don to leave behind his tribal practice, since the Indians that are Don's people and make up Father Bill's congregation suffer from so much deprivation. But as the play begins, Don, too, is delayed in his departure on his motorcycle by the same travel problems that have waylaid the two couples. No one can leave until the mysterious road closure has ended. Before long, it emerges that the closure is due to an accident involving radioactive yellowcake from the nearby atomic testing range.

Lanford was convinced that contemporary culture was so enamored with the thrill of danger that the risk of a catastrophic atomic disaster was titillating, allowing governments to build up ridiculous stockpiles of atomic weapons and to continue testing them, no matter how unnecessary. He thought we've grown to *like* the excitement of living under the threat of nuclear annihilation.

Lanford wrote Father Bill for Helen Stenborg's husband, the impish, charismatic Barnard Hughes. Lanford always admired Barney and was eager to create a rich characterization for him that would defy the cliché of a drunken priest. He wrote the young Indian doctor for the dark-complexioned Danton Stone, who had demonstrated a wide range at Circle Rep, from a rebellious servant in *Mrs. Murray's Farm* to the amusingly slow Weston Hurley in *Fifth of July*. The surly young medical genius would give Danny a wonderful change of pace.

Knocked out by Fritz Weaver's dynamic performance in *A Tale Told*, Lanford crafted the part of Niles Harris for Fritz. This tall, elegant actor effortlessly conveyed the effete refinement of an Ivy League Art Historian, with the quirky explosiveness of a mentally fragile professor in full bloom. Lanford wrote his young wife, Vita, for the ethereally beautiful Nancy Snyder, whose calm and peaceful charm were an essential balance to Niles' instability.

John Lee Beatty's design for the church was a masterpiece of simplicity. Downstage on the left, we see two massive wooden doors that attest to the age of the building. Upstage from the entrance is a small chest-high square window, whose two-foot thickness shows the solidity of the white walls. Just slightly off-center upstage is a corner of the little adobe desert mission, so the central back wall is not quite parallel to the front of the stage and contains the spare elements of an altar. To the right of the altar, a jog in the wall provides a door leading to Father Dougherty's living quarters, shared with Don and their cook, Maria (who is talked about, but not seen). Continuing downstage to the right, the wall arrives at the proscenium with a pair of side garden doors that open into a dusty courtyard. So the sanctuary is seen on a slight angle, with four rows of rough-hewn, wooden, backless benches parallel to the altar, separated by a center aisle.

Because Father Bill serves the Indian community on a rotating basis, traveling from one small mission to another, the room contains no permanent religious icons. The plain wooden table Up Center becomes an altar only when he covers it with a white lace cloth and produces from his traveling bag a small standing cross, a chalice and a silver salver for Communion. The candles lighted near the end of the play as the priest prepares for the service are small votives in glass holders. Almost unnoticed to the left of the great, simply carved entrance doors, outside near the proscenium, is a rudimentary eighteen-inch bell on a stand that the priest rings to summon his parishioners.

As the play opens, the room is in cool shadows, emphasized by the scorching sunlight pouring in at the small window where Don Tabaha stands looking out onto the parking lot. As he sees someone coming, he quickly leaves through the small door to the living quarters.

When Niles and Vita enter, the huge doors swing wide open with an inferno of blinding light from the sweltering midday sun. Dennis Parichy's lighting was praised as being Georgia O'Keefe-like, illuminating the church with unmistakably Southwestern sunlight. He placed a stanchion of brilliant lights blazing from the left wing of the stage. The actors complained to me that they were blinded by the lights and I responded, "Yes, that's right. You are so blinded you'll need to shade your eyes to see where you're going." Dennis' lights made the presence of the desert a haunting reminder of the isolation of the church near the atomic testing range.

Then there were Jennifer von Mayrhauser's exquisitely perfect costumes, each color, each texture, each fabric absolutely right. Vita's simple jersey skirt flowed with her lissome movement. I've never seen an actor who could surpass Nancy Snyder's willowy poise; simply crossing the stage was the epitome of grace.

Toward the end of the play, government helicopters fly overhead to announce the opening of the roads. Chuck London designed the sound of the incredibly close flight over the heads of the audience. It shook the auditorium. Company composer

Norman L. Berman wrote a haunting melody played on a primitive Indian pipe that mourned the loss of friends and longed for a better future.

The entire visual experience, combining the set, lights, costumes and movement was a delicate painting brought to life with Vermeer-like authenticity. Including the sound and music, all the elements came together in a perfection that we achieved only half a dozen times: *The Sea Horse, The Mound Builders, Talley & Son, As Is* and later, *Book of Days*. The seamless work of the cast equaled our utmost accomplishments of ensemble playing: *Balm in Gilead, The HOT L BALTIMORE, Fifth of July* and *A Tale Told*. Altogether, Lanford wrote:

> "This production was by a considerable measure the most beautiful Marshall and I and our design team had so far accomplished."

John Lee Beatty and Dennis Parichy won Miami's Carbonell Award for Best Scenic and Lighting Design.

When it came time to put the production together, Barnard Hughes was not available to travel to Miami to play the priest Lanford had written for him. Fortunately, there was a good solution. I had seen Richard Seff in an Off-Broadway production of *Modigliani* at the Astor Playhouse, playing that artist's agent. I was so impressed with his portrayal that I offered to make him part of Circle Rep. Richard had been an author in his younger days and switched to being an artist's agent for most of his career. Now approaching his "character" years, he returned to acting and was a grateful member of the acting Company. I approached Richard to see if he would agree to fill in as Father William Dougherty. Knowing full well that eventually he would be replaced by Barney, Richard eagerly signed on to create the role in Miami, as well as its successive productions at Lucille Lortel's White Barn Theater in Connecticut and the John Houseman Theater in Saratoga Springs. The only material recompense for this generous artistic contribution was a little pocket cash for understudying Barney when the play moved to Broadway. The artistic experience, however, is a cherished memory, the highpoint of Richard's acting career. He was wonderful in the part and won the Carbonell Award for Best Supporting Actor.

Lanford was always ambivalent about commissions; on the one hand, they were a strong motivating factor; on the other, they became an obligation, which he hated. He was lax in fulfilling his commission, putting off writing until the last possible moment. In April, just six weeks or so before rehearsals were to begin, he had finished only the first act. Needing to kick start inspiration, Lanford decided what was called for was a research trip to New Mexico where he could soak up the Western atmosphere, see Native Americans at close range, and immerse himself in the artistic vibes of Taos. As I've mentioned, Lanford rarely flew, preferring the comforting sway of a railroad car; so he booked his trip on a train from New York to Denver. But Lanford also hated being alone, so he decided to use a portion of his commission money to take along a couple of the actors for whom he was writing roles: Tanya Berezin and Danton Stone. He also asked Clyde Vincent, Circle Rep's vocal coach, to join them, since Clyde had spent considerable time in Taos and would be able to facilitate introductions, especially on the Indian reservations. Tanya, Danton and Clyde flew to Denver, where they picked up Lanford at the train station, rented a car and drove down to Taos. They spent five days there, storing up valuable details to use in creating their characters; and Lanford got the jolt of inspiration he needed to finish the play. I was in London at the time, directing *Talley's Folly*, so I missed this great adventure. I'm very envious.

Lanford finished the first draft just as we began rehearsals. The rehearsal period was only three weeks, a week shorter than usual, so our work felt very rushed. Lanford recalled that we had no complete run-through of the play until the opening performance. But something miraculous occurred when the cast began to play together that opening night, providing a breathtaking experience of seeing a script spring to life. The effect of Circle Rep actors was so natural that the audience could not tell we hadn't been playing it in our repertoire for years. Only Lanford and I understood the nerve-racking reality that lay beneath their apparently relaxed, spontaneous creativity.

Angels Fall premiered at the Coconut Grove Playhouse in Miami, Florida on June 19, 1982. It was directed by Marshall W. Mason, setting by John Lee Beatty, lighting by Dennis Parichy, costumes by Jennifer von Mayrhauser, sound design by Chuck London and original score by Norman L. Berman. The stage manager was Fred Reinglas. Here are the first impressions of the Florida reviewers:

The Miami Herald, June 20, 1982 (Christine Arnold):
"*Angels Fall* is a drama grown from richly textured characters, a play that is sometimes belly-laugh funny and full of conversation that displays the playwright's adept ear for the way very different people speak. Wilson is sometimes called Chekhovian in style. [But] if the play sometimes appears rather aimless, it's a combination of Wilson's gift for evoking realism and the fact that this is the first production of the play, which will open the fall season of New York's Circle Rep. In other words, [it's] a work in progress, and more work is needed. Wilson will do that work along with director Mason, and they may wind up with a wonderful play; Wilson's canvas is already painted with some glorious characters. [The Priest] played by Richard Seff is priceless and endearing. Weaver makes the Professor a cultured and self-tortured man. Marion is exquisitely acted by Berezin. Tarantina is enormously funny. The production values, from the Circle Rep team, are superb."

Miami News, June 21, 1982 (Bill von Mauer):
"*Angels Fall* is an empty piece of posturing nonsense. A good hunk of the audience departed after the first act and, hopefully, went someplace to have a quieting drink. They

needed it. There are worse things in life [than a nuclear accident], and *Angels Fall* is one of them."

The Sacramento Bee, June 15, 1982 (Bill Glackin):
"With shows such as Wilson's *Angels Fall,* Miami's New World Festival of the Arts is going into the record books as an extremely distinguished affair. As in the Wilson plays the public knows best, there is a lot of talk. As usual, the talk is not only good but important. As usual, the people are what the play is about. In Wilson's play, you make friends, you're sorry to see them go when the play is over, and you wish them well. These people are eminently worth knowing. Weaver is very fine. Snyder is an excellent wife. Stone is rock solid, a dour, untrusting, impatient, but still sympathetic figure. Mason's direction is full of insights. Beatty's set is, as usual, wholly believable."

During the run at the Coconut Grove, Lanford created a regrettable stir in the empty lobby, shoving an elderly lady as she was walking out on the production. This is the incident that I think triggered Lanford's resolve to give up drinking. Although she was uninjured, he and the theater were fortunate the lady didn't sue. We played a week in steamy Miami and then returned to cooler climes up north. In July, we were in refreshing Connecticut, capturing the extraordinary ensemble of *Fifth of July* for PBS and Showtime. It was a creative summer after a winter of discontent.

The Mission Continues

While Jeff Daniels was electrifying audiences at Circle Rep with *Johnny Got His Gun* in August of 1982, the cast of *Angels Fall* got back together to play a weekend at Lucille Lortel's White Barn Theater near Westport.

There is an autobiographical passage in *Angel's Fall* in which Lanford wrote about the crucial discovery of what one is meant to do in life. When he went to Chicago, he registered for a writing course at the night school of the University of Chicago. One of his assignments was to write a story that contained some dialogue. Lanford hadn't written more than a couple of lines when he was struck with a blinding self-discovery: he was a playwright. Lanford dramatized that defining moment in *Angels Fall*, when Zappy describes how he realized he was a tennis player:

> "Zappy: I was like in the fifth grade and I was watching these two hamburgers on some practice court, and they took a break and one of them hands me his racket. So I threw up a toss like I'd seen them do and zap! Three inches over the net, two inches inside the line. There wasn't nobody over there, but that was an ace, man."

It was an epiphany that Lanford recognized in his own life:

> "Zappy: That was it. I hit that first ball and I said, 'This is me. This is what I do. What I do is tennis.' And once you know, then there's no way out. You've been showed something. Even if it's just tennis, you can't turn around and say you wasn't showed that. So I went to church and said a novena for those meatballs 'cause they didn't know all the butterflies that was in my stomach, that they'd been my angels. But man, on the way home, anybody had asked me what I did, right there I'd have said, 'I play tennis' Didn't know love from lob, didn't matter. That's what I am. 'Cause once you know what you are, the rest is just work."

Defining one's self by work is a central theme throughout Lanford's writing.

The thematic question in *Angels Fall* is posed by Father Dougherty, reading from the Bible, after describing the end of the world:

> "Seeing then that all these things shall be dissolved, what manner of persons ought ye to be?"

For the priest, it's transparently clear what Don's decision should be; he is obligated morally to stay at home and help his tribe. This was a viewpoint that Lanford fervently shared. He saw Don's chance to go to the clinic as a temptation that must be resisted. When he finished the first draft of the play, which was the script we played at the opening in Miami, the deck was completely stacked against Don; the priest was right and that was that.

I saw the issue of Don's dilemma quite differently. I argued that Lanford needed to even out the contention over this moral decision, because one must consider the potential good Don might do at the clinic, perhaps even discovering a cure for cancer. I told Lanford that as written, the play was little more than a Catholic morality play. He was taken aback by this charge; he had not intended to preach.

Providentially, we had a character on stage that could shore up my side of the debate: the Professor questions the kind of authority the priest represents, a disbelief that has resulted in his "nervous breakdown." One factor that contributes to Niles' crumbling evaluation of reality is the recent suicide of a promising student, afraid he was sexually deviant. Niles ably defends the young doctor's right to decide for himself which is the "moral" choice.

After playing a weekend at the White Barn, we moved on to the Saratoga Performing Arts Center, where we resumed rehearsals after our month-long break and Lanford continued working on the script, incorporating the new elements of conflict, framing this fight over the soul of the young Indian doctor as an even battle, in which everyone was free to agree with either point of view. The debate was well dramatized and engaged the hearts and minds of the audience in a gripping moral conflict. I'm proud of the dramaturgical contribution I made to strengthening the battle in the play and I believe Lanford's revisions make *Angels Fall* one of his most compassionate plays. Overlooked among his *oeuvre*, I think this play and *Talley & Son,* written only months apart, are (as yet) unrecognized paradigms of construction that will be celebrated when they are rediscovered.

Angels Fall opened at the John Houseman Theater in Saratoga Springs, New York on August 19, 1982, with the entire production from the Coconut Grove intact. Here are the insights of the local reviewers:

Albany Times Union, August 24, 1982 (Martin P. Kelly):
"Wilson has peopled the stage with six absorbing characters. All are totally engrossing. Under Mason's staging, [the actors] create a marvelous mosaic of people caught up in crucial moments of their personal lives. Wilson's dialogue crackles and illuminates. Yet, the script has its drawbacks. It's too leisurely in setting the personal conflicts in motion. The set by Beatty is a wonderful replica of the mission church, and the lighting by Parichy evokes the heat and shadows of the desert locale. In all, it is a first-class production of a very promising script due for its New York City premiere in October."

The Glens Falls Post-Star, August 23, 1982 (Bob Rose):
"The New York debut of Wilson's *Angels Fall* at SPAC proves to be a major event. And a happy one too. The play makes some important statements about the role of the individual in the nuclear world. It does so with interesting, appealing characters and resourceful dialogue. Astutely avoiding all stereotypes, Wilson has created what have been aptly termed glorious characters. Weaver brings magnificent dimensions to the art professor. His wife is beautifully played by Snyder. The painter's widow is stunningly portrayed by Berezin. Stone performs superlatively as the stoical medical student. Tarantina gives a vibrant performance as the tennis pro, while Richard Seff as the priest acts with brilliant nonchalance. He makes the priest's remarkable honesty a source of effervescent humor. It is a richly satisfying and very promising play."

The Schenectady Gazette, August 24, 1982 (Dan Dinicola):

"Even though it is still being revised and polished, *Angels Fall* is already a presentation well worth your attendance. Both provocative and entertaining, Circle Rep's presentation is one of the few highlights of the summer's professional drama season. Buttressed by some excellent direction by Mason, *Angels Fall* features both credible characterizations and provocative dialogue. Two superb performances are turned in by Weaver and Seff. Wilson's *Angels Fall* is more than a promising work in progress. Compelling, humorous and intelligent, Circle Rep's production is not only one I recommend highly, but one which should fare well in New York as well."

The Times Record, August 20, 1982 (Doug deLisle):

"Although it's a serious play, it has lots of legitimate humor. The play is over-written, but the playwright has been working hard on the script and has until mid-October to prepare the play for New York. There is enough that already works in the script to give hope that it can be turned into a work of integrity. Mason directs with swift and telling strokes, and the physical production, especially Beatty's detailed set, is class all the way"

The Saratogian, August 20, 1982 (Craig Wilson):

"It is a good play. The characters grow as the evening progresses. And by the end, I didn't want the people to leave. If you want to get lost for a couple of hours and get involved in some problems other than your own, I suggest you take a look at *Angels Fall.* It is one of those plays that will make you laugh, and cry."

Mission in Manhattan

Back in the City, we went back into rehearsal, polishing our summer work and incorporating Barnard Hughes into the production, replacing our very able Richard Seff as Father Dougherty. Throughout this extended journey, rehearsals were an adventure of new discovery from the rich characterizations Lanford created. John Lee's set fit so snugly into the intimacy of Circle Rep that the whole theater felt transformed into a mission.

Angels Fall opened at Circle Repertory Company on October 16, 1982, where It played for thirty-three performances. Here are the New York critics' first impressions:

The New York Times, October 18, 1982 (Frank Rich):
"Mr. Wilson is one of the few artists in our theater who can truly make America sing. Though *Angels Fall* is not a successful play, its unmistakable flaws are often drowned out by the moving sound of its author's tender, democratic voice. There are six characters, all fully realized in the writing and by the exquisite cast assembled by the director Mason. Wilson cannot escape the contrived nature of his plot gimmick. It's too predictable and implausible, as well as sentimental. Yet the human spirits bottled up in the play's artificial enclosure are real. Wilson is a master at confounding our expectations. Wilson's supreme achievement in this play is the academic couple. Miss Snyder, who hasn't worked nearly enough since she created the role of the flipped-out heiress in the original Circle Rep production of *Fifth of July*, is the perfect counterbalance to the dynamic Mr. Weaver. But the whole production is beyond reproach. Mr. Mason's staging suffuses *Angels Fall* with a mood of repose that reinforces the setting's serenity and suggests the ecstasy of inner peace that the characters seek. John Lee Beatty has designed a Spartan adobe mission of dreamlike radiance, and Dennis Parichy has flooded it with Southwestern light worthy of Georgia O'Keefe."

Daily News, October 18, 1982 (Douglas Watt):
"Since Wilson is a gifted and exceptionally deft playwright given the benefit of a first-rate cast directed by

Mason with considerable virtuosity, the evening flows along entertainingly. The talk and the situations are, for the most part, lively and real. All are admirably set forth. The players mesh beautifully under Mason's confident hand. Beatty's broad and evocative set is enhanced by von Mayrhauser's artful costumes and Parichy's lighting (you can practically feel the June heat outside). *Angels Fall* is a neat piece of play carpentry set before us with a fine professional polish."

New York Post, October 18, 1982 (Clive Barnes):
"*Angels Fall* is an exquisitely wrought old-fashioned new play. It is realistic, yet it sings with a sweet, unaffected poetry. Wilson and his long-time director Mason deeply involve us in the action, which in its quiet, understated way becomes a parable of vocation and survival. Wilson has one eye for truth and one eye for detail that give him 20/20 vision. His world is astonishingly real. It is a realism carefully nurtured by the production. Beatty's adobe mission is a small miracle of design and, together with Parichy's uncannily accurate lighting, transports the audience to sun and shelter in New Mexico. The costumes by von Mayrhauser and the sound by Chuck London are, equally, as sensitive as a Geiger counter. The acting is flawless. Fritz Weaver and Danton Stone are outstanding, but the sweetest performance comes from Barnard Hughes. These are people caught in a particular pulse in their lives – and we are invited to stare and consider. It is an invitation worth accepting."

WQXR, October 18, 1982 (Mel Gussow):
"Wilson's new play is a deeply humane consideration of fathers and sons, teachers and students, and mankind facing its own possible extinction. But since Wilson is such a masterful craftsman as well as a theater poet, the apocalyptic aspects of the play are never overstated. The evening has a

naturalness and a confidence that can only come from an artist creating at the peak of his form. Under Mason's unerring direction, the evening begins leisurely, in a beautiful, sunlit set designed by Beatty. Barnard Hughes, in his best performance since *Da,* is an exceedingly endearing figure. In an equally fine performance, Danton Stone has the baleful intensity of the short-fused doctor. As in his *Fifth of July,* the author completely envelops us in the lives of representative but individual Americans and, as in *The Mound Builders,* he is discussing a public issue with his customary fair-mindedness and intelligence. [It's] a compelling group portrait – a memorable new play from a major American playwright."

The New York Times, October 31, 1982 (Walter Kerr):
"Our plays are growing articulate again. Wilson's agreeable and ultimately rather touching get-together at the Circle Rep is an artifice of sorts. Its people have little to do but talk about themselves, but being products of Wilson's fertile imagination, they talk well. It's the lively self-description, together with the selves involved, that keep us listening."

The New Yorker, November 1, 1982 (Edith Oliver):
"With the years, Wilson grows ever more proficient, and if at times he disturbs my own willing suspension of disbelief or seems somewhat glib in writing here about the most important subject on earth, his play in all its detail, is constantly absorbing. About the performance, I have no reservations whatever; under the deft direction of Mason, who has come to function as Wilson's alter-ego, it is first rate. Beatty has, as usual, designed a remarkably effective setting on the tiny stage."

New York Magazine, November 1, 1982 (John Simon):
"The wonder of it is that Wilson writes with such insight and tact, such respect for his flawed but flavorous characters, such sprightly dialogue, and such intelligent decency that the absence

of plot, the slight contrivedness, the problems that nuzzle triteness take on a crisp cleanliness, as of a bed of freshly laundered sheets. We slip into this play as between ozone-exhaling linen, and feel refreshed, renewed. Wilson's range, both in his *oeuvre* and in this relatively slight play, is imposing. He has a sense of all kinds of places and activities, and uncovers both their extraorinariness and their ordinariness with acuity and joy; and best of all he knows people of every stripe, in the manner of someone with the rare gift of observation. And not only observation, but also synthesis and dramatic confrontation. Matters are enormously helped by Mason's masterly direction, which seems totally self-effacing yet is always there, not missing a trick. Beatty's mission could not be more genuine, sacred, and inviting; Parichy's oblique lighting captures the fugitive afternoon like a fly in amber; and von Mayrhauser's costumes are subtly, understatedly revealing. The acting ensemble could hardly be improved on. Snyder's performance is astounding: she is precariously commanding, anxiously smiling, and deeply moving. *Angels Fall* has its little blemishes, but it puts you absolutely *there*, into its problems, into the ways of caring and coping, into people touched by the holiness of a place. It is a play you may find yourself – unusually – loving."

Daily News, November 1, 1982 (Rex Reed):

"*Angels Fall* is one of those rare evenings of theatrical fireworks that no serious theater enthusiast can afford to miss. Wilson is our most important contemporary writer for the theater, and this play is one of his finest."

The Village Voice, October 26, 1982 (Julius Novick):

"That famous Circle Rep ensemble is very much in evidence. Wilson has dramatized [the characters'] interactions so deftly, and Mason has directed such a full and mellow production, that *Angels Fall* is a warm, funny, touching, highly satisfying theatrical evening."

The Star-Ledger, October 18, 1982 (William A. Raidy):
"Wilson's play isn't particularly profound but it is an infinitely moving – and involving – work. *Angels Fall,* splendidly directed by Mason, is a vastly human play that touches the heart, reaffirming the glory of life, even when it is lived – as it must be in this age – in confusion."

Angels Fall was named among the Ten Best Plays of 1982 on lists by Mel Gussow (*WQXR*), Clive Barnes (*New York Post*), Douglas Watt and Don Nelson (both of the *Daily News*).

Flying Uptown

Despite Frank Rich's reservations about the play, he continued to bring attention to *Angels Fall* as the autumn progressed:

The New York Times, November 11, 1982 (Frank Rich):
"One can see top ensemble acting by any standard from the sextet who populate Lanford Wilson's flawed *Angel's Fall*."

There was growing anticipation about an extended run of the play. We had to find a producer to head a transfer, so we turned once again to Elliott Martin, who'd moved *Red Ryder* to commercial success eight years before. I was more than usually active (aided by my agent, Irv Schwartz of The Lantz Office, who shared my belief in the play) in pulling together the elements we need for a Broadway move.

We had two legitimate Broadway stars in Tony Award-winners Bernard Hughes and Fritz Weaver. I talked to my good friend Lucille Lortel (known fondly as the Queen of Off-Broadway), who was a member of our Board. Since she'd presented the play in her White Barn Theater, Lucille felt a proprietary connection to the production and she agreed to invest $50,000 in the move. The Shubert Organization, owners of seventeen Broadway theaters, came on board, matching Lucille's contribution, and suggesting she double it, which she did and so did they. The Kennedy Center presumably put in another investment, but the overall budget for moving the play to Broadway was under $300,000; there was no leeway for an adequate advertising budget.

> *The New York Times,* December 17, 1982 (Carol Lawson):
> "Lanford Wilson's play *Angels Fall*, which recently ended a successful run at the Circle Rep and which was headed for another Off-Broadway theater, has had a sudden change of course. The play is rerouted to Broadway, where it will reopen next month. The exact opening dates and the theater, which will be one of the Shubert houses, cannot be announced yet. The production will move uptown intact. The producers are Circle Rep, Lucille Lortel, the Shubert Organization, the Kennedy Center, and Elliot Martin. Wilson sounds not only confident, but utterly exuberant about the uptown prospects for *Angels Fall*. "The writing is as good as anything I've ever done," he said. "I don't think I've ever had a show that audiences liked so much, except maybe *Talley's Folly*. If *Fifth of July* could run over a year, I'm optimistic about *Angels Fall*."

The one full-page ad the producers took out for *Angels Fall* was the one announcing our move to Broadway. Here are the quotes they used to announce the transfer:

> "Lanford Wilson truly makes America sing. *Angels Fall* can be loved for its rich writing and generosity of spirit. Marshall W. Mason's exquisite production suggests the ecstasy of inner peace the characters seek. One is grateful to be among them!"
> —Frank Rich, *The New York Times*
>
> "*Angels Fall* is brisk and forthright and funny."
> —Walter Kerr, *The New York Times*

"One of the year's best! *Angels Fall* sings with sweet, unaffected poetry. Exquisitely wrought, astonishingly real, the acting is flawless."

—Clive Barnes, *New York Post*

"*Angels Fall* glows! Slip into this play and feel refreshed and renewed. A play you may find yourself loving."

—John Simon, *New York Magazine*

"Touches the heart! *Angels Fall* is infinitely moving. Vastly human, a splendidly directed play that reaffirms the glory of life! Fritz Weaver is brilliant."

—William A. Raidy, *Newhouse Newspapers*

"Enormously rewarding! Lanford Wilson is unmatched in capturing both the humor and cry from the heart of his contemporaries."

—Edwin Wilson, *The Wall Street Journal*

"Warm, funny, touching! *Angels Fall* is a highly satisfying, absorbing, theatrical evening."

—Julius Novick, *The Village Voice*

"Winning and eloquent! An engaging, comic and touching play about individual responsibility and personal fulfillment."

—John Beaufort, *Christian Science Monitor*

"One of the year's best! Lively and entertaining. Barnard Hughes is a delight!"

—Douglas Watt, *New York Daily News*

"One of the year's best! A deeply human consideration of fathers and sons, teachers and students, and mankind facing its own possible extinction, *Angels Fall* is a memorable play by a major American playwright at the peak of his form. Barnard Hughes givers his best performance since *Da*."

—Mel Gussow, *The New York Times*

"A warm, touching, comic look at the way we live now. A rewarding evening of theater."

—Howard Kissell, *Women's Wear Daily*

"Solidly entertaining! Pulitzer Prize playwright Lanford Wilson is in fine form. *Angels Fall* is full of affection and outstanding performances."

—Jay Sharbutt, *Associated Press*

"Theatrical fireworks!"

—Rex Reed

"One of the best plays in town!"

—Liz Smith

With an ad that quoted praise like this, one would think a Broadway audience would line up to buy tickets. But such was not to be the case.

Angels on Broadway

Angels Fall opened on Broadway at the Longacre Theater on January 18, 1983. It was produced by Elliot Martin, Circle Repertory, Lucille Lortel, the Shubert Organization and The Kennedy Center. Here's the critics' second look at the play:

New York Post, January 24, 1983 (Clive Barnes):
"*Angels Fall* has arrived on Broadway in its original production and with its original cast intact from Circle Rep. It is playing at the Longacre Theater, and it is a thousand times welcome – for this is assuredly one of the season's best plays. It sings with a sweet, unaffected poetry. The acting is flawless. This is just the kind of play that should be on Broadway – and one worth waiting for. It is exquisitely wrought, astonishingly real."

The New York Times, February 3, 1983 (Walter Kerr):
"*Angels Fall* has been successful enough at the Circle Rep to make a quite justified leap to Broadway. The talk is good. And lively."

The New York Times, February 6, 1983 (Frank Rich):
"*Angels Fall* is to be savored for the intelligence and cleareyed compassion that can be found in every line Wilson

writes, and for the high quality of the production. Under the loving direction of the playwright's longtime collaborator, Mason, the entire cast exemplifies American acting at its best. The exquisite production suggests the ecstasy of inner peace the characters seek. One is grateful to be among them."

The Daily News, January 5, 1983 (Don Nelson):
"Circle Rep has been on the side of the angels this year. *Angels Fall*, after generally fine notices at Circle Rep is flying north to Broadway. But this is more than just another Off-Broadway to Broadway move. The comedy-drama represents the thirty-seventh collaboration between Mason and Wilson. It also marks Wilson's third play to reach Broadway in the last four seasons. Justice at last for a playwright who seemed doomed to a permanent Off-Broadway existence and a smaller audience than he deserved. Wilson's skill at drawing human beings and his poetic tonality lend fresh perspective."

New York Magazine, February 7, 1983 (John Simon):
"Last November, I wrote enthusiastically about *Angels Fall*, which has now been moved unimpaired to Broadway. I am truly happy to report my undiminished pleasure at re-seeing the play. [It] is the best American play on Broadway this season. *Angels Fall* is a tender and moving experience, often marvelously droll, consistently but unforcedly dramatic, a lovely place to spend a couple of hours, whose sustaining aftertaste will linger in the consciousness a long, long time. Beatty's New Mexican mission is so clean and humble and holy that it may well produce religious conversions; Parichy's lighting you all but feel on and under your skin as it progresses from white heat to golden enlightenment. Wilson writes very likely the best dialogue in America today. How well Danton Stone smolders and mocks; Brian Tarantina [is]

excellent; Fritz Weaver is enchanting. Tanya Berezin does a dazzling balancing act with superiority and edginess; her performance is both lancet and poultice. Barnard Hughes is perfect down to the last little detail, and perfection is something you want to see, not read about in a column. And Nancy Snyder has gifts that are uncanny. And Mason has moved, disposed, and paced actors and words with shrewd and limitless diversity – and what eloquent pauses he and Wilson have wrought!"

The New Yorker, January 31, 1983 (Brendan Gill):
"Now in the winter of Broadway's discontent, it's a comfort to be able to salute an excellent play. *Angels Fall* opened last week at the Longacre Theater, for what should prove to be a lengthy visit. It is the particular good fortune of *Angels Fall* to be directed by Wilson's friend and colleague at Circle Rep, Mason, and to be enacted by a cast every member of which reads his lines to perfection and then, remaining silent, is so intensely present as to strike us as indispensable. The little rough-timbered adobe church trembles with the collision of six mingled contrarieties. The admirable setting, lighting and costumes are by, respectively, Beatty, Parichy (how did he manage to carry that fierce sunlight by hand all the way from New Mexico to West Forty-eighth Street?), and von Mayrhauser."

With this kind of extraordinary reception from the press, it seems incredible that *Angels Fall* lasted only sixty-four performances on Broadway, closing the week the Tony nominations were announced. We were nominated for Best Play and Best Director, but no Tony voters saw it because they were not yet invited by the producers. In his introduction to the play, Lanford blamed a lack of publicity for the premature closing. He recounts that he got a rare grin from notoriously dour Bernard Jacobs, head of the Shubert Organization, when he noted that word of mouth may not be the most effective way of advertising a play, but it is certainly the cheapest.

One annoying thing that couldn't be helpful to the box office was in the weekly listing of *The New York Times*, where they summarize *The Times* reviews. The editors chose to sum up Frank Rich's critique beginning: "Although the play is not a success ... ". After several weeks of this, I wrote *The Times* pointing out that some would imagine a play that has transferred to Broadway is in fact enjoying some success. As I questioned, what is their definition of success? The editors apparently saw the sense in my objection, because they changed the summary, eliminating the derogatory evaluation. It's the only time I've seen the arbiters of art concede a point and make a change.

Walter Kerr wrote a rebuttal to Frank Rich's characterization of *Angels Fall* as a genre play, in which the characters are artificially trapped in a situation wherein they undergo confessions and changes forced by the entrapment. *The Desperate Hours* and *When You Comin' Back, Red Ryder?* are two plays that adhere to this formulaic structure. Even *The Tempest* could be seen as a play of this "rats trapped in a trap" genre, but nobody would complain about Shakespeare's dramaturgy. Besides, as Mr. Kerr pointed out, two of the characters (Father Bill and Don) *live* here and so are not trapped; Marion and Zappy are free to return to Ernie's estate if they so chose; and even Niles and Vita could leave to seek more comfortable accommodations if they wanted to. Nobody is literally trapped in the church, so the charge of a genre play is inaccurately applied to *Angels Fall*. Nevertheless, Lanford accepted the designation of it as a genre play and considered that a flaw. So, as proud as he was of the production, Lanford always considered *Angels Fall* a bit of a stepchild in his body of work. As you may surmise, this is not an assessment I share.

"Adieu, Adieu, Remember Me"

On July 9, 1986, twenty days shy of his fiftieth birthday, Rob Thirkield, our inspirational founder and patron and my best friend, took his own life by jumping through the window of his high-rise apartment. He was the last in a long series of suicides in my life: Joe Cino, Zita Litvinas, Jim Tuttle, among others. Looking back, it seemed incredible that none of us saw this coming. Rob's choice of the plays he directed suggested a dark side: *Ghost Sonata*, *Exiles*, *Lulu* – all appear as obvious signs of a hidden pain. But Rob was the last person on earth I ever expected would end this way. He was cheerful, generous and encouraging to all who knew him. His devotion to openness, trust and self-forgiveness buoyed the artists he taught through stormy periods of self-doubt. He saved so many others, but he could not save himself.

In 1979, Rob realized that commercial success was changing Circle Rep into an institution that no longer could afford the kind of experimentation and training of young artists that characterized the theater when we began in 1969. He talked to me about his desire to resuscitate that spirit of adventure; he wanted to start a new program called The Lab within Circle Rep's auspices. I thought it sounded like a terrific idea and encouraged him to realize his vision. Rob's creation of The Lab became a vital component of the Company, serving as our developmental engine. Many productions in The Lab were splendid examples of our ongoing creativity, providing Circle Rep with a second stage. The Lab's most prominent success was William M. Hoffman's *As Is*, which went on to acclaim on our main stage and transferred to Broadway, where it received the Drama Desk Award for Best Play of 1985, as well as three Tony nominations for Best Play, Best Actor (Jonathan Hogan) and my fifth Tony nomination for Best Director. But the remarkable thing about The Lab was not its results, but its opportunities. It was perhaps the most vibrant element of the theater in its last fifteen years. After the first year under Rob's leadership, we hired R. Stuart White to become the Artistic Director of The Lab until his death from AIDS a year later. He was succeeded by Daniel Irvine who served from 1981 to 1985 and then by Michael Warren Powell. The Lab (later called Circle East) is the only part that survived the end of Circle Rep in 1996. At its peak, The Lab was training ground for more than 300 participants. After handing off responsibility for The Lab to Stuart, Rob formed his own company at the Byrdcliffe Theater in Woodstock, where he presented fascinating productions of experimental interpretations of classics. I was always warmly welcomed there and I enjoyed seeing where Rob was taking his artistic life, unfettered by the demands of an institution, which Circle had become.

With a suicide, survivors are always left with feelings of guilt: could I have done anything differently to prevent this tragedy? Ultimately, I think no one can be responsible other than the person who makes that choice. The reasons for suicide remain a mystery locked inside the mind of the victim. Nothing can really explain it, even a final note. Rob's read: "I can no longer stand the pain." His artistic family at Circle Rep deeply grieved his loss; but his inspiration lingers beyond the demise of the theaters he founded. I wear his memory in my heart of hearts. "Rest, rest perturbed spirit."

Bridge to Come

Circle Repertory Company transformed theater in America. It set a template that theaters like Manhattan Theater Club, Playwrights Horizons, Second Stage and even Circle Rep itself followed to continue changing the American Theater landscape. An innovative paradigm was established, as Clive Barnes noted in his headline for *The HOT L BALTMORE*: "Herald of a New Pattern."

What nobody so far has been able to emulate consistently is the artistry that produced "writing, acting, and direction meshing into one glorious whole," as Michael Billington of *The Observer* described it in 1978. That is the legacy of Circle Rep to the art of theater. Gratefully, isolated examples still astonish: the admirable ensemble of John Logan's *Red*, directed by Michael Grandage, with exquisite performances by Alfred Molina and Eddie Redmayne brought that play vividly to life in a world created by Christopher Oram's set and costumes, Neil Austin's lighting and Adam Cork's sound design. *Red* was as good as anything we ever did.

But no subsequent theater has been able to match Circle Rep's consistency in year after year of ensemble superiority. Fortunately, a number of our productions are preserved at the Library of

Performing Arts at Lincoln Center in the Lucille Lortel Collection, a video archive of contemporary American theater.

With the production of *Angels Fall*, the transcendent years at Circle Rep drew to a close. It was not the end of Circle (or of its excellence), but the theater had to transform in order to survive.

Survive, we did, and grew stronger. The 1984–85 seasons proved particularly productive. We joined forces with Chicago's Steppenwolf Theater Ensemble to co-produce a collaboration between the two Companies to stage Lanford's *Balm in Gilead*. During my sabbatical, I'd gone to Chicago to see their production, and I was thrilled with what I saw. For twenty years, people had been of urging me to remount *Balm*, but superstitious about the unlikely prospect of equaling our first work together, a monumental landmark of early off-off-Broadway, I had always demurred. Suddenly, here was a vibrant production alive on stage in Chicago that would relieve me of the need to revive it. I suggested we import the Steppenwolf production to New York, replacing half the cast with Circle Rep actors. It was a copasetic combination. Somehow this incredible economic challenge was met by Richard Frankel and Steppenwolf's management, and on May 31, 1984, the united Circle Rep/Steppenwolf production opened. It was a huge success, playing 109 performances at Circle and then transferring to a commercial run at the Minetta Lane Theater for an additional 142 performances. Here's a summary of a typical review:

The New York Times, June 1, 1984 (Frank Rich):
"The play caused a sensation at the Cafe La Mama in 1965; witnesses say that the doors had to be locked to keep out excess theatergoers. Until one witnesses the stunning revival of *Balm in Gilead* at the Circle Rep, it's hard to imagine how the excitement of two decades ago could be rekindled today. Yet the electricity that must have swept through La Mama – that of discovering original theatrical talent – still courses through the new [production] almost from start to finish.

"What we discover here is an imaginative young director out of Chicago's Steppenwolf Theater Ensemble and the actors he's brought with him. The director is John Malkovich [with such] Steppenwolf veterans as Gary Sinise, Terry Kinney, and Laurie Metcalf, whose twenty-minute Act II monologue should in itself prove one of the year's most memorable theatrical events. In concert with the Circle Rep's own fine young actors – such as Danton Stone, Jonathan Hogan and Brian Tarantina (here in full drag) – these Chicagoans have given Wilson's play a contemporary beat. Malkovich and his designer, Kevin Rigdon, have transformed the entire theater into Wilson's forlorn cafe. But it's Malkovich's choreography of his huge company that is crucial. We are completely locked into a seething nocturnal community with its own rituals, laws, loyalties, manners and language. We're moved by the way a young team of inspired stage artists has linked arms with Wilson to make yesterday's new theater new once more."

The following spring, only a month after *Balm in Gilead* closed, we premiered Bill Hoffman's groundbreaking *As Is*, which opened at Circle Rep on February 27, 1985, playing sixty-two performances before it transferred to Broadway's Lyceum for another 285 performances. Here's a summary of *The Times* review:

The New York Times, March 11, 1985 (Frank Rich):
"Hoffman has turned a tale of the dead and the dying into the liveliest new work to be seen at the Circle Repertory Company in several seasons. Far from leaving us drained, *As Is* is one of the few theatrical evenings in town that may, if anything, seem too brief. He reaches out to examine the impact of AIDS on hetero- and homosexual consciences as well as to ask the larger questions (starting with, "Why me?") that impale any victims of terminal illness. It's a feat that Hoffman accomplishes with both charity and humor. In

mocking obsessive promiscuity with light wit, the playwright can gracefully bid such behavior a permanent farewell without adopting a hectoring moralistic tone. Hoffman devotes more attention to exploring both the present panic and solidarity of a group that has found itself rightly "terrified of every pimple." So fluent is Mason's direction of the overlapping scenes that we don't notice the play's begged questions or superficial examinations of character until we're out of the theater. Mason may arrange the cast's choral configurations too pretentiously, yet his staging is mostly inventive. The acting could not be better. Jonathan Hogan gives the breakout performance of his career. Jonathan Hadary's conflicted, at times comically whiny Saul is just as compelling, as are the performances of Ken Kliban and Lou Liberatore in multiple roles. Claris Erickson makes her [character] moving: 'My job is not to bring enlightenment, only comfort,' is how she describes her mission to the dying and their loved ones. Mr. Hoffman's play, as much as is possible under the grim circumstances, brings a stirring measure of both."

Circle Rep was honored with a Drama Desk Award for Best Ensemble for *Balm in Gilead* (amazingly, our first) and John Malkovich beat me out for their award as Best Director.

And within a month of *As Is* receiving the Drama Desk Award for Best Play, we took our abstract production of Edward Albee's *Who's Afraid of Virginia Woolf?* to play at the National Theater of Japan in Tokyo.

And upon our return, we opened *Talley & Son* at Circle Rep, as I've already described. Altogether, a very productive sixteen months; but, perhaps, no longer transcendent: excellence earned by perseverance.

These last three events followed my return from my two-year sabbatical. As the classical repertory of *Richard II/Jedediah Kohler* was ending, I had discovered financial irregularities were routinely happening. I brought my findings to the attention of the Board of Directors and Porter van Zandt was dismissed. For leadership, we installed Richard Frankel as Managing Director. Richard was promoted to producing head after three years as our Press Representative. It was the first step in what developed into a sterling career as one of Broadway's foremost producers. Richard took over running the theater just as I went on sabbatical, so he helped guide B. Rodney Marriott and Tanya Berezin through their stewardship of Circle Rep in my absence. After his three years as Managing Director, Richard moved into the commercial theater, starting with *Penn & Teller, Love Letters* and *Angels in America.*

Traditionally, the seventh year in a career is taken off to replenish the worker's well-being, both mentally and physically. The sabbatical usually is taken in order to pursue a project, such as writing a book or traveling extensively for research. In my case, it was to give myself a chance to fulfill my childhood dreams of directing a movie, following in the steps of my artistic hero, Elia Kazan. In the normal timing of a sabbatical, mine would have occurred the seventh year, the year after we moved Circle Rep to the Sheridan Square Playhouse, elevating our theater to Off-Broadway status. I didn't take the seventh year off; if fact, I spent it directing *Knock Knock,* leading Circle Rep through its first Broadway transfer. Having missed the timing for a traditional sabbatical, I found myself at the fourteenth year needing to take two years away. The first year of the sabbatical was spent directing *Angels Fall* from its premiere in Miami in June through its Broadway closing the following March. I was hoping in the second year to complete my work on directing a movie of Patricia Nell Warren's book *The Front Runner.* The rights to the book belonged to Jerry Wheeler, who hired me to direct the film. Without going into detail, I spent a span of years trying to get this film made, without success.

It had been my hope that we would be able to parlay the stage success of Circle Rep into the medium of film. The Showtime taping of *Fifth of July* was as close as we came to fulfilling this goal. As artistic director, I lacked the savvy of the leaders of the Steppenwolf Theater

Company (John Malkovich, Gary Sinise, Joan Allen and Laurie Metcalf, for example), who ably leapt from the stage to the screen.

It was not to be my destiny. I returned to Circle Rep in the fall of the sixteenth season, that dream unrealized. But look at the dream I returned to.

Transcendence

From 1970 to 1983, the first thirteen years of Circle Rep's existence, the world changed dramatically. The awakening that was summoned by John F. Kennedy's election and foretold by Bob Dylan brought tumultuous forces into play. The power of hallucinogenic drugs paralleled advances in technology; many of America's youth discovered new dimensions of spirituality while many of their brothers braved the sacrifices of a senseless war, whose brutal deaths were broadcast nightly on television. Assassinations and unthinkable crimes coincided with mass suicides, shaking our convictions to the core. The beautiful, safe world of our childhood that characterized the first two centuries of our young country was permanently shattered. A profound sense of unrest put us on a path that led with apparent inevitability to the advent of terrorism at the end of the century.

The idealism of Circle Rep is a lens through which these forces that changed our times can be perceived. Provoked by Alvina Krause's challenge to create an artistic theater that was morally responsible, we found allies who shared an intense desire to make the art of theater an important antidote to a civilization spinning out of control. Circle Rep's focus on the human experience made our plays about real people, buffeted by uncontrollable circumstances.

Our first play, *A Practical Ritual to Exorcise Frustration after Five Days of Rain*, was a comic metaphor of a fragile humanity floundering in a flood of anarchic elements. Next, we turned to Chekhov's insights in *Three Sisters* to illuminate an upheaval in our county that mirrored the tumultuous prelude to the Russian revolution, desperate for Chekhov's wisdom as the security of the past was changing. Resuscitating the time-tested system of rotating rep, our own revolutionary artistic approach honored tradition while breaking boldly into experimentation that startled conventional concepts of how theater could address the problems of our times.

Using perceptive writers to create plays for specific actors to illuminate the present age, we erased the division between script and production so that the action of the play became the experience of the audience. Lanford Wilson's *The HOT L BALTIMORE* brought that concept intro three-dimensional life; it was more than a "herald of a new pattern," as Clive Barnes proclaimed, creating a new avenue for plays created free of commercial pressure off-off-Broadway to transfer into the commercial arena; it was also a seamless embodiment of Harold Clurman's dictum that the true play in the theater is when the text becomes indistinguishable from the acting, and, I might add, the other elements of production. It was recognized with major awards and became a record-setting commercial success for a three-year run.

We followed this achievement with two other extraordinary plays within the same year: *When You Comin' Back, Red Ryder?* and *The Sea Horse*, showing that our approach to changing the way theater was done was no fluke, but hinted at profound principles on which Circle Rep was based. The terrorism implicit in *Red Ryder* was eerily predictive of the pervasive feature of today's world, while *Sea Horse* showed how difficult it is to break free of the past for an uncertain future.

Our elevation to the professional venue of Off-Broadway with our move to the venerable Sheridan Square Theater in the Village established Circle Rep as an institution that indeed was the primary source of new plays in the New York Theater. We kicked off that enterprise with the premiere of Tennessee Williams' long-neglected first play, *Battle of Angels*, adding America's foremost playwright to our arsenal of writers. Lanford's *The Mound Builders* reflected on the clash between understanding our history and the irresistible onslaught of commercial enterprise. Corinne Jacker's *Harry Outside* dramatized a man whose genius has convinced him that he must escape the pressures of society to fulfill his artistic vision. Julie Bovasso's *Down by the River Where Waterlilies Are Disfigured Every Day* used an absurd world to suggest the madness of contriving political machinations, on the cusp of Nixon's Watergate.

Jules Feiffer's *Knock Knock* showed how two guys trying to escape the world must be rescued from their philosophic dead end by the ridiculous notion of following an inspired lunatic in the form of Joan of Arc to create a new world by emigrating to other planets. This production took audiences on a rollicking ride of entertainment that required Circle Rep's world to expand to the established standard of success, Broadway. We continued to utilize the foremost writers of our time with David Storey's *The Farm*, which dramatized a family impoverished by the struggle to dig out a life from the hostile soil. Then, Albert Innaurato's *Gemini* illustrated how the difficult search for one's sexuality could triumph over the limitations of traditional family values, at the time of Anita Bryant's crusade for the contrary. Its move to Broadway showed that Circle Rep's rise to the reputed top of American theater was no accident and it became the fourth longest-running straight drama in Broadway history, playing for nearly four years. *Gemini* enlarged the appeal of the Broadway theater to a previously untapped "bridge and tunnel" crowd.

At this stage of our development, Circle Rep had become an important supplier for the American Theater repertoire, as regional theaters expanded our influence throughout the country. Lanford Wilson's *Fifth of July* exposed how the Vietnam War had ravaged not only the resources of our nation, but our spirit as well. It was, perhaps, the definitive depiction of that war-torn decade, as Frank Rich characterized it. Coincidentally, it introduced us to the Talleys, who would reveal how the American family was altered by war; the romance of Matt and Sally in *Talley's Folly* was set against the backdrop of a global conflict that put us in grave danger of prosperity, in ways from which we've never recovered. *Talley & Son* showed us a changed country that was no longer recognizable to the soldiers who'd fought to save our way of life.

As we thrived, we were joined by more of America's foremost writers, like David Mamet and Sam Shepard who used the Circle Rep's artistic riches to shed light on America's continuing struggle to live up to our best ideals. We were also the debut stage in New York for new important playwrights like William Mastrosimone, Jim Leonard, Marsha Norman, Beth Henley, David Ives, Kenneth Lonergan, Howard Ashman, Timothy Mason and John Bishop.

The world transformed from the innocence of the Sixties to the materialism of Reagan's Eighties. *Angels Fall* questioned how we ought to live given the conflicts inherent in contemporary life. When we produced *Angels Fall* in 1983, the transcendent quality that characterized our beginnings and thirteen years of growth still radiated with a fading cosmic glow.

Circle Rep would continue to make important contributions to the art of theater over the next fourteen years, introducing important artists with vivid dissections of our on-going moral dilemmas. Our artists prolonged our tradition of remarkable collaborations: Paula Vogel and Anne Bogart with *The Baltimore Waltz;* Jon Robin Bates and Joe Mantello with *Three Hotels*, a personal and agonizing examination of American business practices in third world countries; Craig Lucas and Norman René carried forth an ideal writer/director collaboration through the dark hilarity of *Reckless* and *Prelude to a Kiss* (with mesmerizing performances by Alec Baldwin and Mary Louise Parker). William Hoffman's *As Is* was the first play about AIDS and its transfer to Broadway and winning awards helped audiences to understand that this was not someone else's problem, but ours. Larry Kramer's *The Destiny of Me* chronicled the autobiographical progression of a young man (played by John Cameron Mitchell) into a prophet and a leader in the global struggle against the plague of AIDS (played by Jonathan Hadary).

In addition to our important writers, Circle Rep introduced some of the most accomplished actors of our generation: William Hurt, Jeff Daniels, Kathy Bates, Christopher Reeve, Lindsay Crouse, Conchata Ferrell, Brad Dourif, John Dossett, Debra Monk, Cherry Jones and Joe Mantello among many others; they brought the art of acting to new heights, elevating America's awareness of what fine native-grown talent we possessed. Their influence has been worldwide.

Additionally, Circle Rep spawned new theater organizations to carry on its vision of theater, whicht continue decades later to contribute to American Theater. Our Jeff Daniels founded The Purple Rose Theater in Chelsea, Michigan, which continues to premiere new American plays, performed by a company of dedicated actors. Our Carole Rothman (along with our Robyn Goodman) created The Second Stage, a theater with important contributions to the New York Theater, and whose continual growth is an inspiration. They are soon moving into the Helen Hayes, the Broadway theater Clive Barnes thought would be a perfect home for Circle Rep. And our Robert LuPone co-founded (with Bernard Telsey and William Cantler) the invaluable MCC Theater, who are the principal tenant of Circle Rep's old part-time home at the Lucille Lortel Theater. Our legacy lives on.

Ultimately, it might be asked whether any theater can truly affect the tides of history. It's an issue difficult to assess, like trying to prove a negative. Without the insights that Circle Rep and other theaters of our time provided, would our current affairs be in even worse array than they are? I think an argument can be made that without plays like *Angels in America* and *The Normal Heart*, less progress would have been made in understanding what was at stake in the war against AIDS. I think without plays like *As Is* or *Fifth of July*, we might never have reached the powerful evolution of understanding that has led to marriage equality. I believe the exposure of the motives and consequences of war had an effect on a re-evaluation of the wisdom of the wars in Iraq and Afghanistan.

We no longer live in transcendent times, but we are the beneficiaries of the enlightenment those years inspired. We have transformed into a nation and a world, for better or worse, that moves forward with uncertainty, guided to some extent by the lessons of the past. I'd like to think that Circle Rep's role in the transcendent years has contributed to our understanding of our human predicament.

Of course, the past is useful only to the degree that it can influence the present. The era of the transcendent years may have passed, but the illumination they initiated may be an inspiration to those who will shape the future of the theater and our civilization. We can fervently hope so.

Acknowledgements

Memories alone will not suffice when writing a history, so I am deeply grateful to these members of Circle Repertory Company who generously shared their recollections of events the author could not have reconstructed without their help:

Tanya Berezin, Patricia Carey, Stephen de Fluiter, Jeff Daniels, Brad Dourif, Conchata Ferrell, Stephanie Gordon, Trish Hawkins, John Heuer, Jonathan Hogan, Judith Kirtley, Ken Kliban, Zane Lasky, Sharon Madden, Claris Nelson, Marshall Oglesby, Burke Pearson, Joyce Reehling, and Terry Schreiber.

I also thank Lisa Bishop and Jay Broad for providing forgotten details.

A great thanks to Russel Lunday, Lisi Tribble, and Laura Crow for their early readings of an evolving manuscript; their encouragement spurred me on to complete what sometimes seemed a monumental task. Special thanks to my spouse Daniel Irvine for his meticulous corrections for the final proof of the manuscript, which he finished on Valentine's Day; a gift of love indeed.

Thanks to Jeffrey Sweet for guiding me to my persistent agent, Susan Schulman, who in turn guided me to the white-gloved care of Lauren Simpson for Goodreads.

Finally, thanks for the memories themselves to all who joined me on the remarkable journey that was Circle Rep, and to the readers who have waited patiently to relive vicariously the adventure. I guess I owe a special thanks to all the critics whose assessments of Circle Rep are quoted here; their documentation of sustained excellence tells a story that otherwise might not be believed.

About the Author

Marshall W. Mason is the Founding Artistic Director of New York's Circle Repertory Company, which *The New York Times* designated "the chief provider of new American plays." His artistic partnership with Pulitzer Prize-winner Lanford Wilson spanned over forty years and is the longest collaboration between a playwright and director in the history of the American Theater. He directed twelve plays on Broadway (including *Gemini, Burn This, The Seagull* and *Redwood Curtain*) that earned him five Tony nominations for Best Director (*Knock Knock, Talley's Folly, Fifth of July, Angels Fall* and *As Is*). Off-Broadway, he was honored with five Obie Awards for Distinguished Direction (*The HOT L BALTIMORE, Battle of Angels, The Mound Builders, Knock Knock* and *Serenading Louie*), plus a sixth Obie for Sustained Achievement. Memorable productions include *The Sea Horse, Talley & Son, The Destiny of Me* and *Sunshine*. He has directed at major regional theaters throughout the United States, as well as productions in London and Tokyo. He is the author of *Creating Life on Stage: A Director's Approach to Working with Actors* (Heinemann Press). He was the Chief Drama Critic for Phoenix's *New Times*, for which he received an Arizona Press Club Award. He is Professor Emeritus of Arizona State University and is past president of the Stage Directors and Choreographers. He is the recipient of the Theater World Award, the Margo Jones Award, the Erwin Piscator Award and a Special Millennium George Abbott Award as one of "the most influential and innovative directors of the 20th century." In 2015 he was elected to the Theater Hall of Fame and in 2016 he received the Tony Award for Lifetime Achievement in the Theater.

Made in United States
North Haven, CT
15 August 2022